THE COLLECTED COUR
THE ACADEMY OF EUROP

Series Editors:

PROFESSOR NEHA JAIN
PROFESSOR CLAIRE KILPATRICK
PROFESSOR SARAH NOUWEN
PROFESSOR JOANNE SCOTT
European University Institute, Florence

Assistant Editor:

JOYCE DAVIES
European University Institute, Florence

Volume XXVIII/3

The UK's Withdrawal From the EU
A Legal Analysis

THE COLLECTED COURSES OF
THE ACADEMY OF EUROPEAN LAW

Edited by Professor Neha Jain, Professor Claire Kilpatrick,
Professor Sarah Nouwen, and Professor Joanne Scott

Assistant Editor: Joyce Davies

The Academy of European Law is housed at the European University Institute in Florence, Italy. The Academy holds annual advanced-level summer courses focusing on topical, cutting-edge issues in Human Rights Law and The Law of the European Union. The courses are taught by highly qualified scholars and practitioners in a highly interactive environment. General courses involve the examination of the field as a whole through a particular thematic, conceptual, or philosophical lens or look at a theme in the context of the overall body of law. Specialized courses bring together a number of speakers exploring a specific theme in depth. Together, they are published as monographs and edited volumes in the Collected Courses of the Academy of European Law series. The Collected Courses series has been published by Oxford University Press since 2000. The series contains publications on both foundational and pressing issues in human rights law and the law of the European Union.

The UK's Withdrawal from the EU

A Legal Analysis

MICHAEL DOUGAN

OXFORD

UNIVERSITY PRESS

OXFORD
UNIVERSITY PRESS

Great Clarendon Street, Oxford, OX2 6DP,
United Kingdom

Oxford University Press is a department of the University of Oxford.
It furthers the University's objective of excellence in research, scholarship,
and education by publishing worldwide. Oxford is a registered trade mark of
Oxford University Press in the UK and in certain other countries

Public sector information reproduced under Open Government Licence v3.0
(http://www.nationalarchives.gov.uk/doc/open-government-licence/open-government-licence.htm)

Published in the United States of America by Oxford University Press
198 Madison Avenue, New York, NY 10016, United States of America

British Library Cataloguing in Publication Data
Data available

Library of Congress Control Number: 2021937978

ISBN 978-0-19-883347-5 (hbk.)
ISBN 978-0-19-883348-2 (pbk.)

DOI: 10.1093/oso/9780198833475.001.0001

Printed and bound by
CPI Group (UK) Ltd, Croydon, CR0 4YY

For my parents, Tommy and Eilish Dougan

Preface

This book is based on the General Course of the Academy of European Law entitled 'The UK outwith the EU and the EU without the UK' which I delivered at the European University Institute in Florence in July 2017. The usual process of subsequently converting the course materials into a research monograph for publication turned out to be unusually complicated and significantly delayed, thanks to the unusual complications and significant delays involved in the actual process of UK departure from the Union. It was only in January 2020, when the UK's withdrawal agreement was finally ratified, that I was able to confirm the precise scope and detailed subject matter of this book.

By that stage, the situation had changed so much since July 2017, that the original General Course materials had become almost entirely obsolete. Several topics that I had originally planned to cover now needed to be cut out or drastically reduced, while the vast majority of the text for the remaining content had to be written almost entirely afresh. Of course, that is a familiar occupational hazard for many legal researchers—though the added challenge of trying to compile a weighty monograph amid the disruption of the global pandemic and national lockdowns was rather more unexpected.

I am very grateful to both the European University Institute and Oxford University Press for their great patience and kind assistance. I would also like to acknowledge the support of the Liverpool Law School as I undertook the significant preparatory work involved in this book. For several years, my life was utterly dominated by Brexit activities of all sorts and in all sorts of places; the Liverpool Law School offered me the enormous time and flexibility such intensive yet protracted research and impact work so mercilessly demands. Sincere thanks also to the many colleagues and good friends, elsewhere in the UK and across the Union, who contributed to this project—with helpful comments and discussions, bountiful encouragement and camaraderie, as well as the fruits of their own labour and research, which enriched my understanding and deepened my knowledge.

I owe particular gratitude to the UK's burgeoning pro-European movement, in its myriad configurations and wonderfully varied guises. Since 2016, my impact engagement activities—through my online presence, in person at countless events, and during the pandemic via regular 'zoom talks'—have brought me into direct contact with tens of thousands of people, from a boggling array of backgrounds and preoccupations, who are nevertheless united in their commitment to the ideals of European peace and solidarity, cooperation and integration. Their questions regularly challenged me, their observations often informed me, and their dedication constantly inspired me.

It would be incomplete of me not to mention another important source of motivation in completing this book. Whether through the regular torrents of abuse spewed out by its activists, or at the occasional events when I shared a platform with one of its mouthpieces, the Leave movement consistently reminded me—through its dishonesty, ignorance and bigotry—of the supreme importance of affirming and defending one's own professional and personal values, come what may, against those who wish to undermine the achievements and reverse the progress of liberal social market democracy.

Thanks go above all, of course, to my family—for their boundless love, their innate good sense, and their robust humour, all of which are shared with great generosity. I could burst with pride, that our wee house in West Belfast has surely produced more talent and humanity than one might find in the entire UK Cabinet. And where would I be in life, without Little Monty and Bestfriend Wezl? At least 'that bloody Brexit book' didn't entirely stop us eating homemade florentines and watching *Medici*.

On so many levels, Brexit is a tale of trauma, division, and senseless damage. Of course, Europe will not only survive, but press ahead with its historical vocation to protect peace and promote prosperity. We can only hope that the UK will in due course learn its necessary lessons, sort out its profound problems and prove itself worthy of one day returning to its European home.

Michael Dougan

Liverpool
December 2020

Contents

Contents

Table of Cases

For the benefit of digital users, indexed terms that span two pages (e.g., 52– 53) may, on occasion, appear on only one of those pages.

Table of Legislation, International Agreements and International Instruments

For the benefit of digital users, indexed terms that span two pages (e.g., 52– 53) may, on occasion, appear on only one of those pages.

EUROPEAN UNION

Treaties and Other Primary Law

OTHER INTERNATIONAL AGREEMENTS/ INSTRUMENTS

List of Abbreviations

AFSJ	Area of Freedom, Security and Justice
CFSP	Common Foreign and Security Policy
CJEU	Court of Justice of the European Union
CSDP	Common Security and Defence Policy
CTA	Common Travel Area
EAW	European Arrest Warrant
EBA	European Banking Authority
ECHR	European Convention on Human Rights
EDF	European Development Fund
EEA	European Economic Area
EFTA	European Free Trade Association
EMA	European Medicines Agency
EU(W)A	European Union (Withdrawal) Act
EU(WA)A	European Union (Withdrawal Agreement) Act
FTA	Free Trade Agreement
MFF	Multiannual Financial Framework
OLAF	European Anti-Fraud Office
PINI	Protocol on Ireland/Northern Ireland
SEM	Single Electricity Market
TEU	Treaty on European Union
TFEU	Treaty on the Functioning of the European Union
VCLT	Vienna Convention on the Law of Treaties
WA	Withdrawal Agreement
WTO	World Trade Organization

1

Introduction

On 23 June 2016, the United Kingdom held a national referendum, in which 51.9 per cent of those who participated voted to leave the European Union, on a turnout of 72.2 per cent.[1] On 29 March 2017, the British Government delivered formal notice to the European Council of the UK's intention to leave the EU—thus initiating a period of intensive and often controversial negotiations over the precise terms of departure.[2] In due course, the final withdrawal package was approved by the competent institutions of each party and the United Kingdom left the European Union at midnight CET on 31 January 2020.[3]

This book will explore the overall constitutional framework governing the departure of a Member State from the Union, together with the more specific legal and political factors that shaped the particular experience and outcomes of the UK's own withdrawal negotiations. We will also offer a more detailed analysis of key elements within the UK's final withdrawal package: for example, concerning the future protection of those EU and UK citizens whose existing free movement rights were suddenly uprooted by Brexit; addressing the serious challenges posed by UK withdrawal for the open frontier that exists between the Republic of Ireland and Northern Ireland; and examining the tentative plans for a new form of future relationship between the Union and the UK in fields such as trade and security.[4]

In this introductory chapter, Section 1 will provide a brief overview of the background to and context of the UK's referendum on membership of the Union. Section 2 will then explain in greater detail the scope of this book and the structure of the analysis to follow.

1. Explaining the UK's Referendum on Leaving the EU

We will not specifically investigate, but simply take it for granted that many readers are sufficiently familiar with the broader political and empirical factors and debates that led to the UK's withdrawal from the EU: the gaping chasm between the reality of the UK as a leading Member State versus the distorted portrayal/perception of Union

---

[1] See further: https://www.electoralcommission.org.uk/who-we-are-and-what-we-do/elections-and-referendums/past-elections-and-referendums/eu-referendum/results-and-turnout-eu-referendum.
[2] See HMG, *Prime Minister's notification letter to President of the European Council* (29 March 2017).
[3] And Euratom: Art 1 Withdrawal Agreement (hereafter: WA) as published at OJ 2019 C 384 I.
[4] Note that we will not explore the UK's separate negotiations and agreements (e.g. on trade continuity or the protection of citizens' rights) with the EFTA–EEA states or with Switzerland—save for passing references where these are directly relevant also to the EU–UK Withdrawal Agreement, e.g. in Chapter 6 on linking the various agreements together for the purposes of facilitating the smooth cross-border coordination of national social security systems.

The UK's Withdrawal from the EU. Michael Dougan, Oxford University Press. © Michael Dougan 2021.
DOI: 10.1093/oso/9780198833475.003.0001

membership among large parts of the British media/public opinion; the alleged origins of the 2016 referendum as a tool primarily of internal Conservative Party management and electoral posturing; a referendum campaign in which the lacklustre Remain effort was pitted against the systematic dishonesty of the Leave movement; and extensive academic as well as journalistic and political efforts both to explain the factors behind, and interpret the significance of, Leave's narrow victory in 2016. Nevertheless, it is worth saying a few words about each of those key themes—if only to provide some important context for our own subsequent study, though without purporting to offer any sort of comprehensive or rigorous cross-disciplinary analysis.

Among the vast efforts that have been made to explain the causes behind the Leave vote in 2016, some commentators have suggested that the greatest weight and importance should be attached to essentially long-term and aggregate political trends.[5]

On the one hand, the UK was undoubtedly a leading Member State within the EU—one of the 'Big Three' (along with Germany and France) that exercised a major and often decisive influence over both the Union's general evolution and the direction of many of its core policies. At the same time, the UK was also accorded a degree of special treatment within the EU that made its constitutional and legal position quite exceptional compared to the great majority of other Member States—including a permanent derogation from participation in the Single Currency and a privileged relationship of opt-out and opt-in provisions related to the Area of Freedom, Security and Justice.[6] Moreover, that combination of leadership and exceptionalism was a consistent British policy over a considerable period of time—from the era of Prime Ministers Thatcher and Major, through to Prime Ministers Blair and Brown. Indeed, in many ways, the emergence in the 1990s and 2000s of a general consensus that the Union's vocation should be to serve as a 'constitutional order of sovereign states' (rather than aspire to sovereignty in its own right) amounted to a triumph of British policy in and for Europe.[7]

On the other hand, perceptions of the UK's status and role within the Union could not have been more different when viewed through the distorted and distorting lens of much of the domestic British political and public debate. In the early years of UK membership, Euroscepticism was perhaps more associated with the left wing (as demonstrated in the campaign surrounding the 1975 referendum on whether the UK should remain within the European Communities).[8] However, throughout the 1980s, antagonism towards European integration emerged as a powerful force on the right wing—including a staunchly Europhobic faction within the Conservative Party. Far from marking a victory for mainstream Conservatism, the conclusion of Prime Minister Major's parliamentary battles over approval of the Treaty on European Union 1992 only illustrated how radicalized and uncompromising that faction had become.

---

[5] See further, e.g. Warlouzet, 'Britain at the Centre of European Cooperation 1948–2016', 56 *Journal of Common Market Studies (JCMS)* (2018) 955; Carl, Dennison, and Evans, 'European but not European Enough: An Explanation for Brexit', 20 *European Politics* (2018) 282.

[6] See, in particular, Protocols No 15 and 19–21.

[7] The phrase 'constitutional order of states' is most closely associated with Professor Sir Alan Dashwood QC, e.g. in A. Dashwood (ed.), *Reviewing Maastricht: Issues for the 1996 IGC* (1996).

[8] That (first) referendum was won by 'Remain' with 67 per cent of the votes cast.

And subsequent years only saw the phenomenon intensify. Across the Union, the Treaty of Lisbon 2007 may have been regarded as a triumph for an essentially British vision of European integration—but within the UK itself, it was commonly denounced as a federalist plot to destroy the nation state, a conspiracy theory illustrated by all manner of deceptions, from secret deals to abolish the pound sterling to plans for conscription into a European army. The fuel for populist rhetoric about anti-democratic elites only grew stronger when the Labour Government decided not to hold a referendum on approving the Lisbon Treaty (despite the Government's previous promise to do so in respect of the defunct Treaty establishing a Constitution for Europe).[9]

However, it was under the Cameron-led governments that Europhobia was finally embraced as official state policy. Adoption of the European Union Act 2011—with its unprecedented requirements to hold national referenda prior to almost any further attempt at Treaty amendment, as well as in respect of a wide range of decisions already provided for under the existing Treaties—effectively imposed a unilateral British veto on the Union's further constitutional evolution through primary law reform.[10] The *Review of the Balance of Competences between the UK and the EU*—the most extensive evaluation undertaken by any Member State into the nature and implications of its own Union membership—was supposedly launched at the insistence of Tory Europhobes seeking evidence of just how damaging the EU really was to the British economy and society. When the official reports from various sectors started appearing in print, describing a reality in which Union membership generally made a valuable and important contribution to British law and policy, the Review was promptly denounced as a 'Whitehall whitewash' and effectively buried alive.[11]

Politicians and commentators have offered different explanations for the long-term growth in power and influence of the British Europhobic faction—and, just as importantly, of its relationship to broader public opinion towards Union membership as eventually expressed in the 2016 referendum. Some of those explanations are keen to stress the underlying power of British exceptionalism and its natural antagonism towards continental plans for greater cross-border integration: either in a rather smugly self-righteous way (as with Theresa May's attempt to explain Brexit, with the benefit of hindsight, on the grounds that the British are historically and culturally a race simply set apart from other Europeans);[12] or in a rather more self-critical manner (for example, among those who argue that the UK has never truly reconciled itself to the reality of its status as a middle-ranking post-imperial power, but instead harbours and indeed feeds continuing delusions of global grandeur).[13] From such perspectives, it is arguable that the Europhobic faction merely gave political expression to views that

[9] See further, e.g. Dougan, 'The Treaty of Lisbon: Winning Minds, Not Hearts', 45 *Common Market Law Review (CMLRev)* (2008) 617.
[10] See further, e.g. Dougan and Gordon, 'The European Union Act 2011: "Who Won the Bloody War Anyway?"', 37 *European Law Review (ELRev)* (2012) 3; Craig, 'The European Union Act 2011: Locks, Limits and Legality', 48 *CMLRev* (2011) 1915.
[11] See further, e.g. House of Lords European Union Committee, *The Review of the Balance of Competences between the UK and the EU* (HL140 of 25 March 2015).
[12] E.g. in her 'Florence Speech': see Theresa May, *Florence Speech: A New Era of Cooperation and Partnership between the UK and the EU* (22 September 2017).
[13] A perspective which is obviously more common on the centre and left of UK political commentary!

were much more prevalent and indeed effectively latent within the UK population at large.

Other explanations accept the long-term trajectory of British antagonism towards their own membership of the Union but, rather than attribute such antagonism to some inherent (positive or negative) character trait of the post-war British, argue that it is the deliberately manufactured product of various political choices and powerful social forces. For example, one might argue that mainstream British politicians failed, consistently, over a period of several decades to engage with the UK public about the true nature of the Union and the actual implications of British membership. On the contrary: as was also the experience in other Member States, the relatively complex and distant institutions of European integration grew to provide a convenient source of domestic political capital, as governments claimed sole credit for Union-level decisions while seeking easy 'Brussels scapegoats' for their own national failures.[14] The void of public discourse and understanding created by so-called responsible politicians was ripe for filling by an increasingly confident and virulent Europhobic movement—and in the British situation, their cause was actively aided and abetted by the predominantly right-wing media, with its frequent populist misinformation and barely-concealed xenophobia.[15]

Although those explanations might differ in their search for the underlying cause of (widespread) British antagonism towards Union membership, what they have in common is that they do not regard the outcome of the 2016 referendum as any real surprise. On the contrary: according to this analysis, the vote to leave the Union was a product of essentially long-term factors, as a result of which right wing political Europhobia in fact reflected or at least gave more effective expression to the underlying views of a significant part of the British population, such that it was probably only a matter of time before the UK eventually withdrew from the Union anyway.

By contrast: other commentators have argued that Brexit should not be regarded as the natural or inevitable consequence of some long-term or inherent antagonism between the UK and the Union; rather, when it comes to explaining the outcome of the 2016 referendum, the greatest weight and significance should be attached to a series of more short-term and immediate political and social contingencies and factors. In effect, the Leave campaign was victorious primarily because it happened to be in the right place at the right time. Had the referendum been held under appreciably different short-term or immediate circumstances, the outcome could have been very different.

Thus, for example, various commentators have stressed the significance of the post-Maastricht civil war within the Conservative Party—pitching its essentially pro-Union mainstream against its Europhobic hard right. To that internal struggle was added the electoral threat posed to the Conservative Party (at least in local and European elections, though hardly in general elections to the Westminster Parliament) of the United Kingdom Independence Party under the latter's unashamedly populist–jingoist

---

[14] A phenomenon that the Treaty of Lisbon consciously sought to help counter, by explicitly providing for the Council's deliberations and votes on draft Union legislation to be held in public: see Art 16(8) TEU.

[15] Though consider, e.g. Copeland and Copsey, 'Rethinking Britain and the European Union: Politicians, the Media and Public Opinion Reconsidered', 55 *JCMS* (2017) 709.

leadership.[16] It has often been said that Tory leaders consistently believed the only way to end that civil war, and defeat the real/perceived electoral threat from UKIP, was to borrow the language and policies of Euroscepticism for themselves—thereby making the fundamental error of failing to appreciate that political ideologues are generally uninterested in compromise, but only grow more convinced and more confident with every concession to their cause.

It is certainly true that the Cameron governments (the first in coalition with the Liberal Democrats, the second as a majority Tory-only administration) were keen to brandish their Eurosceptic credentials. Readers may recall the European Council meeting of December 2011.[17] At the height of the global financial crisis, the vast majority of Member States agreed upon the need to adopt various measures they believed to be crucial to restoring confidence in the embattled Eurozone. Moreover, in order to give those measures increased force and credibility, there was a widespread preference for enshrining them into primary Union law. However, the Cameron Government publicly announced that it would veto any attempt at Treaty reform—even though the UK would not itself be directly affected by the relevant proposals—allegedly on the grounds that the other Member States would not acquiesce in the UK's (essentially ulterior) demand for the City of London to be granted various special concessions and exemptions from EU financial services regulation.[18]

Cameron's attempt to placate his backbench Europhobes (and dampen the electoral appeal of UKIP at the Tories' expense) culminated in his 'Bloomberg speech' of January 2013—in which he called for changes to the UK's existing terms of Union membership, and indeed for a broader range of reforms applicable to the Union as a whole, followed by a national referendum to decide whether the UK should then remain a Member State on those renegotiated terms or instead leave the Union altogether.[19] That approach was then contained in the Conservative Party manifesto for the 2015 general election. However, with the opinion polls generally pointing to another hung parliament, which would in turn likely lead to another Tory–Liberal Democrat coalition, it was widely assumed that Cameron's promise of a major EU membership renegotiation, followed by a national referendum on withdrawal, was never seriously intended or expected to be implemented in practice.[20]

---

[16] See, e.g. Craig, 'Brexit: A Drama in Six Acts', 41 *ELRev* (2016) 447; Gormley, 'Brexit: Nevermind the Whys and Wherefores? Fog in the Channel, Continent Cut Off!', 40 *Fordham International Law Journal* (2017) 1175.

[17] See further, e.g. Editorial Comments, 'Some thoughts concerning the Draft Treaty on a Reinforced Economic Union', 49 *CMLRev* (2012) 1.

[18] Consider also the UK Government's decision to make use of the UK's power (under Art 10 of Protocol No 36) to repudiate all existing Third Pillar instruments on police and judicial cooperation in criminal matters, then seek to opt back in again to a more selected group of Union measures. See HMG, *Letter from the Permanent Representative of the UK to the Presidents of the Justice and Home Affairs Council* (24 July 2013); HMG, *Letter from the Prime Minister to the President of the Council* (20 November 2014); Council Decision 2000/365 concerning the request of the United Kingdom to take part in some of the provisions of the Schengen *acquis*, OJ 2000 L 131/43 (as amended); Council Decision 2004/926 on the putting into effect of parts of the Schengen *acquis* by the United Kingdom, OJ 2004 L 395/70 (as amended).

[19] See https://www.gov.uk/government/speeches/eu-speech-at-bloomberg.

[20] Note that the era of the Cameron Governments coincides with a period when the senior UK judiciary were also adopting a more critical approach towards the status of EU law within the domestic legal system—though there is unlikely to have been any direct connection/influence between the two developments.

Whether or not that is true, after Cameron won the 2015 general election with a working majority in the House of Commons, he decided to press ahead with his project of renegotiation followed by a membership referendum. But even under this line of analysis, the outcome of any popular vote remained far from being a foregone conclusion: for many commentators, the Leave victory in 2016 still owed much to a series of additional short-term and immediate political factors.

For example, it is argued that Cameron and the mainstream Conservative Party seriously mismanaged their own 'renegotiation and referendum' policy. The primary legislation required to authorize the referendum left open important questions, or at least created ambiguous perceptions, about the proper constitutional status and authority of the outcome; while the Government refused to include safeguards (that would have been entirely reasonable, given the significance of the proposed decision) such as a minimum threshold of support for change, or the need for positive endorsement of withdrawal by each constituent territory of the UK.[21] The Government was also accused of raising unrealistic expectations about what the UK was likely to achieve in any renegotiation exercise—particularly in fields of fundamental importance to the Single Market, such as the free movement of workers, thereby allowing the Leave campaign to dismiss the 'new deal' agreed between the UK and the remaining Member States in February 2016 as a failure and a fraud.[22]

In any case, Cameron's sudden conversion from outspoken Eurosceptic to committed champion of Union membership was surely never going to feel like a sincere and convincing political strategy. And the referendum campaign itself revealed the full extent of the Government's inadequate preparations for a serious and informed public debate about such important yet complex questions. If anything, the official Remain campaign often appeared unable to explain basic facts or arguments about the value and significance of Union membership. Its focus on the likely negative economic impacts of withdrawal instead allowed its opponents to dismiss the Government as practitioners of 'Project Fear'.[23]

But the short-term and immediate failures that opened the path to a Leave victory were not just those of mainstream Conservatism. For its part, the Labour Party is also alleged to have badly mishandled its usually pro-European policies and messaging during the crucial years before the 2016 referendum. Certainly, some of the Labour Party's decisions and experiences in government appear to have dented its willingness to act as a strong advocate of Union membership or at least to counter the populist narratives peddled by right-wing Europhobic politicians and their tabloid allies. After all, it was a Labour Government that had decided to proceed to the 2004 'Big Bang'

Consider, e.g. *R (HS2 Action Alliance) v Secretary of State for Transport* [2014] UKSC 3; *Pham v Secretary of State for the Home Department* [2015] UKSC 19.

[21] European Union Referendum Act 2015.

[22] Decision of the Heads of State or Government, meeting within the European Council, *Concerning a New Settlement for the United Kingdom within the European Union* (19 February 2016).

[23] The allegation was particularly associated with the Conservative Government's claim that a Leave victory in the referendum would lead immediately to a major recession and an emergency budget—claims which may not have proved altogether baseless, if the Prime Minister had kept to his promise of notifying the European Council of the UK's intention to withdraw, immediately after the result on 23 June 2016: see further the discussion in Chapter 3.

enlargement without imposing any significant transitional restrictions on the free movement of persons from the newly acceded Member States in central and eastern Europe;[24] and it was a Labour Government that had finalized, then decided to ratify, the Treaty of Lisbon without first holding a national referendum and regardless of its own previous promises in respect of the Constitutional Treaty.[25] But in addition, the Labour Party also seemed increasingly concerned about the prospect of UKIP making significant electoral inroads into traditional working class strongholds, particularly in the Midlands and the North of England.[26] And the election of Jeremy Corbyn as party leader signalled an appreciable cooling by the most senior Labour team towards Union membership: it is certainly fair to observe that, for many pro-European campaigners in the UK, Corbyn and his closest allies appeared disappointingly lukewarm in their own support for Remain.[27]

Another set of influential short-term and immediate factors working in favour of a Leave victory that should, in itself, be considered far from inevitable concerns the state of the Union's own well-being, confidence, and public perception. After all, the UK referendum was held in the midst of a series of apparently interminable 'crises' that hardly allowed the Remain campaign to project the image of a Union firmly in control of its own destiny and capable of offering effective solutions to the challenges facing its citizens. Instead, it handed Leave populists ready fuel for their narrative of a weak organization teetering on the brink of collapse. Consider the impact of the global financial crisis, and the emergence of its successor sovereign debt crises, with their destabilizing effects on the Single Currency; or the onset of the migration crisis, that saw unprecedented numbers of third country nationals arriving at the Union's borders, calling into question the fundamentals or at least the capacities of the Area of Freedom, Security and Justice and of the Schengen system, while becoming mixed up with existing political concerns and public fears about internal security and the fight against terrorism. If the Leave campaign were the beneficiaries of a particularly lucky set of circumstances, at least part of that luck rested upon the coincidence of a Union experiencing its own multiple misfortunes.[28]

If some commentators regard the Leave victory as the natural culmination of long-term political trends, while others believe 2016 was more a matter of bad timing under particularly unfortunate circumstances, yet another body of research offers a rather different approach to explaining the referendum result, focusing less on the 'supply side' of the entire debate (i.e. centred around the plans, tactics and failings of political parties and leaders) and more on the 'demand side' of the 2016 vote (i.e. focusing on the actual voters and their various characteristics, motivations, and preferences). Indeed, an enormous amount of effort has been invested in the collection and analysis

---

[24] See further, e.g. Dougan, 'A Spectre is Haunting Europe ... Free Movement of Persons and the Eastern Enlargement' in C. Hillion (ed.), *Enlargement of the European Union: A Legal Approach* (2004).

[25] See further, e.g. Dougan, 'The Treaty of Lisbon: Winning Minds, Not Hearts', 45 *CMLRev* (2008) 617.

[26] See further, e.g. K. Tournier-Sol and C. Gifford (eds), *The UK Challenge to Europeanization: The Persistence of British Euroscepticism* (2015).

[27] Though consider the analysis provided at https://www.theguardian.com/commentisfree/2016/jul/04/evidence-blame-jeremy-corbyn-brexit-remain-labour-conservative.

[28] A fact implicitly recognized by the Union itself, e.g. already in European Council, *Statement from Informal Meeting at 27* (29 June 2016) as well as the *Bratislava Declaration* (16 September 2016).

of data concerning voting patterns that might reveal how far particular economic, so-cial, or cultural factors influenced or can explain the outcome of the referendum.

For example, there is a common perception that simple geography played a deci-sive role in the outcome of the referendum. True enough, there are certainly some important geographical facts about voting patterns in 2016: Scotland and Northern Ireland voted Remain; England and Wales voted Leave. But beyond that, the rele-vance of geography has perhaps suffered from certain popular and media distortions. For example, it is not uncommon to hear the (misleading) claim that cosmopolitan London and its liberal southern satellites are to be pitched against the more insular, Leave-dominated population living in the North of England. It might be more accu-rate to argue that urban dwellers across England were generally more likely to support Remain, while the inhabitants of smaller towns and villages across the English coun-tryside were more likely to vote Leave.[29]

Geography is not the only characteristic that has been cited as a reliable or at least relevant indicator of voting behaviour in the 2016 referendum. A host of other factors have been suggested, with stronger or weaker data to support their claim to coincide with and therefore shed light upon the 'demand side' of the Leave victory: for example, socio-economic factors such as age (younger = more likely to vote Remain) or edu-cation (fewer qualifications = more likely to vote Leave);[30] as well as cultural values such as views on immigration (pro- tends to indicate a Remain supporter) or capital punishment (pro- on this issue is more likely to mean a Leave voter).[31] In each case, of course, any patterns suggested by the data only pave the way for much more com-plex and controversial questions about how those factors specifically and qualitatively relate to voter preferences about the distinct issue of EU membership: *why* might an urban dweller be more likely to have supported Remain; *why* does support for the death penalty often coincide with having voted Leave?[32]

A vast effort has therefore been invested in explaining the long- and short-term causes behind the Leave vote in 2016. But another body of work has been devoted to a rather different line of enquiry. Regardless of the objective factors that might cred-ibly explain the Leave campaign's electoral victory, what might that victory actually tell us about the British population's preferences concerning the UK's future relation-ship to the EU, in ways that the competent public decision-makers and authorities can translate into a meaningful agenda for concrete action? Again, for present purposes, it should suffice to summarize a range of relevant views.

---

[29] Note that many of the major English cities voted with a majority for Remain (including Bristol, Leeds, London, Liverpool, Manchester and Newcastle); while the Leave vote tended to predominate in non-metropolitan areas. But there were, of course, exceptions: e.g. Birmingham and Nottingham voted (narrowly) for Leave; while South Lakeland (Cumbria) and Cotswold-South West voted for Remain. See the detailed breakdown of results available via https://www.electoralcommission.org.uk/who-we-are-and-what-we-do/elections-and-referendums/past-elections-and-referendums/eu-referendum/results-and-turnout-eu-referendum.

[30] See further, e.g. Curtice, 'Why Leave Won the UK's EU Referendum', 55 *JCMS* (2017) 19.

[31] See further, e.g. Kaufmann, 'It's NOT the economy, stupid: Brexit as a story of personal values' available via https://blogs.lse.ac.uk/politicsandpolicy/personal-values-brexit-vote/.

[32] Consider, e.g. https://www.centreforcities.org/blog/casting-towns-bastions-brexit-ignores-reasons-referendum-result-address/.

In the first place, and particularly for many Leave campaigners, the referendum re-sult offered a clear popular mandate for a concrete course of future action. Of course, depending on which Leave campaigner one might listen to, the nature and detail of that mandate/action might still vary considerably. But this was certainly the interpre-tation adopted by the UK Government itself. After an initial period of confusion and uncertainty in the months immediately following the vote on 23 June 2016, when it appeared simply that 'Brexit means Brexit', Prime Minister Theresa May announced that the referendum had in fact given expression to the popular demand that the UK must 'take back control'. In a series of public speeches and announcements, May would elaborate further upon this idea, explaining how the Leave victory reflected the British sense of political alienation from the institutions and trajectory of the EU and a pop-ular desire for national renewal outside the structures and confines of European in-tegration.[33] In time, the May Government's interpretation of the referendum indeed settled into a relatively focused political agenda for concrete future action: the vote in 2016 was a solemn instruction from the British people, that the UK must take back control of its laws, its borders and its money. And true enough: it was on the basis of that mandate that the UK eventually approached its formal withdrawal negotiations with the EU.[34]

On the one hand, it may well be true that issues such as 'immigration' and 'sover-eignty' played a significant role, not just in the political tactics of the Leave campaign itself, but also in the calculations that motivated significant numbers of Leave voters themselves.[35] On the other hand, it perhaps feels less convincing to argue that many Leave voters were conscious of, let alone driven by, constitutional and legal issues quite so specific as those identified by the May Government: for example, the potential for the Court of Justice of the European Union (CJEU) to exercise its jurisdiction under the Treaties in a manner that might create binding interpretations or obligations for the UK as a third country.[36] And it is also open to contestation, whether the UK Government was justified in translating tangible voter concerns about 'immigration' or 'sovereignty' into much broader and more fundamental policy decisions—such as the need for the UK to leave not only the EU, but also the entire Customs Union as well as the Single Market—particularly without any evidence that voters had weighed their specific concerns against the considerable countervailing costs or problems.[37]

In any case, there are other objections to the UK Government's interpretation of the Leave victory as a clear and direct mandate for the Conservative Party's own particular policy agenda. Of course, and as we shall mention shortly, there are obvious concerns about the objective political or moral integrity of converting the complex and varied motivations behind the Leave vote into a monolithic and coherent policy message.

---

[33] In particular: Theresa May, *Lancaster House Speech: The Government's Negotiating Objectives for Exiting the EU* (17 January 2017); Theresa May, *Florence Speech: A New Era of Cooperation and Partnership between the UK and the EU* (22 September 2017).

[34] See further the detailed discussion and references in Chapters 4 and 5.

[35] See further, e.g. A. Glencross, *Why the UK Voted for Brexit: David Cameron's Great Miscalculation* (2016).

[36] Consider, e.g. HMG, *The United Kingdom's Exit from and New Partnership with the European Union* (Cm 9417 of 2 February 2017).

[37] Again, consider HMG, *The United Kingdom's Exit from and New Partnership with the European Union* (Cm 9417 of 2 February 2017).

One might also object to the very proposition that responsible politicians should so readily pander to popular opinions—on an issue such as EU immigration—when the hard scientific data and evidence quite simply contradicts what many voters naively or stubbornly chose to believe. And, of course: the UK Government's decision to pursue a relatively hard-line interpretation of the referendum result entirely ignored the fact that the Leave victory was actually a relatively narrow one; it would have been equally, indeed arguably much more, appropriate to extract a mandate and craft an agenda that sought to accommodate the views and concerns also of the very large numbers of voters who supported Remain.

In the second place, for many commentators, the Leave vote—while it might contain a basic instruction from a majority of British voters that the UK should cease to be a Member State of the EU—otherwise told us little that can be described as specific or useful about the alternative relationship that instead needed to be constructed between the two parties for the future. Of course, that is not to deny that the Government needs to consider and formulate a new policy, so as to provide a concrete basis for the myriad choices and actions necessary to carry out the 2016 instruction in a practical and responsible manner. The point is simply that the Leave victory could not *in itself* provide a plausible basis or justification for those subsequent choices and actions. To pretend otherwise was, in effect, to create a smokescreen of 'popular legitimacy' that merely served to reduce transparency and evade accountability for an entire series of subsequent political calculations.

After all, many politicians have lamented the fact that—in their rush to hold the referendum —the Cameron Government made no serious attempt to communicate to the public what the implications of a Leave vote might be, when it came to the range of alternative relationships the UK might seek to build with the EU, let alone inviting the public to indicate a preference of their own for the future. For its part, the Leave campaign was, without any shadow of a doubt, an unholy alliance of highly divergent and, in many respects, mutually contradictory political movements: from radical leftists who regard the Union as a capitalist conspiracy to destroy socialism, to hard neo-liberals who believe the EU is a socialist conspiracy to undermine capitalism; from those who believe an introverted and protectionist EU is holding the UK back from its natural vocation to be a truly open and dynamic player on the global scene, to those who want the UK to close itself off from the forces, institutions and processes of international cooperation and/or globalization—not forgetting, of course, a good smattering of bigots, xenophobes and proto-fascists thrown into the mix, just for good measure.

Against that background, the crucial fact is that the 2016 ballot paper asked nothing about what of sort of 'leave' voters might actually want: for example, membership of the European Economic Area; perhaps to be even closer to the EU, with a full customs union too; a more distant but still relatively proximate relationship, based on a tight network of agreements providing for meaningful cooperation across a broad spectrum of policies; or a more stand-offish approach based on limited degrees of economic and security cooperation across a more narrow range of sectors; or an abrupt severance of bilateral ties and a preference instead for relations to be mediated essentially through default multilateral agreements and organizations. As a result, the Leave victory in itself can hardly be interpreted as a clear and specific mandate for *any* particular future relationship between the EU and UK as a third country. Indeed, one might legitimately wonder whether—if voters had originally been asked in 2016 to support what emerged as the May and then the Johnson Government's plans for only a very distant future EU–UK relationship—then a coalition of Remain supporters and 'soft Leavers' might instead have decisively rejected any such vision.[38]

In the third place, one might also argue that the Leave victory in itself could tell us little useful about how the UK's withdrawal should actually take place, or the terms of its future relationship to the EU, because the result was almost certainly influenced by various extraneous factors that had little (if anything) to do with the issue voters were actually being asked to decide upon. In that respect, we should not act too surprised: it would tally with an extensive political science literature confirming that that experience is entirely typical of referenda across many European democracies—including (indeed especially) those concerned with questions of national engagement with the EU.[39]

For example: one might agree with the May Government's basic assertion that 'immigration' played a significant role in motivating many people to vote 'Leave' but without also endorsing the suggestion that those voters were specifically or primarily concerned about the situation of EU citizens exercising their reciprocal free movement rights under the Treaties. After all, national statistical data had consistently confirmed that EU citizens make up only a minority of the total number of foreign nationals living in the UK—the rest being third-country nationals whose entry, residence, and associated rights fall almost entirely within the competence of the UK authorities and outside the scope of Union law.[40]

Similarly: one might again agree with the May Government's basic claim that the Leave vote involved a popular rebellion against distant elites who seemed uninterested in the concerns and problems of ordinary people—yet still feel entitled to suggest that such sentiments were directed as much against the institutions and political leaders of the UK state, as against those of the EU itself. After all, many commentators have discussed long-running problems of public confidence in the UK's domestic political structures (fuelled by scandals such as that over the abuse by MPs of their parliamentary expenses). Moreover, it is pertinent to recall that the EU membership referendum took place in the wake of a serious economic downturn in the UK itself, against the immediate backdrop of severe cutbacks in public spending and services at the instigation of the British authorities (another important contextual point in the argument about the referendum being held in a particular 'time and place').[41] According to this

---

[38] As indeed, they arguably did by depriving the Conservative Party of its parliamentary majority at the General Election in 2017: see further the discussion in Chapter 4.

[39] See further, e.g. F. Mendez, M. Mendez, and V. Triga, *Referendums and the European Union: A Comparative Inquiry* (2014). Also, e.g. Taggart, 'Questions of Europe: The Domestic Politics of the 2005 French and Dutch Referendums and their Challenge for the Study of European Integration', 44 *JCMS Annual Review* (2006) 7; Arnull, 'Ireland and the Lisbon Treaty: All's Well That Ends Well?' in A. Arnull, C. Barnard, M. Dougan and E. Spaventa (eds), *A Constitutional Order of States: Essays in EU Law in Honour of Alan Dashwood* (2011); Snell, 'European Union and National Referendums: Need for Change after the Brexit Vote?', *European Business Law Review* [2017] 767.

[40] See further the discussion and references in Chapter 7.

[41] I.e. the 'austerity' programme adopted by the Conservative-led governments in 2010 and 2015, in the wake of the global financial crisis and the UK's related public debt problems.

analysis, while the Leave victory might well contain important lessons about the views and preferences of many British voters, it is less obvious that those lessons can point us in a clear and specific direction when it comes to making fundamental decisions about future EU–UK relations.

For any or all such reasons, one might well argue that there is limited value in any analysis that focuses on the 'demand side' of the referendum debate, i.e. on the understanding, preferences and intentions of Leave voters, who were clearly motivated by wide range of factors and can be assumed to have supported a diverse range of potential outcomes, making it hard to interpret the '51.9 per cent' outcome as any sort of coherent agenda for the future. But in the fourth place, another substantial body of opinion has argued for the Leave vote—its significance, its interpretation, and its utility as a reference point for taking future political decisions about EU–UK relations—to be assessed having regard also to its 'supply side' characteristics, i.e. based on the conduct and intentions of those who provided leadership to the campaign for UK withdrawal from the EU.

Here, we refer of course to the assessment—particularly widespread among Remain supporters, but amenable to plentiful objective scientific analysis and verification—that the Leave victory was procured through a campaign characterized by deliberate and widespread political dishonesty.[42] Basic constitutional, legal, factual, and empirical evidence about the nature and structure of the EU, its institutions and competences, its policies and plans, the role of the UK as a Member State and the domestic impact of Union membership—all were systematically distorted, in campaign materials and public debates, through major speeches and across social media, often far beyond any meaningful relationship to reality.[43] Indeed, the present author has described the Leave campaign as guilty of 'dishonesty on an industrial scale' and written about how the core tactics employed by the Leave campaign reflect those employed by other political movements gathered together under the banner of 'post-truth populism' and identified as an international phenomenon afflicting not just the UK, but a range of other Western democracies as well.[44]

Building on such criticisms, an alternative view can therefore be proposed. It was (only ever at best) inappropriate even to attempt to interpret the Leave victory as a legitimate, let alone coherent, agenda for subsequent political decisions about EU–UK relations. Even if one felt obliged to 'respect the referendum result',

---

[42] Compounded, e.g. by a lack of reliable independent sources of objectively verifiable information; as well as allegations of 'false balance' in the mainstream media which failed to challenge (indeed actively legitimated) political misinformation—to say nothing of the aggressive Europhobic propaganda disseminated by the tabloid and right-wing media. See further, e.g. I. R. Lamond and C. Reid, *The 2015 UK General Election and the 2016 EU Referendum: Towards a Democracy of the Spectacle* (2017); Organ, 'Legal Regulation of Campaign Deliberation: Lessons from Brexit', 7 *Politics and Governance* (2019) 268.

[43] For a worked-out detailed example, focusing on Leave claims about the 'amount of UK law imposed by the EU', consider Dougan, 'Faux Research in the Service of Ideological Deceit during the 2016 EU Referendum Campaign: The Legal Surreality of Leave's 'Sovereignty' Statistics', Issue 118 *Radical Statistics* [2017] 21. Consider also, e.g. the financial claims examined in House of Commons Treasury Committee, *The Economic and Financial Costs and Benefits of the UK's EU Membership* (HC122 of 27 May 2016).

[44] See, in particular, https://www.youtube.com/watch?v=ic8A7KXFkKY. Also: https://www.thelacanianreviews.com/the-charlatans-little-box-of-tricks/.

responsible political leaders should have felt free to debate and define the national future without reference to the blatant lies and idle fantasies of the Leave campaign itself. Indeed, for many Remain campaigners, the punishment for the Leave campaign's conduct should have extended much further: in their eyes, the Leave victory was so tarnished by tactics that should be regarded as antithetical to any functioning liberal democracy that the entire referendum should be treated as exercising little or no moral and political authority, even when it came to answering the essential question of whether the UK should actually decide to withdraw from the Union at all.[45] However, it is perhaps fair to point out that the latter argument perhaps assumes rather than proves that the Leave campaign and its tactics actually exercised a real and decisive influence over the real-life preferences and decisions of millions of individual voters. Moreover, our revulsion at Leave's eager resort to the full-blooded tactics of post-truth populism, should not blind us to the fact that the Remain side also had its campaign problems—including accusations of inaccurate scaremongering about the immediate economic consequences of a Leave victory—though it should be stressed that such failings were (relatively speaking) much more minor in scale and degree.

What should we make of all those competing and overlapping perspectives, interpretations and explanations? For present purposes, the key point is that we do not need to make any particular choice for or against any one viewpoint or another. Suffice to say: the fact that Leave won a majority of the votes cast in the referendum on 23 June 2016 was undoubtedly the product of a complex array of factors, both long and short term, as well as more immediate to the referendum campaign itself; equally, when it came to making the necessary political decisions about the concrete implications to be drawn from the Leave victory, the latter proved readily amenable to various competing, often contradictory, sometimes even polar-opposite, interpretations. Conversely, in the months following the referendum, there was a real danger that the relatively narrow and deeply divisive result in favour of Leave would be both simplified and instrumentalized—providing the basis for fabricating some clear and decisive 'will of the people' that could then be consecrated with a constitutional and political authority, as well as a long-lingering shelf-life, that could not possibly be justified or sustained within the UK's (albeit by then tumultuous and fractious) parliamentary system of representative democracy.

And that seems as good as any a launchpad for our critical legal analysis of what came next: the UK's actual constitutional decision to withdraw from the EU; the complex and controversial negotiations between the two parties to settle the precise terms of British departure from the Union; and initial discussions about how future EU–UK relations might be reshaped into the longer term.

---

[45] Prominent Remain campaigners immediately questioned the political authority of the referendum result not only on the grounds of the Leave campaign's dishonesty but also, e.g. because of the narrowness of the final result and the lack of any credible victors' plan for the future; consider, e.g. https://www.theguardian.com/politics/commentisfree/2016/jun/26/second-referendum-consequences-brexit-grave.

2. Structure of the Analysis to Follow

Chapter 2 opens our substantive discussion with the legal framework for withdrawal as a matter of Union law and, in particular, under the process laid down by Article 50 of the Treaty on European Union (TEU). Once the relevant State has taken the decision to leave the Union, in accordance with its own domestic constitutional requirements, the relevant State should notify its intention to the European Council. After that, the primary objective of Article 50 TEU is to provide the legal basis for an agreement between the relevant State and the Union, aimed at delivering a smooth and orderly (rather than chaotic and disruptive) withdrawal. As we will explore, the objective of an orderly departure from the Union in fact requires various unilateral measures by each party, as well as the Article 50 TEU negotiations over appropriate bilateral arrangements. Moreover, even when it comes to those negotiations, the drafting of Article 50 TEU is relatively sketchy: various important questions are left open by the text and need to be addressed through further legal and political action. In any case, Article 50 TEU also foresees, or at least allows for, other outcomes to the withdrawal process: including a 'no deal' departure in the event that negotiations end in failure; or unilateral revocation by the relevant State of its original notice of intention to leave. But for all its faults and limitations, Article 50 TEU was still the primary legal basis upon which UK withdrawal was expected to proceed.

In Chapter 3, we undertake a detailed consideration of various additional legal and political factors that were to shape the UK withdrawal process as it unfolded in accordance with Article 50 TEU. Looking first at the situation of the Union, there are interesting questions to address about the allocation of roles and responsibilities across the various Union institutions—particularly the European Council, Council, Commission, and European Parliament—some of which are explicit in the text of Article 50 TEU, while others only emerged through political practice. Of particular importance is the Council's early decision to exclude any possibility that the withdrawal agreement should call not only for approval by the Union's own institutions, but also for Member State ratification through the latter's domestic institutions—the first indication that Article 50 TEU is to be treated as an 'exceptional' competence or legal basis, capable of deviating from some of the ordinary principles one would otherwise expect to follow under Union constitutional law. We will also introduce the core legal and political principles laid down by the European Council in its Guidelines of April 2017—which served to structure and steer the Union's overall approach to the negotiations under Article 50 TEU,[46] supplemented by modest but still important contributions by the CJEU in its fledgling 'Brexit caselaw'.[47]

Looking secondly at the situation of the UK, we will begin by sketching out how an initial period of turmoil and uncertainty after the referendum gave way to significant decisions by the May Government about the UK's basic political preferences for withdrawal and its future relationship with the EU—preferences that were to prove

---

[46] See European Council (Article 50), *Guidelines following the United Kingdom's notification under Article 50 TEU* (29 April 2017).

[47] E.g. Case T-458/17, *Shindler* (EU:T:2018:838); Case C-327/18, *R O* (EU:C:2018:733); Case C-621/18, *Wightman* (EU:C:2018:999); Case C-661/17, *M A* (EU:C:2019:53).

the source of many subsequent troubles and, in the end, to be both unsustainable and undeliverable. At the same time, the UK also faced the first of its 'Brexit constitutional crises': the Supreme Court was called upon to decide that it was Parliament (not the Government, and certainly not the referendum itself) that held the legitimate authority to take any final decision on UK membership of or departure from the Union.[48] Moreover, the UK's position, right at the threshold of formal Article 50 TEU negotiations, was decisively affected by the Prime Minister's decision to call an early general election in June 2017 in which the Conservative Party lost its parliamentary majority and the Government thenceforth acted as a minority administration. Among the many consequences of that outcome was the fact that Parliament enacted a novel procedure—under section 13 of the European Union (Withdrawal) Act 2018— requiring the House of Commons to grant its prior approval to any deal agreed with the Union, prior to formal ratification by the Government itself.

Having set out the basic legal and political framework for withdrawal, Chapter 4 then proceeds to examine the conduct of the negotiations themselves. Above all, we will consider the EU–UK dispute over the basic scope, sequence and timing of the various strands of talks that needed to be undertaken between the parties in order to deliver an orderly withdrawal and establish a new relationship into the future. That dispute was resolved by unilateral decision of the European Council: Article 50 TEU can provide the legal basis only for an agreement addressing the immediate consequences of the very act of withdrawal; though once sufficient progress had been made with those negotiations, preliminary and preparatory discussions could then begin about the shape of future relations between the Union and the relevant State—even if formal negotiations were only possible after withdrawal itself had been completed.[49]

Within that framework, the two parties identified a provisional agenda for the 'separation challenges' that needed to be addressed under Article 50 TEU, including how to protect the status of EU and UK citizens who had already made use of their rights to free movement; and how to avoid the creation of a 'hard border', particularly for the movement of goods, across the island of Ireland. Subsequent negotiations were marked by regular moments of deadlock, breakthrough, frustration, and resolution— nevertheless culminating in political endorsement of a 'First Withdrawal Package' in November 2018. That package consisted of a legally binding (First) Withdrawal Agreement on delivering an orderly withdrawal; together with a non-binding (First) Political Declaration expressing the parties' mutual understanding of their future relations.[50]

However, the First Withdrawal Package ultimately failed to secure the approval of the House of Commons under the 'section 13' procedure. Chapter 5 explains the efforts undertaken by the May Government to persuade MPs to support her Brexit deal, including various additional political statements and supplementary agreements relating (in particular) to the border arrangements affecting Ireland and Northern Ireland; as well as requests to the European Council that the effective date of

---

[48] See *Miller* [2017] UKSC 5.
[49] See European Council (Article 50), *Guidelines following the United Kingdom's notification under Article 50 TEU* (29 April 2017).
[50] Published at OJ 2019 C 66 I.

UK withdrawal be delayed while the British approval process continued. Eventually, however, May was replaced as Prime Minster by Boris Johnson, who came to office insisting upon a fundamental renegotiation of the UK's withdrawal package. Even if many commentators doubted the sincerity of his intentions, fresh talks did result in political endorsement of a revised 'Second Withdrawal Package' in October 2019.[51]

Under that new deal, Johnson secured significant changes to the Irish border arrangements now contained in the Second (and final) Withdrawal Agreement, that would effectively lead to the partial legal and economic segregation of Northern Ireland from the rest of the UK; together with a revised Second (and final) Political Declaration, making clear that the UK wanted to pursue only a relatively distant future relationship with the Union—opening the way for the British both to diverge from existing or future EU regulatory standards and to pursue their own independent trade policy in relations with other third countries. Despite continuing parliamentary resistance, and another delay to the due date of departure, many commentators believed that Johnson would eventually have been able to pass that revised deal through the House of Commons. But instead, Johnson insisted on (and the main opposition parties eventually agreed to) holding another general election—in December 2019—at which the Conservative Party won a safe parliamentary majority. The Government was then able to abolish the troublesome 'section 13' procedure altogether and directly adopt the necessary legislation to implement the Second Withdrawal Package in domestic law.

So far, our analysis has worked through the legal and political framework and process for UK withdrawal. The remainder of our discussion will then focus on the substantive content of the final Withdrawal Package of October 2019. To begin with, Chapter 6 provides an overview of the legally binding Withdrawal Agreement: for example, its general structure; the main governance institutions and decision-making procedures; illustrations drawn from the various 'separation provisions' aimed at winding-up the lingering remnants of UK membership; the rules governing interpretation of the treaty as well as the system for dispute settlement; and the unusually prescriptive provisions concerning the internal legal status and effects of the Withdrawal Agreement, particularly within the UK legal system.

However, the bulk of our attention in Chapter 6 will be reserved for consideration of the post-withdrawal, status quo transition period provided for under the Withdrawal Agreement whereby, for a period of 11 months after becoming a third country, the UK was nevertheless treated as if it were still a Member State for a vast range of legal and regulatory purposes. That transition period was central, indeed crucial, to the objective of delivering an orderly withdrawal—not least by giving each party more time to undertake the necessary legal and logistical preparations for the full consequences of Brexit. But the transition period also raises various interesting legal questions of its own—not least the issue (once again) of how far Article 50 TEU should be interpreted as an 'exceptional' competence or legal basis, that permits the Union institutions to do or agree to things that appear unorthodox as a matter of standard EU rules and/or practices.

---

[51] Published at OJ 2019 C 384 I.

In Chapter 7, we embark upon a more detailed explanation and critique of the provisions of the Withdrawal Agreement dealing with one of the most important problems raised by UK departure from the Union: the treatment of millions of EU citizens and UK nationals who exercised their rights to free movement under the Treaties before the end of the transition period, and for whom Brexit had created a prolonged period of horrible uncertainty and anxiety about their future residency status, family unification, employment rights, and social protection.

Part Two of the Withdrawal Agreement contains the legal regime intended to guarantee the continued protection of citizens' rights in both the UK and across the Member States. However, while Part Two undoubtedly offers a significant degree of certainty and an important array of safeguards for EU citizens and UK nationals, we will explain how the provisions also suffer from various shortcomings and problems. Some of those are attributable to various 'red lines' demanded by the UK Government: for example, the power to insist that individuals falling within the potential scope of Part Two must nevertheless proactively register with the national authorities for a new immigration status in order to qualify for any future protection of their intended rights. Other issues are the result of approaches and choices supported more or at least equally by the Union itself: for example, the fact that individuals will only qualify for future protection under Part Two if the necessary qualifying periods of past residency can be considered 'lawful' as a matter of existing Union free movement law—thus incorporating familiar concerns about legal exclusion of the economically and socially most vulnerable and precarious.

In Chapter 8, we offer another detailed analysis of another of the major problems created by Brexit and addressed in the Withdrawal Agreement: the danger that UK withdrawal might lead to the creation of a 'hard border' across the island of Ireland—a prospect that would not only threaten serious economic, social, and logistical damage to both the Republic of Ireland and Northern Ireland; but also pose a severe challenge to political stability and cross-community support for the peace process underpinned by the 'Good Friday Agreement'.[52] When it came to the movement of people, the challenges were relatively straightforward to resolve—being essentially a bilateral issue between the Republic and the UK, with the latter's government accepting the importance of maintaining the existing Common Travel Area arrangements and therefore an open immigration border between the two territories. However, when it came to the movement of goods, the challenges were much more difficult, particularly given the UK's decision to leave not just the EU, but also the Customs Union and the Single Market: customs and regulatory controls must take place somewhere; if not across the island of Ireland, then the UK had to decide on an alternative location.

The solution contained in the Protocol on Ireland/Northern Ireland would succeed in avoiding a 'hard border' across the island of Ireland, while also protecting the integrity of the Customs Union and the Single Market, and paying due respect to the Johnson Government's insistence that Northern Ireland should remain formally part of the UK customs territory. But even if the Protocol works as planned, its arrangements involve certain important compromises. For the Union, the Protocol means

---

[52] Belfast (or Good Friday) Agreement of 10 April 1998.

accepting that part of the EU's own external frontiers will essentially be policed and enforced by the authorities and officials of a third country. For the British, the Protocol provides for Northern Ireland to be subject to different customs and regulatory arrangements from the rest of the UK and consequently for the erection of various barriers to trade in goods with Great Britain. For Northern Ireland itself, the Protocol imposes a novel and untested, but surely cumbersome and costly, 'dual customs regime' whereby all goods entering the territory must be allocated for the payment of EU tariffs or UK tariffs or neither. However, at the time of writing, there are tangible grounds for concern that the Johnson Government does not actually intend to facilitate full and effective application of its own agreement—being willing instead to undermine years of complex and difficult negotiations with the Union and, indeed, risk provoking a border crisis in Ireland that could directly threaten political stability in the North.

Our final substantive, Chapter 9, turns its attention away from the legally binding Withdrawal Agreement and instead towards the Political Declaration on future relations between the Union and the UK in fields such as trade and security. The revised Political Declaration of October 2019 foresees only a relatively shallow relationship between the two parties—certainly as compared to the years of UK membership of course, but even when set against other models for third country relations that had been proposed and discussed during the referendum campaign and thereafter. But the Political Declaration was never intended to be legally binding or enforceable. And within weeks of the UK's withdrawal from the Union, the Johnson Government published new plans that made clear it did not regard itself even as morally bound by its own revised Political Declaration: the already distant relationship foreseen in October 2019 was no longer distant enough for the new UK regime.

When formal negotiations on future relations finally commenced, the two parties were soon divided by fundamental disagreements on a range of key issues: for example, the nature of the 'level playing field' commitments required to ensure fair competition under any free trade agreement; the relationship between continuing access by EU fishing fleets to UK waters (on the one hand) and continuing access by UK fish suppliers to the EU market (on the other hand); as well as the nature of the UK's safeguards for fundamental rights protection, based on the European Convention on Human Rights (ECHR), as an essential prerequisite for cooperation with the Union in various fields of security, policing and anti-terrorism. Yet despite the obstacles that lay across the path to reaching a meaningful agreement, the Johnson Government absolutely refused to request an extension to the post-withdrawal, status quo transition period (as provided for under the Withdrawal Agreement) in order to create more time for the negotiations. That remained true, even despite the onset of the global health and economic crisis caused by the Covid-19 pandemic, thereby risking an abrupt 'no deal Brexit' on 1 January 2021, in the midst of an already deeply challenging situation. At the time of writing, negotiations are continuing, but the problems remain considerable.

After that extensive discussion, Chapter 10 will offer only relatively brief overall concluding remarks, including some reflections on other important issues raised by UK withdrawal, but not falling directly within the mandate of this book: for example, the idea that the UK is now set to embark upon the unprecedented process of 'de-Europeanizing' its domestic legal system by not only eliminating many of the rules and institutions of European integration itself, but also fundamentally reshaping many of the internal relationships (between the institutions of central government, as well as in relations with the devolved authorities in Scotland and Wales) that emerged during the period of UK membership. We also provide some thoughts on the converse phenomenon of 'de-Britishizing' the Union legal order, in terms of removing not only UK participation in the Union's various institutions, bodies, and agencies, but also UK influence over the content and direction of important fields of Union policy-making and (not least) the British power to control amendments to Union primary law and therefore the future constitutional evolution of the EU as a whole. Ultimately, Brexit Britain should be understood, by itself as much as by the rest of the world, as a fascinating but tragic experiment into the pitfalls of poor governance and the dangers of post-truth populism. If those lessons are learned well and help to save others from the temptation to pursue a similar fate, or at least serve to steel the determination of mainstream liberal social market democracy to confront and defeat its sworn enemies, then perhaps the UK's self-inflicted trauma will have served some useful purpose.

Before closing this introductory chapter, it seems appropriate to make three short observations.

First, it is easy to be critical of the events that dominated UK political life, and, to a lesser extent, the attention also of the Union, between 2016 and 2020, and also of the outcomes of the negotiations between the two parties over the terms of British withdrawal and the pathway to an alternative future relationship. But it is also worth bearing in mind that such criticism has benefited much from hindsight: we can now see and understand much more clearly the main challenges, the key variables, the available solutions, and their various advantages and drawbacks. But it is fair to recall that, at the time these events were actually unfolding, things were often nowhere near so clear or obvious. The problems were often completely unprecedented, the factors often only revealed themselves over time, and the answers generally emerged through learning and with improvisation. Our criticisms may well be fully justified, particularly where the final outcomes were indeed the result of deliberate political calculations that defied available evidence and analysis of their likely weaknesses and problems. But otherwise, we should be prepared to acknowledge that a great many very able people invested considerable time and effort in trying to deliver what they sincerely believed to be reasonable and workable outcomes under uncertain and difficult circumstances.

Secondly, and continuing the theme of justified criticism, the present author is happy to reiterate that he regards the UK's withdrawal from the Union as an historic and deeply unfortunate mistake, procured in part by political campaigners whose post-truth tactics are the very antithesis of the values of academic science and whose ulterior preferences and goals (in as much as they can be coherently identified) appear equally incompatible with the fundamental values of liberal social market democracy. One of the most unpleasant trends during and since the UK referendum campaign is that any academic who uses their training, qualifications, skills, knowledge, and experience to express support for the arguments made by pro-European politicians, or to challenge the claims issued by anti-Union campaigners, is immediately attacked and dismissed as 'partisan', 'activist', 'biased'. No doubt some readers will say exactly the same about this book. But it is *not* partisan to reach and express professional evaluations and judgments based on objective, evidence-based, rational analysis. On the contrary: to pretend that two sides to an argument are equal, when that is simply and patently untrue, is *in fact* and *in itself* deeply biased, since it gives credit and credibility to views that deserve neither. Indeed: in these dangerous times, to adopt an artificial stance of 'academic neutrality' amounts to an act of self-censorship that not only betrays our basic scientific vocation but also facilitates (however passively or unintentionally) the populist attack on our fundamental values.

Thirdly, this research project (like every other) needed an appropriate cut-off date before which relevant events and materials would be taken into account, but after which no further developments would be incorporated into the text or discussion. The long, tortured and uncertain process of Brexit has already forced the author (and his patient colleagues at the European University Institute and Oxford University Press) into repeated postponements of the target delivery date for a completed manuscript. Only once UK withdrawal had actually taken place, on the basis of a concrete legally binding agreement, were we able to settle on a definite date for completion and also to identify the deadline for taking account of new developments. The latter deadline was chosen as 30 June 2020, i.e. the final date, as laid down in the Withdrawal Agreement, for the EU and the UK to agree on any extension to the post-withdrawal, status quo transition period. The decision not to extend the UK's transitional arrangements at least provided a more concrete context for our analysis of the Withdrawal Agreement itself. As for the Political Declaration, it was obvious that developments would continue to drag on beyond the final date for submission of the manuscript so that particular element of our discussion would in any case have to finish on an inflection of speculation and suspense. The eventual outcome of the EU–UK negotiations will surely provide the opportunity for another book by another colleague.

2

Article 50 TEU: The Quest for an Orderly Withdrawal and the Possibility of Alternative Denouements

1. Introduction

This chapter examines the basic legal framework for withdrawal as governed by Article 50 TEU. As Section 2 explains, Article 50 TEU was introduced by the Treaty of Lisbon 2007, based on proposals previously drawn up by the Convention on the Future of Europe, so as to provide an explicit process for managing a Member State's decision to leave the Union. Once the relevant State has taken the decision to withdraw, in accordance with its own domestic constitutional requirements, the relevant State should notify its intention to the European Council. After that, the primary objective of Article 50 TEU is to provide the legal basis for an agreement between the relevant State and the Union aimed at delivering a smooth and orderly (rather than chaotic and disruptive) departure.

However, Section 3 highlights three main qualifications to the proposition that Article 50 TEU provides an effective legal basis for delivering an orderly withdrawal from the Union. In the first place, in addition to whatever bilateral arrangements might be agreed between the two parties under Article 50 TEU, any 'orderly departure' also requires the adoption of various purely unilateral measures by both the relevant State and the Union so as to prepare their respective internal legal systems for the full consequences of departure. In the second place, even when it comes to the bilateral negotiations provided for under the Treaties, the drafting of Article 50 TEU is relatively sketchy: several important questions are left open by the Treaty text and can only effectively be addressed through further legal elaboration and concrete political action. In the third place, Article 50 TEU also foresees, or at least allows for, other outcomes to the withdrawal process than a negotiated, orderly departure: including the relevant State leaving with 'no deal' in the event of the negotiations simply ending in failure; or, indeed, the possibility of unilateral revocation by the relevant State of its original notice of intention to leave.

2. Article 50 TEU and the Framework for an Orderly Withdrawal

The question of whether and how a Member State might leave the European Union had been the subject of discussion and speculation well before the issue was eventually

The UK's Withdrawal from the EU. Michael Dougan, Oxford University Press. © Michael Dougan 2021.
DOI: 10.1093/oso/9780198833475.003.0002

addressed by the Treaty of Lisbon 2007.[1] Until the latter's entry into force in 2009, the Treaties themselves failed to make any express provision for or about withdrawal. On the one hand, it was widely assumed that the possibility of leaving the Union should nevertheless be considered inherent in the sovereign prerogatives of each Member State as a matter of public international law. On the other hand, from the perspective of constitutional and legal certainty, it remained unfortunate that Union law itself prescribed no particular procedure and laid down no particular conditions to clarify and govern the possible withdrawal of a Member State.[2]

Those omissions were addressed during the constitutional reform process initiated by the Member States in December 2000. At the same time as concluding the Treaty of Nice, the Member States decided to adopt a 'Declaration on the Future of the Union' highlighting the need for a more thorough reflection upon the EU's constitutional framework.[3] The European Council held in Laeken in December 2001 then agreed a 'Declaration on the Future of the European Union' laying down more precisely the parameters for this process of constitutional reflection, and establishing a 'Convention on the Future of Europe' charged with preparing proposals for consideration at a future intergovernmental conference.[4] The Convention—composed of representatives of the Member States, the European Parliament, the national parliaments and the Commission—commenced its work in February 2002 and culminated in the presentation of a draft Treaty establishing a Constitution for Europe (or Constitutional Treaty) to the European Council in July 2003.[5] That text provided the basis for further negotiations between the Member States, leading eventually to the signature of the final Treaty establishing a Constitution for Europe (or Constitutional Treaty) on 29 October 2004.[6]

On its own terms, the Constitutional Treaty represented a very far-reaching set of proposals for reform of the Union's primary legal instruments.[7] It would have reconstituted the Union upon an entirely new and much simplified set of legal foundations. Most of the existing EU Treaties would have been repealed and replaced in their entirety; the 'pillar structure' introduced at Maastricht would have been dismantled; the European Community abolished as a distinct legal entity. Instead, there would have been a unitary European Union, based upon a single foundational text, and possessing its own legal personality. The Constitutional Treaty would also have carried out a multitude of more detailed reforms to many aspects of the Union's functioning and activities: for example, as regards the structure of and relations between the institutions, the

---

[1] See further, e.g. Łazowski, 'Withdrawal from the European Union and Alternatives to Membership', 37 ELRev (2012) 523.

[2] See further, e.g. Dashwood et al., 'Draft Constitutional Treaty of the European Union and Related Documents', 28 ELRev (2003) 3.

[3] See European Council, *Presidency Conclusions of 8 December 2000*.

[4] See European Council, *Presidency Conclusions of 14 December 2001*.

[5] OJ 2003 C 169. For analysis, see e.g. Dougan, 'The Convention's Draft Constitutional Treaty: Bringing Europe Closer to its Lawyers?', 28 ELRev (2003) 763; Kokott and Ruth, 'The European Convention and its Draft Treaty Establishing a Constitution for Europe: Appropriate Answers to the Laeken Questions?', 40 CMLRev (2003) 1315.

[6] OJ 2004 C 310. For analysis, see e.g. Dashwood, 'The EU Constitution: What Will Really Change?' 7 *Cambridge Yearbook of European Legal Studies* (2004/2005) 33.

[7] See further, e.g. A. Arnull, A. Dashwood, M. Dougan, M. Ross, E. Spaventa, and D. Wyatt, *Wyatt and Dashwood's EU Law* (5th ed, 2006) Chapter 11.

range of competences exercised by and legal instruments available to the Union, and the protection of human rights and fundamental freedoms.

Among the reform proposals drawn up by the Convention on the Future of Europe and included in the draft Constitutional Treaty was an express provision for the possibility of withdrawal from the Union. However, the relevant proposals were introduced relatively late in the Convention's working life and without having been subject to its standard process of detailed deliberation and debate among dedicated working groups. Instead, a draft 'withdrawal clause' was first presented to the Convention by the governing Praesidium on 2 April 2003.[8] The Praesidium's draft withdrawal clause then underwent several amendments within the Convention, before emerging as a firm proposal for inclusion in the draft Constitutional Treaty as presented to the Member States.[9] The subsequent intergovernmental conference agreed further adaptations to the draft Constitutional Treaty as a whole, and the proposed withdrawal clause in particular, before settling on the agreed text of the final Constitutional Treaty—which was then to be submitted for national ratification across the Member States.[10]

With hindsight, some of the discussions suggested by the publicly available documentation concerning the drafting of the Constitutional Treaty appear particularly relevant to the UK's eventual experience of withdrawal. For example: the Praesidium's introduction to, and more detailed commentary on, the initial draft withdrawal clause of April 2003 seemed to envisage that any withdrawal agreement between the Union and the withdrawing State should not only resolve the immediate issues required to ensure an orderly departure, but also seek to establish the new legal framework that would govern future relations between the Union and the withdrawing State—though without making any such agreement an actual condition for withdrawal, so as not to void the concept of voluntary withdrawal of its substance.

However, the actual text of the draft withdrawal clause provided that the Union should conclude an agreement with the relevant State 'setting out the arrangements for its withdrawal, taking account of the framework for its future relationship with the Union'. That text that does not clearly support the interpretation apparently intended by the original drafters, but instead suggests a clearer distinction between (on the one hand) an agreement on the immediate arrangements for departure, to be concluded under the proposed withdrawal clause and (on the other hand) any subsequent treaty on future relations between the Union and the withdrawing State. That drafting was preserved into the final version of the withdrawal clause as contained in the draft Constitutional Treaty and endorsed by the Convention in July 2003. As we shall see, this question—of whether the withdrawal clause itself could provide an appropriate legal basis for an agreement establishing, not only the immediate conditions for withdrawal, but also new terms for the Union's future engagement with its former Member State—proved critical to decisions about the proper scope, sequence and timing of withdrawal negotiations between the Union and the UK.[11]

---

[8] CONV 648/03.
[9] Article 59 in draft Treaty establishing a Constitution for Europe of 18 July 2003: CONV 850/03.
[10] Article I-60 in final Treaty establishing a Constitution for Europe 2004, OJ 2004 C 310.
[11] See, in particular, Chapter 4.

The Constitutional Treaty was to be ratified by the High Contracting Parties in accordance with their respective constitutional requirements, with a view to entering into force on 1 November 2006. However, the new agreement was rejected by popular referenda in France (on 29 May 2005) and the Netherlands (on 1 June 2005). In June 2007, the European Council agreed to declare the Constitutional Treaty dead and approved the mandate for another intergovernmental conference charged with drafting an alternative 'Reform Treaty'.[12] That Reform Treaty was to shed the form, language and symbols of a 'European Constitution', in favour of having another amending Treaty, similar in nature to the Treaties of Amsterdam and Nice; but within this new garb, it was to preserve as many as possible of the technical reforms proposed under the old Constitutional Treaty which were intended to improve the Union's effectiveness, efficiency, and accountability. The Reform Treaty—which became known as the Treaty of Lisbon—was signed by the Member States on 13 December 2007 and (notwithstanding some additional ratification problems, particularly though not solely in Ireland) entered into force on 1 December 2009.[13] Thus, after nearly a decade of complex negotiations and often bitter disputes, the reform process initiated at Nice and Laeken had succeeded in providing a new constitutional and legal framework for the institutions and activities of the European Union.[14]

Among the provisions carried over from the defunct Constitutional Treaty into the Treaty of Lisbon was, of course, the introduction of an explicit withdrawal clause in Article 50 TEU:

1. Any Member State may decide to withdraw from the Union in accordance with its own constitutional requirements.
2. A Member State which decides to withdraw shall notify the European Council of its intention. In the light of the guidelines provided by the European Council, the Union shall negotiate and conclude an agreement with that State, setting out the arrangements for its withdrawal, taking account of the framework for its future relationship with the Union. That agreement shall be negotiated in accordance with Article 218(3) of the Treaty on the Functioning of the European Union.[15] It shall be concluded on behalf of the Union by the Council, acting by a qualified majority, after obtaining the consent of the European Parliament.
3. The Treaties shall cease to apply to the State in question from the date of entry into force of the withdrawal agreement or, failing that, two years after the notification referred to in paragraph 2, unless the European Council, in agreement with the Member State concerned, unanimously decides to extend this period.

---

[12] See European Council, *Presidency Conclusions of 23 June 2007*.

[13] Consolidated texts of the post-Lisbon TEU and TFEU (as well as their Protocols and Declarations) were published as OJ 2010 C 83 (though subsequently updated in the light of further, albeit more minor, Treaty amendments).

[14] See further, e.g. Dougan, 'The Treaty of Lisbon 2007: Winning Minds, Not Hearts', 45 *CMLRev* (2008) 617.

[15] Art 218(3) TFEU: 'The Commission ... shall submit recommendations to the Council, which shall adopt a decision authorising the opening of negotiations and, depending on the subject of the agreement envisaged, nominating the Union negotiator or the head of the Union's negotiating team'.

4. For the purposes of paragraphs 2 and 3, the member of the European Council or of the Council representing the withdrawing Member State shall not participate in the discussions of the European Council or Council or in decisions concerning it. A qualified majority shall be defined in accordance with Article 238(3)(b) of the Treaty on the Functioning of the European Union.[16]

5. If a State which has withdrawn from the Union asks to rejoin, its request shall be subject to the procedure referred to in Article 49.[17]

As the CJEU held in the *Wightman* case, Article 50 TEU pursues two objectives: first, it enshrines the sovereign right of a Member State to withdraw from the European Union; and secondly, it establishes a procedure to enable such withdrawal to take place in an orderly fashion.[18] And within the context of Article 50 TEU, the Treaties assume that an 'orderly withdrawal' should be facilitated primarily by means of an international agreement between the Union and the relevant State. Any such withdrawal agreement would need to address and settle the various 'separation challenges' which are inherent in the very act of leaving the EU (having regard, as Article 50 TEU explicitly states, also to the likely nature of the longer-term future relationship between the Union and the relevant State). And many of those 'separation challenges' had already been anticipated and discussed well before the organization and outcome of the UK's 2016 referendum: for example, determining the relevant State's outstanding financial commitments and liabilities towards the Union; defining the future status of natural and legal persons who had already made use of their rights to free movement between the Union and the relevant State before the latter's departure; and (in the specific context of the UK's decision to leave the EU) addressing the acute problems that withdrawal would inevitably entail for the maintenance of an open land border across the island of Ireland.

3. Limitations of the Article 50 TEU Vision of a Negotiated Orderly Withdrawal

The process of delivering an orderly withdrawal through the medium of a negotiated agreement, within the specific sense envisaged under Article 50 TEU, commenced when the UK finally delivered its notification of intention to withdraw on 29 March

---

[16] Art 238(3)(b) TFEU: 'the qualified majority shall be defined as at least 72% of the members of the Council representing the participating Member States, comprising at least 65% of the population of these States'.

[17] Art 49 TEU: 'Any European State which respects the values referred to in Article 2 and is committed to promoting them may apply to become a member of the Union. The European Parliament and national Parliaments shall be notified of this application. The applicant State shall address its application to the Council, which shall act unanimously after consulting the Commission and after receiving the consent of the European Parliament, which shall act by a majority of its component members. The conditions of eligibility agreed upon by the European Council shall be taken into account. The conditions of admission and the adjustments to the Treaties on which the Union is founded, which such admission entails, shall be the subject of an agreement between the Member States and the applicant State. This agreement shall be submitted for ratification by all the contracting States in accordance with their respective constitutional requirements'.

[18] Case C-621/18, *Wightman* (EU:C:2018:999), at para 56.

2017,[19] paving the way for formal negotiations with the Union to begin on 19 June 2017.[20] In Chapter 3, we will explore many of the key legal and political factors that shaped the processes of notification and negotiation right from their very outset: both as regards the Union (the detailed allocation of decision-making responsibilities across the institutions, combined with the clear articulation of core principles to guide the negotiations); and concerning the UK (which was afflicted by serious political instability, while being forced to experiment with novel institutional arrangements, having failed to make adequate preparations for such contingencies in advance of the referendum itself).

At this point, however, it is important to emphasize and explore three key qualifications to the basic assumption underpinning Article 50 TEU and its quest for an orderly withdrawal based on a negotiated agreement: first, the fact that an orderly withdrawal also requires various *unilateral* measures by both the Union and the relevant State in order to prepare their respective legal systems for the full *internal* consequences of departure; secondly, the problem that Article 50 TEU itself is drafted in only relatively sketchy terms, even when it comes to the task of agreeing on a joint solution to shared 'separation challenges', thus leaving open various important questions about its correct interpretation and application; and thirdly, the possibility that the Article 50 TEU process might end, not in an orderly withdrawal based upon a negotiated settlement, but in some other outcome—whether a 'no deal' departure, or perhaps even a decision by the relevant State to 'revoke and remain'.

A. Unilateral as well as Agreed Preparations for an Orderly Withdrawal

Regardless of any agreement designed to address the various 'separation challenges' posed by withdrawal, the latter prospect will, in any event, require certain unilateral measures by the relevant State, the Union institutions and the remaining Member States, so as to prepare their respective internal legal orders for those consequences which are inherent in or inevitable from the very act of departure.[21]

In the case of the Union, the formal consequences of the UK's withdrawal for the maintenance of a fully functioning internal legal system proved to be relatively limited in nature and extent. Perhaps the most high-profile act of internal preparation for Brexit was the physical relocation to the remaining Member States of those Union regulatory agencies previously based in the UK: the European Medicines Agency moved to The Netherlands, the European Banking Authority to France, and the Galileo Security Monitoring Centre back-up site to Spain.[22] Less obvious but of at least

---

[19] HMG, *Prime Minister's Notification Letter to President of the European Council* (29 March 2017).

[20] See Commission, *Terms of Reference for the Article 50 TEU negotiations* (19 June 2017).

[21] There are also important questions about the impact of a Member State's withdrawal from the Union, upon existing external agreements and relationships with third countries/international organizations as governed by Union law: see further Chapter 4.

[22] See Regulation 2018/1718 amending Regulation 726/2004 as regards the location of the seat of the European Medicines Agency, OJ 2018 L 291/3; Regulation 2018/1717 amending Regulation 1093/2010 as regards the location of the seat of the European Banking Authority, OJ 2018 L 291/1; Commission Implementing Decision 2018/115 amending, as regards the location of the Galileo Security Monitoring

equal importance for the integrity of the Union legal order, the Commission under-took a screening exercise aimed at identifying which existing Union regulatory regimes would need to be formally amended so as to reflect the fact of UK departure.[23] For example: the UK would need to be allocated to the appropriate list, both of those countries whose nationals are required to be in possession of a visa when crossing the external borders of the Member States, and of those countries whose nationals are exempt from any visa requirement for stays of no more than three months.[24]

Beyond those limited adaptations, the Union's working assumption appears to have been that references to the UK in primary and all remaining secondary Union law could effectively be treated as defunct pending their formal amendment or repeal in due course. For example: it was obvious that Protocol No 15 to the Treaties, containing the UK's permanent right to derogate from participation in the Single Currency, no longer served any meaningful purpose and was effectively devoid of further legal effects.[25]

It is worth noting that (unlike Article 49 TEU on the accession of new Member States) Article 50 TEU does not provide an explicit legal basis for any withdrawal agreement between the Union and the relevant State (or indeed for the Union institutions themselves) to implement any adjustments to the Treaties (or to secondary Union law) even if such changes are directly entailed by the relevant State's departure. The Commission's programme of necessary regulatory adaptations, as well as any future efforts to eliminate lingering references to the UK from the Union legal system, were and will have to be undertaken according to the procedure/s ordinarily applicable under the Treaties for amendment of the relevant provisions—according to their status within the hierarchy of norms and in accordance with the applicable legal basis/bases.

By contrast, the task facing the UK was significantly more daunting. After all, the UK legal system had evolved for over 45 years under the influence of and in combination with Union law.[26] For the UK as much as for any other Member State, EU law had come virtually to dominate certain regulatory sectors, while others remained largely untouched. And as we know: in some fields, the EU develops a systematic and coherent legal framework, while elsewhere its interventions prove to be more ad hoc and limited; many EU measures set out general objectives or principles, which the Member States are expected to translate into more concrete rules, rights and duties using essentially national concepts and instruments; Member States (including the UK during its period of membership) have often decided to 'gold plate' their basic EU

Centre, Implementing Decision 2016/413 determining the location of the ground-based infrastructure of the system established under the Galileo programme and setting out the necessary measures to ensure that it functions smoothly, OJ 2018 L 20/14.

[23] See, in particular: COM(2018) 556 Final/2; COM(2018) 880 Final; COM(2018) 890 Final; COM(2019) 195 Final; COM(2019) 276 Final; COM(2019) 394 Final.
[24] See, e.g. COM(2018) 556 Final/2—referring to Regulation 2018/1806 listing the third countries whose nationals must be in possession of visas when crossing the external borders and those whose nationals are exempt from that requirement, OJ 2018 L 303/39.
[25] On the UK's special position under the AFSJ, and its potential relevance to Ireland's continuing rights as a Member State, see further Chapter 8.
[26] See further, e.g. S. de Mars, EU Law in the UK (2020).

obligations by extending the latter's scope of application or adding additional substantive content; and, of course, many EU measures offer the Member States a range of options, derogations and exclusions during the process of incorporation and/or transposition into national law.

The highly intertwined relationship between EU and UK law therefore posed a major internal challenge for the British: that of preparing their domestic legal system for the very act of withdrawal, without creating damaging regulatory vacuums or intolerable legal uncertainty. After all, if the UK were simply to have waltzed out of the EU (as many Leave campaigners seriously argued it should) without any adequate preparations to safeguard basic regulatory continuity, the internal consequences would have been disastrous, creating a state of outright legal chaos and administrative malfunction across the country. Large tracts and indeed whole sectors of regulation would simply have disappeared since huge numbers of domestic implementing measures, as well as directly effective regulations and Treaty provisions, would no longer have enjoyed a valid legal basis or existence under UK law. Another considerable range of existing legislative frameworks, while they might not have simply disappeared altogether, would still have been rendered unworkable or nonsensical: for example, because it would no longer have been possible to identify any competent decision-maker or because the flow of crucial information from the Union institutions or competent authorities in other Member States would have ceased.

As a direct result, huge numbers of both public and private relationships might immediately and without notice have become subject to entirely different rules (if one could even have managed to identify which rules applied at all). Regardless of one's view on the overall merits or shortcomings of Brexit, and entirely besides the negotiations taking place between the EU and the UK under Article 50 TEU to address their mutual 'separation challenges', the goal of an orderly withdrawal clearly demanded that the UK legal system also provide an effective internal mechanism for preserving regulatory continuity and legal certainty so as to protect the finality of public decisions, safeguard the effectiveness of state administration and guarantee the stability of private relationships.[27]

The UK Government's strategy for tackling those essentially internal challenges was first sketched out in its White Paper on *The United Kingdom's Exit from and New Partnership with the European Union* (February 2017);[28] then described in greater detail in the White Paper on *Legislating for the United Kingdom's Withdrawal from the European Union* (March 2017).[29] The basic plan can be summarized as follows. Legal continuity and legal certainty would be best served by existing EU law remaining, in principle, part of the UK legal system: either by retention (where EU rules are already implemented into UK law) or by incorporation (where EU rules are not already so implemented). However, that initial presumption of retention/incorporation should be subject to various important exceptions and limitations. For example, EU-derived

---

[27] See further, e.g. Dougan, 'The Charter's Contribution to Human Rights in the UK Before and After Brexit' in A. Iliopoulou Penot and L. Xenou (eds), *La charte des droits fondamentaux, source de renouveau constitutionnel européen?* (2020).

[28] Cm 9417.

[29] Cm 9446.

rules should no longer enjoy primacy over subsequent domestic legislation, while continued legal recognition for the Charter of Fundamental Rights should be rejected entirely. Moreover, even as regards those EU-derived instruments which were to be retained as a matter of domestic UK law, there would still need to be an extensive programme of legislative adaptation, to ensure that the relevant rules remained operational outside their original context of EU membership: for example, by replacing references to Union decision makers with a suitable domestic alternative. Such amendments should be implemented largely by means of secondary legislation adopted by the Government (albeit subject to parliamentary oversight).

Those plans together provided the basis for the European Union (Withdrawal) Bill as presented to the Westminster Parliament on 13 July 2017.[30] The Bill was widely regarded as perhaps the most important item of constitutional legislation to be presented to the UK legislature, certainly since 1972, if not for considerably longer and it raised some very difficult (if not altogether troubling) questions about the nature and functioning of UK democracy.[31] The House of Commons and the House of Lords proposed hundreds of amendments, while the UK Government became embroiled in serious disputes with the administrations in Scotland and Wales over the Bill's impact upon devolved powers.[32] The legislative process took significantly longer than the Government had planned or hoped, but the final European Union (Withdrawal) Act was eventually adopted on 26 June 2018.[33] In accordance with the Government's original plans, the 2018 Act immediately initiated a further titanic regulatory process whereby huge numbers of secondary instruments, aimed at 'correcting' retained EU measures for the post-withdrawal era, were proposed, scrutinized and adopted.[34]

Following Theresa May's replacement as Prime Minister by Boris Johnson and the latter's victory in the general election of December 2019, the 2018 legislation was promptly and substantially amended by the European Union (Withdrawal Agreement) Act 2020. Those amendments were partly required so as to adapt the UK's purely internal system of retention, incorporation and adaptation, to the final terms

---

[30] Available at https://publications.parliament.uk/pa/bills/cbill/2017-2019/0005/18005.pdf.

[31] Consider, e.g. House of Lords Select Committee on the Constitution, *The 'Great Repeal Bill' and Delegated Powers* (HL123 of 7 March 2017); House of Lords Select Committee on the Constitution, *European Union (Withdrawal) Bill: Interim Report* (HL19 of 7 September 2017); House of Lords Delegated Powers and Regulatory Reform Committee, *European Union (Withdrawal) Bill* (HL22 of 28 September 2017); House of Commons Procedure Committee, *Scrutiny of Delegated Legislation under the European Union (Withdrawal) Bill: Interim Report* (HC386 of 6 November 2017); House of Commons Exiting the European Union Committee, *European Union (Withdrawal) Bill* (HC373 of 17 November 2017).

[32] In fact, the Scottish Parliament withheld its consent to adoption of the European Union (Withdrawal) Act 2018 but, after the UK Supreme Court ruling in *Miller v Secretary of State of Exiting the European Union* [2017] UKSC 5, devolved consent to Westminster legislation affecting devolved powers is to be treated merely as a political expectation rather than a legally enforceable requirement.

[33] See further, e.g. Elliott and Tierney, 'Political Pragmatism and Constitutional Principle: The European Union (Withdrawal) Act 2018', *Public Law* [2019] 37.

[34] See https://www.gov.uk/eu-withdrawal-act-2018-statutory-instruments. Note also the work of the House of Commons European Statutory Instruments Committee (https://www.parliament.uk/business/committees/committees-a-z/commons-select/european-statutory-instruments/) and of the House of Lords Secondary Legislation Scrutiny Committee (https://www.parliament.uk/business/committees/committees-a-z/lords-select/secondary-legislation-scrutiny-committee/). And note further, e.g. House of Commons Procedure Committee, *Scrutiny of Delegated Legislation under the European Union (Withdrawal) Act 2018* (HC1395 of 9 July 2018).

of the Withdrawal Agreement reached with the EU under the auspices of Article 50 TEU. For example, the extensive obligations applicable to the UK during the post-withdrawal, status quo transition period required the effective postponement of the UK's deadline for calculating precisely which EU-derived rules were to be retained/incorporated under domestic law; as well as the precise date for entry into force of the myriad adaptations to which those rules would in turn become subject.[35] However, the Johnson Government also insisted upon a range of additional amendments to the 2018 Act, not strictly required for the purposes of domestic implementation of the Withdrawal Agreement itself, but instead reflecting the new regime's desire to weaken still further the future status of EU-derived rules within the UK legal system once the transition period had expired.[36]

Moreover, it was always understood that the 2018 Act provided only a baseline solution to the problems of regulatory continuity and legal certainty posed by Brexit. In sectors such as customs, trade, agriculture, fisheries, and immigration, the option of simply retaining or replicating EU rules (even in some substantially amended or adapted form) was simply not a realistic means of plugging the legislative gap directly resulting from the very act of withdrawal. The UK would instead have to design, adopt, and implement entirely new policies and regulatory frameworks to govern such fields—and do so in time for withdrawal, or at least for the end of the transition period.[37]

Furthermore, even our brief summary of the internal regulatory preparations required simply to stabilize each party's own legal system in readiness for the inevitable consequences of withdrawal, needs to be read in the context of the much broader practical and logistical challenges facing a wide range of public and private actors both across the Union and within the UK—all of whom were expected to ready themselves and their activities for the full consequences of treating the UK (and its natural or legal persons or residents) as a third country (and its citizens as third country nationals) in accordance with whatever legal regime would govern their future relations after withdrawal had been completed. Consider, for example, the need for massive investment in infrastructure and staff to cope with the large-scale introduction of customs procedures, including the challenge of suitably adapting port facilities at those sites engaged in handling significant volumes of EU–UK trade; as well as the particular burdens of unfamiliar border bureaucracy that would inevitably fall upon small and medium-sized undertakings previously accustomed to the relative luxury of free movement across the Internal Market.[38]

---

[35] See the provisions of European Union (Withdrawal) Act 2018 (as amended), especially sections 1A and 1B.

[36] See the provisions of European Union (Withdrawal) Act 2018 (as amended), especially section 6.

[37] Consider the 'Brexit Bills' in the Government's legislative agenda (Queen's Speech) of 21 June 2017. At the time of writing, certain of the Government's planned 'Brexit Bills' have already been enacted into legislation (e.g. the Haulage Permits and Trailer Registration Act 2018, the Sanctions and Anti-Money Laundering Act 2018, the Nuclear Safeguards Act 2018 and the Taxation (Cross-Border Trade) Act 2018); while others remain to be adopted by Parliament in due course (e.g. in the fields of agriculture, fisheries, trade and immigration, and social security coordination).

[38] See, e.g. the Commission's myriad sectoral notices on preparing for the full impact of UK withdrawal, available via https://ec.europa.eu/info/european-union-and-united-kingdom-forging-new-partnership/future-partnership/getting-ready-end-transition-period_en.

B. Overcoming the Sketchy Drafting of Article 50 TEU

Our second key qualification to the Treaties' primary assumption of an orderly withdrawal based on a negotiated settlement, is that the procedure for delivering that specific outcome, as established by Article 50 TEU, as well as its interaction with the relevant State's sovereign right to withdraw, are only sketchily described by the written text of Article 50 TEU itself. Many important issues potentially raised by the overall process of departure from the Union are left wholly or partially unanswered. That might well reflect the relatively unsatisfactory manner (limited deliberation and scrutiny) by which the core provisions of the withdrawal clause emerged and evolved during and after the Convention on the Future of Europe. But it also reflects the simple fact that (like so much law) Article 50 TEU cannot foresee and provide for every potential eventuality. Moreover, it is inevitable that a provision which has never been used before cannot draw upon past practice and precedent to help inform and answer our current problems and questions. As a result, for much of the period following the 2016 referendum, events were throwing up important questions but with few clear answers already to hand.[39]

For example, precisely which form should a 'decision to withdraw' from the Union actually take? Might it even be presumed from events in the relevant Member State; or at the very least, must it be formally communicated by the competent authorities to the Union institutions and remaining Member States? Even then: how far should the Union be expected to double-check that the authorities which delivered a formal communication of intention to withdraw, were indeed 'competent' to do so as a matter of domestic constitutional law within the relevant State? Should it be possible for the relevant State to deliver a conditional notification of its intention to withdraw, thereby explicitly leaving open the possibility (right from the outset) of changing its mind unilaterally in the event of certain contingencies occurring (or failing to occur)? Should an apparently unconditional notification of intention to withdraw be treated as final and binding, or might such notification be rescinded, if and when the relevant Member State subsequently changes its mind and decides to remain? And in the latter situation: may such revocation be made unilaterally by the relevant Member State, or does it remain subject to the agreement also of certain Union actors and (if so) precisely which actors, according to which procedures and subject to which conditions?

The fact that the text of Article 50 TEU fails to offer explicit or compelling answers to so many of the key questions raised by withdrawal means that we must search elsewhere for solutions. But that search creates a potentially difficult constitutional and political challenge. On the one hand, the inherent uncertainty of Article 50 TEU could be interpreted to mean that the Treaty drafters consciously intended the Union's political institutions to play a central role in elaborating the more detailed procedure, scope, and conditions for delivering an orderly departure. By design and by necessity, operationalizing Article 50 TEU calls for significant political discretion and

---

[39] See further, e.g. J. Carmona, C.-C. Cîrlig and G. Sgueo, *UK Withdrawal from the European Union: Legal and Procedural Issues* (In-Depth Analysis commissioned by the European Parliamentary Research Service, PE 599.352 of March 2017); Eeckhout and Frantziou, 'Brexit and Article 50 TEU: A constitutionalist reading', 54 *CMLRev* (2017) 695.

judgment—not least in defining and pursuing the Union's values and objectives, as well as its non-negotiable red lines. That applies when setting the overall agenda, when conducting the appropriate negotiations, in reaching a suitable agreement, and when it comes to making adequate preparations for a wide range of potential outcomes.

On the other hand, the Union remains an organization governed by the rule of law and Article 50 TEU must still be located within a broader system of constitutional principles. Even allowing for the importance of political discretion in steering and managing the withdrawal process, the Union's conduct should still comply with certain fundamental legal rules and expectations—such as the principle of conferred powers in relations between the Union and its Member States, the principle of inter-institutional balance in relations between the Union institutions inter se, and the protection of fundamental rights and basic principles of good governance (under the Charter of Fundamental Rights and/or the general principles of Union law) in relations with citizens and other natural or legal persons.

For example: although Article 50 TEU envisages the negotiation of a withdrawal agreement to make arrangements for the relevant State's departure, the Treaty text gives no indication whatsoever about what precise range of 'separation challenges' might need to be addressed. Quite legitimately, the Union institutions need to exercise a considerable political judgment in drawing up the necessary agenda. But what happens if their choices about what to address, in order to deliver an orderly withdrawal, appear relatively arbitrary: say, making provision to wind down the Union rules applicable to the movement of goods between the Single Market and the territory of the relevant State at the point of withdrawal; but failing to make any comparable provision to govern the very similar problems and challenges affecting the movement of services?[40]

Or again: Article 50 TEU seems to direct the Union institutions to reach an agreement with the relevant State 'setting out the arrangements for [the latter's] withdrawal', thereby leaving longer-term relations in fields such as trade and security to be negotiated and settled by the Union and its erstwhile Member State after the latter's departure and in accordance with the Union's ordinary external relations competences. As we shall see further, particularly in Chapter 4, that is precisely the interpretation endorsed and pursued by the Union institutions. But it still raises the question: how far might the Article 50 TEU agreement legitimately seek to address certain 'separation challenges' that are admittedly immediate in nature, by making provision for arrangements that would nevertheless and in fact endure for a very considerable period of time, potentially even on an indefinite basis, thus blurring the distinction between the Union's specific power to arrange the relevant State's 'orderly withdrawal' and its general competences to agree on a new 'future relationship'?

A final example is what happens if the proposed Article 50 TEU agreement tackles the 'separation challenges' involved in delivering an orderly withdrawal by proposing solutions that fall outside our normal understanding of the Union's own exclusive competences under the Treaties and touch instead upon those competences shared between the Union and its Member States? In particular, notwithstanding the requirement in Article 50 TEU for approval by a super-majority in the Council acting with

---

[40] On which: see further the discussion in Chapters 4 and 6.

the consent of the European Parliament, would it be open to any Member State, in such circumstances, to insist that the withdrawal agreement must also be ratified at the domestic level by the national and (where applicable) regional parliaments? That is what our ordinary expectations under Union constitutional law would lead us to assume, but such an interpretation would surely alter the entire dynamic of the Article 50 TEU process and potentially even endanger the chances of successfully delivering its core objective of an orderly, negotiated withdrawal.[41]

The fact that the Treaty framework governing withdrawal was both novel and underdeveloped would therefore inevitably compel the Union institutions to make the choices and decisions necessary to convert Article 50 TEU into a genuinely operational legal process and properly effective legal basis. And we shall see, the peculiar UK experience of withdrawal has already helped to illuminate and resolve many of the questions and choices originally left open by the bare text of Article 50 TEU, even if some other important issues were not specifically explored (or at least definitively settled) during the process of UK departure per se. But it is important, at the outset of this study, to highlight an additional body of considerations that also bear upon the Union's interpretation and application of Article 50 TEU. While such choices and decisions may have been prompted under the immediate pressure of managing the urgent UK situation, they were also capable of producing impacts and creating precedents for a broader range of situations and from a wider array of perspectives than the 'Brexit crisis' itself.

The point is true most obviously when it comes to the prospect of another withdrawal. Of course, that is something which neither the Union institutions nor the remaining Member States want. On the contrary, they may well hope that the problematic process undergone by the UK will act as a powerful deterrent to any future government minded to advocate the withdrawal of its own Member State. But the possibility cannot be ruled out that another State may eventually decide that it also wishes to leave the Union. In interpreting and applying Article 50 TEU in relations with the UK, the relevant Union actors may not have had any previous experience to call upon. But their decisions and actions were not merely ad hoc responses to a series of discrete enquiries. They constituted a series of interconnected legal and political factors that together have now created an identifiable body of 'withdrawal law and practice' whose principles and limits will also shape the conduct and outcomes of any subsequent departures.

Yet the UK experience is capable of creating precedents in other ways too. Consider the Union's relations with a wider range of third countries and other international organizations. The Union may well insist in its external relations that the 'four freedoms' are indivisible and there can be no 'cherry-picking' from amongst the various elements of the Single Market.[42] But how far might it decide to depart from that insistence (for example) in the context of negotiating a new relationship with a former Member

---

[41] On which: see further the discussion in Chapter 3.
[42] In the UK context, e.g. European Council (Article 50), *Guidelines of 29 April 2017* and *Guidelines of 23 March 2018*; European Parliament, *Resolution on the framework of the future EU-UK relationship* (14 March 2018). But also (say) in the Swiss context, e.g. Council, *Conclusions on a homogenous extended single market and EU relations with Non-EU Western European countries* (16 December 2014), especially at para 45.

State, so as to protect the Union's own interests against significant economic disruption or disadvantage? And in that case: how much more difficult might it then become, in discussions with other third countries, for the Union to offer a principled defence of the supposed indivisibility of the four freedoms and the sacred integrity of the Single Market? Not that precedents need only be restrictive or inconvenient; they can also be creative and open up new possibilities for cooperation. For example: the departure of an existing Member State might well prompt the Union to consider designing alternative pathways to external engagement with its own regulatory bodies and agencies—offering not just former Member States but also other third countries greater opportunities for joint collaboration and participation than those which had hitherto been available.[43]

The immediate uncertainties and challenges involved in managing the particular UK experience of withdrawal are not only capable of creating important legal and political precedents for any future possible departure of another Member State, or for the conduct of the Union's external relations with a broader range of other third countries. The Union's handling of the UK's departure is also capable of stimulating knock-on consequences for the development of the Union's own internal constitutional principles. After all, the choices which need to be made about the interpretation and application of Article 50 TEU need to be resolved by reference to, and anchored securely within, the wider Union legal order.

In the first place, the sovereign right of the relevant State to withdraw from the Union needs to be balanced against the equally legitimate interests of the Union institutions and the remaining Member States in preserving and protecting their common interests. Yet the very act of engaging in that delicate balancing exercise may in itself provoke considerable debate about precisely what the Union's common interests are and how they should best be defended. As Hillion has argued, the withdrawal of one Member State effectively forces the others to articulate what their Union membership really means: its fundamental values; its unique characteristics; the special privileges of membership; the particular obligations that accompany them.[44] And the legacy of that self-reflective process of debate and articulation—the tangible products of a more focused and refined legal definition and political understanding of what Union membership actually means—could form a lasting part of the Union's constitutional law and discourse long after the relevant State's withdrawal has been completed.

In the second place, that process of constitutional debate about the impact of withdrawal upon the Union's own legal order includes deciding how far the highly unusual circumstances of a Member State's departure from the Union should nevertheless be treated fully in accordance with the principles and limitations which are already familiar from the rest of Union law or, instead, how far the legal basis for withdrawal provided for under Article 50 TEU should be construed and applied somehow as an exceptional Union competence capable of deviating from our ordinary constitutional expectations. The Union is already familiar with such challenges—not least from

---

[43] See further, e.g. House of Commons Library Briefing Paper, *EU Agencies and Post-Brexit Options* (No 7957 of 28 April 2017).

[44] Hillion, 'Withdrawal under Article 50 TEU: An Integration-Friendly Process', 55 *CMLRev Special Issue* (2018) 29.

experiences such as the Eurozone crisis or the migration crisis—both of which called for novel legal solutions to extreme political challenges in a way that prompted many scholars to voice reservations over the degree to which law must serve the interests of realpolitik even in the midst of a potentially existential crisis.[45] Withdrawal presents a similar dilemma: just how exceptional a legal basis and competence might the apparently bland and vague terms of Article 50 TEU need and/or prove to be in order to allow the Union institutions to act flexibility and appropriately in the defence of their strategic interests under novel and complex circumstances, even if that comes at the expense of clarity, predictability, and respect for supposedly fundamental legal principles?

C. The Possibility of Alternative Outcomes to the Article 50 TEU Process

Our final key qualification to the basic assumption underpinning the Treaties' quest for an orderly withdrawal, is the possibility that the Article 50 TEU process will eventually produce some other outcome than a negotiated settlement. Two alternative potential denouements were much discussed within the UK context: the risk of a 'no deal Brexit'; and the possibility of a British decision to 'revoke and remain'.

(i) 'No Deal Brexit'
It remained a substantial possibility, throughout the period after June 2016, that the UK might leave the Union without any negotiated settlement in place to minimize the full impacts of withdrawal. Indeed, once the relevant State has delivered its formal notification of intention to depart from the Union, a 'no deal exit' becomes the default outcome as provided for under Article 50 TEU. Every other possibility involves taking some more positive action in order to dislodge the countdown to a 'no deal exit': concluding a withdrawal agreement; requesting and agreeing to an extension; revoking the original notification of intention to depart. At some points in the EU–UK negotiations, the chances of outright failure appeared to be so high that a 'no deal Brexit' even felt like the most likely outcome to the Article 50 TEU process.[46] Indeed, certain commentators believed that a 'no deal Brexit' was actually the *preferred* outcome of a significant proportion of the parliamentary Conservative Party and (at least for some time) of the Johnson Government when it first assumed power in July 2019.[47] In any case, both the Union and the UK were forced to undertake contingency plans aimed at mitigating the adverse impacts of any potential 'no deal' outcome.

---

[45] See further, e.g. Ruffert, 'The European Debt Crisis and European Union Law', 48 *CMLRev* (2011) 1777; de Gregorio Merino, 'Legal Developments in the Economic and Monetary Union during the Debt Crisis: The Mechanisms of Financial Assistance', 49 *CMLRev* (2012) 1613; Chiti and Gustavo Teixeira, 'The Constitutional Implications of the European Responses to the Financial and Public Debt Crisis', 50 *CMLRev* (2013) 683.

[46] Consider, e.g. Commission, *Statement by the European Commission on the vote on the Withdrawal Agreement in the House of Commons* (29 March 2019).

[47] See further Chapter 5.

As for the Union, the European Council had already declared, in its Guidelines from April 2017, that national authorities, businesses, and other stakeholders should take all the necessary steps to prepare for the consequences of UK withdrawal: although the Union would strive to reach an agreement, it must also prepare itself to handle the situation should negotiations eventually fail.[48]

In and of itself, 'no deal' implied, from the Union's perspective, two main specific and particular sets of consequences. In the first place, the Union and its Member States would need to resolve the shared 'separation challenges' arising from UK withdrawal, which should ideally have been addressed through mutual agreement, instead through the adoption of purely unilateral and therefore inherently sub-optimal measures. For example, Union and/or national decisions would need to be taken concerning the future status and treatment of those UK nationals currently exercising free movement rights across the EU27—but without the benefit (say) of cross-border cooperation with the UK authorities on important matters such as social security coordination in fields like the aggregation and exportation of pensions. In the second place, the Union, its Member States, and all other relevant public and private sector actors would need to be ready and able to engage with the UK and its natural and legal persons or residents, on the basis of the ordinary Union and domestic rules applicable to third countries and third country nationals, far sooner and much more abruptly than would have been the case under a more orderly, negotiated withdrawal—particularly in the absence of a status quo transition period, of the sort negotiated between the parties, designed to provide significant extra time to make the necessary legal, infrastructural, logistical, and other practical adjustments.

The Union anticipated that the combined result of those twin sets of 'no deal' challenges would be significant disruption: for example, the sudden replacement of Single Market integration with WTO terms of trade; the immediate introduction of systematic customs tariffs and regulatory checks on trade in goods; far-reaching changes in the legal framework applicable to fields ranging from financial services and data sharing to immigration and security cooperation. The disruption entailed by a 'no deal Brexit' would inevitably prove to be highly differentiated across the Member States. The hammer would fall hardest on Ireland. Serious disruption was also to be expected in those regions and sectors characterized by particularly close relations with the UK for reasons of trade infrastructure and/or cross-border trade and supply chains—the latter proving also that the adverse consequences of a 'no deal Brexit' would often fall largely upon the shoulders of private sector actors.

For those reasons, the European Council repeatedly called upon the Union institutions, the Member States and all other stakeholders to intensify their joint and several preparations for all potential eventualities, including the possibility of the UK leaving in a disorderly fashion without any withdrawal agreement (in general) or transition period (in particular).[49] In response, the Commission created and regularly updated a 'contingency action plan' to deal with the threat of a 'no deal Brexit'.[50] In particular, the

---

[48] European Council (Article 50), *Guidelines of 29 April 2017.*

[49] See further the discussion and references in Chapters 4 and 5.

[50] See, in particular, Commission, *Preparing for the UK's withdrawal from the EU on 30 March 2019: Implementing the Commission's Contingency Action Plan,* COM(2018) 890 Final.

Commission distinguished between preparedness measures (which would be needed in any case as a result of UK withdrawal) and contingency measures (which would only be required in the event of a 'no deal' outcome to the Article 50 TEU process).

Insofar as such contingency measures required action at the Union level, they were to be governed by a clear set of principles: for example, contingency arrangements should not replicate the terms either of existing Union membership or of the proposed transition period; they would be entirely unilateral in nature, temporary in duration and limited in scope; they must respect the division of competences between the Union and its Member States; and they should not act as a substitute for timely preparations that could and should have been undertaken by relevant stakeholders. On that basis, the Commission prepared various draft Union measures for the protection of vital interests in fields such as financial services, air transport, climate policy, the status of Erasmus students, social security coordination for citizens affected by UK withdrawal, the maintenance of Union budget commitments, and access to financial assistance for Member States exposed to particular difficulties as a result of a disorderly UK departure.[51]

When it came to the UK, the governments of Theresa May and then Boris Johnson offered a very different assessment of what a 'no deal Brexit' might entail. Already, in her 'Lancaster House speech' of 17 January 2017, the Prime Minister had adopted the official line that 'no deal is better than a bad deal'.[52] A range of parliamentary enquiries concluded that the Government was unable to produce any reliable analysis to support its claim that 'no deal' would be anything other than a seriously damaging and deeply undesirable outcome for the UK.[53] Academic analyses reinforced that assessment.[54] Nevertheless, 'no deal is better than a bad deal' remained a regular refrain in the UK Government's approach to the Article 50 TEU process.[55]

In and of itself, 'no deal' would have entailed the same two groups of specific and particular consequences for the UK just as much as it would have done for the EU: the British would need to find unilateral and therefore sub-optimal solutions to the 'separation challenges' arising from its own withdrawal; and all relevant public and private sector actors would need to be ready and able to engage with the EU as third country authorities and nationals without any status quo transition period during which to complete the necessary legal, infrastructural, logistical, and other practical

---

[51] See further, e.g. COM(2019) 195 Final; COM(2019) 276 Final; COM(2019) 394 Final.

[52] Theresa May, *Lancaster House Speech: The Government's Negotiating Objectives for Exiting the EU* (17 January 2017).

[53] E.g. House of Commons Foreign Affairs Committee, *Article 50 Negotiations: Implications of 'No Deal'* (HC1077 of 12 March 2017); House of Commons Exiting the EU Committee, *The Government's Negotiating Objectives: The White Paper* (HC1125 of 4 April 2017); House of Commons Exiting the EU Committee, *The Progress of the UK's Negotiations on EU Withdrawal* (HC372 of 1 December 2017); House of Lords EU Committee, *Brexit: Deal or No Deal* (HL46 of 7 December 2017); House of Commons Exiting the EU Committee, *The Progress of the UK's Negotiations on EU Withdrawal—June to September 2018* (HC1554 of 18 September 2018); House of Commons Exiting the EU Committee, *Response to the Vote on the Withdrawal Agreement and Political Declaration: Assessing the Options* (HC1908 of 28 January 2019); House of Commons Exiting the EU Committee, *The Consequences of No Deal for UK Business* (HC2560 of 19 July 2019).

[54] Consider, e.g. Baetens, ' "No deal is better than a bad deal"? The fallacy of the WTO fall-back option as a post-Brexit safety net', 55 *CMLRev Special Issue* (2018) 133.

[55] E.g. Theresa May, *Brexit Negotiations Statement* (21 September 2019).

adjustments. But in the case of the UK, it was safe to assume that those combined 'no deal' challenges would result in an even more serious degree of disruption and damage than that anticipated for the EU.

After all, as we have just seen, the UK faced an enormous task even to stabilize its legal system for the act of withdrawal without causing significant regulatory vacuums and widespread uncertainty, potentially affecting entire sectors of the economy and society and further unsettling relations between London and the devolved administrations in Scotland and Wales.[56] Similarly, the prospect of having to provide unilateral, sub-optimal solutions to 'separation challenges' such as the land border across the island of Ireland, went far beyond mere logistical headaches and economic disruption, posing instead the prospect of political crisis and social disorder, capable of threatening peace and stability in Northern Ireland and beyond. In addition, the UK faced the herculean task of undertaking an extensive programme of external negotiations with third countries and international organizations: for example, so as to regularize its membership of bodies such as the World Trade Organization; and to clarify, replicate or rebuild the UK's rights and obligations under a vast range of existing international agreements covering a wide array of sectors and partners.[57]

The UK Government published and periodically updated its assessment of British preparations for a 'no deal Brexit'—summarizing the state of the UK's legislative and regulatory adaptations in order to safeguard legal continuity and legal certainty; describing plans for broader public sector preparations through significant investments in staffing and infrastructure; and advising private sector actors to consult various technical notices offering more detailed guidance about the steps one should take to prepare for a 'no deal Brexit'.[58] More specific publications also outlined the UK's plans to deal unilaterally with various 'separation challenges': for example, concerning the treatment of existing lawfully resident Union citizens as well as the interim status of new arrivals from the EU (pending the adoption and implementation of a new immigration regime in due course).[59] The UK also offered regular updates on its progress in addressing the external consequences of a 'no deal Brexit': for example, the successful conclusion of 'continuity agreements' with a range of third countries, designed to replicate (subject to various amendments and adjustments) existing EU agreements in fields such as customs cooperation and trade preferences.[60]

---

[56] On which, consider the controversies surrounding the project to create a 'UK internal market' as discussed in Chapter 10.

[57] On which, see the discussion in Chapter 4. See further, e.g. the contributions by Messenger, 'Membership of the World Trade Organization' and Cremona, 'UK Trade Policy' in M. Dougan (ed.), *The UK After Brexit: Legal and Policy Challenges* (2017); Mariani and Sacerdoti, 'Brexit and Trade Issues', *European Journal of Legal Studies: Special Issue* [2019] 187.

[58] HMG, *UK Government's Preparations for a 'No Deal' Scenario* (first published 23 August 2018 and periodically updated thereafter). See also, e.g. HMG, *Implications for Business and Trade of a No Deal Exit on 29 March 2019* (26 February 2019).

[59] See, in particular, Department for Exiting the European Union, *Citizens' Rights—EU citizens in the UK and UK nationals in the EU* (6 December 2018; updated 28 March 2019); and (as regards new EU arrivals) Home Office, *European Temporary Leave to Remain in the UK* (28 January 2019). Also, e.g. Department for Exiting the European Union, *Citizens' Rights—UK Nationals in the EU: Policy Paper* (4 April 2019).

[60] Details of such 'continuity agreements' were published by the Department for International Trade; regular updates on the overall position as regards the impact of withdrawal on the UK's external relations/international agreements were provided by the Department for Exiting the European Union. See further, e.g.

However, something closer to the true extent of the UK's vulnerabilities in the event of a 'no deal Brexit' was revealed when the Westminster Parliament forced the Johnson Government to publish (on 11 September 2019) its infamous 'Operation Yellowhammer' report (dated 2 August 2019).[61] This document discussed the possibility of the UK experiencing shortages of certain foodstuffs and medicines; serious disruption to various supply chains; price rises for essential commodities such as fuel; disproportionate impacts upon those in lower socio-economic groupings; and the potential for civil disorder breaking out among certain sections of society. After such startling revelations, the Government's claim that 'no deal is better than a bad deal' was greeted with even greater scepticism than before. In fact, a collapse in the Article 50 TEU negotiations leading to a disorderly withdrawal posed a serious risk that the UK might experience outright legislative, regulatory, and administrative malfunction (whether generalized or at least affecting certain sectors of its economy)—a truly remarkable position for any developed society not only to find itself in, but seriously to contemplate inviting into practice.

(ii) 'Revoke and Remain'

If the chaos and disruption of a 'no deal Brexit' represented one alternative finale, as compared to an orderly withdrawal based on a negotiated agreement, the other main possible outcome available under Article 50 TEU was that the UK might change its mind altogether and seek to remain within the Union. Indeed, for a considerable time after the UK referendum in June 2016, one of the most common questions raised about Article 50 TEU was whether a notification of intention to depart should be treated as unconditional and irreversible or whether the relevant State should be able to halt the withdrawal process and remain a Member State on its current constitutional terms and conditions.[62]

In some instances, that question was framed in terms of how far Article 50 TEU might allow the relevant State to submit from the very outset only a conditional notification, whereby its intention to withdraw should be considered to lapse automatically upon the materialization of certain future contingencies. Such conditionality could be explicit: for example, if the relevant State were to notify its intention to withdraw, provided that its national parliament later either approved the proposed separation agreement or endorsed leaving the Union without any agreement, failing which the original notification should automatically and without further ado be treated by all concerned actors as having lapsed. But it was also argued that ex ante conditionality could, in some cases, even be treated as implicit in the relevant State's original notification of

---

House of Commons International Trade Committee, *Continuing Application of EU Trade Agreements After Brexit* (HC520 of 7 March 2018).

[61] Available via https://assets.publishing.service.gov.uk/government/uploads/system/uploads/attachment_data/file/831199/20190802_Latest_Yellowhammer_Planning_assumptions_CDL.pdf.

[62] See further, e.g. Eeckhout and Frantziou, 'Brexit and Article 50 TEU: A Constitutionalist Reading', 54 *CMLRev* (2017) 695; I. Papageorgiou, *The (Ir-)revocability of the Withdrawal Notification under Article 50 TEU* (In-Depth Analysis commissioned by the AFCO Committee of the European Parliament, PE 596.820 of January 2018); Tsiliotis, 'The Irrational Brexit and the Revocability of the Withdrawal Notification of the United Kingdom to the European Council', *Public Law* [2018] 659.

intention to withdraw. For example, imagine that the constitutional arrangements of the relevant State envisaged certain subsequent domestic requirements (such as parliamentary, regional or even popular support) in order to approve the outcome of the Article 50 TEU negotiations. Compliance with such requirements could be considered, from the very start, a necessary condition for fully implementing the original but essentially conditional decision to leave the Union.

The UK did not make its March 2017 notification explicitly conditional on any factors or requirements. Prominent legal voices did argue that the UK notification should nevertheless be treated as implicitly conditional upon subsequent parliamentary approval of either the proposed agreement or a 'no deal' departure.[63] However, that argument was neither accepted by the UK Government nor tested in the UK courts. Instead, attention focused on the alternative scenario: having expressed its initial intention to withdraw in apparently absolute and unconditional terms, would it be possible for the relevant State subsequently to change its mind, revoke its original notification under Article 50 TEU and thereby halt the entire process in its tracks?

On the one hand, the text of Article 50 TEU makes no express provision for ex post revocation by the relevant State. Indeed, the language of withdrawal appears mandatory in nature: the Treaties *shall* cease to apply to the relevant State after submission of its notification of intention to leave—the only question being whether such departure takes effect either on the date of entry into force of the negotiated separation agreement, or by default after two years, or subject to some specified delay as decided by unanimous agreement between the relevant State and the European Council.

On the other hand, the text of Article 50 TEU does not explicitly rule out the possibility of ex post revocation by the relevant State and it is arguable that the possibility of revocation should be treated as implicit in Article 50 TEU. After all, the Treaties refer only to an initial expression by the relevant State of its 'intention' to withdraw, then provide for a period potentially lasting several years before withdrawal itself actually occurs, during which there should be a process of detailed negotiations about the more precise terms of departure. It is perfectly possible that, during the passage of such time and over the course of those negotiations, especially when faced with the reality of the choices it once made and the future alternatives actually available to it, the relevant State's intentions will change in favour of remaining a Member State on its current constitutional terms and conditions.[64]

The latter argument focuses attention on a different question: assuming revocation is possible in principle, how far might Union law impose procedural and/or substantive conditions upon revocation in practice?

Certain actors and commentators (including the European Parliament at an early stage in the Article 50 TEU process) took the view that revocation by the relevant State should be possible only with the consent of the Union itself.[65] In the first place,

---

[63] See, in particular, the so-called 'Three Knights Opinion' by D. Edward, F. Jacobs, J. Lever, H. Mountfield and G. Facenna, *In the Matter of Article 50 of the Treaty on European Union* (10 February 2017) available via https://www.bindmans.com/uploads/files/documents/Final_Article_50_Opinion_10.2.17.pdf.

[64] Consider, e.g. F. Alabrune, *Note pour le Cabinet du Ministre au sujet de Brexit/Article 50 TUE* (Department of Legal Affairs, Ministry of Foreign Affairs and International Development, Paris, 21 June 2016).

[65] See, e.g. European Parliament, *Resolution on negotiations with the UK following its notification that it intends to withdraw from the European Union* (2017/2593 of 5 April 2017). Note also Commission, *Article 50*

conditional revocation would prevent the relevant State from engaging in abusive behaviour: seeing that its withdrawal negotiations are not proceeding according to plan,
and unable to guarantee that the European Council would unanimously agree to a de-
ferral of the due departure date, the relevant State might be tempted to revoke its original notification simply as a means of 'stopping the ticking clock', only then to submit
a fresh notification and begin the Article 50 TEU process all over again. In the second
place, even though the relevant State was entitled unilaterally to initiate the process
of withdrawal, once notification had been served under Article 50 TEU, the Treaties
made clear that the subsequent process was a more multilateral one, engaging each of
the Union's main political institutions and affecting the interests of every remaining
Member State. Conditional revocation would offer legal recognition for the multilateral character of the post-notification withdrawal process—not least of the fact that
the Union and its Member States would now suffer considerable disruption and incur
considerable costs as a direct consequence of the relevant State's previously unilateral
behaviour. Both citizens and taxpayers had a legitimate interest in the Union and its
Member States directly shaping all possible outcomes from the withdrawal process
laid down in their Treaties.

However, other actors and commentators advocated that revocation by the relevant
State should be possible even on a unilateral basis.[66] In the first place, advocates of
conditional revocation had to confront a difficult but nevertheless serious problem: in
the absence of any clear and explicit rules, how do we decide precisely which institutions or actors should be required to consent to a proposed revocation, and according
to what process, and indeed subject to what potential terms, conditions, or limits? For
example: should it require a decision of the European Council or the Council; and if
so, acting by unanimity or by (super) qualified majority vote? Should the European
Parliament have any direct input or even be required also to consent to the proposed
revocation? Should the competent institutions (whoever they may be) be entitled to
refuse a proposed revocation on any political grounds? Or would they be required to
justify their decision by reference to (as yet unidentified) criteria accepted as legitimate under Union law? In the second place, the argument in favour of recognizing an
implicit possibility of revocation rests upon the idea that an intention to leave is not
the same as a definitive decision to leave: it is perfectly possible to change one's mind
according to evolving circumstances, particularly over the significant period of time
provided for under the Treaties between original notification and the proposed date
of final departure. During that period, the relevant State remains a Member State with
(almost) its full rights and obligations under Union law. To deny the possibility of the
relevant State changing its mind and being entitled unilaterally to revoke its original
notification, and instead offer the Union institutions and/or the other Member States
a power of veto over the possibility of remaining within the Union, would convert

---

of the Treaty on European Union: Q&A (29 March 2017): once triggered, Article 50 TEU cannot be *unilaterally* reversed.

[66] See, e.g. the analysis by S. Peers, 'The Case For Unilateral Revocability of the Article 50 Notice' available
via http://eulawanalysis.blogspot.com/2018/01/can-article-50-notice-of-withdrawal.html.

Article 50 TEU from a voluntary withdrawal clause into a compulsory expulsion mechanism—something not provided for under the Treaties.[67]

It was not until relatively late in the UK withdrawal experience that those questions were the subject of direct judicial consideration. In the 2016–2017 *Miller* litigation before the High Court of England and Wales, and then the UK Supreme Court, it was accepted for the sake of argument, by both the parties and the judges, that notification under Article 50 TEU could neither be made conditionally nor subsequently rescinded. But the specific legal questions about the possibility of revocation under Article 50 TEU were not argued, considered, or pronounced upon in any direct or authoritative manner.[68]

The issue was left for subsequent litigation and the opportunity arose with the *Wightman* case.[69] The dispute involved a petition for judicial review before the Scottish Court of Session seeking a declaration specifying whether, when, and how an Article 50 TEU notification could be unilaterally revoked and (for that purpose) asking the domestic judges to make a preliminary reference to the CJEU for definitive clarification of the Union legal position. The Government argued that the petition should be refused on the grounds that, since the UK had no intention of revoking its notification of intention to withdraw, the issue was entirely hypothetical. That argument succeeded at first instance.[70] However, the decision was overturned on appeal. The question of revocation was indeed uncertain and its answer would have the concrete effect of clarifying which options were open to MPs in the House of Commons when it came to casting their votes for or against approval of any proposed withdrawal package under the process provided for by section 13 of the European Union (Withdrawal) Act 2018.[71] In particular, an authoritative answer to the claimant's question would clarify whether MPs were being asked by the UK Government to choose simply between the latter's proposed withdrawal package and a 'no deal' departure; or whether there was in fact a third option, of revocation and remaining within the Union.[72]

Nevertheless, the Government continued to resist the possibility of a preliminary reference through the UK courts—until the Supreme Court finally rejected the Government's arguments in November 2018.[73] Yet even before the CJEU, the UK's sole argument was that the Scottish request for a preliminary ruling should be treated as purely hypothetical and therefore entirely inadmissible.[74] However, the Court found the reference perfectly admissible: Union law operates on the basis of a presumption of relevance for preliminary reference requests; the national court had stated that there

[67] And indeed explicitly dismissed as a possibility during the Convention on the Future of Europe—as noted by the CJEU itself in Case C-621/18, *Wightman* (EU:C:2018:999).

[68] See, in particular, *Miller v Secretary of State for Exiting the European Union* [2016] EWHC 2768 and *R (on the application of Miller) v Secretary of State for Exiting the European Union* [2017] UKSC 5.

[69] Case C-621/18, *Wightman* (EU:C:2018:999). See further, e.g. the annotation by Cuyvers, 56 *CMLRev* (2019) 1303.

[70] See *Wightman v The Advocate General* [2018] CSOH 8.

[71] See further the analysis in Chapters 3 and 5.

[72] See *Wightman v The Advocate General* [2018] CSIH 18.

[73] See *Wightman v Secretary of State for Exiting the European Union*, UKSC Order of 20 November 2018, available via https://www.supremecourt.uk/docs/in-the-matter-of-secretary-of-state-for-exiting-the-european-union-v-wightman-and-others.pdf.

[74] Case C-621/18, *Wightman* (EU:C:2018:999), especially at paras 20–36.

THE QUEST FOR AN ORDERLY WITHDRAWAL

was a question of law representing a genuine and live issue of considerable practical importance which had given rise to a dispute between the parties. That was especially persuasive, given that one petitioner and two interveners in the case were MPs entitled to vote under section 13 of the European Union (Withdrawal) Act 2018, for whom an answer to the questions posed in the preliminary reference would indeed clarify the options open to them in exercising their parliamentary mandates.

Since the UK made no submissions on the substantive questions concerning interpretation of Article 50 TEU, it was left instead to the Commission and the Council to argue against the applicants' claim that the UK's notification of intention to withdraw was capable of subsequent and unilateral revocation. The Commission and Council essentially argued for conditional revocability, subject to the unanimous consent of the European Council, on the grounds that this was necessary to prevent the relevant State from engaging in abusive conduct in circumvention of the time limits for withdrawal laid down in the Treaties.

The Court began its substantive analysis[75] by recalling that the Treaties provide the basic constitutional charter of the Union: the latter's 'new legal order' stems from an independent source of law, capable of having primacy over national law and characterized by the direct effect of a whole series of Union provisions; that new legal order gives rise to a structured network of principles, rules, and mutually interdependent relations binding together the Union and its Member States as well as the Member States inter se. Against that background, Article 50 TEU should be interpreted according to its wording, its context, and its origins.

To begin with, as regards the wording of Article 50 TEU, the text does not explicitly address the issue at hand: it neither expressly prohibits nor expressly authorizes the possibility of revocation. However, Article 50 TEU does refer to an 'intention'—which, by its very nature, is neither definitive nor irrevocable. Moreover, Article 50 TEU provides for the relevant State to take a sovereign decision to withdraw in accordance with its own constitutional requirements—alone and without acting in concert with the Union institutions or the other Member States. The sovereign nature of the right of withdrawal enshrined in Article 50(1) TEU supports the conclusion that the relevant State has a right to revoke the notification of its intention to withdraw for as long as a withdrawal agreement has not entered into force; or (if no such agreement is concluded) for as long as the two-year period provided for under Article 50(3) TEU (possibly extended with the unanimous agreement of the European Council) has not yet expired. In the absence of any express provision governing revocation, the latter should be treated as subject to the rules laid down in Article 50(1) TEU to govern withdrawal itself: revocation may be decided upon unilaterally, in accordance with the constitutional requirements of the relevant State, thus reflecting a sovereign decision by that State to retain its status as a member of the Union, a status which is not in any relevant way suspended or altered by the original notification.[76]

Next, as regards the context of Article 50 TEU, it should be recalled that the preamble to the Treaty on European Union refers to an 'ever closer union among the peoples of Europe'. Both Article 49 TEU on the possibility of accession and its counterpart

---

[75] Which essentially followed the Opinion of AG Campos Sánchez-Bordona (EU:C:2018:978).
[76] Subject to the specific institutional restrictions laid down in Art 50(4) TEU.

Article 50 TEU on the possibility of withdrawal, demonstrate that the Union is composed of States which have freely and voluntarily committed themselves to the values contained in Article 2 TEU. Union law is based on the fundamental premiss that each Member State shares with all the other Member States (and recognizes that those Member States share with it) those same values. The withdrawal of a Member State is liable to have a considerable impact upon the rights of all Union citizens—not only nationals of the withdrawing State but nationals of all the other Member States as well. Given that no Member State can be forced to accede to the Union against its will, neither can any Member State be forced to withdraw from the Union against its will. Yet if notification were to lead inevitably to withdrawal at the end of the period laid down in Article 50(3) TEU, a Member State could indeed be forced to leave the Union despite its wish (as expressed in a democratic process in accordance with its own constitutional requirements) to reverse its original decision to withdraw and remain a Member State. Such a result would be inconsistent with the aims and values of the Treaties—not least with the purpose of creating an 'ever closer union' among the peoples of Europe.

Finally, as regards the origins of Article 50 TEU, the latter provision largely adopts the wording of the withdrawal clause first set out in the draft Treaty establishing a Constitution for Europe. During the drafting of that clause, amendments were proposed to allow the expulsion of a Member State, to avoid any risk of abuse of the new withdrawal procedure, and to make a withdrawal decision more difficult in practice. All such proposed amendments were rejected on the express grounds that Union law should ensure the voluntary and unilateral nature of the decision to withdraw.

Those combined factors also provided the basis upon which the Court felt able to reject the Commission/Council proposal, for revocation to be subject to the unanimous consent of the European Council: such a requirement would indeed transform the relevant State's unilateral sovereign right to revoke into a conditional right to remain subject to a prior approval procedure—a result that would be incompatible with the principle that no Member State can be forced to leave the Union against its will. Although the Court did not directly address the argument that the Union institutions and remaining Member States have a legitimate interest in controlling the outcome of the Article 50 TEU process, based not least upon the already considerable disruption and costs imposed by the relevant State's conduct thus far, that argument was directly rebutted by the Advocate General: whatever the burdens incurred in preparing for a potential withdrawal, they would be far less than the costs of an actual withdrawal. In effect, unilateral revocation would represent a net saving of energy and resources, compared to seeing the withdrawal process through to its conclusion as originally planned.

As a result of all those considerations, the Court concluded that Article 50 TEU should be interpreted to mean that the original notification of an intention to withdraw does not lead inevitably to actual withdrawal. A relevant State which reverses its previous decision to withdraw in accordance with its domestic constitutional requirements is then entitled unilaterally to revoke its original notification of intention to leave—though only for as long as the withdrawal agreement concluded under Article 50(2) TEU has not yet entered into force or (if no such agreement has been concluded) for as long as the period calculated in accordance with Article 50(3) TEU has not yet expired.[77]

The judgment in *Wightman* was of enormous political as well as legal significance, revealing to the UK (parliament and population) that the choice being offered in the Article 50 TEU process[78] was not necessarily a binary one between accepting the Government's proposed withdrawal package or inevitably leaving the Union without any negotiated agreement. Instead, the Court in *Wightman* confirmed that the possibility of the UK opting to revoke its original notification and remain a Member State on its current constitutional terms and conditions was equally legally robust—a position then regularly and explicitly affirmed by the European Council at key points in the legal and political process that followed the *Wightman* ruling itself.[79]

However, the Court's apparent generosity in *Wightman* was not entirely without limits. The Court's insistence that any decision by the relevant State to revoke its original notification under Article 50 TEU must be submitted in writing to the European Council provides an obvious and not especially controversial instance. Much more importantly, the Court also stressed that any decision to revoke must be unequivocal and unconditional: its purpose is to confirm the relevant State's membership of the Union, under terms that are unchanged as regards its status as a Member State, and to bring the Article 50 TEU withdrawal procedure to an end. By those means, the Court sought to provide reassurance that the power of revocation could not be abused by the relevant State for purely strategic or ulterior purposes. Nevertheless, it is unfortunate that the ruling in *Wightman* failed to elaborate any further on the precise nature of or process for this Union law safeguard against potential abuse of the power to revoke. One assumes that, in practice, it would fall to the European Council to decide that a purported revocation by the relevant State failed to meet the criteria identified in *Wightman* by reason of some lingering degree of equivocation or conditionality—thereby rendering the purported revocation non-existent for the purposes of Union law; though also entitling the relevant State to challenge the European Council's assessment by means of judicial review before the CJEU itself.

On the one hand, the Court's qualifications in *Wightman* effectively mean that the ability to revoke is not in fact *entirely* unilateral: the Union may still decide that the power of revocation is being used for improper purposes or under inappropriate conditions—entitling them to ignore the purported revocation and proceed with withdrawal in accordance with the terms of Article 50 TEU. On the other hand, the Court has chosen to characterize the power of the Union institutions to act against any potential abuse of the power to revoke in a very particular manner. This is not an essentially political judgment, to be made in the context of a prior requirement for positive consent to a requested revocation, thereby offering the competent Union actors

---

[77] Note that the CJEU regarded its analysis as being corroborated by the relevant provisions of the Vienna Convention on the Law of Treaties (to the effect that, if a treaty authorizes withdrawal, a notification of withdrawal may be revoked at any time before it actually takes effect): see Case C-621/18, *Wightman* (EU:C:2018:999), at paras 70–71.

[78] As well as for the purposes of the 'meaningful vote' by the House of Commons, on approval of any proposed withdrawal package, as required under section 13 European Union (Withdrawal) Act 2018: see further Chapters 3 and 5.

[79] E.g. European Council (Article 50), *Conclusions of 10 April 2019*.

a wide discretion to determine the course of action that best suits their collective or indeed individual interests—of the sort which would be difficult later to scrutinize or control by means of judicial review. Instead, this is an essentially legal assessment, to be made in the context of a subsequent decision effectively to veto a purported revocation, thereby requiring the competent Union actors to exercise their discretion according to a predetermined set of objectively verifiable criteria—of the sort that is eminently amenable to scrutiny and control through the courts.

The Court's choice to juridify the Union's subsequent response to a purported unilateral revocation by the relevant State nevertheless raises some difficult questions. For example, the Court restricted the ability of the competent Union actors to reject a purported revocation to certain specified grounds/circumstances—which naturally focuses our attention on precisely what nature or degree of equivocation or conditionality (on the part of the relevant State, concerning its continued Union membership) could legitimately be regarded as objectionable for the purposes of Article 50 TEU as interpreted in *Wightman*. At one extreme, it would obviously be acceptable for the competent Union actors to reject a purported revocation in circumstances where the relevant State was indeed rather blatantly seeking to 'reset the clock' in order simply to gain more time: either to negotiate a more favourable withdrawal agreement with the Union; or to prepare itself for the full consequences of its intended withdrawal from the Union. At the other extreme, one may doubt that the Court in *Wightman* intended to inhibit the prerogative of each Member State—including one once minded to leave but now keen to remain—to propose and indeed lobby for future changes to its current terms of Union membership (whether on its own initiative or in the context of a broader discussion about constitutional and/or policy reform).

Between those two extremes, the borderline may be more difficult to define and more controversial to police. Consider a situation in which the relevant State changes its mind through a second referendum on Union membership—but votes once again by only a narrow margin, with Leave advocates vowing to continue their campaign and seek another mandate for withdrawal as soon as possible. Should a unilateral decision to revoke in such circumstances be considered sufficiently unequivocal and unconditional? Or imagine that the competent Union actors sought to extract certain political guarantees from the relevant State as a condition for accepting its purported revocation, for example, to the effect that its parliament would not authorize another referendum on Union membership for some minimum period of time. Would such efforts be compatible with the objective criteria for responding to a purported unilateral revocation under Article 50 TEU as interpreted in *Wightman*?[80]

4. Concluding Remarks

An orderly withdrawal on the basis of a negotiated settlement may have been the preferred outcome envisaged under the Treaties, but Article 50 TEU was certainly capable

---

[80] Even assuming they were at all enforceable in practice, not only as a matter of Union law, but also as a matter of domestic constitutional law—particularly in the UK, given the doctrine of parliamentary sovereignty.

of ending in alternative outcomes: a 'no deal Brexit'; or a UK decision to 'revoke and remain'. However, each of those alternative possibilities was effectively ruled out following the Conservative Party victory in the UK's general election of December 2019. At that point, it became clear that there would indeed be a deal; but there would be no second referendum to verify whether withdrawal on the terms proposed by the Johnson Government still reflected the will of the UK population.

And so, in the end, Article 50 TEU fulfilled its primary purpose of producing an orderly withdrawal based on a negotiated settlement. But as we have seen, Article 50 TEU itself provided only one (albeit an important) part of that overall process and eventual outcome. The parties' relative success in delivering a smooth departure also crucially depended upon their respective unilateral and internal plans and preparations. Moreover, in various respects, the sketchy text offered by Article 50 TEU actually managed to raise more questions than it provided answers—intentionally or otherwise—leaving crucial parts of the withdrawal negotiations to be determined through the subsequent exercise of discretion and judgment.

Thus, the final Withdrawal Package of October 2019 must also be explored through a much broader lens than the strict terms of Article 50 TEU itself. In that regard, the UK's eventual deal was of course the natural product of a certain amount of logical deduction and responsible management: conscientious civil servants identifying relevant issues and working out appropriate solutions informed by insight and experience. However, the final Withdrawal Package was also the direct result of various additional legal and political choices and factors, affecting both the EU and the UK, which together had a decisive impact upon the agenda of the Article 50 TEU negotiations as well as the more detailed contents of the parties' ultimate agreement. Those choices and factors provide the focus for our next chapter.

3

Legal and Political Factors at Work Within the Article 50 TEU Process

1. Introduction

Having set out the basic constitutional framework for withdrawal from the Union under Article 50 TEU in Chapter 2, we will now provide a detailed examination of various additional legal and political choices and factors, that were to shape the specific UK withdrawal process as it unfolded in practice.

Section 2 concerns the situation of the Union and its Member States. Here, there are basic questions to address about the allocation of roles and responsibilities across the various Union institutions—some of which are explicit from the text of Article 50 TEU, whilst others only emerged through political practice—including the central and ongoing importance of the European Council to strategic management of the entire Brexit process; as well as the determination of the European Parliament to convert its eventual power of consent over any withdrawal treaty into a more tangible parliamentary influence over the negotiations as they unfolded.

However, Section 2 also explores several other key legal and political issues. For example, we will consider the Council's decision (taken relatively early in the entire Article 50 TEU process) to exclude any possibility that the withdrawal agreement should call not only for approval by the Union's own institutions, but also for Member State ratification through the latter's domestic institutions—the first concrete indication that Article 50 TEU was to be treated as an exceptional competence or legal basis, capable of deviating from some of the ordinary principles one would expect to follow under Union constitutional law.

We will also introduce the core principles laid down by the European Council in its foundational 'Brexit Guidelines' of April 2017. Those Guidelines served to structure and guide the Union's overall approach to negotiations under Article 50 TEU: both highlighting the basic legal parameters imposed upon Brexit by Union law (for example) by adapting the duty of sincere cooperation to the unprecedented context of withdrawal; and also affirming the Union's overriding political interest in preserving its own unity and safeguarding the integrity of core EU policies (an interest explicitly elevated above the immediate goal of delivering an orderly UK departure). For its part, the CJEU also had the opportunity to make modest but still important contributions to this debate: for example, concerning the impact of the UK's notification of its intention to leave the Union, upon the fundamental principles (such as mutual trust and mutual recognition) that underpin core Treaty policies concerning the Single Market and the Area of Freedom, Security and Justice.

The UK's Withdrawal from the EU. Michael Dougan, Oxford University Press. © Michael Dougan 2021.
DOI: 10.1093/oso/9780198833475.003.0003

Section 3 then shifts attention to the situation of the UK. We begin by sketching out how the initial period of turmoil and uncertainty that occurred immediately after the referendum, gave way to the adoption of several highly significant decisions by the May Government about the UK's basic political preferences for withdrawal and its future relationship with the EU—preferences that were to prove the source of many subsequent troubles and, in the end, to be both unsustainable and undeliverable. At the same time, the UK also faced the first of its 'Brexit constitutional crises': the Supreme Court was called upon to decide that it was the Westminster Parliament (not the UK Government, and certainly not the referendum itself) that held the legitimate authority to take any final decision on UK membership of or departure from the Union.

Even having overcome those twin political and constitutional challenges—deciding who was entitled formally to embark upon the withdrawal process and defining (however unconvincingly) what Brexit should eventually look like—the UK's position, right at the threshold of its own Article 50 TEU negotiations, was to be rocked by one further and fateful decision: the Prime Minister's gamble of calling an early general election in June 2017. Thanks to that election, the Conservative Party lost its existing parliamentary majority and the Government thenceforth acted as a minority administration. Among the many consequences of that outcome was the enactment of a novel legal requirement that would directly impact upon the entire Brexit process (at least until its eventual repeal in 2020 by the electorally triumphant Johnson regime): the House of Commons must grant its prior approval to any deal agreed with the Union, prior to formal ratification by the UK Government itself.

For simple reasons of relative size and risk exposure, the Union was always going to be the dominant party in the Article 50 TEU process. But the legal and political choices made by the Union served positively to reinforce its natural position of strength; whereas those pursued by the UK only had the effect of rendering a difficult situation even more challenging.

2. Legal and Political Factors Affecting the EU

As the Court observed in *Wightman*, Articles 50(2) and (3) TEU set out the procedure to be followed if and when a Member State decides to withdraw from the Union. That procedure consists of: first, notification to the European Council of the intention to withdraw; secondly, negotiation and conclusion of an agreement setting out the arrangements for withdrawal, taking into account the future relationship between the State concerned and the Union; and thirdly, the actual withdrawal from the Union on the date of entry into force of that agreement or (failing that) two years after notification to the European Council—unless the latter (in agreement with the relevant State) unanimously decides to extend that period.[1] This section will explore the Union's legal

---

[1] Case C-621/18, *Wightman* (EU:C:2018:999), at para 51.

and political position during the period immediately before and after UK notification of its intention to withdraw under Article 50 TEU.

A. The Union's Initial Preparations for UK Notification Under Article 50 TEU

Needless to say, the linear series of events set out in Article 50 TEU should not be taken to suggest that—pending notification of the relevant State's sovereign decision to withdraw—the Union institutions and/or the other Member States are simply passive observers waiting for the completion of an essentially domestic constitutional process.

Immediately after the UK's 2016 referendum there were certain urgent problems to deal with: for example, amending the future order of presidencies of the Council, so as to exclude the UK from the groups-of-three rotation system.[2] But in addition, the Union institutions set about identifying certain ground-rules for how the overall process for the UK's anticipated withdrawal should be interpreted and managed as a matter of Union law and practice—thereby starting to provide rapid answers to some of the questions which had been left open by the bare text of Article 50 TEU itself.[3] For example, the Union institutions were quick to rule out any suggestion that the UK's decision to withdraw could be assumed simply from the outcome of the referendum, that the UK's notification of its intention to leave (for the purposes of Article 50 TEU) could be deemed already to have been submitted, and thus that the timescales for withdrawal as laid down in the Treaties were to be treated as already underway. Far from it: it was clearly assumed that 'triggering Article 50 TEU' would require the explicit communication of a formal decision by the UK Government to the European Council.[4]

Until then, moreover, the EU27 made clear that there would be no negotiations with the UK in relation to its potential withdrawal.[5] Instead, the Union institutions concentrated their attention on making various internal preparations for an eventual UK notification and thenceforth the commencement of formal withdrawal negotiations as envisaged under Article 50 TEU: for example, by identifying key personnel to act as the necessary institutional representatives.[6]

---

[2] See Council Decision 2016/1316 amending Decision 2009/908 laying down measures for the implementation of the European Council Decision on the exercise of the Presidency of the Council and on the chairmanship of preparatory bodies of the Council, OJ 2016 L 208/42.

[3] See the discussion in Chapter 2.

[4] See, e.g. European Council, *Informal meeting of Heads of State or Government of 27 Member States as well as Presidents of European Council and European Commission* (29 June 2016); European Council, *Informal meeting of Heads of State or Government of 27 Member States as well as Presidents of European Council and European Commission* (15 December 2016).

[5] See, e.g. European Council, *Informal meeting of Heads of State or Government of 27 Member States as well as Presidents of European Council and European Commission* (29 June 2016); European Council, *Informal meeting of Heads of State or Government of 27 Member States as well as Presidents of European Council and European Commission* (15 December 2016).

[6] Including the identification of Michel Barnier as lead negotiator; and of Guy Verhofstadt as Brexit spokesperson for the European Parliament.

B. Basic Roles of the Union Institutions as Laid Down
in Article 50 TEU

The UK delivered its formal notification of intention to withdraw on 29 March 2017.[7] Article 50 TEU then identifies a basic allocation of roles among the Union institutions in the negotiation and conclusion of a withdrawal agreement between the Union and the relevant State.

The process begins when the European Council (acting by consensus) draws up guidelines for handling the intended withdrawal—for which purpose, Article 50 TEU explicitly provides that the relevant State shall be excluded from the necessary discussions and decision-making. In the case of the UK, the European Council adopted its initial guidelines on 29 April 2017.[8]

Next, the Commission must make recommendations to the Council, concerning the appointment of the Union's negotiating team and the mandate under which that team should conduct the negotiations.[9] The Council must then adopt a formal decision to open the negotiations and appoint the Union negotiator—again, for which purpose, Article 50 TEU explicitly provides that the relevant State should be excluded from the necessary discussions and decision-making. In the case of the UK, the relevant Council decision was adopted on 15 May 2017 and included appointment of the Commission itself as Union negotiator.[10]

Formal talks with the UK commenced on 19 June 2017 (after another delay created, as we shall see, by the British Government's decision to call an early general election).[11] Naturally, the Council and the Commission maintained a close working relationship throughout the process. For example, an ad hoc Working Party on Article 50 TEU held regular meetings;[12] while additional negotiating directives were proposed and adopted as the discussions proceeded.[13]

Article 50 TEU provides that the withdrawal agreement per se shall be concluded on behalf of the Union by the Council, acting by a qualified majority, after obtaining the consent of the European Parliament. For those purposes, however, Article 50(2) TEU cross-refers to the more detailed procedure laid down in Article 218(3) of the Treaty on the Functioning of the European Union (TFEU): the Union negotiator should propose a formal decision by the Council to authorize the signing of the agreement; then propose a further formal decision by the Council to conclude the agreement (having obtained the consent of the European Parliament). Moreover, Article 50(4) TEU defines a qualified majority for the purposes of the Council's decisions on signature and conclusion by reference to Article 238(3)(b) TFEU: at least 72 per cent of Member

---

[7] HMG, *Prime Minister's notification letter to President of the European Council* (29 March 2017).

[8] European Council (Article 50), *Guidelines following the United Kingdom's notification under Article 50 TEU* (29 April 2017).

[9] COM(2017) 218 Final.

[10] Council Decision authorizing the opening of negotiations with the United Kingdom of Great Britain and Northern Ireland for an agreement setting out the arrangements for its withdrawal from the European Union (22 May 2017).

[11] See Commission, *Terms of Reference for the Article 50 TEU negotiations* (19 June 2017).

[12] See Council Decision 2017/900, OJ 2017 L 138/138.

[13] E.g. COM(2017) 830 Final; Council Decision supplementing the Decision of 22 May 2017 (29 January 2018).

States; comprising at least 65 per cent of the population. As usual, the UK is excluded from the Council's discussions and eventual decisions on signature and conclusion.

By contrast, the European Parliament may consent to the agreement acting by simple majority; and for those purposes, the MEPs representing constituencies in the UK are not excluded from either the relevant debates or the final vote. Thus, even within the context of the withdrawal of a Member State, the Treaties adopt the usual 'unitary' understanding of the electoral mandate of the European Parliament: MEPs represent the interests of Union citizens as a whole, rather than the interests of their own Member State or indeed solely the interests of their own particular constituents.[14] The same underlying understanding is reflected in the fact that all MEPs, even those from non-participating Member States, are entitled to vote on measures relating to the Single Currency, the Area of Freedom, Security and Justice or the adoption and implementation of enhanced cooperation initiatives.[15] Given the size and complexion of the UK's parliamentary representation, that 'unitary' approach to voting within the European Parliament, even as regards the participation of UK MEPs in a vote of consent over the UK's own proposed withdrawal agreement, was not without potentially significant political consequences.[16]

Article 50 TEU makes explicit provision only for the negotiation and conclusion of a withdrawal agreement, i.e. a legally binding international agreement that sets out the arrangements for the relevant State's withdrawal. By contrast, Article 50 TEU does not make explicit provision as regards any other elements that might make up the overall withdrawal package agreed between the Union and the relevant State. Yet as we know, besides their formal Withdrawal Agreement (WA), the EU and the UK also negotiated and adopted a Political Declaration setting out the parties' common understanding about the framework for their future relationship, intended to provide the basis for conducting future negotiations in fields such as trade and security, after the withdrawal process had been completed and the UK had become a third country.[17]

Notwithstanding the lack of express provision in Article 50 TEU to govern the negotiation and approval of additional documents, it appears to have been assumed (and certainly happened in practice): first, that the Commission would undertake initial discussions with the UK with a view to presenting a draft political declaration for consideration by the European Council;[18] that additional negotiations would then take place between the UK and the remaining Member States with a view to finalizing the text of that political declaration;[19] and that endorsement would then be granted

---

[14] See further, e.g. Curtin and Fasone, 'Differentiated Representation: Is a Flexible European Parliament Desirable?' in B. de Witte, A. Ott and E. Vos (eds), *Between Flexibility and Disintegration: The Trajectory of Differentiation in EU Law* (2017).

[15] See further, e.g. Dougan, 'The Unfinished Business of Enhanced Cooperation: Some Institutional Questions and their Constitutional Implications' in A. Ott and E. Vos (eds), *Fifty Years of European Integration: Foundations and Perspectives* (2009).

[16] E.g. if the European Parliament had eventually been much more sceptical about the final terms agreed with the UK, the sizeable contingent of UKIP MEPs from the UK itself might have held the balance of power over granting consent to the proposed treaty.

[17] OJ 2019 C 384 I. See further Chapter 9.

[18] Consider, e.g. the Joint Report by the Commission and the UK (TF50 (2018) 54); followed by publication of a draft (First) Withdrawal Package (14 November 2018).

[19] Consider, e.g. the more detailed text of the proposed (First) Political Declaration, as presented to the European Council for approval at its meeting on 25 November 2018.

directly by the European Council (in keeping with the convention of acting by consensus, even when not specifically required to do so by the Treaties).[20]

However, the Council and (more importantly) the European Parliament were still able indirectly to express their opinion on the final version of the Political Declaration as endorsed politically by the European Council (and the UK Government). After all, the Withdrawal Agreement itself contains explicit reference to the text also of the Political Declaration. In particular, Article 184 WA refers to the Political Declaration as a reference point for the parties' mutual obligation to proceed using best endeavours and in good faith with negotiations over the framework for their future relationship. Through their respective powers to approve or reject the Withdrawal Agreement itself, the Council and (more importantly) the European Parliament were therefore able to endorse or object to the UK's entire withdrawal package, consisting also of the proposed Political Declaration.

C. Union-Level Institutional Dynamics Less Obvious from the Text of Article 50 TEU

We know that Article 50 TEU is a 'bare bones' provision that leaves important and legitimate (if often uncertain) scope for political discretion and judgment in its interpretation and application.[21] That point is well illustrated by the way in which the formal institutional roles envisaged by Article 50 TEU itself evolved alongside additional informal practices and understandings about the way in which decisions should in practice be reached at the Union level (as well as about the potential for other stakeholders to influence the conclusion of any withdrawal agreement). Thus, beyond the basic system of institutional responsibilities laid down in Article 50 TEU, several features of the Union's approach to withdrawal, perhaps not so immediately obvious from the bare text of the Treaties, nevertheless proved central to the conduct and outcome of the EU–UK negotiations.

First, the role and influence of the European Council were far from exhausted by adoption of the initial guidelines foreseen under Article 50 TEU. On the contrary: those very guidelines declared that the European Council would remain permanently seized of the Article 50 TEU situation:[22] for example, reviewing the state of play at regular points in the negotiations;[23] deciding whether sufficient progress had been achieved to justify broadening or deepening the agenda;[24] adopting additional guidelines to determine the scope and conduct of the withdrawal discussions;[25] and granting political approval to the proposed withdrawal package as a whole and

---

[20] Note that Art 15(4) TEU only requires consensus for 'decisions' of the European Council (in the particular sense of Art 288 TFEU).

[21] See further, e.g. Eeckhout and Frantziou, 'Brexit and Article 50 TEU: A Constitutionalist Reading', 54 *CMLRev* (2017) 695.

[22] A point already made, e.g. in European Council, *Informal meeting of the Heads of State or Government of 27 Member States as well as the Presidents of the European Council and the European Commission* (15 December 2016), Annex at para 1.

[23] E.g. European Council (Article 50): meetings of 20 October 2017, 29 June 2018 and 17 October 2018.

[24] E.g. European Council (Article 50): meeting of 15 December 2017.

[25] E.g. European Council (Article 50): meetings of 15 December 2017 and 23 March 2018.

in prelude to initiating the formal procedure for approval of the withdrawal agreement under Union law.[26] In particular, although the bare text of Article 50 TEU offers the European Council no formal role in the Union's final approval of any withdrawal agreement, it was obvious in practice that no proposed text could realistically proceed to formal approval by the Council and European Parliament without having already secured prior political endorsement within the European Council. Needless to say, such continuous oversight of a major event in the Union's constitutional life falls squarely within the European Council's mandate: to provide the Union with the necessary impetus for its development and define its general political directions and priorities.[27]

Secondly, not only the European Council but also the European Parliament made an important contribution to the conduct of negotiations with the UK under the Article 50 TEU process.[28] In fact, the European Parliament made it clear almost from the very moment of the 2016 referendum result that it wished to use the requirement for its eventual consent to any agreement as leverage to play an active and influential role in shaping the terms of UK withdrawal.[29] And indeed, by passing well-timed resolutions expressing its own (often detailed and frequently critical) assessment of the negotiations, the European Parliament sought to exercise significant influence over the formulation of Union positions, not only by the Commission, but also by the European Council (in adopting its periodic assessments and guidelines) and the Council (in settling the detailed negotiating directives and liaising with the Commission via the ad hoc Working Party).[30] As Michel Barnier publicly acknowledged: the European Parliament set the political direction for the Brexit negotiations, alongside the European Council, by adopting very precise negotiating directives and through the power of final say over any eventual agreement.[31]

Thirdly, the basic institutional responsibilities for the conduct of withdrawal negotiations, as laid down in Article 50 TEU itself, were supplemented by the additional input not only of Union actors such as the European Parliament, but also of the Member States themselves. In particular, the withdrawal negotiations quickly identified certain issues which were to be considered of major concern to specific Member States. The prime example is the extraordinary economic and political impact of the UK's departure upon Ireland; but important issues were also raised by Cyprus as regards the future of the UK's Sovereign Base Areas in that Member State; and by Spain when it came to the treatment of Gibraltar in the context of UK withdrawal. The Union

---

[26] E.g. European Council (Article 50): meetings of 25 November 2018 and 17 October 2019.

[27] Art 15(1) TEU. Though consider, e.g. D. Curtin, *Executive Power of the European Union: Law, Practices and the Living Constitution* (2009).

[28] See further, e.g. P.-T. Stoll, *The Role and Powers of the European Parliament in the Brexit Process* (In-Depth Analysis commissioned by the IMCO Committee of the European Parliament, PE 602.054 of June 2017).

[29] E.g. European Parliament, *Resolution on the decision to leave the EU resulting from the UK referendum* (28 June 2016).

[30] In particular: European Parliament, *Resolution on negotiations with the UK following its notification that it intends to withdraw from the European Union* (5 April 2017); plus subsequent resolutions of 3 October 2017, 13 December 2017, 14 March 2018 and 18 September 2019.

[31] See, e.g. Commission, *Speech by Michel Barnier at the Plenary Session of the European Parliament on the state of play of negotiations with the United Kingdom* (3 October 2017).

institutions sought to respect the importance and sensitivity of those special national interests when making political judgments about the overall progress and outcomes of the negotiations. For example, in the case of Ireland, the Commission maintained a regular dialogue with the Irish government;[32] while the European Council President held bilateral meetings with the Taoiseach throughout the Article 50 TEU process.[33]

Just as importantly, even if no Member State held a formal veto over conclusion of the withdrawal agreement as a matter of Union law, it is arguable that the Union in practice acted only with the consent of certain Member States—the latter effectively being offered a de facto blocking power by their peers over further progress in the relevant discussions. In some cases, that de facto veto was surely of a relatively limited nature and extent. For example, the EU27 were willing to agree that Spain's positive consent was required specifically on the question of whether Gibraltar should be included within the territorial scope of the proposed transition period under the withdrawal agreement (and indeed for Gibraltar to be the subject of any potential future agreements between the Union and the UK).[34] In one situation, however, the de facto veto offered to a Member State by its peers appears to have been more far-reaching in nature and extent. In particular, so central was the question of how to manage the Irish border, both to the interests of the Republic of Ireland as a Member State, and to the separation challenges that needed to be addressed within the withdrawal negotiations, that Ireland's satisfaction (or otherwise) with the proposed solutions was generally assumed to be critical for progress with the overall discussions and to political endorsement of the entire withdrawal package.[35]

Besides those exceptional situations justified by the engagement of fundamental national interests, recognized as such and deferred to by their peers, the question arises: did any Member State enjoy a de facto power to veto the Union's approval of the withdrawal agreement as a whole and for less compelling reasons of national discontent? The point was never tested in practice, even during the fraught experience of the UK negotiations. On the one hand, it could be argued that, since no proposed text could realistically proceed to formal approval and ratification without the European Council's explicit endorsement, and since the European Council had a longstanding practice of acting only by consensus, Union approval of any draft withdrawal agreement effectively depended upon the prior unanimous support of every Member State—a point reinforced (as we shall see) by the Union's determination to maintain a united front in its approach towards the UK's withdrawal throughout the entire

---

[32] Consider, e.g. Commission, *Joint Statement by President Jean-Claude Juncker and Taoiseach Leo Varadkar* (6 February 2019); *Statement following President Jean-Claude Juncker's phone call with Taoiseach Leo Varadkar* (3 October 2019); *Von der Leyen in Ireland: Our Mutual Solidarity is Here to Stay* (15 January 2020).

[33] Consider, e.g. European Council, *Remarks by President Donald Tusk after his meeting with Taoiseach Leo Varadkar* (1 December 2017); *Remarks by President Donald Tusk after his meeting with Taoiseach Leo Varadkar* (8 March 2018); *Remarks by President Donald Tusk after his meeting with Taoiseach Leo Varadkar* (4 October 2018).

[34] Consider, e.g. European Council (Article 50), *Guidelines of 29 April 2017,* at para 24; Council Decision supplementing the Council Decision of 22 May 2017 (29 January 2018), Annex at para 5; European Council (Article 50), *Guidelines of 23 March 2018,* at para 1.

[35] Consider, e.g. European Council, *Remarks by President Donald Tusk after his meetings with Taoiseach Leo Varadkar* (1 December 2017 and 8 March 2018).

Article 50 TEU process. On the other hand, it would undoubtedly have remained constitutionally possible for the Commission to propose signature and conclusion of a draft withdrawal agreement by super-qualified majority within the Council, acting with the consent of the European Parliament, notwithstanding the objections of certain Member States within the European Council and indeed the active opposition of their voting representatives in Council—for example, in the (unlikely) event that Spain were to have sought to 'veto' endorsement of the entire withdrawal package for reasons not only unrelated to its legitimate concerns about the status of Gibraltar, but also considered by its peers to be politically unreasonable in nature.

D. The Involvement of National Institutions in Approval of Any Proposed Withdrawal Agreement?

In setting out the procedure for concluding and approving any proposed withdrawal agreement with the relevant State, Article 50 TEU describes only the roles of the relevant Union institutions. But how far might the domestic institutions of the Member States also have a role to play in finalizing the terms of the relevant State's withdrawal from the Union (even despite the absolute silence of the Treaties on any such possibility)?

In that regard, it is useful to begin by recalling the normal rules governing the existence and nature of Union external competences: the fundamental principle of conferral; the distinction between exclusive and shared Union competence; and the possibility of mixity.[36] The latter arises where either an agreement involves shared competences and the Member States insist upon mixity as a political choice (which is the more common explanation);[37] or an agreement contains provisions falling altogether outside the Union's powers so that mixity becomes a positive constitutional requirement (though that is somewhat rarer).[38] Either way, mixed agreements need to be agreed and ratified also by the Member States themselves.[39] Even though the Treaty of Lisbon broadened the scope of the Union's exclusive external competences,[40] and the Court has since played its part in confirming their expansive interpretation,[41] rulings such as the *Opinion on the Singapore Free Trade Agreement* remind us that Union competences in general, and exclusive competences in particular, still have their limits

---

[36] See further, e.g. A. Dashwood, M. Dougan, B. Rodger, E. Spaventa and D. Wyatt, *Wyatt and Dashwood's EU Law* (6th ed, 2011) Chapter 27.

[37] As with the EU-Ukraine Association Agreement or the Comprehensive Economic and Trade Agreement with Canada.

[38] See further, e.g. P. Koutrakos (ed.), *Mixed Agreements Revisited: The EU and Its Member States in the World* (2010).

[39] Subject to the possibility of a Council decision pursuant to Article 218(5) TFEU for provisional application by the Union of an international agreement before its entry into force. See further, e.g. van der Loo and Wessel, 'The non-ratification of mixed agreements: legal consequences and solutions', 54 *CMLRev* (2017) 735.

[40] Arts 3(1) and 3(2) TFEU; but particularly in the field of the common commercial policy under Art 207 TFEU.

[41] On Art 207 TFEU, e.g. Case C-414/11, *Daiichi Sankyo* (EU:C:2013:520); Case C-137/12, *Commission v Council* (EU:C:2013:675); Case C-389/15, *Commission v Council* (EU:C:2017:798). Though note rulings such as Opinion 3/15, *Marrakesh Treaty* (EU:C:2017:114).

and therefore the possibility of mixity remains an important element of Union external relations law.[42]

Against that background, it was evident from the earliest stages in discussions about UK withdrawal that any agreement designed to address the 'separation challenges' raised by a Member State's departure would soon extend beyond issues generally accepted to fall within the Union's exclusive powers and into matters usually regarded as falling within competences shared between the Union and the Member States (or even reserved exclusively to the Member States alone)—such as the future treatment of existing UK migrants across the EU27 after they are reclassified as third country nationals for the purposes of Union and national immigration law.[43] Moreover, as the Article 50 TEU negotiations progressed, it became even more obvious that the proposed EU–UK withdrawal agreement would inevitably cover issues ordinarily considered to be matters of shared Union–Member State competence. That was particularly true in light of the UK's request for a wide-ranging 'status quo' transition period, which was designed to govern the future (even if only temporary) treatment of the UK, not only by the Union institutions but also the Member States, for all manner of regulatory and administrative purposes, across almost all possible spheres of activity falling under the Treaties.[44]

The question therefore arose: what is the nature of the Union competence created under Article 50 TEU and, in particular, how far does it deviate from our normal constitutional expectations concerning mixed agreements? As a matter of principle, it was possible to identify (at least) three interpretations, each suggesting a different role for national institutions in the ratification of any Article 50 TEU withdrawal agreement.

First, Article 50 TEU could be treated as a sui generis power which has ousted the ordinary possibilities of mixity, even as regards matters falling within the scope of shared competences. Instead, the Member States have effectively delegated to the Union institutions sole power to negotiate and conclude the agreement under Article 50 TEU, as regards all necessary arrangements relating to the relevant State's withdrawal, regardless of whether the subject matter would normally be considered to fall within Union or national exclusive or shared competence. As such, matters such as the future treatment of current UK migrants, or the adoption of wide-ranging status quo transitional provisions, could all be dealt with under the withdrawal agreement and in accordance with the Article 50 TEU procedure alone.

Secondly, it could instead be argued that Article 50 TEU simply cannot displace the normal division of competences between the Union and its Member States in the field of external relations. The withdrawal agreement is therefore an ordinary international agreement, capable of qualifying as a mixed agreement in accordance with the ordinary principles of Union constitutional law. As such, the Member States retain their right to assert the prerogative of national ratification as regards issues falling within fields of shared competence—precisely such as the future treatment of existing UK migrants and/or the creation of a status quo transitional regime.

---

[42] Opinion 2/15, *Singapore Agreement* (EU:C:2017:376). Note the clarification in Case C-600/14, *Germany v Council* (EU:C:2017:935).

[43] On citizens' rights under the Withdrawal Agreement, see further Chapter 7.

[44] On the transition period under the Withdrawal Agreement, see further Chapter 6.

The third and final interpretation argues that Article 50 TEU is indeed intended to exclude any possibility of mixity, since the Treaty drafters clearly sought to deny any single Member State the power of veto over the terms of the relevant State's withdrawal from the Union. But at the same time, in the absence of any clear indication to the contrary, nor can Article 50 TEU have the effect of expanding Union competences at the expense of legitimate national powers. The logical conclusion is that the withdrawal agreement under Article 50 TEU can only deal with issues falling under exclusive Union competences. In order to deal with issues covered by shared competences (such as current UK migrants or the transitional period), the Union would need to rely on alternative legal bases in order to reach an agreement with the UK—and that agreement could indeed be mixed.

As usual, it would ultimately be for the Court of Justice to clarify the applicable legal principles and pronounce on the correct interpretation of Article 50 TEU. But in the absence of judicial guidance, it fell to the Union's political institutions to spell out their understanding of the nature of Union competence under Article 50 TEU.

Of course, one can understand the principled motivations underpinning all three of the potential interpretations set out above. But in sheer practical terms, the second interpretation (apply our normal constitutional expectations also to the specific context of Article 50 TEU and allow for the possibility of mixity as well as the prospect of national ratifications) would have inevitably rendered the challenge of agreeing an orderly withdrawal from the Union within the limited time available considerably more cumbersome and uncertain.[45] Similarly, the third interpretation (restrict the legitimate scope of the Article 50 TEU competence to exclusive Union matters then search for alternative legal bases to address other withdrawal-related issues) would have enormously complicated the constitutional framework for withdrawal—even assuming that the Union could identify any alternative legal bases for reaching agreements to address (non-exclusive) withdrawal-related issues. After all: under either interpretation, there would have been the potential for any Member State parliament (or indeed regional parliament, even a popular referendum) to cause significant delays and/or disruption to the process and/or terms of the relevant State's withdrawal from the Union.

For those reasons, it was surely unsurprising that the Union's political institutions adopted our first potential interpretation of the Article 50 TEU competence. In particular, the Council in its negotiating directives from May 2017 explicitly endorsed the Commission's proposed understanding that Article 50 TEU gives the Union an *exceptional* horizontal power to negotiate all the matters necessary to arrange the terms of withdrawal—exceptional at least to the extent that it empowers the Union alone to reach agreement with the UK, on behalf of the remaining Member States, even as regards issues which would normally be seen as falling within shared competence.[46]

---

[45] Again, as with the EU–Ukraine Association Agreement (consider the impact of the negative Dutch referendum) or the Comprehensive Economic and Trade Agreement with Canada (consider the impact of regional parliamentary ratification in Belgium).

[46] See Commission, *Recommendation for a Council decision authorising the Commission to open negotiations on an agreement with the UK setting out the arrangements for its withdrawal from the European Union*, COM(2017) 218 Final.

The Council also stressed that this exceptional power was of a one-off nature and strictly for the purposes of arranging withdrawal; it would not affect in any way the distribution of competences between the Union and the Member States as regards future instruments in the areas concerned.[47] Otherwise, however, the exceptional power conferred upon the Union under Article 50 TEU was sufficient to avoid any possibility of the withdrawal agreement being treated as a mixed one, requiring individual national ratifications, in addition to the Union-level endorsement explicitly provided for under Article 50 TEU itself. And indeed, the Commission thereafter conducted the entire withdrawal negotiations on the assumption that, when it came to calculating the time required for approval of the Article 50 TEU agreement, it was necessary to factor in the requirements of the European Parliament, the Council, the UK Government and the Westminster Parliament—omitting any consideration or possibility of domestic ratification procedures also by any other Member State.[48]

The purpose of the political agreement expressed by the Council is clear: to prevent any single Member State from wielding a veto over the terms of departure for a withdrawing country, at least through the medium of insisting upon the need also for domestic level ratifications, in addition to the approval procedures laid down at the level of the Union directly by and under the Treaties.[49] The problem was that that political agreement remained vulnerable to challenge by a disgruntled Member State should the unity of the EU27 have broken down at any stage in the negotiations (for example) over the treatment of the Irish border or the transitional status of Gibraltar. It also remained possible that dissent could well up from other stakeholders, not least at the national constitutional level, if parliaments or regional assemblies did not agree with the political preference expressed by their national government within the Council—a preference which may well be justified by reasons of convenience in the conduct and conclusion of the Article 50 TEU negotiations but undoubtedly came at the potential expense of national competence and prerogatives.

In the end, no Member State or national institution directly challenged the Union's claim to exclusive competence over all arrangements relating to the UK's orderly withdrawal under Article 50 TEU. It is worth noting that, not only the domestic institutions of the Member States themselves, but also other important stakeholders were offered very limited opportunities for direct engagement with the Union's own internal process for handling the UK's withdrawal. For example, despite their clear and obvious interest in the outcome of both the negotiations on the immediate challenges of withdrawal (such as the protection of existing migrant citizens' rights) and the discussions on longer-term relations between the Union and the UK (including potential terms of participation in and/or access to the Single Market) the European Free Trade Association–European Economic Area (EFTA–EEA) states were not formally

---

[47] Council Decision of 22 May 2017.

[48] E.g. Commission, *Déclaration presse par Michel Barnier suite à l'adoption d'une recommandation visant à entamer les discussions relatives à la phase suivante du retrait ordonné du Royaume-Uni de l'Union européenne* (20 December 2017).

[49] See further, e.g. Editorial Comments, 'Withdrawing from the 'ever closer union'?', 53 *CMLRev* (2016) 1491; Eeckhout and Frantziou, 'Brexit and Article 50 TEU: A Constitutionalist Reading', 54 *CMLRev* (2017) 695.

included in any of the Union's internal decision-making processes or in the actual withdrawal negotiations with the UK.[50]

E. The European Council's 'Core Principles': Legal and Political Considerations Informing the Withdrawal Process

The overwhelming impetus behind the formulation and advancement of the Union's negotiating objectives and interests was therefore provided by the Union institutions themselves. And at that Union level, primary responsibility for making the judgments and exercising the discretion required to operationalize Article 50 TEU in practice, not least by formulating a coordinated Union response to the prospect of UK withdrawal, fell squarely upon the shoulders of the European Council.

In that regard, the initial Guidelines adopted in April 2019 (even if they were far from the last word on negotiations with the UK) assumed a position of central importance in the entire withdrawal process, in so far as they identified a series of 'core principles' which would be treated as applicable to any and all negotiations conducted under the auspices of Article 50 TEU.[51] For present purposes, those 'core principles' can be divided into two main categories: those which were essentially legal in character, seeking to clarify and elaborate on the constitutional implications of withdrawal; and those which were primarily political in nature, seeking to articulate the key negotiating interests of the Union and its remaining Member States. The former usefully provided certain minimum rules and criteria to help guide the Union's handling of the Article 50 TEU process; but only the latter can fully explain the Union's (surprisingly coherent and relatively successful) approach to the UK withdrawal negotiations.

(i) Core Legal Principles Identified by the European Council's
      April 2017 Guidelines
Right from the outcome of the 2016 referendum and the realization that the Union now needed to prepare in earnest for its first ever withdrawal, it was clear that there would be certain legal and technical limits to what the Union could possibly offer or agree to with the UK. For example: as an organization endowed with only attributed competences, governed by the rule of law, and obliged to respect various fundamental principles and rights, it was obvious that the Union could not offer or agree to terms which it lacked the necessary power to deliver—such as political or journalistic suggestions that the UK could be offered or negotiate 'associate member status' of the Union, when no such phenomenon exists under the Union's current constitutional arrangements.[52] Similarly: the possibilities for involvement of a third country in a whole range of Union policies, programmes and bodies/agencies is dependent upon fulfilling the necessary criteria for participation in accordance with the opportunities available

---

[50] See further, e.g. Hillion, 'Brexit means Br(EEA)xit: The UK Withdrawal from the EU and its Implications for the EEA', 55 *CMLRev* (2018) 135.
[51] European Council (Article 50), *Guidelines of 29 April 2017*. The key themes were already evident from European Council, *Statement from Informal Meeting at 27* (29 June 2016).
[52] See further, e.g. Dashwood, 'The Limits of European Community Powers', 21 *ELRev* (1996) 113.

under the relevant Union legislative frameworks.[53] Moreover, from a technical perspective, negotiating workable terms of involvement or participation is not merely a matter (as so often assumed, certainly in the UK political and public debates) of the relevant third country simply following the same or at least comparable substantive rules to that of the Union itself; they also depend upon the existence of appropriate institutions and processes for operationalizing the relevant rules and frameworks for cooperation, together with adequate guarantees for implementation and enforcement within each territory.[54]

Such legal and technical issues also featured prominently in the European Council's April 2017 Guidelines. The latter's 'core principles' sought to express and articulate certain legal values or norms—often derived and adapted from the existing caselaw of the Court of Justice—that should govern and influence both the conduct and the outcomes of the UK withdrawal process.

Some of those 'core principles' imposed relatively clear and identifiable substantive legal limits on what the Union could possibly agree to under any negotiated withdrawal deal. For example, the European Council stressed that the Union must preserve its own autonomy as regards both decision-making and the role of the CJEU—an obvious reference to the constitutional principles developed by the Court in its caselaw which are designed to protect the Union legal order from external interference, particularly in the context of external agreements with third countries and/or other international organizations.[55] Those principles were recalled in all of the relevant Union negotiating papers and are reflected in the final provisions of the Withdrawal Agreement concerning legal interpretation by/dispute settlement between the Union and the UK.[56]

In other cases, the European Council's 'core [legal] principles' were less prescriptive and more flexible in character—being aimed primarily at influencing the Union's handling of the Article 50 TEU process, when it came to the mutual conduct of the Union institutions and the remaining Member States, by articulating certain minimum standards of loyal cooperation among the relevant actors. For example, the April 2017 Guidelines agreed that there should be no separate negotiations by individual Member States on matters pertaining to the UK's withdrawal.[57] Again, that implicitly referenced the special obligations of action and abstention which the Court had previously extracted from the general duty of loyal cooperation, in situations where the Commission has submitted proposals to the Council which (even if not yet finally adopted) represent the point of departure for concerted action by the Union institutions. In particular, the Court has previously held that the adoption of a decision to negotiate a multilateral agreement on behalf of the Union marks the start of collective Union action at the international level and requires, if not a duty of abstention by the Member States, at least a duty of close cooperation between the Member States and

---

[53] See further, e.g. House of Commons Library Briefing Paper, *EU Agencies and Post-Brexit Options* (No 7957 of 28 April 2017).

[54] See further, on these issues, Chapter 9.

[55] See the detailed analysis and references in Chapter 9.

[56] See the detailed analysis and references in Chapter 6.

[57] European Council (Article 50), *Guidelines of 29 April 2017*, at para 2.

the Union institutions in order to facilitate the achievement of the Union's tasks and to ensure coherence and consistency in the Union's international affairs.[58]

Another important part of the European Council's 'core [legal] principles' was again directed at managing the Article 50 TEU process, but this time as regards relations with the UK as a withdrawing State, by identifying certain minimum standards of loyal cooperation between the UK (on the one hand) and the Union and its remaining Member States (on the other hand). Indeed, the April 2017 Guidelines represent an important initiative to adapt and clarify the proper interpretation and application of the general duty of sincere cooperation as contained in Article 4(3) TEU, specifically as regards the unprecedented situation in which the UK continued to be a Member State but was also actively engaged in proceeding towards its own eventual withdrawal.

The European Council's starting point was that (until withdrawal) the UK would remain a Member State with its full rights and obligations; in principle, the Union should seek to maintain the principle of 'business as usual' for the entire EU28.[59] The European Council thus correctly anticipated the basic legal approach towards the UK's membership of the Union, even after formal notification of its intention to withdraw, which was subsequently confirmed by the Court in rulings such as *Wightman*: the status of Member State is not suspended or altered by the act of notification; the relevant State enjoys all of the rights and remains bound by all of the obligations laid down in the Treaties.[60] The only explicit exceptions provided for under the Treaties are to be found in Article 50(4) TEU, which decrees that the UK should not participate in discussions or decisions of the European Council or the Council specifically under Article 50(2)–(3) TEU, i.e. those concerning the adoption of the necessary withdrawal guidelines, the negotiation and conclusion of any withdrawal agreement or the extension of the final date of actual withdrawal.

However, the full implications of withdrawal for the general duty of sincere cooperation, as well as the aspiration to maintain 'business as usual' among the EU28, sometimes proved more difficult to interpret and apply in practice than the April 2017 Guidelines or the Court in *Wightman* might have appeared to suggest or assume. In fact, the UK experience highlighted several situations in which the Union was challenged to adapt the usual legal expectations of sincere cooperation to the novel political realities of withdrawal.

For example, the European Council expressed its expectation that the UK would recognize the need for the EU27 to meet and discuss inter se various matters relating to the UK's withdrawal.[61] Such formulation suggested that the exclusion of the UK from various Union-level discussions relating to its eventual withdrawal would not be limited to the relatively small number of specific situations identified in Article 50(4) TEU. Far from it: the April 2017 Guidelines suggest a potentially wider range of institutional situations or procedures in which the EU27 might wish to discuss a

---

[58] E.g. Case C-266/03, *Commission v Luxembourg* (EU:C:2005:341); Case C-433/03, *Commission v Germany* (EU:C:2005:462). See further, e.g. Neframi, 'The duty of loyalty: Rethinking its scope through its application in the field of EU external relations', 47 *CMLRev* (2010) 323.

[59] European Council (Article 50), *Guidelines of 29 April 2017*, at paras 25 and 27.

[60] Case C-621/18, *Wightman* (EU:C:2018:999), at para 59 and para 73. Also, e.g. Case C-327/18, *R O* (EU:C:2018:733); Case C-661/17, *M A* (EU:C:2019:53).

[61] European Council (Article 50), *Guidelines of 29 April 2017*, at para 26.

broader array of substantive matters, nevertheless raised or affected by the UK's decision to leave the Union, without the presence or participation of British representatives. That practice appears to have evolved, not just within Union institutions such as the Commission and the Council but also across a wider range of Union bodies and agencies—and seems not to have been considered incompatible with the UK's status as a continuing Member State under the terms laid down in Article 50 TEU and confirmed by the Court in *Wightman*.[62]

Conversely, the European Council explicitly recognized the need (especially in the context of international relations) to take into account the specificities of the UK as a withdrawing State—thus acknowledging that there should be an additional space for the UK Government to prepare for the consequences of its own withdrawal in the external sphere.[63] However, eyebrows were raised when the UK not only negotiated but signed a series of international agreements with third countries, intended to preserve some of the terms and conditions of trade which currently applied between the parties under existing international agreements already concluded between the EU and the relevant third countries—doing so even before the effective date of withdrawal and thus while the UK was still a full Member State of the Union.[64] Of course, the UK may have felt that—given its obvious national interest in preserving existing trade conditions across the global economy, particularly when faced with continuing uncertainty about the prospects for approving any withdrawal agreement with the Union itself—this was precisely the type of situation where the EU27 should (as they had themselves suggested) take into account the specificities of the UK within the context of international relations.[65] But it is not at all obvious that the relevant core principles identified by the European Council in its April 2017 Guidelines were ever intended to exempt the UK from clear and legally binding obligations imposed under the Treaties concerning the division of competences between the Union and its Member States—or indeed, whether those Guidelines were at all legally capable of having such an effect (even if it had been intended or envisaged) as a matter of Union constitutional law.[66]

---

[62] The practice was recognized and reaffirmed by the European Council (Article 50), *Conclusions of 10 April 2019*.

[63] European Council (Article 50), *Guidelines of 29 April 2017*, at para 26.

[64] In particular, the UK signed several 'continuity agreements' with third countries even before formal British withdrawal from the Union, e.g. the Trade Agreement between the United Kingdom of Great Britain and Northern Ireland (of the one part) and the Republic of Colombia, the Republic of Ecuador and the Republic of Peru (of the other part) of 15 May 2019.

[65] On the UK's preparations for its own post-Brexit external relations in general and the negotiation of third country 'continuity agreements' in fields such as trade in particular, see also the discussion in Chapter 2 and Chapter 6.

[66] The answer, of course, most certainly being 'no': mere guidelines adopted by the European Council, or indeed by any other Union institution, body or agency, would not be capable of amending or abrogating legally binding Union acts—least of all the Treaties themselves. Note that issues of loyal cooperation in relation to the UK as a withdrawing State, and indeed as a third country under the final Withdrawal Agreement, were to resurface later in the Brexit process: see further, e.g. the discussion in Chapter 5 about sincere cooperation during the period of extended UK membership; and in Chapter 8 about UK implementation of the border plans contained in the final Protocol on Ireland/Northern Ireland.

(ii) Core Legal Principles Also Explored and Clarified by the CJEU

It was not only in the political but also in the judicial sphere that situations arose in which the full implications of UK withdrawal for the European Council's core principles concerning the duty of sincere cooperation and the principle of 'business as usual' had to be tested and worked through. In particular, the Union courts were invited to explore the implications of the UK's intended departure from the Union legal order for the full and proper functioning of the principle of mutual recognition for national decisions and the presumption of mutual trust between the Member States—principles which together lie at the foundation of so much Union activity in fields such as the Single Market and the Area of Freedom, Security and Justice.[67]

Consider the dispute in *R O*.[68] In 2016 and before the referendum, the UK authorities issued European Arrest Warrants (EAWs) in respect of the defendant for alleged crimes consisting of murder and rape. R O was arrested in Ireland and remanded in custody based on those UK-issued EAWs. However, after the UK delivered its formal notification of intention to leave the Union in March 2017, the defendant objected to his judicial surrender by the Irish authorities on the grounds that it was highly probably he would remain in prison in the UK after the latter's withdrawal took effect in March 2019; and that it remained uncertain precisely which future rules or protections would govern his future detention in the UK as compared to the existing rights he enjoyed under Union law—such as the restrictions on further extradition as laid down in the EAW Framework Decision;[69] or the protections against inhuman and degrading treatment as contained in the Charter of Fundamental Rights.[70] In effect, the defendant argued that UK notification had irreparably eroded the principle of mutual trust, which lies at the basis of the system of mutual recognition underpinning the operation of the EAW, such that the UK's request for his judicial surrender should not now be executed.

On a reference from the Irish courts, the Court of Justice held that mere notification by a Member State of its intention to withdraw from the Union does not have the consequence that another Member State must refuse to execute an EAW or postpone the latter's execution pending clarification of the law that will be applicable in the issuing Member State after withdrawal.

According to the Court, EU law is based on the fundamental premiss that each Member State shares with all the other Member States a set of common values on which the European Union is founded. That premiss implies and justifies the existence of mutual trust between the Member States that those values will be recognized

---

[67] See further, e.g. Cramér, 'Reflections on the Roles of Mutual Trust in EU Law' in M. Dougan and S. Currie (eds), *50 Years of the European Treaties: Looking Back and Thinking Forward* (2009); Möstl, 'Preconditions and Limits in Mutual Recognition', 47 *CMLRev* (2010) 405; Lenaerts, 'La vie après l'avis: Exploring the principle of mutual (not blind) trust', 54 *CMLRev* (2017) 805; Xanthopoulou, 'Mutual Trust and Rights in EU Criminal and Asylum Law: Three Phases of Evolution and the Unchartered Territory Beyond Blind Trust', 55 *CMLRev* (2018) 489; Maiani and Migliorini, 'One Principle to Rule Them All? Anatomy of Mutual Trust in the Law of the Area of Freedom, Security and Justice', 57 *CMLRev* (2020) 7.

[68] Case C-327/18, *R O* (EU:C:2018:733). See further, e.g. Sáenz Pérez, '*R O*: Brexit means nothing has changed ... yet', 44 *ELRev* (2019) 548. Consider also the ruling in Case C-661/17, *M A* (EU:C:2019:53).

[69] Framework Decision 2002/584 on the European arrest warrant and the surrender procedures between Member States, OJ 2002 L 190/1 (as amended).

[70] In particular: Art 4 CFR.

and that EU law implementing them will be respected. The principle of mutual trust between the Member States requires each of them, save in exceptional circumstances, to consider all the other Member States to be complying with EU law and particularly with the fundamental rights recognized by EU law. Those principles apply within the specific legal framework created in respect of judicial surrenders pursuant to the EAW. Moreover, the mere act of notification under Article 50 TEU does not have the effect of suspending the application of Union law in the relevant Member State: Union law, including the provisions of the EAW Framework Decision and its underlining principles of mutual trust and mutual recognition, continue in full force and effect within the relevant Member State until the time of its actual withdrawal from the Union.

Against that background, refusal to execute an EAW issued by the UK, based simply on the latter's notification under Article 50 TEU, would be equivalent to unilateral suspension of the EAW Framework Decision in respect of an existing Member State. Moreover, notification under Article 50 TEU cannot be regarded in itself as an exceptional circumstance capable of justifying a refusal to execute an EAW issued by the UK. The position would be different only if the competent judicial authorities in Ireland had substantial grounds to believe that the defendant would be at risk, following UK withdrawal, of being deprived of the rights recognized under the EAW Framework Decision or the Charter of Fundamental Rights. For those purposes, however, the Irish courts had to take into account the fact that the UK would remain bound by and continue to implement various relevant provisions of international law (including the European Convention on Human Rights and the European Convention on Extradition 1957) which together provided many of the same protections as did Union law itself under the Charter and/or the EAW Framework Decision. As such, there appeared to be no concrete evidence suggesting that the defendant would be deprived of the opportunity to assert his relevant rights and protections before the UK courts even after the UK's eventual withdrawal from the Union.

Moreover, that finding was not affected by the fact that, after the date of withdrawal and in the absence of a suitable agreement between the Union and the UK, the defendant's rights could no longer form the subject of a preliminary reference to the Court of Justice itself. After all, recourse to the preliminary ruling system had not always been possible in respect of the EAW, even as regards the national courts and tribunals of the Member States themselves: it was only on 1 December 2014 that the Court gained full jurisdiction, in accordance with the Lisbon Treaty reforms, to interpret the EAW Framework Decision (despite the latter's deadline for national transposition having already expired on 31 December 2003).

It is easy to sympathize with the Court's decision in *R O*, that the UK's notification of intention to withdraw from the Union should not, in itself, upset the continued functioning of the European Arrest Warrant. After all, to have decided otherwise could have wreaked havoc not only with the system of cross-border judicial surrenders per se, but also with a much broader range of primary and secondary Union law regimes that depend on comparable presumptions of mutual recognition and mutual trust, across the remainder of the Area of Freedom, Security and Justice but also the field of application of the Single Market. Moreover, though admittedly with the benefit of hindsight, such havoc would have proved even more troublesome, in the light of the subsequent ruling in *Wightman*, having regard to the possibility that the UK might well revoke its original notification of intention to withdraw and decide to remain a Member State after all.[71]

Nevertheless, the judgment in R O is also amenable to criticism. For example, it is difficult to reconcile R O with other judgments in which the Court seemed to conceive of the Union as a 'special legal space' which offers its own particularly robust system of guarantees to the fundamental rights of its own citizens—especially in relations with third countries that do not participate in the same legal order or subscribe to the same standards of judicial protection; and specifically when it comes to requests for the extradition of a Union citizen to face trial or punishment outside the Union's own territory.[72] Against that background, it might appear rather generous of the Court in R O to accept the prospect of continued UK compliance with 'ordinary' international standards of fundamental rights protection in general, and extradition processes in particular, as effectively equivalent to the Union's supposedly special and superior guarantees. Indeed, not just generous, but positively naïve: the Court based its reasoning on a positive legal assumption that the UK would continue to adhere to international fundamental rights standards such as those enshrined in the European Convention on Human Rights (ECHR)—despite the fact that there was no compelling legal basis for, let alone concrete guarantee underpinning that assumption. On the contrary: concerns that the Court was risking the fundamental rights of Union citizens for the sake of rather flimsy guarantees that the UK would maintain (only lower) standards of protection were subsequently reinforced, when the Johnson Government reneged upon its promise (as contained in its very own Political Declaration) to make explicit provision for continued UK membership and domestic implementation of the ECHR within any future agreement on EU–UK trade and security relations.[73]

(iii) Core Political Priorities Identified by the European Council's April 2017 Guidelines

We have seen how the UK's withdrawal process was to be governed and influenced by a range of provisions and factors: the general institutional framework provided by Article 50 TEU as supplemented by the additional roles exercised by/afforded to the European Council, the European Parliament and the Member States; together with the broader legal and technical constraints imposed under Union law—including several of the 'core principles' set out by the European Council in its April 2017 Guidelines, which sought to establish minimum standards for the conduct of the withdrawal process as well as certain restrictions upon its potential outcomes. But that institutional and legal framework still left very considerable room for political discretion to define more fully the Union's interests in and approach towards negotiations with the UK following notification of its intention to withdraw.

Once again, right from the outcome of the 2016 referendum, it was possible to identify various political limits to what the Union could possibly offer or agree to with the UK within the context of the Article 50 TEU negotiations.

---

[71] On which: see the discussion in Chapter 2.

[72] Consider, e.g. Case C-182/15, *Petruhhin* (EU:C:2016:630); Case C-247/17, *Raugevicius* (EU: C:2018:898).

[73] See further the detailed discussion in Chapter 9.

Those political limits derived at least partly from the individual national interests of the remaining Member States. Naturally, each Member State was bound to calculate and promote its specific concerns arising from UK withdrawal: the potentially fundamental adverse economic and political implications for Ireland provide the supreme example; though one also thinks of Spain's particular interest in the future status and treatment of Gibraltar. National agendas might align along certain regional lines. For example, it was arguable that UK withdrawal threatened specific economic consequences for a relatively small number of Member States (such as Belgium, the Netherlands, France and Germany) which had evolved highly integrated business supply chains, consumer markets and/or logistical infrastructure based on UK membership; whereas another contingent of Member States (especially in central and eastern Europe) might be worried less about the domestic trade implications of UK withdrawal and more concerned about making adequate provision for the future treatment of their own nationals already resident in the UK pursuant to Union free movement law. Obviously, the national interests of each Member State could also pull in different directions across different policy sectors (France might have some economic incentive to capitalize on the downgrading of the UK as an international business hub, yet still desire a strong UK commitment to European security and defence); and might well evolve over time according to changing national political pressures (not least as a consequence of domestic elections, for example in Italy, that might suddenly produce a radically different government).

Altogether, such factors made it difficult to identify a clear and coherent 'Brexit policy' defined primarily by reference to the individual national interests of a stable coalition of Member States. But that only increased the importance attached to the main alternative (or rather additional) source of political limits to what the UK could possibly be offered/expect in its own withdrawal negotiations: the collective interests of the remaining Member States working together in and with the Union institutions. And those collective interests were articulated, above all, in the European Council's April 2017 Guidelines—whose 'core principles' not only explored certain legal issues around the Article 50 TEU process, but also identified the key political considerations that would guide the Union's overall approach to and management of the UK's withdrawal.

In particular, the April 2017 Guidelines contained the seeds of the Union's four key shared negotiating objectives; expressed, moreover, in a clear order of priority. First, the Union attached overriding importance to preserving its own unity within and between the Union institutions and the 27 remaining Member States. The unprecedented decision of the UK to leave cannot endanger the solidarity or indeed the survival of the Union as a whole. To that end, every competent actor should present a common front in the Article 50 TEU process—going above and beyond whatever formal institutional roles might be prescribed under the Treaties and surpassing whatever basic legal requirements might derive from the duty of sincere cooperation. Thus, the European Council proclaimed that the Union should approach the negotiations with unified positions and engage with the UK exclusively through the channels provided for under Article 50 TEU.[74] And indeed, many commentators marvelled at

---

[74] European Council (Article 50), *Guidelines of 29 April 2017*, at para 2.

the relative discipline and success of the Union institutions as well as the remaining Member States in approaching the UK withdrawal negotiations with a high degree of mutual coordination and consensus—both from the outset and throughout the entire process.[75]

Secondly, and of almost equal importance, the Union and its Member States must protect the cohesion of the EU legal order as a whole and of the Single Market in particular. The UK cannot be allowed to enjoy better treatment by leaving the Union than it enjoyed as a (particularly privileged) Member State or indeed as compared to the situation of the remaining Member States. Such concessions could call into question the very principle of Union membership based on the reciprocity of a particularly far-reaching network of rights and obligations. It would also risk destabilizing the Union's existing relations with a wider range of third countries, who might legitimately question why they should be denied comparable forms of 'special treatment'. So (for example) the European Council recalls that no third country can enjoy the same rights and benefits as a Member State; any agreement with the UK must be based on a balance of rights and obligations that ensures a level playing field and preserve the integrity of the Single Market.[76] Again, those political imperatives arguably go beyond the strict legal or technical limits inherent in constitutional principles such as those protecting the autonomy of Union law.[77] The Union can insist (for example) on treating the four freedoms as indivisible for the purposes of discussions with the UK over their future economic relationship—entirely regardless of whether or not such indivisibility is strictly required as a matter of Union law.[78]

The Union's remaining two negotiating objectives were to be pursued entirely subject to that initial pair of overriding political aims. So, thirdly, the Union would seek to deliver the UK's withdrawal in a smooth and orderly (rather than chaotic and damaging) manner—as far as possible, preserving legal certainty and minimizing disruption for public authorities, private businesses, and individual citizens. Thus (for example) the April 2017 Guidelines provide that the Article 50 TEU negotiations should be carefully phased so as to prioritize reaching an agreement that addresses the immediate challenges posed by the very fact of UK withdrawal.[79] Moreover, those talks should be conducted transparently and as single package, so that nothing is agreed until everything is agreed and no individual items are to be settled separately.[80] Fourthly, and finally, the Union's longer-term objective is to reach a future relationship with the UK that will succeed (if at all possible) in keeping its erstwhile Member State still firmly within the Union's own legal orbit and sphere of influence. So (for example) the April 2017 Guidelines insist that, once formal negotiations over a new EU–UK

---

[75] See further, e.g. Van Middelaar, 'Brexit as the European Union's "Machiavellian Moment"', 55 *CMLRev Special Issue* (2018) 3; Laffan, 'How the EU27 Came to Be', 57 *JCMS* (2019) 13.

[76] European Council (Article 50), *Guidelines of 29 April 2017*, at para 1.

[77] See the more detailed discussion of these issues in Chapter 9.

[78] Further, on the integrity of the Single Market as political and legal phenomena, e.g. Editorial Comments, 'Is the "Indivisibility" of the Four Freedoms a Principle of EU law?', 56 *CMLRev* (2019) 1189.

[79] European Council (Article 50), *Guidelines of 29 April 2017*, at paras 4–5.

[80] European Council (Article 50), *Guidelines of 29 April 2017*, at para 2.

relationship commence, the Union's clear desire is to have the UK as a close partner into the future.[81]

Those four political objectives effectively governed the Union's entire subsequent interpretation and application of Article 50 TEU as a legal basis for managing the process and outcomes of UK withdrawal. The Union was always going to be the dominant party in the negotiations. But the EU's natural position of strength was considerably reinforced and amplified by the (perhaps surprising) determination and success of both the Union institutions and the remaining Member States in defending and promoting their shared fundamental political interests as expressed in the April 2017 Guidelines.[82]

3. Legal and Political Factors Affecting the UK

Having examined the key legal and political factors relevant to framing the EU's approach to the Article 50 TEU process, it is now time to explore those affecting the UK's initial engagement with the framework for its own withdrawal. That requires us to step back once again to events and developments immediately following 23 June 2016. After all, Article 50 TEU foresees and requires a decision by the relevant State, in accordance with its own constitutional requirements, to withdraw from the Union. As the Court of Justice observed in *Wightman*, the relevant State is not required to take that decision in concert with the other Member States or with the Union institutions; the decision to withdraw is for the relevant State alone to take and depends solely on its sovereign choice.[83] So how would the UK's political leadership react to the referendum result? In particular: how (if at all) would the popular vote to leave be translated into a constitutionally valid decision to withdraw, which could then provide the basis for formally notifying the European Council of the UK's intention to leave the Union? And what core principles would guide the UK's engagement with the EU when it came to negotiations over the immediate 'separation challenges' as well as the prospects for their future relationship?

In answering those questions, it is (again) useful to separate the politics from the law. Political factors certainly shaped the timing of the UK's formal decision to leave and its subsequent communication to the European Council, whereas legal principles eventually revealed which institutions were constitutionally responsible for taking those actions. However, the fact that the two forces eventually produced a coordinated result—in the form of the Prime Minister's constitutionally valid letter to the President of the European Council, delivered on 29 March 2017, just within the Government's publicly announced deadline—was as much a matter of coincidence as of design.

---

[81] European Council (Article 50), *Guidelines of 29 April 2017*, at paras 1 and 18.

[82] The unity of the EU27 was a point repeatedly stressed by key Union actors throughout the Article 50 TEU process, e.g. European Council, *Report by Donald Tusk to the European Parliament on October European Council meetings* (24 October 2017).

[83] Case C-621/18, *Wightman* (EU:C:2018:999), at para 50.

A. The UK's Political Situation Leading up to Notification

Let's begin with the politics. Before the referendum, Prime Minister Cameron had indicated that the Government would notify the UK's intention to withdraw, directly after a victory for the Leave campaign on 23 June 2016.[84] But even if Cameron had ever genuinely planned to do so, his previous intentions were entirely overtaken by immediate developments—not least Cameron's own resignation as Prime Minster, leading in due course to his replacement by Theresa May and the constitution of a radically different ministerial and Cabinet team. Also, there were significant changes to the central civil service, for example, with new departments created for Exiting the European Union and for International Trade.[85] It was therefore only on 2 October 2016 that the new Prime Minister announced (at the Conservative Party conference in Birmingham) that the UK would submit its notification of intention to withdraw from the Union before the end of March 2017.[86]

(i) Immediate Political Challenges Facing the UK

May's Government was clearly politically committed to leaving the EU: 'Brexit means Brexit'.[87] Moreover, various Union actors were keen to minimize the damaging atmosphere of uncertainty surrounding the UK position, by pressing for notification under Article 50 TEU to be delivered as quickly as possible.[88] So why was there a planned period of up to 9 months between the referendum outcome and formal commencement of the Article 50 TEU process for UK departure? Besides the initial delay attributable to immediate turmoil in the UK's political leadership, several other factors help to explain the Prime Minister's announced timescale. Together, they reveal the fact that the UK's political capacity, to prepare for and then commence the process for its own withdrawal from the Union, was relatively weak and unstable.

In the first place, it appeared that the UK Government had failed to make any significant bureaucratic or diplomatic preparations for the possibility of a Leave victory in the referendum. The state institutions now faced the enormous task of calculating (let alone acting on) the true implications of withdrawal for virtually every aspect of law, administration, the economy, and society. For those purposes, serious questions were soon raised also about the gap between what was available and what was required in terms of the UK's capacities to deal with many of the challenges likely to arise from withdrawal (say) in fields such as international trade negotiations or customs border management.[89] The UK evidently needed more time simply to identify, build, and

---

[84] E.g. speaking in the House of Commons on 22 February 2016.

[85] As well as the other immediate political and institutional consequences of the UK referendum outcome, also at the level of the Union itself, e.g. resignation of the UK Commissioner and the decision to exclude the UK from the rotating presidency of the Council.

[86] See, e.g. 'Brexit: Theresa May to trigger Article 50 by end of March' at https://www.bbc.co.uk/news/uk-politics-37532364.

[87] See, e.g. 'No second referendum if Theresa May becomes PM' at https://www.bbc.co.uk/news/av/uk-politics-36764525.

[88] E.g. European Parliament, *Resolution on the decision to leave the EU resulting from the UK referendum* (28 June 2016).

[89] Consider, e.g. House of Commons Exiting the European Union Committee, *The Process for Exiting the European Union and the Government's Negotiating Objectives* (HC815 of 14 January 2017).

mobilize the enormous and diverse resources that would be required to implement its own decision to leave the Union with even a minimum level of competence.[90]

In the second place, the UK was deeply divided about how to respond to the referendum result and how (if at all) to implement the Leave vote. That was true not only for the general population (as revealed in the June 2016 outcome) but also for Parliament (within, not just across, the two main political parties), as well as for the Government (and indeed the Cabinet). The UK's political leaders not only lacked any clear vision for what might come next in terms of relations with the Union itself—whether the immediate issues involved in the very act of withdrawal, or the longer-term question of the UK's future place in the European order—but were also subject to highly contradictory pressures that rendered the task of formulating a workable and coherent plan even more difficult.

As we saw in Chapter 1, Remain supporters argued that the referendum result had been only a very narrow one and could dispute its very legitimacy given the controversial nature of the Leave campaign. Leave supporters might have had the weight of (a slim majority of) popular support behind them—but even between themselves, they could offer only a range of mutually incompatible manifestos. Some advocated the certainty and continuity of a negotiated withdrawal, leading to a relatively close future framework between the Union and the UK.[91] Others pressed for a unilateral departure, either dismissing or swallowing the risks of short-term disruption, leading to only a much more distant EU–UK relationship.[92] It must have seemed tempting to hark back to some of the key referendum promises of the victorious Leave campaign—whether about retaining the benefits of Single Market membership after withdrawal, or about the nirvana of trading just as easily if not better as a World Trade Organization (WTO) member than as a Member State of the Union—but those could only ever provide a very risky basis for Government policy, given that such promises were bound to prove undeliverable in practice. Once again, the UK evidently needed more time simply to articulate a credible and coherent policy position that could provide the basis for its own withdrawal discussions with the Union under Article 50 TEU.

Against that background, one might at least feel grateful for the fact that Cameron did not keep his word about triggering the Article 50 TEU process immediately after the referendum outcome—a promise that would have initiated a time-constrained process, involving fundamentally important internal challenges as well as external negotiations, which the UK was singularly ill-prepared to manage successfully. But the question remained: having delayed the prospect of notification until the end of March 2017, would the new May Government prove able to use that extra time so as to develop a more workable plan for managing the withdrawal process?

---

[90] Consider, e.g. National Audit Office, Report by the Comptroller and Auditor General, *Implementing the UK's Exit from the European Union: The Department for Exiting the European Union and the Centre of Government* (HC593 of 17 November 2017). Also, e.g. J. Owen, L. Lloyd and J. Rutter, *Preparing Brexit: How Ready is Whitehall?* (Institute for Government, June 2018).

[91] What became known in popular discussion as a 'soft Brexit'.

[92] What became known in popular discussion as a 'hard Brexit'.

(ii) A Policy Goal Emerges: 'To Have One's Cake and Eat It'
The first significant indications emerged from the Prime Minister's 'Lancaster House Speech' on 17 January 2017, in which she described the Government's '12 objectives' for Brexit.[93] In fact, several of those objectives were primarily concerned with internal UK matters, rather than with negotiations or relations with the EU. In particular, the Prime Minister rightly emphasized the importance for the UK of beginning its internal preparations for the inevitable impact of withdrawal upon its own domestic constitutional and legal system: for example, the need to deliver clarity during the overall process of departure, not least by ensuring continuity and certainty across the UK legal system; a desire to strengthen the UK's own union between England, Scotland, Wales and Northern Ireland, particularly as a range of regulatory powers were 'returned from Brussels'; and explicit promises to protect existing workers' rights under UK law, even without the minimum guarantees expected under Union law.

But the Lancaster House Speech did also begin to sketch out the Government's thinking on a range of more externally facing challenges that would need to be addressed as a result of withdrawal from the EU. For example, there was a strong emphasis on the idea that leaving the Union should lead to the UK gaining control over its own laws; a stated desire to maintain the Common Travel Area with the Republic of Ireland; a robust assertion of the need for UK control over immigration; an aspiration to reach agreement on protecting the rights of existing migrant UK and Union citizens; an ambition to secure the freest possible trade with the Union in the future; the prize of also negotiating new trade agreements with the rest of the world; and recognition of the importance of maintaining cross-border cooperation with the Union in broader fields such as security and science.

Perhaps the most important objective of all was the Government's proposed timescale for delivering those various promises and ambitions:

> I want us to have reached an agreement about our future partnership by the time the 2-year Article 50 process has concluded. From that point onwards, we believe a phased process of implementation, in which both Britain and the EU institutions and member states prepare for the new arrangements that will exist between us will be in our mutual self-interest. This will give businesses enough time to plan and prepare for those new arrangements ... For each issue, the time we need to phase-in the new arrangements may differ ... But the purpose is clear: we will seek to avoid a disruptive cliff-edge ...

Soon after the Lancaster House Speech, on 2 February 2017, the Government published its White Paper on 'The UK's Exit from and New Partnership with the European Union', which was essentially concerned with elaborating in greater detail, together with additional nuance and certain qualifications, upon each of the 12 objectives already described by the Prime Minister.[94] For example, when it came to the UK gaining

---

[93] Theresa May, *Lancaster House Speech: The Government's Negotiating Objectives for Exiting the EU* (17 January 2017).

[94] HMG, *The United Kingdom's Exit from and New Partnership with the European Union* (Cm 9417 of 2 February 2017).

control over its own laws, the White Paper admitted that Parliament has always remained sovereign, throughout the period of UK membership of the EU.[95] So the real meaning of this particular 'Brexit objective' was that laws would be fully made in the UK and the CJEU would no longer have jurisdiction within the UK.[96] Similarly, on relations with the Republic of Ireland, the White Paper set out the goals of having as seamless and frictionless a border as possible between Northern Ireland and the Republic; preserving the reciprocal special treatment of UK and Irish nationals within Ireland and the UK (respectively); respecting the citizenship choices available to the people of Northern Ireland; and maintaining the Common Travel Area whilst also protecting the integrity of the UK's future immigration system.

At a superficial glance, the objectives listed in the Lancaster House Speech/February 2017 White Paper might read like a rather meandering stream of consciousness about some of the main challenges posed by UK withdrawal. Nevertheless, it is possible to extract some underlying themes about the UK's initial political approach to its own withdrawal process, particularly as regards those externally facing 'Brexit objectives' more directly concerned with EU–UK relations.

In the first place, the Government lays down some of its infamous 'red lines', i.e. major decisions about the nature of EU–UK relations, which seek to rule out particular options and close down potential avenues, apparently taken with little parliamentary or public debate, and certainly with only limited governmental understanding of their full significance and implications. Several such 'red lines' were of particular importance: for example, the insistence on ending the free movement of persons between the EU and the UK; the promise to cease making 'vast contributions' towards the EU budget; and the rejection of any continuation of CJEU jurisdiction in respect of the UK. After all, such 'red lines' necessarily implied that the UK would not only be withdrawing from the EU, but would also be leaving the Customs Union, and indeed positioning itself outside the Single Market.[97]

On its face, 'taking back control of our borders, money and laws' (to use the phrase which came to define just how 'Brexit means Brexit') therefore meant that withdrawal should lead to a much more distant EU–UK relationship.[98] Yet at the same time, the Government declared that it still wanted to create a close and bespoke relationship with the Union into the future—a relationship that would apparently replicate many of the same benefits as membership of the EU, particularly in delivering a high degree of frictionless trade across multiple sectors of the economy, though without the UK having to abide by the same obligations and disciplines as are expected of the Member States themselves. From that really rather unrealistic expectation came

---

[95] Suggesting, bizarrely, that the actual problem has been: 'it has not always felt like that' (see para 2.1).

[96] Suggesting, again bizarrely, that one of the key goals of the entire project of UK withdrawal from the EU, was for the British to be able to rely on different dispute settlement mechanisms in their future relationship with the Union (see paras 2.3–2.10).

[97] See further, on the general evolution of the UK's preferences for its future relationship to the EU, Chapter 9.

[98] The phrase even provided the title for a subsequent UK Government publication, explaining the contents of the First Withdrawal Package as agreed in November 2018: see HMG, *EU Exit: Taking back control of our borders, money and laws while protecting our economy, security and Union* (Cm 9741 of 28 November 2018).

the well-known and pithy summary of the UK's initial approach to its own withdrawal negotiations: 'we want to have our cake and we want to eat it'.[99]

In the second place, it is noteworthy that both the Lancaster House Speech and the February 2017 White Paper concentrate almost entirely on longer-term questions about a new framework for future EU–UK trade and cooperation. The Government has much less to say about the nature of or its attitude towards the more immediate 'separation challenges' raised by UK withdrawal from the Union. True, the Speech/White Paper offer relatively positive but essentially generalized statements about protecting existing migrant citizens' rights; they show some (though only limited) awareness of the major challenges likely to arise for the Irish border; and they flag up other urgent tasks such as managing the impact of withdrawal upon international agreements and relations between the UK and other third countries/international organizations. But the Government says almost nothing about several of the other key questions which would eventually take central stage in the negotiations under Article 50 TEU and form core elements of the First Withdrawal Agreement as endorsed by EU and UK political leaders in November 2018: for example, the 'divorce bill' that should settle the UK's financial liabilities and commitments as a Member State; or the broad range of 'separation issues' required to wind down the UK's outstanding involvement in a large number of Union frameworks, processes, and programmes.

The assumption underlying the Speech/White Paper appears to be that, since the new EU–UK future relationship will be negotiated and concluded under the auspices of the Article 50 TEU process, then gradually brought into force during the post-withdrawal 'implementation period', concerns about the immediate separation challenges involved in the act of leaving the Union are of relatively less importance or urgency.

As we shall explore in greater detail in Chapter 4, the UK's appreciation of the scope, sequence and timing of discussions under Article 50 TEU differed radically from that of the Union institutions and the remaining Member States—with profound consequences for the conduct and outcomes of the withdrawal process. But for now, suffice to observe that the UK's initial attempt to define the withdrawal agenda almost entirely around discussions about future relations with the Union, was surely a direct reflection of its own internal political priorities and troubles.

To some degree, the calculation was evidently influenced by rational self-interest: given that many businesses were expressing serious concerns about the uncertainty created by the referendum outcome and the urgent need for clarity about the long-term conditions for trade and economic development, the Government was evidently keen to offer explicit reassurance, i.e. that the legal bases for future EU–UK relations would be agreed and implemented as soon as possible and entail only a minimal level of disruption to many existing commercial relationships. But the Lancaster House Speech and February 2017 White Paper perhaps also reflect a deeper truth about the UK's political starting point towards its own withdrawal: since Brexit constitutes an existential national crisis of identity and vocation, characterized

---

[99] See, e.g. 'A brief history of having cake and eating it: How an old expression became one of the key phrases of Brexit' available at https://www.politico.eu/article/a-brief-history-of-having-cake-and-eating-it/
.

by profoundly different preferences and visions right across society, it is perhaps not surprising to find that the 'big picture' questions around the UK's future place in the European and wider world order attracted greater British attention than the more detailed and technical problems involved in the very act of withdrawal.

B. The UK Legal Debate About Competence to Notify

Those were some of the main political factors that help explain the delay between the initial outcome of the 2016 referendum, the subsequent formulation of something approaching an official Government plan for handling the withdrawal process, and then the eventual delivery of the UK's formal notification of its intention to leave the Union. But running directly parallel to those political debates, crucial legal considerations were also at work. In particular, the 2016 referendum led directly to a serious dispute about what the UK's 'constitutional requirements' even were for the purposes of Article 50 TEU and (in particular) over which institution was actually competent to take and/or communicate a formal decision that the UK should leave the EU.

(i) Locating the Legitimate Constitutional Power to Notify

Of course, in the minds of many Leave supporters, the formal decision to withdraw had already been taken through the outcome of the referendum on 23 June 2016. The only remaining question was about who should communicate that decision to the European Council—but that was to be considered a purely technical matter. Indeed, some Leave campaigners even argued that, having already decided through and by the referendum to leave, the UK should now implement that decision in an entirely unilateral manner, simply by repealing the European Communities Act 1972, and without even engaging the EU institutions as provided for through the Article 50 TEU process.[100]

Such assumptions were deeply flawed. It is true that, as a matter of political discourse and public perception, the significance of the 2016 plebiscite sometimes appeared confused. For example: the legal status of the referendum outcome had not been explicitly addressed in the authorizing legislation of 2015;[101] and the Government had clearly indicated that it would regard the result as politically binding (regardless of its strict legal status);[102] yet a parliamentary briefing paper from June 2015 had pointed out that (regardless of political assurances) the referendum should be considered merely advisory in nature.[103] But whatever the political confusion or public expectation, the parliamentary researchers had expressed the constitutional position accurately: in itself, the 2016 referendum could only have the status of a glorified opinion poll; its outcome

---

[100] A position robustly criticized, e.g. in House of Lords Select Committee on the Constitution, *The Invoking of Article 50* (HL44 of 13 September 2016).
[101] See the European Union Referendum Act 2015.
[102] Not least in the Conservative Party's 2015 manifesto for the general election.
[103] See House of Commons Library Briefing Paper, *European Union Referendum Bill 2015-16* (No 7212 of 3 June 2015), at p 25.

did not of itself have any particular legal status and could not in itself constitute a formal decision of the UK state to withdraw from the EU.[104]

The purely advisory status of the 2016 referendum provided the basis for a vocal campaign by many Remain supporters to argue for the UK's political leaders simply to ignore the outcome on the grounds either that the whole process had been so deeply flawed or that the outcome would be so deeply damaging (or both) that the popular preference should not be implemented.[105] However, that was never very likely to happen. Even if its outcome was not binding as a matter of law, there was a widespread political commitment to respecting or at least implementing the Leave victory.[106] The real question was which institution should be considered responsible for acting upon the popular desire for withdrawal as expressed in the referendum, by converting its non-binding outcome into a legally valid decision to leave the EU?

The Government position was clear: the formal decision to leave, and subsequent notification of that decision under Article 50 TEU, fell entirely within the Government's own autonomous powers. Under UK constitutional law, the royal (executive) prerogative power to conduct foreign affairs includes the power both to contract and to terminate international treaties. For those purposes, the EU Treaties were no different from any other international agreement. As such, both the decision to withdraw and its notification under Article 50 TEU could validly be made by the Government alone and without any need for authorization from, or the consent of, Parliament. That constitutional understanding was evidently the basis upon which the Prime Minister had announced the Government's decision to implement the result of the 2016 referendum, that the UK would indeed leave the European Union, and that the Government would formally notify its intentions to the European Council by the end of March 2017.[107]

However, the Government position was far from universally shared. The alternative analysis was that a formal decision for the UK to leave the European Union could only be taken by or under the authority of Parliament—not by the Government acting autonomously in the exercise of its executive powers. In the absence of explicit parliamentary authorization, any purported decision by the Government that the UK should leave the Union, and/or any purported notification by the Prime Minister of the UK's intention to withdraw under Article 50 TEU, would be invalid as a matter of domestic constitutional law. The main argument in favour of this analysis was that, under UK constitutional law, it was well established that the royal prerogative could not be exercised in a manner that would change existing domestic legislation or the common law. Yet a decision to withdraw from the EU would (eventually but inevitably) lead to significant changes to the UK legal system through, for example, the elimination of the rights associated with Union citizenship, such as the right to free movement or to stand and vote in European and local elections.[108] On that basis, the

---

[104] See also, e.g. House of Commons Library Briefing Paper, *Brexit: What Happens Next?* (No 7632 of 30 June 2016).

[105] See the overview provided in Chapter 1.

[106] Not only the Conservative Party in Government, but also by the leadership of the Labour Party in Opposition.

[107] In particular: Theresa May, *Lancaster House Speech: The Government's Negotiating Objectives for Exiting the EU* (17 January 2017).

[108] In accordance with Arts 21 and 22 TFEU.

Government was not entitled to take for itself any decision either to withdraw or to notify under Article 50 TEU. It could only do so after obtaining appropriate parliamentary authorization—lacking which, the Prime Minister's speeches, promises and timescales lacked any constitutional validity.

The internal UK debate was further complicated by disagreement over what role (if any) the devolved institutions might play in the withdrawal process—particularly if the basic constitutional starting point was that the decision lay within the power of the Westminster Parliament rather than the UK Government alone. Indeed, given that both the latter institutions seemed sure to support withdrawal in principle, the potential for the devolved governments to participate in the decision-making process had perhaps greater political significance than the contest between the central UK institutions themselves.[109]

True, each of the devolved authorities found itself in a very different position after the referendum. The Scottish Government was strongly anti-Brexit and represented a population that was equally pro-Remain; whereas the Welsh Government was also strongly anti-Brexit but represented a population that had voted firmly for Leave. The population of Northern Ireland had voted clearly for Remain but lacked any effective political leadership from its non-functioning Executive.[110] But even Scotland alone had the potential to reshape the debate about how best to respond to the 2016 referendum outcome—assuming that the Scottish authorities were afforded any meaningful role or say in the process as a matter of UK constitutional law. On the one hand, the UK Government argued that foreign affairs is a reserved competence, so there should be no formal role for the devolved administrations in any decision by the central UK authorities to withdraw from the EU.[111] On the other hand, the Scottish Government argued that any proposed UK legislation that would affect the competences of the devolved administrations required the latter's consent under the Sewell Convention, which was now enshrined in the applicable devolution statutes—thus affording the devolved administrations an effective veto over any final decision (at least by the Westminster Parliament) over UK membership of the EU.[112]

Given such uncertainty and contestation, it was inevitable that the courts would be called upon to clarify and settle the constitutional position. The initial judicial response consisted of two High Court judgments. To begin with, the Northern Ireland High Court delivered its ruling in *McCord's Application*, which was focused on the devolution issues, but also made certain assumptions about the balance of power between Westminster and Whitehall.[113] The court held: (first) that nothing in the legislation providing for Northern Ireland's devolved constitutional settlement would prevent the UK Government from giving notification of the UK's intention to withdraw from the EU under Article 50 TEU based on the exercise of the Government's prerogative powers alone; and (secondly) even if UK parliamentary authorization was required for a valid decision/notification of withdrawal, the central UK authorities

---

[109] See further, e.g. Craig, 'Brexit, A Drama: The Interregnum', 36 *Yearbook of European Law* (2017) 3.

[110] See further, e.g. House of Lords European Union Committee, *Brexit: Devolution* (HL9 of 19 July 2017); Hunt, 'Devolution' in M. Dougan (ed.), *The UK After Brexit: Legal and Policy Challenges* (2017).

[111] See, e.g. Schedule 5 to the Scotland Act 1998.

[112] See, e.g. section 28(8) Scotland Act 1998 (as amended by Scotland Act 2016).

[113] *McCord's Application* [2016] NIQB 85.

were not legally bound by any constitutional convention according to which Northern Ireland's devolved institutions were asked to consent to UK wide-legislation capable of impinging upon devolved matters.

Shortly after the ruling in *McCord's Application*, the English High Court delivered its ruling in *Miller v Secretary of State for Exiting the European Union*, which was more directly concerned with the contest between UK Government and UK Parliament.[114] The court acknowledged that the residual legal competences of the Crown making up the Government's prerogative powers indeed included the conduct of international relations in general and the making or unmaking of international treaties in partic-ular. But the court also agreed that those prerogative powers cannot be used to change domestic law (whether statute or common law). Thus, the executive power to make or unmake treaties as a matter of international law cannot confer new rights on in-dividuals, or deprive individuals of their existing rights, without the intervention of Parliament to give effect to such changes as a matter of domestic law. Since the parties in *Miller* had agreed (for the sake of the proceedings) that a notification of intention to withdraw under Article 50 TEU could not be made conditionally or subsequently withdrawn, the court accepted that, once notification had been given, it would inevi-tably result in the UK's withdrawal from the EU.[115] As a result, the very notification of the UK's intention to withdraw under Article 50 TEU would give rise to various legal effects as a matter of domestic UK law, particularly as regards those rights which had been created pursuant to the European Communities Act 1972: for example, directly effective rights derived from EU secondary measures; directly effective rights derived from EU primary law (such as free movement rights, including those enjoyed by UK citizens in the other Member States); the right to stand and vote in European parlia-mentary elections etc.

The Government had argued that the domestic legal effects of all such EU rights pursuant to the European Communities Act 1972 in fact presupposed that the UK was and remained a Member State of the European Union in the first place; and Parliament had intended that prior question about Union membership to remain a matter of international relations under the direct responsibility of the Government. As such, if the Government were to exercise its prerogative powers so as to withdraw from the EU treaties and render the UK no longer a Member State, then there would no longer be any more EU-based rights upon which the European Communities Act could confer legal effects under domestic UK law—but that is an outcome entirely compatible with the underlying intentions of Parliament when it adopted the 1972 legislation. However, the High Court rejected that argument. There must be a strong constitutional presumption that (unless Parliament expressly provides otherwise) the exercise of the royal prerogative should not be able to alter domestic UK law. That is es-pecially true having regard to the special status which the European Communities Act 1972 undoubtedly holds within the UK constitutional order: having conferred such a privileged status upon EU law within the domestic legal system, Parliament cannot

---

[114] *Miller v Secretary of State for Exiting the European Union* [2016] EWHC 2768.

[115] Even if the date of eventual withdrawal were to be delayed for a further period of time. On the actual legal position as a matter of Union law, see the ruling in Case C-621/18, *Wightman* (EU:C:2018:999) and the discussion in Chapter 2.

have intended that the Government should be able to take that status away again using nothing more than its residual executive powers.

The High Court in *Miller* acknowledged that its counterpart in Northern Ireland had reached a different assessment of the relationship between Westminster and Whitehall, but politely observed that the ruling in *McCord's Application* was clearly focused primarily on the devolution issues raised by UK withdrawal and had perhaps not explored the royal prerogative questions in comparable detail. In any event, it did not take long for the two High Court rulings to be considered side by side in the Supreme Court, which delivered its ruling in *R (on the application of Miller) v Secretary of State for Exiting the European Union* on 24 January 2017.[116]

The majority ruling (agreed by 8 of the 11 Justices involved in the proceedings) endorsed the finding of the English High Court that a decision to withdraw/notification under Article 50 TEU reached by exercise of the royal prerogative alone would be capable improperly of altering domestic law by changing the existing rights and obligations which were created under EU law and incorporated into the UK legal system by the European Communities Act 1972. However, the Supreme Court went even further: a decision to withdraw, and/or notification under Article 50 TEU, by exercise of the royal prerogative alone would also alter (remove) one of the very sources of law (EU law) recognized within the UK legal system. Such an alteration would amount to a fundamental change in the UK's existing constitutional arrangements—and that also lay outside the scope of the Government's autonomous executive powers. For those twin reasons, a decision to withdraw and/or notification under Article 50 TEU requires positive statutory authorization from Parliament.[117]

At the same time, however, the Supreme Court endorsed the principal conclusion of the Northern Ireland High Court in *McCord's Application* that constitutional conventions are not enforceable before the courts, including the Sewell Convention on the need for the consent of the devolved administrations to UK-wide legislation which was capable of impinging upon devolved matters. That conclusion was not affected by express inclusion of the Sewell Convention in the relevant devolution statutes themselves—provisions which were intended merely to codify the relevant constitutional convention, but not to give it any novel legal effects.[118]

Thus, the Supreme Court decided that the UK Government could not decide upon and notify the UK's withdrawal from the EU in the exercise of its prerogative powers. Those decisions required explicit statutory authorization from Parliament, which could be granted, regardless of the consent or opposition of the devolved administrations in Scotland, Wales and Northern Ireland; though the Supreme Court deliberately

---

[116] *R (on the application of Miller) v Secretary of State for Exiting the European Union* [2017] UKSC 5.

[117] The minority dissenting judgment (endorsed by the remaining three Justices) was more sympathetic towards the Government's core argument that the existence of EU law as a source of law within the UK legal system was premised upon the UK's continuing membership of the EU in the first place. It was true that withdrawal from the EU would remove the entire content of Union law as provided for in the European Communities Act. But even so, the 1972 legislation does not prevent withdrawal from being decided upon by the Government under the exercise of prerogative powers alone: the European Communities Act only addressed the question of the content of EU law within the UK legal system; it did not address the prior question of the UK's very membership of the EU in the first place.

[118] *R (on the application of Miller) v Secretary of State for Exiting the European Union* [2017] UKSC 5.

refrained from offering any further guidance as to the nature or content of the legislation that would be required to give effect to its judgment.[119]

The *Miller* ruling was greeted with dismay by many Leave campaigners and delight by many Remain supporters—the former perhaps fearing and the latter hoping that, once the formal power to make a final decision about withdrawal was removed from the largely pro-Brexit Government and granted to the largely pro-Remain Parliament, MPs would refuse to endorse the (marginal) outcome of the (deeply contested and purely advisory) referendum. But that was never a very realistic expectation: it was always clear that, if called upon to do so, a majority of MPs would vote to implement the Leave victory (even though they might not support or even respect it) so as not to be accused of involvement in the 'elite conspiracy' to 'undermine democracy' by defying the 'will of the people'. Indeed, from another perspective, the outcome of the *Miller* litigation could actually be viewed as potentially damaging to the Remain cause: a clear parliamentary vote in favour of withdrawal (however reluctant) could end up conferring a degree of democratic credibility, as well as constitutional legitimacy, upon the decision for the UK to leave the EU that such decision could never derive from the 2016 referendum result alone.

Be that as it may, immediately after the Supreme Court judgment in *Miller*, the Government initiated the process of seeking parliamentary authorization for the UK's withdrawal. The European Union (Notification of Withdrawal) Bill was published on 8 February 2017. Various attempts at amendment (for example, seeking to protect the rights of existing migrant EU citizens within the UK, or to guarantee a stronger role for Parliament also as regards the conduct and conclusion of the forthcoming EU–UK withdrawal negotiations) proved unsuccessful.[120] The European Union (Notification of Withdrawal) Act 2017 was therefore adopted on 16 March 2017. Its sole substantive provision (Section 1) stated that:

(1) The Prime Minister may notify, under Article 50(2) of the Treaty on European Union, the United Kingdom's intention to withdraw from the EU.
(2) This section has effect despite any provision made by or under the European Communities Act 1972 or any other enactment.

After several months during which the Government had been making important political commitments based upon uncertain or even non-existent legal foundations, politics and law finally fell back into tandem with each other. Strictly speaking, Parliament had still not decided—explicitly and for itself—that the UK should withdraw from the EU. If indeed many MPs viewed *Miller* as a poisoned chalice, they did at least succeed in passing it along into one final pair of hands: under the terms of the European Union (Notification of Withdrawal) Act 2017, Parliament delegated the power, both to decide on the path of withdrawal and to communicate that decision

---

[119] See further, e.g. Young, '*R (Miller) v Secretary of State for Exiting the European Union: Thriller or Vanilla?*', 42 *ELRev* (2017) 280; and the various analyses contained in *Public Law* [2017] *Brexit Special Extra Issue.*
[120] See the full list of documents concerning the Bill's passage through the UK Parliament available via https://services.parliament.uk/Bills/2016-17/europeanunionnotificationofwithdrawal/documents.html.

to the European Council under Article 50 TEU, to the Prime Minister. On that basis, Theresa May submitted her formal letter to the President of the European Council on 29 March 2017:

> I hereby notify the European Council in accordance with Article 50(2) of the Treaty on European Union of the United Kingdom's intention to withdraw from the European Union ... [and] from the European Atomic Energy Community.[121]

As the High Court confirmed in the subsequent *Webster* case: the Supreme Court in *Miller* had held that any decision to withdraw required parliamentary authorization, but left it to Parliament to determine what precise form such legislation should take; the 2017 Act was intended to give effect to *Miller* and did so by conferring the power to take the final withdrawal decision upon the Prime Minister. In effect, Theresa May's letter of 29 March 2017 constituted both the formal decision of the UK to withdraw and the official notification of that decision as expected under Article 50 TEU. Through *Miller*, the 2017 Act, and the March letter, the UK had exercised its sovereign right to decide to withdraw from the EU. No additional domestic constitutional requirements remained to be satisfied.[122]

(ii) Other Legal Challenges to the UK's Decision to Withdraw

It is worth noting that *Miller* was not the only judicial challenge exploring the legality of the UK's process for, and eventual decision about, withdrawing from the EU. For example: even before the 2016 referendum itself had taken place, the claimants in *Shindler* sought to challenge the propriety of its 2015 authorizing legislation, on the basis that the electoral franchise (as defined under section 2 of the European Union Referendum Act) was incompatible with Union law. It was argued that, by excluding from the franchise those UK nationals who had lived abroad for more than 15 years, the 2015 Act constituted a restriction on the claimants' rights of free movement law in other Member States that had to be objectively justified. In the claimants' view, that restriction could not be considered proportionate to any legitimate public interest objective.[123] However, the Court of Appeal held that (unlike other examples in the caselaw where a home state was found to have restricted the exercise of its own nationals' free movement rights) a decision whether or not to withdraw from the EU altogether, in accordance with the relevant State's own constitutional requirements, could not fall within the scope of Union law: that was a decision about whether EU law should continue to apply within the national legal system at all (not merely about the effective operation of EU law within the Member State). Article 50 TEU had left that decision entirely to the relevant State and the latter's choices were not subject to any restrictions or scrutiny under the Treaties.[124]

---

[121] HMG, *Prime Minister's Notification Letter to President of the European Council* (29 March 2017).
[122] *Webster* [2018] EWHC 1543 (Admin).
[123] See *Shindler* [2016] EWHC 957 (Admin).
[124] See *Shindler* [2016] EWCA Civ 469. Note that, according to the Court of Appeal, even if the situation did fall within the scope of the Treaties, there would be no restriction on the right to free movement, i.e. because the latter requires a proper deterrence to exercise of the right to free movement either now or in the future (not just some sort of disadvantage for having already exercised the right to free movement).

Other (unsuccessful) judicial challenges to the legality of the UK's internal withdrawal process were brought after the 2016 referendum and indeed even after the March 2017 decision/notification of intention to leave the Union.[125] For example: the claimants in *Shindler* continued their campaign to impugn the terms and conduct of the 2016 referendum, but this time before the EU courts and by seeking annulment of the Council decision authorizing the opening of withdrawal negotiations with the UK under Article 50 TEU.[126] In effect, the applicants relied upon the same arguments as they had before the Court of Appeal, albeit in the hope that the General Court would reach a different conclusion on the merits: the UK's restricted voting franchise constituted an unlawful restriction on the exercise of Union free movement rights and, as such, there was no valid UK decision to withdraw in accordance with its own national constitutional requirements, which in turn rendered the entire process under Article 50 TEU (including the relevant Council decision) unlawful.

However, the General Court held the action to be inadmissible.[127] As non-privileged applicants seeking to challenge a Union measure which was not addressed to them, the claimants had to demonstrate direct concern, i.e. that the contested measure directly affected their legal situation. However, the relevant Council decision had legal effects only as regards relations between the EU and its Member States and as between the Union institutions themselves. That Council decision was not to be confused with the UK's prior decision/notification of its intention to withdraw under Article 50 TEU. After all, it was that notification (not the subsequent Council decision) which had set the clock running for the Treaties to cease to apply to the UK. Moreover, the contested decision did not in itself alter the legal situation of UK citizens resident in other Member States: the Council's decision was merely a preparatory act towards any final withdrawal agreement—so annulment of that preparatory decision would have no impact on the applicants' legal situation, since it would not (for example) entail annulment of the UK's notification or suspension of the time limits applicable under Article 50 TEU.

It is understandable that citizens who were deeply unhappy not just with the final outcome but also with the very process and indeed legitimacy of the UK's decision to withdraw from the EU should seek to use any means available—including the legal system and the courts—to express their objections and seek to advance their interests. Most such judicial challenges ended in failure that was entirely predictable or even inevitable. The Supreme Court's ruling in *Miller* appears to stand out as an important exception.[128] It is certainly true that *Miller* represents an important victory for those who defend the constitutional role and authority of Parliament relative to that of the executive. But it is less obvious that *Miller* represents a satisfactory outcome for the

---

[125] E.g. *Webster* concerned an application for permission to apply for judicial review against the ongoing conduct of Article 50 TEU negotiations, on the basis that there had been no valid 'decision to withdraw' under UK law and so the EU–UK negotiations were also to be treated as invalid under Article 50 TEU itself. However, the High Court refused permission on the grounds that the application was 'hopeless and, for that matter, Totally Without Merit' (Judgment of 12 June 2018).

[126] Council Decision authorizing the opening of negotiations with the United Kingdom of Great Britain and Northern Ireland for an agreement setting out the arrangements for its withdrawal from the European Union (22 May 2017).

[127] Case T-458/17, *Shindler* (EU:T:2018:838).

[128] Along with the litigation culminating in the ruling in Case C-621/18, *Wightman* (EU:C:2018:999).

constitutional role and authority of the devolved administrations relative to that of the central UK authorities. And of course, *Miller* proved only a Pyrrhic victory for those Remain supporters who had looked to Parliament in the hope of challenging the conduct and/or the outcome of the 2016 referendum. However, it is arguable that the legacy of *Miller* lived on in more indirect ways, setting the 'constitutional mood music' which would influence other important questions about the legal framework governing the withdrawal process within the UK—not least (as we shall see very shortly) when it came to the debate about which institution should have the final say over the outcomes of the EU–UK negotiations under Article 50 TEU.[129]

C. The 2017 General Election and its Impact on the UK's Initial Negotiating Position

On 1 April 2017, the UK looked set to commence its formal negotiations for withdrawal from the European Union. From a legal perspective: the Supreme Court ruling in *Miller,* followed by the European Union (Notification of Withdrawal) Act 2017, had together settled the question of which institution was constitutionally entitled to adopt the UK's sovereign decision to leave the European Union. From a political perspective: whatever its various merits or shortcomings, the rudimentary plan set out in the Lancaster House Speech and the February 2017 White Paper did at least provide the Government with some basis for discussions with the EU.

However, the UK position was about to become significantly more unfavourable even before formal negotiations under Article 50 TEU could begin. On 18 April 2017, and to widespread surprise in the UK and across the EU, the Prime Minister called an early general election, to be held in June 2017. She perhaps calculated that it would deliver an increased Conservative majority in the House of Commons that could in turn provide greater democratic endorsement and a stronger parliamentary base for her withdrawal plans as set out in the Lancaster House Speech and the February 2017 White Paper, with direct and commensurate benefits not only for her domestic political position, but also as regards the popular mandate the Government could call upon in its negotiations with the EU. If so, those calculations were seriously misjudged or at least badly backfired: the election produced a hung Parliament in which the Government lost its previous Commons majority—reduced from 331 to 318 seats out of 650.[130]

That outcome could have been interpreted as a sign that the public had recoiled from the Government's proposal for a relatively distant future relationship between the Union and the UK as set out in the Lancaster House Speech and February 2017

---

[129] And also other important constitutional litigation about the centrality of Parliament within the UK's unwritten constitutional system: consider, e.g. the judgment of the UK Supreme Court in *Miller v Prime Minister* [2019] UKSC 41 concerning Boris Johnson's unlawful prorogation of Parliament—discussed further in Chapter 5.

[130] See, in particular, https://www.electoralcommission.org.uk/who-we-are-and-what-we-do/elections-and-referendums/past-elections-and-referendums/uk-general-elections/results-and-turnout-2017-uk-general-election. See further, e.g. Hobolt, 'Brexit and the 2017 UK General Election', 56 *JCMS Annual Review* (2018) 39.

White Paper and might thus have prompted the Prime Minister to rethink her plans, perhaps by seeking a new cross-party consensus that would support a different (closer) relationship between the EU and the UK as the basis for conducting imminent negotiations under Article 50 TEU. Instead, Prime Minister May preferred to focus her efforts on maintaining the fragile coalition between moderates and extremists within her own Conservative Party—forming a minority administration that was, moreover, only propped up in power in the House of Commons through the support of the 10 MPs of the Democratic Unionist Party (DUP).[131]

On paper, a chastened May Government remained committed to its basic 'cake and eat it' approach towards withdrawal: seeking a 'deep and special partnership' with the Union, but subject to various UK 'red lines' about the terms on which that partnership could ever operate. We know that that approach was never particularly realistic. But the political shenanigans resulting from the 2017 general election now directly impacted upon the UK's preparations for the commencement of negotiations under Article 50 TEU in ways that rendered the inherent tensions of the Government's approach even more acute.

In the first place, consider the Government's newfound dependence upon the voting support of the DUP. The latter is a highly partisan (loyalist), if not altogether sectarian (Protestant) political party from Northern Ireland: dogmatic about upholding Northern Ireland's position within the UK; opposed to closer relations with the Republic of Ireland; located on the hard right of the political spectrum, particularly on social and moral questions; and strongly Europhobic, having campaigned for Leave in the 2016 referendum and notwithstanding the fact that a majority of the population in Northern Ireland voted otherwise. Yet this rather unsavoury and certainly unrepresentative political force was now offered an entirely disproportionate influence over the entire UK withdrawal process, particularly when it came to addressing the serious challenges posed specifically for relations between Northern Ireland and the Republic (in general) and the maintenance of an open land border for persons and goods (in particular). As we shall see throughout the rest of this book, the UK Government's room for manoeuvre in negotiating effective solutions to such challenges was seriously constrained for as long as it needed the DUP's votes in the Commons.[132]

Secondly, consider the fact that the May Government now found itself even more vulnerable than before to the political demands of its own cabal of hard right Europhobes within the Conservative Party itself, particularly the self-styled 'European Research Group' (ERG), which was often accused of acting as a 'party with a party', determined to pursue its own policy agenda with ideological fervour. In particular, the Conservative Party members of the ERG appeared to pressurize a now weakened and vulnerable Government into adopting more extreme positions in the negotiations under Article 50 TEU—ultimately with a view to producing only a distant future relationship between the EU and the UK, if necessary, even by leaving without any

---

[131] In particular: Confidence and Supply Agreement between the Conservative and Unionist Party and the Democratic Unionist Party (26 June 2017).

[132] See especially the discussion in Chapter 8 of negotiations between the EU and the UK aimed at avoiding a 'hard border' across the island of Ireland.

agreement between the two parties, either on the immediate separation challenges or as to the longer-term.[133]

Indeed, the 2017 general election contributed to a political dynamic (or at least rhetoric) in favour of pursuing 'Brexit at any cost': the UK's overriding priority was to deliver on the 'will of the people' to leave the EU—and for many Leave campaigners, that meant withdrawal regardless of any negotiated agreement and irrespective of the costs or damage. Certainly, the Government itself continued to reiterate that 'no deal would be better than a bad deal'—an objectively untenable position that only added another damaging dimension to the UK's already difficult political position by encouraging hardline Leave campaigners to oppose any and every negotiated outcome to the withdrawal process, as well as significant numbers of UK citizens to believe that a 'no deal Brexit' was indeed to be considered even a tolerable (let alone desirable) destination.[134]

D. The 2017 General Election and its Impact on Constitutional Responsibilities towards the Article 50 TEU Process

If the UK's approach to its own withdrawal was already handicapped by a lack of responsible preparations, a state of extraordinary internal disunity, and a series of political miscalculations and contradictions, the 2017 general election directly contributed to another chain of events that would only make the Government's position even more awkward: the amendment of its flagship European Union (Withdrawal) Bill by a fragmented and fractious Parliament, so as to include an explicit legal obligation for the Government to submit the provisional outcomes of its Article 50 TEU efforts for prior approval by the House of Commons, before the UK could formally conclude any negotiated withdrawal.[135]

It need not have been so. The usual position under UK constitutional law is that the negotiation, conclusion and ratification of international agreements constitutes a royal (executive) prerogative power vested in the Government.[136] Parliament plays only a limited role in that process, focused on two main stages. To begin with, there is some scope for parliamentary scrutiny of international agreements after their conclusion but before their formal ratification by the Government. The process is governed by Part 2 of the Constitutional Reform and Governance Act 2010. Both Houses of Parliament are entitled to vote on the final text of a proposed international agreement prior to its ratification. However, those votes take the form of a 'negative resolution procedure': each House must actively express its opposition to the proposed treaty,

---

[133] See further, e.g. C. Grant, *The Brexit Negotiations: An Assessment of the Legal, Political and Institutional Situation in the UK* (In-Depth Analysis commissioned by the AFCO Committee of the European Parliament, PE 583.130 of March 2017).

[134] On the prospect of a 'no deal Brexit', see the more detailed discussion and references contained in Chapter 2.

[135] The European Union (Withdrawal) Bill, as originally published on 13 July 2017, is available via https://publications.parliament.uk/pa/bills/cbill/2017-2019/0005/18005.pdf.

[136] Further, e.g. House of Commons Library Briefing Paper, *Parliament's Role in Ratifying Treaties* (No 5855 of 17 February 2017).

failing which the Government may proceed freely to ratification.[137] Moreover, the power of objection offered by the negative resolution procedure may only be exercised on a 'take it or leave it' basis: there is no direct mechanism by which Parliament can seek to reopen negotiations on the proposed text with a view to its amendment. In any event, the effect of a negative resolution is simply to delay (not to prevent) ratification, though in the case of the House of Commons, the possibility of adopting serial negative resolutions offers the ability (at least in theory) of creating a potentially indefinite delay to ratification.[138]

Besides that essentially marginal role in the prior approval of international agreements, Parliament's main responsibility is in fact to implement treaties into UK domestic law *after* their ratification has been completed, where such domestic implementation is required in order for the UK to comply with its obligations under the relevant agreement. As a dualist state, the Government can negotiate, conclude, and ratify international agreements that become binding upon the UK under international law; but insofar as such agreements require changes to domestic UK law, they need to be implemented by primary legislation or under delegated powers created by primary legislation. It is only through such acts of domestic implementation that the UK's international legal obligations are translated into a cognizable source of binding rights and obligations for the purposes of the domestic legal order and before the UK courts.[139]

Absent any other constitutional or legal developments, that is the system one would have expected to apply also to the EU–UK withdrawal agreement negotiated under Article 50 TEU.[140] In particular, the Supreme Court's judgment in *Miller* may have insisted that Parliament initially authorize the decision of the UK to notify its intention to leave the Union; but the *Miller* ruling did not require any different kind or additional degree of parliamentary involvement in the subsequent process of negotiating and approving a withdrawal agreement under Article 50 TEU.

Arguably, however, *Miller* did have an important indirect impact upon the broader legal and political debate about whether the standard constitutional opportunities for parliamentary involvement in the approval and implementation of international agreements were really sufficient in the extraordinary circumstances of the UK's withdrawal from the EU. The divided and fractious character of the UK's post-referendum politics had already generated a campaign for greater parliamentary input into the Article 50 TEU process—a campaign which explicitly drew upon the victorious Leave campaign's rhetoric of 'taking back control' and 'restoring parliamentary sovereignty', while also highlighting an unfavourable contrast with the much more extensive powers offered to the European Parliament by the alleged 'anti-democratic' European

---

[137] By contrast, under a 'positive resolution procedure', proposed governmental measures require the active approval of the relevant chamber/s.

[138] See sections 20–25 Constitutional Reform and Governance Act 2010.

[139] Note that the devolved administrations have no formal role in the negotiation/conclusion of international agreements by the central UK authorities though they may well be closely involved in/responsible for their subsequent domestic implementation.

[140] See, e.g. House of Lords European Union Committee, *Scrutinising Brexit: The Role of Parliament* (HL33 of 22 July 2016); House of Lords European Union Committee, *Brexit: Parliamentary Scrutiny* (HL50 of 20 October 2016).

Union.[141] The *Miller* judgment surely added further fuel to that campaign—not least by highlighting the centrality of Parliament in limiting the prerogative powers of Government and the case for enhanced democratic control of executive decisions that would alter the very constitutional fabric of the UK.

Whatever the precise combination of factors, they together generated intense pressure upon the Government to offer Parliament a more influential role in the process of approving the Article 50 TEU agreement, above and beyond the usual expectations of UK constitutional law. And so, in its White Paper of February 2017, the Government promised to 'ensure that the UK Parliament receives at least as much information as that received by members of the European Parliament ... The Government will then put the final deal that is agreed between the UK and the EU to a vote in both Houses of Parliament'.[142]

That was a highly significant concession. Yet its full import was counter-balanced by various other considerations. In the first place, it was unclear what precise legal status the Government intended such parliamentary votes to carry. Would these be advisory votes, carrying significant political weight but not formally binding upon the executive? And would the House of Lords be offered a vote on the same terms and with the same potential effects as the House of Commons? In the second place, the Government appeared to envisage that any parliamentary vote on the withdrawal agreement would be on a 'take it or leave it' basis: either Parliament could accept the final treaty as it stood and the UK would leave the EU on the basis of that deal; or Parliament could reject the Government's proposed withdrawal agreement—in which event (assuming such a vote was to be treated as legally binding and/or politically compelling) the UK would simply leave the EU with no deal in place.

It is also worth noting that, while the Government was prepared to offer a greater parliamentary say over approval prior to ratification, the Government also proposed to limit parliamentary involvement in the subsequent process of implementing the Article 50 TEU agreement into UK law—the very domain which ordinary constitutional principles told us should be the primary concern of Parliament itself. In particular, the Government's proposed European Union (Withdrawal) Bill envisaged the delegation of far-reaching powers from the legislature to the executive, specifically so as to implement the withdrawal agreement into domestic law, including the power to amend and repeal existing primary legislation, subject only to limited parliamentary scrutiny or control.[143]

Viewed in that context, the February 2017 White Paper's promises of greater parliamentary involvement in the approval of any Article 50 TEU agreement were therefore more ambiguous and less generous than they appeared.[144] However, given the loss of its Commons majority in the June 2017 general election, the UK Government

---

[141] I.e. given that Art 50 TEU requires the consent of the European Parliament before the Council may conclude a proposed withdrawal agreement between the Union and the relevant State.

[142] HMG, *The United Kingdom's exit from and new partnership with the European Union* (Cm 9417 of 2 February 2017), at paras 1.11–1.12.

[143] See Clause 9 of the European Union (Withdrawal) Bill as originally published on 13 July 2017.

[144] A fact confirmed by subsequent divergences in the interpretation of what had been promised/was now envisaged, even among leading Government figures: see, e.g. 'Theresa May and David Davis at odds over vote on final Brexit deal' (*The Guardian*, 25 October 2017).

was eventually forced into accepting further concessions: during the passage of the European Union (Withdrawal) Bill through Parliament, the Government's original plans for domestic scrutiny of the Article 50 TEU outcomes were altered quite considerably and in several key ways.

First, there was strong support in Parliament for enshrining the White Paper's essentially political promises in a more binding legislative form—setting out in more detail both the process for and the legal effects of any vote on approval prior to ratification in each of the Commons and the Lords. Secondly, Parliament also expressed its desire that any vote should be 'meaningful'—not merely a 'take it or leave it' choice between accepting the Government's proposals or leaving the EU without any agreement; but offering parliamentarians the opportunity to shape potential outcomes in a more flexible and influential manner. Thirdly, Parliament further decided that its approval should be required not just for the formal withdrawal treaty being negotiated under Article 50 TEU to deal with the immediate challenges of separation/transition; but also for the non-binding political declaration designed to sit alongside the withdrawal agreement and setting out the basis for subsequent negotiations on the future EU–UK relationship. A vote would only be 'meaningful' if it allowed Parliament to express its views not just on separation and transition, but also on a sufficiently developed template for the future EU–UK relationship.

The anticipated role of the Westminster Parliament in formally approving any withdrawal package that might be agreed politically between the UK Government and the responsible Union institutions was largely the result of those various promises, pressures and concessions. Until its repeal by Parliament itself at the initiative of the Johnson Government, following the latter's victory in the general election of December 2019, section 13 of the European Union (Withdrawal) Act 2018 provided that any withdrawal agreement under Article 50 TEU could be ratified only if three distinct processes were completed by 'exit day'.[145]

In the first place, under section 13(1), the Government was obliged to lay before each House of Parliament: a statement that political agreement had been reached between the EU and the UK; a copy of the negotiated agreement on separation/transition; plus a copy of the political declaration on the framework for the future EU–UK relationship. The House of Lords was offered only a marginal role: it should hold a debate, on a Government motion to take note of the withdrawal package.[146] However, the House of Commons was to have a much greater say: it must positively approve the withdrawal package, by a resolution on a Government motion.[147]

If and when the Commons were to vote to approve the text of a withdrawal package, whether at a first or subsequent attempt under section 13(1), that would trigger the second stage in the approval process under section 13 of the European Union

---

[145] Originally anticipated to be 29 March 2019 but revised in the light of subsequent extensions to the effective date of UK withdrawal, as requested by the British Government and agreed to by the European Council: see the detailed discussion in Chapter 5.

[146] A requirement that would also be deemed fulfilled if the relevant debate were not concluded within a certain period of time.

[147] Under section 13(2): so far as practicable, the relevant Commons motion should be debated and voted on before the European Parliament had reached a decision concerning its consent to the withdrawal agreement in accordance with Art 50 TEU.

(Withdrawal) Act 2018: before the formal withdrawal agreement under Article 50 TEU can be ratified, Parliament must adopt primary legislation which contains provision for the implementation of that agreement directly into UK law.[148] In other words: Commons approval of the withdrawal package would need to lead swiftly to publication of an additional European Union (Withdrawal Agreement) Bill;[149] the latter would also have to be adopted in time for 'exit day' so as to allow for the smooth ratification and entry into force of the proposed Article 50 TEU withdrawal treaty.[150]

Commons approval of the Government's proposed withdrawal package would also trigger the third and final process for UK ratification of the Article 50 TEU agreement. Section 13(14) provided that the relevant provisions of the European Union (Withdrawal) Act 2018 should not affect the operation of Part 2 of the Constitutional Reform and Governance Act 2010 in relation to the withdrawal agreement. Thus, alongside the adoption of additional primary legislation so as to implement any withdrawal agreement into UK law, the proposed treaty would still have to be scrutinized in compliance with the normal constitutional procedures applicable to international agreements: the possibility of negative resolutions by both the Lords and the Commons, which would have the effect of delaying formal ratification, repeatedly and indeed potentially indefinitely in the case of the Commons though not of the Lords.[151]

We will explore several more detailed questions about the interpretation and application of the section 13 process in due course: for example, the procedures that should apply in the event of the Commons voting against the Government's proposed withdrawal package.[152] For now, suffice to say that Parliament's success in enacting the amended European Union (Withdrawal) Act 2018, in the face of objection and resistance from the minority May Government, decisively changed the institutional dynamics of the UK's engagement in the Article 50 TEU process. For a while at least, the Westminster Parliament's role in the approval of any proposed withdrawal package was very considerably strengthened—certainly as compared to our normal constitutional expectations under UK law, but also as compared to the May Government's initial intentions under the February 2017 White Paper, and indeed even as compared (formally at least) to the corresponding powers of the European Parliament as a matter of EU law under Article 50 TEU.[153]

---

[148] Note that the May Government was obliged to alter its original plans for domestic implementation of any withdrawal agreement, partly due to substantial parliamentary opposition to the proposal for sweeping delegated powers under the European Union (Withdrawal) Bill, but also given the Union's insistence that key parts of the proposed withdrawal agreement (including those concerning citizens' rights) must be enshrined and protected under UK law, and not merely by secondary measures, but through primary legislation. See further, e.g. Joint Report from the EU and UK negotiators (8 December 2017) and Joint Technical Note on Citizens' Rights (TF50 (2017) 20).

[149] The May Government published its provisional plans as HMG, *Legislating for the Withdrawal Agreement between the UK and the EU* (Cm 9674 of 24 July 2018); but did not eventually publish its formal legislative proposals before Theresa May was replaced by Boris Johnson as Prime Minister.

[150] In due course, the Johnson Government published its initial legislative proposals for implementing the final Withdrawal Agreement into domestic UK legislation, even before the House of Commons had given its prior approval to the proposed Withdrawal Package in accordance with section 13: see European Union (Withdrawal Agreement) Bill 2019 as published on 21 October 2019.

[151] See above.

[152] See the more detailed discussion in Chapter 5.

[153] Note, however, that the devolved authorities in Scotland, Wales and Northern Ireland were not afforded any greater constitutional influence over approval of the outcomes of the Art 50 TEU negotiations.

In fact, as we shall see in Chapter 5, the requirement that the Government hold and win a 'meaningful vote' on its proposed withdrawal package in the House of Commons, paved the way for months of political turmoil in the UK, including the premature demise of Prime Minister May, as well as deep uncertainty across the broader Union about the eventual outcome of the whole Brexit debacle. Small wonder that the first priority of the Johnson Government, after winning the December 2019 general election, was to use its newfound Commons majority in order simply to abolish the section 13 process altogether, clearing the path for formal ratification of its own revised Withdrawal Agreement under the exercise of ordinary executive powers, while still adopting the necessary legislative framework for its domestic implementation into UK law through a now-compliant Parliament.[154]

E.   Other Parliamentary Attempts to Influence the Ongoing Negotiations Under Article 50 TEU

Earlier in this chapter, we made the point that the European Parliament was able to maximize its influence, not only over final approval of the withdrawal agreement, but also during and over the negotiations themselves—and did so not only by relying upon the pre-emptive influence afforded by its ultimate power of consent to the terms of UK withdrawal directly under Article 50 TEU, but also by benefiting from the strong political desire of the Union institutions and the EU27 to act in close concertation with each other throughout the UK withdrawal process.

By contrast, the Westminster Parliament appeared less able to translate its eventual power of approval under section 13 of the European Union (Withdrawal) Act 2018 (even while it existed) into an effective tool for on-going influence over the conduct and progress of the Article 50 TEU negotiations. That was partly due to the inability of the House of Commons to produce any clear and stable majority in favour of any particular outcome to the EU–UK talks, capable of rivalling the agenda being pursued by the Government itself. But it should also be explained by the unwillingness of Prime Minister May to engage in any meaningful efforts at building parliamentary support for the UK's negotiating position, virtually until a finalized withdrawal package had been already agreed with the Union.[155]

Nevertheless, Parliament did seek to use certain other means at its disposal, in an attempt to exercise a greater-than-usual say over the more detailed course of the negotiations even as the latter were underway—albeit that the tools were usually quite blunt and some of the results appear to be of dubious effectiveness and/or consistency.

In particular, parliamentary amendments to various 'Brexit Bills' ostensibly dealing with domestic UK preparations for withdrawal from the Union, in fact sought to

Consultative arrangements such as the Ministerial Forum on EU Negotiations held regular meetings, but were heavily criticized (particularly by the Scottish Government) for affording the devolved institutions no appreciable say over the withdrawal process.

---

[154] See the revised European Union (Withdrawal Agreement) Bill 2019 as published on 19 December 2019 and subsequently adopted as the European Union (Withdrawal Agreement) Act 2020.

[155] On which: see further the discussion in Chapter 5.

influence/constrain certain Government choices/decisions within the context of the Article 50 TEU negotiations, by either insisting upon or ruling out particular policy preferences and options. Several such amendments made their way into the European Union (Withdrawal) Act 2018 as originally adopted. Some were only ever of cosmetic importance. For example, section 18 obliged a minister to lay before each House of Parliament (before the end of 31 October 2018) a written statement outlining the Government's steps to negotiate an agreement, as part of the framework for future EU–UK relations, for the UK to participate in a customs arrangement with the EU.[156] Other amendments had slightly more bite. For example, section 17 obliged the Government to seek to negotiate a reciprocal agreement with the EU under which (post-withdrawal) an unaccompanied child who has made an application for international protection in one party's territory may (if it is in that child's best interests) come to the other party's territory in order to join a relative who is lawfully resident (or has made a pending protection claim) there.[157]

Other parliamentary attempts to influence the course of the negotiations were more legally robust but could hardly be described as a coherent programme for finding effective solutions to complex problems. For example, section 10 of the European Union (Withdrawal) Act 2018 (as originally enacted) sought to shield Northern Ireland from some of the worst potential adverse effects of UK withdrawal from the Union, by giving legal force to various commitments already offered by the UK Government during the course of its negotiations with the Union. In particular, when exercising any powers conferred under the 2018 Act, the Government (or devolved administration) was obliged to act in a way that was compatible with the terms of the Northern Ireland Act 1998 and that paid due regard to the commitments the UK had already made towards Northern Ireland in its negotiations with the Union.[158] In addition, various legal bases under the 2018 Act, conferring delegated powers related to withdrawal, were not to be understood as authorizing anything that could diminish North-South cooperation under the Good Friday Agreement; or that could create or facilitate border arrangements between Northern Ireland and the Republic of Ireland after 'exit day', involving physical infrastructure that did not exist before exit day and are not in accordance with an agreement reached between the UK and the EU.[159]

However, whatever utility those statutory obligations might have enjoyed was undermined by subsequent amendments to the Taxation (Cross Border Trade) Act 2018—amendments which were designed by Europhobic MPs precisely so as to reduce significantly the (already limited) room for manoeuvre in finding a negotiated solution that would avoid a 'hard border' across the island of Ireland—thereby

---

[156] That provision was subsequently repealed by section 36 of the European Union (Withdrawal Agreement) Act 2020.

[157] That provision was subsequently amended by section 37 of the European Union (Withdrawal Agreement) Act 2020.

[158] In particular: under the Joint Report from the EU and UK negotiators (8 December 2017). See further, on the problems facing Northern Ireland, the detailed discussion in Chapter 8.

[159] Consider, in particular, section 8 (deficiencies), section 9 (WA implementation), section 23(1) (consequentials) and section 23(6) (transitionals) of the European Union (Withdrawal) Act 2018 (as originally enacted).

contradicting the spirit, even if not the letter, of section 10 of the European Union (Withdrawal) Act 2018.

Thus, section 54 of the Taxation (Cross Border Trade) Act 2018 provided that it would be unlawful for Her Majesty's Customs and Revenue to account for any duty etc, collected by HMCR, to the government of a country or territory outside the UK, unless the Treasury confirmed arrangements under which that government would account to HMCR for those duties etc, collected in that country or territory, on a reciprocal basis. That amendment sought effectively to kill off one of the key proposals of the UK Government for avoiding a hard border in Ireland through an agreement on the future EU–UK trading relationship. As we shall see in Chapter 4, under the 'Chequers Plan' of July 2018, the UK had proposed creating a new and borderless customs arrangement with the EU under which the UK would simultaneously apply both the EU's customs system and its own potentially divergent customs regime to third country goods entering the national territory.[160] To make the scheme appear more palatable, the UK proposed collecting and accounting for all relevant EU customs duties etc on goods entering the UK territory but destined for the EU market, though without expecting the Member States to perform the same onerous and costly functions on behalf of the UK itself in respect of goods entering the EU territory but destined for the UK market.[161] Regardless of whether that plan was ever practically feasible, by enacting section 54 and insisting upon reciprocity as a precondition for agreeing to any such customs arrangement, Parliament effectively killed off any realistic chance of the EU ever agreeing to the Government's proposals.[162]

Even more important was section 55 of the Taxation (Cross Border Trade) Act 2018: it shall be unlawful for the Government to enter into arrangements under which Northern Ireland forms part of a separate customs territory to Great Britain. The primary purpose of that amendment was to help undermine the EU's opening proposals for a 'backstop solution' that would prevent the return of a hard border in Ireland under any circumstances and especially in the absence of any suitable agreement on the future EU–UK trading relationship. As we shall discuss further in Chapter 8, those EU proposals were premised upon Northern Ireland effectively remaining within the Customs Union and relevant parts of the Single Market, thereby avoiding the need for customs or regulatory controls in relations with the Republic, but requiring various customs and regulatory barriers instead between Northern Ireland and Great Britain. However, the UK Government declared itself implacably hostile to any such plan on the grounds that it would undermine the UK's own constitutional, economic and territorial integrity for Northern Ireland to be treated any differently from Great Britain. The enactment of section 55 gave the Government convenient statutory backing for its hostility towards the EU's opening proposals, in favour of an alternative 'backstop' proposal, under which the whole of the UK would effectively remain within the

---

[160] HMG, *The Future Relationship between the United Kingdom and the European Union* (Cm 9593 of 17 July 2018).

[161] HMG, *The Future Relationship between the United Kingdom and the European Union* (Cm 9593 of 17 July 2018), especially at para 17: 'the UK is not proposing that the EU applies the UK's tariffs and trade policy at its border for goods intended for the UK'.

[162] See further, on the evolution of the UK's preferences concerning its future relationship with the EU, Chapter 9.

Customs Union. The latter proposal provided the basis for the relevant provisions of the First Withdrawal Agreement, as politically endorsed by the UK Government and the European Council in November 2018.[163]

Moreover, the influence of section 55 did not end there. The replacement of Theresa May with Boris Johnson prompted the UK Government to ditch its own previous 'backstop' proposal based on a UK-wide customs arrangement with the Union. But many commentators suspected that the continuing statutory strait-jacket imposed on the Article 50 TEU negotiations by section 55, remained an important factor in the design of new British proposals for dealing with the border between Northern Ireland and the Republic. Those proposals, which were based on the idea that Northern Ireland should be simultaneously subject to large tracts of EU customs law, whilst also remaining formally part of the UK customs territory in compliance with the statutory direction contained in section 55, were eventually enshrined in the Second Withdrawal Agreement of October 2019, on the basis of which UK withdrawal actually occurred in January 2020.[164]

4. Concluding Remarks

In comparison to the Union, for simple and inescapable reasons of relative size and power, the UK was always going to occupy a weaker position in the Article 50 TEU process. But the UK's natural disadvantage was considerably reinforced and amplified by the lack of responsible preparations for its own withdrawal, the abject disunity of its political class, the self-inflicted fragility of its governing administration, and the blatant contradiction of its official negotiating objectives.

It is hardly a desirable position to find oneself in: attempting to conduct a major course of international negotiations with a naturally stronger counterpart; with no clear, consistent or realistic plan for identifying and pursuing one's own interests; concentrating considerable time and effort in maintaining a fragile and ultimately incompatible coalition of domestic support which cannot even guarantee a working parliamentary majority; yet still ultimately obliged to secure Commons approval for the fruits of one's negotiating efforts; despite having deliberately sought to exclude Parliament from participating in or influencing ongoing talks in any meaningful or constructive manner.

The Government's approach to domestic political management appeared to be: avoid confessing that its 'cake and eat it' policy was unsustainable; refuse to admit that a 'no deal Brexit' would in fact be disastrous for the UK; refrain from disclosing the true nature of the negotiation challenges ahead; and decline to explain the compromises required to achieve a successful outcome. Yet such tactics could not be sustained indefinitely. When reality finally arrived, the combination of (first) a mutually

---

[163] Albeit with Northern Ireland still treated separately from Great Britain, as regards relevant regulatory elements of the Single Market: see the provisions of the original Protocol on Ireland/Northern Ireland contained in the First Withdrawal Package and published at OJ 2019 C 66 I.

[164] See the detailed discussion of the final agreement concerning management of the border between the Republic of Ireland and Northern Ireland, as well as the latter's relationship with the rest of the UK, in Chapter 8.

incompatible governing coalition, (secondly) a jilted and hostile opposition and (thirdly) the need nevertheless to secure positive parliamentary approval for the outcome of negotiations, virtually guaranteed a political implosion. Nevertheless, that was the basis upon which the UK took its sovereign decision to withdraw from the Union and was now expected to embark upon withdrawal negotiations in accordance with the legal process laid down in Article 50 TEU.

4

Framing the Article 50 TEU Negotiations and Agreeing the First Withdrawal Package

1. Introduction

It took nearly a year from the referendum on 23 June 2016 for withdrawal talks under Article 50 TEU formally to commence on 19 June 2017.[1] Nevertheless, the two parties hoped that a withdrawal package could still be concluded and approved in time for the UK's planned departure on 31 March 2019.[2] As we know, that hope eventually proved misplaced.[3] Even allowing for the benefit of hindsight, which permits us now to see more clearly than was possible at the time the various challenges that needed to be ad-dressed, it is still fair to say that the UK experience of negotiating (let alone approving) satisfactory terms of departure from the Union proved to be more difficult and tor-tuous than many people expected. Yet having regard to the various legal and political choices and factors discussed in Chapter 3, it perhaps becomes easier to understand the relative confusion and frustration that marked so much of the negotiations during the Prime Ministerial tenancy of Theresa May.[4]

This chapter will examine the conduct and progress of the negotiations under Article 50 TEU, culminating in political endorsement by the European Council and the May Government of the 'First Withdrawal Package' of November 2018.[5]

In Section 2, we consider how—right from the very outset of the Article 50 TEU negotiations—the Union and the UK had to confront a series of interlinked questions about how to frame the entire process: the basic range of issues that would need to be addressed in the context of withdrawal and the precise sequence and timing of those various strands of discussions, having regard also to the necessary calculations about the overall period of time available for completing the negotiations and approving their eventual outcome.

The EU–UK dispute over scope, sequence and timing, which senior UK ministers had foretold would escalate into a major international row, was in fact quickly re-solved by unilateral decision of the European Council: Article 50 TEU can provide the legal basis only for an agreement addressing the immediate consequences of the very act of withdrawal. Once sufficient progress had been made with those negotiations,

---

[1] See Commission, *Terms of Reference for the Article 50 TEU negotiations* (19 June 2017).
[2] See European Council (Article 50), *Guidelines of 29 April 2017*, at para 7.
[3] See further Chapter 5.
[4] For regular analysis of the withdrawal process, see the Editorial Comments of the *Common Market Law Review*, e.g. 53 *CMLRev* (2016) 875; 53 *CMLRev* (2016) 1491; 54 *CMLRev* (2017) 1309; 54 *CMLRev* (2017) 1613; 55 *CMLRev* (2018) 1; 56 *CMLRev* (2019) 611; 56 *CMLRev* (2019) 1447. Also: 55 *CML Rev Special Issue on Brexit* (May 2018).
[5] Published at OJ 2019 C 66 I.

The UK's Withdrawal from the EU. Michael Dougan, Oxford University Press. © Michael Dougan 2021.
DOI: 10.1093/oso/9780198833475.003.0004

preliminary and preparatory discussions could begin about future relations between the Union and the relevant State—but formal negotiations were only possible after withdrawal itself had been completed. As we shall see, the solution adopted by the European Council was instrumental in structuring the conduct of the negotiations and (again with the benefit of hindsight) proved decisive in promoting their eventual success—at least judged by the objective of delivering a negotiated, orderly withdrawal.

Section 3 then proceeds to consider the parties' joint efforts to address the various 'separation challenges' that needed to be settled under Article 50 TEU: for example, how to protect the status of EU and UK citizens who had already made use of their rights to free movement; and how to avoid the creation of a 'hard border', particularly for the movement of goods, across the island of Ireland. After the European Council decided that 'sufficient progress' had been achieved on those 'separation challenges' that had been designated a political priority by the Union, bilateral talks were then initiated, in the form of preliminary and preparatory discussions, about the terms of the future relationship between the Union and the UK.

As we shall see: both the separation negotiations and the future relationship discussions were marked by regular moments of deadlock, breakthrough, frustration, and resolution. In particular, several major stumbling blocks emerged, generally driven primarily by the May Government's (mis-)management of domestic UK political tensions: for example, posturing about the methodology for calculating the UK's financial settlement towards the Union; and arguments about political governance, dispute settlement and legal interpretation of the withdrawal treaty. However, the central knot that needed to be untangled concerned the mutually interdependent questions (first) of how to manage the border between the Republic of Ireland and Northern Ireland and (secondly) of how closely the UK as a whole might eventually remain tied to the Union in the fields of trade and security. Nevertheless, all relevant obstacles were indeed overcome and the Article 50 TEU process did result in joint political agreement on the 'First Withdrawal Package'—a legally binding (First) Withdrawal Agreement aimed at delivering an orderly withdrawal, together with a non-binding (First) Political Declaration expressing the parties' mutual understanding for their future relations—that the Union and the UK Government could then present for formal approval via their respective internal processes.

2. Some Fundamental Questions that Needed to be Answered about the Scope, Sequence and Timing of Negotiations

Right at the dawn of the EU–UK withdrawal negotiations, the parties had to reach a provisional understanding of several key issues: first, the basic scope, sequence and timing of talks under the auspices of Article 50 TEU; secondly, a working agenda for the range of challenges that had to be settled in order to deliver an orderly departure; and thirdly, a clear calculation of the time available in order to complete the necessary negotiations. Obviously, those issues were mutually interdependent. For example, choices made about the basic scope, sequence and timing of talks concerning the UK's withdrawal would inevitably have a direct and significant influence upon the more precise range of 'separation challenges' likely to find themselves up for discussion under the Article 50 TEU process. But in addition, the particular combination of answers to those questions about scope and sequencing, agenda, and timings, as worked out by and between the Union and the UK, would raise some interesting legal questions about the nature of Article 50 TEU as an 'exceptional Union competence' and its constitutional limits as a legal basis.

A. The Basic Scope, Sequence and Timing of Talks Under the Auspices of Article 50 TEU

Let's begin by considering the basic scope, sequence and timing of the UK's withdrawal negotiations, which was perhaps the single most important among the myriad legal and political factors that shaped the conduct and outcomes of the entire Article 50 TEU process.

It was evident from soon after the 2016 referendum that UK withdrawal would entail three distinct if inter-related sets of discussions. First, the 'separation challenges' involved in ensuring that the very act of the UK's withdrawal from the Union took place in an orderly fashion and under conditions which produced the minimum necessary disruption and uncertainty for public and private actors. Those included major challenges such as the future treatment of existing Union citizens and UK nationals within the UK and across the EU27 (respectively); reaching a financial settlement of the UK's liabilities and commitments arising from its period of Union membership; and how to handle the unique implications of UK withdrawal for Ireland, particularly when it came to protecting the peace settlement in Northern Ireland.

Secondly, the 'future relationship' between the Union and the UK which would govern their mutual relations after the immediate process of withdrawal had been completed (preferably in an orderly fashion). That relationship would likely be multi-faceted: from trade in goods and services, data protection, security and foreign policy cooperation to environmental protection and scientific research. In each case, however, the fundamental question was similar: would the future EU–UK relationship be relatively close or instead relatively distant; with all that that choice inevitably entails for the substantive and institutional terms of their ongoing engagement?

Thirdly, there was the possibility of negotiating some form of 'transition period' which would help smooth the way between the immediate priority of delivering an orderly withdrawal and the eventual entry into force of the framework for the future EU–UK relationship. Again, even here, there was evidently much to talk about. For example: what policy fields should any such transition period cover? On the basis of which substantive rules and institutional structures should it operate? And for precisely how long should it last? And in case it proved too short for its intended purpose, should there be a power to extend the duration of any transition period?

However, if there was general agreement about the basic range of short- and long-term issues raised by the UK's withdrawal, more serious differences in understanding arose concerning the precise sequence and timing of those various sets of discussions. As we saw in Chapter 3, the UK Government's preferences were made clear in its

White Paper from February 2017: there should be single (or at least parallel) negotiations covering both the immediate separation challenges and the future relationship, to be concluded and ratified before the effective date of UK withdrawal; followed
by a phased implementation of the new arrangements—allowing public and private
actors to prepare for the introduction of new regulatory regimes which had already
been agreed and were simply awaiting entry into force.[6] It is worth pointing out that
the Cameron Government had previously expressed a more hesitant and ultimately
different view on this issue: '[i]t is unclear from the terms of Article 50 how far the
arrangements for the UK's future relationship with the EU would be included in a
withdrawal agreement. But it is likely that the scope of those arrangements would require the negotiation of a separate agreement with the EU.'[7] Nevertheless, the May
Government confidently set out its rather different understanding—an approach then
consistently reflected in subsequent UK official statements.[8]

On a generous interpretation, one might argue that the Government was merely
seeking to be efficient: since an agreement on plans (say) for an ambitious future EU–
UK relationship could in itself resolve many of the more immediate challenges posed
by the very act of withdrawal, it surely made sense to concentrate time and effort on
negotiating that future relationship right from the very outset. However, such efficiency could easily morph into a false economy. For example, if the parties were unable to reach agreement on anything other than a more distant future relationship, the
various 'separation challenges' would remain as pressing as before and yet may have
received significantly less time and attention than they truly deserved. In any case, the
UK Government's preferred approach to timing and sequencing could also be seen
as a logical extension of its 'cake and eat it' philosophy towards the entire Article 50
TEU process—particularly in seeking to reassure businesses and investors that the economic impacts and disruptions of withdrawal would be minimal. Moreover, the UK's
plans on timing and sequencing can also be interpreted as a natural reflection of Brexit
as a national existential crisis of identity and future: the purpose of withdrawal is to
redefine the UK's place in Europe and indeed the world, so the objective of the withdrawal negotiations must be to contribute to that process of fundamental redefinition,
rather than the relative mundanities of citizens' rights, divorce bills and Irish borders.[9]

What about the EU's understanding? According to the European Council's April
2017 Guidelines, the main purpose of the Article 50 TEU negotiations was to ensure
an orderly withdrawal so as to reduce uncertainty and (to the extent possible) minimize disruption. The process should therefore commence with a 'first phase' aimed
at providing as much clarity and certainty as possible on the immediate effects of
UK withdrawal; as well as settling the UK's disentanglement from the Union and the

---

[6] HMG, *The United Kingdom's Exit from and New Partnership with the European Union* (Cm 9417 of 2
February 2017).
[7] HMG, *The Process for Withdrawing from the European Union* (Cm9216 of 29 February 2016), at para 3.6.
[8] E.g. HMG, *Prime Minister's Notification Letter to the European Council President* (29 March 2017);
Department for Exiting the European Union, *Legislating for the United Kingdom's Withdrawal from the
European Union* (Cm 9446 of 7 March 2017). And indeed, commanded broader parliamentary support, e.g.
House of Commons Exiting the EU Committee, *The Process for Exiting the European Union* (HC815 of 14
January 2017).
[9] See the discussion in Chapter 3.

rights/obligations derived from the UK's commitments as a Member State. By contrast, any agreement on the future EU–UK relationship could be finalized and concluded only *after* the UK's withdrawal. However, an overall understanding of that future relationship could and should be identified during a 'second phase' of the Article 50 TEU negotiations. To that end, the Union would be ready to engage in preliminary and preparatory discussions with the UK, as soon as the European Council were to decide that sufficient progress had been made on the 'first phase' issues. Finally, to the extent necessary and legally possible, the Article 50 TEU negotiations might also seek to determine transitional arrangements—provided the latter were in the Union's interests—in order to provide a bridge towards some foreseeable future relationship. Such transitional arrangements must be clearly defined, limited in time, and subject to effective enforcement mechanisms. Moreover, in so far as it involved a prolongation of the Union *acquis*, transition would require existing Union rules, instruments, and structures to apply.[10]

The European Council's approach to the question of sequence and timing was evidently and radically different from that of the UK Government. But the European Council's plan was fully supported by other Union actors;[11] and (unsurprisingly) was subsequently confirmed in the Council's negotiating directives for the Commission from May 2017.[12] The UK Government suggested that a major row over sequence and timing could consume the negotiations just as soon as they had (finally) started.[13] However, the Union position on sequence and timing was accepted as the basis for the Article 50 TEU process at the very first meeting between the UK Government and the Commission on 19 June 2017,[14] though it was only with Theresa May's 'Florence Speech' in September 2017 that the UK finally reconciled itself to the reality of the situation and began to work more faithfully within the parameters laid down by the Union institutions.[15]

The dispute over sequence and timing proved fundamental to the entire Article 50 TEU process. Its resolution had far-reaching consequences not only for the conduct but also the eventual outcomes of the UK withdrawal negotiations: by concentrating time and attention on agreeing a legal text that would resolve the immediate separation challenges in an orderly manner; by ruling out any possibility of the future EU–UK relationship being formally negotiated (let alone concluded) before withdrawal had already taken place; by conjuring into existence the need for a political declaration that would nevertheless outline the parties' mutual understanding and aspirations for what that future relationship might consist of; and by creating the pressing need for an appropriate transitional regime, more wide-ranging in scope and more onerous in character than either party had originally envisaged, so as to bridge the inevitable gap

---

[10] European Council (Article 50), *Guidelines of 29 April 2017*, at paras 4–6.

[11] E.g. European Parliament, *Resolutions of 28 June 2016* and *5 April 2017*.

[12] Council Decision authorizing the opening of negotiations with the United Kingdom for an agreement setting out the arrangements for its withdrawal from the European Union (15 May 2017).

[13] See, e.g. https://www.ft.com/content/01396086-38ae-11e7-821a-6027b8a20f23.

[14] See Commission, *Terms of Reference for the Article 50 TEU negotiations* (19 June 2017).

[15] Theresa May, *Florence Speech: A New Era of Cooperation and Partnership between the UK and the EU* (22 September 2017). Contrast, e.g. with David Davis, *Comments at the 3rd round of EU–UK negotiations* (31 August 2017) and *Update to the House of Commons* (5 September 2017).

which would arise between the act of withdrawal and the subsequent conclusion of a new relationship.

We will consider all of those consequences in greater detail in due course. For now, let's focus on the rationale behind the decisions on sequence and timing under Article 50 TEU that were taken and then effectively imposed by the European Council. In Chapter 3, we suggested that the European Council's April 2017 Guidelines contained both legal principles which were intended to reiterate and clarify the basic framework governing a Member State's withdrawal from the Union; and more political choices that reflected the EU27's fundamental priorities, interests, and objectives under the Article 50 TEU process. Those political choices often assumed the prior existence, but then far exceeded the actual demands, of the underlying legal principles. Yet sometimes the two overlapped and led to the same conclusion—and that was certainly true in the case of sequence and timing, where the European Council's guidelines were not only a direct product of its fundamental political choices about how to manage the UK's withdrawal, but also reflected a clear understanding of the procedural requirements imposed by Union constitutional law.

Starting with the politics, the European Council's preferences on sequence and timing were a natural consequence of its four-tiered objectives for UK withdrawal. Maintaining the unity of the Union and protecting the integrity of its legal order were to be taken as givens. After that, the priority was to deliver a smooth and orderly withdrawal that would minimize disruption and uncertainty. That job done, the Union would then seek a new relationship that would keep the UK tied as closely as possible to the Union into the future.[16] In other words: the European Council was expressing a pragmatic desire to prioritize the urgent need to reach agreement on the short-term (and hopefully less taxing) problems posed by withdrawal, within the limited time actually available for negotiations under Article 50 TEU; rather than risk all the parties' time and energy being dissipated on addressing the longer-term (and potentially more difficult) challenge of defining the UK's new European future.

After all, empirical experience tells us that a wide-ranging cooperation agreement between the Union and any external partner is likely to take some considerable time to negotiate, conclude, and ratify. That seems particularly true in the case of an ex-Member State, where the scope and depth of potential cooperation may well be considerable; yet the political circumstances surrounding relations with the Union are also likely to be especially complex and acutely sensitive. In the UK's case, the Government's plans for sequence and timing never felt particularly realistic: it seemed certain that the time required between notification and final settlement of the future relationship would exceed the two years available by default under the Treaty withdrawal process. From the Union's perspective: to have adopted the UK's approach to sequence and timing might therefore have incorporated a substantial risk of outright failure into the entire withdrawal negotiations from their very outset.

And in that regard, it is worth pointing out that subsequent events undoubtedly proved the European Council's initial political evaluation to be entirely sound. By November 2018, the two parties managed to agree the first version of the legal text of

---

[16] See further the discussion in Chapter 3.

an agreement that would address the immediate separation challenges raised by with-drawal (as well as provide for a far-reaching transitional regime) but only after con-siderable delay and uncertainty even in the conclusion of the negotiations themselves; to say nothing of the UK's subsequent difficulties in trying and failing to complete the necessary internal approval processes; and that text then had to be renegotiated and revised in order to satisfy the demands of the new UK Government led by Boris Johnson.[17]

On future relations, however, the Union and the UK could do nothing more than agree a relatively short, sketchy and ambiguous political declaration—identifying the basic range of issues that subsequent negotiations should cover and expressing certain bland and/or vague aspirations about the sorts of outcomes those negotiations might produce. Even that document remained the subject of deep contestation within the UK, and subsequently underwent important revisions of its own in late 2019.[18] But at least with the text of the final Withdrawal Agreement, the European Council had done its part in protecting against the worst uncertainty and disruption associated with the very act of departure. Had the UK Government's approach prevailed, it is dif-ficult to see how negotiations about the future relationship could possibly have been concluded within the time available. In fact, it is easy to imagine that the 'Article 50 TEU guillotine' would have fallen upon the negotiations with no provision in place even to deliver an orderly withdrawal.

Not that such sober political calculations were perceived and appreciated as such in much of the febrile UK discourse: the Union's stance on sequence and timing was frequently cited by Leave campaigners as concrete evidence of Brussels' delib-erate plan to make life as difficult as possible for the UK in order to prove the point that 'Brexit doesn't pay'.[19] For example, the former Secretary of State for Exiting the European Union would regularly bemoan the UK Government's failure (in which he presumably shared, as the minister directly responsible at the time) to challenge and overturn the agenda imposed by the European Council through its April 2017 Guidelines.[20]

However, the April 2017 Guidelines on sequence and timing were not merely a (pragmatic and sensible) political choice. They were also the product of certain basic legal principles, designed to find an interpretation of Article 50 TEU that would fit satisfactorily within the wider constitutional framework of the EU legal system. After all, under the principle of conferred powers, every Union action requires an iden-tifiable legal basis under the Treaties containing appropriate competence for the proposed measures.[21] Article 50 TEU clearly provides a legal basis conferring com-petence for the Union to reach an agreement with the UK covering the arrangements for the latter's withdrawal.[22] But could Article 50 TEU also provide a legal basis for the

---

[17] See further Chapter 5.

[18] See further Chapter 5.

[19] Or to bribe the UK into conceding less favourable withdrawal terms: see, e.g. 'David Davis: EU is trying to drag out Brexit talks to get more money' (*The Guardian*, 17 October 2017).

[20] See, e.g. https://www.politico.eu/article/how-uk-lost-brexit-eu-negotiation/.

[21] Arts 4 and 5 TEU.

[22] Even if the precise scope/nature of that competence remained open to debate and contestation: see the discussion on mixity in Chapter 3 and on the transition period in Chapter 6.

Union to conclude a single (or separate) agreement also covering the future relationship with the UK? If not, which Treaty provisions might provide an alternative legal basis for the Union to reach a parallel agreement on that future relationship, i.e. also to be concluded before withdrawal had actually taken place and thus while the UK still remained a Member State?

On the question of whether Article 50 TEU was capable of acting as a legitimate legal basis for a single (or at least parallel) agreement(s) covering both separation and future, the European Council's core principles reflected a solid legal understanding that the treaty governing the nuts-and-bolts of withdrawal was to be considered separate and distinct from any agreement on the longer-term EU–UK relationship. After all, the very text of Article 50 TEU explicitly distinguishes between (on the one hand) 'an agreement ... setting out the arrangements for [the relevant State's] withdrawal' and (on the other hand) 'the framework for [the relevant State's] future relationship with the Union': the former agreement is to be negotiated and concluded simply 'taking account of' (not addressing or incorporating or otherwise giving concrete legal expression to) the latter framework.[23] As we saw in Chapter 2, early commentary on the draft withdrawal clause had indeed suggested that the withdrawal agreement should directly settle both the separation issues and the future relationship; but the actual text of the proposals, as well as the final version of Article 50 TEU, did not actually reflect that discussion and suggested instead that the two issues were indeed to be handled separately.[24]

Besides its clear text, additional constitutional considerations argued against the proposition that Article 50 TEU could provide an appropriate legal basis for an agreement covering also the future relationship between the Union and the withdrawing State. In particular, the Lisbon Treaty drafters decided that conclusion of a withdrawal agreement under Article 50 TEU should be possible with the support of a (super-)majority in the Council. As we have seen, the Council further agreed that Article 50 TEU conferred an exceptional competence upon the Union institutions alone to conclude any withdrawal treaty (even as regards areas falling within shared competence, with no possibility of ratification also by domestic institutions).[25] That approach and understanding may well have been constitutionally tolerable in respect of an agreement dealing only with the immediate and inherent challenges of withdrawal. But it would not be nearly so persuasive or sustainable in the case of a wide-ranging cooperation agreement between the Union and an external partner intended to last far into the future. To interpret Article 50 TEU as a valid legal basis not only for separation issues but also the future relationship, exempted from the normal constitutional rules governing issues such as mixity, and without any compelling textual or contextual reason for doing so other than political convenience for the withdrawing State, would directly override our standard

---

[23] In French: 'en tenant compte du cadre de ses relations futures avec l'Union'. Similarly, e.g. in Spanish: 'teniendo en cuenta el marco de sus relaciones futuras con la Unión'.

[24] In particular: the original proposals contained in CONV 648/03; their amended version in CONV 850/03; and their final version in OJ 2004, C 310.

[25] See the discussion in Chapter 3.

expectations concerning the division of competence between the Union and its Member States.

If Article 50 TEU could not provide an appropriate legal basis for the Union to conclude a single agreement also covering its future relationship with the UK, that left the question: which Treaty provisions might provide an alternative legal basis for the Union to reach a parallel agreement on that future relationship before withdrawal had actually taken place? Here, the problem was more straightforward, since the relevant Treaty texts leave little room for ambiguity: all of the relevant alternative provisions and legal bases provided for under the Treaties make clear that the Union can negotiate and conclude agreements 'with third countries'.[26] For that reason, the European Council adopted the view that the Union institutions could not legitimately exercise their existing external relations competences so as to engage in (let alone conclude) formal negotiations with an existing Member State— even one which has notified its intention to withdraw under Article 50 TEU, but which otherwise remains a Member State subject to all of the relevant provisions of Union law.[27]

Of course, that is not to deny a tangible political and even legal connection between negotiation of the withdrawal agreement and consideration of the future relationship. After all, Article 50 TEU specifically directs that separation should be agreed 'taking account of' the framework for future relations. And of course, a withdrawing State that wants to maintain close ties with the Union into the future might well agree immediate terms of departure very different from a withdrawing State that is minded to pursue only much looser or more distant relations. The European Council was therefore entirely justified in foreseeing a more informal dialogue about future relations in the form of preliminary and preparatory discussions within the context of the Article 50 TEU process—allowing for diplomatic preparations that would pave the way for more formal negotiations after the UK's departure had been completed.

For those combined reasons, there are strong grounds for arguing that the European Council's approach to the sequence and timing of negotiations was not only politically more realistic and empirically grounded, but also legally more robust than the alternative interpretation championed by the UK. Ultimately, however, the issue was decided at the political rather than the legal level: the Court was never called upon to clarify the precise nature of the Union's competences under Article 50 TEU. The Court in *Wightman* did have occasion to observe that Article 50 TEU pursues the objective of establishing a procedure 'to enable ... withdrawal to take place in an orderly fashion';[28] but it is difficult to read that dictum as a conscious endorsement of the April 2017 Guidelines (or a deliberate refutation of the February 2017 White Paper) specifically on the issue of sequence and timing or the inter-relationship between negotiations on separation and discussions on future relations.

---

[26] E.g. Arts 216 and 218 TFEU.

[27] With the exception of the circumstances prescribed in Art 50(4) TEU.

[28] Case C-621/18, *Wightman* (EU:C:2018:999), at para 56.

B. A Provisional Withdrawal Agenda Under and Beyond
Article 50 TEU

The European Council's phased approach to the basic scope, sequence and timing of negotiations under Article 50 TEU had an important and immediate consequence: the need to identify a more precise 'first phase' agenda for negotiations to deliver the UK's orderly withdrawal from the Union, including which items should be considered sufficiently important as to require 'sufficient progress' on their resolution before moving on to commence 'second phase' talks also concerning a possible framework for future EU–UK relations.

As we saw in Chapter 3, the UK's White Paper from February 2017 (having concentrated attention on future relations as well as various essentially domestic objectives) had relatively little to offer by way of a detailed agenda for negotiations on the immediate issues raised by the very act of withdrawal. Once again, the initiative was seized largely by the Union: the European Council had already identified many of the key separation challenges in its April 2017 Guidelines;[29] that list was then elaborated upon in greater detail by the Council in its negotiating directives for the Commission as adopted in May 2017.[30]

(i) Priority Separation Issues

To begin with, the Union declared that three separation issues were to be considered priority tasks—such that the Article 50 TEU process could proceed to 'second phase' talks only if 'sufficient progress' were achieved on these particular items.

The first priority issue was to agree a regime for protecting the status of those EU citizens and UK nationals who were currently living or working in the UK and the EU27 (respectively) pursuant to the free movement rights offered under Union law during the period of UK membership.[31] We will explore this issue—the scale and nature of the challenge, the regime proposed under the final Withdrawal Agreement, together with its potential shortcomings and problems—in greater detail in Chapter 7. For now, suffice to note that both parties claimed to regard the question of protecting existing citizens' rights as one of paramount importance—especially since it was clear that several million people, who had moved across the UK and the EU27 in good faith to build their lives, careers, families and friendships, were plunged into a state of deep uncertainty and anxiety about their future treatment and prospects.

Addressing that challenge would now require the two parties to negotiate a system for identifying precisely which range of EU and UK citizens (as well as their associated family members) should be protected in accordance with the withdrawal regime—and conversely, who might be excluded from the potential scope of the new system. The two parties would also need to define the full content of the future rights that would be vested in those protected individuals—covering fields such as residency, employment

---

[29] European Council (Article 50), *Guidelines of 29 April 2017*.
[30] Council Decision authorizing the opening of negotiations with the United Kingdom of Great Britain and Northern Ireland for an agreement setting out the arrangements for its withdrawal from the European Union (22 May 2017).
[31] European Council (Article 50), *Guidelines of 29 April 2017*, at para 8.

and social advantages; as well as principles for cooperation in related fields such as the mutual recognition of professional qualifications and the cross-border coordination of social security benefits. Last but not least, the EU and the UK would have to agree on any special provisions to determine how all these citizens' rights guarantees would be interpreted and enforced in practice within the parties' respective legal systems.

The second priority issue was for the two parties to agree a methodology for calculating a 'single financial settlement' between the Union and the UK designed to ensure that the latter fulfilled the various budgetary commitments it had already undertaken as a Member State.[32] We will not explore this particular issue in any greater detail, either here or in subsequent chapters: despite its undoubted political and practical importance, it is of relatively little legal interest, save to those with a specialist focus on the law surrounding the Union budget.[33] Suffice to say that, as a Member State, the UK had made various promises to contribute to the funding of a whole range of Union programmes, schemes, and projects, many of which would remain in the process of being delivered and/or their accounts settled even beyond the projected date of UK departure. It was therefore necessary to determine precisely which commitments the UK would still be obliged to fulfil and according to what overall time scale.[34]

Yet that was far from a self-executing task. Given the very different methodologies that could be employed in order to identify and calculate the projected UK share of relevant liabilities, receipts, and assets, estimates of the UK's 'divorce bill' might range from 10 billion euros up to 100 billion euros—though the UK Government itself estimated a 'divorce bill' of around £35 billion to £39 billion.[35] Such methodological choices inevitably meant that the question of how to calculate the single financial settlement was as much a political as a technical matter. For example, the Union had a strong interest in minimizing the potential damage that UK withdrawal might inflict upon its own spending plans or the remaining Member States; and also treated satisfactory resolution of the 'divorce bill' as a fundamental requirement in building the mutual trust considered essential for negotiating any withdrawal agreement (let alone an ambitious future relationship).[36] In the UK, however, Leave campaigners both within and outwith the Government were inflamed by the prospect of a substantial 'divorce bill'—either because they failed to comprehend or at least accept that the UK could possibly suffer any financial consequences as a result of its sovereign decision to withdraw; or because they saw in the 'divorce bill' a sufficiently simple yet emotive issue through which to whip up populist resentment against the EU as a means of influencing or even derailing the Article 50 TEU negotiations.[37]

---

[32] European Council (Article 50), *Guidelines of 29 April 2017*, at para 10.

[33] Though see the outline commentary offered, on the relevant provisions of the final Withdrawal Agreement, in Chapter 6.

[34] See further, e.g. House of Lords European Union Committee, *Brexit and the EU Budget* (HL125 of 4 March 2017); Commission, *Position Paper on Essential Principles on Financial Settlement* (12 June 2017).

[35] See further, e.g. House of Commons Committee on Public Accounts, *Exiting the EU: The Financial Settlement* (HC973 of 27 June 2018). Note also: House of Lords European Union Committee, *Brexit: The Financial Settlement* (HL7 of 23 October 2019).

[36] A point frequently made by Michel Barnier, e.g. Commission, *Speaking points by Michel Barnier at the press conference following the second round of Article 50 negotiations with the United Kingdom* (20 July 2017).

[37] E.g. https://www.theguardian.com/politics/2017/jul/11/european-leaders-can-go-whistle-over-eu-divorce-bill-says-boris-johnson.

The third and final priority issue identified by the European Council in its April 2017 Guidelines was to recognize the unique challenges facing Ireland as a consequence of the UK's intended withdrawal from the Union.[38] This is an issue we will most definitely return to in greater detail: Chapter 8 will explain the various ways in which UK withdrawal created potential problems, for both Northern Ireland and the Republic, and then explore and critique the solutions proposed under the final Withdrawal Agreement. Suffice for now to observe that the challenges are myriad and profound: Northern Ireland has been identified as the UK region that will suffer the very worst consequences of withdrawal; while among the remaining Member States of the Union, the Republic surely stands to be most seriously and adversely affected by the UK's departure.[39]

But the key issues relate to the threat that UK withdrawal from the Union would lead directly to the erection of a 'hard border' across the island of Ireland—with all the damaging economic, social and political consequences that implies. In the first place, how far might the UK Government's decision to end the free movement of persons and impose immigration restrictions on EU nationals affect the survival or operation of the Common Travel Area with the Republic—and thereby lead to the imposition of immigration controls at the Northern Irish frontier? In the second place, how far might the UK Government's insistence upon leaving not just the Union but also the Customs Union and the Single Market, lead to the creation of a customs and regulatory border between the UK and the EU as a whole and/or the imposition of a physical frontier for the movement of goods between Northern Ireland and the Republic in particular?

(ii) Remaining Withdrawal Agreement Issues

Besides the three 'priority' topics of citizens' rights, the financial settlement, and the unique circumstances facing Ireland, the European Council and the Council identified a range of other issues that would need to be addressed explicitly in any negotiated treaty, in order to deliver a smooth and orderly UK withdrawal.

In particular, it was clearly understood that the Article 50 TEU agreement should seek to safeguard legal certainty for public and private actors by addressing a wide array of situations in which the UK's outstanding involvement in various Union institutions, instruments, and procedures would need to be wound down.[40]

---

[38] European Council (Article 50), *Guidelines of 29 April 2017*, at para 11.

[39] See further, e.g. House of Lords EU Committee, *Brexit: UK-Irish Relations* (HL76 of 12 December 2016).

[40] See, e.g. European Council (Article 50), *Guidelines of 29 April 2017*, at paras 9, 14 and 16. The Commission published a series of more detailed 'position papers' setting out the Union's negotiating stance on these 'other separation challenges', covering, e.g. the functioning of the Union institutions, agencies and bodies (TF50 (2017) 6); ongoing Union judicial and administrative procedures (TF50 (2017) 5); goods placed on the market under Union law before withdrawal (TF50 (2017) 7/2); judicial cooperation in civil and commercial matters (TF50 (2017) 9/2); ongoing police and judicial cooperation in criminal matters (TF50 (2017) 8/2); nuclear materials and safeguard equipment (TF50 (2017) 3/2); customs related matters needed for an orderly withdrawal (TF50 (2017) 13/2); ongoing public procurement procedures (TF50 (2017) 12/2); intellectual property rights (TF50 (2017) 11/2); use of data and protection of information obtained or processed before withdrawal (TF50 (2017) 14/2). Likewise, the UK Government published its own 'position papers' on many of the corresponding topics, covering, e.g. privileges and immunities (13 July 2017); ongoing Union judicial and administrative proceedings (13 July 2017); continuity in the availability of goods for the EU and the UK (21 August 2017); nuclear materials and safeguards issues (13 July 2018); confidentiality and access to documents (21 August 2017).

That was true in many fields of the Single Market: for example, the treatment of UK/ EU goods already lawfully placed on the EU/UK market (particularly those subject to ongoing market surveillance regimes which called for cross-border cooperation between the competent national authorities); or the status of large numbers of intellectual property rights which had already been granted, or were in the process of being recognized, at the point of UK withdrawal. Similar challenges arose in other fields, such as the Area of Freedom, Security and Justice (AFSJ). Even if the UK's constitutional relationship to the AFSJ was governed by a complex series of opt-out/opt-in provisions, it remained the case that the UK did participate in various Union measures designed to improve cross-border cooperation in both civil and criminal matters; so the parties would have to decide (for example) what to do with any European Arrest Warrants, seeking the judicial surrender of individuals between the UK and the EU27, which were still live at the point of the UK's formal departure from the Union.

However, such 'other separation issues' also covered a much broader category of potential situations. For example: what should happen to the various Union proceedings, involving UK authorities and/or natural and legal persons, which were either outstanding as at the effective date of withdrawal or still capable of arising based on facts which had occurred before the UK's formal departure? That could arise in the judicial sphere (preliminary references, enforcement proceedings etc) but also in the administrative realm (competition and state aid investigations, regulatory proceedings in fields such as chemicals or medicines). At what stage might proceedings be deemed to have progressed sufficiently that they should now be completed in accordance with the applicable Union rules; and if so, what should be the precise legal status and effects of any Union ruling or decision, particularly within the UK legal system?

Similarly, the Union expected special rules to be agreed in order to protect its own future interests within the UK. That included a new regime on diplomatic privileges and immunities for the EU and its civil servants, covering immediate tasks such as the integrity of Union buildings and offices; as well as longer-term issues, such as the handling and storage of confidential information that the UK had previously received in its capacity as a Member State, or the future obligations of UK nationals who had previously worked as public servants at the Union institutions. Moreover, the European Council and the Council highlighted the particular questions raised by UK withdrawal not only from the Union but also from Euratom: for example, concerning UK guarantees that it would be capable of meeting its international obligations as regards civil nuclear materials even after withdrawal; settling issues about the ownership and/or use of existing nuclear materials located within the UK and/or across the EU27; and determining the legal status of existing contracts for the cross-border supply and/or use of nuclear materials as between the UK and the Union.

On top of both the 'priority separation issues' and those 'other separation issues', the Union agenda for negotiations under Article 50 TEU drew particular attention to the situation of the UK's Sovereign Base Areas in Cyprus.[41] In particular, several thousand Cypriot nationals lived and/or worked in the UK's remaining military bases on the island of Cyprus. The flow of people, goods, and services had worked smoothly while

---

[41] European Council (Article 50), *Guidelines of 29 April 2017*, at para 12.

the UK and Cyprus were both Member States, in accordance with the relevant EU free movement rules and regulatory standards. But UK withdrawal meant identifying and agreeing a replacement legal regime to ensure the continued smooth functioning of both the UK's military bases and the lives and livelihoods of the Cypriot nationals who lived and/or worked there.

Last but not least, the Union's negotiating agenda included the unavoidable question of how any agreement to deliver a smooth and orderly withdrawal would be governed and operationalized.[42] We will explore the governance structures and principles of the final Withdrawal Agreement in greater detail in Chapter 6. Suffice for now to recall that the two parties needed to devise appropriate political and administrative institutions and processes (for example) to implement and amend the agreement as required; acceptable judicial or other dispute settlement structures (in particular) to resolve disagreements between the parties about interpretation and application of the agreement; effective means of enforcement (for example) through a system of sanctions or other penalties designed to address situations of proven non-compliance; and potentially, provisions to determine the more precise implementation measures for/ legal effects of the agreement within the internal legal system of each party, including whether and how far the treaty should be considered enforceable before domestic courts/administrative authorities at the suit of natural and legal persons.

(iii)   Issues Outside Article 50 TEU per se but that would Benefit
        from Mutual Coordination

So far, we have considered various separation challenges placed directly on the agenda for negotiations between the Union and the UK with a view to the inclusion of appropriate provisions within the withdrawal agreement envisaged under Article 50 TEU. However, the European Council and the Council also explicitly identified several other challenges that should be discussed during talks with the UK. These challenges also arose as a direct consequence of the UK's intended departure from the Union but they were not to be considered matters for negotiation and agreement between the two parties as such. Instead, they were issues to be decided unilaterally by the competent Union institutions without any need for agreement with or the consent of the UK. Nevertheless, the European Council and the Council evidently believed that satisfactory resolution of these issues would be facilitated by some degree of cooperation with the UK within the broader context of the Article 50 TEU withdrawal discussions.

In the first place, the Union would decide unilaterally upon the relocation of its existing regulatory agencies from the UK to the territory of a remaining Member State. As we noted in Chapter 2, the main bodies involved were the European Banking Authority (EBA) and the European Medicines Agency (EMA) (both based in London); but relocation was also required for the Galileo Security Monitoring Centre back-up site (based in Swanwick). At first, the UK Government suggested that withdrawal need not lead to relocation of the EBA or the EMA—no doubt motivated not only by the economic losses of the agencies themselves, but also by the dissipation of their broader network effects, including an inevitable diminution in the opportunities for regulatory

---

[42] European Council (Article 50), *Guidelines of 29 April 2017*, at para 17.

influence which the presence of the EBA and EMA had previously offered to public and private actors within the UK.[43] Unsurprisingly, the Union dismissed those UK suggestions and arranged its own internal bidding process for relocating the EBA and EMA, ultimately deciding that the former should move to Paris and the latter should be rehomed in Amsterdam;[44] while the Galileo Security Monitoring Centre back-up site was destined to relocate to Spain.[45] Nevertheless, the issue was still included on the agenda for talks under Article 50 TEU, simply because the UK would be expected to facilitate the smooth relocation of the agencies back to the Union territory.[46]

In the second place, the Union declared (again unilaterally) that, upon withdrawal, the UK would no longer be covered by international agreements concluded by the Union, or by the Member States on the Union's behalf, or by the Union and its Member States acting jointly.[47] It should be said immediately that the precise impacts of UK withdrawal upon the Union's existing international agreements with third countries and other international organizations is a specialist and complex topic which has produced considerable comment and analysis. There was much speculation (for example) about how far it would be necessary to distinguish between the impact of withdrawal upon agreements which had been concluded pursuant to exclusive Union competences (where the UK's immediate exclusion from future scope of application seemed obvious and inevitable); and those situations instead involving mixed agreements covering shared competences and which had been ratified by the Member States as well as by the Union itself (in respect of which certain commentators argued that the legal position was much less straightforward and automatic UK exclusion was far from obvious).[48]

Suffice for present purposes to observe that, even before the Article 50 TEU negotiations formally commenced, the Union had already taken a unilateral decision to exclude the UK from vast tracts of its existing international agreements—effectively obliging the UK to undertake case-by-case negotiations to rebuild and/or regularize its own external relations with large numbers of other third countries and international organizations.[49] However, the Union did recognize that—in its own interests—there

[43] See, e.g. 'London battles to keep hold of two main EU agencies' (*The Financial Times*, 16 April 2017).

[44] See Regulation 2018/1718 amending Regulation 726/2004 as regards the location of the seat of the European Medicines Agency, OJ 2018 L 291/3; Regulation 2018/1717 amending Regulation 1093/2010 as regards the location of the seat of the European Banking Authority, OJ 2018 L 291/1.

[45] Commission Implementing Decision 2018/115 amending, as regards the location of the Galileo Security Monitoring Centre, Implementing Decision 2016/413 determining the location of the ground-based infrastructure of the system established under the Galileo programme and setting out the necessary measures to ensure that it functions smoothly, OJ 2018 L 20/14.

[46] European Council (Article 50), *Guidelines of 29 April 2017*, at para 15. Originally, the EU had hoped that the UK would also cover the costs of agency relocation; but that demand was not maintained as the two parties finalized the methodology for calculating the 'single financial settlement'.

[47] European Council (Article 50), *Guidelines of 29 April 2017*, at para 13.

[48] See further, e.g. Wessel, 'Consequences of Brexit for International Agreements Concluded by the EU and its Member States', 55 *CMLRev Special Issue* (2018) 101. Though in the case of some such agreements, it was clear that UK withdrawal from the EU effectively meant UK exclusion from the relevant treaty too: consider, e.g. Sif Tynes and Haugsdal, 'In, Out or In-Between? The UK as a contracting party to the Agreement on the European Economic Area', 41 *ELRev* (2016) 753.

[49] As mentioned in Chapter 2. Consider, e.g. the British programme of 'continuity agreements' (especially though not exclusively in the field of trade) whereby the UK sought to negotiate the post-Brexit continuation of existing EU–third country FTAs (subject to appropriate amendments). See further, e.g. House

should still be some form of dialogue with the UK on the possibility of adopting a common approach towards certain third countries/international bodies, particularly in relation to international commitments which had been contracted before withdrawal but which would remain binding upon the UK, as well as about how to ensure that the UK continued to honour those commitments.[50]

By way of example, consider the position of the UK within the WTO.[51] Of course, even as a Member State of the EU, the UK was also a party to the WTO in its own right. However, many of the relevant negotiations and agreements concerning the precise terms and conditions of WTO membership were conducted and concluded by the EU on behalf of its Member States. Withdrawal would therefore leave the UK with certain gaps and deficiencies that would need to be addressed in order for the UK to operate as a fully independent WTO member. It was clear that some of those challenges would be resolved more satisfactorily through coordinated action by the EU and the UK (rather than by purely unilateral measures or initiatives). An obvious case concerned tariff rate quotas, i.e. reduced customs duties for a specified quantity of imports, above which higher taxes are to become payable. Those quotas were negotiated by the EU and applied to the Member States collectively; there was therefore a strong case for the EU and UK to find a common solution about how to divide the existing tariff rate quotas between the two parties into the future, then present that solution to the remaining members of the WTO for endorsement. And indeed, on 11 October 2017, the EU and UK submitted joint proposals to the WTO in order to help regularize the UK's terms and conditions of membership, including a formula for dividing the existing tariff rate quotas between the Union of 27 Member States and the post-withdrawal UK.[52]

The relocation of EU agencies from the UK, and the impact of withdrawal upon existing international agreements and obligations, provide examples of separation issues which the Union intended to resolve on an essentially unilateral basis, outside the context of any negotiated settlement under Article 50 TEU, but preferably still involving some degree of cooperation from the UK in order to deliver a smooth and orderly departure. Of course, all of that is besides the remaining preparations that each party would be obliged to undertake—again on a unilateral basis, but this time without any need for or expectation of mutual cooperation or involvement—simply in order to prepare their respective domestic constitutional and legal systems for the immediate and inevitable consequences of UK withdrawal. And as we discussed in Chapter 2: in the event that the Article 50 TEU negotiations ended without delivering a negotiated withdrawal, such internal preparations would have to be intensified and supplemented

---

of Commons International Trade Committee, *Continuing Application of EU Trade Agreements After Brexit* (HC520 of 7 March 2018).

[50] European Council (Article 50), *Guidelines of 29 April 2017*, at para 13. See further, e.g. Cremona, 'The Withdrawal Agreement and the EU's International Agreements', 45 *ELRev* (2020) 237.

[51] See further, e.g. Messenger, 'Membership of the World Trade Organization' in M. Dougan (ed.), *The UK After Brexit: Legal and Policy Challenges* (2017); Luca, 'The Impact of Brexit on the UK's Membership of the WTO', *Journal of International Banking Law and Regulation* [2017] 479.

[52] See Joint Letter from the Union and the UK to other WTO members (11 October 2017). Note that those proposals were quickly rejected by a range of States (including, e.g. the USA, Canada and New Zealand) on the grounds that the EU–UK plan did not offer sufficient future market access.

by additional unilateral contingency measures designed to mitigate some of the worst immediate impacts of a 'no deal Brexit'.

(iv) Withdrawal as an Evolving Agenda

The European Council and the Council had therefore sketched out a relatively detailed agenda for the 'first phase' withdrawal discussions with the UK that were about to be conducted under the auspices of the Article 50 TEU process: the 'priority separation issues' of citizens' rights, the single financial settlement and the challenges facing Ireland; 'other separation issues' such as ongoing proceedings, the situation in Cyprus and governance structures for any withdrawal agreement; plus several additional challenges that would be addressed on an essentially unilateral basis but could nevertheless benefit from a degree of mutual coordination between the Union and the UK.

Yet the Union never intended that list to be exhaustive or final in nature. The Union's initial agenda was intended to spell out only a first tranche of immediate separation issues arising from the very act of UK withdrawal. Other 'first phase' questions were to be identified and addressed as the Article 50 TEU negotiations progressed.[53] In that regard, several new topics did indeed arise during the course of the negotiations and eventually found their way directly into the legal text of the final Withdrawal Agreement. An obvious example is the treatment of Gibraltar. Although the European Council in its April 2017 Guidelines had addressed the position of Gibraltar as regards post-withdrawal negotiations on the future EU–UK relationship, those Guidelines did not suggest Gibraltar would be the subject of any specific provision in the Article 50 TEU withdrawal agreement itself.[54] However, as the negotiations themselves progressed, it became clear that Spain also harboured particular concerns about the immediate situation surrounding Gibraltar, leading eventually (for example) to the incorporation of a dedicated protocol into the text of the final Withdrawal Agreement.[55]

However, it is also important to stress that several issues which had been tentatively identified as apt for inclusion among the 'separation issues' to be negotiated under Article 50 TEU were not the subject of any explicit provision under the final Withdrawal Agreement—apparently for the simple reason that the parties ran out of time to discuss and agree on them. For example, that proved true in the case of the cross-border provision of services, where the Union and the UK never addressed or made specific provision for the problems of legal certainty created by the very act of withdrawal, despite the fact that such problems are surely comparable in nature and importance to those arising and indeed addressed in fields such as cross-border trade in goods or transnational civil and criminal cooperation.[56]

---

[53] European Council (Article 50), *Guidelines of 29 April 2017*; Council Decision authorising the opening of negotiations with the United Kingdom of Great Britain and Northern Ireland for an agreement setting out the arrangements for its withdrawal from the European Union (22 May 2017).

[54] European Council (Article 50), *Guidelines of 29 April 2017*, at para 24.

[55] See further Chapter 6. See further, e.g. House of Lords European Union Committee, *Brexit: Gibraltar* (HL116 of 1 March 2017).

[56] See Council Decision of 22 May 2017, at Annex, para 10. Further, e.g. Mariani, 'La protection des citoyens et des opérateurs économiques à la suite de la sortie du Royaume Uni de l'Union européenne: Régimes transitoires et droits acquis', 123 *Revue Générale de Droit International Public* (2019) 653.

C. Calculating the Time Available in Order to Complete the Necessary Negotiations

Having determined that the Article 50 TEU negotiations should focus on reaching an agreement on the 'separation challenges' required to deliver an orderly withdrawal, and having identified at least a provisional agenda of what those issues should more precisely consist of, the EU and the UK were obliged to take into account one further but equally crucial factor: the method laid down in Article 50 TEU for calculating the effective departure date of the relevant State, once the latter has delivered formal notification of its intention to withdraw from the Union, on the basis of which the parties must realistically plan the timescales available not only to negotiate but also to approve any agreement.

For that purpose, Article 50(3) TEU provides that the Treaties shall cease to apply to the relevant State from the date of entry into force of its withdrawal agreement; or 'failing that', the Treaties will cease to apply to the relevant State two years after notification of its intention to withdraw. The rather vague words 'failing that' are not explicitly defined in the Treaties. But we can safely assume they are intended to cover a scenario in which the two parties are unable to agree any negotiated terms of withdrawal; as well as a situation in which the proposed agreement fails to secure the necessary institutional approvals in the Union and/or the relevant State.

In any case, Article 50(3) TEU explicitly allows the default 'two year' period for calculating the effective date of withdrawal to be extended, i.e. where the European Council, together with the relevant State, unanimously agrees to that effect. During any agreed extension to its period of membership, the relevant State will remain fully bound to its rights and obligations under the Treaties,[57] subject to the specific institutional qualifications contained in Article 50(4) TEU, and to any relevant adaptations to the duty of sincere cooperation required to reflect its peculiar status as a withdrawing State.[58]

By and large, the EU legal framework governing the date of withdrawal appears clear and precise. But it is not altogether devoid of ambiguity and potential uncertainty—particularly when it comes to the precise options available for extending the relevant State's effective period of Union membership in accordance with Article 50(3) TEU.

Of course, there are a variety of political reasons why a withdrawing State might seek to extend its effective period of Union membership by a certain period of time: for example, if negotiations towards a withdrawal agreement are still ongoing but there are reasonable chances of reaching a successful conclusion; if the processes for approving and/or implementing an agreed withdrawal settlement have experienced delays or setbacks but again there are reasonable chances of overcoming those obstacles; if efforts at a negotiated withdrawal have clearly failed but both parties agree there would be merit in having additional time to prepare for the full consequences of a 'no deal' departure; or if the relevant State is open to the possibility of changing its mind, revoking its intention to withdraw and remaining a Member State, but now needs additional time to organize and work through the appropriate constitutional processes.

---

[57] Case C-621/18, *Wightman* (EU:C:2018:999).
[58] See the discussion in Chapter 3.

In each of those situations, the process for arranging the necessary additional time before the effective date of withdrawal might well appear clear from the text of Article 50(3) TEU: a unanimous decision of the EU27 in the European Council, acting in agreement with the relevant State.

However, there is at least one scenario where the process for identifying an extended date of withdrawal is less obvious and potentially more controversial. Imagine that the withdrawal agreement as negotiated under Article 50 TEU were to propose a date for its own entry into force *beyond* the two year anniversary of the relevant State's original notification of its intention to withdraw—perhaps by several months but perhaps even by several years—and to do so, not after a formal postponement unanimously endorsed by the European Council as envisaged explicitly under Article 50 TEU, but simply following (super-)majority agreement within the Council acting with the consent of the European Parliament. Such an agreement would effectively amount to an extended period of Union membership for the relevant State, potentially delivered without the unanimous consent of the remaining Member States.

One hastens to add that that scenario did not actually arise in practice during the UK experience of withdrawal. It was understood relatively early in the Article 50 TEU process that the proposed and preferred date of entry into force of any withdrawal agreement should in principle coincide with the departure date calculated by default under Article 50(3) TEU, i.e. at 00.00 (CET) on 30 March 2019.[59] On the one hand, it was never seriously proposed that the withdrawal agreement and therefore a negotiated UK withdrawal might take place at any time *before* the default date provided for directly under Article 50(3) TEU. Under the circumstances, it seems to have been taken for granted that the available timeframe for negotiations was relatively challenging even as it stood. On the other hand, various Union actors did express reservations about allowing the withdrawal agreement to provide a date for its own entry into force any *later* than the default date laid down in the Treaties—though such reservations were apparently based not on legal concerns about the appropriate interpretation of Article 50 TEU, but rather on political concerns (for example) about ensuring the smooth operation of the elections to the European Parliament which were due to be held in May 2019.[60]

Nevertheless, and as we shall see in more detail in Chapter 5, the UK Government did eventually deem it necessary several times to request a temporary extension to the UK's period of membership. However, those requests were handled directly by the European Council, following the procedure provided for under Article 50(3) TEU. It was therefore by unanimous agreement among the EU27 that the UK's effective date of departure was eventually delayed until 00.00 (CET) on 31 January 2020; and it was, at the same time, through agreement within the Council (acting with the consent of the European Parliament) that that departure took place on the basis of a negotiated settlement.[61] Indeed, given the Union's core political objectives for the Article 50 TEU process, chief among them maintaining the unity and cohesion of the Union and its Member States in the face of the UK's intended withdrawal, it would

---

[59] See, e.g. European Council (Article 50), *Guidelines of 29 April 2017*, at para 7.
[60] See further the discussion in Chapter 5.
[61] See, in particular, European Council Decision 2019/1810, OJ 2019 L I 278/1.

have been surprising if the Union institutions or its remaining Member States had followed any other potential route for approving an extension to the effective period of UK membership.

That said, it is still relevant to consider the question, which remained at least a remote possibility throughout the experience of the UK's negotiations under Article 50 TEU, and could well arise once again in the future context of another Member State deciding to leave: might the withdrawal agreement itself propose a date of entry into force beyond the default departure date as calculated under the Treaties; but without such an extension of Union membership having been unanimously approved by the European Council as foreseen under Article 50(3) TEU; and instead finalized merely within the Council, acting by super-QMV, with the consent of the European Parliament, as provided for under Article 50(2) TEU?

After all, it would only take a change in political circumstances to make that question much more real. Imagine, for example, that the Union's institutional unity breaks down during the final stages of the withdrawal process, so that genuine differences of opinion emerge about the proposed date as well as the final terms of withdrawal. Some Member States might be minded to agree an extended period of membership eventually leading to a negotiated departure; others might prefer the relevant State to leave, with an agreement but if necessary without one, in any case by the default date of two years after its original Article 50 TEU notification. In that scenario, it is perfectly possible to envisage a dispute in which the majority of Member States are prepared to approve a withdrawal agreement in Council (supported by the European Parliament) containing a date of entry into force beyond the two year anniversary of the relevant State's original notification of intention to leave, while a minority argue that this constitutes an unlawful attempt to bypass their power of veto within the European Council as regards any decision to extend the effective membership of the relevant State.

The problem is that, even though they are evidently difficult to reconcile with each other from a procedural and institutional perspective, both possible routes to an extension of Union membership are nevertheless theoretically possible under the bare text of Article 50 TEU itself. Is there any more compelling legal reasoning that helps determine whether Article 50(3) TEU should in fact be considered an *exclusive* means of postponing withdrawal?

One interpretation of Article 50(3) TEU would be that the negotiated agreement cannot by itself simply extend the actual date of withdrawal beyond the two-year anniversary of the relevant State's original notification of intention to leave without such an extended period of membership having first been approved unanimously by the Member States meeting within the European Council. The rationale is that Article 50(3) TEU intends 'two years' to act as the outer limit to the relevant State's permissible period of continuing Union membership, unless that period is extended using the only process explicitly provided under the Treaties for that very purpose.

However, the alternative interpretation is that Article 50 TEU expresses a clear preference for withdrawal to take place on the basis of an agreement. The Treaties explicitly allow such an agreement to define its own date of withdrawal without any express limits on the range of permissible dates; and the Treaties explicitly provide for that agreement to be adopted by the Member States if necessary acting by super-QMV rather than unanimously. The words 'failing that' as used in Article 50(3) TEU make clear that the alternative system for calculating the effective date of withdrawal (two years after original notification, unless extended by unanimous agreement) is precisely that: an alternative system, to be invoked only by default and in the absence of an agreed departure. But the clear intention of the Treaties is to give preference and priority to a negotiated withdrawal, even if the latter is based on a date of entry into force (and thus a prolongation of Union membership) falling beyond the two-year anniversary of the original Article 50 TEU notification (and agreed without the unanimous consent of the Member States).

D. More Questions About Article 50 TEU as an 'Exceptional Union Competence'

From the very outset, the course of the Article 50 TEU negotiations was therefore framed by a particular combination of interconnected limits and expectations, informed not only by various political preferences but also by certain legal considerations: a primary focus on the 'separation challenges' raised by UK withdrawal; a phased approach to negotiations together with a mechanism for assessing progress centred on the guiding role of the European Council; and a potentially flexible timetable/deadline for delivering a negotiated departure or otherwise terminating the withdrawal process.

But that particular combination of limits and expectations also focused attention on a further line of legal enquiry that we have already encountered at several points before now: just how far, and in what ways, should Article 50 TEU be considered an 'exceptional Union competence' and treated as a legal basis that deviates from our ordinary expectations under Union constitutional law?

On the one hand, we know from Chapter 3 that the Council chose to endorse the Commission's proposal whereby Article 50 TEU should be treated as conferring upon the Union an exclusive competence to conclude any withdrawal agreement with the relevant State—notwithstanding the possibility or indeed inevitability that such an agreement would involve matters falling within shared Union–Member State competences and would normally qualify as a mixed agreement amenable also to national ratification processes.[62] On the other hand, we have just seen how the European Council limited the material scope of any such withdrawal agreement to dealing only with those 'separation challenges' required for an orderly departure, in accordance with the explicit terms of the Treaties themselves—thus excluding any possibility that the Union's exceptional powers under Article 50 TEU might intrude into the broader system of Union external competences, including when it came to negotiating the Union's future relationship with the relevant State after its own withdrawal had been completed and as a third country.[63]

---

[62] Council Decision authorising the opening of negotiations with the United Kingdom of Great Britain and Northern Ireland for an agreement setting out the arrangements for its withdrawal from the European Union (22 May 2017).

[63] European Council (Article 50), *Guidelines of 29 April 2017*.

Those decisions—even if only established at the political level, not as yet confirmed judicially by the CJEU—at least sought to clarify the outer parameters of what Article 50 TEU offers as a legal basis. But even within that framework, several important issues about the precise nature and limits of the Union's competence under Article 50 TEU remained to be addressed, particularly having regard to the European Council's pronouncements also about the scope, sequence and timing of the EU–UK withdrawal negotiations. As we shall see in subsequent chapters, such issues certainly proved relevant in practice to the UK withdrawal experience—though again, they were not directly brought before the CJEU for resolution and thus their proper constitutional status and significance for now remains obscure.

In the first place: what happens if the relevant State asks for certain privileges for the purposes of arranging its own withdrawal, which the Union institutions would not normally be entitled to offer or grant under their ordinary Treaty competences—such as the benefit of certain Union rules, or membership of certain Union bodies, not currently provided for or available in respect of the authorities or nationals of third countries?

In the UK context, that issue was thrust into constitutional prominence by the European Council's decision to reject the British proposal for parallel negotiations covering both separation issues and future relations, in favour of a strict division between pre-withdrawal negotiations on separation issues and post-withdrawal talks concerning the future relationship. That decision focused the parties' attention on the need to negotiate adequate transitional provisions, to bridge the inevitable gap between the very act of withdrawal and the subsequent entry into force of new arrangements to govern EU–UK relations into the longer-term. And, in due course, it became clear that such transitional provisions would be based on a general principle of preserving the status quo—in effect, treating the UK (together with its natural and legal persons, whether nationals or residents, public bodies or private actors) just as if it were still a Member State for all manner of regulatory and administrative purposes. As we shall see in Chapter 6: it is difficult to reconcile the proposal for a post-withdrawal, status quo transition period with the ordinary constitutional principles governing Union competences—unless one regards Article 50 TEU as conferring an exceptional power upon the Union also for those specific purposes.

In the second place, the proposition that Article 50 TEU confers an exceptional competence (Union exclusivity, no mixity) albeit within a limited field of application (to deliver an orderly withdrawal) begs the question: where precisely do we draw the line when it comes to issues or problems that might be raised or sparked by the immediate act of withdrawal (and thus appear to fall within the legitimate scope of Article 50 TEU) but whose effective management might involve arrangements with the potential to endure for a considerable or potentially even indefinite period of time (and therefore seem to pertain instead to future relations with the relevant State and thus to the Union's ordinary external powers)?

In the UK context, that question arose with particular force in respect of discussions over how to prevent the return of a 'hard border' for the movement of goods between Northern Ireland and the Republic of Ireland. On the one hand, the problem itself is undoubtedly a direct and immediate product of the UK's choices about its own withdrawal from the Union, as well as its extraction from the Customs Union and the

Single Market, thus qualifying as a 'separation challenge' within the scope of Article 50 TEU. On the other hand, the solution which the parties adopted under the final Withdrawal Agreement—entailing the close alignment of Northern Ireland to a wide range of Union regulatory regimes and the involvement of Union officials in an array of activities relating to the application and enforcement of those rules—is consciously intended and anticipated to be a lasting arrangement (subject to periodic review by the competent devolved institutions within Northern Ireland itself). As we shall see in Chapter 8: the conclusion of detailed arrangements that will govern the Union's future relations with a third country on a permanent or at least indefinite basis, can comfortably be reconciled with the constitutional division of labour correctly identified and insisted upon by the European Council at the very outset of the UK withdrawal process, only if Article 50 TEU is again construed as an exceptional legal basis intended to make legitimate provision for those specific and unique purposes.

3. From the Opening of Negotiations to the First Withdrawal Package

Having clarified all those important questions about the scope, sequence and timing of negotiations and discussions under Article 50 TEU, we will now offer a critical commentary on the conduct of the EU–UK talks that resulted in political endorsement of the First Withdrawal Package in November 2018. This commentary is not merely a matter of contributing to the historical record (however important a job that may well be, in and of itself). In addition, the terms upon which the UK eventually left the Union—and which will continue to play an important role in EU–UK relations for some considerable time to come—can only be fully understood when located and evaluated within the context of the unfolding Article 50 TEU process.

A. Initial Deadlock

At the commencement of formal EU–UK negotiations on 19 June 2017, the Union's position on the scope, sequence and timing of Article 50 TEU proceedings was presented as a fait accompli, and appeared to have been accepted as such by the UK Government: first phase talks would now concentrate on certain priority separation issues; only sufficient progress on those topics could lead to second phase discussions also about the tentative outlines for a future relationship. On that basis, the two parties established various working groups, agreed common principles about transparency and access to documents, and looked set to embark upon substantive negotiations over the summer.[64]

However, it soon became clear that matters were not going to progress nearly so smoothly as the two parties may have hoped. The July 2017 talks allowed each side to present their overall positions, initiate discussions on the priority issues of citizens'

---

[64] See Commission, *Terms of Reference for the Article 50 TEU negotiations* (19 June 2017).

rights, Ireland/Northern Ireland and the single financial settlement, and begin consideration of the 'other separation issues' identified by the European Council and the Council.[65] But already in August 2017, it seemed clear that progress was going to be much slower than expected across all of those fields.[66] The essential problem was that, in practice, the UK had not genuinely accepted the Union's approach to the sequence and timing of negotiations.

On the Union side, there was clear frustration from the Commission that the UK had not brought forward any detailed proposals on key issues such as Ireland/ Northern Ireland or the single financial settlement—matters as regards which, the Union declared, swift and satisfactory progress would help build mutual trust and confidence in the negotiations.[67] On the UK side, the Government resumed its public protests against the Union's decisions over scope, sequence and timing—suggesting that talks should immediately begin on the framework for future EU–UK relations and insisting that 'separation issues' such as the financial settlement and Ireland/ Northern Ireland were inherently linked to and therefore best addressed within that broader context.[68] If anything, the UK appeared to be approaching the Article 50 TEU talks according to its own very different and indeed disconnected understanding of their actual agenda and appropriate pace—publishing a series of position papers on different aspects of the future relationship, while still revealing little about its appreciation of the more immediate separation challenges.[69]

Even at the time—let alone with the benefit of hindsight—the UK's insistence upon fighting an already lost battle with the Union over the sequence and timing of negotiations seems utterly perplexing. It should have been crystal clear that the UK would be leaving the Union without having negotiated let alone concluded any agreement on their future relationship—and it was on that critical basis that the May Government should have been planning (administratively), conducting (diplomatically) and explaining (publicly) discussions under Article 50 TEU. Instead, the UK's behaviour produced an effective deadlock in the negotiations almost as soon as they had managed to get underway. And of course, the slow pace of progress right from the very outset of the talks succeeded only in immediately exposing the lack of realism and fragility underlying the UK Government's entire approach. Only the most loyal and optimistic spokesperson could dare suggest that the plans and timescales set out in the February 2017 White Paper were still on course for delivery.[70]

---

[65] See the statements delivered by the EU and UK negotiators after their monthly talks on 20 July 2017.

[66] See the statements delivered by the EU and UK negotiators after their monthly talks on 31 August 2017.

[67] E.g. Commission, *Speech by Michel Barnier at the press conference following the third round of Article 50 negotiations with the United Kingdom* (31 August 2017); *Speech by Michel Barnier in front of the Committees of Foreign Affairs and the Committees of European Affairs of the Italian Parliament* (21 September 2017).

[68] E.g. HMG, *David Davis' comments at third round of UK–EU negotiations* (31 August 2017).

[69] E.g. in August and September 2017, the UK Government published a series of 'Future Partnership Papers' on issues such as future customs arrangements; enforcement and dispute resolution; the exchange and protection of personal data; providing a cross-border civil judicial cooperation framework; collaboration on science and innovation; foreign policy, defence and development; and security, law enforcement and criminal justice.

[70] HMG, *The United Kingdom's exit from and new partnership with the European Union* (Cm 9417 of 2 February 2017).

B. The 'Florence Speech' in September 2017

In an attempt to break the deadlock, the UK Prime Minister delivered her 'Florence Speech' on 22 September 2017.[71] The speech was widely seen (even at the time) as an important moment in the Article 50 TEU process.[72] Its significance is justified for three main reasons. In the first place, the UK Government finally accepted—in reality, not by just paying lip-service—the full implications of the Union's approach to the sequence and timing of the negotiations. In fact, the Florence Speech was essentially an admission of failure by the UK Government in respect of its core negotiating strategy as set out in the February 2017 White Paper: the Prime Minister conceded that the scope and pace of negotiations lay entirely within the power of the EU27 and admitted that there was no prospect whatsoever of reaching a comprehensive package, covering both the immediate terms of withdrawal and the framework for a future relationship, within the short time available.[73]

In the second place, the UK recognized that it must therefore genuinely engage in the process prescribed by the European Council, in particular, by delivering 'sufficient progress' on the three 'priority separation issues' identified in the April 2017 Guidelines and the Council's May 2017 negotiating directives. In particular, within the Florence Speech itself, the Prime Minister explicitly promised that the UK would honour the financial commitments it had undertaken as a Member State and also pay its fair share for participation in any future cooperation programmes with the Union. Otherwise, however, it should be observed that the Florence Speech offered little by way of detail to advance negotiations on the other two 'priority separation issues'. There were merely some warms words about the UK valuing the contribution of existing migrant Union citizens; while almost nothing concrete was said about how to resolve the considerable challenges facing Ireland/Northern Ireland.

In the third place, having accepted both the failure of its own negotiating strategy and the need (in principle at least) to engage more constructively with the Union's settled agenda for the Article 50 TEU process, the UK now had to formulate and propose a fundamental change in its withdrawal plans. In her Florence Speech, the Prime Minister formally requested a post-withdrawal, status quo transition period so as to allow further time for the two parties to negotiate and finalize an agreement on their future relationship. The Prime Minister still employed her previous language of an 'implementation period' but it is clear that, under and after the Florence Speech, this now meant something radically different from what was intended in the White Paper of February 2017.[74] This was not about merely phasing in the application of a deal on future relations which the two parties would have already concluded by the date of UK departure. Instead, the Prime Minister was suggesting that the withdrawal agreement

---

[71] Theresa May, *Florence Speech: A New Era of Cooperation and Partnership between the UK and the EU* (22 September 2017).

[72] See further, e.g. Editorial Comments, 'Theresa's Travelling Circus: A Very British Entertainment Trips Its Way From Florence To Brussels', 54 *CMLRev* (2017) 1613.

[73] Though British grumbling about scope, sequence and timing continued for another while yet, e.g. David Davis, *Update to the House of Commons* (17 October 2017).

[74] Though for a considerable time, the UK Government still referred to transition as the 'implementation period' (and even insisted upon an explicit reference in the Agreement itself: see Art 126 WA).

should provide for a period of 'around 2 years' during which the UK would no longer be a Member State, and would therefore have no further representation in the Union institutions, but would continue to abide by almost all of the EU's laws and obligations, in return for maintaining the status quo as regards Single Market access and other forms of cross-border cooperation.

For those reasons, the Florence Speech should indeed be considered a significant step in the Article 50 TEU process. Not only did it mark a first attempt by the UK Government to recalibrate its negotiating strategy along more realistic lines in accordance with the Union's decisions on the scope, sequence and timing of withdrawal discussions. It also paved the way for the Article 50 TEU agenda between the two parties to crystallize into a more precise form and one that would essentially remain in place for the remainder of the negotiations:

- the need to reach a formal agreement on the immediate separation challenges (especially citizens' rights, the single financial settlement and Ireland/Northern Ireland) involved in delivering an orderly withdrawal by the UK from the Union;
- the challenge of agreeing an outline for how EU–UK relations might be conducted into the future, in fields ranging from trade relations and environmental standards to security cooperation and foreign policy, which would provide the basis for subsequent negotiations after withdrawal had been completed;
- the task of settling the terms for a post-withdrawal, status quo transition period which would offer more time for a smooth adjustment to life after UK departure and possibly also help bridge the gap before the eventual conclusion of a new future relationship with the Union; and
- the desire to continue cooperating as appropriate in finding common solutions to address other withdrawal challenges, for example, as regards the implications of UK departure for existing EU external agreements with third countries and international organizations.

Obviously, those objectives were still without prejudice to each party undertaking the necessary unilateral preparations for the full consequences of withdrawal as regards its own internal legal order (including the possibility that 'no deal' would necessitate additional contingency measures to mitigate the worse immediate consequences of any such outcome).

Public response to the Florence Speech by various key Union actors was relatively warm: it was interpreted and welcomed as an important change in tone from the UK and an attempt by the Prime Minister to inject much-needed momentum into the Article 50 TEU process.[75] But when monthly discussions resumed between the Commission and its UK counterparts, it soon became clear that the Florence Speech was still not going to translate directly into any major breakthrough, in terms of offering effective solutions to the more detailed stumbling blocks that were actually holding up progress in the negotiations. Significant differences and some very wide gaps remained between the Union and the UK on both citizens' rights and Ireland/

---

[75] E.g. Commission, *Statement by Michel Barnier* (22 September 2017); *Introductory Remarks by Michael Barnier at the press conference following the General Affairs Council (Article 50)* (25 September 2017).

Northern Ireland, while discussions on a methodology for calculating the single financial settlement remained at the level of technical discussions rather than political negotiations.[76]

The European Council had hoped to evaluate, at its planned meeting in mid-October 2017, whether 'sufficient progress' had been achieved as regards the 'priority separation issues' as to justify proceeding to the 'second phase' of negotiations. However, on 3 October 2017, the European Parliament expressed its view that the Florence Speech had not yet led to tangible changes in the UK's position or to concrete proposals that would address outstanding difficulties.[77] Soon after, Michel Barnier as Union chief negotiator announced that he was unable to recommend a finding of 'sufficient progress' to the European Council.[78] It was little surprise that the European Council meeting on 19–20 October 2017 concurred with those negative assessments.[79] However, the prospect that even its recalibrated ambitions and revised timescales risked slipping further and further away from delivery, did seem to incentivize the UK Government to focus its attention on finding workable solutions to the problems standing in the way of progress on the 'priority separation issues'—paving the way for a breakthrough in December 2017.[80]

C. Breakthrough in December 2017

On 8 December 2017, the Commission and the UK Government published a Joint Report summarizing progress made in the Article 50 TEU negotiations.[81]

The two parties had reached a political agreement around all three of the Union's priority first-phase separation challenges. First, there was a detailed scheme for the future protection of the status of existing Union citizens and UK nationals exercising their free movement rights under the Treaties. That scheme was sufficiently worked out as to be apt for translation into a more precise legal text, identifying which categories of people would be protected, the processes they might have to follow in order to obtain protection, the substantive rights which would be granted into the future, and various principles to ensure consistent interpretation and effective enforcement.[82]

Secondly, the Joint Report also contained a detailed agreement on the methodology to be used for calculating the UK's single financial settlement: a list of the components that would be taken into account; principles for calculating the value of the financial settlement and the modalities of payment; arrangements for continued UK participation in Union programmes under the current Multiannual Financial Framework; and

---

[76] See the statements delivered by the EU and UK negotiators after their monthly talks on 28 September 2017 and on 12 October 2017.

[77] European Parliament, *Resolution on the state of play of negotiations with the United Kingdom* (3 October 2017).

[78] See Commission, *Press statement by Michel Barnier following the fifth round of Article 50 negotiations with the United Kingdom* (12 October 2017).

[79] European Council (Article 50), *Conclusions of 20 October 2017*.

[80] Consider the concluding remarks by the Union and the UK negotiators after the sixth round of negotiations under Article 50 TEU (10 November 2017).

[81] Joint Report from the EU and UK negotiators (8 December 2017).

[82] To be read alongside the Joint Technical Note on Citizens' Rights (TF50 (2017) 20).

specific arrangements covering bodies and actions such as the European Investment Bank, the Facility for Refugees in Turkey, and the European Development Fund.

Thirdly, the Joint Report contained a series of commitments about how to resolve the challenges facing Ireland/Northern Ireland: for example, upholding existing protections against non-discrimination; respecting the citizenship choices available to those in Northern Ireland; and maintaining the Common Travel Area between the UK and Ireland so as to avoid a 'hard border' for the movement of persons with Northern Ireland. But the most important commitment was the UK's promise to avoid the creation of a 'hard border' for the movement of goods between Ireland and Northern Ireland in all circumstances and thus even in the event that the issue was not resolved through some subsequent EU–UK agreement (either on the two parties' overall future relationship or at least making specific future provision for Ireland/Northern Ireland).[83] However, the full implications and precise details of that UK promise were still left to be thrashed out during the remainder of the Article 50 TEU process.

In addition to detailed provisions on the three priority separation issues, the Joint Report identified progress towards an agreement between the Union and the UK on various 'other separation issues' for inclusion in the planned withdrawal agreement: for example, as regards the treatment of goods already on the market; security cooperation in the field of cross-border crime; the winding down of UK participation in a range of ongoing Union procedures; and the extraction of the UK from the Euratom regime on civil nuclear energy.

The Joint Report was at pains to highlight several general features of this political agreement. It constituted a single and coherent package.[84] Although it remained true that 'nothing is agreed until everything is agreed', nevertheless the commitments contained in the Joint Report should be reflected in any final withdrawal agreement in their full detail, though without prejudice to any appropriate adaptations in the event of subsequent agreement on a transitional regime and/or to reflect the results of upcoming discussions on the framework for a future EU–UK relationship.[85] On those points, the UK went even further, noting that it had agreed to the Joint Report 'on the condition of an overall agreement under Article 50 [TEU] on the UK's withdrawal, taking into account the framework for the future relationship, including an agreement as early as possible in 2018 on transitional arrangements'.[86]

On the basis of the Joint Report, the Commission felt able to report to the European Council that sufficient progress had now been achieved in the first phase negotiations, including as regards the trio of priority separation issues identified in the April 2017 Guidelines and the May 2017 negotiating directives.[87] For its part, the European Parliament adopted a resolution endorsing the Commission's findings—something it was not strictly required or expected to do, but reflecting MEPs' desire to be fully

---

[83] To be read alongside Prime Minister, *Open Letter on Commitments to Northern Ireland* (8 December 2017).

[84] Joint Report from the EU and UK negotiators (8 December 2017), at para 4.

[85] Joint Report from the EU and UK negotiators (8 December 2017), at para 5.

[86] Joint Report from the EU and UK negotiators (8 December 2017), at para 96.

[87] See COM(2017) 784 Final.

involved in the Article 50 TEU process, with a view to providing consent to the text of any final withdrawal agreement.[88]

On 15 December 2017, the European Council (in its Article 50 TEU formation) adopted additional guidelines concerning the UK's withdrawal from the Union.[89] The Joint Report indeed demonstrated that progress had been achieved as to justify moving the negotiations into a second phase. Thus, while work should continue with a view to reaching final agreement over the separation issues, the European Council laid down a new set of principles concerning the UK's request for a post-withdrawal, status quo transitional regime; and indicated that it would soon publish additional guidelines to enable preliminary and preparatory talks on the framework for a future EU–UK relationship. The European Council's stated objective was to agree a definitive legal text covering separation and transition, together with a political declaration on future relations that would accompany the new treaty. It was generally understood that those twin documents would need to be finalized by (around) October 2018 in order to leave sufficient time to secure the necessary institutional approvals on each side.[90]

D. Tangible Progress Alongside Persistent Obstacles

After the European Council meeting in December 2017, the two parties made surprisingly rapid progress in agreeing the terms of the UK's proposed post-withdrawal, status quo transitional regime. Initially, the UK Government had once again threatened to brew up a series of major rows over domestically sensitive issues: for example, whether any changes to existing EU rules or indeed entirely new Union measures adopted during the transition period would also become automatically binding upon the UK; or whether EU nationals arriving in the UK during the transition period would do so pursuant to existing Union free movement rules and indeed whether such new arrivals should also become entitled to future protection under the proposed citizens' rights provisions.[91] In the end, however, the UK capitulated on almost every point of apparent disagreement with the Commission's negotiating directives and proposals.[92]

Further progress was reflected in the publication of two key documents. The first was the Commission's draft Withdrawal Agreement of 28 February 2018, which represented an attempt to translate the political agreement reached in the Joint Report, as well as in subsequent negotiations, into a workable legal text.[93] The second document was a revised and colour-coded draft Withdrawal Agreement, jointly published by the

---

[88] European Parliament, *Resolution on the state of play of negotiations with the United Kingdom* (13 December 2017).

[89] European Council (Article 50), *Guidelines for Brexit Negotiations* (15 December 2017).

[90] In particular: by the European Parliament in accordance with Article 50 TEU and by the Westminster Parliament under section 13 European Union (Withdrawal) Act 2018.

[91] See, e.g. David Davis, *Teesport Speech: Implementation Period—A Bridge to the Future Partnership between the UK and EU* (26 January 2018); HMG, *Draft Text for Discussion: Implementation Period* (21 February 2018).

[92] See the detailed discussion in Chapter 6.

[93] TF50 (2018) 33 of 28 February 2018.

Commission and the UK on 19 March 2018, in an effort to represent more accurately the current state of negotiations over separation and transition.[94] The joint text was divided into: green to represent settled agreement at both a political and legal level (for example, provisions on the transitional regime, the protection of citizens' rights and the methodology for calculating the single financial settlement); yellow to indicate political agreement in principle but subject to formulating more appropriate legal text (which was true for many of the 'other separation issues'); and white to say that there was neither political nor legal agreement on the proposed text and the relevant issues thus remained subject to further negotiations (for example, much of the text of a proposed Protocol on Ireland/Northern Ireland and significant parts of the draft governance provisions).

Another sign of momentum in the Article 50 TEU process was the fact that, in late March 2018, the European Council adopted a third set of guidelines, this time specifically concerning the principles that should guide preliminary and preparatory discussions about the framework for a future EU–UK relationship.[95] Even as regards the 'other separation issues', which had perhaps dipped in relative political importance within the overall agenda of the withdrawal negotiations, there was evidence of slow but steady progress to complete the work done in the Joint Report and reflected in the colour-coded draft Withdrawal Agreement. For example, on 19 June 2018, the two parties produced a joint statement confirming that another set of points had been finalized and their draft texts converted from white or yellow into green.[96]

However, all that tangible and indeed considerable progress could not disguise the fact that several serious and persistent obstacles had arisen in the Article 50 TEU discussions. Three deserve specific mention.

In the first place, particular elements of the draft withdrawal agreement remained matters of deep contestation between the Union and the UK. Perhaps the most striking example concerned the challenge of designing an appropriate dispute settlement mechanism.[97] The Commission had originally proposed that the Court of Justice should act as the primary dispute settlement body under the new treaty—even after expiry of the planned post-withdrawal, status quo transition period and even in situations where an authoritative role for the CJEU was not strictly required or justified by the familiar constitutional requirement to defend the autonomy of Union law.[98] That proposal was rejected by the UK Government, which insisted that dispute settlement in respect of the withdrawal agreement (in the period following expiry of the transitional regime) should be entrusted to an independent arbitration panel (with

---

[94] TF50 (2018) 35 of 19 March 2018.

[95] European Council (Article 50), *Guidelines of 23 March 2018*. Note also Commission, *Topics for discussions on the future framework at forthcoming meetings* (TF50 (2018) 36); *EU/UK Possible Framework for the Future Partnership Discussions* (TF50 (2018) 37).

[96] Joint Statement on progress of negotiations under Article 50 TEU (19 June 2018): see TF50 (2018) 52.

[97] Though there were others, e.g. the question of protected indications of origin for foodstuffs remained problematic until near the end of the May Government's negotiations in November 2018.

[98] See Commission, *Position Paper on Governance* (12 July 2017). On the caselaw concerning the autonomy of Union law, see the detailed discussion and references in Chapter 9.

suitable restrictions to accommodate the CJEU's sole jurisdiction over the definitive interpretation of Union law).[99]

In the second place, there was deep disagreement between the two parties about how best to operationalize the UK's promise (in the December 2017 Joint Report) that there would be no 'hard border' for the movement of goods between Ireland and Northern Ireland in any circumstances and regardless of any subsequent EU–UK agreement to resolve the situation. In the Commission's view, that promise required the withdrawal agreement to include an 'all-weather backstop': legally binding commitments from the UK that would prevent the emergence of a 'hard border' for goods; to be activated and remain in force unless and until replaced by a future agreement making suitable alternative arrangements to deliver the same objective.[100] The Commission's draft Withdrawal Agreement of February 2018 contained proposals for just such a 'backstop' in its Protocol on Ireland/Northern Ireland—essentially providing that Northern Ireland should remain both within the Customs Union and subject to all relevant elements of the Single Market, thereby eliminating the need for customs or regulatory checks on the movement of goods to and from the Union in general and the Republic in particular.[101] However, the reaction of the UK Government (supported by its DUP allies) was openly hostile: the Commission proposal would create a significant difference in regulatory treatment between Northern Ireland and the rest of the UK and lead to the expansion/imposition of checks on goods between Northern Ireland and Great Britain; such effects would pose a direct and unacceptable threat to the constitutional and economic integrity of the UK.[102]

In the third place, there was an almost complete lack of clarity about the UK's vision for its future relationship with the Union. As we know, the February 2017 White Paper had laid down a series of 'red lines' that were intended to define the limits of future UK association/cooperation with the Union but also called for a deep and special partnership between the two parties that would effectively replicate (at least for the UK) many of the existing benefits of Union membership.[103] That 'cake and eat it' policy was also evident in the Florence Speech from September 2017 and reflected in many of the May Government's sectoral publications exploring different potential facets of the UK's future relationship with the Union.[104] Now that the European Council had set out its guiding principles for preliminary and preparatory discussions on the future relationship, it was clear that the UK's 'cake and eat it' policy was not going to succeed. The UK needed to decide whether it wanted a relatively close relationship, based on significant

---

[99] See HMG, *Technical Note on Implementing the Withdrawal Agreement* (13 July 2017). Note also: HMG, *Future Partnership Paper on Enforcement and Dispute Resolution* (23 August 2017). See further the discussion in Chapter 6.

[100] Consider, e.g. Commission, *Remarks by Michael Barnier at the press conference on the Joint Report from the Negotiators of the European Union and the United Kingdom* (8 December 2017); *Press statement by Michel Barnier following this week's round of Article 50 negotiations (6th-9th February)* (9 February 2019).

[101] See TF50 (2018) 33.

[102] See, e.g. https://www.bbc.co.uk/news/uk-politics-43224785; Theresa May, *Letter to Donald Tusk* (19 March 2018). Also: House of Commons Northern Ireland Affairs Committee, *The Land Border between Northern Ireland and Ireland* (HC329 of 16 March 2018). See further the discussion in Chapter 8.

[103] HMG, *The United Kingdom's exit from and new partnership with the European Union* (Cm 9417 of 2 February 2017).

[104] Theresa May, *Florence Speech: A New Era of Cooperation and Partnership between the UK and the EU* (22 September 2017).

commitments and obligations; or whether it wanted only a relatively distant relationship, with correspondingly fewer rights or benefits.[105]

As regards both the Irish 'backstop' and the future EU–UK relationship, the primary cause of the serious blockage in negotiations and discussions under Article 50 TEU was therefore the same: the UK flatly rejected the Union's proposals (both the Commission's 'backstop' plan and the European Council's March 2018 guidelines), yet consistently failed to bring forward any credible alternative plans of its own, despite the fact that various Union actors repeatedly stressed that the onus was firmly on London to offer effective solutions to problems which were ultimately of London's own making.[106] As the European Council observed on 29 June 2018: important parts of the withdrawal agreement remained subject to further negotiation; no substantial progress had yet been made on the 'Irish backstop'; and on future relations, the Union still awaited realistic and workable proposals from the UK—based on the latter's current 'red lines' and the Union's correspondingly limited offer, or on a revised UK position that would allow the Union to reconsider its offer in line with its established principles.[107]

E. The UK's 'Chequers Plan' of July 2018

That is not to suggest that the UK simply did or proposed nothing at all. To be more precise: the Government's entire withdrawal policy had been based on making irreconcilable commitments to different domestic factions, within the governing administration as well as its parliamentary party and indeed to the country at large. As a result, the UK's attention seemed to be focused primarily on formulating positions that were sufficiently vague and ambiguous as still to be capable of pacifying the fractious home audience—without necessarily worrying very much about whether those positions offered effective solutions to the real negotiating problems that had arisen under the Article 50 TEU process and which would be politically acceptable to the competent Union institutions as well as the remaining Member States.

To illustrate the problem, it is worth selecting an example to explore in greater detail. The most obvious candidate is the UK's supposedly make-or-break attempt to put together a more coherent and more detailed blueprint for the future EU–UK relationship—purporting to put real flesh on the bones of the February 2017 White Paper, while rejecting the 'false choices' suggested by the European Council, by demonstrating just how the Government's various 'red lines' could indeed be reconciled with the desire for a 'deep and special partnership'. That blueprint was outlined

---

[105] European Council (Article 50), *Guidelines of 23 March 2018*. See further the discussion in Chapter 9.
[106] Consider, e.g. Commission, *Statement by Michel Barnier following his working lunch in London with David Davis* (5 February 2018); *Speech by Michel Barnier at BusinessEurope Day 2018* (1 March 2018); European Council, *Remarks by President Donald Tusk after his meeting with Taoiseach Leo Varadkar* (8 March 2018); Commission, *Speech by President Juncker at the Plenary Session of the European Parliament on the guidelines on the framework of future EU-UK relations* (13 March 2018); *Déclaration par Michel Barnier devant la session plénière du Parlement européen sur les négociations Article 50 avec le Royaume-Uni* (13 March 2018); *Speech by Michel Barnier at Hannover Messe* (23 April 2018).
[107] See European Council (Article 50 TEU), *Conclusions of 29 June 2018*.

in the 'Chequers Statement' of 6 July 2018;[108] then described in greater detail in the 'Chequers White Paper' of 12 July 2018.[109]

As an attempt to preserve unity within the Government and Conservative Party, the 'Chequers Plan' was only and at best a partial success—given that it directly prompted several ministerial resignations and considerable consternation among backbench MPs.[110] But in so far as the Chequers Plan was ever intended to convince the Union that the UK had a credible plan for a very different (mould- and ground-breaking) future relationship, it can only be considered an abject failure.[111]

Future EU–UK trade relations lay at the centre of the Chequers Plan, with trade in goods specifically providing its flagship proposals. In the first place, the Government advocated a 'free trade area for goods' based on a common rulebook which would see the UK continue to apply certain EU rules governing trade in goods, though not all such rules: only those necessary to avoid literal border checks between the EU and the UK. In the second place, the UK suggested a 'facilitated customs arrangement' between the EU and the UK. The latter would adopt its own regime for tariffs on other third country goods as well as its own regulatory standards for a whole range of sectors falling outside the common rulebook of the 'free trade area for goods'; but would also and simultaneously continue to apply and enforce the Union's entirely separate tariff system and potentially divergent product regulations at the very same UK borders.

It is fair to say that, in other contexts, the Chequers Plan suggested the UK had finally dropped some of its more unrealistic demands for 'special treatment' in future relations with the EU. For example, in the field of financial services, the Government appeared to accept that, if the UK refuses to play by the Union's own rules, then privileged Single Market access for UK businesses would almost certainly come to an end. But in the field of trade in goods, the Chequers proposals fitted entirely into the 'cake and eat it' mould inherited from the Lancaster House Speech, the February 2017 White Paper, and the Florence Speech: the UK could pursue an independent trade policy with the rest of the world and 'take back control' of its own policy choices; but without creating new and economically harmful barriers to trade between the UK and the EU27.

Moreover, the Chequers proposals on trade in goods were particularly important because they also represented the Government's main initiative to avoid the reintroduction of customs and regulatory controls on the border between Northern Ireland and the Republic. A few weeks before producing the Chequers White Paper, the Government had in fact published its own proposals for the 'backstop', as an alternative to the Commission's original plans as laid out in the draft Withdrawal Agreement of February 2018.[112] But by their own explicit admission, the UK's proposals were

---

[108] Available via https://assets.publishing.service.gov.uk/government/uploads/system/uploads/attachment_data/file/723460/CHEQUERS_STATEMENT_-_FINAL.PDF.

[109] HMG, *The Future Relationship between the United Kingdom and the European Union* (Cm 9593 of 12 July 2018). See further the discussion in Chapter 9.

[110] Including the resignations of David Davis (Secretary of State for Exiting the EU) and Boris Johnson (Foreign Secretary).

[111] Consider, e.g. Commission, *Press Statement by Michel Barnier following the July 2018 General Affairs Council* (20 July 2018); *Statement by Michel Barnier at the press conference following his meeting with Dominic Raab* (26 July 2018).

[112] See HMG, *Technical Note on Temporary Customs Arrangement* (7 June 2018).

focused solely on the question of customs tariffs and enforcement, failing entirely to address the equally important subject of regulatory controls on the movement of goods across the Irish border. And even as regards customs tariffs and enforcement, the Commission immediately produced a response that systematically dismantled the Government's proposals and described their multiple flaws.[113] Against that background, the UK now seemed to be hoping that the Chequers Plan could not only lay the foundations for future trade relations between the EU and the UK as a whole, but also reduce the political sensitivities surrounding the 'backstop' which still needed to be negotiated and included in the final withdrawal agreement under Article 50 TEU.[114]

However, as an effective solution to the actual problems facing the Union and UK negotiators, it did not take long before the Chequers proposals for a 'free trade area for goods' and 'facilitated customs arrangements' were also dismissed as fanciful and unworkable. For example, the Chequers proposals for a 'facilitated customs arrangement' did not appear to differ in any significant respect from customs proposals which the Government had first published in summer 2017 and which had been criticized as speculative, untested, and undeliverable—not least since they implied a massive increase in bureaucracy, requiring vast quantities of goods to be categorized, tracked, and verified throughout the various processes of manufacture within, import into, and export from the UK, so as to ensure that they were subject to the correct tariffs and marketed in accordance with the appropriate regulatory standards.[115]

Even besides the question of whether the UK's proposals appeared credible from a regulatory and logistical perspective, the Chequers Plan was objectionable on more fundamental political grounds. After all, the UK was proposing to 'take back control' of its borders and money, by expecting the Union to surrender control over its own borders and money to a third country, in effect, allowing the UK to collect the Union's own income and enforce the Union's own public policy regulations.[116] Moreover, the UK proposals raised immediate accusations of cherry-picking. Why should the UK enjoy special treatment through continued participation in the free movement of goods, while being free to reject the parallel systems governing natural persons, legal persons, services, and capital (to say nothing of other common policies in fields such as agriculture or external commercial relations)? Why should the EU27 have to submit their state aid plans to independent, external scrutiny by the Commission, while the UK would be allowed (under the Chequers Plan) to scrutinize and approve its own state aid projects for itself? Why should the EU27 have to submit to binding dispute settlement by the Court of Justice and give priority to their Union law obligations within their national legal systems, while the UK would be subject only to an international arbitration system and remain free to respect or reject supposedly common obligations at its own discretion?

---

[113] See TF50 (2018) 39.

[114] See, e.g. HMG, *Prime Minister's Belfast Speech* (20 July 2018).

[115] See HMG, *Position Paper on Northern Ireland and Ireland* (16 August 2017) and HMG, *Future Customs Arrangements* (16 August 2017).

[116] A point already before made by the Union negotiator, e.g. Commission, *Speech by Michel Barnier on German Employers' Day* (29 November 2017). Note that the UK was already accused by the Commission of failing to discharge such responsibilities fully and effectively, even as a Member State, let alone as a third country: see Case C-213/19, *Commission v United Kingdom* (pending).

At the very least, the Chequers Plan posed an obvious question: why should the EU offer special privileges of market access to the UK, when the latter was openly threatening to use its newfound third country status so as to create competitive advantages for its own industries—advantages which could then be immediately and unfairly directed back against the EU economy? But more fundamentally: the Chequers Plan constituted a direct challenge to the Union's entirely legitimate political imperative of ensuring that any agreement with a third country does not pose an external threat to the smooth functioning of the Union's own internal trade system. After all, the Single Market is a complex, multi-faceted, interdependent trade bargain: it grants extensive rights and opportunities but at the price of corresponding obligations. Every Member State accepts that bargain as a whole, regardless of reservations about individual elements within it. If a third country is allowed to disaggregate, unravel, or pick-and-chose between the elements of the Single Market, it risks undermining not just the internal cohesion but also the very legitimacy of the EU itself.[117]

Viewed from the perspective of the Union and its Member States, what ultimately made the UK's Chequers proposals so unrealistic is that the UK wanted to be treated as special—not just compared to the Union's existing treatment of other third countries, but even as compared to how the Member States are prepared to treat each other within the context of their shared Union membership. However, we should stress again that (perhaps) the primary objective of the Chequers exercise was not to offer a serious plan for resolving the very real negotiating obstacles which still persisted between the Union and the UK; but rather to sustain for as long as possible the UK's own fragile coalition of interests by avoiding their widely divergent preferences and mutual antagonisms spilling over into overt hostility and rebellion.[118]

F. The Salzburg Summit and its Aftermath

The fact that the Chequers Plan offered no breakthrough, either in discussions about a credible framework for the future EU–UK relationship particularly as regards trade, or over the need to negotiate a workable 'backstop' to prevent the creation of a 'hard border' for goods across the island of Ireland, was explicitly confirmed by the European Council at its informal summit in Salzburg on 19–20 September 2019.[119]

That conclusion could not have come as a surprise to any informed observer of or commentator on the Article 50 TEU process. The fact that the UK Government reacted with apparent shock and public anger is probably best interpreted as a rather cynical attempt to deflect attention away from responsibility for its own continuing problems (both domestic and in the negotiations) by seeking to scapegoat 'Brussels'.[120]

[117] See further, e.g. M. Dougan, *The Institutional Consequences of a Bespoke Agreement with the UK Based on a 'Close Cooperation' Model* (European Parliament, Policy Department for Citizens' Rights and Constitutional Affairs, at the request of the Constitutional Affairs Committee: PE 604.962 of May 2018). And also the discussion in Chapter 9.
[118] Which is not to suggest that the position of the Labour Party in Opposition was any clearer or more satisfactory: see further the discussion in Chapter 5.
[119] Informal Summit of the Heads of State or Government meeting in Salzburg (19–20 September 2018).
[120] E.g. HMG, *PM Brexit Negotiations Statement* (21 September 2018). Contrast with European Council, *Statement by Donald Tusk on the Brexit Negotiations* (21 September 2018).

The tense political situation was not helped by the tendency of certain UK politicians, even senior Government figures, to pander to their domestic supporters by treating the negotiations as some form of high stakes poker game between sworn adversaries: for example, suggesting that the UK should now threaten to renege on due payments under the single financial settlement as a means to pressurize the EU into offering improved future trading terms within the context of the future relationship;[121] and clinging to the dangerous mantra that 'no deal is better than a bad deal' (often linked to the equally bizarre assumption that 'they need us more than we need them') despite the overwhelming evidence of how deeply damaging any such outcome would be not only to the EU27 but especially for the UK itself.[122]

Against that background, we can discern during this troubled period, over the summer and autumn 2018, two distinctive sets of developments/debates. In the first place, there was a genuine and earnest acceleration of preparations for a breakdown in negotiations leading to a UK departure on 29 March 2019 without any withdrawal agreement in place. For example, at its meeting in June 2018, the European Council had expressed serious concern at the lack of progress under Article 50 TEU and exhorted the Commission as well as the EU27 to increase their preparations for a potential collapse of the talks.[123] In response, the Commission set out its plans to go beyond unilateral 'preparedness measures', i.e. those which were required in any event to prepare the Union and its Member States for the consequences of UK withdrawal; and embark upon a programme of unilateral 'contingency measures', i.e. those which might be required to ameliorate the more immediate adverse consequences of a chaotic UK departure.[124]

For its part, the UK Government also began to plan and advise more explicitly for the possibility of a 'no deal Brexit'.[125] That included progressing the legislative and regulatory changes needed to preserve basic standards of regulatory continuity and legal certainty across the UK legal system as a whole as well as in specific sectors likely to be particularly affected by withdrawal from the Union: for example, immigration policy, agriculture, and fisheries. But the challenges were not merely legal. The Government also identified the need for significant investments in institutions, personnel, and infrastructure, as well as extensive contingency planning to cope with immediate logistical challenges in fields such as food and medical supplies, all required to ensure that public as well as private sector actors were sufficiently prepared for the short-term impacts of a potential 'no deal' outcome. That was besides the hefty programme of

[121] See, e.g. Dominic Raab, *Commons Statement on the Future Relationship between the UK and the EU* (12 July 2018). Also, e.g. https://www.politico.eu/article/brexit-theresa-may-uk-to-eu-play-fair-or-we-wont-pay-our-bill/amp/; https://www.politico.eu/article/raab-britain-to-refuse-paying-divorce-bill-without-trade-deal/. Note (and contrast with) House of Lords European Union Committee, *Brexit: The Financial Settlement* (HL7 of 23 October 2019).

[122] See, e.g. Theresa May, *Brexit Negotiations Statement* (21 September 2019). On the likely impacts of a 'no deal Brexit' upon the UK, see further the discussion and references in Chapter 2.

[123] European Council (Article 50), *Conclusions of 29 June 2018*.

[124] See, in particular, Commission, *Preparing for the UK's withdrawal from the EU on 30 March 2019: Implementing the Commission's Contingency Action Plan*, COM(2018) 890 Final. On the Union's unilateral preparations, particularly for a 'no deal Brexit', see the discussion and references in Chapter 2.

[125] See, in particular, HMG, *UK Government's Preparations for a 'No Deal' Scenario* (first published 23 August 2018 and periodically updated thereafter). Also, e.g. Dominic Raab, *Statement to Parliament* (4 September 2018); and *Update on EU Exit Negotiations* (9 October 2018).

Government measures needed to regularize key parts of the UK's international relations and commitments in fields such as trade, transport, and security.[126]

In the second place, the sense of uncertainty and confusion surrounding the Article 50 TEU process during the summer/autumn of 2018 prompted fresh reflection and debate about the precise legal and political nature of the withdrawal package that the two parties might once have hoped to conclude but which they might now have to reconsider and even redesign. In particular, the question arose: what if the Union and the UK were able to conclude a legally binding text dealing with the immediate separation challenges posed by withdrawal and containing a detailed transitional regime to apply immediately after the UK's departure; but (at best) their mutual understanding of the framework for future relations managed to consist of no more than a sketchy outline in a non-binding political declaration; or (at worst) the future relationship would be left entirely undefined by the date of withdrawal because the two parties could not agree even on such a thin political sketch?

Such an outcome was apparently to be considered positively objectionable by the UK. The British Government had adopted the robust position that any withdrawal deal under Article 50 TEU must be treated as a complete package covering separation, transition, and future relations: if any one element of the deal were lacking, then there would be no deal at all.[127] Indeed, that 'all or nothing' position was effectively incorporated into UK law under the European Union (Withdrawal) Act 2018. Section 13 provided that any withdrawal agreement between the EU and the UK could be ratified only if (inter alia) the House of Commons gave its prior approval to a withdrawal package consisting of *both* the formal treaty on separation/transition *and* the political declaration on the framework for future relations.[128]

However, whatever the political preferences, 'negotiating red lines' or even domestic legal constraints adopted unilaterally by the UK, it was surely never the case—as a matter of EU constitutional law—that the conclusion of a valid withdrawal treaty under Article 50 TEU should be treated as dependent also upon the prior or simultaneous adoption of any particular legal or political instrument defining the parties' mutual understanding of how their future relationship might evolve. After all, Article 50 TEU merely requires the negotiation and conclusion of an agreement 'taking account of' the framework for future relations between the Union and the relevant State—language so flexible as to be capable of covering any of a wide array of valid potential reference points, from a detailed common plan to create a close post-withdrawal partnership, through to a unilateral understanding that the future will consist of only loose and distant relations.

Nevertheless, the prospect of a workable agreement on separation and transition, but without any (or at least any credible) political declaration on future relations, still appeared potentially uncomfortable for the Union. As we know, the European Council's April 2017 Guidelines foresaw that the withdrawal agreement under Article

---

[126] On the UK's unilateral preparations, particularly for a 'no deal Brexit', see the discussion and references in Chapter 2.

[127] See, e.g. Joint Report from the EU and UK negotiators (8 December 2017)—including the UK's position as set out in para 96.

[128] See further the discussion in Chapter 3 and Chapter 5.

50 TEU might contain transitional arrangements in order to provide a bridge towards some foreseeable future relationship between the Union and the UK.[129] As the risk increased that there might be no agreed (or at least no clear) blueprint for the future, the question arose: should the withdrawal agreement nevertheless still make provision for a wide-ranging and far-reaching transitional regime, when the latter might no longer provide a bridge towards some foreseeable future relationship in any genuine and meaningful way?

In such a scenario, one might have assumed that the Union's political preferences would again evolve in a relatively pragmatic manner. Even if it were not possible to describe the proposed transition period as any sort of bridge to a reasonably clear alternative vision for EU–UK relations, the benefits of providing public and private actors with additional time to prepare for the full consequences of withdrawal, and the Union and UK negotiators with additional time at least to try to define the future in more concrete terms, still justified the inclusion of transitional provisions within the final Article 50 TEU agreement.[130] It is doubtful that the legal framework under Article 50 TEU could or should have added anything more substantial or specific to those essentially political judgments and choices. After all, a transition period designed primarily to deliver more time for public and private preparations (regardless of its value as a bridge to the future) is still capable of contributing to the underlying Article 50 TEU objective of enabling withdrawal 'to take place in an orderly fashion'.[131]

G. From Apparent Despair to Apparent Success

The European Council meeting in mid-October 2018 had long been anticipated as the 'crunch moment' in the Article 50 TEU process, i.e. as the date when the two parties hoped and planned to have concluded their negotiations, paving the way for high level endorsement of both the final text of a legally binding withdrawal agreement and the contents of a political declaration on the future relationship, thus opening the path for the Union and the UK to undertake their respective domestic approval and ratification processes.[132]

However, as the anticipated deadline approached, it was clear that negotiations remained mired in disagreement over exactly the same list of problems as they had been for many months already: outstanding issues concerning appropriate governance and dispute settlement mechanisms; an acceptable 'backstop' model for Ireland/Northern Ireland; and the more detailed terms of a political declaration on future relations.[133]

---

[129] European Council (Article 50), *Guidelines of 29 April 2017*, at paras 4–6.

[130] See further, e.g. Dougan, 'An airbag for the crash test dummies? EU-UK negotiations for a post-withdrawal "status quo" transitional regime under Article 50 TEU', 55 *CMLRev Special Issue* (2018) 57.

[131] Case C-621/18, *Wightman* (EU:C:2018:999), at para 56.

[132] See, e.g. Commission, *Press point by Michel Barnier in advance of his meeting with Dominic Raab* (19 July 2018); *Press statement by Michel Barnier following the General Affairs Council* (Article 50) (18 September 2018).

[133] Consider the (often brief, often terse) press statements by the Union and/or UK negotiators delivered after the negotiation rounds/meetings conducted across July, August and September 2018. Also, e.g. Commission, *Speech by Michel Barnier at the closing session of Eurochambre's European Parliament of Enterprises 2018* (10 October 2018).

The European Council meeting on 17 October 2018 therefore concluded that 'not enough progress has been achieved'; while at the same time confirming the readiness of the EU27 to convene an additional European Council meeting, if and when the Union negotiator were to report that 'decisive progress has been made'.[134]

The very real prospect of total failure succeeded in concentrating minds. For the next several weeks, Commission and UK negotiators engaged in intensive discussions to resolve their remaining differences. Commentators noted sourly that the UK finally appeared to be negotiating genuinely with the EU rather than playing to its own deeply divided domestic audience. Be that as it may, the parties' final efforts paid off. On 14 November 2018, the Commission and the UK Government published a Joint Report which confirmed: first, that the two parties had reached an agreed text for the withdrawal treaty; and secondly, that they had also agreed the outline for a political declaration on the future EU–UK relationship—though the latter still needed to be converted into a more substantial document over the coming days.[135] Publication of that draft withdrawal package led (almost inevitably) to fresh political turmoil in the UK.[136] But it also prompted some (perhaps more unexpected) problems among the EU27. For example, Spain effectively accused the UK of acting in bad faith, by seeking to use certain final changes to the text of the draft withdrawal agreement so as to circumvent the European Council's existing principle that called for Spanish consent before any agreement on future relations between the EU and the UK could apply to the territory of Gibraltar.[137]

Notwithstanding the UK's domestic turmoil and the EU's own political snags, Theresa May's Government signalled its collective satisfaction with the proposed fruits of the Article 50 TEU negotiations,[138] allowing the draft withdrawal package to be endorsed at a political level by the European Council meeting on 25 November 2018.[139] We will refer to the deal of November 2018 as the 'First Withdrawal Package'. After all, the May Government eventually failed to secure its domestic approval and ratification, the succeeding Johnson Government then requested the reopening of negotiations, and revisions agreed between the Union and the UK in due course created the 'Second Withdrawal Package' of October 2019.[140] However, those subsequent revisions—while very important in and of themselves—were effectively limited to defined parts of the texts that had previously been agreed under the May Government

---

[134] European Council (Article 50), *Conclusions of 17 October 2018*.

[135] Joint Report by Commission and UK (TF50 (2018) 54); together with publication of a revised draft Withdrawal Package (TF50 (2018) 55). Note also: Commission, *Statement by Michel Barnier* (14 November 2018); European Council, *Remarks by President Donald Tusk after his meeting with Michel Barnier* (15 November 2018). A full draft of the Political Declaration was first published by the General Secretariat of the Council on 22 November 2018: see XT 21095/18.

[136] See, e.g. https://www.theguardian.com/politics/2018/nov/15/theresa-may-vows-to-see-brexit-plan-through-on-day-of-turmoil.

[137] See, e.g. https://www.theguardian.com/politics/2018/nov/19/brexit-eu-ministers-prepare-to-end-45-years-of-difficult-marriage; https://www.theguardian.com/world/2018/nov/22/spain-accuses-uk-of-treachery-over-gibraltar-brexit-deal.

[138] See Prime Minister, *Statement on Brexit* (14 November 2018). Note also: Prime Minister, *Statement on Brexit Negotiations* (15 November 2018).

[139] See European Council (Article 50), *Conclusions of 25 November 2018*.

[140] See further Chapter 5.

in November 2018.[141] Otherwise, most of the substantive elements of the First Withdrawal Package survived intact into the Second Withdrawal Package and provided the formal basis upon which the UK finally left the Union on 31 January 2020.

The First Withdrawal Package was secured only through some late and significant concessions and compromises by each party. It consisted of two main elements.[142] First, the text of a formal (First) Withdrawal Agreement for the purposes of Article 50 TEU. That relatively lengthy agreement was intended to be a legally binding treaty, providing for an orderly departure of the UK from the Union. Article 185 of the First Withdrawal Agreement defined its planned date of entry into force—and therefore the effective date of a negotiated UK withdrawal—as 00.00 (CET) on 30 March 2019, i.e. the same date as would have been provided for directly under Article 50(3) TEU even in the absence of any agreement. As well as horizontal provisions on matters such as governance structures, interpretation of the agreement, and dispute settlement/legal enforcement, the main body of the First Withdrawal Agreement made substantive provision for a post-withdrawal, status quo transition period; the future protection of existing Union citizens and UK nationals exercising free movement rights under the Treaties; a single financial settlement of the UK's liabilities and commitments arising from Union membership; and the smooth management of a wide range of 'other separation issues' created by the very act of UK departure.

The First Withdrawal Agreement also contained three Protocols, covering Ireland/Northern Ireland, the UK's Sovereign Base Areas in Cyprus, and Gibraltar. The Protocol on Ireland/Northern Ireland was by far the most substantial and (at least from an overall perspective) the most significant since it contained a substantially revised model for the 'backstop' guarantee that there would be no return to a 'hard border' across the island of Ireland as regards the movement of goods. That revised 'backstop' was based on the UK's own significantly updated proposals. To begin with, the two parties agreed that the whole of the UK should remain in a 'single customs territory' with the EU and subject to extensive Union law obligations as regards trade within and outside that 'single customs territory', as well as in terms of regulatory standards to guarantee a level playing field between EU and UK businesses. But in addition, Northern Ireland would remain subject to a wide-ranging body of Union regulatory standards covering fields such as product specifications, agricultural production, food safety, and the provision of state aid. As a consequence, certain checks would be required on the movement of goods between Northern Ireland and Great Britain—though the First Withdrawal Agreement would not otherwise prevent the UK from guaranteeing unfettered (if essentially one way) access for Northern Irish products to the market in Great Britain.

Secondly, the Union and the UK also agreed the much shorter text of a (First) Political Declaration outlining their mutual understanding of the principles that should underpin the framework for their future relationship. It remained the case that that future relationship should be formally negotiated and concluded only after the UK's withdrawal from the Union had been completed. Nevertheless, the First

---

[141] In particular: the Protocol on Ireland/Northern Ireland; and the Political Declaration on future EU–UK relations.

[142] Published at OJ 2019 C 66 I.

Political Declaration was explicitly referenced in the text of the First Withdrawal Agreement: the latter included a commitment by both parties to use their best endeavours, in good faith, to take the necessary steps to negotiate expeditiously the legal agreements governing their future relationship, and to conduct the relevant procedures for the ratification or conclusion of those agreements, with a view to ensuring that the latter would apply (to the extent possible) as from the end of the planned transition period.[143]

In themselves, the substantive terms of the First Political Declaration were not intended to be legally binding or enforceable. Indeed, it was hard to see how they ever could have been: the document was essentially a future negotiating agenda, consisting primarily of a series of political aspirations and potential options, almost none of which could be described as self-standing or self-executing, and many of which were expressed only in relatively vague and/or decidedly ambiguous terms. It was therefore clear that the UK Government had failed to make good on its longstanding promises about offering a detailed plan for the future relationship, let alone one which would be virtually ready for conversion into a precise legal text and finalized shortly after the effective date of withdrawal.

On their face, even the sketchy provisions of the First Political Declaration suggested that the future EU–UK relationship would in due course be determined (on the one hand) by the UK Government's 'red lines' on issues such as ending the free movement of persons, terminating the jurisdiction of the CJEU and pursuing an independent trade policy; and (on the other hand) by the logical implications of those 'red lines' for the Union's approach to the UK as a third country, effectively seeking only a relatively distant relationship at least in the field of trade.

But in practice, the apparent implications of the First Political Declaration were muted by the provisions of the proposed Protocol on Ireland/Northern Ireland and the 'backstop' plan to prevent the return of a hard border for the movement of goods across the island of Ireland. For at least the foreseeable future, and regardless of the plans outlined in the First Political Declaration, the UK would in practice remain much more closely aligned to the Union across a significant number of key policy fields. Under any scenario, there would be no 'cake and eat it' outcome for the UK of the sort proposed in the Chequers Plan from July 2018.

Besides the First Withdrawal Package as politically endorsed by the European Council in November 2018, it is important to note various additional materials that were intended to supplement the main elements of the deal as agreed between the EU27 and the UK Government.

In the first place, even at the time of endorsing the First Withdrawal Package, the European Council adopted various unilateral statements, intended to reflect the Union's own understanding of certain provisions within its proposed Withdrawal Agreement and/or Political Declaration. In particular, the minutes of the European Council meeting on 25 November 2019 recorded various formal statements by the remaining Member States: for example, stressing the importance they attach to the UK respecting the commitments it has undertaken in the First Withdrawal Package;

---

[143] Art 184 of the First Withdrawal Agreement. Note also the provisions on future EU–UK relations contained in the original version of the Protocol on Ireland/Northern Ireland.

stressing the need to reach a future agreement on EU–UK fishing rights as a matter of priority; and recalling the principles that should govern the potential application of any future agreements between the Union and the UK to the territory of Gibraltar.[144] Even if not forming an integral part of the First Withdrawal Package and not strictly binding upon both parties, such unilateral statements and measures were nevertheless intended (at least on the Union side) to be relevant to the context in which that withdrawal package would in due course be interpreted and applied.

In the second place, the First Withdrawal Agreement itself envisaged that each party would adopt various internal measures for its more concrete and detailed implementation into their respective legal systems. That included appropriate measures: to ensure compliance with a range of concrete legal obligations, for example, concerning the terms of the transition period as well as management of the various separation issues;[145] to make important discretionary choices about the more precise terms for domestic implementation of various elements of the First Withdrawal Agreement, not least in the field of citizens' rights protection;[146] and to make provision for the internal allocation of roles and responsibilities as required for operationalizing the First Withdrawal Agreement, for example, as regards who would represent each party on the Joint Committee and how those representatives would be held accountable for their decisions.[147]

In the third place, during the months following their initial agreement on a draft deal in November 2018, the Union and the UK Government proceeded to issue various additional documents directly related to the First Withdrawal Package. Some such texts were intended to clarify the parties' understanding of their proposed agreement but without actually changing its substantive terms: for example, the 'Strasbourg Deal' agreed between the Union and the UK in March 2019 with a view to reiterating their joint intention to treat the 'Irish backstop' as a purely temporary arrangement and their mutual determination to replace it as swiftly as possible with a more durable future relationship.[148] Other subsequent texts did indeed formally amend the First Withdrawal Package, in particular, by extending its projected date for entry into force, in the light of subsequent decisions adopted by the European Council in accordance with Article 50(3) TEU so as to extend the UK's intended withdrawal date beyond 30 March 2019.[149] We will recount the adoption and explore the significance of those supplementary acts in greater detail in Chapter 5.

[144] Available via https://www.consilium.europa.eu/media/37102/xt20017-en18.pdf.
[145] E.g. decisions by particular Member States about the continued applicability of the European Arrest Warrant to the UK during the transition period, in accordance with Art 185 of the First Withdrawal Agreement.
[146] E.g. decisions by particular Member States about whether to introduce a system of compulsory registration, or instead rely on a merely declaratory system, in respect of UK nationals falling within the protective scope of Part Two of the First Withdrawal Agreement.
[147] See, e.g. the Commission's proposals as contained in COM(2018) 834 Final.
[148] 'Strasbourg Deal' of 11 March 2019: Instrument Relating to the Withdrawal Agreement; Joint Statement Relating to Political Declaration. Note also HMG, *Unilateral Declaration Concerning the Northern Ireland Protocol* (12 March 2019).
[149] European Council Decision 2019/476, OJ 2019 L I 80/1; European Council Decision 2019/584, OJ 2019 L 101/1; European Council Decision 2019/1810, OJ 2019 L I 278/1.

For the sake of completeness, it is also worth recalling a range of issues which were raised during the course of the Article 50 TEU process, but as regards which the First Withdrawal Package failed to make any explicit provision. That includes various 'separation issues' that were not included within the scope of the European Council's initial negotiating guidelines or indeed the Council's opening negotiating mandate for the Commission but (as we discussed above) which it seems to have been assumed the parties would return to and address at some subsequent point in the Article 50 TEU process, with a view to including appropriate provisions within the final withdrawal settlement. If that was indeed the plan or at least the expectation, it was frustrated by events and the passage of time: no relevant further guidelines, additional directives, or final negotiations were issued, adopted, or undertaken. And so the First Withdrawal Agreement failed explicitly to address important questions (for example) about how to wind down situations of cross-border service provision as between the Union and the UK (including the treatment of posted workers) that might remain outstanding as at the end of the transition period.[150]

4. Concluding Remarks

After around 18 months of often difficult negotiations, the Union and the UK had finally settled on detailed proposals for delivering an orderly withdrawal and had also managed to agree at least the framework for subsequent talks on their future relationship. But that turned out to be the easy part. Now the First Withdrawal Package had to be approved through the two parties' respective internal procedures. Yet the very act of agreeing a text that finally spelled out the meaning of Brexit in black and white (though still also plenty of grey) terms, provided the inevitable catalyst for Theresa May's unhappy governing coalition to unravel and implode—thereby heralding a new period of chaos as her Government tried and failed to steer its deal through the parliamentary approval process provided for under section 13 of the European Union (Withdrawal) Act 2018. That next phase in the Article 50 TEU process will be examined in Chapter 5.

---

[150] See further, e.g. Mariani, 'La protection des citoyens et des opérateurs économiques à la suite de la sortie du Royaume Uni de l'Union européenne: Régimes transitoires et droits acquis', 123 *Revue Générale de Droit International Public* (2019) 653.

5

Rejection, Revision, and Approval of the Withdrawal Package

1. Introduction

Once a withdrawal deal is finalized, it has to be approved by the competent authorities within both the Union and the relevant State. In the context of the UK, after provisional agreement had been reached on the First Withdrawal Package in November 2018, attention thus focused on its political stewardship through the formal approval processes of both the Union and the UK.

The two experiences could not have been more different. When it came to the Union, the Commission had conducted the Article 50 TEU negotiations under mandate from and/or in close coordination with all relevant Union decision-makers. One could therefore feel confident that whatever agreement was provisionally reached with the UK was virtually guaranteed to be formally approved by the competent Union institutions. And so, after the entire First Withdrawal Package was politically endorsed unanimously by the European Council, the other Union institutions proceeded with the steps required for formal conclusion (in particular) of the First Withdrawal Agreement.[1] Acting upon a Commission proposal,[2] a decision to sign the draft treaty was adopted by the Council on 11 January 2019;[3] the Union negotiator also adopted a further proposal on the basis of which the Council could later conclude the agreement, after having obtained the consent of the European Parliament.[4]

When it came to the UK, as we mentioned in Chapter 3, and will now explain in greater detail here in Section 2, the exceptional nature of the UK's decision to leave the Union created pressure for greater (Westminster) parliamentary control over the outcome of the Article 50 TEU negotiations than would normally be the case under domestic law as regards the scrutiny and approval of international agreements. The Government's vague promise that Parliament would have a say over any agreement was converted, after the general election of June 2017 and by a coalition of opposition and rebellious backbench votes, into a formal requirement under section 13 of the European Union (Withdrawal) Act 2018 that the House of Commons must positively approve the entire First Withdrawal Package, and that Parliament must also enact

---

[1] See further Chapter 3.
[2] See COM(2018) 833 Final.
[3] See Council Decision 2019/274 on the signing, on behalf of the European Union and of the European Atomic Energy Community, of the Agreement on the withdrawal of the United Kingdom of Great Britain and Northern Ireland from the European Union and the European Atomic Energy Community, OJ 2019 L 471/1.
[4] See COM(2018) 834 Final.

The UK's Withdrawal from the EU. Michael Dougan, Oxford University Press. © Michael Dougan 2021.
DOI: 10.1093/oso/9780198833475.003.0005

primary legislation for its domestic implementation, even before the Government could proceed to formal ratification of the First Withdrawal Agreement per se.

Against that background, we will then consider the efforts undertaken by the May Government to persuade MPs to support her Brexit deal—including various additional political statements and supplementary agreements relating, in particular, to the border arrangements affecting Ireland and Northern Ireland (Section 3), as well as requests to the European Council that the effective date of UK withdrawal be delayed while the British approval process continued (Section 4). Eventually, however, Theresa May was replaced as Prime Minster by Boris Johnson, who came to office insisting upon a fundamental renegotiation of the UK's withdrawal package, even if many commentators at the time doubted the sincerity of his intentions (Section 5). Under renewed pressure from the opposition parties and backbench rebels in the Westminster Parliament, the Johnson Government eventually engaged in a fresh bout of intensive talks that resulted in political endorsement of a revised 'Second Withdrawal Package' in October 2019.[5]

As Section 6 explains, under that new deal, Johnson secured significant changes to the Irish border arrangements that would effectively lead to the partial legal and economic segregation of Northern Ireland from the rest of the UK, together with revisions to the Political Declaration, making clear that the UK wanted to pursue only a relatively distant future relationship with the Union—opening the path for the British both to diverge from existing or future EU regulatory standards; and to pursue their own independent trade policy in relations with other third countries. Despite continuing parliamentary resistance, and another delay to the due date of departure, many commentators believed that Johnson would eventually have been able to pass that revised deal through the House of Commons. But instead, in Section 7, we will see how Johnson insisted on (and the main opposition parties eventually agreed to) holding another general election—in December 2019—from which the Conservative Party won a safe parliamentary majority. The Johnson Government was then able to abolish the troublesome 'section 13' procedure altogether and directly adopt the necessary legislation to implement the Second Withdrawal Package (insofar as that was required) into domestic law.[6]

2. The Legal Framework Governing UK Approval of the First Withdrawal Package

Section 13 of the European Union (Withdrawal) Act 2018 (EU(W)A 2018), as originally enacted, laid down the process for approval of the First Withdrawal Package and ratification of the First Withdrawal Agreement. Chapter 3 described the background to those provisions and summarized the main requirements imposed under the 2018 legislation. In this section, we will explore in greater detail some of the key features of, including several relevant disputes that arose in relation to, the section 13 approval process.

---

[5] Published at OJ 2019 C 384 I.
[6] European Union (Withdrawal Agreement) Act 2020.

As we know, section 13 EU(W)A 2018 stated that any withdrawal agreement under Article 50 TEU could be ratified only if three distinct processes were completed by 'exit day'. First, under section 13(1), the Government must lay before each House of Parliament a statement that political agreement had been reached between the EU and the UK, a copy of the negotiated agreement on separation/transition, plus a copy of the political declaration on the framework for the future EU–UK relationship. The House of Lords was offered only a relatively marginal role: it should hold a debate, on a Government motion, to take note of the withdrawal package.[7] However, the House of Commons was to have a much greater say: it must positively approve the withdrawal package, by a resolution on a Government motion.[8]

Secondly, if and when the Commons votes to approve the text of a withdrawal package, still before the formal withdrawal agreement under Article 50 TEU can be ratified, Parliament must then adopt primary legislation which contains provision for the implementation of that agreement directly into UK law.[9] That necessity was incumbent upon the UK in any case, thanks to the terms of the First Withdrawal Agreement concerning the latter's intended legal status and extensive legal effects within the UK legal system.[10]

Thirdly, Commons approval of the proposed withdrawal package would also trigger the final parliamentary procedural requirement for UK ratification of the Article 50 TEU agreement. Section 13(14) provided that the relevant provisions of the EU(W)A 2018 did not affect the operation of Part 2 of the Constitutional Reform and Governance Act 2010 in relation to any withdrawal agreement. Thus, any withdrawal agreement must still be scrutinized in compliance with the normal constitutional procedures applicable to international treaties, raising the possibility of negative resolutions by both the Lords and the Commons, which would have the effect of delaying formal ratification, repeatedly and indeed potentially indefinitely in the case of the Commons (though not of the Lords).[11]

Beyond that basic three-hurdled scheme, section 13 EU(W)A 2018 also set out various procedures to be followed in a range of scenarios where the Government failed to present, or to obtain Commons approval for, a negotiated withdrawal package. In particular, sections 13(3)–(6) governed the situation where the Commons rejects the Government's proposed withdrawal package. The Government must (within 21 days) make a statement setting out how it intends to proceed in relation to the withdrawal negotiations under Article 50 TEU; then make arrangements for a motion in neutral

---

[7] With explicit time-limits, beyond which the condition is deemed to be fulfilled, even if the Lords debate has not actually been concluded.

[8] Under section 13(2) European Union (Withdrawal) Act 2018: so far as practicable, the Commons motion should be debated and voted on before the European Parliament decides on its consent to the withdrawal agreement under Art 50 TEU.

[9] Note that the May Government had already published its outline plans for domestic implementation of any withdrawal agreement: see HMG, *Legislating for the Withdrawal Agreement between the UK and the EU* (Cm 9674 of 24 July 2018).

[10] In general but also as regards specific provisions (e.g. Part Two on citizens' rights): see further Chapter 6.

[11] See further, e.g. House of Commons Library Briefing Paper, *Parliament's Role in Ratifying Treaties* (No 5855 of 17 February 2017).

terms (within seven days of that statement) to the effect that the Commons has considered the Government position.[12]

Those provisions—both the initial section 13(1) Commons resolution on a Government motion to approve the withdrawal package, and any subsequent section 13(6) Commons vote on a motion in neutral terms following rejection of the proposed deal—prompted considerable debate in the UK about their full legal nature and potential consequences.[13] On the one hand, having already conceded considerable power to the Commons under section 13 as a whole, the Government was keen to limit any further scope for Parliament to challenge executive control over the more detailed process for approving its proposed withdrawal package. On the other hand, many parliamentarians were determined to ensure that the votes provided for under section 13 were genuinely 'meaningful'. They should not be limited to a simple 'take it or leave it' choice between accepting or rejecting the Government's proposed deal (especially since rejection on such terms would risk the UK leaving the Union with no agreement at all). The relevant votes should instead allow the Commons to express more flexible preferences, and to provide more specific instructions, which could well force the Government to rethink its withdrawal strategy (including seeking to reopen negotiations with the EU and/or to postpone the planned date of withdrawal).

Thus, for example, there was considerable argument about whether a Government motion under section 13(1) for initial Commons approval of the withdrawal package should be capable or incapable of amendment. The Government argued that any possibility of amendment would risk producing a parliamentary resolution expressing only qualified or conditional support for the withdrawal package, which could in turn cause confusion and uncertainty about the extent of the Government's mandate lawfully to proceed with ratification of the Article 50 TEU treaty.[14] However, the House of Commons Exiting the European Union Committee took the view that it was entirely proper for Parliament to be able to amend a Government motion under section 13(1): in itself, that could not have the effect of changing the withdrawal package as agreed politically between the Government and the EU; but it would provide the Commons with an opportunity to direct the Government to change its approach—opening up alternative pathways, such as efforts at renegotiation and/or an extension of the planned date of withdrawal, rather than leading inexorably towards a 'no deal Brexit'.[15] In the end, the Government conceded that a motion under section 13(1) was indeed amendable.[16]

---

[12] Note that section 13 also provided for certain scenarios which did not in the end materialize, e.g. if the Government had failed to reach any political agreement with the EU on the withdrawal treaty and/or political declaration.

[13] See further, e.g. R. Hogarth and H. White, *Voting for Brexit: Parliament's consideration of the withdrawal deal and future framework* (Institute for Government, April 2018).

[14] See the discussion in House of Commons Committee on Exiting the European Union, *Parliamentary scrutiny and approval of the Withdrawal Agreement and negotiations on a future relationship* (HC 1240 of 28 June 2018).

[15] House of Commons Committee on Exiting the European Union, *Parliamentary Scrutiny and Approval of the Withdrawal Agreement and Negotiations on a Future Relationship* (HC 1240 of 28 June 2018).

[16] See further, e.g. House of Commons Procedure Committee, *Motions under Section 13(1) of the European Union (Withdrawal) Act 2018* (HC 1664 of 16 November 2018). Also, e.g. https://ukandeu.ac.uk/wp-content/uploads/2018/09/Brexit-endgame-A-guide-to-the-parliamentary-process.pdf.

Similar arguments surrounded the question whether, in the event of the Government's proposed withdrawal package being rejected by the Commons, any subsequent Government motion in neutral terms for the purposes of section 13(6) should in itself be amendable. Again, the issue revolved around whether Parliament should be limited simply to considering or noting the Government's intentions about how to proceed; or how far Parliament should instead be entitled to express its more detailed views and potentially offer more specific political instructions concerning the Government's handling of the unfolding situation. The House of Commons Exiting the European Union Committee pointed out that, under ordinary parliamentary rules, the requirement for a debate in neutral terms would normally lead the Speaker to regard the motion as unamendable; but thanks to a decision of the House of Commons on 4 December 2018, those ordinary procedures were to be disapplied in this particular case, paving the way for any debate on a section 13(6) motion in neutral terms also to allow for amendments.[17] Moreover, the House of Commons further decided on 9 January 2019 that, in the event of a decision not to approve the proposed withdrawal package under section 13(1), the Government should table its additional section 13 motion within just three sitting days.[18]

Through the section 13 provisions, the Westminster Parliament's upcoming role in approval of the First Withdrawal Package had been very considerably strengthened (certainly as compared to the normal constitutional expectations under UK law, but also as compared to the Government's initial intentions under the February 2017 White Paper). Moreover, the fact that the Westminster Parliament had been unable to translate its eventual power of approval under section 13 (or indeed its other statutory attempts to steer the terms of UK withdrawal)[19] into an effective tool for exercising ongoing influence over the conduct and outcomes of the Article 50 TEU negotiations themselves, only sharpened the political significance and the high stakes invested in the 'meaningful vote' which would ultimately have to be held in the House of Commons.

3. Initial Attempts to Approve the First Withdrawal Package Under Section 13

In the period between political endorsement of the First Withdrawal Package by the European Council in November 2018 and the UK's planned date of withdrawal on 29 March 2019, the Government introduced two formal motions for approval of the First Withdrawal Package pursuant to section 13 EU(W)A 2018. Both motions were heavily defeated. In this section, we will explore those initial attempts to secure parliamentary approval for the Government's negotiated deal—including the various

---

[17] See House of Commons Committee on Exiting the European Union, *Progress of the UK's Negotiations on EU Withdrawal: The Withdrawal Agreement and the Political Declaration* (HC 1778 of 9 December 2018), at paras 109–110.

[18] See House of Commons Committee on Exiting the European Union, *Response to the vote on the Withdrawal Agreement and Political Declaration: Assessing the Options* (HC 1902 of 16 January 2019), at para 5.

[19] See the detailed discussion of this issue in Chapter 3.

domestic and EU-level initiatives and assurances by which the Government sought to clarify and/or supplement the First Withdrawal Package itself, in an attempt to render it more palatable to a deeply sceptical House of Commons.

A. The First 'Meaningful Vote' Under Section 13

Even accepting that the UK Government had negotiated and concluded the First Withdrawal Package without much apparent concern for whether it would be approved by the House of Commons, as required under section 13 EU(W)A 2018, the eventual scale of parliamentary opposition to the First Withdrawal Package, when it was finally put to a vote in January 2019, proved much stronger even than many commentators had expected. We will now briefly explore the reasons for the Commons' opposition.

As we know, the question of the UK's withdrawal from the Union was the source of deep divisions across Parliament and within the two main political parties.[20] But even after losing its majority in the early general election of June 2017, the Government decided not to approach the question of withdrawal as a fundamental change in national policy best addressed through an attempt to forge some workable and sustainable cross-party consensus. Instead, the UK's opposition parties were largely excluded from any participation in or indeed meaningful engagement with the negotiations under Article 50 TEU and (unsurprisingly) in due course declared themselves opposed to the First Withdrawal Package—albeit for different reasons. The position of several of the smaller parties was relatively clear and consistent. For example, the Liberal Democrats objected to the very principle of UK withdrawal from the Union and were in favour of a second referendum so as to campaign for Remain.[21] The Scottish National Party also argued against UK withdrawal altogether, but alternatively in favour of the closest possible future EU–UK relationship; while insisting upon the option of differentiated treatment for Scotland even if the rest of the UK took a different path and affirming their eventual preference for Scottish independence and Union membership in its own right.[22]

However, the stance adopted by the Labour Party was more complex. Having supported Remain in 2016, albeit under the rather lukewarm leadership of Jeremy Corbyn, Labour then committed to implementing the outcome of the referendum in its 2017 manifesto.[23] Yet the Government's decision to exclude Labour from any meaningful participation in the Article 50 TEU process, together with the progressive realization that the Government's 'cake and eat it' policy would not materialize, let alone alleviate the long-term damage posed by UK withdrawal, permitted the Labour Party to occupy a more ambiguous and flexible policy space. On the one hand, it was clear that a large majority of Labour MPs, members, and voters continued to oppose British

---

[20] See further Chapter 1.
[21] Though in due course, the Liberal Democrats changed policy in favour of a simple revocation of the UK's notification of intention to withdraw (even without any second referendum to confirm it).
[22] See, in particular, the Scottish Government's White Paper, *Scotland's Place in European* (20 December 2016).
[23] Available via https://labour.org.uk/wp-content/uploads/2017/10/labour-manifesto-2017.pdf.

withdrawal and remained supportive of Union membership. On the other hand, a significant minority did support Brexit—whether out of apparent conviction,[24] or out of supposed respect for the 'will of the people'.[25] Labour's task was to avoid alienating ardent Leave supporters, by claiming to respect the 2016 ballot and its outcome; while seeking to appeal to uncommitted opinion by arguing for a close future EU–UK relationship that would minimize disruption as regards trade and security; but hoping also to retain the support of Remain voters, by keeping open the option of a further referendum should the Government fail to deliver an acceptable withdrawal deal.

In March 2017, Labour formulated a series of 'six tests' for identifying and supporting an acceptable withdrawal package as negotiated by the Government—including the proposition that any deal should deliver exactly the same benefits as membership of the Single Market and the Customs Union.[26] Those tests were so incompatible with Conservative policy (and indeed so unrealistic even on their own terms) that they appeared doomed to fail right from the outset—thus guaranteeing Labour's opposition to whatever deal the Government brought back for parliamentary approval. At its party conference in September 2018, the Party then sought to articulate the further implications of such opposition.[27] In the first place, Labour would argue for a general election with a view to forming a Labour government—though it was unclear whether Labour would fight any such election merely by offering a new approach to the withdrawal negotiations, or instead arguing for a reversal of the decision to leave. In the second place, if no general election were to take place, Labour would keep all options on the table, including support for a second public vote—though it was again unclear precisely which options might be offered, and which outcome Labour might ultimately campaign for, in any second referendum. On that basis, Labour perhaps hoped to make maximum political capital out of the Conservatives' deep divisions and problems over UK withdrawal while avoiding the adoption of any firm policy of its own, for fear of provoking comparable internal political dissent and/or significant public and voter alienation. In any event, the clear implication was that Labour would oppose whatever withdrawal package this Government eventually brought before Parliament for approval.

The Government's apparent insouciance about securing cross-party support for its negotiating strategy and approval of any final withdrawal package might have been more comprehensible if the Conservative Party was both united in its vision for UK withdrawal and capable of commanding a stable majority in the House of Commons. But in the real world, the Government's decision to rely primarily upon the votes of Conservative MPs, supplemented by the support of the DUP, never appeared anything other than reckless.

[24] E.g. as with the so-called 'Lexiters'—self-proclaimed enemies of the 'neo-liberal' EU and its plan to destroy socialism in Europe.

[25] Particularly in the case of those Labour MPs who were elected by constituencies that had strongly voted for Leave in the 2016 referendum.

[26] See, in particular, https://www.chathamhouse.org/sites/default/files/events/2017-03-27-StarmerPREP.pdf. And later, e.g. https://labour.org.uk/wp-content/uploads/2018/09/Theresa-Mays-failed-Brexit-plan-STRICTLY-EMBARGOED-UNTIL-2230-Monday-24-September.pdf.

[27] See, in particular, https://labourlist.org/2018/09/labours-brexit-composite-motion-in-full/.

After all, we know that the Cabinet, the Government, and the Tory parliamentary party were all deeply split over the question of UK withdrawal and future relations with the EU. That fragile coalition had been held together partly by the Government's 'cake and eat it' approach to the Article 50 TEU negotiations: the strategy of promising different things to different people had at least served to keep internal party tensions tolerably under control. But now that the First Withdrawal Package was finally put on the table, the Conservatives' latent tensions and divisions were bound to resurface—especially on the hard Europhobic right, which (any competent observer would have concluded long before) showed no serious interest in compromise with more moderate views and indeed many of whom made plain their preference for a 'no deal' departure as quickly as possible.[28] Moreover, the Government's parliamentary vulnerability was reinforced by its dependence upon the support of the DUP, which stood not only on the hard Europhobic right, but also expressed its own uncompromising opposition to any proposals which might be perceived (rightly or wrongly) as a threat to the position of Northern Ireland within the United Kingdom.

In short, publication of the First Withdrawal Package in November 2018 finally focused attention squarely and inescapably upon the problems, tensions, and divisions afflicting the UK's body politic.[29] It was now clear beyond any doubt that not every Leave campaign or May Government promise or fantasy was going to be kept or delivered. It was equally apparent that the Government's proposed deal faced substantial opposition from a range of parliamentary sources motivated by a variety of policy perspectives. Indeed, initiating the section 13 approval process was bound to precipitate a period of open political crisis.

The warning signs were clear to read even before debate on the First Withdrawal Package opened in the Commons on 5 December 2018—with the Government already suffering a series of defeats, of which perhaps the most important was being declared in contempt of Parliament for failing to release in full the Attorney General's legal analysis of the Irish backstop provisions contained in the First Withdrawal Agreement.[30] That defeat was not merely of symbolical but also of considerable substantive importance, since the Attorney General's legal advice came to occupy a prominent role in the parliamentary process to come. For now, it was disclosed that (in a letter dated 13 November 2018) the Attorney General had advised the Government that the backstop could endure indefinitely in international law and (in particular) could not be brought to an end in the absence of a subsequent agreement between the EU and the UK *even if* the two parties believed that talks had broken down and there was no prospect of reaching an agreement on their future relationship.[31]

That opinion galvanized the opposition of both the Tory hard right and the DUP: the supposedly negative effects of the proposed backstop (tying the UK to the

---

[28] For an earlier insight into their long-term thinking, consider, e.g. the letter to Prime Minister Theresa May of 16 February 2018 sent by John Penrose and endorsed by many of the leading Tory Europhobes in the European Research Group.

[29] See further, e.g. Birkinshaw, 'Brexit's Challenge to the UK's Unwritten Constitution', 26 *European Public Law* (2020) 29.

[30] In a vote in the House of Commons on 4 December 2018.

[31] Attorney General's Legal Advice of 13 November 2018. Note the rather slippery account offered by Theresa May, *Prime Minister's Statement on the Special European Council* (26 November 2018).

Customs Union, hindering its pursuit of an independent trade policy, subjecting Northern Ireland to distinct regulatory treatment) could be maintained in place unless and until the EU itself agreed that a suitable alternative had been found to replace them—moreover, with no guarantee that such an alternative would be any less objectionable (in the eyes of its detractors) than the backstop itself. When the scale of the parliamentary opposition even among its own backbenchers and supporters became clear, the Government aborted the section 13 vote that was scheduled to take place on 11 December 2018.[32] That in turn prompted a failed attempt by the Tory hard right to oust Theresa May as Conservative Party leader and Prime Minister on 12 December 2018.[33]

Nevertheless, the Government decided that its best chance of securing the passage of the First Withdrawal Package through the Commons was to reaffirm its previous strategy of regarding 'delivering Brexit' as a responsibility bestowed almost exclusively upon the Conservative Party, and therefore to win over its own hard-line backbenchers (as well as the DUP) by seeking and offering additional reassurances about the operation and implications of the backstop. Domestically, the Prime Minister had promised towards the very end of 2018 to give further consideration to the potential role of Parliament in the operation of the backstop.[34] That led (on 9 January 2019) to the announcement that Parliament should hold the power to choose between two options contained in the First Withdrawal Agreement: of either entering the backstop on 1 January 2021; or of instead requesting an extension to the post-withdrawal, status quo transition period.[35] At the same time, the Government sought to comfort the DUP by publishing specific incentives for Northern Ireland: for example, guaranteeing extensive rights of access to the market in Great Britain for Northern Irish goods; and bolstering the potential role of the devolved institutions in Belfast in the future functioning of the backstop.[36]

Furthermore, the Government persuaded the Union itself to provide additional assurances surrounding the backstop. After its meeting on 13 December 2018, the European Council (acting in its reduced Article 50 TEU formation) affirmed the EU27's determination to reach agreement on the future EU–UK relationship as quickly as possible and their expectation that (if it were even required at all) resort to the backstop should be on a temporary basis and only for as long as strictly necessary.[37] However, such sentiments failed to impress the Tory rebels and their DUP allies: after all, expressions of political determination or expectation did not change the legally binding text of the First Withdrawal Agreement itself.

In a further effort, the Government then engaged in an Exchange of Letters between the UK Prime Minister and the Presidents of the European Council and the European

---

[32] See Prime Minister, *Statement on exiting the European Union* (10 December 2018).

[33] See,e.g.https://www.theguardian.com/politics/2018/dec/12/theresa-may-defeats-leadership-challenge-by-83-votes.

[34] See Prime Minister, *Statement on the European Council* (17 December 2018).

[35] See,e.g. https://www.theguardian.com/politics/2019/jan/09/mps-to-get-final-say-on-brexit-backstop-theresa-may-confirms.

[36] See HMG, *Commitments to Northern Ireland and its Integral Place in the United Kingdom* (9 January 2019).

[37] See European Council (Article 50), *Conclusions of 13 December 2018*.

Commission as published on 14 January 2019.[38] Those letters sought to build on the previous European Council conclusions and provide additional mutual reassurances about the temporary nature of the proposed backstop and the joint commitment to delivering an agreement on the future relationship: for example, by clarifying that the European Council had undertaken solemn commitments, which would constitute part of the context in which the legal text of the First Withdrawal Agreement should eventually be interpreted; by suggesting the possibility of provisional application for the relevant parts of any new agreement on future EU–UK relations, should national ratifications still be pending at the end of the transition period; by promising to consider the potential role of technology and other customs facilitations in replacing the backstop; and indeed recalling that any new arrangements need not replicate the content of the backstop itself (provided they still delivered the underlying objective of avoiding a hard border).[39]

Those various domestic and EU-level assurances did nothing to dampen parliamentary opposition. The House of Lords expressed its (non-binding) opposition to the First Withdrawal Package on 14 January 2019. The following day, the Government's motion seeking approval of the First Withdrawal Package for the purposes of section 13 EU(W)A 2018 was defeated in the House of Commons by 230 votes—reputedly the worse defeat suffered by any UK government in the modern era.[40]

B. The Second 'Meaningful Vote' Under Section 13

The Union expressed its regret at the outcome of the vote in the House of Commons.[41] Domestically, the May Government's massive defeat prompted immediate and dramatic political responses—including the Labour Party's unsuccessful attempt to pass a 'no confidence' motion through the House of Commons on 16 January 2019.[42] Underneath the political noise and drama, however, the UK's basic options remained virtually unchanged.

In the first place, the UK could leave the Union as planned on 29 March 2019 without any agreed withdrawal package. That 'no deal' outcome remained the default position both as a matter of UK law (under the EU(W)A 2018) and Union law (pursuant to Article 50 TEU). However, a 'no deal' departure on 29 March 2019 was not legally compelled: Article 50 TEU made provision for an agreed extension of the UK's

---

[38] Exchange of Letters between the UK Prime Minister and the Presidents of the European Council and the European Commission (14 January 2019).

[39] Note the advice of the UK Attorney General on the Exchange of Letters (14 January 2019), i.e. in effect: politically useful and potentially relevant to future interpretation; but no actual effect on the fundamental legal obligations contained in the Protocol. Consider also: Prime Minister, *Statement in the House of Commons* (14 January 2019).

[40] See, e.g. https://www.theguardian.com/politics/2019/jan/15/theresa-may-loses-brexit-deal-vote-by-majority-of-230.

[41] E.g. Commission, *Statement by President Juncker on the outcome of the Meaningful Vote in the United Kingdom House of Commons* (15 January 2019).

[42] See,e.g.https://www.parliament.uk/business/news/2019/parliamentary-news-2019/commons-debate-motion-of-no-confidence-in-hm-government/.

period of Union membership; while the 2018 Act explicitly allowed for amendments to the definition of 'exit day' under UK law.

On the one hand, a 'no deal' withdrawal was generally regarded as a highly undesirable outcome, not least for the UK, which would be deprived of its post-withdrawal, status quo transition period (despite the inadequate state of its domestic preparations for the direct consequences of its own departure from the Union); be required to devise unilateral solutions to the immediate separation problems, which were meant to be provided for under the proposed withdrawal agreement; and witness a major setback to negotiations with the Union over establishing a new economic and security relationship into the future.[43] For those reasons, there was strong parliamentary opposition to any 'no deal' departure, for example, as expressed in a vote in the House of Commons on 29 January 2019.[44]

On the other hand, it was clear that a significant number of Conservative and DUP MPs viewed the prospect of a 'no deal' outcome very differently: some simply did not believe that such difficult problems would ever materialize and dismissed them as a 'Remainer plot' to frustrate Brexit; others seemed to accept that the problems might be genuine but nevertheless regarded them as a price worth paying to 'deliver Brexit' according to the Government's promised timescale; while many argued that keeping alive the possibility of simply walking away from the Union table in fact constituted the UK's strongest negotiating card and should not be surrendered. Apparently beholden to such views among her rebellious backbenchers and allies, the Prime Minister repeatedly refused to rule out a 'no deal' outcome to the Article 50 TEU process.[45]

But perhaps more importantly, simply opposing a 'no deal' outcome did not in itself solve the problem of what should take its place. If the UK were genuinely not willing to leave the Union without a negotiated settlement, then it still had to propose a viable alternative from among the two remaining options. And so, in the second place, that might mean revoking the UK's original intention to withdraw. Just a few weeks before the Government's (first) crushing defeat in the Commons under section 13, the Court of Justice in *Wightman* had confirmed that the relevant State is entitled unilaterally to revoke its previous notification under Article 50 TEU at any time before the effective date of its departure from the Union, provided that such revocation represents a settled decision to remain on the relevant State's current terms and conditions of membership.[46]

Needless to say, the *Wightman* ruling was cheered by Remain supporters for confirming that revocation was indeed a viable legal option legitimately available to the UK. However, it was unclear how the possibility of revocation might be operationalized as a matter of domestic constitutional law. By analogy with the previous Supreme Court ruling in *Miller*, there was a strong argument that revocation was a decision reserved for Parliament, to be actioned through the adoption of appropriate primary legislation: choosing to remain in the EU, having already decided to depart, would be

[43] See further the discussion in Chapter 2.
[44] See, e.g. https://www.parliament.uk/business/news/2019/parliamentary-news-2019/house-of-commons-debates-brexit-next-steps/.
[45] E.g. in statements to the House of Commons on 21 January 2019, 12 February 2019 and 26 February 2019.
[46] Case C-621/18, *Wightman* (EU:C:2018:999). See further the discussion in Chapter 2.

another decision of constitutional stature entailing a reconfiguration (or least reaffirmation) of the very sources of law recognized within the UK legal order.[47] But it was also possible to suggest that revocation could be decided upon by the Government on its own initiative and account. Given that the power to decide on and notify the UK's withdrawal had been delegated by Parliament to the executive under the terms of the European Union (Notification of Withdrawal) Act 2017, perhaps the power to decide on and notify the UK's revocation of its former intention could also be regarded as having been conferred directly upon the Government;[48] though such an approach could never have provided more than a temporary convenience, given that any decision to remain would soon require significant changes also to domestic primary law—not least through repeal of the EU(W)A 2018 and other related 'Brexit legislation'.[49]

However, the UK debate was clearly proceeding on the basis of a very different assumption about the process for the UK to change its mind about leaving the Union. Almost regardless of the strict position as a matter of domestic constitutional law, it was widely understood that any decision to revoke and remain would only be regarded as politically legitimate, by large sections of the British population, if such a decision were approved through a second referendum.[50] Moreover, the debate about how to operationalize the power of revocation as a matter of constitutional law and/or practice appeared rather premature compared to the state of political and public opinion. After all, the Prime Minister consistently ruled out either any Government decision to revoke and remain, or the organization of a second referendum on Union membership.[51] As for Parliament, there was also only limited support in the House of Commons for the option of revocation—whether directly through the adoption of primary legislation, or indirectly by means of a second referendum.[52]

If the UK was unwilling to leave without a negotiated agreement, but was also unprepared to revoke its original notification under Article 50 TEU, then that left only one final option: in the third place, to overcome the massive parliamentary opposition expressed on 15 January 2019 and somehow manage to approve a withdrawal package. That option appeared to depend upon the Government offering/securing sufficient changes or at least additional assurances as to meet the concerns of enough MPs to deliver a Commons majority. And for that purpose, the Government could opt to take one of two main avenues.

First, the Government could seek to build cross-party support for revisions to the proposed political declaration, so as to aspire to a much closer future relationship between the Union and the UK—in particular, by committing to negotiate some form of permanent Customs Union together with some model for continued Single Market membership. It was widely assumed that such an approach would be capable

---

[47] R (on the application of Miller) v Secretary of State for Exiting the European Union [2017] UKSC 5.

[48] See the discussion in Chapter 3.

[49] Including, e.g. the Haulage Permits and Trailer Registration Act 2018, the Sanctions and Anti-Money Laundering Act 2018, the Nuclear Safeguards Act 2018 and the Taxation (Cross-Border Trade) Act 2018.

[50] Indeed, many people (particularly on the Leave side) would probably not have regarded a decision to Remain as politically legitimate even after a second referendum.

[51] E.g. Prime Minister, Commons Statement (21 January 2019).

[52] See above on the position, e.g. of the Liberal Democrats, the Scottish National Party, and the Labour Party.

of commanding cross-party support in the House of Commons—not least since a much closer future EU–UK relationship was explicitly supported by the Labour Party.[53] There was also little doubt that—even though it regarded the text of the First Withdrawal Agreement itself as closed—the European Council would be prepared to revisit the text of the First Political Declaration were the UK to change its longstanding 'red lines' and propose a different model for the future relationship.[54]

However, agreeing to a permanent Customs Union and any form of Single Market membership would have constituted a radical departure from the Government's longstanding policy promises and no doubt have provoked an outright crisis threatening the very survival of the administration and indeed the Conservative Party.[55] Surely for that reason, the Prime Minister may well have gone through the motions of engaging in preliminary cross-party discussions about finding greater consensus on how to move forward, but the fact that the Government appeared adamant that the fundamentals of the First Political Declaration, as based on the Conservative Party's 'red lines', were not up for renegotiation, effectively ruled out any serious prospect for cross-party cooperation.[56]

That left no choice but to take the second avenue: the Government decided to redouble its efforts to win over the hard-right Tory rebels and the DUP, by concentrating on securing changes to the Irish backstop provisions of the First Withdrawal Agreement. In a statement to the House of Commons on 21 January 2019, the Prime Minister announced that she considered the backstop to be the main source of parliamentary opposition to her proposed withdrawal package.[57] On 29 January 2019, the Prime Minister then decided to support a backbench amendment to a Government motion, calling for replacement of the backstop with alternative arrangements designed to prevent the return of a hard border on the island of Ireland.[58] Having engineered a direct parliamentary attack on its very own withdrawal package, the Government nevertheless believed it had secured a domestic mandate to demand 'legally binding changes' to the existing backstop provisions—not only by resuming talks over the viability of technological and other customs facilitations, but also by insisting upon a fixed time-limit on and/or a right of unilateral exit from the backstop.[59]

---

[53] See the discussion above. Note Jeremy Corbyn's letter to Theresa May of 6 February 2019, setting out the terms on which the Labour Party would support the Conservative Government on approval of the Withdrawal Agreement.

[54] Note the European Council (Article 50), *Conclusions of 13 December 2018*, especially at paras 1–2. Also, e.g. Commission, *Speech by Michel Barnier at the European Economic and Social Committee* (23 January 2019); HMG, *Joint Statement on behalf of the Prime Minister and President Juncker* (7 February 2019).

[55] See the discussion in Chapters 3 and 4. Note Theresa May's reply to Jeremy Corbyn of 11 February 2019, rejecting the Labour Party's terms for supporting the First Withdrawal Agreement; and Prime Minister, *Statement to the House of Commons on Brexit* (12 February 2019).

[56] See, e.g. Prime Minister, *Statement to the House* (16 January 2019); https://www.theguardian.com/politics/2019/jan/16/no-10-rules-out-customs-union-before-cross-party-talks-begin; Prime Minister, *Statement to the House of Commons on Brexit* (21 January 2019).

[57] See Prime Minister, *Statement to the House of Commons on Brexit* (21 January 2019).

[58] The so-called 'Brady amendment': see, e.g. https://www.parliament.uk/business/news/2019/parliamentary-news-2019/house-of-commons-debates-brexit-next-steps/. See also: Prime Minister, *Statement to the House of Commons* (29 January 2019).

[59] Commons statement on 12 February 2019 available at https://www.gov.uk/government/speeches/pms-statement-to-the-house-of-commons-on-brexit-12-february-2019. Note that similar proposals had been flagged up by the UK Government before, during the previous Art 50 TEU negotiations, e.g. Dominic

Needless to say, this looked like a very odd avenue to proceed along. The Union had already decreed the text of the First Withdrawal Agreement (including the backstop) closed to further renegotiation.[60] Moreover, the backstop had assumed its final form— a UK-wide de facto customs union together with Northern Ireland-specific provisions on regulatory alignment—only at the dogged insistence of the UK itself.[61] It was difficult to imagine which 'alternative arrangements' the UK might now propose that had not already been exhaustively considered over the previous near two years of discussions under Article 50 TEU.[62] Last but far from least: it was blindingly obvious that any UK demand for either a fixed time-limit on or a unilateral power of exit from the backstop would mean the latter provisions were no longer to be considered any sort of proper 'backstop' at all.[63]

Those far-reaching objections notwithstanding, the Government engaged in a series of discussions with the Commission about revisiting the existing backstop provisions.[64] The outcome of those discussions was the so-called 'Strasbourg Deal', reached between the UK and the Commission on 11 March 2019.[65] This new package of measures was published just hours before the Government sought Commons approval for the First Withdrawal Package for a second time under section 13 EU(W)A 2018— though the Strasbourg Deal was not formally endorsed by the EU27 until a meeting of the European Council (acting in its Article 50 TEU formation) held on 21 March 2019.[66]

The 'Strasbourg Deal' consisted of two texts agreed jointly by the Commission and the UK Government: an 'Instrument relating to the [First] Withdrawal Agreement' and a 'Joint Statement relating to the [First] Political Declaration'. They contain no new substantive content that goes beyond the existing provisions of the First Withdrawal Package, as supplemented by the UK Government's previous public assurances about the impact of the backstop on Northern Ireland,[67] as well as the Exchange of Letters

---

Raab, *Statement following negotiation round Thursday 26 July* (26 July 2018); Theresa May, *Statement on Brexit* (15 October 2018); Prime Minister, *Statement on European Council* (22 October 2018).

[60] E.g. European Council (Article 50), *Conclusions of 13 December 2018*, at para 1.

[61] See the detailed discussion in Chapter 8.

[62] Note that ardent Leave campaigners insisted on technological solutions to the Irish border problem, despite the lack of evidence from international practice to demonstrate their feasibility: consider, e.g. L. Karlsson, *Smart Border 2.0: Avoiding a Hard Border on the Island of Ireland for Customs Control and the Free Movement of Persons* (European Parliament, Policy Department for Citizens' Rights and Constitutional Affairs: PE 596.828, November 2017); House of Commons Northern Ireland Affairs Committee, *The Land Border between Northern Ireland and Ireland* (HC329 of 16 March 2018).

[63] Consider, e.g. Commission, *Speeches by President Juncker and Chief Negotiator Barnier at the Plenary Session of the European Parliament on the Occasion of the Debate on the United Kingdom's Withdrawal from the EU* (30 January 2019).

[64] Consider, e.g. HMG, *Joint Statement on behalf of the Prime Minister and President Juncker* (7 February 2019); Commission, *Joint Statement on behalf of President Juncker and Prime Minister May* (20 February 2019). Alongside continuing overtures to the DUP, offering further domestic assurances about the involvement of Northern Ireland's devolved institutions in the operation of the 'backstop', e.g. Prime Minister, *Speech in Belfast* (5 February 2019).

[65] 'Strasbourg Deal' of 11 March 2019: Instrument relating to the Withdrawal Agreement; Joint Statement relating to Political Declaration.

[66] European Council (Article 50), *Conclusions of 21 March 2019*, at para 2.

[67] In particular: HMG, *Commitments to Northern Ireland and its Integral Place in the United Kingdom* (9 January 2019).

between the UK Prime Minister and the Presidents of the European Council and the European Commission.[68] In fact, the Commission and the UK Government merely set out further details about how best to pursue their common aspiration to replace the existing backstop with alternative arrangements as soon as possible, but without offering any guarantees as to the outcome of their future negotiations, and without purporting to alter the underlying obligations contained in the First Withdrawal Agreement in general or the backstop provisions in particular.

To be more precise: the Joint Instrument was intended to express the parties' mutual understanding of the appropriate interpretation of certain provisions of the First Withdrawal Agreement. Indeed, the Joint Instrument was explicitly described as a clear and unambiguous statement by the parties of what they had agreed under the proposed treaty.[69] As such, it was said to constitute a 'document of reference' to be made use of if any issue were to arise as regards implementation of the First Withdrawal Agreement and which (to that effect) 'has legal force and a binding character'. In fact, most of the provisions of the Joint Instrument merely restated what was already obvious from, inherent in, or to be considered possible under the existing terms of the First Withdrawal Agreement itself: for example, the sorts of behaviour that should be considered a failure to act in good faith; the sorts of temporary remedies that should be considered possible in the event of an established instance of non-compliance; or the sorts of subsequent agreement that could (in accordance with the proposed Protocol on Ireland/Northern Ireland) lead in principle and in due course to replacement of the backstop. Beyond its potential but limited utility as a relevant reference point for future interpretation of certain provisions of the First Withdrawal Agreement, it was clear that the Joint Instrument did not seek to amend or alter the text of the proposed treaty in any way.

The remaining provisions of the Joint Instrument set out various (essentially procedural) intentions and aspirations concerning the detailed planning and conduct of subsequent negotiations towards an agreement on the parties' future relationship in general and/or on the Irish border question in particular. In that regard, the relevant provisions of the Joint Instrument shared much in common with the Joint Statement, which supplemented the First Political Declaration by expressing similar (essentially procedural) intentions and aspirations concerning subsequent negotiations on the future relationship: for example, committing to commence formal talks as soon as UK withdrawal were to become effective; and aiming to have the necessary agreements in place by the end of the transition period. Within the framework of Article 50 TEU, it was possible for the Joint Statement to be politically endorsed by the European Council alone—though since it was adopted before the European Parliament had consented to, and the Council had finally concluded, the First Withdrawal Agreement, the Joint Statement could also be regarded as subject to indirect approval by the Union's twin legislative institutions. In any event, as regards form (in the case of the Joint Statement) and content (also as regards the relevant provisions of the Joint Instrument) it was

---

[68] In particular, Exchange of Letters between the President of the European Council, the President of the Commission and the UK Prime Minister (14 January 2019).

[69] In the sense of Art 31 of the Vienna Convention on the Law of Treaties.

clear that these essentially procedural and politically contingent commitments would not be legally enforceable as regards the outcome of any future negotiations.

In addition to the Joint Instrument and the Joint Statement, the Prime Minister announced that the UK Government would publish a separate Unilateral Declaration to the Withdrawal Agreement to the effect that, if the backstop were to come into force and discussions on the future relationship were to break down, leaving no prospect of a subsequent EU–UK agreement, there would be nothing to prevent the UK from instigating measures that would ultimately disapply the backstop.[70] At first glance, that announcement appeared remarkable: the UK Government appeared to be openly threatening to breach its clear obligations under a legally binding international agreement, even before that agreement had been finally approved and ratified. However, the final text of the Unilateral Declaration proved to be more ambiguous and arguably entirely ineffectual: the UK expressed its understanding that—if there was no prospect of replacing the backstop with an alternative agreement *and* that situation is attributable to a breach by the Union of its obligation to act in good faith—then nothing in the First Withdrawal Agreement would prevent the UK from instigating measures that could ultimately lead to disapplication of the backstop—though apparently only in accordance with the procedures laid down in the First Withdrawal Agreement itself *and* on condition that the UK would still avoid the return of a hard border on the island of Ireland.[71] In any case, although the Union did not positively object to the text of the Unilateral Declaration, the European Council (acting in its Article 50 TEU formation) did repeatedly remind the UK that any unilateral statements or actions it might make or undertake should be fully compatible with both the letter and the spirit of its own proposed withdrawal agreement.[72]

The UK Government made much of the idea that the Strasbourg Deal was 'legally binding' and had thus delivered on the Prime Minister's promises regarding renegotiation of the existing backstop provisions. But regardless of their superficial legal form or status, the substantive contents of the Strasbourg Deal could not be described as legally significant.[73] After all, neither the Joint Instrument nor the Joint Declaration did anything to prevent the backstop being activated and remaining operational on a potentially indefinite basis (subject to mutual agreement between the parties for its amendment, replacement, or removal). The Prime Minister had therefore failed to secure any legally binding or enforceable time-limit, or to deliver any mechanism by which the UK would be entitled unilaterally to terminate the backstop.[74]

That general assessment was shared by the Attorney General in his revised legal advice of 12 March 2019: the Joint Instrument, read together with the UK's Unilateral Declaration, might well reduce the risk of the UK being indefinitely and involuntarily detained within the backstop insofar as that situation is brought about by bad faith on

---

[70] See Prime Minister, *Press Statement in Strasbourg* (11 March 2019).

[71] HMG, *Unilateral Declaration concerning the Northern Ireland Protocol* (12 March 2019).

[72] E.g. European Council (Article 50), *Conclusions of 21 March 2019*, at para 4; and *Conclusions of 10 April 2019*, at para 4.

[73] See further, e.g. http://eulawanalysis.blogspot.com/2019/03/briefing-paper-legal-analysis-of.html.

[74] Indeed: the Joint Instrument effectively acknowledges that underlying reality, in its discussion of compliance with/enforcement of the parties' commitments to seek to replace the existing 'backstop' with alternative arrangements.

the part of the Union; but the legal risk remained unchanged that if, through no such demonstrable failure but simply because of intractable differences, such a situation does indeed arise, the UK would have no internationally lawful means of exiting the backstop save by agreement with the EU.[75]

Perhaps it was clear even to the Government that any serious attempt at renegotiation of the Irish backstop was doomed to failure—partly because the Union would never agree to substantial changes and partly because minor concessions would never satisfy the hard-right Tory rebels or the DUP. In parallel with its discussions with the Commission over the backstop, the Government therefore embarked upon a series of domestic initiatives—projects designed not to alter the existing terms of the First Withdrawal Package in any meaningful way, but rather to persuade a wider group of MPs to change their minds and support the same deal when it returned for a second Commons vote under section 13.

That parallel strategy was first unveiled during the Prime Minister's statement to the House of Commons on 21 January 2019.[76] In that statement, the Government announced that the UK would waive the fee demanded from existing Union citizens when applying for 'settled status' in the UK as a precondition for acquiring future protection of their residency and other rights as provided for under the First Withdrawal Agreement.[77] But in addition, the Prime Minister promised to consider the options for greater parliamentary involvement in negotiations over the future EU–UK relationship;[78] and to address MPs' concerns about the future protection of workers' rights and environmental standards after the UK's withdrawal from the Union.[79] Those initiatives were clearly intended to win over Labour MPs representing constituencies that voted Leave in the 2016 referendum and who might be more inclined to support the Government's deal in order to 'deliver Brexit'.[80]

It was never clear that the Government's promises stood much chance of success. After all, many MPs surely felt that Parliament positively *deserved* to have some meaningful input into crucial negotiations and fundamental decisions about the very basis for the UK's future international relations with a major economic and strategic partner. Moreover, given the nature of the UK constitution and the centrality of the principle of parliamentary sovereignty, executive promises or even statutory procedures seeking to uphold existing regulatory standards in fields such as employment or environmental law were inherently vulnerable to any future change in Government policy capable of being translated into primary legislation. In any event, the Government's persuasive powers were perhaps hindered rather than helped by the announcement (on 4 March 2019) of a 'Stronger Towns Fund' promising modest sums for investment

---

[75] See Attorney General's Revised Legal Advice of 12 March 2019.

[76] See Prime Minister, *Statement to the House of Commons on Brexit* (21 January 2019).

[77] See further Chapter 7.

[78] On which, see also the Prime Minister's Commons statement of 12 February 2019.

[79] On which, see also the Prime Minister's Commons statements of 12 and 26 February 2019; together with HMG, *Protecting and Enhancing Worker Rights after the UK Withdrawal from the European Union* (6 March 2019).

[80] Note: these efforts were also referenced in the Strasbourg Deal itself, e.g. in para 5 of the Joint Statement, the EU notes the UK's intention to ensure that the latter's social, employment and environmental standards do not regress from those in place at the end of the transitional period and to provide Parliament with the opportunity to consider future changes in Union law in these areas.

in deprived communities across England, which was immediately decried as a blatant attempt to bribe Labour MPs in Leave-voting constituencies into supporting the Prime Minister.[81]

If the Prime Minister's carrots appeared rather unappetizing, perhaps the Government's sticks would be more effective, i.e. at frightening MPs into supporting the proposed withdrawal deal simply because the alternative outcomes were even more unpalatable. On the one hand, the Prime Minister's consistent refusal to rule out a 'no deal' withdrawal—despite acknowledging, even herself, what a damaging outcome that would be—was surely intended to apply additional pressure not only to wavering Labour MPs but also to the small group of Conservative MPs inclined to vote alongside the Liberal Democrats and Scottish Nationalists in favour of a second referendum. On the other hand, the Government appeared simultaneously to be threatening the hard-right Tory rebels and the DUP that their continued rejection of the First Withdrawal Package might well lead to a significant delay in the UK's departure from the Union, or to some sort of renegotiation that could deliver a much closer future relationship with the EU, or perhaps even risk a future parliamentary or popular decision to cancel Brexit altogether.[82]

Despite (indeed, perhaps even because) of those various Government initiatives to win whatever support it could muster for a second Commons vote on its proposed withdrawal package, the UK's political atmosphere remained febrile and unstable. For example, simmering internal tensions within both the Labour Party and the Conservatives led to the defection of several MPs to form The Independent Group—which in due course evolved into a new political party, Change UK, espousing a clear pro-European message and campaigning for a second referendum.[83] Or again, having promised to allow a new Commons debate on Brexit on 14 February 2019,[84] but then postponed any firm date for another attempt at approval under section 13,[85] the Government was defeated on a vote of continued support for its handling of the withdrawal negotiations with the EU—a largely symbolic humiliation, but delivered thanks to the abstention of Europhobic Tory MPs, underlining just how fragile the Government's parliamentary authority had become.[86]

On 26 February 2019, the Prime Minister announced that the second 'meaningful vote' under section 13 would be held in the Commons on or by 12 March 2019.[87] But in addition, if the Government lost again, it would ask the Commons to vote the very next day on whether the UK should leave the EU without any negotiated settlement. If the Commons also refused to endorse a 'no deal' outcome, then it would be asked the following day to vote once more, this time on whether the UK should request an

---

[81] See, e.g. https://www.gov.uk/government/news/16-billion-stronger-towns-fund-launched.

[82] See, e.g. Prime Minister, *Speech in Grimsby* (8 March 2019).

[83] In due course, Change UK failed to elect any MPs in the general election of December 2019 and effectively disappeared from the British political horizon.

[84] In a statement on 29 January 2019, the Government promised to bring forward a new section 13 motion, based on a new agreement, or otherwise to hold another Commons debate, on 14 February 2019.

[85] In a statement on 12 February 2019, the Government announced that there would be another vote (whether for approval of a revised deal or on another Government motion) by 26/27 February 2019.

[86] See, e.g. https://www.parliament.uk/business/news/2019/february/house-of-commons-debates-new-motion-on-brexit-next-steps/.

[87] Prime Minister, *Statement in Commons* (26 February 2019).

extension of its Union membership in accordance with the facility provided for under Article 50(3) TEU. In the end, the second approval vote under section 13 was indeed held on 12 March 2019—just hours after publication of the Strasbourg Deal and the Attorney General's revised legal advice on the backstop. The Government was again defeated by a (reduced but still massive) majority of 149—and the UK's political crisis entered a new phase.[88]

4. Delays to Departure

As we saw in Chapter 4, Article 50(3) TEU provides that the Treaties shall cease to apply to the relevant State from the date of entry into force of its withdrawal agreement; or 'failing that', the Treaties will cease to apply to the relevant State two years after notification of its intention to withdraw. Article 185 of the First Withdrawal Agreement, as politically endorsed by the European Council in November 2018, defined the agreement's proposed date of entry into force as 00.00 (CET) on 30 March 2019, the same as that which would have been calculated by default under Article 50(3) TEU even in the absence of any negotiated departure.[89]

At this stage, it remained possible but increasingly unlikely that the UK would leave the Union on 30 March 2019 by default and without any withdrawal deal in place. Having already indicated its opposition to such an outcome in the past, on 13 March 2019, the House of Commons voted resoundingly against a 'no deal' UK departure.[90] In fact, the Government had sought to limit the effect of that motion only to the immediate days and weeks—but MPs voted against leaving without a withdrawal agreement under any circumstances.[91]

Yet every other possible course of action now required more time than the existing deadline of 30 March 2019 allowed: whether that be for somehow approving the First Withdrawal Package and adopting the necessary implementing measures; or negotiating a different withdrawal package, perhaps recalibrating the future relationship as sketched out in the proposed political declaration; or indeed reconsidering the entire withdrawal decision and deciding to revoke the UK's original Article 50 TEU notification (presumably following a second referendum).[92] In recognition of that fact, on 14 March 2019, the House of Commons voted in favour of the Government asking for an extension to the UK's period of membership as provided for under Article 50 TEU.[93] It was therefore anticipated that the Prime Minister would duly submit a formal extension request to the European Council for consideration at its forthcoming meeting on 20–21 March 2019.

---

[88] See, e.g. https://www.parliament.uk/business/news/2019/march/key-brexit-vote-as-meaningful-vote-returns-to-the-commons/.

[89] See the discussion in Chapter 4.

[90] See, e.g. https://www.parliament.uk/business/news/2019/march/house-of-commons-to-vote-on-no-deal-brexit/.

[91] The so-called 'Spellman amendment', which was passed by 312 votes to 308 votes.

[92] See further, e.g. House of Commons Exiting the EU Committee, *Response to the 12 March 2019 Vote on the Withdrawal Agreement and Political Declaration: Next Steps for Parliament* (HC2073 of 13 March 2019).

[93] See further, e.g. https://www.parliament.uk/business/news/2019/march/house-of-commons-to-vote-on-article-50-extension/.

In this section, we will consider the legal framework as well as the political calculations then surrounding any extension of UK membership pursuant to Article 50(3) TEU; and explore the twin decisions reached by the European Council, in response to requests made by the May Government, to delay the due date of UK withdrawal.

A. Legal Framework and Political Calculations Surrounding Extension

As a matter of Union law, the legal process for requesting an extension is relatively straightforward: Article 50(3) TEU provides for the date of withdrawal to be postponed based on unanimity within the European Council acting with the agreement of the relevant State.[94] As a matter also of UK law, the position was relatively uncomplicated. As the Prime Minister acknowledged in her Commons statement on 26 February 2019, any proposed extension to the UK's membership under Article 50 TEU would require amendments to the UK's existing withdrawal legislation.[95] In particular, the European Union (Withdrawal) Bill as published in 2017 had proposed conferring a delegated power on the Government to define the UK's precise date of departure from the Union ('exit day') as the withdrawal process itself evolved—thereby mimicking under domestic law the inherent flexibility as to the effective date of withdrawal which was already provided for under Article 50 TEU. However, as the draft legislation passed through Parliament, the Government agreed to the demands of Europhobic MPs to enshrine a more precise date in the final statute. Section 20(1) of the European Union (Withdrawal) Act 2018 therefore defined 'exit day' as 23.00 (GMT) on 29 March 2019. Nevertheless, sections 20(3)–(4) provided that, if the Treaties were to cease to apply to the UK, in accordance with Article 50(3) TEU, on a different date from that laid down in section 20(1), the Government could exercise a delegated power to amend the definition of 'exit day' in order to ensure that the latter date reflects the actual date that the Treaties are to cease to apply to the UK.[96]

In both the Union and the UK, the prospect of extension was regarded as an essentially political (rather than any sort of legal) problem.

Let's begin with the UK. The Government had been adamant, throughout almost the entire period after notification of the UK's intention to withdraw, that the UK would leave the Union (preferably on the basis of a negotiated agreement, but without one if necessary) on 30 March 2019. The first official indication that the Government was prepared to consider an extension under Article 50 TEU came with the Prime Minister's announcement on 26 February 2019 that there might well be a Commons vote on the issue—if the First Withdrawal Package were not approved at its second attempt under section 13 *and* if MPs were not willing to support a 'no deal' departure either.[97] Nevertheless, the Government seems to have conceived such an extension only

---

[94] Even if there might also be a need for certain additional or subsequent steps, e.g. to formally revise the date of entry provided for under the withdrawal agreement before its final conclusion by the Council with the consent of the European Parliament.

[95] Prime Minister, *Statement to the House of Commons* (26 February 2019).

[96] Note that exercise of those delegated powers was subject to parliamentary scrutiny in accordance with para 14 of Schedule 7 (i.e. subject to positive approval from both the Commons and the Lords).

[97] Prime Minister, *Statement to the House of Commons* (26 February 2019).

on very specific terms. Its strategy was clearly to bring the same withdrawal package back for a third attempt at approval under section 13 as soon as possible—so that any brief delay to the withdrawal date would serve the sole purpose of completing the necessary implementation and ratification processes.

That may well have been the Government's strategy but by now it was equally clear that the Government's authority and capacity to deliver its own policy preferences were in the process of disintegrating. On 18 March 2019, the Speaker of the House of Commons ruled that the Government could not simply bring the same motion back to the chamber again for yet another vote under section 13 EU(W)A 2018. To do so would contravene a long-established parliamentary convention against repeat attempts to pass the same measure. According to the Speaker, 'if the Government wish to bring forward a new proposition that is neither the same nor substantially the same as that disposed of by the House on 12 March, that would be entirely in order. What the Government cannot legitimately do is to resubmit to the House the same proposition or substantially the same proposition as that of last week . . .'.[98]

The Speaker's intervention appeared fatal to the Government's strategy of staging a third section 13 approval vote on the First Withdrawal Package in time for the upcoming European Council meeting. However, the Government had not specified exactly what its position would be, in precisely such a scenario where the First Withdrawal Package remained unapproved by 20 March 2019. The Prime Minister had merely repeated her previous warnings that (in such circumstances) any extension would likely be for a longer period and require UK participation in the European Parliament elections.[99] Moreover, it was reported that the possibility of requesting any longer extension under Article 50 TEU would threaten to inflame serious internal political disagreements within the Cabinet.[100] It was surely an unenviable position, albeit one largely of her own making: the Commons would not endorse her deal, but was equally opposed to 'no deal'; the situation required more time, but there were apparent limits to what her own party might support.

Not only in the UK, but also from the Union's perspective, the prospect of extension was politically charged. That was true for two main reasons. First, various Union actors had expressed reservations about the prospects of an extension. True, a short extension could in some circumstances be useful to the Union: for example, if the prospects for a negotiated withdrawal collapsed, so that UK withdrawal was inevitable, but the Union, its Member States and citizens/businesses would appreciate additional time to complete their preparedness and contingency plans.[101] Beyond that, it was argued that the Union should be prepared to consider a more substantial extension only if the latter were a necessary consequence of a significant and welcome change in UK policy: such as precisely to hold a second referendum with a substantial possibility

---

[98] See https://hansard.parliament.uk/commons/2019-03-18/debates/AB031E78-C906-4833-9ACF-291998FAC0E1/Speaker'SStatement.

[99] See, e.g. Prime Minister, *Statement in the House of Commons* (13 March 2019). Consider also: HMG, *EU Exit: Parameters of Extending Article 50* (14 March 2019).

[100] See,e.g.https://www.theguardian.com/politics/2019/mar/19/brexit-may-to-ask-eu-for-brexit-extension-as-uk-slides-into-political-crisis.

[101] On which, see further the discussion in Chapter 2.

of a remain victory.[102] Otherwise, however, various Union voices cautioned against agreeing to an extension request where the latter's purpose was simply to allow the UK Government additional time and opportunity to drag out the Article 50 TEU process in a vain attempt either to seek substantial concessions from the EU27 or to exhaust the House of Commons into accepting the proposed withdrawal package, thereby prolonging the damaging state of 'Brexit uncertainty' already inflicted upon the entire Union for several years.[103]

Secondly, the UK situation was further complicated by the fact that elections to the European Parliament were due to commence on 23 May 2019 with the resumption of legislative business then scheduled for 1 July 2019. Depending on the purpose and duration of any proposed delay to the UK's effective date of withdrawal, those European parliamentary elections could be seen as either a matter of indifference, a blessing, or a curse. Indifference would arise where both the Union and the UK might envisage only a short extension, whether to complete the approval/implementation process for a negotiated withdrawal or to finalize preparations for a 'no deal Brexit', with the UK still leaving by 22 May or (at the very latest) in June 2019 and without having participated in the European electoral process. A blessing would occur in the (admittedly rather particular) situation where the UK proposed an extension for the sole purpose of holding a second referendum, with that domestic process to be completed before 22 May or (at the very latest) in June 2019, the UK also having committed to participate (as necessary) in the European parliamentary elections: if Remain were victorious, the UK could immediately affirm its Union membership and still be prepared to send a full complement of newly elected MEPs to sit in the European Parliament; whereas if Leave won again, the UK could depart immediately without having to elect any MEPs or at least without the latter ever taking up their seats.

The curse would afflict virtually every other possible scenario, in which the UK might seek to prolong its Union membership beyond 22 May 2019. On the one hand, the prospect of the UK failing to participate in the European parliamentary elections was legally problematic. Such a scenario would directly contradict the Court's assertion in *Wightman* that, until the actual date of withdrawal and with only very limited exceptions, the UK remained a full Member State of the Union.[104] In particular, the Treaties offered no appropriate mechanism for suspending the UK's due participation in the forthcoming elections—prompting widespread concerns that any delay to the UK's departure without its full participation in the ballot could wreak havoc with the Union's own institutional framework and functioning, by calling directly into question the very constitutional legitimacy of the newly constituted European Parliament.[105]

---

[102] See, e.g. https://www.theguardian.com/world/2019/feb/27/spanish-pm-warns-may-brexit-delay-with-no-plan-not-reasonable-or-desirable.

[103] See, e.g. https://www.theguardian.com/world/2019/mar/12/credible-justification-needed-to-delay-brexit-says-donald-tusk. Note also, e.g. Commission, *Statement by Michel Barnier at the European Parliament Plenary Session* (13 March 2019); *Press Statement by Michel Barnier following the General Affairs Council (Article 50)* (19 March 2019).

[104] Case C-621/18, *Wightman* (EU:C:2018:999).

[105] See further, e.g. https://acelg.blogactiv.eu/2019/03/14/the-complications-of-a-brexit-delay-that-runs-into-the-european-parliament-elections-by-leonard-besselink-and-bastian-michel/.

On the other hand, even the idea of the UK actually taking part in the elections as a withdrawing State posed all manner of political difficulties. At the very least, the Union would have to postpone its plans partially to redistribute the UK's seats among the remaining Member States, in an effort to address various distortions in the existing system of parliamentary representation.[106] Going further, it was understandable that many Member States might object to the prospect of the UK returning a full set of MEPs (even if only on a temporary basis): the latter were bound to include yet another cohort of Farage-led agitators whose contribution to European parliamentary business was minimal, if not altogether negative, and whose avowed objective was to disrupt the good functioning of the wider Union at every opportunity.[107] That prospect was all the more unwelcome given that, for several governments, the 2019 elections were being framed explicitly as a 'battle for the soul of Europe'—a battle in which the UK risked offering a greater boost to the hard-right populists than to more mainstream political groupings.[108]

B. First Extension Request and Decision

Against that complicated political background, the Prime Minister submitted her first request for an extension under Article 50 TEU on 20 March 2019: the UK was seeking a prolongation of its Union membership only until 30 June 2019 and only for the purposes of approving the existing withdrawal package and ratifying/implementing its withdrawal agreement.[109]

In other words, the Government seemed to be reaffirming its previous strategy, simply regardless of the adverse political circumstances ranged against it both at home and within the EU. After all, the chances of securing parliamentary consent to the First Withdrawal Package at any point in the foreseeable future appeared slim: the Prime Minister had failed to articulate any credible plan for dealing with the situation where her strategy had clearly failed; in any event, the Government had deliberately omitted any request for a longer date of the sort that might offer time and space to find a more radical alternative solution; and last but far from least, the suggested date of 30 June 2019 posed a direct challenge to the smooth conduct of the European elections. Indeed, so peculiar was the Prime Minister's request that some commentators perceived it to be little more than a deliberate attempt to shift political responsibility for a 'no deal' outcome (if indeed that should occur) away from the UK authorities and onto the Union's own shoulders.

---

[106] In accordance with European Council Decision 2018/937 establishing the composition of the European Parliament, OJ 2018 L 165/1.

[107] Concerns eventually borne out by the success of Farage's new-style Brexit Party in the 2019 European elections.

[108] E.g. French President Macron described the 2019 European elections as part of an 'existential fight' for the future of the EU: see https://www.france24.com/en/20190521-macron-jumps-eu-campaign-warning-existential-risk.

[109] Available via https://assets.publishing.service.gov.uk/government/uploads/system/uploads/attachment_data/file/787434/PM_to_President_of_the_European_Council.pdf.

If 'passing the blame' was indeed part of the UK's political calculations, the Union managed the situation adroitly. Effectively ignoring the contents of the Prime Minster's letter, the EU27 instead set out the terms for an alternative extension scenario under Article 50 TEU.[110] In the event that the First Withdrawal Agreement was approved in the House of Commons by 29 March 2019 at the latest, the period provided for in Article 50(3) TEU would be extended until 22 May 2019. However, in the event that the First Withdrawal Agreement remained unapproved by the House of Commons by 29 March 2019 at the latest, the period provided for in Article 50(3) TEU would instead be extended until 12 April 2019. In that event, the UK was expected to indicate a way forward before 12 April 2019. In either case, a special European Council (in its Article 50 TEU formation) meeting was scheduled for 10 April 2019 to take stock of developments and (if necessary) to consider any further UK proposals.

The substantive contents of the conclusions were translated (with the agreement of the UK) into a formal European Council decision under Article 50(3) TEU.[111] The preamble to that First Extension Decision is noteworthy, insofar as it indicates the collective thinking of the EU27, already in anticipation of the UK failing to approve the First Withdrawal Package by 29 March 2019, but still being reluctant to depart on 12 April 2019 without any deal in place, and thus likely to return with an alternative plan or at least a further extension request. In the first place, the EU27 observe that, if the UK is still a Member State on 23–26 May 2019, it will be under an obligation to hold elections to the European Parliament in accordance with Union law (with the UK expected to give notice of the poll by 12 April 2019 in order to hold such elections). In the second place, the EU27 reaffirm that any extension would exclude reopening the proposed Withdrawal Agreement (though nothing in the First Extension Decision rules out redrafting the proposed Political Declaration). In the third place, the EU27 also recall that any unilateral commitment, statement or other act by the UK must be compatible with the letter and the spirit of the First Withdrawal Agreement.

C. Making Good Use of the Extra Time Available?

In the light of the First Extension Decision, the definition of 'exit day' under the European Union (Withdrawal) Act 2018 was amended to reflect the European Council's terms for a delay to the UK departure.[112] But the main question was: how would the Government and Parliament now use the limited window of extra time that had just been granted by the EU27? The short answer was: by engaging in a ping-pong of parallel processes that ultimately yielded no tangible progress by the deadline the European Council had set for a meaningful UK response.

To start with, the Prime Minister returned from the European Council and immediately confirmed that the Government remained committed to securing approval for its existing withdrawal package while admitting that there was as yet insufficient support for the Government to be confident of winning any third vote under section 13.

---

[110] European Council (Article 50), *Conclusions of 21 March 2019*.
[111] European Council Decision 2019/476, OJ 2019 L I 80/1.
[112] See European Union (Withdrawal) Act 2018 (Exit Day) (Amendment) Regulations 2019.

Nevertheless, the Government still declared itself opposed to all other options: for example, the proposed process of holding 'indicative votes' in the Commons as a means of testing the views of MPs; any longer extension under Article 50 TEU that would entail UK participation in the European elections; and most of all, halting Brexit altogether either through direct revocation or following a second referendum.[113]

Despite the Government's avowed hostility, the House of Commons nevertheless voted to take temporary control of its own internal proceedings in order to conduct a first round of 'indicative votes' in the hope that MPs might be able to identify an alternative solution to the UK's political impasse capable of commanding a workable parliamentary majority.[114] However, when the votes were held on 27 March 2019, they yielded no conclusive outcome: of the eight possible strategies presented to MPs, none managed to secure majority support. Several came close: for example, a proposal to renegotiate the First Political Declaration so as to commit the UK to negotiate a permanent and comprehensive UK-wide customs union with the EU;[115] and a call for the Commons not to allow implementation and ratification of any withdrawal agreement or framework for the future EU–UK relationship unless and until those were approved in a confirmatory public vote.[116] Others fell far short: for example, a proposal to renegotiate the First Political Declaration so as to provide for the UK's EFTA/EEA membership, for a 'comprehensive customs arrangement' to last until replaced by an alternative agreement that would guarantee both frictionless trade and no hard border in Ireland, together with full and fair enforcement of the Union's free movement rules on work-seekers and economically inactive persons;[117] and inevitably also the standard Europhobic call for the UK to simply leave with no deal on 12 April 2019.[118]

Both Government and Parliament appeared stuck. Yet the terms of the First Extension Decision required the House of Commons quickly to approve the First Withdrawal Agreement, if the UK were to be guaranteed any extension of membership until 22 May 2019. The Government therefore announced plans to hold another vote on the First Withdrawal Agreement on 29 March 2019. It is worth stressing that this was not a valid motion for approval of the entire First Withdrawal Package as required under section 13 EU(W)A 2018—the Speaker having reiterated the need for the Government to make substantial changes to its proposition before any such third vote could be held.[119] Instead, this was a motion specifically for approval of the First Withdrawal Agreement and solely for the purposes of complying with the European Council's conditions for extension under Article 50(3) TEU. Even still, the Government treated it as a crucial test of how far the Commons might have shifted opinion since the previous section 13 vote and, in particular, how many hard right

---

[113] Prime Minister, *Statement on the European Council* (25 March 2019).
[114] See, e.g. https://www.parliament.uk/business/news/2019/march/whats-next-for-brexit-house-of-commons-holds-indicative-votes/.
[115] For: 264; Against: 272.
[116] For: 268; Against: 295.
[117] For: 188; Against: 283.
[118] For: 160; Against: 400.
[119] See, e.g. https://www.theguardian.com/politics/2019/mar/27/andrea-leadsom-government-intends-to-revive-theresa-may-brexit-deal-this-week.

Tories might have fallen into line behind the First Withdrawal Package, out of fear that a longer delay could lead to a closer EU–UK relationship or even a second referendum.

In a sign of just how desperate the Government was to win the backing of Europhobic MPs, Theresa May even committed herself to stepping down as Prime Minister if the Commons now approved the First Withdrawal Agreement.[120] But it was all in vain: the Government was defeated once again, this time by 58 votes—thus sacrificing the conditional possibility of an extension until 22 May 2019 and obliging the UK to bring forward a new plan, for consideration by the European Council at its upcoming meeting on 10 April 2019, or face a 'no deal' departure on 12 April 2019.[121]

The Government's latest failure gave another opportunity for Parliament to show whether it could offer an any more constructive way forward. The House of Commons again assumed temporary control of its own business in order to conduct a second round of 'indicative votes' (held on 1 April 2019).[122] This time, four options were presented to MPs. The previous proposal for renegotiation of the First Political Declaration with a view to negotiating a permanent and comprehensive UK-wide customs union with the EU was again narrowly defeated;[123] as was the renewed call for the Commons to refuse implementation and ratification of any withdrawal package unless and until the latter was approved in another referendum.[124]

MPs also rejected a revised proposal to renegotiate the First Political Declaration so as to provide for UK membership of EFTA and the EEA, together with terms relating to frictionless agri-food trade across the EU–UK border, plus a 'comprehensive customs arrangement' which also gave the UK a say on future EU trade deals (to be replaced by alternative arrangements that would maintain frictionless trade and prevent a hard border in Ireland).[125] The final unsuccessful option sought to ensure that the UK would revoke its original notification of intention to withdraw under Article 50 TEU rather than actually embark upon a 'no deal' departure which MPs had refused positively to endorse —in which event, the Government would be obliged to organize a public inquiry to explore whether any future EU–UK relationship could command majority support in a public referendum on whether to re-trigger Article 50 TEU and renegotiate the terms of departure on the basis of such a model.[126]

Two rounds of 'indicative votes' had therefore yielded no alternative plan clearly capable of commanding majority support among MPs. The initiative passed back from the Commons to the Government and, on 2 April 2019, the Prime Minister announced plans to request a second extension under Article 50 TEU—to be as short as possible and only for the purpose of ensuring an orderly withdrawal.[127] But in addition, the Prime Minister invited the Leader of the Opposition to talks with a view

---

[120] See, e.g. https://www.theguardian.com/politics/2019/mar/27/theresa-may-to-resign-before-next-phase-of-brexit.

[121] Of course: ruling out any realistic possibility that the May Government would simply revoke its original notification of intention to leave the Union.

[122] See, e.g. https://www.parliament.uk/business/news/2019/april/house-of-commons-holds-second-round-of-indicative-votes/.

[123] For: 273; Against: 276.

[124] For: 280; Against: 292.

[125] For: 261; Against: 282.

[126] For: 191; Against: 292.

[127] Prime Minister, *Statement on Brexit* (2 April 2019).

to agreeing a common plan for a negotiated departure from the Union (working on the assumption that the terms of the First Withdrawal Agreement had been settled and so focusing only on potential changes to the First Political Declaration). If the Conservative and Labour leaders could agree on a model for the future EU–UK relationship (albeit one that still 'delivers on the referendum') it could be presented for approval in the Commons then brought for discussion to the European Council. If not, the two leaders might at least agree on a series of options for the future EU–UK relationship that could then be tested in the Commons in a fresh series of 'indicative votes'—with the Government promising to abide by the outcome, provided that the Opposition agreed to do the same. Either way, the Government would then bring forward draft legislation for implementing the First Withdrawal Agreement into domestic law with a clear timetable for it to be adopted before 22 May 2019—thereby ensuring that the UK did not take part in the European elections.

On that basis, the Prime Minister formulated another extension request for submission to the European Council while discussions commenced between the Conservative and Labour leaderships with a view to identifying a common plan or at least an agreed range of options. Backbench MPs did, however, have another (if ultimately rather pointless) moment of independent power: a bill was rushed through the House of Commons, and then the House of Lords, forcing the Government to seek a further extension under Article 50 TEU in accordance with a date chosen by the Prime Minister but subject to amendment by MPs. In the end, MPs did not challenge the Prime Minister's second extension request. The original bill had also proposed that, if the European Council were to counter-suggest a different date to that requested by the Prime Minister, the Government would have to seek additional Commons approval before acceding to that alternative date. However, that draft provision was deleted from the final version of the European Union (Withdrawal) Act 2019.[128] When the time came, the European Council did indeed propose an alternative extension and the UK Government was obliged to accept it as a fait accompli.

D. Second Extension Request and Decision

On 5 April 2019, Theresa May wrote to the President of the European Council requesting a second extension under Article 50 TEU. Having summarized the approach announced in her statement of 2 April 2019, she argued that talks with Labour, whether they led to an agreed plan or instead a series of options, would still require more time. The UK recognized this additional delay might overlap with the European parliamentary elections and (if so) the UK would respect its legal obligation to participate, though the Government was determined to complete the UK's departure before then. The Prime Minister therefore proposed (once again) an extension until 30 June 2019—but with the actual date of withdrawal capable of being brought forward, possibly and preferably even to before 23 May 2019.[129]

---

[128] As adopted on 8 April 2019.

[129] Available via https://assets.publishing.service.gov.uk/government/uploads/system/uploads/attachment_data/file/793058/PM_letter_to_His_Excellency_Mr_Donald_Tusk__1_.pdf.

The UK's second extension request was always bound to be more controversial within the Union than the first. Already, on 3 April 2019, the Commission President had argued that 12 April 2019 should be treated as the absolute deadline for the UK to approve the First Withdrawal Agreement on the basis of a sustainable majority. If that deadline was met, the Union should be prepared to grant another short extension until 22 May 2019—during which time, there could be discussions over and amendments to the First Political Declaration. But otherwise, the Union should not offer the UK any further short extension that would risk endangering the integrity of the European elections and undermining the smooth functioning of the Union's own institutions. Moreover, if that meant a 'no deal' departure, the Union should still insist that the UK address the Union's same three priority separation issues (protecting citizens' rights, paying the financial settlement and safeguarding the Irish border) as a strict condition for rebuilding trust into the future.[130]

The UK's second extension request certainly prompted intense discussions among the EU27 at their meeting on 10 April 2019. Once again, many commentators regarded the UK's actions and intentions with suspicion: despite having made no appreciable progress with the extra time it had already been given, and still lacking any credible alternative plan to deal with the situation, the UK had effectively repeated the same extension date as before and did so regardless of the fact that it would raise the same problems and objections (not least for the European elections). Perhaps by this stage the Government was genuinely devoid of any meaningful capacity or fresh imagination to manage its own predicament. Or maybe it simply calculated that, with 'no deal' still very much a live possibility, any refusal by the Union to accede to the UK's request for an extension could more easily be portrayed as an outcome inflicted upon the British against their will.[131]

Whatever the true motivations of the UK Government, the EU27 once again responded by effectively ignoring the dates suggested by the Prime Minister and devising its own alternative extension mechanism.[132] The European Council was prepared to offer an extension to allow for ratification of the First Withdrawal Agreement but only for as long as necessary: until 31 October 2019 at the latest, though if the Withdrawal Agreement were to be ratified before that date, the UK's departure should take place on the first day of the following month. However, no extension could be allowed to undermine the regular functioning of the Union and its institutions: if the UK remains a Member State on 23–26 May 2019 but has not yet ratified the First Withdrawal Agreement before then, the UK must hold European parliamentary elections in accordance with Union law. If the UK fails to live up to that obligation, its withdrawal will take place on 1 June 2019.

Besides the details of the new extension, the European Council offered several additional conclusions. First, the EU27 reiterated that there could be no reopening of the

---

[130] Available via https://ec.europa.eu/commission/presscorner/detail/en/SPEECH_19_1970. Similarly, e.g. Commission, *Speech by Michel Barnier at the EPC Breakfast* (1 April 2019). But contrast with, e.g. European Council, *Report by Donald Tusk to the European Parliament on March European Council Meetings* (27 March 2019).

[131] See further, e.g. Editorial Comments, 'When the music finally stops, who'll be left holding the Brexit parcel?', 56 *CMLRev* (2019) 611.

[132] European Council (Article 50), *Conclusions of 10 April 2019*.

First Withdrawal Agreement; while any unilateral commitment, statement, or other act by the UK should be compatible with the letter and the spirit of that text and must not hamper its implementation. Secondly, while the additional extension cannot be used to start negotiations on the future EU–UK relationship, if the UK's position were to evolve, the European Council would be prepared to reconsider the terms of the First Political Declaration (though only in accordance with the positions and principles laid down in its previous guidelines and statements). Thirdly, the European Council emphasized that, during the additional extension, the UK will remain a Member State with full rights and obligations under the Treaties. That includes the right to revoke its original Article 50 TEU notification at any time. Fourthly, the EU27 noted the UK's commitment to act in a constructive and responsible manner throughout its additional extension, in accordance with the duty of sincere cooperation, and expected the UK to fulfil that commitment and duty in a manner that reflected its situation as a withdrawing State—in particular when it came to participation in the Union's decision-making processes.

As we saw in Chapter 3, the prospect of a Member State's withdrawal from the Union raised questions about how far the legal duty of sincere cooperation might be called upon, and indeed might need to be specially adapted, so as to help manage such an exceptional situation.[133] The issue of whether and how to define further the implications of the UK's commitment to and duty of sincere cooperation now appears to have prompted particular discussion among the EU27. The question arose, how far could and should the Union seek to impose certain enhanced obligations or terms of conditionality upon the UK during any additional period of membership: for example, whereby the UK should recuse itself from certain institutions, bodies, or meetings; and/or abstain from voting on certain Union measures or decisions. Any such proposals would have raised difficult questions not just of politics (based on concerns about the de facto creation of second-class membership and the potential precedent it could set for situations beyond a delayed withdrawal under Article 50 TEU) but also of law (given the clear terms of the Court's ruling in *Wightman* and the self-evident need to reconcile any purported form of conditionality with the relevant institutional and procedural provisions of the Treaties).[134]

In the end, the EU27 refrained from articulating any more specific terms of sincere cooperation for the UK during its prolongation of membership. But the European Council's conclusions do provide that, in addition to the relevant European Council and Council meetings specifically identified in Article 50 TEU itself, the EU27 and the Commission (where appropriate together with other Union institutions, bodies, offices, and agencies) should continue to meet separately at all levels to discuss matters related to the situation after the UK's withdrawal—thus confirming the position already taken by the Union throughout the Article 50 TEU process.[135]

The European Council's formal decision on the terms of the second extension under Article 50 TEU was adopted (with the agreement of the UK) on 11 April 2019: the

---

[133] As first addressed in European Council (Article 50), *Guidelines following the United Kingdom's notification under Article 50 TEU* (29 April 2017).

[134] Case C-621/18, *Wightman* (EU:C:2018:999).

[135] See further the discussion in Chapter 3.

date of withdrawal is extended until 31 October 2019; but the extension will cease to apply on 31 May 2019 in the event that the UK has not held elections to the European Parliament in accordance with Union law and has not ratified the First Withdrawal Agreement by 22 May 2019.[136] On the same day, the definition of 'exit day' under the European Union (Withdrawal) Act 2018 was amended for the purposes of domestic UK law;[137] while the Commission and UK Government agreed to a small number of technical amendments to the text of the First Withdrawal Agreement so as to reflect the decision of the European Council.[138]

The European Council declared that it would remain seized of the matter and re-view progress at its next meeting in June 2019.[139] But in the meantime, the EU27 had managed to sidestep whatever potential traps had been laid out (deliberately or oth-erwise) by the Prime Minister: offering enough flexibility in terms of both the date of withdrawal and the possibility of revisiting the First Political Declaration as to provide the British with more time to solve their domestic political crisis; but without either reopening the First Withdrawal Agreement or endangering the autonomy and integ-rity of the Union institutions; yet still keeping the door open for the UK to change its mind, revoke, and remain a Member State. The underlying message was unmistak-able: the UK must take responsibility for the consequences of its own decisions or inactions.[140]

5. The Demise of Theresa May and her Replacement by Boris Johnson

Between the European Council's Second Extension Decision of April 2019 and elec-tions to the European Parliament in June 2019, the UK's political attention centred on the Prime Minister's call for talks between the Conservative and Labour party leaderships—aimed at thrashing out an agreed solution to the current impasse that stood a reasonable chance of being approved in the House of Commons; or at least identifying a range of options that could be presented to MPs on the understanding that their choice would then be respected by the Government and the Opposition.[141]

At first glance, the UK Government might have appeared finally to have given up on pandering to the hard-right Tories and DUP, and have sought instead to build a new cross-party consensus capable of delivering the parliamentary majority required

---

[136] European Council Decision 2019/584, OJ 2019 L 101/1.

[137] See the European Union (Withdrawal) Act 2018 (Exit Day) (Amendment) (No 2) Regulations 2019.

[138] See the Exchange of Letters between the EU and the UK setting out the limited technical changes to the Withdrawal Agreement to reflect the extension of the Article 50 period (11 April 2019) available (together with a revised text of the First Withdrawal Agreement) via https://ec.europa.eu/commission/publications/exchange-letters-between-eu-and-uk-setting-out-limited-technical-changes-withdrawal-agreement-reflect-extension-article-50-period-11-april-2019_en.

[139] European Council (Article 50), *Conclusions of 10 April 2019*, at para 9.

[140] Though note also the more optimistic message expressed by Donald Tusk, *Report and Concluding Remarks to the European Parliament on the Special European Council (Art 50) meeting on 10 April* (16 April 2019).

[141] See also Theresa May, *Commons statement* (11 April 2019).

for a negotiated withdrawal.[142] And indeed, perhaps one should not be unduly cynical: even though previous offers of cross-party talks seem to have been conducted only on the Prime Minister's terms, this latest initiative could well have been her first genuine attempt to find a workable path forward based on political compromise.

But even on the most generous assessment, the prospects for success of those cross-party talks never seemed much better than bleak. The reason for such pessimism was not because the Conservative and Labour leaders were actually so very far apart in their viewpoints on many of the key issues. After all, both Theresa May and Jeremy Corbyn proclaimed themselves committed to respecting the outcome of the 2016 referendum; and neither the First Withdrawal Agreement in general nor the proposed Irish backstop in particular were the subject of serious dispute between the two sides. The main difference in perspective lay rather upon the prospect of redrafting the First Political Declaration on future EU–UK relations: for example, how could Labour's preference for a full EU–UK customs union possibly be reconciled with the Tories' desire for an independent UK trade policy?

Moreover, even if the two party leaders managed to hammer out some vague formula capable of reconciling their apparently contradictory Brexit aspirations, May and Corbyn would each only run the risk of provoking outright rebellion within their respective parties in both Parliament and across the country at large: significant concessions towards the Labour position might finally split the already warring Tories; endorsing Brexit (at all, but especially without promising a second referendum, to chose between any proposed deal or remaining in the Union) could be an equally damaging path for Labour to pursue.

Against that background, it was widely and not unreasonably assumed that the Government's invitation to parley was motivated also and in at least equal measure by the expectation that cross-party talks might in themselves accelerate within Labour the same open conflict as was already engulfing the Tories: both parties would share in the blame for whatever outcome emerged; if it came to it, both parties could plunge together in flames into the Brexit abyss. Conversely, it was easy to imagine that Labour's enthusiasm to engage in cross-party talks was also and in at least equal measure aimed at avoiding precisely any such outcome: being seen to talk in good faith, while articulating principled reasons for resisting agreement with an uncompromising Government, could allow Labour to escape being saddled with responsibility for the failure of cross-party talks, while also ensuring that Brexit remained firmly a Tory policy.

In the end, six weeks of Tory–Labour talks indeed failed to produce any tangible results (let alone the elusive parliamentary breakthrough longed for by the Prime Minister). In particular, the Conservative leadership's suggestion of negotiating a temporary EU–UK customs union, but with any future government remaining free to end such an arrangement and instead pursue an entirely independent trade policy, still fell far short of the Labour Party's demand for a much closer framework of future EU–UK

---

[142] See Prime Minister, *Statement on Brexit* (2 April 2019) available at https://www.gov.uk/government/speeches/pm-statement-on-brexit-2-april-2019; also, e.g. Prime Minister, *Statement on the European Council* (11 April 2019) available at https://www.gov.uk/government/speeches/pm-statement-on-european-council-11-april-2019.

relations. Faced with the imminent prospect of elections to the European Parliament in which the Conservatives were expected to suffer humiliating losses, Theresa May made one final attempt to secure approval for her withdrawal package by making a series of additional promises to her various tribes of domestic opponents and seeking to sell the combined result as a 'New Brexit Deal'.[143]

It is clear from the nature of those promises that the primary goal of May's last-ditch plan was, once again, to win over the Tory rebels and their DUP allies. For example, the Government would come under a legal obligation to seek to find 'alternative border arrangements' that could prevent the UK ever having to implement the Irish backstop; if that backstop were indeed activated, Great Britain would remain in regulatory alignment with Northern Ireland (i.e. the EU) so as to avoid the imposition or expansion of checks across the Irish Sea; and the devolved authorities in Northern Ireland would have to consent to new EU regulatory standards being added to the existing alignment obligations contained in the backstop.

But in addition, Theresa May's 'New Brexit Deal' contained certain elements aimed at retaining/attracting the support of Labour MPs willing to break ranks and support the First Withdrawal Package: for example, a new 'Workers' Rights Bill' that would ensure UK employment standards remained at least as favourable as those provided for under EU law; as well as a guarantee that there would be no change in the UK's environmental protection standards, overseen by a new and independent Office of Environmental Protection. As usual, however, the political value of the Prime Minister's various offerings was undermined by the legal reality of the UK constitution: even promises which might be 'entrenched in law' for the time being, were ultimately unenforceable against any future government with a working Commons majority.

Perhaps the most important elements in May's 'New Brexit Deal' were those with a more short-term focus on identifying immediate steps to resolve the current parliamentary impasse. In the first place, the Prime Minister offered a legal obligation to secure approval from the House of Commons both for the Government's negotiating objectives on the future EU–UK relationship and for any proposed treaties governing that relationship; coupled with a further legal duty for the Government to seek as close to frictionless trade as possible with the EU specifically in the field of goods (while still placing the UK outside the Single Market). For those purposes, Parliament itself would decide (during the process of adopting the implementing legislation required under section 13 EU(W)A 2018 and therefore before the UK's actual withdrawal from the EU) whether the UK should prioritize pursuing its own independent trade policy or instead remaining in some form of customs union with the EU.

In the second place, the Prime Minister even sought to attract the (before now largely elusive) support of parliamentary campaigners for a second referendum: if the Commons were to vote to approve her withdrawal package, the draft legislation which was then required under section 13 for the purposes of implementing the First Withdrawal Agreement into domestic law would include a requirement for the Commons to vote on whether to hold another popular vote, which (if supported by

---

[143] See, in particular, Theresa May, *Speech on New Brexit Deal* (21 May 2019); and Prime Minister, *Statement on New Brexit Deal* (22 May 2019).

the Commons) would then have to be held before the Government could proceed to final ratification. Nevertheless, the Prime Minister made clear that she herself remained deeply opposed to holding any second referendum.

The Prime Minister suggested that, in order not to ask the Commons to approve a withdrawal package MPs had already twice rejected, she would seek the EU's agreement to revise the First Political Declaration so as to reflect the terms of her 'New Brexit Deal'. Commons approval of a revised withdrawal package, in accordance with section 13 EU(W)A 2018, could then pave the way for adoption of the necessary implementing legislation, with a view to the UK's withdrawal from the EU finally taking place by the end of July 2019.

However, the Conservative Party's electoral humiliation in the European parliamentary elections, held in the UK on 23 May 2019, dealt the final and fatal blow to Theresa May's authority and position.[144] On 24 May 2019, she announced her own resignation as leader of the Conservative Party with effect from 7 June 2019; and then as Prime Minister of the UK, once the process of finding a new Tory leader had been concluded.[145]

It is understandable that the Union's attention during this particular period was focused largely on managing its own constitutional affairs, rather than indulging the latest political pandemonium in London. In particular, the EU27 had to digest the outcome of the European Parliament elections and negotiate the appointment of key Union officeholders; including another President of the European Council, the next President of the Commission, and indeed the entire college of new Commissioners, as well as the High Representative of the Union for Foreign Affairs and Security Policy.[146]

But of course, there was still enough time and space to register the fact that a major change had occurred in British politics and a new period of uncertainty was about to begin: for example, on 12 June 2019, the Commission published its latest assessment of the Union's 'no deal' contingency plans, noting that such an outcome remained undesirable yet very much possible, particularly given the domestic political situation in the UK.[147] Michel Barnier continued to remind his UK counterpart that a withdrawal agreement remained the best vehicle for delivering an orderly UK departure and creating the necessary trust for negotiating an ambitious future relationship with the Union.[148] But EU27 leaders expressed their frustration with the interminable chaos afflicting the UK and voiced reservations about the wisdom of prolonging the uncertainty still further by offering London any more extensions under Article 50(3) TEU.[149]

---

[144] The Tories won less than 10 per cent of the UK vote and took only 4 seats in the European Parliament. See further, e.g. Vasilopoulou, 'Brexit and the 2019 EP Election in the UK', 58 *JCMS Annual Review* (2020) 80.

[145] Prime Minister, *Statement in Downing Street* (24 May 2019).

[146] Leading to political approval of a new 'senior leadership team' as announced by the European Council on 2 July 2019: see European Council, *Conclusions of 30 June–2 July 2019*.

[147] See COM(2019) 276 Final (together with Annexes I and II). Note also: House of Commons Exiting the EU Committee, *The Consequences of No Deal for UK Business* (HC2560 of 19 July 2019).

[148] See, e.g. Commission, *Reply from* Michel Barnier, *Chief Negotiator, to Steve* Barclay, *Secretary of State for Exiting the European Union, on citizens' rights* (18 June 2019).

[149] E.g. https://www.theguardian.com/politics/2019/jun/20/eu-wont-negotiate-on-boris-johnson-brexit-plan-says-dutch-pm-mark-rutte.

6. Renegotiating the Withdrawal Package (Even if Only Under Duress)

The new leader of the Conservative Party, Boris Johnson, replaced Theresa May as UK Prime Minister on 24 July 2019. Johnson immediately made clear that he was determined to reprise his 2016 role as 'Brexiter-in-Chief' and to bring about a decisive change in the UK's political orientation: the UK would be leaving the EU on 31 October 2019, 'no ifs or buts';[150] to do otherwise would cause 'a catastrophic loss of confidence in our political system'.[151]

In practice, several of Johnson's initial acts in office were essentially theatrical devices designed to appease his core support base by reinforcing his 'do or die' promise to ensure that UK withdrawal finally occurred by 31 October 2019.[152] For example, on 18 August 2019, the Government decided to adopt the secondary legislation required under the European Union (Withdrawal) Act 2018 that would make formal provision for repeal of the European Communities Act 1972—rather disingenuously portrayed as 'a clear signal to the people of this country that there is no turning back—we are leaving the EU as promised on October 31, whatever the circumstances'.[153] Similarly, the UK announced that its ministers and other officials would cease to attend 'most EU meetings' with effect from 1 September 2019, in order that the UK could concentrate its resources on more pressing domestic tasks, and making exceptions only for meetings where the British had a 'significant national interest' in the outcome of discussions.[154] Shortly afterwards, the UK Government also confirmed that, since the UK would be leaving the EU on 31 October 2019 'whatever the circumstances', the UK would not be nominating a candidate for the Commission; though this was not intended to prevent the EU from proceeding to appoint its new College of Commissioners with effect from 1 November 2019.[155]

Alongside the domestic theatrics, however, Johnson did outline his thinking around the Article 50 TEU process in a statement to the House of Commons.[156] He would prefer that the UK left the EU on 31 October 2019 on the basis of a negotiated settlement. But the terms of the First Withdrawal Package were unacceptable: no country that valued its independence and self-respect could agree to the backstop; the latter provisions could not be saved by some sort of time-limit but must now be abolished altogether. Without engaging in any more detailed discussion or providing any more specific evidence, Johnson asserted that the problems surrounding the Irish border

---

[150] Boris Johnson, *First Speech as Prime Minster* (24 July 2019).

[151] Boris Johnson, *Statement on Priorities for the Government* (25 July 2019).

[152] See, e.g. https://www.politicshome.com/news/article/boris-johnson-vows-to-deliver-brexit-do-or-die-by-31-october.

[153] See https://www.gov.uk/government/news/brexit-secretary-signs-order-to-scrap-1972-brussels-act-ending-all-eu-law-in-the-uk (press statement of 18 August 2019).

[154] See https://www.gov.uk/government/news/uk-officials-will-stop-attending-most-eu-meetings-from-1-september (press statement of 20 August 2019).

[155] Seehttps://www.gov.uk/government/news/the-uk-will-not-nominate-a-new-commissioner-to-the-eu (press statement of 23 August 2019) and Letter from the UK's Permanent Representative to the EU https://assets.publishing.service.gov.uk/government/uploads/system/uploads/attachment_data/file/827315/Nomination_of_a_Commissioner_-_FINAL.pdf>> (23 August 2019).

[156] Prime Minister, *Statement on Priorities for the Government* (25 July 2019).

should be dealt with in negotiations over the future EU–UK relationship and could be solved through 'other arrangements' without all or any part of the UK remaining in either the Customs Union or the Single Market. Moreover, if the EU were unwilling to reopen the text of the First Withdrawal Agreement for renegotiation, then the UK would indeed leave without any agreement—with Johnson explicitly threatening (for example) also to renege on the UK's financial liabilities arising from its period of Union membership.

If Johnson's statement in the Commons was somewhat lacking in specifics, his subsequent letter to the President of the European Council did at least offer greater insight into the UK's revised strategic thinking.[157] To begin with, Johnson criticizes the backstop which had been proposed and supported by his predecessor as 'anti-democratic and inconsistent with the sovereignty of the UK': that backstop would lock the British into its provisions on a potentially indefinite basis; create a substantial regulatory border between Northern Ireland and Great Britain; and subject Northern Ireland to external rules and bodies over which its people had no control. But Johnson goes further: given his regime's emphasis on the UK's future freedom to diverge from EU rules, Johnson now explicitly renounces the Government's solemn commitment, as contained in the Joint Report of December 2017, to avoid a 'hard border' across the island of Ireland (if needs be) through full alignment with relevant EU customs and regulatory standards.[158] For those reasons, the existing backstop provisions cannot form part of any revised withdrawal agreement. In its place, Johnson called for a legally binding commitment that neither the UK nor the EU would impose any form of infrastructure, checks or controls at the border between Ireland and Northern Ireland. Instead, the two parties should explore alternative ways of managing their customs and regulatory differences—hoping to find and implement creative solutions before the end of the proposed transition period and as part of the future EU–UK relationship, while remaining ready to look constructively at what should happen if such arrangements were not fully in place within that projected timescale.

In other words: the EU and the UK should place their joint faith in discovering some 'border management' system of the sort Leave campaigners had fantasized about for several years already, yet without any objective basis in technological or logistical reality; while at the same time subscribing to an unspecified body of commitments, to be called upon when the proposed transition period expired and no credible 'border management' system had materialized, so as seamlessly to integrate their distinct customs and regulatory territories—but having ruled out any lawful recourse to the traditional tools of border checks and controls across the island of Ireland, so as to protect the integrity of the Customs Union and the Single Market.

Small wonder many commentators regarded Johnson's proposals as seriously lacking in credibility. Indeed, many observers believed that Johnson's real strategic objectives were implied rather than expressed in his letter to the European Council President: to do no more than pretend to engage in serious negotiations with the EU with a view to revising the existing withdrawal package; but, in practice, to proceed on the basis that the UK would leave the Union on 31 October 2019 without

---

[157] Prime Minister, *Letter to Donald Tusk* (19 August 2019).
[158] See Joint Report from the EU and UK negotiators (8 December 2017), at para 49.

any negotiated settlement—not as some default or undesirable outcome, but as the Government's positively preferred course of action.

A reasonable range of evidence can be called upon to support the hypothesis that procuring a 'no deal Brexit' was indeed Johnson's strategy in the period immediately after assuming office.[159] After all, his repeated promise that the UK would leave on 31 October 2019 'do or die', coupled with the wilfully amateurish if not altogether preposterous nature of his proposals for renegotiation of the First Withdrawal Agreement, already suggested that this was not intended as a serious attempt to reopen the Article 50 TEU process with a view to securing a meaningful change in the UK's terms of withdrawal. But in addition, the UK media reported various accusations that the new UK Government had secretly promised the hard-line Europhobes of the Tory Party's European Research Group that, in return for their support, Johnson would (by one means or another) ultimately favour their preferred 'no deal' outcome to the entire Brexit process.[160] Moreover, the UK Government's domestic claims that good progress was being made in renegotiations with the EU were publicly contradicted by the Commission, which insisted that the British had failed to bring forward any formal proposals that could provide the basis for further discussions. Indeed, as late as 18 September 2019, both the Commission President and its Chief Negotiator confirmed that the UK Government had merely explained and reiterated its objections to the existing backstop provisions, but without yet providing any more concrete proposal that could provide the basis for their replacement.[161]

Perhaps most significant, certainly from a legal perspective, was Johnson's decision (constitutionally requested of the Queen on 27 or 28 August 2019) to prorogue the Westminster Parliament for an extended period of time, lasting from 9 or 12 September 2019 until 14 October 2019. That decision was supposedly motivated by the need to prepare for a new Queen's Speech setting out the Government's revised legislative agenda. But in practice, Johnson's decision to shut down Parliament was widely attributed to his desire to suppress any further scrutiny of or interference in his Brexit plans.

In particular, it was clear both that the House of Commons was increasingly sceptical of Johnson's claim to be making good progress in his renegotiation efforts and that MPs remained as determined as ever to prevent the Government leading the UK towards a 'no deal' exit. Indeed, a cross-party alliance of MPs were actively planning to introduce legislation forcing the Prime Minister to request a further extension of the UK's planned departure date in accordance with Article 50(3) TEU, rather than risk reaching 31 October 2019 without the guarantee of any agreement on the terms for an

---

[159] Note also earlier reports that Johnson sought to pressurize Theresa May into pursuing a 'harder Brexit', e.g. 'Michael Gove and Boris Johnson send secret Brexit letter to May' (*The Guardian*, 12 November 2017); and that was even before Johnson's resignation from Government after publication of the 'Chequers Plan' in July 2018.

[160] See, e.g. https://www.thelondoneconomic.com/politics/erg-mps-reveal-how-johnsons-deal-paves-way-for-no-deal-brexit-next-year/19/10/; https://www.theguardian.com/politics/2020/sep/08/brexiter-tory-mps-urge-pm-to-ditch-withdrawal-agreement-if-no-deal.

[161] See Commission, *Discours du Président Juncker et du Négociateur en chef de la Commission européenne Barnier sur le retrait du Royaume-Uni de l'Union européenne lors de la session plénière du Parlement européen* (18 September 2019) available via https://ec.europa.eu/commission/sites/beta-political/files/speech-19-5610_fr.pdf.

orderly withdrawal.[162] So the fact that an extended prorogation would now coincide precisely with the period of time during which the Government and/or Parliament might make crucial decisions about the terms or date of UK withdrawal (together with the manner in which Johnson used his public statement explaining prorogation as an opportunity to denounce MPs for plotting to frustrate his Brexit plans and undo the outcome of the 2016 referendum) only fuelled speculation that the Government's primary aim was improperly to silence Parliament, rather than innocently to afford the Prime Minister time to unveil his revised statutory agenda.[163]

Johnson's decision to prorogue Parliament was subsequently declared unlawful by the UK Supreme Court, on 24 September 2019, in a unanimous judgment containing some of the strongest criticism of a Prime Minister's behaviour in the legal records:

> Nowhere is there a hint that the Prime Minister, in giving advice to Her Majesty, is more than simply the leader of the Government seeking to promote its own policies; he has a constitutional responsibility [to have regard to all relevant interests, including the interests of Parliament] ... It is impossible for us to conclude, on the evidence which has been put before us, that there was any reason—let alone a good reason—to advise Her Majesty to prorogue Parliament for five weeks, from 9th or 12th September until 14th October. We cannot speculate, in the absence of further evidence, upon what such reasons might have been. It follows that the decision was unlawful.[164]

In the meantime, MPs had already progressed with their plans to scupper the prospect of a 'no deal Brexit' on 31 October 2019: draft legislation was introduced and swiftly adopted into law (on 9 September 2019) as the European Union (Withdrawal) (No 2) Act 2019. The core provisions of this legislation provided that if, by 19 October 2019, the Commons had failed either to approve the conclusion of a withdrawal agreement under Article 50 TEU, or to endorse the UK's withdrawal without any such agreement, then the Prime Minister must (using a pre-drafted form of words) request a further extension of the UK's membership of the EU from the European Council, in accordance with Article 50(3) TEU, until 31 January 2020. If the European Council were to offer another date, the Prime Minister would be obliged to accept that offer, if the Commons voted also to approve it (though the Government could still decide to agree to an alternative extension even without such explicit Commons approval).

The Government's reaction was furious: Johnson thenceforth preferred to describe the European Union (Withdrawal) (No 2) Act 2019 as the 'Surrender Act'—directly accusing MPs of undermining the UK's efforts at renegotiating the existing withdrawal package by denying the Government its 'trump card' of threatening to walk away from further talks and thereby inflict a calamitous 'no deal Brexit' upon the EU27 [sic].[165]

---

[162] What was ultimately to become the 'Benn Act': the European Union (Withdrawal) (No 2) Act 2019.

[163] Consider, e.g. Prime Minister, *Statement* (2 September 2019).

[164] *Miller v Prime Minister* [2019] UKSC 41, at paras 60–61.

[165] See, e.g. https://www.theguardian.com/politics/2019/sep/29/ex-minister-rejects-allegations-rebels-colluded-with-eu-to-stop-no-deal.

If it were not clear already that such bluster and swagger were seriously mis-placed, the publication in quick succession of the latest EU and UK 'no deal contingency plans' should have provided the necessary reality check. On the one hand, on 4 September 2019, the Commission produced another detailed set of papers reviewing and refining the advanced state of EU preparations.[166] On the other hand, and as we already mentioned in Chapter 2, on 11 September 2019, the UK Government was obliged (by parliamentary fiat and only in the face of dogged resistance) to release its 'Operation Yellowhammer' report outlining official assessments over the likely impact of a 'no deal Brexit'.[167] Even allowing for a delay of several weeks between its original preparation and eventual public disclosure, 'Operation Yellowhammer' made sobering reading. For example, the Government anticipated serious disruption to cross-border trade and supply chains, with the potential for shortages in key sectors such as medicines, medical supplies and fresh food stuffs, as well as price rises for basic commodities, such as fuel; such impacts would have a disproportionate effect upon low-income groups and, more generally, the Government expected to see both protests and counter-protests as well as a rise in public disorder and community tensions. Far from passing a 'Surrender Act', any rational person might have thought that Parliament had in fact done the Government a massive favour by providing both the impetus and the time for serious EU–UK talks in order to avoid such a disastrous 'no deal' outcome.

Whatever the circumstantial evidence might suggest, nevertheless and at least for our purposes, it must remain a matter of conjecture whether the incoming Johnson Government indeed only intended to engage in a sham renegotiation exercise while privately steering the UK deliberately towards a 'no deal Brexit' on 31 October 2019. But it is certainly safe to say that, regardless of the Prime Minister's original plans, Parliament's successful initiative to rule out any such denouement now significantly increased pressure on the Government to undertake serious talks with the EU.[168] And indeed, on 2 October 2019, Johnson published the UK's long-awaited proposals for a revised Protocol on Ireland/Northern Ireland.[169]

In the first place, Johnson proposed that Northern Ireland should indeed remain in alignment with EU standards for those purposes strictly required to avoid regulatory checks between the Republic and Northern Ireland—though with a much-reduced set of 'level playing field' commitments to guarantee free and fair competition; and also subject to a periodic 'consent mechanism' involving the devolved institutions in Belfast. In the second place, however, Northern Ireland would constitute an integral part of the UK's customs territory, entirely separate from that of the EU and the

---

[166] See COM(2019) 394 Final. Note also the Commission–UK 'Exchange of Letters' (September 2019) in which the Union negotiator ruled out any prospect of agreeing 'no deal mini deals': available via https://ec.europa.eu/commission/publications/exchange-letters-between-steve-barclay-and-michel-barnier_en.

[167] Available via https://assets.publishing.service.gov.uk/government/uploads/system/uploads/attachment_data/file/831199/20190802_Latest_Yellowhammer_Planning_assumptions_CDL.pdf.

[168] Note HMG, *PM Meeting with President of the European Commission* (Press Release of 16 September 2019).

[169] Prime Minister, *Letter to Commission President (together with Explanatory Note)* (2 October 2019) available via https://assets.publishing.service.gov.uk/government/uploads/system/uploads/attachment_data/file/836115/PM_letter_to_Juncker_WEB.pdf. Note also: Prime Minister, *Commons Statement on Brexit Negotiations* (3 October 2019).

Republic. Customs checks and procedures would therefore inevitably be required, but both parties should undertake never to employ them at or on the border itself. Instead, and harking back to previous UK proposals, Johnson argued that such checks and procedures should be managed through reliance (for example) on electronic filing, physical inspections at trading premises and mutual recognition of 'trusted trader' schemes. In the third place, Johnson confirmed that his new Government was also seeking substantial changes to the First Political Declaration: post-withdrawal negotiations should proceed on the basis of a significantly more distant future relationship between the EU and the UK, particularly in the field of trade, so that the UK enjoyed the autonomy both to diverge from EU regulatory standards and to pursue a wholly independent trade policy.

The Commission was quick to point out that Johnson's proposals suffered from various weaknesses—most of which should already have been familiar to anyone who had followed the course of the Article 50 TEU negotiations thus far: for example, the fact that existing technologies and other forms of mutual cooperation were simply not an adequate substitute for more traditional tools of border security and management at any developed economy's customs frontier; and the proposition that the Union should be satisfied with a much looser set of commitments from the UK as regards future economic relations without adequate guarantees against unfair competition and social, fiscal or environmental dumping.[170]

Indeed, the problems perhaps went even further than the Commission itself had stated: not only did the proposed 'consent mechanism' create inherent and ongoing uncertainty over the regime governing the Irish border for all relevant parties and stakeholders; but, in addition, the UK Government appeared to suggest that the necessary consent must be provided on a cross-community basis—thus effectively handing the DUP a unilateral veto over both the initial entry into force and thereafter the continued application of any revised backstop.[171]

Whatever their shortcomings, the British proposals nevertheless succeeded in providing a basis for concrete and intensive negotiations with the Commission. On 17 October 2019, the two parties announced that they had reached provisional agreement on a revised (Second) Withdrawal Package.[172]

The Second Withdrawal Package contained two main and indeed closely inter-related changes as compared to the arrangements that had previously been agreed under Theresa May. In the first place, the Commission and the UK negotiated significant amendments to the border plans that would apply under the Protocol on Ireland/Northern Ireland. Much to the horror of Johnson's former DUP allies,[173] Northern Ireland would be aligned to a wide array of EU customs and regulatory standards; those EU rules would be applied and enforced primarily by UK officials but with significant roles also for the EU's own institutions and agencies; while Northern Ireland would simultaneously remain part of the UK's own customs territory and as such

---

[170] See, e.g. Michel Barnier, *Statement at the European Parliament Plenary Session* (9 October 2019).
[171] See further the detailed discussion in Chapter 8.
[172] Published at OJ 2019 C 384 I.
[173] See, e.g. Democratic Unionist Party, *Statement from the DUP* (17 October 2019) opposing the revised Protocol (inter alia) on the grounds that it would not be beneficial to the economic well-being of Northern Ireland and would weaken the union with Great Britain.

subject to a complex and essentially experimental 'dual customs regime'; and those arrangements would no longer be temporary but should instead provide a permanent solution to the Irish border problem;[174] though subject to a revised 'consent mechanism' which did not, however, depend upon cross-community agreement and therefore deprived the DUP of any formal power of veto.[175] Otherwise, it should be stressed, the vast majority of the Second Withdrawal Agreement was completely identical to the text of the First Withdrawal Agreement.

In the second place, the Commission and the UK also settled upon various changes to the Political Declaration that foretold a significantly more distant future EU–UK relationship than even Theresa May had suggested. Much to the delight of Johnson's hard-line Tory supporters, the core of the future EU–UK economic relationship would be a more traditional free trade agreement; that agreement would still aim to deliver 'zero tariffs and quotas' on cross-border trade in goods, though still subject to certain social, fiscal and environmental obligations designed to ensure free and fair competition; but in those as well as in other fields, the UK insisted upon retaining greater discretion to diverge from EU regulatory standards and pursue its own independent trade policy.[176]

Yet just as important as the revised text of the Second Political Declaration per se, was the fact that its translation into an operable international treaty would no longer be subject to the strait-jacket effectively imposed by Theresa May's previous Irish backstop arrangements, under which the UK's future conduct would in practice have been constrained by its far-reaching obligations to maintain customs and regulatory alignment with the EU. With Northern Ireland now subject to a highly specific and potentially permanent regime to avoid a 'hard border', the rest of the UK would now be free to translate the Second Political Declaration into a genuinely more abrupt and decisive break away from its former EU partners.

It is worth noting that the Second Withdrawal Package, consisting of the mutually agreed texts of the revised withdrawal agreement and political declaration, was again supplemented by certain additional measures. In particular, the UK published a unilateral declaration (which was nevertheless explicitly referred to in the text of the new Protocol on Ireland/Northern Ireland) setting out in greater detail the modalities of the 'consent mechanism' involving the devolved institutions in Belfast.[177] Moreover, the European Council subsequently made clear that it still regarded the unilateral statements previously recorded in the minutes from its meeting in November 2018 to endorse the First Withdrawal Package, as relevant to the Union's understanding of and approach to negotiations over the future EU–UK relationship in accordance with the Second Political Declaration.[178]

---

[174] See, e.g. Michel Barnier, *Remarks at the press conference on the Commission Recommendation to the European Council to endorse the agreement reached on the revised Protocol on Ireland/Northern Ireland and revised Political Declaration* (17 October 2019).

[175] See further the detailed discussion in Chapter 8.

[176] See further the detailed discussion in Chapter 9.

[177] See HMG, *Declaration Concerning the Operation of the 'Democratic Consent in Northern Ireland' Provision of the Protocol on Ireland/Northern Ireland* (19 October 2019). Note also the brief 'legal opinion' published by the UK Government on 17 October 2019.

[178] See European Council (Article 50), *Conclusions of 13 December 2019*, at para 2.

However, the revisions that were provisionally agreed between the Commission and the UK on 17 October 2019 now also effectively rendered redundant certain other measures which had previously been adopted in order to supplement the First Withdrawal Package. In particular, the fact that the new arrangements to govern the Irish border were both highly specific to Northern Ireland and also supposed to be permanent in nature, without any pressure or expectation that they should be replaced as quickly as possible by an alternative UK-wide agreement, meant that the political assurances previously secured by Theresa May were now otiose, that is, the Exchange of Letters from January 2019 and the Strasbourg Deal from March 2019.[179]

7. Approval of the Second Withdrawal Package

On 17 October 2019, the Commission recommended that the European Council should politically endorse the revised texts of the Second Withdrawal Package.[180] The European Council duly obliged that very same day and invited the other competent Union institutions to proceed with the steps required for conclusion of the Second Withdrawal Agreement.[181] Once again, it was clear that both the consent of the European Parliament and formal approval by the Council were virtually guaranteed to be granted in due course.[182] The real question was whether Boris Johnson would now succeed where Theresa May had repeatedly failed, in steering the Second Withdrawal Package to domestic approval within the UK.

As one might expect, Johnson lauded the Second Withdrawal Package as a 'great deal' for the UK and the chance to 'get Brexit done'.[183] Indeed, his revised withdrawal package provided for a 'real Brexit'.[184] But insofar as the Prime Minister still genuinely hoped to complete the processes of approval, implementation, and ratification in time for the UK's projected withdrawal on 31 October 2019, the House of Commons once more managed to defy him. A fresh statement that political agreement on a withdrawal package had been reached, together with a motion for its approval in the Commons in accordance with section 13 EU(W)A 2018, were published by the Government on 19 October 2019. However, MPs succeeded in amending that motion before passing it: the Commons 'withholds approval unless and until implementing legislation is passed'.

By voting to delay further approval of the Second Withdrawal Package, the Commons succeeded in triggering the obligations incumbent upon the Prime Minister pursuant to the European Union (Withdrawal) (No 2) Act 2019. It is important to recall that, for a period of several weeks already, speculation had been rife that

---

[179] See the detailed discussion above.
[180] See Letter from Commission President to President of the European Council (17 October 2019) together with accompanying texts.
[181] See European Council (Article 50), *Conclusions of 17 October 2019*.
[182] See Commission, *Proposal for a Council Decision amending Decision 2019/274 on the signing, on behalf of the European Union and of the European Atomic Energy Community, of the Agreement on the withdrawal of the United Kingdom of Great Britain and Northern Ireland from the European Union and the European Atomic Energy Community*, COM(2019) 880 Final.
[183] Prime Minister, *Press Conference at European Council* (17 October 2019).
[184] Prime Minister, *Statement in the House of Commons* (19 October 2019).

the Government was seeking some means of evading or nullifying Johnson's statutory obligation to request another extension from the European Council. Indeed, many commentators noted ruefully that the British media and public appeared to be engaged in a serious debate about whether Prime Ministers must really obey the rule of law. But in the end, albeit with continuing protestation,[185] and arguably with little regard for proper diplomatic protocol,[186] Johnson did indeed comply with the terms of the European Union (Withdrawal) (No 2) Act 2019.

But despite having now requested another extension to the UK's membership of the EU, Johnson made clear that he would still seek to complete ratification of the Second Withdrawal Agreement in time for the UK to leave on 31 October 2019. Two routes remained open for him to do so, both of which were initiated on 21 October 2019. In the first place, the Government sought to introduce another motion for Commons approval of the Second Withdrawal Package in accordance with section 13 EU(W)A 2018. However, that initiative failed immediately: the Speaker of the House of Commons decided not to allow a vote on the latest section 13 motion, because it would breach the convention against asking MPs to vote again on essentially the same question.[187] In the second place, the Government introduced to Parliament the European Union (Withdrawal Agreement) Bill—as now demanded by the Commons before MPs should be asked again to approve the Second Withdrawal Package; and in any case as required directly under section 13 itself before the Government could proceed to ratification.[188] However, the Bill sought to fast-track the process for ratification of the Second Withdrawal Agreement by simply abolishing the existing approval procedure under section 13 EU(W)A 2018 and disapplying the ordinary process for parliamentary scrutiny of proposed international agreements under Part Two of the Constitutional Governance and Reform Act 2010.[189]

Otherwise, the draft legislation was aimed primarily at laying down the statutory framework required for implementing the Second Withdrawal Agreement into domestic law: for example, making detailed provision for the continuing application of EU law during the proposed transition period and adjusting the future legal status of EU-derived rules within the UK legal system thereafter; enshrining the main citizens' rights provisions of the Second Withdrawal Agreement into primary legislation; and conferring wide-ranging powers upon the Government to implement various other elements of the Second Withdrawal Agreement. In addition, it is important to note that the draft legislation provided for various mechanisms of enhanced parliamentary oversight and control of the Government's future Brexit plans: for example, requiring prior approval from the House of Commons before the Government could agree to

---

[185] E.g. Prime Minister, *Statement in the House of Commons* (19 October 2019, i.e. second statement, issued after the Commons vote).

[186] The UK's official extension request of 28 October 2019 was sent to the President of the European Council, unformatted and unsigned, accompanied by a cover letter from the UK's Permanent Representative to the Union—though the Prime Minister himself also sent a separate letter, effectively exhorting the EU27 not to agree to his own extension request: see https://assets.publishing.service.gov.uk/government/uploads/system/uploads/attachment_data/file/842622/20191028_HE_Mr_Donald_Tusk.pdf.

[187] See Statement from Speaker of the House of Commons (21 October 2019) available via https://www.parliament.uk/business/news/2019/october/statement-from-the-speaker-of-house-of-commons/.

[188] Text available via https://publications.parliament.uk/pa/bills/cbill/2019-2019/0007/20007.pdf.

[189] See Clauses 32 and 33 of the Bill as published on 21 October 2019.

any extension of the proposed transition period (in accordance with the facility provided for in the Second Withdrawal Agreement).[190]

In particular, recall that Theresa May had promised Parliament the power to approve both her Government's negotiating objectives for, and any proposed agreements related to, the future EU–UK relationship.[191] Similarly, when introducing his Second Withdrawal Package to the Commons, Johnson had promised that 'Parliament should be at the heart of decision-making' as the UK develops its approach to the future EU–UK relationship.[192] The European Union (Withdrawal Agreement) Bill now provided that the Government's negotiating objectives must be consistent with the content of the Second Political Declaration; those objectives must be approved in advance by the House of Commons; the Government must undertake subsequent negotiations with the EU with a view to achieving those objectives; and the Government may not ratify any proposed treaty principally concerned with the future EU–UK relationship unless that treaty is approved in advance by the House of Commons.[193]

On 22 October 2019, the House of Commons voted for the Bill to proceed to second reading stage but not in accordance with the Government's massively accelerated legislative timetable. It was now clear that Johnson stood no chance whatsoever of 'getting Brexit done' on 31 October 2019, though nor was he willing to step aside and let another preside over (what he had regularly portrayed as) this terrible betrayal of public trust and British democracy. Instead, the European Council (with the agreement of the UK Government) adopted a Third Extension Decision: the UK's projected date of withdrawal is further postponed, in accordance with Article 50(3) TEU, until 31 January 2020; though the Second Withdrawal Agreement might still be ratified and enter into force (and the UK might therefore still leave the Union) before that date.[194]

Shortly afterwards, the European Council (acting in its Article 50 TEU formation) adopted a supplementary declaration in which it called upon the UK to proceed to ratification of the Second Withdrawal Agreement; excluded any further renegotiation of that text in the future; reiterated that any unilateral statement or act by the UK should be compatible with the letter and spirit of the Second Withdrawal Agreement; called upon the UK to fulfil its continuing Treaty obligations as a Member State (including by nominating a candidate for appointment to the Commission); reminded the UK of its ongoing duty of sincere cooperation during the extended period of its Union membership; and insisted upon the right of the remaining Member States, as well as the Union's institutions, bodies, and agencies etc, to meet separately to discuss matters related to the situation after the UK's departure (over and above those meetings from which the UK was explicitly excluded in accordance with Article 50 TEU).[195]

Johnson may not have 'got Brexit done' by his very own 'do or die' deadline but by this stage it was nevertheless evident that Johnson stood a strong chance of eventually

---

[190] See Clause 30 of the Bill as published on 21 October 2019.
[191] See the discussion above.
[192] See Prime Minister, *Statement in the House of Commons* (19 October 2019).
[193] See Clause 31 of the Bill as published on 21 October 2019.
[194] European Council Decision 2019/1810, OJ 2019 L I 278/1. This was followed by the necessary changes also in UK law: see European Union (Withdrawal) Act 2018 (Exit Day) (Amendment) (No 3) Regulations 2019.
[195] European Council (Article 50), *Declaration of the European Council (Art 50)* (29 October 2019).

succeeding where May had repeatedly failed: even though his new approach to the Irish border had cost him the support of the DUP,[196] his more hard-line stance on future EU–UK relations had won him back the more extreme Tory rebels; and it seemed likely that sheer 'Brexit fatigue' would now persuade enough moderate Conservatives as well as several Labour MPs also to support the Government's proposals. Yet rather than continue with the search for parliamentary approval of his revised withdrawal package, Johnson instead pressed along a different route: he called for another UK general election. As Johnson expressed his intention to the President of the European Council: 'I am seeking a General Election in December to ensure the election of a fresh Parliament which is capable of resolving the issue in accordance with our constitutional norms'.[197]

In fact, Johnson had already been calling for a fresh general election for some time—surely in the expectation that it would save him from the inconvenience of trying to run a minority administration, by delivering a sizeable Tory majority in the Commons. However, the Fixed Term Parliaments Act 2011 effectively gave the opposition parties a veto over Government attempts to call an early election and Johnson had lost several previous votes to that end in the Commons.[198] But now the main UK opposition parties were persuaded to acquiesce—perhaps hoping that voters would swing against the Conservatives altogether; or at least do so in sufficient numbers as to make a second referendum on EU membership part of any future coalition talks. On 29 October 2019, the Government introduced the Early Parliamentary General Election Bill and, the next day, it was supported by the House of Commons, paving the way for an election to be held on 12 December 2019.[199]

If those were indeed their calculations, the UK opposition parties could not have been more wrong. The Conservatives won 43.6 per cent of the popular vote on 12 December 2019, which translated into an 80-seat majority in the House of Commons. Moreover, it is fair to say that the Tories were now a very different political movement from previous generations: almost entirely purged of moderate pro-Europeans; significantly more right wing in orientation. For his part, Johnson's gamble had paid off handsomely: at this point, and really for the very first time since June 2016, Brexit became inevitable.

An emboldened and empowered Johnson Government now set about ratifying the Second Withdrawal Agreement, at the same time as back-pedalling on several of the promises or undertakings it had made only just before victory in the 2019 general election. Consider the European Union (Withdrawal Agreement) Bill as revised and republished on 19 December 2019.[200] Once again, the draft legislation sought simply

---

[196] See DUP statement of 17 October 2019. Also, e.g. https://www.theguardian.com/politics/2019/oct/17/dup-boris-johnson-brexit-deal.

[197] Prime Minister, *Letter to President of the European Council* (28 October 2019) available via https://assets.publishing.service.gov.uk/government/uploads/system/uploads/attachment_data/file/842622/20191028_HE_Mr_Donald_Tusk.pdf.

[198] In particular: Commons votes on 4 September 2019; on 9 September 2019; and on 28 October 2019. Note also Boris Johnson's letter to Jeremy Corbyn (24 October 2019) offering more time to debate the European Union (Withdrawal Agreement) Bill in return for the Labour Party's support in calling for a general election to be held in December 2019.

[199] See the Early Parliamentary General Election Act 2019.

[200] Available via https://publications.parliament.uk/pa/bills/cbill/58-01/0001/20001.pdf

to abolish the troublesome section 13 approval process altogether, provide merely for domestic implementation of the Second Withdrawal Agreement in those situations where it was positively required, and otherwise clear the path for the Government to ratify in accordance with its ordinary executive treaty-making powers.[201] But going further, the revised Bill abandoned Johnson's previous pledge that Parliament must sit at the heart of domestic debate and decision-making about the future shape of EU–UK relations—deleting any requirement for prior Commons consent either to a proposed extension of the transition period, or to the Government's future relationship negotiating objectives, or indeed to the ratification of any draft treaty/treaties on the future relationship reached between the Union and the UK.[202]

If those were worrying signs of the direction of political and constitutional travel within the UK, the Union itself should also have found serious cause for concern in the behaviour of the Johnson Government after its victory in the 2019 general election. The revised European Union (Withdrawal Agreement) Bill already sought to render ineffective, in advance, certain provisions of the Second Withdrawal Agreement which Johnson himself had recently endorsed and which his Government was now seeking to ratify. For example, a statutory direction sought explicitly to rule out any possibility, under any circumstances, of the UK Government agreeing to extend the post-withdrawal, status quo transition period beyond 31 December 2020 (in accordance with the facility provided for under the Second Withdrawal Agreement, which itself had been introduced at the request of the UK Government under Theresa May).[203]

Moreover, the Prime Minister soon began publicly to misrepresent important elements of the Second Withdrawal Package—not just elements he had inherited from his predecessor, but obligations specifically relating to the provisions he himself had insisted upon including in the revised texts. In particular, Johnson repeatedly claimed that, under the new Protocol on Ireland/Northern Ireland, there would be no checks or formalities of any kind on trade between Northern Ireland and Great Britain—a claim that was directly contradicted by the explicit text of the Protocol itself and became the source of increasing concern that Johnson was not merely acting in breach of the UK's duty of sincere cooperation (not to make claims or acts incompatible with the letter or spirit of the Second Withdrawal Agreement) but might indeed be actively plotting to sabotage the smooth functioning of his very own 'great new Brexit deal'.[204]

Whatever the concerns about Johnson's post-election conduct, a now-compliant Parliament duly adopted the European Union (Withdrawal Agreement) Act 2020 virtually without amendment.[205] That paved the way for formal signature of the Second

---

[201] See Clauses 31 and 32 of the Bill as published on 19 December 2019.

[202] Contrast the revised Bill with the previous version of 21 October 2019, especially Clauses 30 and 31. And of course, with the May Government's plans, e.g. HMG, *Legislating for the Withdrawal Agreement between the UK and the EU* (Cm 9674 of 24 July 2018); Prime Minister, *Commons Statement on New Brexit Deal* (22 May 2019).

[203] See Clause 33 of the Bill as published on 19 December 2019. Note also, e.g. Clauses 34 and 35 on the terms of UK participation in the Joint Committee. See further the discussion in Chapter 6.

[204] See further the discussion and detailed references in Chapter 8.

[205] Note that attempts in the House of Lords to amend the legislation (e.g. so as to provide proper documentation to EU citizens registered under the EU Settlement Scheme) came to nothing. Note also that the devolved parliaments in Scotland and Wales refused to provide their consent to the legislation but were ignored by the Westminster Parliament.

Withdrawal Agreement by the UK Government;[206] as well as the granting of its consent by the European Parliament and final conclusion of the Second Withdrawal Agreement by the Council.[207]

The United Kingdom thus left the European Union at 00.00 (CET) on 31 January 2020.[208] Prime Minister Johnson hailed it as a moment 'when the dawn breaks and the curtain goes up on a new act in our great national drama'.[209] The UK witnessed some (perhaps surprisingly small-scale) celebrations by Brexit supporters. Many Remain campaigners held somewhat sadder vigils of their own. The Presidents of the European Council, the European Parliament and the Commission expressed the Union's deep regret at the UK's departure, but also reaffirmed their own collective determination to continue working together as nations, institutions, and peoples.[210] The present author was too inebriated, having a delightful time in a Parisian café with his family and friends, to pay this historic moment the respect it did not deserve.

8. Concluding Remarks

Despite knowing it would one day have to face the House of Commons as a minority administration, the May Government still conducted key parts of the Article 50 TEU negotiations in apparent detachment from the question: would any final deal eventually command sufficient support in the Westminster Parliament? But it would be wrong to blame the UK's international humiliation on any single choice or moment of miscalculation. The approval crisis of 2018–2019 was the result of many factors working in tandem and in accumulation: for example, a referendum arranged with virtually no planning for its consequences; a Leave campaign dominated by blatant lies and undeliverable fantasies; a government keen to react swiftly but without considered reflection as to the likely consequences of its decisions and actions; a Prime Minister that rejected the path of cross-party consensus-building in favour of pandering to extreme factions; an opposition, both official and by rebellion, that was incapable of mustering the political cohesion and willpower to offer any better alternative of its own; and a consistent failure to appreciate the true weakness of the UK's position, certainly relative to that of the united and determined Union of 27.

Whatever the precise causes, the period between November 2018 and May 2019 surely provided some extraordinary political drama as the Prime Minister's authority collapsed and evaporated. Perhaps the nadir of Theresa May's time in office came with her 'speech to the nation' on 20 March 2019.[211] That event was widely criticized for suggesting that it was fractious and rebellious MPs, not the Government and its loyal

---

[206] On 24 January 2020.

[207] On 29 and 30 January 2020 (respectively). See, in particular, Council Decision 2020/135 on the conclusion of the Agreement on the withdrawal of the United Kingdom of Great Britain and Northern Ireland from the European Union and the European Atomic Energy Community, OJ 2020 L 29/1.

[208] And Euratom: Art 1 of the final Withdrawal Agreement.

[209] Prime Minister, *Address to the Nation* (31 January 2020).

[210] See https://www.consilium.europa.eu/en/press/press-releases/2020/01/31/a-new-dawn-for-europe-op-ed-article-by-presidents-charles-michel-david-sassoli-and-ursula-von-der-leyen/Joint   op-ed   (31 January 2020).

[211] Available at https://www.gov.uk/government/speeches/pm-statement-on-brexit-20-march-2019.

supporters, who were entirely responsible for the UK's political imbroglio; and indeed for seeking to pit 'The People' against Parliament in a potentially inflammatory manner. Certainly, if one believes the newspaper reports, this speech may well have exacerbated the already poisonous atmosphere that was producing assaults, abuse, and threats against MPs.[212]

Commentators now and in the future might spend a few merry moments answering the largely rhetorical question: has Boris Johnson's time and conduct as Prime Minister restored to that Great Office of State some of its lost dignity and integrity, and rekindled within the battered UK political system some of its old democratic and parliamentary spirit? But whatever the other legacies of his political career and leadership tenure, there is one achievement (so to speak) that Johnson can certainly be credited with: negotiating a (modestly revised) Withdrawal Package that eventually proved capable of passing through the UK's domestic approval process and ultimately allowed Article 50 TEU to fulfil its primacy vocation—to furnish the legal basis for a negotiated, orderly withdrawal of the UK, as relevant State, from the Union of which it had been a leading member for nearly five decades.

Having spent the last four chapters examining the overall constitutional framework for, as well as the more precise legal and political factors affecting the progress and conclusion of, the UK's withdrawal negotiations, our next four chapters will shift attention to the final Withdrawal Package itself—beginning with a general analysis of the Withdrawal Agreement (Chapter 6), before moving on to more focused discussion of the key topics of citizens' rights (Chapter 7) and the Irish border (Chapter 8), then embarking upon an exploration of the Political Declaration and early negotiations over the future EU–UK relationship (Chapter 9).

---

[212] See further, e.g. https://www.theguardian.com/politics/2019/mar/21/mps-told-to-take-simple-steps-to-avoid-abuse-amid-brexit-tensions. And more broadly, e.g. https://www.theguardian.com/politics/2019/apr/22/brexiters-language-worsens-threats-against-mps-nicky-morgan.

6
Withdrawal Agreement: General Provisions

1. Introduction

This chapter provides an overview of the legally binding Withdrawal Agreement as finally concluded between the EU and the UK. Section 2 contains a general overview of the structure of the treaty and its main governance institutions and decision-making procedures but stresses above all the fundamental distinction that runs throughout the Withdrawal Agreement, between the provisions applicable during the transition period and those which are to apply only after its expiry.

Section 3 then concentrates on the terms of the post-withdrawal, status quo transition period itself: for a period of 11 months after becoming a third country, the UK was nevertheless to be treated as if it were still a Member State for a vast range of legal and regulatory purposes. That transition period was central, indeed crucial, to the objective of delivering an orderly withdrawal—not least in giving each party more time to undertake the necessary legal and logistical preparations for the full consequences of Brexit. But the transition period also raises various interesting legal questions of its own—not least the issue (once again) of how far Article 50 TEU should be interpreted as an 'exceptional' competence or legal basis, that permits the Union institutions to do or agree to things that appear unorthodox as a matter of standard EU rules and/or practices.

Section 4 then deals with the provisions of the Withdrawal Agreement that become relevant primarily after expiry of the transition period, when the UK discovers for the first time what it truly means to be a third country. We provide some key illustrations from the various 'separation provisions' that are aimed at winding-up the lingering remnants of UK membership; explain the rules governing interpretation of the treaty; and discuss the system for dispute settlement through independent arbitration, but also subject to several forms and instances of continuing jurisdiction for the CJEU itself. Finally, Section 5 addresses the (unusually prescriptive) provisions determining the internal legal status and effects of the Withdrawal Agreement, particularly within the dualist legal system of the UK, where the traditional constitutional principle of parliamentary sovereignty poses particular problems for the Withdrawal Agreement's objective of providing entrenched protection for many of the latter's rights and provisions.

2. Overview of the Withdrawal Agreement

A. Structure of the Withdrawal Agreement

The Withdrawal Agreement begins, as one would expect, with a Preamble. That text largely signposts the main issues addressed by the Union and the UK so as to deliver on

The UK's Withdrawal from the EU. Michael Dougan, Oxford University Press. © Michael Dougan 2021.
DOI: 10.1093/oso/9780198833475.003.0006

their objective of an orderly withdrawal; as well as noting the accompanying Political Declaration on future Union–UK relations; and stressing the need for the two parties to proceed swiftly with formal negotiations, if the necessary treaties governing their future relationship are to be ready for implementation by the end of the transition period provided for under the Withdrawal Agreement itself.

Although the Preamble is not, of course, a direct source of legally binding provisions, it does nevertheless contain some interesting statements about the parties' understanding and intentions, which might prove to be of potential relevance to future interpretation of the Withdrawal Agreement. For example, the Preamble states that 'pursuant to Article 50 TEU … and subject to the arrangements laid down in this Agreement, the law of the Union … in its entirety ceases to apply to the United Kingdom from the date of entry into force of this Agreement'. As we shall see shortly, that statement is arguably relevant to the question of whether Article 50 TEU can still provide a valid legal basis for the Union to conclude additional agreements with the UK, even after withdrawal itself has taken place and the UK has formally become a third country in relation to the Union.[1]

Besides its preamble, the main body of the Withdrawal Agreement comprises six parts. Part One is entitled 'Common Provisions'. It establishes basic definitions; determines the territorial scope of the Withdrawal Agreement; lays down certain rules and principles for interpreting the Withdrawal Agreement and determining its legal effects within the Union as well as the UK; sets out the parties' duty of good faith in relation to the Withdrawal Agreement; and provides for the cessation of UK access to Union networks, information systems, and databases etc.

Part Two concerns 'Citizens' Rights'. It contains detailed provisions governing the future protection of EU citizens and UK nationals who are exercising free movement rights pursuant to Union law as at the end of the transition period, in fields such as residency, family life, employment, the recognition of professional qualifications, equal treatment, and social security.

Part Three is entitled 'Separation Provisions'. It contains a series of distinct titles, each addressing the consequences of UK withdrawal for a particular range of acts, procedures, statuses, and relationships which are existing and governed by Union law as at the end of the transition period, for example: resolving the customs treatment of goods currently moving between the Union and the UK; addressing the future status and protection of existing Union law-based intellectual property rights; providing for the winding-up of ongoing procedures relating to cross-border police and judicial cooperation in the field of criminal law; prescribing the UK's treatment of personal data and other types of protected (confidential or restricted) information obtained before the end of transition or pursuant to the Withdrawal Agreement; fully extricating the UK from its previous membership of Euratom; detailing the winding-up of ongoing judicial and administrative proceedings involving the Union's institutions, bodies, and agencies

---

[1] See the discussion (below) of how the transition period might be extended beyond 31 December 2020, other than by using the explicit power to decide on an extension provided for under Art 132 WA.

etc; and managing the implications of withdrawal for a range of institutional personnel as well as the Union's immunities and privileges.

Part Four deals with 'Transition'. It makes detailed provision for the post-withdrawal, status quo transitional regime, during which the UK remains bound by the vast majority of its existing rights and obligations under the Treaties, though without any continuing institutional representation or voting powers, and subject to specific adaptions (for example) as regards the Union's external action as well as the allocation of fishing opportunities within the context of the Common Fisheries Policy.

Part Five on 'Financial Provisions' contains the methodology for calculating the single financial settlement by which the Union and the UK agree to honour the mutual commitments undertaken during the period of British membership, for example: as regards the Union's own resources; UK participation in the implementation of Union programmes and activities committed under the 2014–2020 Multiannual Financial Framework (MFF); the activities of the European Investment Bank and European Development Fund; and the UK's commitments under the Facility for Refugees in Turkey.

Part Six consists of 'Institutional and Final Provisions'. As well as making more specific provision for implementation and enforcement (for example) of the citizens' rights' regime, this section of the Withdrawal Agreement establishes the necessary governance rules (including creation of the Joint Committee and specialized committees); lays down the procedure for dispute settlement after expiry of the transition period (primarily through arbitration, subject to oversight by the CJEU as regards the interpretation of Union law); and determines the detailed dates for entry into force of different provisions of the Withdrawal Agreement.

In addition to the main body of the Withdrawal Agreement, the parties agreed the texts of three Protocols and nine Annexes. Those Protocols and Annexes form an integral part of the Withdrawal Agreement itself.[2] The Protocol on Ireland/Northern Ireland is by far the most detailed: it sets out the various commitments designed to address the unique challenges facing the island of Ireland and, in particular, to protect the peace settlement in Northern Ireland from the potentially destabilizing effects of the UK's withdrawal from the Union, including the infamous and now potentially indefinite 'backstop' to prevent the creation of a 'hard border' for the movement of goods between the North and the Republic.

In addition, the Protocol relating to the Sovereign Base Areas of the UK in Cyprus seeks to ensure the continued smooth functioning of relations between the UK's military bases and the local populations who live and work there, particularly in fields (such as agriculture, customs, and taxation) currently administered by the Cypriot authorities and still governed by the relevant provisions of Union law. The Protocol on Gibraltar seeks to facilitate cooperation between the UK and Spain over issues particularly relevant to Gibraltar, such as effective implementation of the citizens' rights provisions specifically concerning frontier workers; and enhanced cooperation as regards

---

[2] Art 182 WA.

tax transparency and the protection of the parties' financial interests (including in respect of criminal activities such as money laundering, fraud and the smuggling of tobacco, alcohol, and petrol). For their part, the Annexes are largely reserved for more detailed technical provisions: for example, they contain the full lists of Union legislation and other legal acts as referred to in specific provisions of the Withdrawal Agreement itself; and also establish the Rules of Procedure for the Joint Committee, the specialized committees, and the dispute settlement arbitration panels provided for under the Withdrawal Agreement.

B. Overall Governance of Withdrawal Agreement

In certain respects, the governance provisions of the Withdrawal Agreement are entirely familiar from standard international practice and caused no particular trouble in the negotiations.[3] Article 164 WA establishes a Joint Committee, comprising representatives of and co-chaired by the Union and the UK, which shall meet at the request of either party and in any event at least once a year. The Joint Committee is responsible for the overall implementation and application of the Withdrawal Agreement. Either the Union or the UK may refer to the Joint Committee any issue relating to the implementation, application, and interpretation of the Withdrawal Agreement.

Article 165 WA also creates various specialized committees: on citizens' rights (under Part Two); on the other separation provisions (dealt with in Part Three); on implementation of the Protocol on Ireland/Northern Ireland; on implementation of the Protocol relating to the UK's Sovereign Base Areas in Cyprus; on implementation of the Protocol on Gibraltar; and on the financial provisions (as contained in Part Five). The specialized committees shall again comprise and be co-chaired by representatives of the Union and the UK, with each party obliged to ensure that its representatives has appropriate expertise with respect to the issues under discussion. Each specialized committee should meet at least once a year—unless the Withdrawal Agreement provides or their co-chairs decide otherwise; and subject to the power of the Union, the UK, or the Joint Committee to request additional meetings. The specialized committees must inform the Joint Committee in advance of their planned activities and then subsequently report on their meetings. In any case, the existence of any given specialized committee shall not prevent the Union or the UK raising any matter directly before the Joint Committee.[4]

The Joint Committee *shall*: supervise and facilitate the implementation and application of the Withdrawal Agreement; decide on the tasks of the specialized committees and supervise their work; prevent problems that might arise in the areas covered by the Withdrawal Agreement or resolve disputes that might arise regarding its interpretation and application;[5] consider any matter of interest relating to an area covered by the Withdrawal Agreement; adopt decisions as provided for under the Withdrawal

---

[3] See further, e.g. Dashwood, 'The Withdrawal Agreement: Common Provisions, Governance and Dispute Settlement', 45 *ELRev* (2020) 183.

[4] See also Annex VIII on the Rules of Procedure of the Joint Committee and Specialised Committees. Note sections 15B–15C EU(W)A 2018 (as amended).

[5] Art 164 WA.

Agreement; make appropriate recommendations to the parties;[6] and adopt amendments to the Withdrawal Agreement in those cases provided for thereunder.[7]

In addition, the Joint Committee *may*: delegate responsibilities to the specialized committees (excluding the power to determine/supervise the tasks of the specialized committees themselves, as well as the power to adopt decisions, make recommendations, or adopt amendments); change the tasks of, establish additional, or dissolve existing specialized committees; adopt decisions amending the Withdrawal Agreement where such amendments are necessary to correct errors, address omissions or other deficiencies, or address situations unforeseen when the Withdrawal Agreement was signed (though that power does not apply in relation to Parts One, Four and Six, is available only for four years after the end of the transition period, and cannot be used to adopt decisions that would amend the essential elements of the Withdrawal Agreement); amend the Rules of Procedure for the Joint Committee and specialized committees as contained in Annex VIII; or take such other action in the exercise of its functions as decided by the Union and the UK.[8]

When adopting decisions and making recommendations under the Withdrawal Agreement, Article 166 WA provides that the Joint Committee must act by mutual consent between the Union and the UK. Decisions of the Joint Committee shall be binding on the parties and enjoy the same legal effects as the Withdrawal Agreement itself. The Union and the UK are obliged to implement those decisions. Although they hold no comparable decision-making powers of their own, the specialized committees are nevertheless authorized to draw up draft decisions or recommendations and refer them for adoption by the Joint Committee.[9]

It is a matter for each party to determine its own internal arrangements for engaging in the work of the Joint Committee, and the specialized committees, in accordance with the terms of the Withdrawal Agreement. In the case of the Union, Council Decision 2020/135 provides that the Commission shall represent the Union within the Joint Committee as well as the various specialized committees—with the possibility of Member State representatives also taking part, as part of the Union delegation, in meetings of particular national interest (including, for example, Irish representatives in the case of the committee meetings relevant to the Protocol on Ireland/Northern Ireland).[10] In that context, the Decision imposes various reporting obligations upon the Commission towards both the Council and the European Parliament, to enable those institutions to exercise their powers and functions in relation to the Withdrawal Agreement as well as under Union law more broadly.[11]

---

[6] Art 166 WA.

[7] E.g. Art 36(4) WA (cross-border social security coordination); Art 172 WA (dispute settlement rules of procedure); Art 181 WA (arbitration panel code of conduct); Art 10(1) Cyprus Protocol (references to Union law in the Protocol).

[8] The Joint Committee shall also issue an annual report on the functioning of the Withdrawal Agreement: Art 164(6) WA.

[9] Art 165(2) WA.

[10] Council Decision 2020/135 on the conclusion of the Agreement on the withdrawal of the United Kingdom of Great Britain and Northern Ireland from the European Union and the European Atomic Energy Community, OJ 2020 L 29/1.

[11] See Art 2 Decision 2020/135.

Decision 2020/135 also makes specific provision for internal Union decision-making concerning (for example) British requests for authorization to allow any new international agreement between the UK and a third country or international organization, despite falling within the Union's own exclusive competence, nevertheless to enter into force or apply during the transition period.[12] In addition, the Decision establishes a procedure whereby Ireland, Cyprus, or Spain can seek authorization from the Council to negotiate bilateral agreements with the UK in fields of exclusive Union competence—where such agreements are deemed necessary for the proper functioning of the Protocol on Ireland/Northern Ireland, the Protocol relating to the Sovereign Area Bases of the UK in Cyprus, or the Protocol on Gibraltar (respectively); and provided the proposed bilateral terms comply with the Withdrawal Agreement and Union law more generally, and would not jeopardize the Union's relevant external objectives or be otherwise prejudicial to the Union's interests.[13]

For its part, the UK's domestic implementing legislation provides that the functions of the British co-chair of the Joint Committee must be exercised personally by a Minister of the Crown;[14] while also seeking to impose various restrictions on the ability of the UK to agree to certain measures within the Joint Committee, even where the relevant decisions fall within the Joint Committee's legitimate powers of decision or recommendation under the Withdrawal Agreement itself—the most prominent example being the explicit statutory prohibition on the UK's ministerial representative within the Joint Committee agreeing to any proposal to extend the duration of the post-withdrawal, status quo transition period.[15]

The Joint Committee held its inaugural meeting on 30 March 2020, albeit under difficult circumstances: due to the impact of the global pandemic and the imposition of lockdown restrictions, the event was conducted by teleconference rather than in person; but the focus remained (as expected) on timely and effective implementation of the Withdrawal Agreement, in particular, as regards the provisions on citizens' rights and the Protocol on Ireland/Northern Ireland.[16] Various specialized committees then also commenced their responsibilities under the Withdrawal Agreement.[17]

But at the time of writing, the most significant meeting between the Union and the UK to have taken place so far, under the auspices of the Withdrawal Agreement, was

---

[12] See Art 3 Decision 2020/135 and further (below) the discussion on external relations during the transition period.

[13] See Art 4 Decision 2020/135.

[14] Section 15B EU(W)A 2018 (as amended).

[15] See section 15A EU(W)A 2018 (as amended)—and see further the detailed discussion (below) on extension of the transition period. Also, e.g. section 10 EU(W)A 2018 (as amended) (statutory limit on Joint Committee recommendations under Art 11(2) PINI); section 15C EU(W)A 2018 (as amended) (UK co-chair of Joint Committee may not consent to use of written procedure under Rule 9(1) of Annex VIII WA).

[16] See Commission, *Agenda of the first meeting of the Joint Committee on 30 March 2020* (25 March 2020) and *Statement following the first meeting of the EU–UK Joint Committee* (30 March 2020).

[17] E.g. Commission, *Statement following the first meeting of the Specialised Committee on the Protocol on Ireland/Northern Ireland* (30 April 2020); Commission and UK, *Joint Statement following the first meeting of the Specialised Committee on Financial Provisions* (19 May 2020); Commission and UK, *Joint Statement following the meeting of the Specialised Committee on Citizens' Rights* (20 May 2020); Commission and UK, *Joint Statement following the meeting of the Specialised Committee on Gibraltar* (27 May 2020); Commission and UK, *Joint Statement following the meeting of the Specialised Committee on the Sovereign Base Areas of the UK in Cyprus* (9 June 2020).

surely the second meeting of the Joint Committee as held on 12 June 2020.[18] As well as carrying on discussions about implementation of the provisions on citizens' rights and Ireland/Northern Ireland, the Joint Committee adopted a formal decision in accordance with Article 164(5) WA in order to correct (some but not all of the) minor technical deficiencies and omissions which had been identified by the Commission in the original text of the treaty;[19] and also recorded the UK's firm decision not to request any extension to the duration of the post-withdrawal, status quo transition period beyond the date of its projected expiry on 31 December 2020.[20]

C. Fundamental Distinction between Transition Period and Thereafter

When it comes to defining the UK's relationship to the Union, as well as the detailed content of the parties' rights and obligations under the Withdrawal Agreement, the latter is predicated upon a fundamental distinction between (on the one hand) the finite period of time before expiry of the post-withdrawal, status quo transition period and (on the other hand) the indefinite period of time which follows thereafter.

That is true, above all, when it comes to the overall nature and terms of the UK's newfound status as a third country after 31 January 2020. The whole point of transition is that, for the vast majority of regulatory purposes, the UK will temporarily retain the rights and obligations of its former Union membership: within the scope of application of the Treaties, neither public nor private natural and legal persons should experience any appreciable difference as, or in their dealings with, UK authorities, nationals, and residents. As we shall see, the Withdrawal Agreement explicitly provides for the possibility that transition might be extended. There is also an interesting legal debate about whether and how it might be possible to recreate the same effect as the Withdrawal Agreement's transition period without relying on that explicit power of extension.[21] However, the UK Government refused to request any extension of the transition period by the deadline provided for under the Withdrawal Agreement and (at the time of writing) appears categorically to rule out otherwise seeking to prolong the effects of the transition period by any other means and under any circumstances.

It therefore appears that, at 00:00 (CET) on 31 December 2020, the transitional arrangements will expire and the UK will finally experience what it really means to become a third country. In particular, the UK will find its relations, not only with the EU but also with every other international actor, governed by whatever bilateral and multilateral arrangements continue to exist or are created de novo under international

---

[18] See Commission, *Agenda of the second meeting of the Joint Committee on 12 June 2020* (8 June 2020).

[19] See Decision No 1/2020 of the Joint Committee established by the Agreement on the withdrawal of the United Kingdom of Great Britain and Northern Ireland from the European Union and the European Atomic Energy Community of 12 June 2020 amending the Agreement on the withdrawal of the United Kingdom of Great Britain and Northern Ireland from the European Union and the European Atomic Energy Community, OJ 2020 L 225/53.

[20] Commission, *Press statement by Vice-President Maroš Šefčovič following the second meeting of the EU-UK Joint Committee* (12 June 2020). See also, e.g. EU–UK Statement following the High Level Meeting on 15 June 2020.

[21] See the discussion (below) about the transition period.

law.[22] Moreover, we will discover whether the 11 months of additional time afforded by transition were indeed sufficient for public and private actors to complete their preparations for the internal consequences of UK withdrawal. And in due course, commentators will be able to assess whether Theresa May was right to warn against the costs of multiple regulatory adaptations of the sort which are now more likely to occur, thanks to the Johnson Government's decision to rule out any extension to the transition period.

Among the international agreements that will continue to govern the UK's future relations with the Union is, of course, the Withdrawal Agreement itself. In particular, many of the Withdrawal Agreement's provisions did indeed enter into force on the very date of UK withdrawal. That is true, for example, of the entirety of Part One (Common Provisions) and Part Four (Transition). However, many of the Withdrawal Agreement's other provisions only become fully applicable and effective as from the expiry of the transition period and, indeed, employ that date as the crucial reference point for defining their own personal and material scope of application.[23]

For example, the great majority of the provisions governing citizens' rights in accordance with Part Two of the Withdrawal Agreement enter into force only from the end of transition and, moreover, largely rely upon that date for the purposes of determining the range of individuals qualifying for future protection.[24] Similarly, the vast bulk of 'other separation provisions' contained in Part Three shall enter into force only upon expiry of the transition period and, once again, generally rely upon that date for the purposes of identifying which acts, procedures, actors, and relationships are to be governed by the substantive provisions on winding-up the remnants of UK membership.[25] Or again, the system of dispute resolution through consultations in the Joint Committee, and potentially recourse to an arbitration panel, is to apply only upon expiry of the transition period (and even then, subject to the continuing jurisdiction of the CJEU as provided for in the Withdrawal Agreement).[26]

3. Transition Period

In Chapters 3 and 4, we discussed how the UK had originally proposed settling the future EU–UK relationship before withdrawal took place, leading to an 'implementation

---

[22] Consider, e.g. the 'continuity agreements' negotiated between the UK and various other third countries with a view to replicating existing EU agreements (particularly in the field of trade) either in the event of a 'no deal' Brexit or upon expiry of the transition period. See further, e.g. House of Commons International Trade Committee, *Continuing Application of EU Trade Agreements After Brexit* (HC520 of 7 March 2018).

[23] For an example of provisions that actually cease to apply upon the expiry of transition (besides Part Four itself): see Protocol on Gibraltar (except Art 1 thereof) in accordance with Art 185 WA.

[24] As well as the associated provisions on enforcement contained in Title I of Part Six. See Art 185 WA and the detailed discussion in Chapter 7.

[25] See Art 185 WA and the more detailed discussion (below). Note also Art 8 WA on ceasing the UK's access to Union networks, information systems and databases; which is nevertheless subject to a series of exceptions, e.g. under Arts 29(2) and 34(2) WA as regards citizens' rights.

[26] See 185 WA and the more detailed discussion (below).

period' during which the new arrangements could gradually be brought into force.[27] By contrast, the European Council insisted that the Article 50 TEU process should focus on the separation challenges involved in arranging an orderly withdrawal, and while the parties might also engage in preliminary and preparatory discussions about their future relationship, formal negotiations on the terms of future EU–UK relations could only begin after withdrawal itself had been completed. Nevertheless, the European Council in its April 2017 Guidelines recognized that its approach to the scope, sequence and timing of negotiations also implied the need for certain transitional provisions, to help ease the shock of withdrawal itself:

> To the extent necessary and legally possible, the negotiations may also seek to determine transitional arrangements which are in the interest of the Union and, as appropriate, to provide for bridges towards the foreseeable framework for the future relationship in the light of the progress made. Any such transitional arrangements must be clearly defined, limited in time, and subject to effective enforcement mechanisms. Should a time-limited prolongation of Union *acquis* be considered, this would require existing Union regulatory, budgetary, supervisory, judiciary and enforcement instruments and structures to apply.[28]

After eventually being forced to admit that it had lost the battle over sequence and timing, the UK was then obliged radically to revise its withdrawal plans and negotiation strategy. In her 'Florence Speech' of September 2017, Theresa May accepted that the UK would be leaving the Union without any agreement on the future relationship and that it might take some time before any new agreements were concluded and ready to enter into force. So the UK now requested a transition period during which the Union *acquis* would be prolonged almost in its entirety even after withdrawal itself had taken place. To be clear, the UK was not here asking for a prolongation of formal membership as provided for under Article 50 TEU, but nor was it any longer envisaging an 'implementation period' in the sense of its previous proposals. Instead, the Florence Speech proposed a post-withdrawal, status quo transitional regime—both a far cry from the UK's original proposals for an 'implementation period', but also going much further even than the European Council itself had envisaged.[29]

Formal discussions about the UK's request for a transition period had to wait until the European Council verified that 'sufficient progress' had been achieved in the 'first phase' negotiations under Article 50 TEU.[30] That assessment reached, the European Council set out its more detailed thoughts on transition in its Guidelines of 15 December 2017.[31] The Commission put forward a recommendation for detailed negotiating directives focused on transition,[32] which provided the basis (though subject to

---

[27] In particular: Theresa May, *Lancaster House Speech: The Government's Negotiating Objectives for Exiting the EU* (17 January 2017); HMG, *The United Kingdom's Exit from and New Partnership with the European Union* (Cm 9417 of 2 February 2017).

[28] European Council (Article 50), *Guidelines of 29 April 2017*, at para 6.

[29] Though for a considerable time, the UK Government still referred to transition as the 'implementation period' (and even insisted upon an explicit reference in the Agreement itself: see Art 126 WA).

[30] See the detailed discussion in Chapter 4.

[31] European Council (Article 50), *Guidelines for Brexit Negotiations* (15 December 2017).

[32] COM(2017) 830 Final.

certain changes) for the Council to adopt supplementary negotiating directives for the Commission.[33] Thereafter, the two parties exchanged views and texts on the terms of transition,[34] with provisional agreement on the draft text of Part Four being reached in March 2018;[35] though subsequent revisions were made during the negotiations that concluded with the First Withdrawal Package (in particular, so as to include a power for the Joint Committee to extend the duration of the transition period).[36]

After outlining the essential provisions contained in Part Four of the final Withdrawal Agreement, we will focus on how far transition might fulfil its various objectives; together with some of the key political and legal controversies raised under Part Four.

A. Legal Provisions Governing Transition Period

The basic principle is set out in Article 127(1) WA: unless otherwise provided for, Union law shall be applicable to and in the UK during the transition period.[37] In order words, the UK may be leaving, but initially at least, very little will actually change. For the duration of the transition period, the UK will largely remain bound by its existing rights and obligations under Union law, just as if it were still a Member State, across the entire scope of Union policy-making. In that regard, the UK's obligations under Part Four include any legislative, administrative, or judicial developments in Union law that might occur during the transition period. Moreover, the continued applicability of Union law to the UK during transition includes not only the substantive rules, but also those Union law methods and general principles governing the interpretation of Union law, as well as the latter's legal effects within the UK legal system.[38]

Notwithstanding the 'status quo' basis for transition, various provisions of Union law as at the date of withdrawal do not apply to the UK during transition: for example, measures not binding upon the UK as a Member State (in fields such as Economic and Monetary Union, the Area of Freedom, Security and Justice, and under enhanced co-operation);[39] and those concerning Union citizens' political rights (citizens' initiatives and voting in local elections).[40] Furthermore, the Withdrawal Agreement describes other situations in which the UK is subject to special treatment: for example, no British participation in any future enhanced cooperation (whether entirely new, or existing but not yet implemented);[41] restrictions on the UK's ability to opt-into additional

---

[33] Decision supplementing the Council Decision of 22 May 2017, together with Annex containing supplementary directives (29 January 2018).

[34] E.g. Commission, *Position Paper (to EU27) on Transitional Arrangements in the Withdrawal Agreement* (7 February 2018); HMG, *Draft Text for Discussion: Implementation Period* (21 February 2018); Commission, *Part Four: Transition* in *Draft Withdrawal Agreement* (TF50 (2018) 33 of 28 February 2018); Commission, *Part Four: Transition* in *Draft Withdrawal Agreement* (TF50 (2018) 33/2 of 15 March 2018).

[35] TF50 (2018) 35 of 19 March 2018.

[36] As published in OJ 2019 C 66 I.

[37] Note also Art 127(6) WA: during transition, references to a 'Member State' in applicable Union law shall generally be understood as including the UK.

[38] Art 127(3) WA.

[39] Art 127(1), second paragraph, subparagraph (a) WA.

[40] Art 127(1), second paragraph, subparagraph (b) WA.

[41] Art 127(4) WA.

AFSJ measures (particularly those measures which do not merely amend, build on, or replace existing AFSJ acts that are already binding on the UK);[42] and British exclusion from Permanent Structured Cooperation under Article 42 TEU (the UK being able to associate only via the Union's own regime on third country cooperation).[43] Part Four also prescribes various restrictions on UK access to certain security-related sensitive information;[44] as well as the exclusion of UK nationals from recruitment as Union officials etc.[45] In addition, Article 185 WA provides the possibility for Member States to cease surrendering own nationals to the UK during transition pursuant to the European Arrest Warrant (in which case, the UK may take reciprocal (in)action). In due course, only Germany, Austria, and Slovenia decided to avail themselves of that particular option.[46]

However, the most extensive deviations from the 'status quo' assumption underpinning transition concern the UK's institutional status under Union law. In accordance with Article 7 WA, the UK is excluded from membership, decision-making, and governance as regards all Union entities and structures during the transition period.[47] There are only limited exceptions: for example, UK representatives may attend meetings of certain Union committees and expert groups etc, on an exceptional and invited basis, where the Member States also take part, and either the discussion concerns individual acts addressed to UK actors, or the UK's presence is necessary and in the Union's interest for the effective implementation of Union law.[48]

Further implications of the UK's institutional non-existence from the point of withdrawal are also spelled out in the Withdrawal Agreement: for example, the UK's parliament cannot issue 'reasoned opinions' objecting to Union proposals on subsidiarity grounds;[49] and the UK is not entitled to submit proposals or requests as if it were still a Member State.[50] Article 130 WA also makes specific provision as regards fisheries: for the purposes of Article 43(3) TFEU, as regards any period falling under transition, the UK will merely be consulted as regards fishing opportunities relating to the UK itself; though the Union commits to maintaining its relative stability keys for the allocation of relevant fishing opportunities.[51]

---

[42] Art 127(5) WA. The UK had requested more extensive opt-in rights as regards AFSJ measures: see HMG, *Draft Text for Discussion: Implementation Period* (21 February 2018).

[43] Art 127(7)(a) WA.

[44] Art 127(7)(b) WA.

[45] Art 127(7)(c) WA.

[46] See Art 4 of Council Decision 2019/274 on the signing, on behalf of the European Union and of the European Atomic Energy Community, of the Agreement on the withdrawal of the United Kingdom of Great Britain and Northern Ireland from the European Union and the European Atomic Energy Community, OJ 2019 L 471/1; leading to Declaration by the European Union (made in accordance with Art 185 WA), OJ 2020 L 29/188. The Agreement contains other specific derogations from the 'status quo' principle underpinning transition, e.g. in Part Five on the financial settlement.

[47] Art 128(1) WA.

[48] Art 128(5) WA. See also Art 34(1) WA on administrative cooperation as regards social security coordination.

[49] Art 128(2) WA.

[50] Art 128(3) WA. See also Art 128(4) WA on the ECB/ESCB; Art 128(6) WA on lead authorities for risk assessments etc under Union law; Art 129(7) WA on operational leadership under the CFSP/CSDP.

[51] The UK had requested the need for prior EU–UK agreement on the UK's fishing quotas (see HMG, *Draft Text for Discussion: Implementation Period* (21 February 2018)) but this was refused.

Despite its institutional exclusion, the UK remains bound by the duty of sincere co-operation throughout the transition period.[52] In addition, Part Four of the Withdrawal Agreement contains provisions on supervision and enforcement during transition.[53] Under Article 131 WA, the Union's institutions, bodies, and agencies etc shall have their powers under Union law in relation to UK authorities, natural and legal persons and residents etc (for example, as regards Commission competition and state aid investigations).[54] In particular, the CJEU shall have jurisdiction as provided for in the Treaties: thus allowing (say) for enforcement proceedings against the UK and preliminary references from British courts; also (during transition) as regards interpretation and application of the Withdrawal Agreement itself.[55] Moreover, the Withdrawal Agreement includes a further body of rules on the conclusion of judicial and administrative proceedings still pending at the expiry of the transition period or arising from facts which occurred before the end of transition.[56]

Article 126 WA provides that transition will expire on 31 December 2020 (corresponding to the end of the Union's current MFF). However, Article 132 WA also provides that the Joint Committee might (before 1 July 2020) adopt a single decision extending transition for 'up to one or two years'. However, any extended transition period would have been conducted under somewhat varied terms and conditions: for example, the UK would have been treated as a third country for the purpose of implementing Union programmes and activities under the MFF applicable as from 2021; (without prejudice to Part Five of the Withdrawal Agreement) Union law concerning own resources relating to the financial years covered by any extension would not have applied to the UK after 31 December 2020; the Joint Committee would have had to specify restrictions on the permissible levels of UK agricultural subsidies during any extension; and the Joint Committee would also have had to agree on an appropriate UK contribution to the Union budget to cover any prolongation of its privileged association with the Union. However, as we know, the UK did not in fact request any extension in accordance with Article 132 WA—thus confirming that transition will indeed expire on 31 December 2020.[57]

B. Objectives of Transition and Likelihood of their Delivery

What were the main objectives behind the UK's request for a post-withdrawal, status quo transitional regime and how likely is it that those objectives will be realized in practice? From the UK's perspective, transition might serve four main purposes: two

---

[52] A point specifically reinforced in respect of Union external relations: Art 129(3) WA.

[53] Note that various provisions concerning supervision and enforcement (e.g. UK preliminary references and independent monitoring authority as regards citizens' rights; e.g. dispute settlement via Joint Committee and by arbitration panel) will only apply from the end of transition: Art 185 WA.

[54] Also: Art 95 WA on the binding force and enforceability of Union decisions vis-à-vis the UK.

[55] Also: Art 89 WA on the binding force and enforceability of CJEU rulings vis-à-vis the UK.

[56] See Title X, Part Three; especially Arts 86–87 WA (judicial proceedings) and Arts 92–93 WA (administrative proceedings). See further below.

[57] See, e.g. Commission, *Press statement by Vice-President Maroš Šefčovič following the second meeting of the EU-UK Joint Committee* (12 June 2020). See also, e.g. EU–UK Statement following the High Level Meeting on 15 June 2020.

that were originally acknowledged in the Florence Speech; another that was explicitly added into the mix by the UK Government later in the negotiations; and a final goal that certain more cynical observers (the present author included) have speculated about, based on the words and deeds of certain senior British politicians over the passage of time.

First, Prime Minister May claimed that transition would give both parties more time to plan for the full consequences of the UK's withdrawal, in terms of their respective internal legal and logistical preparations: certainly useful in the EU's case, particularly as regards raising awareness among those public and private actors across the Member States most likely to be affected in practice by the UK's departure;[58] absolutely essential for the UK, given its almost total lack of pre-referendum preparations and the sheer scale of the task facing even just the Government and Parliament simply to ready the UK legal system for the very act of withdrawal.[59] Transition was originally meant to provide a baseline extra 20 months for post-withdrawal planning but in the end, the Article 50 TEU process dragged on for so long, that much of that extra time was made available, simply by repeatedly extending the UK's formal membership, leaving transition itself to supply only an additional 11 months for Brexit preparations.[60] Yet that extra time was still critical for the UK in carrying on with its basic legislative and regulatory planning for life entirely outside the Union.[61]

Secondly, the Florence Speech also made clear that transition was intended to give the parties more time to finalize the terms of their future relationship, so that public and private actors need only experience the expense and inconvenience of a single major regulatory change, i.e. at the end of transition, rather than once at the time of withdrawal and then again upon the entry into force of an agreement on future relations.[62] That original objective is closely related to the UK's third goal for transition, which emerged somewhat later in the negotiations, though both considerations together prompted the British to request the additional power of extension that was eventually enshrined in Article 132 WA.[63] Of course, it was possible that the original fixed-period transition might eventually prove insufficient to negotiate and ratify the agreements required to structure the future EU–UK relationship. But in addition, the UK Government became increasingly concerned that, should transition expire without any future relationship agreement in place, it would not only lead to 'two regulatory changes' but also trigger automatic application of the Irish backstop provisions

---

[58] Consider, e.g. the Commission's numerous 'preparedness' notices available via https://ec.europa.eu/info/brexit/brexit-preparedness/preparedness-notices_en.

[59] See the more detailed discussion in Chapter 2.

[60] I.e. from 1 February 2020–31 December 2020.

[61] E.g. the UK Government only announced its new plans for post-Brexit immigration in February 2020: see Home Office, *The UK's Points-Based Immigration System* (19 February 2020). At the time of writing, Parliament is still to adopt primary legislation setting out the framework for post-Brexit regimes not only as regards immigration but also in fields such as agriculture, fisheries and trade.

[62] Similarly, e.g. David Davis, *Speech at UBS* (14 November 2017); and *Speech to the Suddeutsche Zeitung Economic Summit* (16 November 2017). An objective supported also the Union itself, e.g. Commission, *Press Statement by Michael Barnier following the General Affairs Council (Article 50) on the adoption of negotiating directives on transitional arrangements* (29 January 2018).

[63] Confirmed by the European Council President in remarks to the European Parliament (24 October 2018).

as agreed by Theresa May in November 2018 (in the face of virulent opposition from Europhobic Tories).[64]

Among the measures requested by the UK in order to help avoid such an outcome (and deter a parliamentary rebellion) was the potential to extend transition: if it appeared likely that January 2021 would arrive with no future relationship agreement in place, the UK could at least choose between either further prolonging the status quo, in the expectation of still reaching a prompt new settlement that would deliver only 'one regulatory change' as well as supersede the Irish backstop; or instead allowing transition to expire, thus letting the backstop become operable, and also accepting that 'two regulatory changes' would eventually be needed in due course.[65]

Given the change in political direction heralded by the 2019 UK general election, the nature and importance of those previously interlinked objectives has now changed substantially. Indeed, the previous UK desire for some mechanism to avoid triggering the Irish backstop is no longer even relevant: the old May arrangements have been replaced by a Johnson alternative which the UK Government was happy to sign up to, without any appreciable risk of splitting the Conservative Party.[66] And as for guarding against 'two regulatory changes', we know that the Johnson Government ruled out requesting any extension of the transition period as provided for under Article 132 WA.[67] We must now proceed in the expectation that comprehensive terms for the future Union–UK relationship will be fully settled in time for 1 January 2021. If not, the Withdrawal Agreement and its transition period will only have postponed the dreaded 'regulatory cliff-edge' and Brexit will indeed ultimately entail 'two regulatory changes'—the very twin prospects which had so discombobulated Johnson's predecessor.

Fourthly and finally, many commentators have suggested (drawing not least upon the conduct of various UK politicians within as well as outside government over a sustained period of time) that the post-withdrawal, status quo transition period might serve another useful if rather more cynical purpose: to create significant space and time between the actual act of departure (on the one hand) and the eventual emergence of its true consequences (on the other hand) sufficient to establish a plausible deniability that any negative impacts upon the UK should actually be attributed to leaving the EU; and to limit the extent to which the relevant decision-makers could convincingly be held responsible and accountable in the court of public opinion. 'Brexit got done' on 31 January 2020, so whatever might happen many months later (i.e. when an unextended transition expires, with or without any replacement deal ready to take effect) can hardly be the fault of Brexit or the Brexiters ....[68]

---

[64] See the more detailed discussion in Chapters 4 and 8.

[65] E.g. Theresa May, *Statement on European Council* (22 October 2018).

[66] See the more detailed discussion in Chapters 5 and 8.

[67] Indeed, even going so far as to enshrine its position in primary legislation: section 15A EU(W)A 2018 (as amended) provides that '[a] Minister of the Crown may not agree in the Joint Committee to an extension of the implementation period'. The original provisions setting out a procedure for approving any extension of the transition period were also repealed: see section 36 EU(WA)A 2020.

[68] Note reports about the UK Government's attempts to restrict the official use of words such as 'Brexit' after 31 January 2020, e.g. https://www.theguardian.com/politics/2020/feb/04/no-more-deal-or-no-deal-no-10s-brexit-diktat-to-foreign-office.

Of course, it is now arguable that events have overtaken even that (real or projected) political objective. Since the onset of the global pandemic, it is likely that the UK will find itself experiencing serious economic and social problems across the winter of 2020–2021 due in any event to the health and economic impacts of responding to Covid-19. As such, the projected expiry of the transition period on 31 December 2020, and any additional economic and social disruption resulting from the UK's full conversion to third country status in its relations with the Union, may prove difficult (if not impossible) to disaggregate, either in practice or at least in the public mind, from the existing and ongoing crisis brought about through the pandemic itself. Naturally, cynics might wonder whether the Johnson Government's conscious decision to risk an entirely foreseeable and avoidable 'double impact' of pandemic plus post-transition Brexit, merely magnifies the opportunities for political scapegoating in due course: either the virus, or expiry of the transition period, might be called upon to take the blame, according to the prevailing winds, for whatever problems the UK finds itself grappling with in the early months of 2021.

C. The UK as a 'Vassal State' of the Union?

On the UK side, transition might (partially) serve several (more or less legitimate) political objectives, but it has been controversial chiefly because of the criticism that it reduces the UK to a 'vassal state' of the Union—bound by almost all of the latter's rules but without any say over their adoption.[69] There is obviously some truth in that criticism, though it is usually voiced without any countervailing acknowledgment of the fact that it was the UK Government that proposed transition in its current form, in order to shield fundamental British interests from the consequences of the UK's very own choices.

Nevertheless, perceptions about the one-sided nature of transition were reinforced by the UK's limited success in changing the terms originally proposed by the Commission.[70] For example, the fact that the UK's transitional obligations also cover any legislative, administrative, or judicial developments in Union law that might occur during the relevant period proved particularly contentious within the UK, with Leave activists claiming that the EU might adopt measures deliberately designed to harm British interests.[71] The UK Government therefore tried but failed to secure an explicit mechanism for the Joint Committee to address disputes about the applicability of new Union measures to the UK.[72] Undeterred, the UK Government claimed that the general duty of good faith under Article 5 WA, together with the ordinary powers of the

---

[69] See, e.g. https://www.theguardian.com/politics/2018/jan/24/david-davis-rejects-vassal-state-claim-over-brexit-transition.

[70] Note, e.g. Commission, *Remarques par Michel Barnier au point presse à l'issue du Conseil affaires généraux (Article 50)* (27 February 2018).

[71] A point publicly contested by the UK Government, e.g. David Davis, *Teesport Speech: Implementation Period—A Bridge to the Future Partnership between the UK and EU* (26 January 2018).

[72] See HMG, *Draft Text for Discussion: Implementation Period* (21 February 2018). See instead Art 128(7) WA on limited consultation with the UK as regards certain draft Union acts during transition; and Art 129(5) WA on case-by-case coordination with the UK in respect of Union external relations.

Joint Committee, would be sufficient to meet British concerns about unwanted infra-transition changes to Union law.[73] Yet the obligation to act in good faith is explicitly without prejudice to the application of Union law as prescribed under the Withdrawal Agreement; while the Joint Committee enjoys no power to adapt or offer exemptions from the UK's transitional obligations, including those arising from post-withdrawal developments in Union law.[74] Still undeterred, the UK's domestic implementing legislation now purports to provide for some vague parliamentary 'review' of Union measures adopted or proposed during the transition period and considered to raise matters of 'vital national interest' to the UK.[75]

Another example concerns the free movement of persons. In accordance with its longstanding hostility towards immigration in general, and that of EU citizens in particular, the UK Government tried to insist that the date of actual withdrawal (rather than subsequent expiry of the transition period) should act as the relevant reference point: both for ending the applicability of Union free movement rules to the UK; and also for calculating the range of persons entitled to citizens' rights protection under the Withdrawal Agreement itself.[76] However, the Union remained adamant that the free movement of persons would be maintained during transition along with the rest of Union law, while the relevant date for the purposes of calculating entitlement to protection under Part Two of the Withdrawal Agreement must be the end of transition. Nevertheless, the Union did concede that, even during the transition period, though only on a voluntary basis, the UK could begin rolling out its new 'settled status' scheme for the registration of Union citizens qualifying for protection under the Withdrawal Agreement; and that the UK could then reduce the final deadlines for Union citizens to apply for 'settled status' when the registration requirement subsequently became compulsory, i.e. upon expiry of the transition period.[77]

The UK's demands bore greater fruit in the field of external relations. True, the UK was again soundly rebuffed when it challenged the Union proposal, whereby the British might negotiate, sign, and ratify international agreements in areas of exclusive Union competence, but could only bring such treaties into force during transition with the Council's specific authorization.[78] But the UK did manage to secure certain concessions. For example: as regards new Council decisions under Chapter 2, Title V TEU on the Common Foreign and Security Policy (CFSP), the UK may declare that, for vital and stated reasons of national policy, the UK exceptionally will not apply a particular decision;[79] and the Withdrawal Agreement also provides that, should the

---

[73] E.g. David Davis, *Statement on EU-UK Article 50 Negotiations* (19 March 2018).

[74] See Arts 5, third paragraph and 164 WA.

[75] See section 13A EU(W)A 2018 (as amended).

[76] See HMG, *UK Policy Statement: EU Citizens Arriving in the UK During the Implementation Period* (28 February 2018).

[77] See Arts 18–19 WA and the more detailed discussion in Chapter 7.

[78] Art 129(4) WA. Note the more detailed authorization process provided for under Art 3 of Council Decision 2020/135 on the conclusion of the Agreement on the withdrawal of the United Kingdom of Great Britain and Northern Ireland from the European Union and the European Atomic Energy Community, OJ 2020 L 29/1. Contrast with the UK proposals contained in HMG, *Draft Text for Discussion: Implementation Period* (21 February 2018).

[79] Art 129(6) WA—though the UK must then refrain from action likely to conflict with/impede Union action based on that decision.

EU and the UK manage to conclude a new agreement in the field of CFSP, or the Common Security and Defence Policy (CSDP), during the transition period, that new agreement may displace the need for continued UK adherence to the relevant provisions of Union law.[80]

The UK's (admittedly limited) influence over the terms of its own transition can be seen not only in what the final text of Part Four says, but also in some of the things that text does not say. For example, the Commission had originally proposed that the Union should enjoy additional powers of enforcement vis-à-vis the UK for the duration of the transition period. In particular, if the Union were to consider that the UK had not fulfilled a Union law obligation (as established in a final judgment on enforcement proceedings rendered by the CJEU during the transition period), or if the Union were to consider that the UK had not respected an interim order (again rendered by the CJEU during the transition period), and the situation might jeopardize the functioning of the Single Market or the Customs Union or the Union's financial stability, then the Union should be entitled to suspend certain benefits of the UK's continued participation in the Single Market.[81] However, the UK strongly objected to those Commission proposals and the latter were eventually excluded from the final Withdrawal Agreement.[82]

D. Treating the UK as if it Were Still a Member State?

On the EU side, the transitional arrangements were less politically sensitive, but still raise some interesting constitutional questions.

Needless to say: transition periods are nothing new to Union law. We are used to certain types of transition being enshrined even in primary law: for example, for the gradual extension of full rights and obligations to newly acceded Member States;[83] or to manage the orderly introduction of new institutional arrangements.[84] Transition periods are also an integral part of the practice of Union secondary law (whether laid down directly in legislative acts or created under delegated powers) so as to ensure the smooth replacement of one regime by another without adversely affecting the legitimate rights and interests of natural and legal persons.[85] Moreover, the Court is

---

[80] Art 127(2) WA—though this possibility appears to have been rendered defunct by the Johnson Government's decision not to pursue any new agreement with the Union in the field of CFSP/CSDP: see further the discussion in Chapter 9. Note that the UK sought but failed to secure a similar 'displacement' provision also in respect of AFSJ measures: see HMG, *Draft Text for Discussion: Implementation Period* (21 February 2018).

[81] Provided any such suspension was proportionate, took into account the consequences for natural and legal persons, and was for a maximum period of three months (renewable).

[82] See: Commission, *Position Paper on Transitional Arrangements*, TF50 (2018) 30; proposed Art 165 of the draft Withdrawal Agreement (TF50 (2018) 33/2). Note also Commission, *Press statement by Michel Barnier following this week's round of Article 50 negotiations (6th–9th February)* (9 February 2019).

[83] See, e.g. C. Hillion (ed.), *EU Enlargement: A Legal Approach* (2004).

[84] E.g. as with Protocol No 36 on transitional provisions (implementing the institutional changes agreed under the Treaty of Lisbon 2007).

[85] Particularly in fields such as agricultural policy: consider, e.g. Article 30 of Regulation 404/93 on the common organization of the market in bananas, OJ 1993 L 47/1 as interpreted in rulings such as Case C-442/99, *Cordis v Commission* (EU:C:2001:493) and Case C-312/00, *Commission v Camar* (EU:C:2002:736).

sometimes called upon to evaluate the appropriateness and/or adequacy of national transitional regimes, under the primary Treaty provisions, during the process of investigating the objective justification of prima facie barriers to free movement.[86]

However, such previous experiences seem of little assistance to the very different context of designing a transitional regime for the outright withdrawal of a Member State from the Union legal order.[87] Our attention needs to focus more directly upon Article 50 TEU: what is the nature of this legal basis, and in particular, what are its limits, at least when it comes to transition?

After all, Article 50 TEU adopts the fundamental premiss that the Treaties will cease to apply to the UK at the moment of its withdrawal when it formally becomes a third country.[88] As we mentioned above, that premiss is also reflected in the Preamble to the Withdrawal Agreement itself: 'pursuant to Article 50 TEU ... and subject to the arrangements laid down in this Agreement, the law of the Union ... in its entirety ceases to apply to the United Kingdom from the date of entry into force of this Agreement'. And yet the Union agreed to an ambitious transitional regime based on the wholesale extension of Union law to the UK just as if it were still a Member State (albeit subject to some important, though still limited, institutional and substantive exceptions).

Rather than constructing an entire edifice of free-standing, comprehensive, and detailed EU–third-country cooperation mechanisms that would have given specific legal expression to the two sides' overall political conception of a 'status quo' transition,[89] the Withdrawal Agreement provides that vast tracts of the Treaties, Union legislation and other legal or policy instruments did not actually cease to apply to the UK from the moment of its withdrawal, but instead were extended and applied wholesale to the territory, public authorities, and natural or legal persons of a third country. The consequences of that approach are no less far-reaching and significant for being so disarmingly obvious: across every field of Union activity, third-country phenomena were fully entitled to engage (say) in the exercise of rights, the exchange of information, the allocation of jurisdiction, the mutual recognition of standards and the enforcement of decisions—including under legal frameworks and through processes where such rights and obligations are explicitly reserved for Union actors alone.[90]

On the one hand, there were obviously good practical reasons during the Article 50 TEU negotiations to explain the transitional model chosen by the Union and the UK: given how much was still left to be done, and how little time remained to do it, there was no credible prospect of negotiating and drafting up the sort of free-standing, comprehensive, and detailed cooperation mechanisms that would be required to express a politically ambitious transitional arrangement in terms more legally appropriate to relations between the Union and a third country. Moreover, we know that Article 50 TEU is an unusual legal basis designed to deal with a novel situation: it

---

[86] E.g. Case C-309/02, *Radlberger* (EU:C:2004:799); Case C-320/03, *Commission v Austria* (EU:C:2005:684); Case C-377/07, *STEKO Industriemontage* (EU:C:2009:29).

[87] Especially since, in the case of the UK's withdrawal, the terms of both departure and transition were being negotiated and agreed with no clear and settled alternative end-state in sight.

[88] See also, e.g. Council Decision of 22 May 2017, at paras 6 and 8 of the Annex.

[89] Again, the EEA Agreement providing a potential model in this regard.

[90] See further, e.g. Dougan, 'An airbag for the crash test dummies? EU–UK negotiations for a post-withdrawal 'status quo' transitional regime under Article 50 TEU', 55 *CMLRev Special Issue* (2018) 57.

needs to be interpreted flexibly, in order to deal with the unprecedented circumstances of its operation; and its relatively skeletal text both offers a wide political discretion, and requires significant political elaboration in order to render it fully operational.[91] For those purposes, we also know that the Union institutions already signalled their understanding that Article 50 TEU confers an exceptional competence which might in some respects deviate from our ordinary expectations under Union constitutional law.[92]

On the other hand, even an exceptional power must have its limits. A transitional regime based on the direct and wholesale (even if only temporary) extension of the Union legal order to the territory of a third country represents a highly expansive conception of the competences conferred by Article 50 TEU. Such a conception is not only difficult to square with the explicit text of Article 50 TEU itself—which, moreover, gives no express indication that it was intended to confer upon the Union institutions a substantively exceptional power, capable of derogating from our normal expectations about the constitutional nature and limits of Union competence. It also sits uneasily with myriad other provisions of Union law: for example, by calling for a broader understanding of the beneficiaries of the rights to free movement and equal treatment than that explicitly set out in the relevant Treaty provisions and their implementing legislation;[93] or by expanding the category of privileged applicants, for the purposes of access to judicial review before the Union courts, beyond the restricted categories already expressly identified in the Treaties.[94]

Furthermore, Article 50 TEU explicitly provides a means simply to continue the wholesale application of Union law on a purely temporary basis for the benefit of a Member State which is nevertheless intent on its own departure: the possibility of an extension agreed within the European Council and/or the delayed entry into force of any withdrawal agreement itself.[95] Such explicit mechanisms could have achieved at least some (albeit not all) of the key objectives underpinning the desire for a prolongation of the status quo. But for its own essentially domestic political reasons, the UK chose not to rely on those explicit mechanisms—or at least, relied on them only partially and even then with great reluctance.[96]

Such questions and concerns might now appear more theoretical than real: after all, challenging the Union's very competence to contract such a far-reaching transition regime will soon appear practically pointless or positively mischievous. But it is still relevant and interesting to speculate about how the Court might have responded if it had been asked to verify the legality of the transitional regime against the powers

---

[91] See the more detailed discussion in Chapter 2. And see further, e.g. House of Commons Exiting the EU Committee, *The progress of the UK's negotiations with the EU on withdrawal* (HC372 of 1 December 2017); House of Lords EU Committee, *Brexit: Deal or No Deal* (HL46 of 7 December 2017).

[92] See the more detailed discussion in Chapter 3, particularly as regards the exclusivity of Union competence conferred by Art 50 TEU.

[93] In particular: Directive 2004/38, OJ 2004 L 158/77.

[94] Under Art 263 TFEU.

[95] See the more detailed discussion in Chapters 4 and 5.

[96] E.g. David Davis, *Teesport Speech: Implementation Period—A Bridge to the Future Partnership between the UK and EU* (26 January 2018). See further, e.g. Łazowski, 'Exercises in Legal Acrobatics: The Brexit Transitional Arrangements', 2 *European Papers* (2017) 845.

conferred upon the Union under Article 50 TEU within the overall system of competences created under the Treaties.

Of course, the Court is fundamentally sympathetic to the importance of transition in order to safeguard legal certainty and to protect the rights and interests of individuals: '[i]t must be acknowledged that any transition from one law to another will not be immediate but will take a certain amount of time'.[97] And had it been asked, the Court would surely have been naturally reluctant to interfere in any fundamental way with a transitional regime that enjoyed the support of all relevant and responsible decision-making actors, particularly within the confines of a strictly time-limited process that could scarcely have allowed for any fundamental efforts at redesign, such that judicial objection to the draft withdrawal agreement could have been tantamount to imposing a 'no deal' (or at least a radically different deal) upon both the Union and the UK at relatively short notice—virtually the opposite outcome from the objectives of legal certainty and careful planning that the very notion of transition is meant to deliver.[98]

That said, there is limited authority in the existing caselaw to suggest that the Court might indeed have expressed a degree of scepticism towards institutional attempts to prolong the temporal application of Union law, beyond the date clearly prescribed by the Treaties themselves, by falling back upon a hierarchically inferior legal instrument —or at least one whose legal basis is open to contestation. In particular, *Parliament v Council* concerned the Council's attempt to extend the temporal application of a voluntary beef labelling system beyond the date clearly laid down by the relevant Union regulation. The Court held that the latter could only be amended on a legal basis equivalent to that on which it had been adopted; not (as here) by means of a subordinate measure enacted under powers conferred by the parent regulation itself.[99] Transcribing that principle up one level within the Union hierarchy of norms, one might argue that the range of possible dates upon which the Treaties should cease to apply to the relevant State has been clearly identified by Article 50 TEU and could only be amended by changing the Treaties themselves—not by means of a subordinate international agreement which seeks to extend the temporal application of Union law directly to a State which has by then formally withdrawn and become a third country.

Nor should we overlook the highly pertinent backdrop provided by the landmark *Opinion on ECHR Accession*.[100] Should the special nature of EU membership—based on a particular balance of rights and obligations, supported by ambitious institutional structures, entrenched within a sophisticated constitutional order—not have inclined us against a transitional model which seeks directly to extend that unique ecosystem to a non-Member State, and does so largely because of the latter's own lack of responsible government preparations, combined with its self-generated internal political obsessions, which together conspired to rule out, either the simple prolongation solutions explicitly provided for by the Treaties, or the (admittedly more complex

---

[97] Joined Cases C-159/10 and C-160/10, *Fuchs* (EU:C:2001:508), at para 95. Also, e.g. Case C-309/02, *Radlberger* (EU:C:2004:799).

[98] Contrast, e.g. with the situation surrounding Union accession to the ECHR as addressed in Opinion 2/13, *Accession to ECHR* (EU:C:2014:2454).

[99] Case C-93/00, *Parliament v Council* (EU:C:2001:689).

[100] Opinion 2/13, *Accession to ECHR* (EU:C:2014:2454).

and time-consuming) transitional mechanisms properly called for by its true third country status?

E. Extending Transition Other Than Through Article 132 WA?

Even if the possibility of legal challenge to the status quo basis of the transitional model chosen under the Withdrawal Agreement now appears to be of purely theoretical interest, nevertheless, and at the time of writing, other scenarios remain in play that still raise interesting legal questions about the full nature and extent of the Union's competences under Article 50 TEU. In particular: now that the UK has allowed the deadline of 1 July 2020 to pass without requesting any additional transition, what if changing circumstances (not least the ongoing impact and disruption caused by the global pandemic) were to render the prospect, either of a 'no deal' outcome on 1 January 2021, or even of a major change in mutual relations based on an entirely new set of legal agreements, utterly unpalatable even for the Johnson Government—is there any alternative means by which the Union and the UK could still manage to extend the duration of the transition period?

With the 1 July 2020 deadline now passed, there is no other way to extend the transition period in accordance with the terms of the Withdrawal Agreement itself. For example, the Joint Committee' limited power to amend certain parts of the Withdrawal Agreement under particular circumstances and subject to various caveats could not possibly be used to enact a prolongation of transition after the explicit facility for extension lapses under Article 132 WA.[101] Yet in theory, it should remain possible to create additional transitional time by adopting an entirely new EU—UK treaty that amends the existing Withdrawal Agreement as a matter of public international law. From a UK constitutional perspective, a new treaty amending the existing Withdrawal Agreement could easily be agreed by the Government acting under its prerogative powers (even if that treaty would still then have to be implemented into UK law by primary legislation). But from an EU constitutional perspective, the Union would need to identify an appropriate legal basis directly under the Treaties conferring the competence to conclude any such amending treaty.

The easiest solution would obviously be to rely upon Article 50 TEU itself: a single legal basis, with clear voting rules based on a super-QMV vote in Council acting with the consent of the European Parliament, which the Union's political institutions have declared to be an exclusive Union competence excluding any requirement for or indeed possibility of national ratifications. And after all, an additional treaty extending the transition period would only entail a modification of the existing Withdrawal Agreement: it might seem natural to adopt the amending act on the same legal basis as the primary measure in question.

However, the converse argument is that Article 50 TEU simply cannot provide a valid legal basis for any further agreements between the Union and the UK: the possibilities of Article 50 TEU in relation to the UK were exhausted by the latter's definitive

---

[101] See above for discussion of the Joint Committee's powers under the WA.

act of withdrawal, after which the UK as a third country no longer qualifies as a relevant State (a 'Member State which decides to withdraw') for the purposes of the Union's treaty-making powers under that specific Treaty provision. As the Preamble to the Withdrawal Agreement itself states: 'pursuant to Article 50 TEU ... and subject to the arrangements laid down in this Agreement, the law of the Union ... *in its entirety* ceases to apply to the United Kingdom from the date of entry into force of this Agreement'.[102] And as Article 50(5) TEU suggests (at least in relation to future re-accession, but arguably merely expressing a more general principle): having seen through its intention to leave the Union, the relevant third country should no longer expect to benefit from special privileges or allowances as a matter of the Union's own constitutional law.

On balance, it seems fair to admit that Article 50 TEU itself does not provide an obvious or compelling textual answer to the question of Union competence to conclude additional withdrawal treaties with its former Member State-now-turned third country. Once again, the contest perhaps boils down to pragmatic considerations of obvious mutual convenience *versus* more fundamental issues of legal principle. Among the latter, in particular: there must be some limit, even to exceptional legal bases. Article 50 TEU offers a wide-ranging power to conclude a withdrawal agreement, based on an unusually broad exclusive Union competence, and that withdrawal agreement might well contain provisions for a wide-ranging transitional regime, and indeed the explicit possibility of extending that transition period for an additional period of time. But Article 50 TEU cannot be construed as a power for the Union also to enter into repeat agreements, now with a third country, offering exceptional substantive benefits, delivered through an exceptional ratification process—particularly when the only reason for doing so is because the third country in question, again for essentially domestic political reasons entirely of its own making and choosing, deliberately refused to make use of the extension facility it itself had originally requested.

If Article 50 TEU is not available as a valid legal basis, could an additional extension to the status quo transitional regime (outside the terms of Article 132 WA) be concluded pursuant to the Union's ordinary external competences found elsewhere under the Treaties? The Commission has previously suggested that Article 50 TEU provides the only legal basis available under the Treaties to create a transitional regime following a Member State's withdrawal from the Union.[103] Even if it were possible to recreate the full breadth and depth of the existing transition period other than via Article 50 TEU, any such agreement would surely entail recourse to multiple legal bases corresponding to the full range of Union policies and activities covered by the 'status quo' premiss underpinning Part Four of the Withdrawal Agreement.

Besides requiring unanimous support within the Council itself, such an agreement would also—and this time both inevitably and inescapably—qualify as a mixed agreement: there could surely be no possibility of treating this situation as an exceptional and exclusive Union competence. In order to preserve the possibility of timely ratification, the Member State governments would therefore also need unanimously to waive the possibility of insisting also upon national ratifications. After all, the prospect of

---

[102] Emphasis added.
[103] COM(2017) 830 Final, at p 2.

full-on mixity leading to a barrage of domestic (national as well as regional) approval processes would render the whole exercise entirely pointless.[104]

In short: if the political desire did materialize for an additional treaty amending the existing Withdrawal Agreement so as to prolong the transition period (without the parties' having exercised the explicit power conferred for that purpose under Article 132 WA within the applicable time-limit), and if the Union's legal competence to adopt such a treaty under Article 50 TEU (or some other equally and conveniently self-contained legal basis) were indeed challenged before the CJEU, the latter would be faced with a difficult conundrum. Realistically, there is no compelling answer that can be logically deduced from the Treaty texts or legal principles alone. As in so many other contexts, Article 50 TEU needs to be interpreted in a way that finds constitutionally tolerable solutions to urgent political problems. If the European Council were unanimously to endorse it, with the other Union institutions also happily on board, then it might prove very difficult for the Court to discover, on an ex-post basis, constitutional obstacles of the sort that would entirely frustrate an otherwise workable solution reached under extreme political circumstances.

F. Transition and Existing Union External Agreements?

In any case, for both parties, the agreement on transition created certain common challenges—particularly as regards existing Union external agreements with other third countries/international organizations.

As discussed in Chapter 4, in its Guidelines of April 2017, the European Council declared that, after withdrawal, the UK will no longer be covered by agreements concluded by the Union, or by its Member States on the Union's behalf, or by the Union and its Member States acting jointly.[105] Although estimates for a precise figure differ, this declaration certainly applies to several hundred international agreements across every imaginable field of cross-border cooperation.[106] With a view to reaching a stable solution to the implications of UK withdrawal for the Union's existing external relations, the April 2017 Guidelines refer to the desirability of dialogue between the two parties so as to pursue a possible common approach:[107] we have already mentioned, for example, the joint Union–UK initiative to manage the implications of withdrawal for the parties' respective terms of membership of the WTO.[108]

Otherwise, the UK could hardly escape the need for a case-by-case analysis of its potential legal status, rights, and obligations in relation to each and every relevant international agreement; or the widespread expectation that the British would need

---

[104] See further the discussion of Union external competences, and the additional procedural hurdles associated with mixity, in Chapter 3.

[105] European Council, *Guidelines of 29 April 2017* (Article 50), at para 13.

[106] See further, e.g. e.g. Wessel, 'Consequences of Brexit for international agreements concluded by the EU and its Member States', 55 *CMLRev Special Issue* (2018) 101.

[107] European Council, *Guidelines of 29 April 2017* (Article 50), at para 13.

[108] E.g. consider the frosty reception afforded to the EU–UK joint letter of 11 October 2017 seeking to propose joint solutions to the issues raised by UK withdrawal when it comes to the World Trade Organization. See further, e.g. Messenger, 'Membership of the World Trade Organisation' in M. Dougan (ed.), *The UK After Brexit: Legal and Policy Challenges* (2017).

actively to adjust and rebuild their international legal relations in a large number of situations with a large number of international partners based on an extensive programme of bilateral and multilateral negotiations.[109] For example, alongside its Article 50 TEU negotiations with the Union itself, the UK sought (and in many but certainly not all cases succeeded) to persuade a range of third countries to replicate (subject to various adjustments) the terms of their existing EU trade agreements with the UK, i.e. into the future and on a purely bilateral basis.[110]

But the question also arose: how might the Union's existing external relations, and the parties' joint as well as separate efforts to manage the external impacts of the UK's departure, interact with the Withdrawal Agreement and its post-withdrawal, status quo transition period? On the one hand, Article 129(1) WA states that the UK shall remain bound by existing international agreements concluded by the Union, by the Member States acting on the Union's behalf, or by the Union and the Member States acting jointly.[111] And of course: there was nothing to stop the two parties agreeing to continue applying the terms of existing EU international agreements for the purposes of their own bilateral relations during the transition period (for example) so that the UK would continue to tax and treat third country imports in accordance with the existing Union customs regime.

On the other hand, a footnote to Article 129(1) WA provides that '[t]he Union will notify the other parties to these agreements that during the transition period the UK is to be treated as a Member State for the purposes of these agreements'.[112] Yet a purely bilateral agreement between the Union and the UK was no guarantee that third countries would automatically consent to maintain the legal effects of existing international agreements in their relations with the post-withdrawal UK. Indeed, there might be political and/or economic incentives to do otherwise: for example, if some other third country were to treat withdrawal as a convenient opportunity to exert pressure on and/or renegotiate terms with either the UK or the Union; or indeed, to regard withdrawal as a chance to re-introduce certain barriers to trade in relations with the UK while the latter was obliged to continue offering preferential trade terms in return.[113]

---

[109] See further, e.g. Cremona, 'UK Trade Policy' in M. Dougan (ed.), *The UK After Brexit: Legal and Policy Challenges* (2017). The situation of the EEA Agreement has attracted particular attention: see further, e.g. Sif Tynes and Haugsdal, 'In, out or in-between? The UK as a contracting party to the Agreement on the European Economic Area', 41 *ELRev* (2018) 753; Hillion, 'Brexit means Br(EEA)xit: The UK Withdrawal from the EU and its Implications for the EEA', 55 *CMLRev* (2018) 135.
[110] I.e. the so-called 'continuity agreements' with, e.g. Georgia, Morocco, Israel, and Chile.
[111] Also: Art 129(2) WA making limited provision for UK participation in any bodies etc established by/under such agreements. Note the UK's request for more extensive rights of attendance: see HMG, *Draft Text for Discussion: Implementation Period* (21 February 2018). See also the specific provision relating to fisheries: Art 130(3) WA.
[112] See also Art 3 of Council Decision 2019/274 on the signing, on behalf of the European Union and of the European Atomic Energy Community, of the Agreement on the withdrawal of the United Kingdom of Great Britain and Northern Ireland from the European Union and the European Atomic Energy Community, OJ 2019 L 471/1; together with Commission, *Template for the Note Verbale sent to International Partners after signature of the Withdrawal Agreement* (31 January 2020). Another footnote, to Art 132(1) WA, provides for further notification by the Union in the event of an extension to transition.
[113] I am very grateful to Marise Cremona for pointing out the parallels here with the 'lop-sided' nature of the EU–Turkey customs union agreement (Decision 1/95 of the EC–Turkey Association Council of 22 December 1995 on implementing the final phase of the Customs Union).

The success of the Withdrawal Agreement's approach to existing external agreements therefore always depended upon the parties' ability to persuade their other international partners to acquiesce in the assumptions underpinning the post-withdrawal, status quo transition—a reality publicly acknowledged by both the Union and the UK.[114] For example, Michel Barnier stated shortly after the Council's adoption of the Commission's supplementary negotiating directives on transition: '... we cannot ensure in the Article 50 agreement that the UK keeps the benefits from these international agreements. Our partners around the world may have their own views on this, for instance the 70 countries covered by trade deals'.[115] Similarly, the UK Secretary of State for Exiting the EU conceded that it would clearly be in the interests of the UK, the Union, and the relevant third countries for existing EU agreements to continue to apply also to the UK during any transitional period; and expressed the hope that all parties should therefore agree to that effect, while the UK continues to work on rolling over the legal effects of such agreements into the longer term.[116] More specialist studies will no doubt reveal how far third country partners, in practice, acquiesced in the Union's request to continue treating the UK as if it were a Member State during the transition period.[117]

4. After Transition

After the transition period expires, many of the provisions of the Withdrawal Agreement that were being held in abeyance will finally enter into force and/or become fully operational. In this section, we will provide various examples of the substantive provisions that will settle some of the key 'separation challenges' addressed in the Withdrawal Agreement; as well as the horizontal provisions concerning interpretation of the Withdrawal Agreement and dispute settlement through arbitration and by the CJEU.

A. A New Range of Rights and Obligations

Many of the substantive provisions of the Withdrawal Agreement that will enter into force only upon expiry of the transition period are to be found in Part Three concerning the 'other separation issues' raised by UK withdrawal.[118]

---

[114] See further, e.g. Wessel, 'Consequences of Brexit for international agreements concluded by the EU and its Member States', 55 *CMLRev Special Issue* (2018) 101.

[115] Michel Barnier, *Press Statement on the adoption of negotiating directives on transitional arrangements* (29 January 2018).

[116] David Davis, *Teesport Speech: Implementation Period—A Bridge to the Future Partnership between the UK and EU* (26 January 2018). Also, e.g. HMG, *Technical Note on International Agreements during the Implementation Period* (8 February 2018). Similarly, e.g. House of Lords European Union Committee, *Brexit: The Withdrawal Agreement and Political Declaration* (HL245 of 5 December 2018), at Chapter 3.

[117] The present author is certainly unaware of any major problems or disputes.

[118] Note the discussion, in Chapter 4, about how these general separation challenges figured in the Union's negotiating agenda under Art 50 TEU.

Some of those provisions relate to the internal market. By way of illustration, consider Title I of Part Three concerning goods lawfully placed on the market in the EU or the UK before the end of the transition period. In essence: such goods may be further made available on the EU/UK market and circulate between those markets until reaching their end-user, in accordance with the requirements contained in Articles 34 and 35 TFEU and any applicable Union rules governing the marketing of the relevant goods. However, that basic principle is subject to various exceptions and derogations. For example, it does not apply to the circulation between the Union and UK markets of live animals, germinal products, and animal products, though the movement of live animals or germinal products between a Member State and the UK may still take place in accordance with specific provisions of Union law (provided the date of departure was before the end of the transition period).[119] Moreover, the Withdrawal Agreement provides for cooperation between the competent authorities within the Union and the UK as regards their respective market surveillance activities in respect of goods lawfully placed on the market before the end of transition; together with additional provisions (for example) defining the circumstances in which a Member State or the UK should make available the marketing authorization dossiers of medicinal products which had been authorized by the competent authorities before the end of transition.

Other provisions of Part Three deal with the Area of Freedom, Security and Justice. By way of illustration, consider Title V concerning ongoing police and judicial cooperation in criminal matters, which governs the winding up of various outstanding EU–UK procedures. For example, both in the UK and in the Member States as regards situations involving the UK, Framework Decision 2002/584 shall apply in respect of European Arrest Warrants where the requested person was arrested before the end of the transition period for the purposes of executing a European Arrest Warrant (irrespective of the decision of the executing judicial authority as to whether the requested person should remain in detention or be provisionally released).[120] Similarly, both in the UK and in the Member States as regards situations involving the UK, Directive 2016/681 on the use of passenger name record data for the prevention, detection, investigation, and prosecution of terrorist offences and serious crime shall apply in respect of requests received by the competent national passenger information unit before the end of the transition period, in accordance with the relevant provisions of the Directive concerning the exchange of information between Member States or access to PNR data by Europol.[121]

Part Three also contains provisions addressing certain cross-sectoral 'separation issues'. Consider Title VII on data and information processed or obtained either before the end of the transition period or on the basis of the Withdrawal Agreement itself. For example, Article 71(1) WA provides that Union law on the protection of personal data shall apply in the UK in respect of the processing of personal data of data subjects outside the UK, provided that the personal data in question were either processed under Union law in the UK before the end of the transition period; or are processed in the UK after the end of transition but on the basis of the Withdrawal Agreement.

---

[119]   Listed in Annex II to the WA.
[120]   Art 62 WA.
[121]   Art 63 WA. See Arts 9 and 10 Directive 2016/681, OJ 2016 L 119/132.

That requirement shall not apply to the extent that the relevant processing of personal data is subject to an adequate level of protection as established in an 'adequacy decision' adopted by the Commission in accordance with the relevant Union data protection legislation.[122] However, to the extent that such an 'adequacy decision' ceases to apply, the UK must ensure a level of personal data protection essentially equivalent to that provided under Union law in respect of the processing of personal data of data subjects as referred to in Article 71(1) WA.

Title XII on privileges and immunities addresses some of the detailed diplomatic and personnel consequences of the UK's withdrawal. For example: the guarantee of inviolability provided for under Article 1 of Protocol No 7 on the Privileges and Immunities of the European Union shall apply in respect of the Union's premises and property etc in the UK, used by the Union before the end of transition, until the Union notifies the UK that the relevant premises or property etc are no longer in official use or have been removed from the UK.[123] Or again: former MEPs who draw a pension in that capacity shall be exempted from obligatory affiliation to and payment into the UK social security system, under the same conditions as were applicable on the last day of the transition period, provided those individuals were MEPs before the end of the transition period.[124] Or again: Union rules imposing an obligation of professional secrecy on certain individuals and institutions, bodies, and agencies etc of the Union shall apply in the UK in respect of any information covered by those obligations of professional secrecy, obtained either before the end of the transition period or after that date but in connection with Union activities pursuant to the Withdrawal Agreement. The UK must respect such obligations and ensure they are complied with in its territory.[125]

As well as the range of 'other separation issues' addressed in Part Three, Part Five of the Withdrawal Agreement contains the methodology for calculating the single financial settlement by which the UK will discharge its responsibility for obligations undertaken during its period of Union membership—including obligations that will fully materialize or fall due only after the date of withdrawal itself—covering not just the Union budget in respect of the 2014–2020 MFF, but also (for example) the European Central Bank, the European Investment Bank, the European Development Fund, the EU Trust Funds, and the Facility for Refugees in Turkey.[126] The methodology is underpinned by certain core principles agreed between the Union and the UK during the course of the Article 50 TEU negotiations: that no Member State should pay more or receive less because of the UK's withdrawal from the Union; that the UK should pay its share of the commitments undertaken during its period of Union membership; and that the UK itself should in fact pay neither any more nor any earlier than if it had remained a Member State.[127]

---

[122] Regulation 2016/679, OJ 2016 L 119/1 or Directive 2016/680, OJ 2016 L 119/89.
[123] Art 102 WA.
[124] Art 107 WA. This also applies to persons entitled to survivor's pensions as survivors of former MEPs.
[125] Art 120 WA.
[126] Note the discussion, in Chapter 4, about how the UK's single financial settlement figured in the Union's negotiating agenda under Art 50 TEU.
[127] See, e.g. Joint Report from the EU and UK negotiators (8 December 2017).

On that basis, Part Five contains a series of detailed provisions elaborating precisely how the UK's financial liabilities will be calculated as regards each relevant field of activity, and when the corresponding payments should be made. For example: in accordance with the status quo premiss underpinning the transition period, Part Five generally assumes that the UK will contribute to and participate in the implementation of the Union budget, as well as those Union programmes and activities committed under the MFF 2014–2020, for the years 2019 and 2020; but even afterwards, Union law concerning own resources relating to the financial years until 2020 shall in principle continue to apply to the UK, and all remaining projects falling under the MFF 2014–2020 are to be financed as originally foreseen (including as regards their UK beneficiaries).[128]

Other provisions state that, for example: the UK's paid-in capital in the European Central Bank will be reimbursed to the Bank of England;[129] the UK shall remain liable, as provided for under the Withdrawal Agreement, for financial operations approved by the European Investment Bank before the date of withdrawal (even if the resulting financial exposure is assumed only subsequently);[130] the UK will remain party to the European Development Fund (EDF) until the closure of the 11th EDF and all previous unclosed EDFs and, as such, shall continue to contribute to the payments necessary to honour all relevant commitments (while UK beneficiaries may continue to participate in projects under those EDFs under the conditions that applied before withdrawal);[131] and the UK shall honour the commitments it made while a Member State to any EU Trust Funds created before the date of withdrawal as well as to the Facility for Refugees in Turkey.[132]

B. Interpretation of the Withdrawal Agreement

The Withdrawal Agreement contains various basic principles of interpretation which are binding on the parties individually as well as within the Joint Committee.

First, the instruments that make up 'Union law' as referred to in the Withdrawal Agreement comprise: the existing Treaties (TEU, TFEU, Euratom, and the various Treaties of Accession); the Charter of Fundamental Rights and the general principles of Union law; acts adopted by the Union's institutions, bodies, and agencies etc; international agreements to which the Union is party and those concluded by the Member States acting on behalf of the Union; agreements between the Member States entered into in their capacity as such; acts of the Member States' representatives meeting within the European Council or the Council; and declarations made in the context of those intergovernmental conferences that adopted the Treaties.[133]

---

[128] See Chapter 2 of Part Five WA.
[129] Art 149 WA.
[130] Arts 150–151 WA.
[131] Arts 152–154 WA.
[132] Art 155 WA.
[133] Art 2(a) WA. Note also Art 7(2) WA: unless otherwise provided for in the Withdrawal Agreement, references to the Union include Euratom.

Secondly, references to 'Union law' in the Withdrawal Agreement shall generally be understood as references to Union law (including as amended or replaced) as applicable on the last day of the transition period.[134] There are exceptions to that general rule of interpretation. For example, it does not apply to Part Four on the transition period itself or to Part Five on the single financial settlement; nor does it apply where more specific provisions of the Withdrawal Agreement provide otherwise.[135] In any event, references in the Withdrawal Agreement to Union acts or provisions thereof shall (where relevant) include reference to Union law or provisions thereof that (although replaced or superseded by the act referred to) continue to apply in accordance with that act;[136] while references to provisions of Union law made applicable by the Withdrawal Agreement shall include references to relevant Union acts supplementing or implementing those provisions.[137]

Thirdly, Article 7(1) WA provides that references to the Member States and their competent national authorities in those provisions of Union law made applicable by the Withdrawal Agreement shall include the UK and its competent authorities. However, that general rule of interpretation does not apply to: nomination, appointment, or election of members of the Union institutions, bodies, and agencies etc; participation in decision-making and attendance at meetings of the Union institutions; participation in decision-making and governance of Union bodies and agencies etc; and attendance at meetings of comitology committees and expert groups etc of the Commission and Union bodies and agencies etc (unless otherwise provided for in the Withdrawal Agreement).[138]

Fourthly, Articles 4(3)–(4) WA establish that provisions of the Withdrawal Agreement referring to Union law, or to concepts or provisions thereof, shall be interpreted and applied in accordance with the methods and general principles of Union law itself; and in particular, in conformity with any relevant caselaw of the CJEU delivered before the end of the transition period. There is no explicit provision to govern the relevance of subsequent CJEU caselaw for the parties' interpretation of the Withdrawal Agreement; though the Union's representatives in the Joint Committee would obviously be bound to respect all relevant CJEU jurisprudence when exercising their functions and powers.[139]

Finally, Article 3 WA defines the geographical scope of the Withdrawal Agreement, unless otherwise provided for in the Withdrawal Agreement itself or in Union law made applicable thereunder, particularly when it comes to the various territories

---

[134] Art 6(1) WA.

[135] E.g. in the Protocol on Ireland/Northern Ireland (see the more detailed discussion in Chapter 8); and under the Cyprus Protocol (Art 1(4) thereof). Note that various provisions also govern the potential incorporation into the Withdrawal Agreement of certain future amendments to Union instruments made applicable by the Withdrawal Agreement, e.g. in the Protocol on Ireland/Northern Ireland (see the more detailed discussion in Chapter 8); and under Art 36 WA on future amendments to Union social security legislation (see the more detailed discussion in Chapter 7).

[136] Art 6(2) WA.

[137] Art 6(3) WA.

[138] See, e.g. Art 34(1) WA; Art 1(5) Cyprus Protocol.

[139] However, see the discussion (below) on the internal legal effects of the Withdrawal Agreement, particularly for the UK's judicial and administrative authorities. Note also that the Withdrawal Agreement contains certain specific provisions on dynamic interpretation in accordance with evolving CJEU caselaw, e.g. Art 13(2) Protocol on Ireland/Northern Ireland; Art 1(2) Cyprus Protocol.

associated with the UK: for example, Gibraltar, the Channel Islands, and the Isle of Man to the extent that Union law was applicable to those territories before the date of UK withdrawal;[140] and the various overseas countries and territories listed in Annex II to the TFEU based on their special relations with the UK, where the provisions of the Withdrawal Agreement relate to the special arrangements for association of overseas countries and territories with the Union.

C. Dispute Settlement: Arbitration

Article 5 WA provides that:

> The Union and the United Kingdom shall, in full mutual respect and good faith, assist each other in carrying out tasks which flow from this Agreement.
>
> They shall take all appropriate measures, whether general or particular, to ensure fulfilment of the obligations arising from this Agreement and shall refrain from any measures which could jeopardise the attainment of the objectives of this Agreement.
>
> This Article is without prejudice to the application of Union law pursuant to this Agreement, in particular the principle of sincere cooperation.

Against that background, Article 167 WA states that the parties shall at all times endeavour to agree on the interpretation and application of the Withdrawal Agreement and make every attempt to arrive at a mutually satisfactory resolution of any matter affecting its operation. However, in the event that a dispute does arise, the Union and the UK agree to have recourse only to those procedures provided for under the Withdrawal Agreement itself.[141]

For those purposes, we know from Chapter 4 that dispute settlement proved to be a relatively contentious subject during the Article 50 TEU negotiations. In particular, the Commission originally proposed that the CJEU should act as the primary dispute settlement body under the Withdrawal Agreement as a whole, including as regards the interpretation and application of those provisions applicable after expiry of the transition period.[142] The UK objected on the basis that its 'red lines' included the UK breaking free of the jurisdiction of the CJEU; but, in any case, it would be inappropriate for the court of one party to have jurisdiction over the agreement for both parties. The UK argued instead for an independent arbitral body to settle post-transition disputes arising under the Withdrawal Agreement.[143] Although the Union was ultimately willing to concede that the CJEU would not act as the sole or even primary forum under the Withdrawal Agreement for the settlement of post-transitional disputes, the Union also had its own red lines—including the non-derogable constitutional

---

[140] An issue on which Union law continued to develop even during the Article 50 TEU process: consider, e.g. Case C-267/16, *Buhagiar* (EU:C:2018:26).

[141] Art 168 WA.

[142] See Commission, *Position Paper on Governance* (TF50 (2017) 4 of 12 July 2017).

[143] See, in particular, HMG, *Technical Note on Implementing the Withdrawal Agreement* (13 July 2017); *Future Partnership Paper on Enforcement and Dispute Resolution* (23 August 2017). Note also: House of Lords European Union Committee, *Dispute Resolution and Enforcement After Brexit* (HL130 of 3 May 2018).

principle that the CJEU must enjoy final jurisdiction over the interpretation of Union law in any situation where such interpretation would become binding upon the Union institutions.[144] Given the extent to which the Withdrawal Agreement refers to and depends upon Union provisions and concepts, it was therefore imperative that any dedicated dispute settlement body created for the purposes of this treaty should respect the fundamental requirement to protect the autonomy of Union law, in particular, by creating a preliminary reference mechanism for the delivery of a binding CJEU ruling on the proper interpretation of Union law.[145]

Thus, in the case of disputes arising after expiry of the transition period, the following system shall generally apply.[146] To begin with, the parties shall endeavour to resolve any dispute through consultations in good faith within the Joint Committee in an attempt to reach a mutually agreed solution.[147] If no such solution has been reached by the Joint Committee within three months, either party may request the establishment of an arbitration panel (or sooner, by mutual agreement).[148] The Withdrawal Agreement contains detailed rules on the establishment and composition of an arbitration panel as well as the procedure and time-frames for its proceedings.[149] However, under Article 174 WA, where a dispute submitted for arbitration raises a question about the interpretation of Union law concepts or Union law provisions as referred to in the Withdrawal Agreement,[150] the arbitration panel must request the CJEU to give a ruling on that question—for which purpose, the CJEU shall have jurisdiction and its ruling shall be binding on the referring panel.[151]

Otherwise, Article 175 WA provides that an arbitration panel ruling shall be binding on the parties,[152] which must adopt any measures necessary to comply in good faith, within an agreed and reasonable period of time.[153] If at the end of that period, the complainant considers that the respondent has failed to comply, it may request another arbitration panel ruling (again subject to oversight by the CJEU as regards the binding interpretation of relevant Union law);[154] and may further request the imposition of a lump sum or penalty payment.[155] The respondent's further non-compliance—either

---

[144] See the more detailed discussion of and references to the CJEU caselaw on protecting the autonomy of Union law which is provided in Chapter 9. And see further, e.g. A. F. Fernández Tomás, *The Settlement of Disputes Arising from the United Kingdom's Withdrawal from the European Union* (Study commissioned by the AFCO Committee of the European Parliament, PE 596.819 of November 2017).

[145] Consider, e.g. Commission, *Speech by Michel Barnier at the 28th FIDE Congress* (26 May 2018).

[146] See Art 185 WA on the entry into force of the post-transition dispute settlement mechanism. For disputes arising during the transition period, see the discussion on CJEU jurisdiction (above). For the special dispute settlement provisions applicable under the Withdrawal Agreement even post-transition: see the discussion below.

[147] Art 169 WA.

[148] Art 170 WA.

[149] Arts 171–173 WA. Note Art 181 WA on independence and immunity; Annex IX on Rules of Procedure.

[150] Or a question about whether the UK has complied with its obligations under Art 89(2) WA.

[151] The relevant provisions of Art 161 WA shall apply.

[152] Note also Art 180 WA: the arbitration panel shall make every effort to decide by consensus but may act by majority (though without issuing dissenting opinions). All rulings are binding on the EU and the UK and shall be made public (subject to the protection of confidential information).

[153] Art 176 WA contains detailed provisions on determining a 'reasonable time' for compliance.

[154] Art 177 WA.

[155] Art 178 WA.

with the original arbitration ruling or with an order to make financial settlement—will entitle the complainant to suspend rights and obligations under the Withdrawal Agreement (apart from those contained in Part Two on citizens' rights) or under any other agreement between the Union and the UK (under the conditions provided for therein) in a proportionate manner and on a temporary basis.[156] If by this stage the parties remain in dispute over compliance, either may request a further arbitration panel ruling (still subject to the provisions on CJEU jurisdiction) that may order termination of the complainant's suspension/the respondent's penalty.[157]

As in other international contexts, the Withdrawal Agreement's complex provisions concerning arbitration, enforcement, and compliance should act as a powerful incentive for the parties to avoid post-transition disputes through political dialogue in the Joint Committee. But conversely, if (for the sake of argument) the UK Government were determined to provoke disagreement over interpretation and/or application of the Withdrawal Agreement, the latter's dispute settlement mechanism may well furnish the Union with only a relatively cumbersome and ineffective means of correction or redress.[158]

D. Other Continuing Powers of the CJEU

Although arbitration (subject to oversight by the CJEU as regards the interpretation of Union law) represents the main dispute settlement mechanism provided for under the Withdrawal Agreement, the latter also envisages a continuing role for the Union courts in a range of other post-transition situations.

To begin with, Title X of Part Three WA contains detailed rules on the post-transition winding-up of judicial proceedings under Union law. In particular: Article 86 WA provides that the CJEU shall continue to have jurisdiction in any proceedings (and for those purposes, at all stages) brought by or against the UK before the end of the transition period; as well as to give preliminary rulings on any requests from UK courts or tribunals made before the end of the transition period.[159] Moreover, under Article 87 WA, if the Commission considers that the UK has failed to fulfil an obligation under either the Treaties or Part Four WA before the end of the transition period, the Commission may (within four years of the end of transition) bring the matter before the CJEU.[160] Similarly, if the UK does not comply with a binding decision adopted by a Union institution or agency etc before the end of the transition period, or fails to give legal effect to such a decision as addressed to natural and legal persons residing

---

[156] Art 178 WA. If the respondent considers that the extent of suspension is not proportionate, it may request a temporary standstill pending another arbitration panel ruling.

[157] Art 179 WA.

[158] Note section 13B EU(W)A 2018 (as amended) on UK government reporting obligations to Parliament on Joint Committee dispute resolution consultations, requests for arbitration, and panel requests for an CJEU ruling.

[159] Note Art 86(3) WA on calculating the relevant date of proceedings.

[160] In accordance with either Art 258 TFEU or the second subparagraph of Art 108(2) TFEU. Note Art 87(3) WA.

or established in the UK, the Commission may (within four years from the date of the relevant decision) bring the matter before the CJEU.[161]

All rulings delivered by the CJEU, whether before the end of transition or thereafter in accordance with Article 86 or 87 WA, shall be binding in their entirety on and in the UK.[162] Where the CJEU finds that the UK has failed to fulfil an obligation under the Treaties or the Withdrawal Agreement itself, the UK must take the necessary measures to comply with that judgment.[163]

Title X also contains detailed rules on the winding-up of various administrative proceedings under Union law—the application of which may well lead to the further involvement of the Union courts in the settlement of post-transition disputes. In particular: Article 92 WA provides that the Union's institutions, bodies, and agencies etc shall continue to be competent for administrative procedures initiated before the end of transition concerning compliance with Union law either by the UK itself or by natural or legal persons residing or established in the UK (as well as compliance with Union law relating to competition in the UK).[164] Moreover, Article 93 WA provides that, in respect of aid granted before the end of the transition period, for a period of four years thereafter, the Commission shall be competent to initiate (and conduct) new administrative procedures on state aid concerning the UK.[165] Similarly, for a period of four years after the end of the transition period, the European Anti-Fraud Office (OLAF) shall be competent to initiate (and conduct) certain new investigations in accordance with Regulation 883/2013,[166] for example, in respect of facts that occurred before the end of transition.[167]

All decisions adopted by the Union's institutions, bodies, and agencies etc, whether before the end of transition or thereafter in accordance with Article 92 or 93 WA, and addressed either to the UK or to natural or legal persons residing or established therein, shall be binding on and in the UK.[168] The legality of those Union decisions shall be reviewed exclusively by the CJEU in accordance with Article 263 TFEU.[169] In addition: the Court's continued jurisdiction under Article 87 WA applies in situations where the UK fails to comply with/give effect to such binding Union decisions—again, not just those adopted before the end of the transition period, but also thereafter in accordance with either Article 92 or Article 93 WA.[170]

Besides Title X of Part Three on the winding-up of Union judicial and administrative procedures, the Withdrawal Agreement contains a series of additional provisions on the involvement of the Union courts in the settlement of specific disputes even after

---

[161] Again in accordance with either Art 258 TFEU or the second subparagraph of Art 108(2) TFEU. And again note Art 87(3) WA.

[162] Art 89(1) WA.

[163] Art 89(2) WA; for which purpose, see also Art 89(3) WA. Note also Arts 88 and 90–91 WA.

[164] Art 92 WA contains detailed rules, e.g. on calculating the relevant date of various categories of administrative proceedings. Note, in particular, Art 92(5) WA.

[165] Again, note Art 92(5) WA.

[166] Regulation 883/2013 concerning investigations conducted by the European Anti-Fraud Office, OJ 2013 L 248/1.

[167] Without prejudice to Arts 136 and 138 WA. Note also Art 96 WA, which deals with a range of additional ongoing administrative procedures and obligations.

[168] Art 95(1) WA. Note also Art 94, Art 95(2) and Art 95(4) WA.

[169] Art 95(3) WA.

[170] See the discussion above.

the transition period has expired. In later chapters, we will consider the temporary regime allowing UK courts to continue sending preliminary references to the CJEU in respect of the citizens' rights provisions contained in Part Two of the Withdrawal Agreement;[171] as well as the role of the CJEU in the interpretation and application of the complex border arrangements contained in the Protocol on Ireland/Northern Ireland.[172]

For now, suffice to note that Article 160 WA also provides for the CJEU to continue exercising jurisdiction in accordance with Articles 258, 260 and 267 TFEU in respect of the interpretation and application of specific provisions of Union law as referred to in Part Five of the Withdrawal Agreement concerning the single financial settlement: to be precise, Article 136 WA, i.e. those rules concerning the Union's own resources relating to the financial years until 2020 that continue to apply to the UK from 2021; and Articles 138(1) and (2) WA, i.e. those rules concerning the implementation of Union programmes and activities committed under the 2014–2020 MFF (or previous financial perspectives) that continue to apply to the UK from 2021.[173] Similarly, Article 12 of the Cyprus Protocol provides that, in respect of the UK Sovereign Base Areas and in relation to natural and legal persons residing or established therein, the Union's institutions, bodies, and agencies etc shall have the powers conferred by Union law in relation to the Protocol and provisions of Union law made applicable thereunder—including the CJEU's jurisdiction as provided for under the Treaties.[174]

5. Internal Legal Status of the Withdrawal Agreement

Many treaties deal only with interpretation, dispute settlement, and enforcement under the agreement itself as between the parties and as a matter of public international law. When it comes to the legal effects of the treaty within the internal legal system of each party, that is often left entirely to their respective constitutional rules in accordance with the traditional distinction between monist and dualist systems. However, it is well known that an entirely laissez-faire approach to domestic legal effects can risk certain 'enforcement asymmetries' between the parties—especially in the case of agreements that contain relatively detailed and concrete rights and obligations; and particularly if one side operates a monist system whereas its counterpart acts as a dualist order. Since the Union effectively acts as a monist system, it often insists that an international agreement should contain specific provisions to determine the appropriate legal status of that treaty within each contracting party, sometimes ruling out any direct internal legal effects, but other times insisting upon explicit provisions to ensure such effects, either for the entire agreement or at least as regards parts thereof.[175]

---

[171]   Art 158 WA. Note also Arts 161(2)–(3) WA. See further Chapter 7.
[172]   Art 12 PINI. See further Chapter 8.
[173]   Such jurisdiction is without prejudice to Art 87 WA. Note also Arts 161(2)–(3) WA.
[174]   Note also Art 161(3) WA.
[175]   Contrast, e.g. the sophisticated enforcement provisions of the EEA Agreement with the limited internal legal effects of the EU–Canada agreement. And recall that the CJEU itself sometimes addresses asymmetries through the criteria for direct internal legal effects of particular international agreements, e.g. as with the WTO agreements in Case C-149/96, *Portugal v Council* (EU:C:1999:574) and Case C-377/02, *Van*

The Withdrawal Agreement falls into precisely this category: it contains often very precise and detailed rights and obligations for each party; but without more specific provisions on internal legal effects, the treaty would have been susceptible to serious asymmetries of application and enforcement as between the monist EU and the dualist UK.

On the Union side, Article 216(2) TFEU provides that international agreements concluded by the Union are binding upon the Union institutions and the Member States. In accordance with the well-established caselaw of the CJEU concerning the more precise legal status of international treaties for the purposes of Union law, it is evident that many of the specific provisions of the Withdrawal Agreement are sufficiently clear, precise and unconditional as to be capable of producing direct effect within the Union legal order as well as the domestic legal systems of the Member States.[176] Indeed, it is absolutely clear that the Union institutions positively intended such provisions of the Withdrawal Agreement to be capable of independent application and enforcement by the Union and Member States courts.[177] Those provisions of the Withdrawal Agreement that do vest or leave certain discretionary powers or choices, either to the Union institutions or to the Member States, do not undermine the capacity of the remaining provisions of the Withdrawal Agreement to produce direct effect as a matter of Union law.[178]

To help ensure that the UK adopted the same approach to application and enforcement of the Withdrawal Agreement within its domestic legal system, the Union insisted that the Withdrawal Agreement also contain detailed provisions describing its intended internal legal status and effects within the UK.[179] In particular, Articles 4(1)–(2) WA provide that both the Withdrawal Agreement and Union law made applicable thereunder shall produce, in respect of and within the UK, the same legal effects as they produce within the Union and its Member States. In particular, natural and legal persons must be able to rely directly on any provision contained or referred to in the Withdrawal Agreement which meets the conditions for producing direct effect under Union law. The UK must ensure compliance with that obligation through the adoption of domestic primary legislation, including the required powers of its judicial and administrative authorities to disapply inconsistent or incompatible provisions of national law. Moreover, in addition to the general principle that Union law for the purposes of the Withdrawal Agreement must be interpreted and applied in accordance with the methods and general principles of Union law, and in accordance with CJEU caselaw delivered before the end of the transition period, Article 4(5) WA further

---

Parys (EU:C:2005:121). On enforcement asymmetries in the Union's external relations, see further the discussion in Chapter 9.

[176] I.e. in accordance with the Case 12/86, *Demirel* (EU:C:1987:400) caselaw.

[177] From repeated Union documents, proposals and statements right throughout the Art 50 TEU process.

[178] E.g. any given Member State's decision to introduce a registration scheme for existing UK migrant citizens in accordance with Art 18 WA–on which, see further the discussion in Chapter 7.

[179] E.g. Council Decision authorizing the opening of negotiations with the United Kingdom of Great Britain and Northern Ireland for an agreement setting out the arrangements for its withdrawal from the European Union (22 May 2017); Joint Report from the EU and UK negotiators (8 December 2017).

states that the UK's judicial and administrative authorities shall have 'due regard' to any relevant CJEU caselaw delivered *after* that date.

In addition to those general provisions concerning the domestic legal status of the Withdrawal Agreement within the EU and UK legal orders, the Withdrawal Agreement also contains certain more specific provisions aimed at promoting its own consistent interpretation and application by the competent Union and national authorities, particularly after expiry of the status quo transition period.[180] For example, Article 161 WA provides that, where a court or tribunal of a Member State makes a preliminary reference concerning interpretation of the Withdrawal Agreement, that request shall be notified to the UK, which may then participate in the relevant proceedings before the CJEU in the same way as a Member State.[181] Conversely, Article 162 WA states that, where the consistent interpretation and application of the Withdrawal Agreement so requires, the Commission may submit written observations to the UK courts in pending cases concerning interpretation of the Withdrawal Agreement; with the permission of the relevant court, the Commission may also make oral observations. Moreover, and again in order to facilitate consistent interpretation of the Withdrawal Agreement, though in full deference to judicial independence, Article 163 WA provides for a regular dialogue between the CJEU and the highest UK courts.

The European Union (Withdrawal Agreement) Act 2020 makes domestic provision for the legal effects of the Withdrawal Agreement within the UK legal system. In the first place, the status quo premiss underpinning the transition period is reflected in amendments to the European Union (Withdrawal) Act 2018—effectively postponing repeal of the European Communities Act 1972 and furnishing a legal basis for the continued recognition, application, direct effect, and primacy of Union law as required under Part Four of the Withdrawal Agreement.[182] Only after the expiry of transition will the UK's new regime on 'retained EU law' come fully into effect—seeking to preserve regulatory continuity and legal certainty by converting all existing EU-derived measures into domestic legal acts, albeit subject to a far-reaching programme of amendments and to be governed by a particular legal status and specific principles of interpretation.[183]

In the second place, many of the remaining (particularly post-transition) rights and obligations contained in the Withdrawal Agreement are implemented into UK law directly by or under the European Union (Withdrawal Agreement) Act 2020 itself. For example, the legislation confers extensive executive powers to make secondary legislation in relation to citizens' rights,[184] for implementing the 'other separation provisions' contained in Part Three of the Withdrawal Agreement,[185]

---

[180] E.g. preliminary references as regards Part Two on citizens' rights (Arts 158 and 161 WA); the independent monitoring authority (Art 159 WA); preliminary references as regards elements of Part Five on the financial settlement (Arts 160 and 161 WA); under Arts 12–13 Cyprus Protocol.

[181] Arts 161(1) and (3) WA.

[182] See, in particular, sections 1A, 1B and 8A EU(W)A 2018 (as amended) as well as the corresponding amendments concerning the devolved administrations.

[183] In accordance with the EU(W)A 2018 (as amended). See the more detailed discussion in Chapter 2.

[184] See section 7 (citizens' rights), section 8 (frontier workers), section 9 (restrictions on entry and residence), section 11 (appeals), section 12 (professional qualifications), section 13 (social security), section 14 (equal treatment, etc) of the European Union (Withdrawal Agreement) Act 2020. Note also section 10 on amendments to existing UK immigration legislation relating to powers of deportation.

[185] Section 8B EU(W)A 2018 (as amended) plus corresponding powers for devolved administrations.

and as regards the Protocol on Ireland/Northern Ireland.[186] The 2020 Act also formally establishes the Independent Monitoring Authority for Citizens' Rights;[187] provides a legal basis for settling the UK's financial obligations under Part Five of the Withdrawal Agreement;[188] and implements the provisions of the Protocol on Ireland/Northern Ireland that call for dedicated mechanisms to maintain the provisions of the Good Friday Agreement concerning rights, safeguards and equality of opportunity.[189]

In the third place, section 7A of the European Union (Withdrawal) Act 2018 (as amended) seeks to implement the principle of reciprocal internal legal effects, as between the Union and the UK, contained in Articles 4(1)–(2) of the Withdrawal Agreement:

(1) Subsection (2) applies to—
  (a) all such rights, powers, liabilities, obligations and restrictions from time to time created or arising by or under the withdrawal agreement, and
  (b) all such remedies and procedures from time to time provided for by or under the withdrawal agreement, as in accordance with the withdrawal agreement are without further enactment to be given legal effect or used in the United Kingdom.
(2) The rights, powers, liabilities, obligations, restrictions, remedies and procedures concerned are to be—
  (a) recognised and available in domestic law, and
  (b) enforced, allowed and followed accordingly.
(3) Every enactment (including an enactment contained in this Act) is to be read and has effect subject to subsection (2).
    ....

In addition, section 7C of the European Union (Withdrawal) Act 2018 (as amended) provides that any question as to the validity, meaning or effect of any domestic measure implementing or otherwise falling with the scope of the Withdrawal Agreement (other than Part Four on transition) should be decided in accordance with the Withdrawal Agreement itself;[190] including Article 4 WA on the internal legal effects of the Withdrawal Agreement for the UK, as well as the CJEU's continuing jurisdiction under Article 158 WA (citizens' rights) and Article 160 WA (financial settlement), and the rules governing interpretation and enforcement of the border arrangements contained in the Protocol on Ireland/Northern Ireland.

By those means, the principles of direct effect and primacy should remain part of UK law for a considerable period, even after the transition period has expired, i.e. in respect of those provisions of the Withdrawal Agreement that satisfy the criteria

---

[186] Section 8C EU(W)A 2018 (as amended) plus corresponding powers for devolved administrations.
[187] Section 15 and Schedule 2 EU(WA)A 2020.
[188] Section 20 EU(WA)A 2020.
[189] Section 23 and Schedule 3 EU(WA)A 2020.
[190] Also having regard (inter alia) to the desirability of ensuring consistency between relevant provisions of the UK's withdrawal/separation agreements with the EU, EFTA–EEA states, and Switzerland.

for producing direct effect as a matter of Union law.[191] However, section 38 of the European Union (Withdrawal Agreement) Act 2020 explicitly provides as follows:

(1) It is recognised that the Parliament of the United Kingdom is sovereign.
(2) In particular, its sovereignty subsists notwithstanding—
   (a) directly applicable or directly effective EU law continuing to be recognised and available in domestic law by virtue of [the provisions of the European Union (Withdrawal) Act 2018 concerning the transition period],
   (b) section 7A of that Act (other directly applicable or directly effective aspects of the withdrawal agreement),
   ... and
   (d) section 7C of that Act (interpretation of law relating to the withdrawal agreement (other than the implementation period) ...
(3) Accordingly, nothing in this Act derogates from the sovereignty of the Parliament of the United Kingdom.

In practice, therefore, UK constitutional lawyers may yet have to decide how far the domestic constitutional principle of parliamentary sovereignty has indeed been nuanced or qualified by the UK's clear international obligations—especially in a situation where subsequent primary legislation conflicts with the terms of the Withdrawal Agreement and the traditional principle of implied repeal would normally require the 2020 Act to be set aside rather than the subsequent (contradictory) legislation to be disapplied.[192]

6. Concluding Remarks

This chapter considered the overall structure and scheme of the Withdrawal Agreement; especially the fundamental distinction between EU–UK relations during, then after, the status quo transition period; together with provisions (for example) governing key separation issues, interpretation and dispute settlement, as well as the intended status and effects of the treaty especially for the domestic UK legal system. However, we have reserved two of the most legally and politically important parts of the Withdrawal Agreement for dedicated analyses of their own: the following chapters will now offer a more detailed exploration of the provisions of Part Two concerning citizens' rights; and of the Protocol on Ireland/Northern Ireland.

---

[191] And besides the rules on (qualified) continued primacy for 'retained EU law' in accordance with the EU(W)A 2018 (as amended), especially sections 5–7.
[192] See, e.g. *Madzimbamuto v Lardner-Burke* [1969] 1 AC 645.

7
Citizens' Rights

1. Introduction

This chapter embarks upon a more detailed explanation and critique of the provisions of the final Withdrawal Agreement dealing with one of the most important problems raised by the UK's departure from the Union: the treatment of millions of EU citizens and UK nationals who had exercised their rights to free movement under the Treaties before the end of the transition period. As Section 2 recalls, Brexit created for those individuals a prolonged period of horrible uncertainty and anxiety over their future residency status, family unification, employment rights, and social protection. Moreover, despite the promising rhetoric of both the Union and the UK Government at the outset of the Article 50 TEU process, the actual negotiations over citizens' rights proved more tense and convoluted than expected.

The final legal regime is contained in Part Two of the Withdrawal Agreement. Section 3 demonstrates how those provisions guarantee the continued protection of citizens' rights, in both the UK and across the Member States, based on the existing standards provided by Union free movement law. However, while Part Two undoubtedly offers a significant degree of certainty and an important array of safeguards for EU citizens and UK nationals, this starting assumption does nevertheless lead to certain problems. For example: the fact that individuals will only qualify for future protection under Part Two, if the necessary periods of past residency can be considered 'lawful' as a matter of existing Union free movement law, incorporates into the Withdrawal Agreement regime familiar concerns about the legal exclusion of economically and socially vulnerable or precarious citizens.

Moreover, Section 4 explains how Part Two also deviates from the general baseline provided by existing Union free movement law in several important respects—many of which are attributable primarily to various 'red lines' demanded by the UK Government during the Article 50 TEU negotiations. For example: the UK (and any Member State which also decides to avail itself of the possibility) enjoys the power to insist that individuals falling within the potential scope of Part Two must nevertheless proactively register with the national authorities for a new immigration status in order to qualify for any future protection of their intended rights. There are also various limitations on individual rights ranging (say) from the potential for family unification, through protection against expulsion based on criminal conduct, to future changes affecting the system of cross-border social security coordination. Finally, Section 5 addresses the specific provisions contained in the Withdrawal Agreement relating to the domestic legal status and effects of the citizens' rights regime—particularly within the UK legal system—aimed at ensuring the effective as well as consistent interpretation and application of Part Two.

The UK's Withdrawal from the EU. Michael Dougan, Oxford University Press. © Michael Dougan 2021.
DOI: 10.1093/oso/9780198833475.003.0007

2. Citizens' Rights in the Article 50 TEU Negotiations

Misinformation about the nature and effects of the free movement of persons between the EU and the UK played a prominent role in the Leave campaign during the 2016 referendum. For many people, Nigel Farage's 'Breaking Point' poster campaign of June 2016 remains emblematic of the deliberately misleading and often proudly xenophobic focus on immigration that fuelled a large part of the 'argument for Brexit'.[1]

But at almost every level of the debate, both law and fact were seriously distorted. The movement of EU27 nationals was frequently compounded with that of third country nationals—the latter in fact making up a significant majority of the foreign nationals residing in the UK, with their immigration status falling almost entirely within the competence of the UK authorities themselves.[2] The free movement rights of Union citizens were consistently portrayed as 'unlimited' and 'uncontrolled'— despite the myriad conditions, restrictions, and derogations imposed and permitted under EU law (many of which successive UK governments had chosen not to enforce in full).[3] EU27 nationals were portrayed by turns as benefit tourists seeking to live off the UK welfare system, as an army of low-skilled workers who had stolen native jobs and suppressed wages for all, as the root cause of the UK's long-term and chronic shortage of affordable housing, and as a serious drain on public services who had damaged access to and standards of health care and education—all notwithstanding the fact that empirical data suggested EU27 nationals were more likely to be in employment, to be better qualified, to be paying more tax, and to be claiming less in public benefits than British nationals.[4] It is true that the UK had witnessed a relatively large number of arrivals from the Member States that acceded to the Union in 2004—but it was seldom discussed how that was the direct consequence of the UK Government's own decision not to impose transitional restrictions on the free movement of persons as provided for under the relevant Treaty of Accession.[5] And of course, free movement was portrayed as an essentially one-way street: Leave campaigners appeared less keen to raise and complain about the large numbers of UK nationals who had taken advantage of the reciprocal opportunities to study, work, or retire across the rest of the EU.[6]

After the referendum, hostility towards Union citizens was quickly endorsed by the UK Government and indeed adopted effectively as official policy. Contemptuous

---

[1] See, e.g. https://www.theguardian.com/politics/2016/jun/16/nigel-farage-defends-ukip-breaking-point-poster-queue-of-migrants.

[2] See, e.g. https://www.ons.gov.uk/peoplepopulationandcommunity/populationandmigration/internationalmigration/articles/immigrationpatternsofnonukbornpopulationsinenglandandwalesin2011/2013-12-17.

[3] I.e. particularly in accordance with Directive 2004/38, OJ 2004 L 158/77; and especially in respect of non-economically active EU citizens.

[4] See, e.g. https://www.ippr.org/publications/free-movement-and-the-eu-referendum. Note that similar conclusions have been formulated in other Member States where free movement rights have provided a source of populist agitation: see, e.g. Martinsen and Rotger, 'The fiscal impact of EU immigration on the tax-financed welfare state: Testing the 'welfare burden' thesis', 18 *European Union Politics* (2017) 620.

[5] See further, e.g. Dougan, 'A Spectre is Haunting Europe … Free Movement of Persons and the Eastern Enlargement' in C. Hillion (ed.), *Enlargement of the European Union: A Legal Approach* (2004).

[6] Precise figures being difficult to compile, e.g. given the different recording approaches in different Member States; as well as the suspected incidence of UK nationals continuing to record themselves as officially resident in the UK while actually living abroad.

language about 'citizens of nowhere', promises to 'take back control of our borders' and vows to deal with European 'queue jumpers' became commonplace in British political discourse.[7] Ending the free movement of persons between the UK and the EU27 fast emerged as a central preoccupation of the May Government—one of the British 'red lines' that would be imposed upon the Brexit negotiations:

> The public must have confidence in our ability to control immigration. It is simply not possible to control immigration overall when there is unlimited free movement of people to the UK from the EU ... We will design our immigration system to ensure that we are able to control the numbers of people who come here from the EU. In future, therefore, the Free Movement Directive will no longer apply and the migration of EU nationals will be subject to UK law.[8]

Of course, the UK will eventually pay a significant long-term cost for its pandering to such post-truth populism. In particular, the UK's decision to end free movement, and indeed any more favourable immigration regime with the EU, will inevitably shape the extent of and conditions for broader relations in fields such as trade and security, as well as other fields of cross-border cooperation, not to mention the future life options and choices of UK nationals themselves.[9] After all, the Union treats the free movement of persons as an integral part of any agreement seeking privileged participation in or access to the Single Market;[10] and as a relevant factor in determining the terms for cross-border police and judicial cooperation in the fields of crime and security.[11]

But the immediate question raised by the referendum was: what would happen to the millions of EU27 citizens and UK nationals who had already exercised their free movement rights in good faith? Even on this issue, leading Leave campaigners had been unable to restrain their natural urge to dissemble: such migrants would apparently have no cause for concern after a Leave victory in the referendum, because their existing rights would be automatically protected under the 'Vienna Convention'.[12] Such claims were apparently intended to refer to Article 70 of the Vienna Convention on the Law of Treaties (VCLT), concerning the consequences for acquired rights of the termination of a treaty/a state's withdrawal from a multilateral treaty. However, Article 70 VCLT is entirely irrelevant in the context of the free movement rights of individual citizens, since that provision refers only to the rights and obligations of the contracting parties (i.e. states), so this particular Leave

---

[7] E.g. Theresa May, *Speech at Conservative Party conference* (5 October 2016); *Lancaster House Speech* (17 January 2017); *Speech to CBI* (19 November 2018).

[8] HMG, *The United Kingdom's exit from and new partnership with the European Union* (Cm 9417 of 2 February 2017), at paras 5.3–5.4.

[9] Consider, e.g. House of Lords Economic Affairs Committee, *Brexit and the Labour Market* (HL11 of 21 July 2017); House of Lords European Union Committee, *Brexit: Movement of People in the Cultural Sector* (HL182 of 26 July 2018). See further Chapter 9.

[10] E.g. as in the EEA Agreement; as well as in relations with Switzerland.

[11] E.g. European Council (Article 50), *Conclusions of 23 March 2018*, at para 13.

[12] A claim made publicly, e.g. by Steve Baker MP and by Michael Gove MP.

fabrication was soon proved to be as thoroughly baseless as academic commentators had already explained it to be even at the time.[13]

In reality, the EU Treaties do not contain any explicit 'grandfathering' provisions dealing with the rights and obligations of natural and legal persons in the event of a current Member State's withdrawal from the EU. It was evidently taken for granted that such issues would be addressed within the context of, and appropriate provisions made under, the withdrawal agreement foreseen by Article 50 TEU.[14] So the future situation of existing migrant nationals would be governed by whatever agreement might be negotiated in due course between the EU and the UK; or by default, through a combination of domestic immigration law, respect for a limited range of fundamental rights under the ECHR, and (at least for the remaining Member States) any applicable EU rules (for example) adopted under the immigration competences conferred upon the Union within the Area of Freedom, Security and Justice.[15] Only by such means would it be possible to identify the precise status and rights of millions of people to residency, family life, employment, professional activities, study opportunities, equal treatment, access to public services, coordination of social security benefits etc. Would they maintain their existing standard of treatment? Would they become categorized simply as third country nationals? Or would they become subject to some more bespoke regulatory regime?

We need not recount in detail, but it is still important to stress, the terrible personal and professional costs suffered by those EU citizens and UK nationals whose lives were so directly affected by the UK's decision to leave.[16]

For example: already, before the referendum, commentators had documented many of the problems generated by the UK's official 'hostile environment' immigration policy as it applied to EU nationals—ranging from the imposition of restrictions that were of dubious compatibility with Union law itself, to the daily reality of bureaucratic obstruction and inconvenience in the exercise even of clear legal rights.[17] Now Union citizens living in the UK were subjected to prolonged uncertainty and anxiety about what the future might hold. Large numbers of people rushed to apply for permanent residency—though the UK Government soon changed the application process so as to render it more complex and cumbersome, including allegations that it was imposing additional requirements incompatible with the conditions laid down in Directive 2004/38;[18] while individuals with even minor gaps in their continuity of

---

[13] E.g. evidence submitted by M. Dougan to House of Commons Treasury Committee for purposes of its report, *The Economic and Financial Costs and Benefits of the UK's EU Membership* (HC122 of 27 May 2016); then, e.g. House of Lords EU Select Committee, *Brexit: Acquired Rights* (HL82 of 14 December 2016).

[14] In that regard, the EU Treaties can be contrasted with other international agreements which do contain specific provisions (albeit in greater or lesser detail) for the protection of certain vested/acquired rights in favour of natural and legal persons in the event of termination of the relevant treaty, e.g. as with the EU's bilateral agreement with Switzerland on the free movement of persons (see Art 23 on the acquired rights of individuals). See further, e.g. Donegan and Teo, 'Brexit: Free Movement of Persons', *Journal of International Banking Law and Regulation* [2016] 565.

[15] E.g. under Directive 2003/109 concerning the status of third country nationals who are long-term residents, OJ 2004 L 16/44.

[16] See the personal accounts documented, e.g. in E. Remigi, V. Martin and T. Sykes, *In Limbo* (2017).

[17] See further, e.g. C. O'Brien, *Unity in Adversity: EU Citizenship, Social Justice and the Cautionary Tale of the UK* (2017).

[18] E.g. House of Commons Exiting the EU Committee, *The Government's Negotiating Objectives: The Rights of UK and EU Citizens* (HC1071 of 5 March 2017).

residence, employment, or sickness insurance worried about how that might impact upon their future status and rights.[19] Even those already holding permanent residency were unsure what guarantees that (essentially Union law) status might eventually offer in the post-withdrawal world.[20] Those who fulfilled the criteria could consider instead applying for British citizenship—but that process is equally cumbersome, and significantly more expensive[21]—while there was considerable uncertainty about how various Member States might respond (for example) to own nationals who might seek to acquire UK nationality and/or those holding dual citizenship once the UK had eventually become a third country.[22]

Meanwhile, the media regularly reported on troubling incidents that proved the 'hostile environment' for EU citizens had if anything only intensified: for example, the UK authorities refusing to approve significant numbers of permanent residency applications;[23] 'deportation letters' being sent by the Home Office to longstanding Union citizens;[24] judicial condemnation of a UK programme designed systematically to detain and deport homeless EU nationals regardless of their rights and safeguards under Union law;[25] a recorded rise in the racist abuse of and even attacks upon EU nationals;[26] and widespread evidence of growing private discrimination against Union citizens in sectors such as employment and housing.[27] Against that background, it is hardly surprising to find reported falls in the number of EU nationals moving to the UK and a rise in the number of Union citizens leaving altogether.[28]

Recognizing those serious injustices and seeking to avert further hardship, already, in December 2016, various UK parliamentary committees had begun to call upon the Government to offer unilateral protection to affected EU27 citizens as regards their future immigration status and associated rights.[29] However, for a significant period of time, the Government consistently refused to do so—eventually publishing

---

[19] E.g. House of Commons Exiting the EU Committee, *The Government's Negotiating Objectives: The Rights of UK and EU Citizens* (HC1071 of 5 March 2017).

[20] E.g. House of Commons Exiting the EU Committee, *The Government's Negotiating Objectives: The Rights of UK and EU Citizens* (HC1071 of 5 March 2017).

[21] E.g. in 2018, a single adult application for UK citizenship by naturalization carried a fee of £1330: see further https://www.gov.uk/government/publications/fees-for-citizenship-applications/ fees-for-citizenship-applications-and-the-right-of-abode-from-6-april-2018.

[22] E.g. House of Commons Exiting the EU Committee, *The Progress of the UK's Negotiations on EU Withdrawal: The Rights of UK and EU Citizens* (HC1439 of 23 July 2018).

[23] See, e.g. https://www.theguardian.com/uk-news/2017/feb/27/rejections-eu-citizens-seeking-uk-residency.

[24] See, e.g. https://www.theguardian.com/politics/2017/aug/23/home-office-apologises-for-letters-threatening-to-deport-eu-nationals.

[25] See, e.g. https://www.theguardian.com/uk-news/2017/dec/14/home-office-policy-deport-eu-rough-sleepers-ruled-unlawful.

[26] See, e.g. https://www.independent.co.uk/news/uk/home-news/brexit-eu-referendum-racial-racism-abuse-hate-crime-reported-latest-leave-immigration-a7104191.html; and more generally https://www. theguardian.com/world/2019/may/20/racism-on-the-rise-since-brexit-vote-nationwide-study-reveals.

[27] See, e.g. House of Lords EU Select Committee, *Brexit: Acquired Rights* (HL82 of 14 December 2016).

[28] See, e.g. https://migrationobservatory.ox.ac.uk/resources/briefings/eu-migration-to-and-from-the-uk/.

[29] E.g. House of Lords EU Committee, *Brexit: Acquired Rights* (HL82 of 14 December 2016); House of Commons Exiting the EU Committee, *The Government's Negotiating Objectives: The Rights of UK and EU Citizens* (HC1071 of 5 March 2017); House of Lords EU Committee, *Brexit: UK–EU Movement of People* (HL121 of March 2017).

a unilateral guarantee for Union citizens' rights only in December 2018, i.e. after the First Withdrawal Package had already been concluded and the process for its domestic approval and ratification had formally begun.[30] In the interim, the UK instead insisted that this issue should be addressed only within the context of the Article 50 TEU negotiations. In particular, the February 2017 White Paper expressed the UK's desire for the two parties to reach an agreement offering full guarantees to all relevant UK nationals and EU27 citizens (and indeed suggested that the EU27 were preventing rapid progress on delivering precisely such an agreement).[31]

For their part, UK nationals living across the EU27 experienced a similar state of uncertainty about their future status and rights.[32] Many of their concerns were the same as those afflicting their fellow Union citizens in relation to the UK: for example, about security of residency for themselves and their families; and as regards continued access to economic and other professional activities. However, various analyses also highlighted certain particular worries commonly held by migrant UK nationals: for example, whether they would remain entitled to cross-border health care provision, as well as the maintenance of their existing pension rights, in accordance with the Union's system of social security coordination; and whether they would retain certain rights to free movement, not only within their current host state, but also across the wider Union, so as to retain the option to change their place (say) of work or residency at some point in the future.[33]

Again, the Union institutions received various calls for them to take unilateral action to safeguard the future position of affected UK nationals by providing an unconditional guarantee of their existing rights across the EU27: for example, a series of Citizens' Initiatives were launched, aiming to persuade the Commission to bring forward legislative proposals that would effectively allow UK nationals to retain their existing free movement rights, even if they were to lose their status as Union citizens.[34] But again, the Union consistently refused to offer any such unilateral guarantee to affected UK nationals—also treating the question of citizens' rights as an integral part of the Article 50 TEU negotiations that should be resolved through mutual agreement.

Indeed, the Union maintained that position throughout the entire withdrawal process, even during the days when a 'no deal Brexit' appeared possible or even probable: the Commission was willing to propose certain measures to address specific problems (for example, in the field of cross-border social security coordination) relevant to migrant UK nationals; but otherwise regarded the latter's treatment as falling essentially within the competence of each Member State, merely calling for generosity in the development and implementation of national contingency plans concerning the future status and treatment of relevant individuals.[35]

[30] HMG, *Citizens' Rights: EU Citizens in the UK and UK Nationals in the EU* (6 December 2018); note also Home Office, *European Temporary Leave to Remain in the UK* (28 January 2019).
[31] While suggesting that the EU was preventing progress here: see HMG, *The United Kingdom's Exit from and New Partnership with the European Union* (Cm 9417 of 2 February 2017).
[32] See the personal accounts documented, e.g. in E. Remigi, D. Williams, H. De Cruz, S. Pybus, C. Killwick and P. Blackburn, *In Limbo Too* (2018).
[33] E.g. House of Commons Exiting the EU Committee, *The Government's Negotiating Objectives: The Rights of UK and EU Citizens* (HC1071 of 5 March 2017).
[34] E.g. COM(2017) 2001 Final; COM(2017) 2002 Final.
[35] See, e.g. COM(2018) 880 Final; COM(2019) 276 Final; COM(2019) 394 Final.

And so, in accordance with the common preference of both the Union and the UK, the issue of citizens' rights indeed became central to the Article 50 TEU process. After the UK delivered its formal notification of intention to withdraw under Article 50 TEU, the Union's overall approach to citizens' rights was first articulated in the European Council's April 2017 Guidelines,[36] then fleshed out in the Council's detailed negotiating directives of May 2017.[37] On that basis, the Commission set out its initial negotiating position on citizens' rights in June 2017.[38] In that document, the Commission effectively called for a full guarantee of residency and associated rights for all affected Union citizens and UK nationals, capable of evolving dynamically in the future, along the lines of Union free movement law itself. A short time later, the UK published its own initial negotiating position on citizens' rights.[39] Despite its regular promises not to use individuals as bargaining chips, those UK proposals in fact fell far short of the 'full guarantee to all' that had been suggested in the White Paper of February 2017—basically calling for a limited degree of protection for certain groups of citizens, frozen in time as at the date of UK departure, and incapable of evolving further into the future.[40]

The UK position drew scathing condemnation not only from across the Union but also from within the UK itself.[41] But it at least served as a useful signal that the question of citizens' rights would not prove to be quite so straightforward as the May Government's political sloganeering had previously suggested. On the contrary, regular updates from the Article 50 TEU negotiations revealed serious disputes between the Union and the UK over the precise personal and material scope of protection that should be offered under the proposed withdrawal treaty.[42] So even on this supposedly straightforward and uncontroversial issue, the European Council meeting in October 2017 was unable to identify evidence of 'sufficient progress'.[43]

The UK Government published further details of its plans for citizens' rights;[44] and of course, negotiations with the Union continued under the auspices of Article 50 TEU.[45] In December 2017, consensus was reached on the main principles as well as many of the more detailed provisions that should govern the future protection of citizens' rights.[46] Certain problems still persisted: for example, concerning the impact of the UK's request for a post-withdrawal, status quo transition period upon the

---

[36] European Council (Article 50), *Guidelines following the United Kingdom's notification under Article 50 TEU* (29 April 2017).

[37] Council Decision authorizing the opening of negotiations with the United Kingdom of Great Britain and Northern Ireland for an agreement setting out the arrangements for its withdrawal from the European Union (22 May 2017).

[38] Commission, *Position Paper on Essential Principles on Citizens' Rights* (12 June 2017).

[39] HMG, *Safeguarding the position of EU citizens living in the UK and UK nationals living in the EU* (26 June 2017).

[40] E.g. Theresa May, *PM's Open Letter to EU Citizens in the UK* (19 October 2017).

[41] E.g. Scottish Government, *Protecting the Rights of EU Citizens: Scottish Government Response to UK Government Citizens' Rights Paper* (17 July 2017).

[42] See, e.g. the 'joint technical notes' on citizens' rights published by the Commission and the UK on 20 July 2017 (TF50 (2017) 10); 31 August 2017 (TF50 (2017) 16); and 28 September 2017 (TF50 (2017) 17).

[43] European Council (Article 50), *Conclusions of 20 October 2017.*

[44] E.g. HMG, *Technical Note: Citizens' Rights—Administrative Procedures in the UK* (8 November 2017).

[45] See further Chapter 4.

[46] See Joint Report from the EU and UK negotiators (8 December 2017) and Joint Technical Note on Citizens' Rights (TF50 (2017) 20).

effective date for calculating entitlement to protection under the proposed citizens' rights regime.[47] Moreover, international concern about the UK's 'hostile environment' policies—as exemplified in the appalling 'Windrush Scandal'—caused the European Parliament to pay particular attention to the precise details and planned implementation of the UK's proposed scheme for registering EU citizens who wished to remain within British territory.[48]

Full agreement on the citizens' rights provisions of any withdrawal package was only reached between the parties in late 2018.[49] Even then, right up until final ratification of the Second Withdrawal Agreement in January 2020, millions of EU27 citizens and UK nationals, living in the UK and across the Union, remained uncertain about whether their futures would indeed be governed by the citizens' rights provisions negotiated between the Union and the UK; or instead by the various 'no deal' immigration contingency plans which would have to be adopted unilaterally across 28 different states.[50]

We will now discuss the general scheme on citizens' rights as provided for under Part Two of the final Withdrawal Agreement (together with the special provisions on interpretation and enforcement in this field contained elsewhere in the treaty).[51] However, it is important to note that the text of the Withdrawal Agreement cannot, in practice, be read entirely in isolation. In the first place, the regime on citizens' rights still offers the UK and each of the EU27 certain discretionary choices that need to be made and implemented within their respective national legal systems: for example, whether individuals who should be entitled to protection under the Withdrawal Agreement in principle, nevertheless need to undergo a formal registration process in order to obtain access to their intended rights in practice.[52] In the second place, as regards most of the provisions contained in Part Two, it remains possible for the UK and/or EU27 states to offer more generous treatment to affected individuals as a matter of domestic law.[53] But there is an exception for the rules concerning cross-border social security as contained in Title III of Part Two: as is the case with the main Union legislation governing this entire field, the system is based on the coordination (rather than the harmonization) of national social security systems; its smooth functioning generally presupposes an exhaustive body of legal rules for determining the applicable legislation and operationalizing core concepts such as aggregation and exportation.[54]

---

[47] See further the discussion about free movement and transition in Chapter 6.

[48] See, e.g. Letter from Guy Verhofstadt to Sajid Javid of 30 April 2018. Again, many of the same concerns were expressed within the UK itself, e.g. Letter from Scottish and Welsh Governments to Home Secretary of 15 June 2018; including in the Westminster Parliament, e.g. House of Commons Exiting the EU Committee, *The Progress of the UK's Negotiations on EU Withdrawal—March to May 2018* (HC1060 of 24 May 2018).

[49] See further the discussion about agreement over the terms of the First Withdrawal Package in Chapter 4.

[50] See, in particular, COM(2018) 880 Final; and also the discussion in Chapter 2.

[51] Art 185 WA: with only limited exceptions, the provisions of Part Two (as well as Arts 158–159 WA) are applicable only from the end of transition.

[52] Art 18 WA—discussed in greater detail below.

[53] Art 38(1) WA: 'This Part shall not affect any laws, regulations or administrative provisions applicable in a host State or a State of work which would be more favourable to the persons concerned'.

[54] See Regulation 883/2004 on the coordination of social security systems, OJ 2004 L 166/1 (as amended)—especially Title II on determination of the applicable legislation.

It is also worth noting that separate agreements, protecting relevant citizens' rights, were concluded between the UK and the EFTA–EEA states (as part of the EFTA–EEA Separation Agreement);[55] as well as with Switzerland (under a dedicated Swiss Citizens' Rights Agreement).[56] Although entirely separate and extraneous to the EU–UK Withdrawal Agreement itself, the latter does nevertheless allow those UK/EFTA–EEA and UK/Swiss treaties to be linked specifically to the provisions contained in Title III of Part Two of the Withdrawal Agreement—thus allowing for a smoother system of cross-border social security coordination across all 32 of the relevant States.[57] Otherwise, the UK decided not to negotiate additional 'citizens' rights' agreements with other third countries, even where the latter's nationals benefit from limited immigration rights or privileges as a matter of existing Union external relations law. In particular: the UK refrained from seeking a 'continuity agreement' with Turkey that would commit to upholding the existing migration provisions of the Ankara Agreement; and instead announced that the UK would adopt its own unilateral and specific provisions to govern the future immigration status of Turkish citizens currently living in the UK.[58]

3. EU Law as the General Baseline for Citizens' Rights Protection

The general starting point adopted under the Withdrawal Agreement is that existing Union law should provide the basis for identifying both who is protected into the future and what the content of their rights should be.

A. Qualification and Entitlements

Thus, Article 10(1)(a)–(b) WA identifies for protection those Union or UK citizens who exercised their right to reside in the host state in accordance with Union law before the end of the transition period and continue to reside in the host state thereafter.[59] In this context, 'Union law' of course refers primarily to the detailed legislative regime contained in the Citizens' Rights Directive 2004/38;[60] as well as the various primary rules on the free movement of persons that are contained directly in the Treaties themselves.[61] Specific provision is also made for frontier workers, i.e. those who pursue an economic activity in accordance with Article 45 or 49 TFEU in a state

---

[55] Available via https://www.gov.uk/government/publications/eea-efta-separation-agreement-and-explainer.

[56] Available via https://www.gov.uk/government/publications/swiss-citizens-rights-agreement-and-explainer.

[57] See Art 33 WA.

[58] See, in particular, https://www.gov.uk/government/publications/international-agreements-if-the-uk-leaves-the-eu-without-a-deal/international-agreements-if-the-uk-leaves-the-eu-without-a-deal.

[59] See Art 9(c) WA on the precise definition of 'host state'.

[60] Directive 2004/38, OJ 2004 L 158/77.

[61] E.g. Arts 21, 45 and 49 TFEU on the free movement of citizens, workers and self-employed persons (respectively).

(or states) in which they do not reside.[62] Under Article 10(1)(c)–(d) WA, Part Two shall also apply to UK nationals who exercised their right as frontier workers in one or more Member States, or Union citizens who exercised their right as frontier workers in the UK, in accordance with Union law before the end of the transition period and continue to do so thereafter.[63]

For the rest of their lives, though provided they continue to meet the relevant conditions, those UK and EU27 citizens will enjoy a defined series of rights.[64] In particular, protected citizens shall enjoy the right to continue residing in the host state in accordance with applicable Union law.[65] That means: subject to the limitations and conditions contained in the relevant provisions of the Treaties, i.e. Articles 21, 45 or 49 TFEU; and/or under Directive 2004/38, i.e. concerning residence for up to three months,[66] residence for more than three months as a worker or self-employed person,[67] residence as a student or person of independent financial means,[68] residence under the special conditions applicable to those who retain the status of worker or self-employed person,[69] and the right to permanent residence.[70] The host state may not impose any limitations or conditions for obtaining, retaining, or losing those residence rights, other than those provided for under Part Two. Even in applying the limitations and conditions contained in the Withdrawal Agreement itself, there shall be no discretion other than in favour of the citizen concerned.[71]

Protected citizens are entitled to change status (say) between student, worker, self-employed, and economically inactive person, while still remaining within the scope of Part Two.[72] Individuals who have not already done so must also enjoy the future possibility of acquiring permanent residence in the host state as provided for under Directive 2004/38.[73] Such permanent residence must be based on having accumulated lawful residence in the host state in accordance with Union law, either for a continuous period of five years, or (in relevant situations) for the shorter periods provided for under Directive 2004/38.[74] For those purposes, periods of legal residence or work in accordance with Union law both before and after the end of the transition period shall be taken in account.[75] Otherwise, continuity of residence for the purposes of acquiring permanent residency is to be determined in accordance with the relevant provisions of Directive 2004/38.[76]

---

[62] Art 9(b) WA.
[63] Note also Art 9(d) WA on the corresponding definition of 'State of work'; as well as Art 1, Protocol on Gibraltar.
[64] Art 39 WA.
[65] Art 13(1) WA.
[66] Arts 6(1) and 14 WA.
[67] Arts 7(1)(a) and 14 WA.
[68] Arts 7(1)(b)–(c) and 14 WA.
[69] Arts 7(3) and 14 WA.
[70] Art 16(1) or 17(1) WA.
[71] Art 13(4) WA.
[72] Art 17 WA.
[73] See Arts 11, 15 and 16 WA.
[74] In particular: Art 17 Directive 2004/38.
[75] Arts 15(1) and 16 WA.
[76] In particular: Arts 16(3) and 21 Directive 2004/38. See Arts 11 and 15(2) WA.

Protected citizens residing in the host state are to enjoy a further body of rights re-lating to work: for example, non-discrimination as regards employment conditions; equal treatment as regards social and tax advantages; equal access to educational pro-vision in respect of resident children; and limited residency rights for the primary carer of any direct descendant who remains in education after the worker him/herself has ceased to reside in the host state.[77] There are also specific rights for protected cit-izens residing in the host state as regards self-employment;[78] as well as for employed and self-employed frontier workers as regards their state of work.[79] Furthermore, the Withdrawal Agreement makes limited provision for protected citizens as regards existing decisions on and pending applications for the recognition of professional qualifications—as usual, taking the expiry of the transition period as the reference date for calculating entitlement; and maintaining the effects of recognition as regards the relevant individual's host state/state of work.[80]

More broadly, Article 12 WA contains a general guarantee of non-discrimination on grounds of nationality within the host state/state of work in favour of protected citizens as regards matters falling within the scope of Part Two; while Article 23 WA makes general provision for the equal treatment with own nationals, in accordance with Article 24 Directive 2004/38, of all protected citizens residing within the host state. However, Articles 12 and 23 WA are each explicitly subject to any specific limi-tations or derogations contained in the relevant provisions of Part Two: for example, a host state shall not be obliged, prior to a claimant's acquisition of permanent residency, to grant maintenance aid for studies (in the form of grants or loans) to persons other than workers, self-employed persons, and persons entitled to retain such status.[81]

B. Social Security Coordination

Title III of Part Two of the Withdrawal Agreement contains specific provisions gov-erning the post-transition maintenance of social security coordination between the Union and the UK.[82]

Protected citizens falling within the general personal scope of Part Two are ex-plicitly covered as such also by the social security rules contained in Title III[83] for as long as those individuals continue to have a right to reside in the host state, or a right to work in the state of work, pursuant to the Withdrawal Agreement.[84] But the category of persons potentially able to rely on Title III is in fact broader than the def-inition of protected citizens for the purposes of continued residency in a host state or

---

[77] Art 24 WA.
[78] Art 25 WA.
[79] Arts 24, 25 and 26 WA.
[80] See the detailed rules contained in Arts 27–29 WA.
[81] Art 23(2) WA.
[82] See further, e.g. Commission, *Guidance Note on Citizens' Rights*, COM(2020) 2939 Final of 12 May 2020.
[83] Art 30(3) WA. Note that Arts 30(3) and (5) WA also cover the family members and survivors of pro-tected citizens under Art 10 WA, to the extent that they derive rights and obligations in that capacity under Regulation 883/2004 on the coordination of social security systems, OJ 2004 L 166/1.
[84] Art 30(4) WA.

of maintaining one's economic activity as a frontier worker. In particular, Article 30 WA provides that the social security rules should apply to: all UK nationals or EU27 citizens who are subject to the legislation of a Member State or to that of the UK at the end of the transition period (even without being resident there); all UK nationals or EU27 citizens residing in a Member State or in the UK but who are subject to the social security legislation of the UK or of a Member State at the end of the transition period; and any other UK nationals or EU27 citizens who pursue an economic activity in a Member State(s) or in the UK at the end of the transition period but who are subject to the social security legislation of the UK or of a Member State in accordance with Regulation 883/2004.[85] Those categories of people are to be covered as such by the social security rules contained in Title III, for as long as they continue without interruption to be in one of the abovementioned situations involving both a Member State and the UK at the same time.[86]

As regards those individuals falling within the personal scope of Title III of Part Two, the rules and objectives on cross-border social security coordination contained in Article 48 TFEU, Regulation 883/2004, and the Implementing Regulation 987/2009 are to apply;[87] while the Union and the UK must take due account of various decisions and recommendations adopted by the Administrative Commission for the Coordination of Social Security Systems.[88] In principle, this covers the Union's well-established principles as well as the more detailed provisions of cross-border social security coordination: for example, the rules on applicable legislation to prevent individuals being either excluded from any social security provision or subject to more than one social security system; the principle of equal treatment on grounds of nationality as regards access to and the conditions for social security provision; and the possibilities for cross-border aggregation and exportation as defined for various specific categories of social security benefits.[89]

But in addition, Article 32 WA makes special provision for a range of specific cross-border social security situations, that would not otherwise be covered by the application of the general coordination rules between the Union and the UK because the relevant individuals do not or no longer fall within the personal scope of Title III as defined under Article 30 WA.[90] For example: UK nationals or EU27 citizens

---

[85] Art 30(1) WA, referring to Regulation 883/2004 on the coordination of social security systems, OJ 2004 L 166/1. Note that Arts 30(1) and (5) WA also cover the family members and survivors of relevant UK/Union citizens, to the extent that they derive rights and obligations in that capacity under Regulation 883/2204. Note also that Arts 30(1) and (5) WA and Art 31(3) WA make additional provision for specified categories of TCNs together with their family members and survivors.

[86] Art 30(2) WA.

[87] Art 31(1) WA, referring to Regulation 883/2004 on the coordination of social security systems, OJ 2004 L 166/1 (as amended and as interpreted by the CJEU) and Regulation 987/2009 laying down the procedure for implementing Regulation 883/2004 on the coordination of social security systems, OJ 2009 L 284/1. Note also Art 31(2) WA on definitions.

[88] As listed in Part I of Annex I to the Withdrawal Agreement: see Art 31(1) WA. Note also Art 34 WA on administrative cooperation between the Union and the UK as regards the provisions on social security coordination.

[89] In accordance with the detailed provisions contained in Regulation 883/2004 on the coordination of social security systems, OJ 2004 L 166/1 (as amended and as interpreted by the CJEU).

[90] Note also Art 35 WA on special rules concerning reimbursement, recovery, and offsetting as between the Union and the UK.

who have been subject to the legislation of a Member State or of the UK before the end of the transition period will still be entitled to rely on and aggregate periods of insurance/employment/self-employment/residence, including any rights and obligations deriving from such periods, in accordance with Regulation 883/2004 (say, in order to calculate future entitlement to and the payment of pension benefits).[91] For the purposes of such aggregation, periods completed both before and after the end of the transition period shall be taken into account.[92] Similarly: persons who, before the end of the transition period, had requested authorization to receive a course of planned healthcare treatment in the UK or a Member State shall remain subject to the relevant Union coordination rules until completion of the relevant treatment;[93] while insured persons who are on a temporary stay in the UK or a Member State as at the end of the transition period shall continue to be covered by the relevant Union coordination rules for the purposes of emergency medical cover until the end of their stay.[94]

C. Problems with Relying on EU Law as the Baseline for Protection

The decision to rely on existing Union law as a general baseline for the protection of citizens' rights under the Withdrawal Agreement might sound uncontroversial but it is still potentially problematic. After all, limiting entitlement to protection (in most situations) to economically active and financially independent citizens has the effect of importing into the Withdrawal Agreement many of the familiar criticisms levelled against Union free movement law in general, based on its inherent tendency to reflect and reinforce certain social inequalities.[95]

Of course, such concerns are most obvious when it comes to the potential for total exclusion from any protection under the Withdrawal Agreement of many of the most marginalized citizens—those who clearly fail altogether to fulfil the various constituent requirements imposed under Union free movement law and who therefore have little hope either of qualifying for initial, or of maintaining future, protection under the corresponding terms of Part Two per se.[96] But potential problems arise also for individuals whose residency has indeed been grounded in some form of legitimate economic activity, yet whose specific situation or combination of life events nevertheless still places them in a legally vulnerable position. For example, consider those with 'non-linear' or 'non-standard' migration experiences involving periods of insecure/ irregular work or career breaks due to care responsibilities; as well as those hoping

---

[91] Art 32(1)(a) WA. This also applies to family members and survivors; as well as various categories of TCNs and their family members and survivors.

[92] Note also Art 32(2) WA on the application of the Union coordination rules concerning sickness benefits to persons receiving benefits in accordance with Art 32(1)(a) WA.

[93] Art 32(1)(b) WA.

[94] Art 32(1)(c) WA.

[95] See further, e.g. Thym, 'The Elusive Limits of Solidarity: Residence Rights of and Social Benefits for Economically Inactive Union citizens', 52 *CMLRev* (2015) 17; Nic Shuibhne, 'Limits rising, duties ascending: The Changing Legal Shape of Union Citizenship', 52 *CMLRev* (2015) 889; O'Brien, 'Civis capitalist sum: Class as the new guiding principle of EU free movement rights', 53 *CMLRev* (2016) 937.

[96] In particular: the requirements imposed upon non-economically active persons, to possess sufficient financial resources and comprehensive medical insurance, by Directive 2004/38, OJ 2004 L 158/77.

to rely on the right to free movement in their capacity as work-seekers pursuant to Article 45 TFEU. Such individuals might encounter real difficulties in proving that their historic, current, or continuing residency is lawful, again for the purposes either of qualifying for initial or of maintaining future protection (or at least of calculating continuity of residence) under the Withdrawal Agreement.[97]

Similar problems might well confront those citizens who sincerely believe their residency (for example, as students or retired persons) to be secure on the basis that, as an empirical fact, they have been and/or remain financially independent and have made/ make no claims upon public support from their host state … yet their failure to obtain comprehensive sickness insurance means that their historic, current, or continuing residency actually falls outside the strict scope of Union free movement law, again for the purposes either of qualifying for initial or of maintaining future protection (or at least of calculating continuity of residence) under the Agreement—even though the requirement to obtain comprehensive sickness insurance was never before insisted upon or enforced as such by the competent authorities of the host state.[98]

If a given State were now to enforce the Withdrawal Agreement at face value, that decision could have serious consequences for many individuals whose residency was never previously questioned and who sincerely believed that their status was unproblematic. It is true that Part Two contains certain standards of fair treatment. For example, the Withdrawal Agreement lays down various principles of evidential flexibility when it comes to proving lawful residency under the applicable Union rules;[99] and (as we have seen) the requirement that any discretion in applying the relevant limitations or conditions under Union law shall be exercised only in favour of the applicant.[100] However, such principles and requirements of fair treatment still presuppose that the claimant meets the objective requirements imposed under Union free movement law in the first place.

Nor is it enough to retort that one cannot lose what one never had in the first place. As Spaventa has pointed out, any change in or loss of status under Union law is usually flexible and temporary: one can leave and come back, one might lose a job then find another, one can rectify an irregular situation. But a change in or loss of status under the Withdrawal Agreement is potentially definitive and permanent: failing to qualify for protection, or later ceasing to satisfy the continuing requirements thereof, could well lead to the total loss of protected status with no possibility that it might ever be regained.[101]

Against that background, the fact that the Withdrawal Agreement generally provides only a minimum standard of protection for Union and UK citizens may well

[97] See, e.g. E. Spaventa, *Update of the Study on the Impact of Brexit in Relation to the Right to Petition and on the Competences, Responsibilities and Activities of the Committee on Petitions* (European Parliament, Policy Department for Citizens' Rights and Constitutional Affairs: PE 604.959 of April 2018).
[98] See further, on the vulnerable position of Union citizens within the UK in this regard, e.g. C. O'Brien, *Unity in Adversity: EU Citizenship, Social Justice and the Cautionary Tale of the UK* (2017).
[99] Art 18(1) WA.
[100] Art 13(4) WA.
[101] See E. Spaventa, *Update of the Study on the Impact of Brexit in Relation to the Right to Petition and on the Competences, Responsibilities and Activities of the Committee on Petitions* (European Parliament, Policy Department for Citizens' Rights and Constitutional Affairs: PE 604.959 of April 2018). Note the very limited exception provided for in Art 19(4) WA.

prove to be particularly important.[102] For example, the UK announced that qualification for 'settled status', under its domestic rules implementing the Withdrawal Agreement, would be based primarily on continuous residence, without necessarily demanding full compliance with all the requirements imposed under existing Union free movement rules, as regards (say) comprehensive sickness insurance for economically inactive persons.[103]

However, the interaction between the minimum standards laid down in Part Two (on the one hand) and the exercise of national competence to offer more favourable treatment to individuals (on the other hand) remains legally unclear and could still leave Union/UK citizens in a vulnerable position: for example, when it comes to the continued maintenance of their initial residence status and/or associated rights; or as regards their future qualification for protection under the Union law rules/Part Two provisions concerning permanent residency. In particular, the Withdrawal Agreement fails to specify the precise legal basis and nature of those rights which are conferred through essentially unilateral domestic choices—admittedly more generous than the Withdrawal Agreement, but not strictly grounded in the citizens' rights provisions themselves. The matter will therefore need to be clarified, in due course, following the system of interpretation and dispute settlement laid down under the Withdrawal Agreement.[104]

A strict approach might argue that only legal qualification under the precise terms of Union law counts for the purposes of entitlement to protection under the Withdrawal Agreement. Whatever the host state decides to offer, above and beyond the basic standards guaranteed under Part Two, is entirely a matter for and will ultimately be governed by national law. By contrast, a more generous approach would suggest that, even where it is only on the initiative of the host state itself that the individual is offered protected status, he/she then becomes entitled to the full range of material protections envisaged under the Withdrawal Agreement.

It is certainly possible to cite analogous legal authorities under Union law tending to support either a strict or a more generous view. For example, in the field of free movement law, the CJEU has sometimes found that individuals whose residency is grounded in national immigration competence, rather than in full compliance with Union rules, nevertheless still fall within the scope of the Treaties and remain entitled to equal treatment under Union law;[105] whereas in other rulings, the CJEU has decided that proper compliance with the qualifying conditions imposed under Union law is in fact constitutive of the individual's right to protection under the Treaties.[106] Similarly, where Union law lays down only minimum regulatory requirements while respecting the competence of Member States to enact higher protective standards, the Court usually insists that such more stringent domestic rules fall altogether outside

---

[102] Art 38(1) WA.

[103] Home Office, *EU Settlement Scheme: Statement of Intent* (21 June 2018), at Part 2.

[104] On which: see the discussion in Chapter 6; as well as the provisions particular to citizens' rights discussed further below.

[105] E.g. Case C-85/96, *Sala* (EU:C:1998:217) and Case C-456/02, *Trojani* (EU:C:2004:488).

[106] E.g. Joined Cases C-424/10 and C-425/10, *Ziolkowski and Szeja* (EU:C:2011:866) and Case C-333/13, *Dano* (EU:C:2014:2358).

the scope of the Treaties;[107] but has occasionally proven willing to scrutinize the Member State's own more generous regulatory choices in accordance with the general principles of Union law.[108]

4. Deviations from the EU Law Baseline

Notwithstanding the fact that Part Two takes existing Union free movement law as the baseline for future protection of EU27 and UK citizens, there are various situations where the Withdrawal Agreement provides for certain deviations from that initial Union legal standard.

A. Better Protection

In a few instances, the Withdrawal Agreement in fact foresees higher standards of protection than existing Union free movement rules. For example: once acquired, protected citizens will forfeit their right to permanent residence after five (rather than the normal Union law benchmark of two) consecutive years' absence from the host state—partial compensation for the potentially definitive and permanent consequences of losing protected status under the Withdrawal Agreement.[109]

But the main instance of the Withdrawal Agreement envisaging 'better protection' than that provided by existing Union law concerns British–Irish relations. In principle, the Union's basic approach towards the Article 50 TEU negotiations on citizens' rights was that there should be a single set of rules for all remaining Member States and their nationals (on the one hand) and the UK and its nationals (on the other hand).[110] However, that approach was not easy to reconcile with the longstanding arrangements (linked to the operation of the Common Travel Area (CTA)) whereby the UK and Ireland each guarantee special treatment specifically for each other's nationals (for example) as regards particularly extensive rights of residency; full access to employment and self-employment; full equal treatment with own nationals in fields such as education, healthcare, social security, and social housing; and also the right to vote in national parliamentary elections.[111]

According to the UK and Irish Governments, '[t]hese arrangements reflect the historically close links and cooperation between Ireland and the UK, the many social and economic connections, as well as how the two countries have approached together

---

[107] E.g. Case C-2/97, *Borsana* (EU:C:1998:613); Case C-6/03, *Deponiezweckverband Eiterköpfe* (EU:C:2005:222); Cases C-609–610/17, *TSN* (EU:C:2019:981).

[108] E.g. Case C-71/02, *Karner* (EU:C:2004:181). See further, e.g. de Cecco, 'Room to Move? Minimum Harmonisation and Fundamental Rights', 43 *CMLRev* (2006) 9.

[109] Arts 11 and 15(3) WA. Contrast with Art 20(3) Directive 2004/38, OJ 2004 L 158/77.

[110] See, e.g. Commission, *Position Paper on Essential Principles on Citizens' Rights* (12 June 2017).

[111] See further, e.g. House of Commons Library Briefing Paper, *The Common Travel Area and the Special Status of Irish Nationals in UK Law* (No 7661 of 15 July 2016). On the Common Travel Area, and the border problems raised by Brexit as regards the movement of persons between the UK and Ireland, see the more detailed discussion and references in Chapter 8.

the movement of people across national borders over time'.[112] Of course, it is arguable that those specific CTA-related arrangements are less a matter of brotherly love than a reflection of the fact that there is no easy way for the UK to distinguish between Irish nationals from the Republic and those from Northern Ireland—thus necessitating the treatment of all Irish nationals as effectively equivalent to British nationals. But in any case, it is clear that the specific CTA-related arrangements offer UK and Irish nationals reciprocal rights going beyond those either contained in Union free movement law or envisaged under the Withdrawal Agreement, whether for UK citizens across the rest of the EU, or for other groups of Union citizens within the UK.

The UK Government had already expressed its desire to retain the current CTA-related arrangements on reciprocal special treatment for British and Irish nationals in its White Paper of February 2017.[113] For its part, the Union also expressed its support for the continued maintenance of the special rights to residence and equal treatment etc associated with the CTA.[114] And in due course, the UK and Ireland issued a joint statement expressing their common determination to uphold the existing benefits offered to each other's citizens within the context of the CTA.[115] In order to reflect this shared political understanding, Article 38(2) WA provides that the principle of non-discrimination on grounds of nationality, as set out in Articles 12 and 23(1) WA, 'shall be without prejudice to the Common Travel Area arrangements between the United Kingdom and Ireland as regards more favourable treatment which may result from these arrangements for the persons concerned'.

Even so, the joint understanding of the UK and Ireland about preserving the special rights associated with the CTA, and its legal accommodation within the framework of Part Two of the Withdrawal Agreement, is not without certain complications. For example, within the UK, the relatively secure right to residency enjoyed by Irish nationals as a matter of domestic immigration law means that their future security of residence is not dependent upon Part Two and they are not required to register for 'settled status' within the UK; yet there may still be distinct advantages for particular individuals to engage with the citizens' rights regime as contained in the Withdrawal Agreement and implemented into UK law—say, when it comes to the future legal status of the family members of Irish citizens resident in the UK, where those family members are not themselves British or Irish nationals. As we shall shortly see, the provisions of Part Two on family rights (however truncated compared to ordinary Union free movement law) are still potentially more generous than those applicable to Irish citizens, along with British nationals, under domestic immigration law alone.[116]

---

[112] Memorandum of Understanding between the Government of Ireland the Government of the UK concerning the Common Travel Area and Associated Reciprocal Rights and Privileges (8 May 2019), at para 4.

[113] See HMG, *The United Kingdom's Exit from and New Partnership with the European Union* (Cm 9417 of 2 February 2017), especially at paras 4.6–4.7 and Annex B.

[114] E.g. Commission, *Position Paper on Essential Principles on Citizens' Rights* (12 June 2017).

[115] Memorandum of Understanding between the Government of Ireland the Government of the UK concerning the Common Travel Area and Associated Reciprocal Rights and Privileges (8 May 2019).

[116] See, e.g. Home Office, *EU Settlement Scheme: Statement of Intent* (21 June 2018), at para 2.6, which also makes clear that the eligible family members of an Irish citizen may apply for 'settled status' in accordance with the provisions of Part Two, even if the relevant Irish citizen does not do so him/herself. See further below, on the treatment of the family members of protected Union citizens. Note: the UK extended the possibility of applying for 'settled status' to family members of people in Northern Ireland regardless of whether

The maintenance of the special rights associated with the CTA, alongside and above the regime on citizens' rights contained in Part Two of the Agreement, perhaps poses more difficult challenges for Ireland. After all, as a Member State of the European Union, Ireland's future freedom of action either to treat, or to agree to treat, UK nationals just as it pleases, will be limited by certain specific obligations imposed under Union law, in ways which were perhaps less relevant or at least less obvious in the past.[117]

Some such obligations would provide certain UK nationals with minimum standards of protection under Union law—regardless of what Ireland decides or agrees as a matter of its own immigration competence—even if the nature and extent of the reciprocal benefits agreed between the UK and Ireland mean that such protections are unlikely to be of much relevance in practice. For example, Ireland would be obliged to treat UK nationals who qualify as the protected family members of EU citizens in accordance with the minimum standards expected under Union law.[118] That includes the safeguards offered directly under Union primary law, in addition to the secondary legislation governing the free movement of Union citizens. Consider situations akin to *Ruiz Zambrano*: where the deportation of a UK national who is the primary carer of an Irish child would effectively oblige the latter also to leave the Union territory, that UK national may enjoy certain derived rights of residency and equal treatment within Ireland, notwithstanding that the situation would normally be considered wholly internal and outside the scope of protection afforded under Directive 2004/38.[119]

However, other EU law obligations could pull in the opposite direction—setting certain limits to, and creating certain costs consequent upon, the degree of favourable treatment that Ireland might be able or willing to reserve for UK nationals. For example, Union law reserves the prerogative to scrutinize how far a Member State (such as Ireland) might allow certain third country nationals (such as UK citizens) to vote in elections to the European Parliament.[120] Perhaps more importantly: although there is no general obligation upon Member States always to grant preference to Union citizens over third country nationals in the ordinary exercise of their domestic competences,[121] various provisions of Union law do contain a more specific duty that Member States should not confer more favourable treatment upon third country nationals than they are prepared to offer other Union citizens in particular situations. That is typically the case, for example, when it comes to the power of existing Member States to impose transitional restrictions upon the free movement of workers from newly acceded Member States within the context of EU enlargement treaties.[122]

the latter chose to adopt British or Irish nationality: see HMG, *The UK's Approach to the Northern Ireland Protocol* (CP226 of 20 May 2020), at para 46.

[117] Note that the competence of both countries will, in these matters, also be restricted by the baseline of obligations imposed under the ECHR.

[118] I.e. again in accordance with the provisions of Directive 2004/38, OJ 2004 L 158/77.

[119] Case C-34/09, *Ruiz Zambrano* (EU:C:2011:124)—as interpreted in subsequent caselaw such as Case C-256/11, *Dereci* (EU:C:2011:734).

[120] See, e.g. Case C-145/04, *Spain v United Kingdom* (EU:C:2006:543).

[121] See further, e.g. s. Robin-Olivier, 'The Community Preference Principle in Labour Migration Policy in the European Union' (OECD Social, Employment and Migration Working Papers No 182, 2016).

[122] E.g. Art 14, Part 1 (Freedom of Movement for Persons), Annex V (as regards the Czech Republic) to the Act concerning the conditions of accession of the Czech Republic, the Republic of Estonia, the

Another significant restriction upon Ireland's freedom of manoeuvre will be the principle that international agreements between a Member State and a third country are still required to comply with Union law.[123] That includes the general principle of equal treatment on grounds of nationality: where an international agreement seeks to confer certain benefits upon the nationals of the signatory Member State, the latter must extend those same benefits also to other EU citizens who find themselves in a comparable position.[124] For example, imagine that Ireland were to sign a bilateral agreement with the UK, providing for the coordination of social security contributions and payments between the two countries—something which may well be required in order to make the maintenance of reciprocal residency rights meaningful in practice.[125] In so far as Ireland agrees to take into account periods of social security insurance within the UK, for the purposes of calculating entitlement to Irish benefits, the general principle of equal treatment on grounds of nationality would (in principle) oblige Ireland to do so for all migrant EU citizens, rather than just Irish (and UK) nationals alone.[126]

B. Worse Protection

In other situations, the Withdrawal Agreement allows for restrictions on citizens' rights that would not comply with existing Union free movement law—a point well illustrated by four important examples.

In the first place: the range of family members entitled to rights by association with a protected Union or UK citizen is reduced—particularly as regards the ability of existing but especially future family members to join a protected citizen within the host state after the end of the transition period.

In particular, Article 9(a) WA defines 'family members' for the purposes of Part Two (though without prejudice to the specific definitions applicable under Title III on social security) as follows:

Republic of Cyprus, the Republic of Latvia, the Republic of Lithuania, the Republic of Hungary, the Republic of Malta, the Republic of Poland, the Republic of Slovenia and the Slovak Republic and the adjustments to the Treaties on which the European Union is founded, OJ 2003 L 236/33. Similar provisions have applied to the accession of other Member States, e.g. consider Case C-15/11, *Sommer* (EU:C:2012:371).

[123] Subject to Art 351 TFEU.
[124] E.g. Case C-55/00, *Gottardo* (EU:C:2002:16). The fact that the relevant third country is not obliged to do the same is irrelevant.
[125] Assuming that the UK leaves the general system of cross-border social security coordination under Regulation 883/2004, OJ 2004 L 200/1 without reaching agreement on any comparable replacement with the EU as a whole. See further, e.g. Commission, *The External Dimension of EU Social Security Coordination*, COM(2012) 153 Final.
[126] The full effects of the *Gottardo* principle assume that the issue falls within the scope of Union law, that the relevant situations are comparable, and there is no objective justification for the difference in treatment (such as respecting the balance and reciprocity of a bilateral agreement): see further, e.g. Case C-307/97, *Compagnie de Saint-Gobain* (EU:C:1999:438); Case C-376/03, *D* (EU:C:2005:424).

the following persons, irrespective of their nationality ...

   (i) family members of Union citizens or family members of United Kingdom nationals as defined in point (2) of Article 2 of Directive 2004/38/EC [i.e. spouses,
certain registered partners, direct descendants of the relevant Union or UK citizen or of their spouse/partner who are under 21 or dependent, and dependent
direct relatives in the ascending line of the relevant Union or UK citizen or of
their spouse/partner] ...
  (ii) persons other than those defined in Article 3(2) of Directive 2004/38/EC
[note that the latter provision covers a wider category of family members
who (in the country from which they have come) are dependants or members of the household of the relevant Union or UK citizen, or suffer from serious health issues strictly requiring their personal care by the relevant Union
or UK citizen, as well as a partner with whom the relevant Union or UK
citizen has a durable and duly attested relationship—dealt with separately
under Articles 10(2)-(5) WA, as explained further below] whose presence
is required by Union citizens or United Kingdom nationals in order not to
deprive those Union citizens or United Kingdom nationals of a right of residence granted by this Part'.

However, under Article 10(1) WA, family members as thus defined will only fall within
the personal scope of Part Two where they belong to one of two main categories:

  (e) family members of [protected Union or UK citizens], provided that they fulfil one
of the following conditions:
   (i) they resided in the host State in accordance with Union law before the end
of the transition period and continue to reside there thereafter;
  (ii) they were directly related to a [protected Union or UK citizen] and resided
outside the host State before the end of the transition period, provided that
they fulfil the conditions set out in point (2) of Article 2 of Directive 2004/
38/EC at the time they seek residence under this Part in order to join the
[protected Union or UK citizen];
 (iii) they were born to, or legally adopted by, [protected Union or UK citizens]
after the end of the transition period, whether inside or outside the host
State, and fulfil the conditions set out in point (2)(c) of Article 2 of Directive
2004/38/EC [i.e. are under 21 or dependent] at the time they seek residence
under this Part in order to join the [protected Union or UK citizen] and
fulfil one of the following conditions:
        • both parents are [protected Union or UK citizens];
        • one parent is a [protected Union or UK citizen] and the other is a national
of the host State; or
        • one parent is a [protected Union or UK citizen] and has sole or joint
rights of custody of the child, in accordance with the applicable rules of
family law of a Member State or of the United Kingdom, including applicable rules of private international law under which rights of custody

established under the law of a third State are recognised in the Member State or in the United Kingdom, in particular as regards the best interests of the child, and without prejudice to the normal operation of such applicable rules of private international law;[127]

(f) family members who resided in the host State in accordance with Articles 12 and 13, Article 16(2) and Articles 17 and 18 of Directive 2004/38/EC before the end of the transition period and continue to reside there thereafter [i.e. those with a retained right of residence following the occurrence of a contingency such as the death or departure of, or divorce from, the relevant Union or UK citizen; as well as those with a right of permanent residence].'

Article 10 WA also makes limited provision for a potentially broader category of family members:

'(2) Persons falling under points (a) and (b) of Article 3(2) of Directive 2004/38/EC [i.e. wider family members who (in the country from which they came) were dependants or members of the household of the relevant Union or UK citizen, or suffered from serious health issues strictly requiring their personal care by the relevant Union or UK citizen, as well as a partner with whom the relevant Union or UK citizen has a durable and duly attested relationship] whose residence was facilitated by the host State in accordance with its national legislation before the end of the transition period in accordance with Article 3(2) of that Directive shall retain their right of residence in the host State in accordance with this Part, provided that they continue to reside in the host State thereafter.

(3) Paragraph 2 shall also apply to persons falling under points (a) and (b) of Article 3(2) of Directive 2004/38/EC who have applied for facilitation of entry and residence before the end of the transition period, and whose residence is being facilitated by the host State in accordance with its national legislation thereafter.

(4) Without prejudice to any right to residence which the persons concerned may have in their own right, the host State shall, in accordance with its national legislation and in accordance with point (b) of Article 3(2) of Directive 2004/38/EC, facilitate entry and residence for the partner with whom the [protected Union or UK citizen] has a durable relationship, duly attested, where that partner resided outside the host State before the end of the transition period, provided that the relationship was durable before the end of the transition period and continues at the time the partner seeks residence under this Part.

(5) In the cases referred to in paragraphs 3 and 4, the host State shall undertake an extensive examination of the personal circumstances of the persons concerned and shall justify any denial of entry or residence to such persons.'

---

[127] See Art 9(e) WA on the definition of 'rights of custody'.

And Articles 24(2) and 25(2) WA make specific provision for a particular category of family member, i.e. '*Baumbast* carers': where a direct descendant of a protected Union or UK worker or self-employed person who has ceased to reside in the host state, is in education in that state, the primary carer for that descendant shall have the right to reside in that state until the descendant reaches the age of majority, and after the age of majority if that descendant continues to need the presence and care of the primary carer in order to pursue and complete his or her education.[128]

Nevertheless, the family unification rights offered to protected Union and UK citizens under the Withdrawal Agreement are considerably reduced compared to those normally associated with Union citizenship under ordinary free movement law: for example, individuals who marry a protected Union or UK citizen only after the end of the transition period, will not come within the personal scope of Part Two as protected family members.[129]

In the second place: any given host state may (at its own discretion) make qualification for future protection under Part Two subject to a system of compulsory registration.[130] That is precisely what the UK decided to do through its EU Settlement Scheme: granting 'settled status' to individuals who satisfy the criteria for permanent residency contained in the Withdrawal Agreement; and recognizing 'presettled status' for those who otherwise qualify for protection under the Withdrawal Agreement with a view to acquiring the right of permanent residence in due course.[131] Within the Union, 13 Member States also decided to avail themselves of the possibility to insist that UK nationals seeking future protection for themselves and their family members should undergo a formal registration process.[132] The remaining 14 Member States opted instead for a purely declaratory system that does not require UK nationals to apply or register for a new residence status as a condition for enjoying protected status under the Withdrawal Agreement.[133]

On the one hand, the text of the Withdrawal Agreement suggests that compliance with any such compulsory registration system is constitutive (not merely declaratory) of the very right to future protection under much of Part Two: the host state may require relevant individuals 'to apply for a new residence status *which confers the rights* under [Title II of Part Two concerning residency and associated rights]'.[134] On the

---

[128] See, in particular, Case C-413/99, *Baumbast* (EU:C:2002:493).

[129] Contrast with the relevant provisions of Directive 2004/38, especially Arts 2 and 3. Note that family members qualifying for protection under the Withdrawal Agreement are offered a series of rights: e.g. Arts 13(2)–(4) WA on continuing residency in accordance with applicable Union law; e.g. Art 14 WA on rights of exit and entry; e.g. Arts 11, 15 and 16 WA on acquisition of permanent residence; e.g. Art 22 WA on the pursuit of economic activities in their own right; e.g. Arts 12 and 23 WA on equal treatment with own nationals. However, the Agreement imposes certain restrictions on the ability of family members to change their status under Part Two: see Art 17 WA. Otherwise, the guarantee of 'lifetime protection' applies also to protected family members: see Art 39 WA.

[130] Art 18 WA. Note also Art 26 WA on compulsory documentary certification by frontier workers.

[131] Home Office, *EU Settlement Scheme: Statement of Intent* (21 June 2018).

[132] See further: https://ec.europa.eu/info/sites/info/files/brexit_files/info_site/overview_ms_residence_rights.pdf.

[133] See Art 18(4) WA.

[134] Art 18(1) WA (emphasis added)—an approach also reflected in the drafting of other provisions throughout Part Two. Note also, e.g. HMG, *Technical Note: Citizens' Rights—Administrative Procedures in the UK* (8 November 2017).

other hand, the Withdrawal Agreement states that the purpose of any registration system is to verify whether the applicant is entitled to enjoy the residence rights contained in Title II; where that is the case, the applicant shall have a right to be granted their new residency status under the Withdrawal Agreement.[135] Moreover, Part Two lays down the various specifications with which any compulsory registration system must comply, for example:

- a minimum six-month application deadline from the end of transition for persons residing in the host state before that date;[136]
- for persons entitled to take up residence in the host state after the end of the transition period, an application deadline of either 6 months from the end of transition or 3 months from their arrival (whichever is later);[137]
- provision for the application deadline to be extended automatically by 1 year, where one party notifies the other of technical problems preventing the host state either from registering applications or indeed from immediately issuing certificates of application;[138]
- flexibility by the competent authorities in situations where the applicant had reasonable grounds for failing to meet the deadline for submitting their application, taking into account all the circumstances, and allowing the individual concerned to apply within a reasonable further period of time;[139]
- smooth, transparent and simple administrative procedures, avoiding unnecessary administrative burdens, for which certain controlled fees may be charged;[140]
- detailed rules on appropriate documentation to prove identity, lawful residency and family status etc;[141]
- an obligation on the competent authorities to help applicants prove eligibility/ avoid errors or omissions, including giving the opportunity to provide supplementary evidence/correct deficiencies;[142]
- access to redress procedures (certainly judicial, possibly also administrative) in respect of any decision refusing registration of residency status under the Withdrawal Agreement—covering the legality, factual basis, and (dis)proportionality of such adverse decisions;[143]
- certain presumptions of protection pending the outcome of any application for registration or appeal against a refusal of residency status.[144]

---

[135] Art 18(1)(a) WA.
[136] Art 18(1)(b) WA.
[137] Art 18(1)(b) WA.
[138] Art 18(1)(c) WA.
[139] Art 18(1)(d) WA.
[140] Arts 18(1)(e)–(g) WA. Though no fees can be charged for exchanging existing permanent residence or equivalent documents: Art 18(1)(h) WA. Note that the UK initially planned to impose charges for applications under its EU Settlement Scheme: see Home Office, *EU Settlement Scheme: Statement of Intent* (21 June 2018), at para 1.18. However, the Government later decided to waive those fees: see Theresa May, *Statement to the House of Commons on Brexit* (21 January 2019).
[141] Arts 18(1)(h)–(n) WA.
[142] Art 18(1)(o) WA.
[143] Art 18(1)(r) WA.
[144] Arts 18(2)–(3) WA.

It is worth noting that Article 19 WA allows those states that decide to operate a registration system to begin its operation, albeit on a purely voluntary basis, from the date of withdrawal and during the transition period. However, decisions on residency status must still be taken in accordance with the specifications contained in Part Two; such decisions shall have no effect until after the expiry of the transition period itself; positive decisions may not be withdrawn before the end of the transition period other than in accordance with ordinary Union free movement rules; negative decisions shall not prevent the individual reapplying within the final deadlines set out under the Withdrawal Agreement; and administrative/judicial redress procedures must be available in respect of any negative decision taken during transition.

Useful as all those specifications are in principle, in seeking to structure and constrain the discretion of the host authorities and ensure fair treatment of affected individuals, one might also doubt just how effective some of the Part Two provisions have really proved themselves to be in practice. For example: the impact of the global pandemic reportedly led to significant (albeit temporary) problems with the UK authorities' capacity to process applications for 'settled status' by EU citizens.[145] One might suspect that the same was true in various Member States of the Union as well, given the widespread and severe disruption experienced by many public bodies and services under national lockdown programmes. However, the UK gave no notification to the Union that it had encountered technical problems for the purposes of Article 18 WA and thus there was no activation of the Withdrawal Agreement's provisions on automatic postponement of the UK's application deadlines under its EU Settlement Scheme.

In the third place: the Withdrawal Agreement makes provision for the refusal or termination of residency rights under Part Two based on the personal conduct of the individual applicant or resident.[146] In particular, those states which decide to operate a compulsory registration scheme are entitled to conduct systematic criminality and security checks on all applicants to determine whether any grounds exist for refusing to confer protected status;[147] while all states are entitled to revoke an individual's existing rights of residence and order their expulsion from the national territory on grounds of their personal conduct.[148] For those purposes, Article 20(1)–(2) WA states that personal conduct occurring *before* the end of transition is to be assessed in accordance with existing Union free movement law;[149] but personal conduct occurring *after* the end of the transition period may constitute grounds for refusing or restricting residency within the host state in accordance with national law.[150] That provision has

---

[145] In March 2020, it was reported that the Home Office was notifying applicants for 'settled status' of significant delays to/interruptions in service, due to the impact of the pandemic: see, e.g. https://twitter.com/georgvh/status/1244652925785423873/photo/1.

[146] Or indeed: the refusal or termination of rights of entry, in the case of frontier workers.

[147] Art 18(1)(p) WA—for which purpose, applicants may be required to declare past criminal convictions which appear in their criminal record in accordance with the law of the state of conviction at the time of the application.

[148] Note also Arts 20(3)–(4) WA on restrictions based on abuse of rights or fraudulent behaviour; as well as Art 21 WA on the procedural safeguards that apply in respect of decisions by a host state to restrict the residency rights of protected citizens and their protected family members etc.

[149] In particular: Chapter VI of Directive 2004/38.

[150] Or entry to the state of work, in the case of frontier workers.

raised concerns about the potential imposition upon protected citizens and/or their protected family members of disproportionate immigration penalties for relatively minor criminal offences.[151]

On the one hand, UK nationals and their family members etc would surely remain protected as a matter of Union law, pursuant to the Charter of Fundamental Rights and/or the general principles of Union law, as regards oppressive or disproportionate attempts by a Member State to restrict or revoke their residency rights under the Withdrawal Agreement by reference to domestic immigration law. The Withdrawal Agreement forms an integral part of Union law and national action seeking to derogate from the rights conferred under Part Two would clearly fall 'within the scope of the Treaties' for the purposes of triggering the application of Union fundamental rights and/or administrative law.[152]

On the other hand, there is greater doubt about whether Union citizens and their family members etc would also remain protected as a matter of Union law, and specifically pursuant to either the Charter or the general principles of Union law, as regards an attempt by the UK authorities to restrict or revoke their residency rights under the Withdrawal Agreement, again, on the basis of domestic immigration rules. It is true that Article 4 WA obliges the UK to interpret and apply any provisions of Part Two that refer to concepts or provisions of Union law in accordance with the methods and general principles of Union law itself as well as the caselaw of the CJEU as it stood at the end of the transition period; but it is unclear how far that general principle of interpretation and application might be qualified in practice by the fact that Article 20 WA specifically allows post-transition criminality/personal conduct to be evaluated in accordance with national law rather than Directive 2004/38.[153] In any case, one assumes that Union citizens would remain entitled to at least some degree of protection against oppressive and/or disproportionate penalties, in accordance with domestic UK fundamental rights rules and/or administrative law principles.[154]

In the fourth place, own nationals are generally not covered by the citizens' rights provisions of the Withdrawal Agreement as regards relations with or treatment by their home state. On the one hand, that restriction is of potential significance for certain UK nationals who would otherwise have been entitled to rely on Union law in respect of the UK itself in a range of specific situations. Consider, for example, a British national who has returned to the UK, relying on Union free movement rights to bring their third country national family member (under the *Surinder Singh* caselaw);[155] or the possibility under Union law for UK children residing in the UK to maintain the protected residency status of their primary carer who is a third country national

---

[151] E.g. E. Spaventa, *Update of the Study on the Impact of Brexit in Relation to the Right to Petition and on the Competences, Responsibilities and Activities of the Committee on Petitions* (European Parliament, Policy Department for Citizens' Rights and Constitutional Affairs: PE 604.959 of April 2018).

[152] See further, e.g. Dougan, 'Judicial Review of Member State Action under the General Principles and the Charter: Defining the "Scope of Union Law"', 52 *CMLRev* (2015) 1201.

[153] See further, e.g. E. Spaventa, *Update of the Study on the Impact of Brexit in Relation to the Right to Petition and on the Competences, Responsibilities and Activities of the Committee on Petitions* (European Parliament, Policy Department for Citizens' Rights and Constitutional Affairs: PE 604.959 of April 2018).

[154] I.e. in accordance with the common law principles of judicial review; as well as the Human Rights Act 1998.

[155] Case C-370/90, *Surinder Singh* (EU:C:1992:296).

(under the *Ruiz Zambrano* caselaw).[156] However, the UK indicated that it would uni-laterally offer a degree of protection to such individuals, i.e. in respect of those who have already claimed rights under the relevant provisions of Union law by the end of the transition period.[157]

On the other hand, the exclusion of own national-own state relations from the scope of the Withdrawal Agreement appears much less significant for Union citizens in their relations with the remaining Member States: those who return to their home state from the UK with a non-EU family member, after having previously exercised their free movement rights under Union law, would still be covered by the *Surinder Singh* principle by process of natural and obvious extension; while those children whose residency in their home state would be imperilled by the removal of their (non-Union) primary carer (including a primary carer of British nationality) would remain fully protected as Union citizens directly under the *Ruiz Zambrano* caselaw.[158]

C. Future Restrictions

There are several situations where the Withdrawal Agreement allows for the potential imposition of additional future restrictions on citizens' rights that again would not be permitted under existing Union free movement law.

For example: Article 14 WA confers upon protected individuals a right of exit from and entry to the host state—with a valid passport or national identity card (in the case of Union citizens and UK nationals) or a valid passport (in other cases). However, five years after the end of the transition period, the host state may decide no longer to ac-cept national identity cards for the purposes of entry to/exit from its territory, where such documents do not include a chip that complies with the applicable International Civil Aviation Organisation standards related to biometric identification.

Another example: Article 36 WA deals with future (post-transition) amendments to the Union's cross-border social security coordination system as currently con-tained in Regulation 883/2004 and the Implementing Regulation 987/2009.[159] Given the relative frequency with which those Regulations are amended, and the potentially significant period of time for which they will be applicable in Union–UK situations pursuant to Title III of Part Two, it is crucial for the smooth functioning of the coordi-nation system that relevant legislative changes are incorporated into the Withdrawal Agreement. In principle, therefore, the Joint Committee is obliged to update the list of relevant acts contained in Part II of Annex I to the Agreement, as soon as an amending or indeed replacement provision is adopted by the Union.[160] However, automatic

---

[156] Case C-34/09, *Ruiz Zambrano* (EU:C:2011:124).

[157] Home Office, *EU Settlement Scheme: Statement of Intent* (21 June 2018), at para 6.12.

[158] See further, e.g. Bernard, 'Union citizens' rights against their own Member State after Brexit', 27 *Maastricht Journal* (2020) 302.

[159] See above on social security coordination under the WA.

[160] Art 36(1) WA. Provision is also made for updating the list of benefits and measures relevant to the UK's participation in the coordination system (Art 36(3) WA together with Part III of Annex I); and the list of relevant decisions and recommendations of the Administrative Commission for the Coordination of Social Security Systems (Art 36(4) WA together with Part I of Annex I).

updating is not required in the case of future acts that change the definition of benefits falling within the material scope of Regulation 883/2004; or that alter a cash benefit's amenability to exportation (whether its exportability in principle or as regards the potential duration of its exportability) as compared to its treatment at the end of the transition period. In those situations, the Joint Committee is expected to undertake an assessment (in good faith, within six months of having been notified of the relevant act by the Union) about whether or not to update the list contained in Part II of Annex I.[161]

D. Total Loss of Rights

Last but not least, the Withdrawal Agreement allows for the total loss even by protected individuals of certain rights that are currently provided for under Union free movement law.

A first example: there is no provision in the Withdrawal Agreement for protected individuals to continue to enjoy equal treatment as regards the right to vote or stand as a candidate in local elections within the host state (based on Article 22(1) TFEU). The Union insisted that this should be treated as a bilateral issue for the UK and individual Member States.[162] Perhaps the Union was concerned that including electoral rights within the scope of the agreement would make it more difficult to maintain the position that Article 50 TEU created an exceptional, exclusive Union competence (excluding any possibility of mixity or question about national ratification requirements).[163] In any event, the UK has instead sought to reach bilateral arrangements on maintaining local voting rights with several Member States.[164] As for future European parliamentary elections: the voting rights of protected Union citizens resident in the UK will naturally depend upon the franchise as defined by their Member State of origin; while the potential voting rights of protected UK nationals resident across the EU27 also falls (in principle) within the competence of each Member State—though subject to the limits imposed by Union law, when it comes to the political participation of third country nationals.[165]

A second example: there is no legal basis under the Withdrawal Agreement for the mutual recognition of *future* professional qualifications, even as regards individuals falling within the protective scope of Part Two. The Commission maintained that this matter fell outside the scope of its negotiating mandate as agreed by the Council for the purposes of Article 50 TEU and must be dealt with (if at all) under subsequent negotiations concerning the future EU–UK relationship.[166] The potential inconvenience

[161] Art 36(2) WA.
[162] E.g. TF50 (2017) 10; TF50 (2017) 17, #34. Contrast, e.g. David Davis, *Update to the House of Commons on EU Negotiations* (17 November 2017).
[163] See the detailed discussion in Chapter 3.
[164] E.g. treaties announced with Spain (21 January 2019), Portugal (13 June 2019), and Luxembourg (18 June 2019).
[165] In accordance with rulings such as Case C-145/04, *Spain v United Kingdom* (EU:C:2006:543); subject to the impact of the Lisbon Treaty amendments, e.g. to Arts 10 and 14 TEU and to Arts 20 and 22 TFEU.
[166] E.g. Joint Technical Note on Citizens' Rights, TF50 (2017) 20, #58. Note that the Joint Technical Note of 8 December 2017 identifies other matters raised by the UK but considered outside the scope of the Commission's negotiating mandate: e.g. the professional qualifications of non-residents; the treatment of

for protected individuals of this omission from the Withdrawal Agreement is considerable, should the parties fail in due course to reach agreement on an ambitious system for the future mutual recognition of professional qualifications.[167] As with local voting rights, it might then prove desirable for the UK and particular Member States to establish at least a bilateral recognition regime—not least in the case of Ireland, given the maintenance of the CTA, since the practical value of reciprocal rights of access to employment and self-employment might otherwise be seriously undermined.[168]

A third example: arguing again that the matter fell outside the scope of its negotiating mandate under Article 50 TEU, the Commission also refused to include within the Withdrawal Agreement any provision for protected UK migrants to enjoy onward free movement or associated rights outside their host state and across the rest of the EU.[169] The Council did not extend the Commission's negotiating mandate to cover this issue—even despite repeated calls from the European Parliament for the Union to be more generous towards protected UK nationals;[170] as well as concerns voiced by the Westminster Parliament about failure to make some provision for onward movement in the context of the Article 50 TEU negotiations.[171] Affected British nationals are thus placed in a potentially difficult position—the so-called 'golden cage': their status may well be protected within their chosen state of residence, but they are unable to claim any further free movement under Union law (say, to change residence to, or conduct an economic activity within, another Member State); unless they qualify for certain onward migration rights under the well-established Union rules concerning long-term resident third country nationals.[172]

5. Special Provisions on Interpretation and Enforcement of Part Two

The provisions on governance of the Withdrawal Agreement as a whole are also applicable to Part Two on citizens' rights: for example, the role and powers of the Joint Committee and relevant specialized committee; as well as the potential for dispute settlement through recourse to an independent arbitration panel (subject to the

---

licences and certificates currently recognized across the EU; lawyers practicing under their home title; secondary establishment and cross-border service provision.

[167] On which: see further Chapter 9.

[168] See, in particular, Memorandum of Understanding between the Government of Ireland and the Government of the UK concerning the Common Travel Area and Associated Reciprocal Rights and Privileges (8 May 2019).

[169] See Art 9(c) WA and, e.g. Joint Technical Note on Citizens' Rights, TF50 (2017) 20, #58.

[170] E.g. European Parliament, *Resolution of 13 December 2017*, at para 3; *Resolution of 14 March 2018*, at para 52.

[171] E.g. House of Commons Exiting the EU Committee, *The Progress of the UK's negotiations on EU withdrawal: December 2017 to March 2018* (HC884 of 18 March 2018); House of Commons Exiting the EU Committee, *The Progress of the UK's Negotiations on EU Withdrawal: The Rights of UK and EU Citizens* (HC1439 of 23 July 2018).

[172] In particular: Directive 2003/109 concerning the status of third country nationals who are long term residents, OJ 2004 L 16/44. For an alternative perspective, see Spaventa, 'Mice or Horses? British Citizens in the EU27 after Brexit as 'Former EU Citizens'', 44 *ELRev* (2019) 589.

jurisdiction of the CJEU); with the provisions contained in Part Two of the Withdrawal Agreement being explicitly excluded from the system of potential sanctions for non-compliance etc.[173]

By their very nature, however, issues about consistent interpretation and effective enforcement of the citizens' rights regime are particularly important at the level of its domestic implementation within the UK and across the EU27. In that regard, commentators anticipated that the Withdrawal Agreement would give rise to numerous empirical challenges—particularly as regards the UK, given its relatively poor record on the treatment of Union citizens even before withdrawal, not least through the Government's overt 'hostile environment' policy, as well as the tendency to place the burden of challenging official wrongdoing onto individuals.[174]

For example: it was widely assumed that the EU Settlement Scheme would generate problems simply through the novelty of the system and sheer number of people affected; including particular concerns about uptake by those with only limited prior engagement with the immigration system and/or by relatively vulnerable citizens; and specific reservations about the clarity of the criteria governing the exercise of administrative discretion in those situations (involving the verification of appropriate documentation or the assessment of criminality checks) where the immigration authorities enjoy the power to reject applications.[175] Certainly, instances were reported of Union citizens who had already been living in the UK for several decades now being required to undergo considerable bureaucratic efforts to prove their residency in the UK when applying for 'settled status';[176] while it was reported that the UK Government was forced (under threat of legal action) to amend the detailed guidance it had provided to immigration case workers responsible for processing claims by EU citizens (for example) so as to clarify the criteria for assessing the relevance of past criminal conduct.[177]

The Withdrawal Agreement itself also seeks to address such concerns, for example, by obliging the UK as well as the Member States to disseminate information concerning the rights and obligations of persons falling within the scope of the citizens' rights regime, in particular, by means of awareness-raising campaigns conducted through the media and other communication channels.[178] In addition, the Withdrawal Agreement includes several important legal provisions relating specifically to the consistent interpretation and effective enforcement of Part Two. Those provisions do not go as far as the Commission had proposed in its initial negotiating position on citizens' rights as published in June 2017; but they certainly go further than the UK had originally been prepared to consider in its opening proposals, and in

---

[173] See further Chapter 6.

[174] Concerns expressed by the European Parliament, e.g. Letter from Guy Verhofstadt to Sajid Javid (30 April 2018); as well as the Scottish and Welsh Governments, e.g. Joint Letter to Sajid Javid (15 June 2018).

[175] E.g. House of Commons Exiting the EU Committee, *The Progress of the UK's Negotiations on EU Withdrawal: The Rights of UK and EU Citizens* (HC1439 of 23 July 2018); House of Commons Home Affairs Committee, *EU Settlement Scheme* (HC1945 of 30 May 2019).

[176] See, e.g. https://www.theguardian.com/uk-news/2020/feb/17/italian-man-95-resident-in-uk-for-68-years-told-to-prove-it.

[177] See, e.g. https://www.theguardian.com/politics/2019/mar/06/home-office-amend-registration-rules-vulnerable-eu-citizens-charity-threat-judicial-review.

[178] Art 37 WA.

any case mean that the rights and obligations contained in Part Two benefit from certain additional enforcement mechanisms as compared to various other provisions of the Withdrawal Agreement.[179]

In the first place: the general provisions on consistent interpretation of the Withdrawal Agreement as a whole (including by the UK and its domestic judicial or administrative authorities) apply as much to Part Two as to the rest of the Withdrawal Agreement;[180] but in addition, Article 158 WA provides that, for cases commenced within eight years from the end of the transition period, in which a question arises concerning the interpretation of Part Two, where a UK court or tribunal considers that a decision on that question is necessary to enable it to render judgment, that court or tribunal may send a preliminary reference to the CJEU.[181] However, in the case of decisions about an application for registration under the EU Settlement Scheme, the eight-year time limit begins to run from the date of the scheme's (voluntary) introduction.[182] In any event, the legal effects in the UK of the CJEU's preliminary ruling shall be the same as the legal effects of preliminary rulings delivered pursuant to Article 267 TFEU in the Union and its Member States.[183] In other words, the referring UK court will be bound by the interpretation of Part Two provided by the CJEU, consistently with the expectations laid down by the CJEU in its caselaw on the autonomy of the Union legal order.[184]

The rather arbitrary-sounding deadline of eight years is effectively a pragmatic compromise between the Union's original desire for ongoing dynamic alignment on citizens' rights under the direct guidance of the CJEU *versus* the UK's starting point of declaring a 'red line' over the jurisdiction of the Union courts after the expiry of the transition period.[185] Nevertheless, the Commission hopes that eight years will still manage to provide a realistic period of time for building up a new jurisprudence on citizens' rights under the Withdrawal Agreement, under the judicial leadership of the CJEU, that will be more consistently followed by the UK as well as across the Member States.[186]

In the second place: the general provisions on domestic enforcement of the Withdrawal Agreement (including through the possibility that all relevant provisions

---

[179] Contrast Commission, *Position Paper on Essential Principles on Citizens' Rights* (12 June 2017), at Part IV; with HMG, *Safeguarding the position of EU citizens living in the UK and UK nationals living in the EU* (June 2017), at p 17.

[180] See further Chapter 6. Note, in particular, section 7C EU(W)A 2018 (as amended).

[181] If the transition period were to have been extended by decision of the Joint Committee under Art 132 WA, the eight-year period for making preliminary references would automatically have been extended to run from the end of the revised transition period: Art 158(3) WA.

[182] Art 158(1) WA.

[183] Art 158(2) WA.

[184] E.g. Opinion 1/91, *EEA Agreement* (EU:C:1991:490); Opinion 1/92, *EEA Agreement II* (EU:C:1992:189); Opinion 1/00, *European Common Aviation Area* (EU:C:2002:231); Cases C-402/05 and C-415/05, *Kadi* (EU:C:2008:461); Opinion 1/09, *European and Community Patents Court* (EU:C:2011:123); Opinion 1/17, *CETA* (EU:C:2019:341).

[185] Note other provisions on continuing CJEU jurisdiction even post-transition: e.g. Title X, Part Three on winding up ongoing procedures; Art 160 WA on the financial settlement; Art 13(1) PINI on Irish border arrangements; Art 12 Cyprus Protocol on UK Sovereign Base Area arrangements. See further the discussion in Chapter 6.

[186] E.g. Commission, *Remarks by Michel Barnier at the press conference on the Joint Report* (8 December 2017).

should produce direct effect and enjoy primacy within the UK legal order as much as across the Member States) again apply to Part Two as they do to the rest of the Agreement;[187] but in addition, the latter contains specific rules on access to administrative and judicial procedures in respect of any refusal of or restriction upon residency rights as contained in Part Two.[188] Furthermore, Article 159 WA obliges the UK to establish an independent authority to monitor the implementation and application of the provisions on citizens' rights: enjoying powers equivalent to those of the Commission under the Treaties to conduct inquiries on its own initiative or in response to complaints from individuals; and including the power, following such complaints, to bring legal action before a competent UK court or tribunal with a view to seeking an adequate remedy.

The independent monitoring authority must be operational as from the end of the transition period.[189] More detailed rules concerning its composition and powers are contained in the European Union (Withdrawal Agreement) Act 2020.[190] The Commission as well as the UK's independent monitoring authority shall report annually to the specialized committee on citizens' rights, about the implementation and application of Part Two, including the number and nature of complaints each has received.[191] The Joint Committee may decide (in good faith, no earlier than eight years from the end of the transition period) that the UK may abolish its independent monitoring authority.[192]

Notwithstanding both the general and the particular provisions on consistent interpretation and effective enforcement of Part Two, as contained in the Withdrawal Agreement, there are still legitimate fears about the potential for widespread problems—especially when it comes to the risk of private (rather than public) sector confusion, abuse, and discrimination. Given the novelty and complexity of the new immigration system applicable to protected individuals, it seems inevitable that certain employers, landlords, and other service providers might struggle to interact with, or indeed seek deliberately to exploit, protected UK nationals or Union citizens and their associated family members.[193]

Those risks are only heightened by the fact that the Withdrawal Agreement allows the host state to issue digital-only residence documentation—whether in the case of a compulsory registration scheme such as that adopted by the UK,[194] or as regards Member States that instead decide to confer automatic residency status upon protected

---

[187] See further Chapter 6.

[188] See Arts 18(1)(r) and 19–21 WA.

[189] See Art 185 WA on the date of entry into force of Art 159 WA. Until the IMA assumes its formal functions, the UK Government proposed that implementation of the EU Settlement Scheme would be monitored by the Independent Chief Inspector for Borders and Immigration: see Home Office, *EU Settlement Scheme: Statement of Intent* (21 June 2018), at para 1.9.

[190] In particular: section 15 and Schedule 2 EU(WA)A 2020.

[191] Art 159(2) WA.

[192] Art 159(3) WA.

[193] E.g. House of Commons Exiting the EU Committee, *The Progress of the UK's Negotiations on EU Withdrawal: The Rights of UK and EU Citizens* (HC1439 of 23 July 2018). Concerns shared by the European Parliament, e.g. *Resolution on implementing and monitoring the provisions on citizens' rights in the Withdrawal Agreement* (15 January 2020). Consider also the broader perspective provided by Ahmed, 'Brexit, Discrimination and EU (Legal) Tools', 44 *ELRev* (2019) 515.

[194] Art 18(1) WA.

individuals.[195] In fact, Council Decision 2020/135 confers implementing powers upon the Commission to lay down common features for the residency documents to be issued by Member States under the Withdrawal Agreement.[196] However, the UK Government initially decided then repeatedly insisted that its EU Settlement Scheme would be based on digital-only documentation.[197] In doing so, the Government ignored multiple calls to provide protected individuals with hard-copy proof of status, so as to minimize the potential for misunderstandings and avoid the risk that private sector actors might be positively deterred from engaging with Union citizens and their family members on a fair and equal basis.[198]

In any case, the future status and effective implementation of the citizens' rights regime within the UK remains subject to the vagaries of domestic immigration politics and the constitutional centrality of the principle of parliamentary sovereignty.[199] The Withdrawal Agreement might well insist that the UK recognizes the direct effect and primacy of the various rights and obligations contained in Part Two,[200] and the UK might well have made explicit provision for those internal legal effects through the provisions contained in the European Union (Withdrawal Agreement) Act 2020.[201] But it remains possible that a future regime with a sufficient Commons majority will decide—whether consciously or inadvertently—to deviate from or even repudiate the UK's obligations under the Withdrawal Agreement (in general) and those contained in Part Two (in particular).[202]

In its White Paper of July 2018, the May Government had suggested not only that the special legal status of the citizens' rights provisions of any withdrawal agreement would be enshrined in primary legislation, but also that the future possibility at least of implied statutory repeal would also be excluded, i.e. by means of a statutory requirement that Parliament should activate an 'additional procedural step' in order to repeal any part of the primary legislation implementing the citizens' rights provisions into domestic law.[203] However, the revised plans for implementation of the Withdrawal Agreement which were published by the Johnson Government, and in due course

---

[195] Art 18(4) WA.

[196] See Art 5 Council Decision 2020/135 on the conclusion of the Agreement on the withdrawal of the United Kingdom of Great Britain and Northern Ireland from the European Union and the European Atomic Energy Community, OJ 2020 L 29/1—referring specifically to documents issued in accordance with Arts 18(1), 18(4) and 26 WA.

[197] E.g. Home Office, *EU Settlement Scheme: Statement of Intent* (21 June 2018), at para 7.2.

[198] E.g. House of Commons Exiting the EU Committee, *The Progress of the UK's Negotiations on EU Withdrawal: The Rights of UK and EU Citizens* (HC1439 of 23 July 2018); House of Commons Exiting the EU Committee, *The Progress of the UK's Negotiations on EU Withdrawal: The Withdrawal Agreement and Political Declaration* (HC1778 of 9 December 2018). In particular: by rejecting attempts in the House of Lords to amend the European Union (Withdrawal Agreement) Bill 2019 so as to provide protected Union citizens with a formal residency document. See House of Commons, *European Union (Withdrawal Agreement) Bill: Explanatory Notes on Lords Amendments* (21 January 2020).

[199] Besides which, note also that the European Union (Withdrawal Agreement) Act 2020 confers extensive executive powers to make secondary legislation in relation to citizens' rights: see Part 3 of the 2020 Act.

[200] In particular: Art 4 WA.

[201] In particular: section 7A EU(W)A 2018 (as amended).

[202] Consider also the critical analysis provided by Smismans, 'EU Citizens' Rights Post-Brexit: Why direct effect beyond the EU is not enough', 14 *European Constitutional Law Review* (2019) 443.

[203] See HMG, *Legislating for the Withdrawal Agreement between the UK and the EU* (Cm 9674 of 24 July 2018).

adopted by the Westminster Parliament, offered no such additional procedural safe-guards against future instances of implied (let alone explicit) repeal of the citizens' rights provisions.[204] Far from it. The European Union (Withdrawal Agreement) Act 2020 explicitly provides that the traditional doctrine of parliamentary sovereignty shall subsist in full, notwithstanding any obligations apparently suggesting the contrary, including the principles of direct effect and primacy provided for under the Withdrawal Agreement in general and as regards citizens' rights in particular.[205]

6. Concluding Remarks

Following the inaugural meeting of the Joint Committee on 30 March 2020, the Commission exhorted both the UK and the Member States to ensure the timely and effective implementation of their obligations under the citizens' rights provisions of the Withdrawal Agreement.[206] Similarly, Michel Barnier has repeatedly urged all parties to ensure compliance with the guarantees for EU citizens and UK nationals contained in Part Two, for the purposes of building trust and confidence in negotiations over the future Union–UK relationship.[207]

In May 2020, the UK Government informed the Commission that, as of the end of March 2020, 3.1 million EU citizens had already been granted a recognized residency status within the UK in accordance with Article 18(1) WA; 58 per cent of those individuals were granted 'settled status' (the rest presumably being recognized as holding 'pre-settled status'); those figures were out of a total of 3.4 million applications made thus far under the UK's domestic implementation scheme.[208] However, the Commission has continued to express concerns, for example, about the ability of particularly vulnerable individuals (including the elderly and those with limited digital skills) to engage with the UK's online registration system; as well as widespread reports about unlawful restrictions on the access by lawfully resident Union citizens to basic welfare provision—particularly during the UK's economic and social lockdown as the global pandemic accelerated in spring 2020.[209]

For its part, the UK has also raised various concerns of its own: for example, about whether certain Member States were doing enough to ensure that their own compulsory registration systems would be ready to process applications within the relevant deadlines; as well as to ensure the timely and effective dissemination of clear

---

[204] See the European Union (Withdrawal Agreement) Bill of December 2019; enacted as the European Union (Withdrawal Agreement) Act 2020.

[205] See section 38 EU(WA)A 2020; and further the discussion in Chapter 6.

[206] Commission, *Statement following the first meeting of the EU-UK Joint Committee* (30 March 2020).

[207] E.g. Commission, *Press Statement by Michel Barnier following Round 3 of negotiations for a new partnership between the EU and the UK* (15 May 2020); and *Press Statement by Michel Barnier following Round 4 of negotiations for a new partnership between the EU and the UK* (5 June 2020).

[208] See https://assets.publishing.service.gov.uk/government/uploads/system/uploads/attachment_data/file/885252/200514_Letter_from_Rt_Hon_Michael_Gove_MP_to_VP_Sefcovic.pdf.

[209] E.g. https://ec.europa.eu/info/publications/letter-vice-president-maros-sefcovic-uk-chancellor-duchy-lancaster-rt-hon-michael-gove-28-may-2020_en; Commission, *Press statement by Vice-President Maroš Šefčovič following the second meeting of the EU-UK Joint Committee* (12 June 2020).

information and instructions to those British nationals resident within their territories.[210] The Commission has sought to reassure the UK Government by pointing out (for example) that various Member States are relying on face-to-face registration processes that might admittedly be more time-consuming but are also more effective at addressing concerns around accessibility for vulnerable and marginalized individuals; while the numbers of British nationals that might needed to be processed, in those Member States which had opted for compulsory registration rather than a mere declaratory system, were relatively small compared to the large-scale administrative challenges which the UK itself had had to confront.[211]

As Spaventa has argued, the various gaps and shortcomings of the Withdrawal Agreement when it comes to the protection of citizens' rights might, in some situations, be remedied or at least partially relieved by the intervention of the national courts (under the guidance of the CJEU) using whatever tools of legislative interpretation, administrative law, or broader fundamental rights protection lie at their disposal. But some problems will prove insurmountable even for the most sympathetic and generous of judges.[212]

Moreover, it is one thing to examine and critique the various legal issues and shortcomings raised by the provisions on citizens' rights under the Withdrawal Agreement; or to anticipate and record the various practical obstacles and empirical problems that have arisen, or may yet occur, as Part Two is fully implemented across the UK and the Member States, particularly after expiry of the transition period. But it is equally important to register and reflect upon the deeper sense of personal dislocation and loss that Brexit has inflicted upon large numbers of people across Europe—family, friends, and colleagues who believed that the common institution of Union membership and the shared community of Union citizenship had created new and lasting opportunities, bonds, and identities; but who suddenly found themselves confronted with feelings of disorientation, alienation, and betrayal as their very presence in their host—i.e. their home—state was placed under scrutiny and (in the UK at least) their very right and sense of belonging was called into question. As the *In Limbo* project records from one Dutch national living in the UK: 'I'm in an Un-Settled Status'.[213]

---

[210] See https://assets.publishing.service.gov.uk/government/uploads/system/uploads/attachment_data/file/885252/200514_Letter_from_Rt_Hon_Michael_Gove_MP_to_VP_Sefcovic.pdf.

[211] E.g. https://ec.europa.eu/info/publications/letter-vice-president-maros-sefcovic-uk-chancellor-duchy-lancaster-rt-hon-michael-gove-28-may-2020_en; Commission, *Press statement by Vice-President Maroš Šefčovič following the second meeting of the EU-UK Joint Committee* (12 June 2020).

[212] See Spaventa, 'The Rights of Citizens under the Withdrawal Agreement: A Critical Analysis', 45 *ELRev* (2020) 193.

[213] E. Remigi, V. Martin and T. Sykes (eds), *In Limbo: Brexit Testimonies from EU Citizens in the UK* (2nd ed, 2020), at p 267.

8

Ireland and Northern Ireland

1. Introduction

In this chapter, we offer a detailed analysis of another of the major problems created by Brexit and addressed in the Withdrawal Agreement. Section 2 explains how Northern Ireland (of all the regions of the UK) and the Republic of Ireland (of all the Member States of the Union) are most likely to be adversely affected by UK withdrawal. Section 3 then focuses on the particular danger that Brexit might lead to the creation of a 'hard border' across the island of Ireland—a prospect that would not only threaten serious economic, social and logistical problems for both the Republic and Northern Ireland; but also pose a severe challenge to political stability and cross-community support for the peace process underpinned by the 'Good Friday Agreement'.[1] As Section 4 explains, when it came to the movement of people, the challenges were relatively straightforward to resolve—being essentially a bilateral issue between the Republic and the UK, with the latter's government accepting the importance of maintaining the existing Common Travel Area arrangements and therefore an open persons border between the two territories. However, we will discuss in Section 5 how, when it came to the movement of goods, the challenges were much more difficult—particularly given the UK's decision to leave not just the EU, but also the Customs Union and the Single Market: customs and regulatory controls must take place somewhere; if not across the island of Ireland, then the UK had to decide on an alternative location.

In Section 6, we discuss how the British preference for trying to address the Irish border problem simply through the overall future EU–UK relationship was effectively doomed to failure. However, the two parties agreed to create a 'backstop' that would apply, in default of any alternative arrangements, to prevent a hard border for the movement of goods. Section 7 recalls the initial proposals of both the Union itself and then the May Government—with the latter providing the basis for the backstop contained in the First Withdrawal Package. After the latter's failure to secure domestic approval through the Westminster Parliament, Section 8 focuses on the alternative solution contained in the final Protocol on Ireland/Northern Ireland as renegotiated by the Johnson Government. The revised plans would indeed succeed in avoiding a hard border across the island of Ireland, while also protecting the integrity of the Customs Union and the Single Market and paying due respect to the UK's insistence that Northern Ireland should remain formally part of the British customs territory.

Even if the Protocol works as planned, its arrangements involve certain important compromises. For the Union, the Protocol means accepting that part of the EU's own external frontiers will essentially be policed and enforced by the authorities and

---

[1] Belfast (or Good Friday) Agreement of 10 April 1998.

The UK's Withdrawal from the EU. Michael Dougan, Oxford University Press. © Michael Dougan 2021. DOI: 10.1093/oso/9780198833475.003.0008

officials of a third country. For the British, the Protocol provides for Northern Ireland to be subject to different customs and regulatory arrangements from the rest of the UK and consequently for the erection of various barriers to trade in goods with Great Britain. For Northern Ireland itself, the Protocol imposes a novel and untested, but potentially cumbersome and costly, 'dual customs regime' whereby all goods entering the territory must be allocated for the payment of EU tariffs or UK tariffs or neither. However, as Section 9 explains, at the time of writing, there are tangible grounds for concern that the Johnson Government does not actually intend to facilitate full and effective application of its own agreement and may even be willing to risk provoking an outright border crisis in Ireland.

2. General Challenges Facing Ireland and Northern Ireland as a Result of UK Withdrawal

Of all the regions of the UK, Northern Ireland is likely to be most deeply affected by withdrawal (even though a clear majority of the population there voted Remain in the 2016 referendum).[2] Equally, of all the Member States of the Union, the Republic of Ireland will be most significantly impacted by the UK's departure (even though the Republic's population obviously had no direct say in the 2016 referendum).[3]

The sheer scale and fundamental nature of the challenges facing Ireland and Northern Ireland were soon recognized by various UK actors. For example, the House of Lords concluded in December 2016 that the whole network of tripartite relations— running north and south, east and west—that link together both past and future relations between the Republic, Northern Ireland and the rest of the UK would now face significant challenges.[4] For its part, the May Government also acknowledged that its decision to press ahead with UK withdrawal, and not only from the Union but also from the Customs Union and the Single Market, would pose particular problems for Ireland and Northern Ireland. For example, the White Paper of February 2017 claimed that maintaining the UK's 'strong and historic ties' with Ireland would be an important priority in the Article 50 TEU negotiations, recognized the potential impact of Brexit upon the two states' existing economic and security relations, and noted the particular challenges that would now face Northern Ireland.[5]

As for the Union, taken as a whole, it was clear that it also had a legitimate interest in and particular responsibility for managing the consequences of Brexit across the island of Ireland, not only due to the direct threat to the fundamental interests of one of its own Member States, but also thanks to the Union's important role in brokering and sustaining the peace process centred around the Belfast or Good Friday Agreement

---

[2] 56 per cent of the votes cast on 23 June 2016 were for Remain.

[3] Note that Irish nationals resident in the UK were entitled to vote in the 2016 referendum under section 2 of the European Union Referendum Act 2015.

[4] House of Lords EU Committee, *Brexit: UK-Irish Relations* (HL76 of 12 December 2016). And indeed, at least to some degree, even before the referendum, e.g. House of Commons Northern Ireland Affairs Committee, *Northern Ireland and the EU Referendum* (HC48 of 26 May 2016).

[5] HMG, *The United Kingdom's exit from and new partnership with the European Union* (Cm 9417 of 2 February 2017), at Part 4.

of 1998;[6] as well as the fact that Northern Ireland would in due course contain a sub-stantial and permanent non-resident population of Union citizens under the jurisdiction of a third country;[7] and indeed having regard to the future possibility (however longer-term that might be) of the North seeking to pursue reunification with the Republic and thus being effectively reabsorbed into the Union.[8] For all those reasons, it was unsurprising to find that the 'Irish question' occupied a prominent position in the April 2017 Guidelines of the European Council as well as in the negotiating directives adopted by the Council during May 2017: nothing should be allowed to undermine the objectives and the commitments set out in the Good Friday Agreement; addressing the myriad challenges for the island of Ireland, posed by the UK's decision to leave the Union, would require flexible and imaginative solutions.[9]

And so the question of how to address the impact of withdrawal upon the island of Ireland fast became central to the entire Article 50 TEU process. Unlike most of the other topics addressed in the withdrawal negotiations, which were conducted through bilateral working groups between the Union and the UK, the 'Irish question' was instead handled through the establishment of a 'dialogue' concerning Ireland/Northern Ireland—within which the Union made clear its view that the onus fell on the UK to propose appropriate solutions for the challenges facing the island of Ireland as created by British withdrawal from the Union.[10] As formal talks commenced, each party published their more detailed positions and proposals: in particular, a UK position paper in August 2017;[11] and a statement of guiding principles from the Commission in September 2017.[12] As with citizens' rights, the first major breakthrough came with publication of the Commission–UK Joint Report in December 2017.[13] But in the case of Ireland/Northern Ireland, the Joint Report proved in many respects to be, not the beginning of the end of the relevant negotiations, but only the end of the beginning of the parties' efforts to reach agreement.

Indeed, the political controversies that soon enveloped the 'Irish question' came effectively to dominate the later stages of the Union–UK withdrawal process. As we

---

[6] Belfast (or Good Friday) Agreement of 10 April 1998.

[7] The citizenship rules applicable to Northern Ireland mean that many of its residents have a free choice to be classed as Irish or as dual Irish–UK nationals. Note the relevant recital in the preamble to the Protocol on Ireland/Northern Ireland: 'RECOGNISING that Irish citizens in Northern Ireland, by virtue of their Union citizenship, will continue to enjoy, exercise and have access to rights, opportunities and benefits, and that this Protocol should respect and be without prejudice to the rights, opportunities and identity that come with citizenship of the Union for the people of Northern Ireland who choose to assert their right to Irish citizenship, as defined in Annex 2 of the British–Irish Agreement Declaration on the Provisions of Paragraph (vi) of Article 1 in Relation to Citizenship'.

[8] Similar to the German experience following reunification between the GDR and West Germany in 1990.

[9] European Council (Article 50), *Guidelines following the United Kingdom's notification under Article 50 TEU* (29 April 2017); Council Decision authorizing the opening of negotiations with the United Kingdom of Great Britain and Northern Ireland for an agreement setting out the arrangements for its withdrawal from the European Union (22 May 2017).

[10] E.g. Commission, *Guiding Principles for the Dialogue on Ireland/Northern Ireland* (TF50 (2017) 15 of 20 September 2017), at p 2.

[11] HMG, *Position Paper on Northern Ireland and Ireland* (16 August 2017)—to be read alongside HMG, *Future Partnership Paper on Future Customs Arrangements* (15 August 2017).

[12] Commission, *Guiding Principles for the Dialogue on Ireland/Northern Ireland* (TF50 (2017) 15 of 20 September 2017).

[13] Joint Report from the EU and UK negotiators (8 December 2017).

have seen, the Union's attempts to find a mutually satisfactory resolution hinged upon regular and close discussions with the Irish Government, that de facto offered Ireland a veto over conclusion of any withdrawal package.[14] As for the UK, we know that its engagement in the negotiations was dominated by the need to deliver a solution that could be approved through the Westminster Parliament—taking particular account of the dependence of the minority Conservative Government upon the Commons votes of the hard-line DUP.[15] The effort almost derailed the entire Article 50 TEU process on several occasions. Certainly, it was the failure to find a domestically palatable solution to the Irish border challenges that proved a major factor behind the prolonged troubles and eventual collapse of the May Government.[16]

So what were all these major problems that Brexit would create for Ireland/Northern Ireland, and which were to cause so much effort and trouble in the Article 50 TEU process? For present purposes, the challenges forced upon the island of Ireland by the prospect of UK withdrawal can be divided into two main categories.

In the first place, there were (and remain) certain Brexit challenges facing the island of Ireland that neither the Article 50 TEU negotiations nor the final Withdrawal Agreement itself could do very much to address. Consider, for example, the considerable risks facing Northern Ireland simply through its generally fragile local economy and lower overall levels of income/wealth; as well as its relative dependence upon public sector employment, financial support for its crucial agricultural sector, and the migrant labour supplied by Union citizens. Such factors rendered Northern Ireland particularly sensitive, both to any economic downturn affecting the UK as a whole that might result from or follow Brexit, as well as to any relevant policy changes imposed by the central UK authorities (for example) limiting the immigration rights of EU citizens.[17] But those are risks inherent in the very act of withdrawing from the Union: they cannot be mitigated or excluded by any EU–UK agreement designed to address the immediate separation issues involved in an orderly departure.

Or again, consider the extraordinary degree to which the Republic's own economy has evolved, particularly within the context of common Union membership, to be closely interwoven with that of the UK: from agricultural markets through to manufacturing supply chains and financial service networks, in many respects, the two states have functioned almost as an exemplar of cross-border economic integration. Of course, that renders the Republic especially vulnerable to a damaging economic rupture between the Union and the UK of precisely the sort now being pursued by the Johnson Government.[18] Conversely, one might argue that (at least in the longer-term) it might well be in the Republic's best interests to reduce its exposure to the UK market and become more integrated into the Single Market and, through it, the wider global economy—making the most of its position as a stable, English-speaking member not

---

[14] See the discussion in Chapter 3.

[15] See the discussion in Chapter 4.

[16] See the discussion in Chapter 5.

[17] Further, e.g. House of Commons Northern Ireland Affairs Committee, *Northern Ireland and the EU Referendum* (HC48 of 26 May 2016); J. Temple Lang, *Brexit and Ireland: Legal, Political and Economic Considerations* (European Parliament, Policy Department for Citizens' Rights and Constitutional Affairs: PE 596.825 of November 2017).

[18] See further Chapter 9.

only of the Union, Customs Union, and Single Market but also of the Single Currency. Yet once again, those are problems and challenges inherent in the very act of UK departure from the Union, falling beyond the mandate of any immediate agreement to deliver an orderly departure.

Of course, some of the Brexit headaches which are not (and indeed could never realistically have been) addressed by the Withdrawal Agreement per se, may still be dealt with (more or less directly, more or less successfully) under the auspices of future EU–UK cooperation—either through informal coordination or by means of more binding commitments; whether at a sectoral level or through the general negotiations concerning the overall EU–UK trade and security relationship. For example: both the UK and the Union have indicated their willingness to continue providing significant levels of 'peace funding' to help support economic and social development projects in Northern Ireland;[19] while the Union and the UK have agreed that the particular challenges facing the continued transit of Irish goods through British territory en route to mainland Europe should be alleviated by the UK's continued adherence to the Common Transit Convention,[20] in addition to unilateral measures adopted by the Union to facilitate new sea trade routes directly between the Republic and the rest of the EU.[21]

Or again: consider the impact of UK withdrawal upon police and judicial cooperation between the competent authorities of the UK including Northern Ireland (on the one hand) and of the Republic (on the other hand) in the fight against various forms of cross-border crime, as well as terrorism and other pressing security threats. Existing mechanisms for cooperation were heavily dependent upon their shared Union membership and common access to the instruments and resources provided under Union law—ranging from the availability of the European Arrest Warrant, through access to information databases, to participation in intelligence sharing fora.[22] Negotiations on the future EU–UK relationship should provide the baseline upon which the UK and the Republic must in due course rebuild a new (and inevitably less effective) framework for mutual security cooperation.[23]

In the second place, there were (and remain) other Brexit challenges facing the island of Ireland that the Article 50 TEU negotiations did indeed seek to alleviate. That is especially true for a series of issues related to the Good Friday Agreement. Even if UK membership of the EU is not decisive as such to the very existence of the peace settlement, UK withdrawal certainly creates various problems for the good functioning of key elements of the Good Friday Agreement. The dedicated Protocol on Ireland/Northern Ireland (PINI) annexed to the Withdrawal Agreement seeks to provide (at least partial) solutions to those problems.

---

[19] See the relevant recital from the preamble to the Protocol on Ireland/Northern Ireland: 'RECALLING the Union's and the United Kingdom's commitments to the North South PEACE and INTERREG funding programmes under the current multi-annual financial framework and to the maintaining of the current funding proportions for the future programme'.

[20] See https://www.gov.uk/government/news/uk-to-remain-in-common-transit-convention-after-brexit.

[21] See Regulation 2019/495 amending Regulation 1316/2013 with regard to the withdrawal of the United Kingdom from the Union, OJ 2019 L 85I/16.

[22] Further, e.g. House of Lords EU Select Committee, *Brexit: The Proposed UK-EU Security Treaty* (HL164, of 11 July 2018), at Chapter 7.

[23] See further Chapter 9.

Consider, for example, the importance of Union law in providing firm legal guarantees of non-discrimination (particularly on grounds of religious belief or affiliation) within Northern Ireland—as part of the broader commitment under the Good Friday Agreement to upholding basic fundamental rights and ensuring parity of treatment between the two main communities. The prospect of UK withdrawal from the Union raised fears that those legal guarantees might be seriously undermined—particularly when it comes to the availability of mechanisms for the effective enforcement of equal treatment legislation and the provision of adequate redress to the victims of unlawful discrimination.[24] In order to address such fears, Article 2 PINI provides as follows:[25]

1) The United Kingdom shall ensure that no diminution of rights, safeguards or equality of opportunity, as set out in that part of the 1998 Agreement entitled Rights, Safeguards and Equality of Opportunity results from its withdrawal from the Union, including in the area of protection against discrimination, as enshrined in the provisions of Union law listed in Annex 1 to this Protocol, and shall implement this paragraph through dedicated mechanisms.

2) The United Kingdom shall continue to facilitate the related work of the institutions and bodies set up pursuant to the 1998 Agreement, including the Northern Ireland Human Rights Commission, the Equality Commission for Northern Ireland and the Joint Committee of representatives of the Human Rights Commissions of Northern Ireland and Ireland, in upholding human rights and equality standards.[26]

The Protocol on Ireland/Northern Ireland also makes specific provision for other Brexit-based problems and concerns. For example, Union law has played an indispensable role in facilitating the creation and operation of the Single Electricity Market (SEM). The SEM is a unique form of cooperation that seeks to address the specific characteristics of the island of Ireland, by combining the two participating jurisdictions into a genuinely integrated wholesale energy market—with the aims of encouraging investment, ensuring security of supply, and promoting competition for the benefit of consumers, while also integrating various environmental policy objectives.[27] The SEM was entirely designed around the assumption of common membership by the UK as well as Ireland of the Union's single energy market—so in order to prevent UK withdrawal from wreaking havoc with the legal foundations of the SEM, Article 9 PINI states that those provisions of Union law governing wholesale electricity markets (as listed in Annex 4 to the Protocol) shall apply (under the conditions set out in that Annex) to and in the United Kingdom in respect of Northern Ireland.[28]

---

[24] Further, e.g. D. Phinnemore and K. Hayward, *UK Withdrawal and the Good Friday Agreement* (European Parliament, Policy Department for Citizens' Rights and Constitutional Affairs: PE 596.826 of November 2017); C. McCrudden, *The Good Friday Agreement, Brexit and Rights* (Royal Irish Academy–British Academy Brexit Policy Discussion Paper, 2017).

[25] Art 2 PINI is applicable as from the end of transition: Art 185 WA.

[26] See section 23 and Schedule 3 EU(WA)A 2020.

[27] See the Memorandum of Understanding between the UK and Ireland on the Single Energy Market Arrangements (2006) available via https://www.dccae.gov.ie/documents/SEM%20Memorandum%20of%20Understanding.pdf.

[28] Art 9 PINI is applicable as from the end of transition: Art 185 WA.

Or again, consider the contribution of Union law to the effectiveness of North–South cooperation pursuant to the Good Friday Agreement. The latter identifies various specific fields of cooperation (agriculture, education, environment, health, tourism, and transport) and establishes a series of implementation bodies responsible for managing joint activities in those fields (though cooperation was subsequently extended into additional fields, such as broadcasting and sport).[29] During the Article 50 TEU process, the Union and the UK jointly conducted a detailed 'mapping exercise' of the various sectors covered by North–South cooperation and evaluating the role of Union law in their smooth functioning.[30] In the light of that exercise, the Joint Report of December 2017 noted that 'North–South cooperation relies to a significant extent on a common European Union legal and policy framework. Therefore, the United Kingdom's departure from the European Union gives rise to substantial challenges to the maintenance and development of North–South cooperation.'[31] In order to address those challenges, Article 11 PINI provides as follows:[32]

1) Consistent with the [border arrangements set out in the Protocol and discussed further below] and in full respect of Union law, this Protocol shall be implemented and applied so as to maintain the necessary conditions for continued North–South cooperation, including in the areas of environment, health, agriculture, transport, education and tourism, as well as in the areas of energy, telecommunications, broadcasting, inland fisheries, justice and security, higher education and sport.[33]

   In full respect of Union law, the United Kingdom and Ireland may continue to make new arrangements that build on the provisions of the 1998 Agreement in other areas of North–South cooperation on the island of Ireland.

2) The Joint Committee shall keep under constant review the extent to which the implementation and application of this Protocol maintains the necessary conditions for North–South cooperation. The Joint Committee may make appropriate recommendations to the Union and the United Kingdom in this respect, including on a recommendation from [the] Specialized Committee.[34]

3. The Border Problems Provoked by Brexit

Without calling into doubt the significance of the Protocol provisions on equal treatment, the Single Energy Market, and North-South Cooperation, it is nevertheless true and fair to say that the main 'Brexit problems' created for the island of Ireland

---

[29] See further, e.g. https://www.instituteforgovernment.org.uk/explainers/north-south-cooperation-island-ireland.

[30] The process and its outcomes are reported in Commission, *Negotiations on Ireland/Northern Ireland: Mapping of North-South Cooperation*, TF50 (2019) 63. Note also: HMG, *Technical Explanatory Note: North-South Cooperation Mapping Exercise* (7 December 2018).

[31] Joint Report from the EU and UK negotiators (8 December 2017), at para 47.

[32] Art 11 PINI is applicable as from the end of transition: Art 185 WA.

[33] Note section 10(2)(a) EU(W)A 2018.

[34] However, note the restriction imposed under section 10(3) EU(W)A 2018 (as amended by EU(WA) A 2020).

concern how to maintain the current open border arrangements between Ireland and Northern Ireland after the UK has surrendered its Union membership.[35]

Of course, the existing open frontier between Ireland and Northern Ireland is of considerable economic importance to both territories: not only as regards trade in primary and secondary goods, but also for the cross-border provision of services, as well as the regular movement of significant numbers of frontier workers. The existing border arrangements are also of enormous social importance, especially for the many border communities whose daily lives have been built around the freedom to trade and travel between Ireland and Northern Ireland on a highly integrated local basis. The open border is also a matter of sensible, if not altogether unavoidable, logistics: the prospect of having to secure, patrol and enforce such a complex boundary, punctuated by hundreds of formal and innumerable informal crossing points, amounts to a near-impossible task.[36]

But above all, the open border is of the utmost political significance. The Good Friday Agreement ended (or at least very significantly downgraded) the de facto civil war in Northern Ireland during which thousands were killed, tens of thousands were injured and entire communities were forced from their homes.[37] Widespread social division, often complete segregation, persists between unionists (largely Protestant and wanting Northern Ireland to remain within the UK) and nationalists (largely Catholic and wishing for reunification with the Republic)—but at least those differences can be addressed under the conditions of relative peace and stability created by the Good Friday Agreement. Part of the latter's genius is that it allowed both main communities to feel that the existing constitutional settlement serves their respective interests: unionists were reassured that Northern Ireland would remain part of the UK for as long as a majority of its population so desired;[38] and while nationalists might have to regard reunification as a more distant aspiration, in the meanwhile, one could move freely across the island—with the only obvious difference being the change on road signs from miles to kilometres.

In short, the absence of a physical frontier is a crucial part of the wider political settlement that helps secure and maintain cross-community support for the peace process. The terrible prospect raised by Brexit was that UK withdrawal from the Union might lead to the erection of a hard border across the island of Ireland. At the very least, it was generally assumed that, were any form of physical infrastructure to be mounted along the border between the Republic and Northern Ireland, that infrastructure would fast become the focus of popular protest an/or violent attack. More seriously, it was widely feared that, should the UK's decision to leave the EU (against the clear wishes of a majority of the population within Northern Ireland itself) lead directly to the imposition of a literal barrier between life in the Republic and that in

---

[35] See further, e.g. Dougan, 'The 'Brexit' Threat to the Northern Irish Border: Clarifying the Constitutional Framework' in M. Dougan (ed.), *The UK After Brexit: Legal and Policy Challenges* (2017).

[36] See further, e.g. House of Lords EU Committee, *Brexit: UK-Irish Relations* (HL76 of 12 December 2016); House of Commons Northern Ireland Affairs Committee, *The Land Border between Northern Ireland and Ireland* (HC329 of 16 March 2018).

[37] See further, e.g. D. McKittrick and D. McVea, *Making Sense of the Troubles: A History of the Northern Irish Conflict* (2012).

[38] Note Art 1 PINI (applicable as from the entry into force of the Agreement: Art 185 WA).

Northern Ireland, such an outcome would (quite legitimately) outrage nationalist sentiment and (then inevitably) serve to destabilize the delicate political balance underpinning the Good Friday Agreement.

Against that background, it is unsurprising to find that maintaining (as far as possible) the current open border arrangements was quickly recognized as a key objective by the main political actors in Northern Ireland,[39] by the UK Government,[40] within the Republic,[41] and across the rest of the Union.[42] However, in the public and political discourse both before and after the 2016 referendum, there was often an unfortunate tendency to treat the physical frontier between the Republic and Northern Ireland as a single phenomenon, to be resolved in a single manner: 'the border' must remain open; or 'the border' risks beginning to close. In legal terms, such discourse was always both misleading and unhelpful. In fact, the applicable constitutional framework requires us to identify and address two distinct and separate physical borders: in the first place, the frontier for persons, which hinges upon the continuing existence of the Common Travel Area between the UK and Ireland; and in the second place, the frontier for goods, which is bound up with the UK's intended departure from the Customs Union and the Single Market.

4. The Border for Persons

The question of whether Brexit might result in the erection of a physical frontier for the movement of persons between Northern Ireland and the Republic in fact has little to do with Union law and instead hinges upon the survival of the Common Travel Area between the UK and Ireland.[43] In that regard, it is important to stress that the CTA is not enshrined or codified in any international treaty between those two states. Rather, the CTA has long been based upon a more informal understanding, which is then translated into the particular domestic legislative and administrative arrangements of each state.[44] And whilst one should acknowledge its limitations and weaknesses, the CTA has nevertheless led to the virtual elimination of border controls on persons between Northern Ireland and the Republic.[45] Throughout the 2016

[39] See Letter to the Prime Minster from the First Minister and Deputy First Minister of the Northern Ireland Executive (10 August 2016).
[40] See HMG, *The United Kingdom's exit from and new partnership with the European Union* (Cm 9417 of 2 February 2017), especially at Section 4 and Annex B.
[41] See, e.g. Irish Government, *Ireland and the Negotiations on the UK's Withdrawal from the European Union: The Government's Approach* (May 2017).
[42] See, e.g. European Parliament, *Resolution on negotiations with the United Kingdom following its notification that it intends to withdraw from the European Union* (5 April 2017), at para 20; European Council (Article 50), *Guidelines following the United Kingdom's notification under Article 50 TEU* (29 April 2017), at para 11.
[43] The CTA also extends to the Isle and Man and the Channel Islands.
[44] Further, e.g. Ryan, 'The Common Travel Area between Britain and Ireland', 64 MLR (2013) 831; House of Commons Library Briefing Paper, *The Common Travel Area and the Special Status of Irish Nationals in UK Law* (No 7661 of 15 July 2016).
[45] See, e.g. House of Lords EU Committee, *Brexit: UK-Irish Relations* (HL76 of 12 December 2016), especially at Chapter 3. Note that the CTA also provides for various associated rights, e.g. to residency and in fields such as employment and social security: see further the discussion in Chapter 7.

referendum campaign, fears were expressed about the potential implications of UK withdrawal for the continued operation of the CTA.[46] However, the two states have since voiced their mutual desire to maintain the CTA into the future and regardless of the UK's departure from the Union—while the Withdrawal Agreement itself explicitly recognizes and accommodates that position.

A. Competence Questions Surrounding Maintenance of the CTA

The EU does not enjoy exclusive competence to regulate the external border for the movement of persons. Rather, border policy is a shared competence between the EU and its Member States: both are entitled to regulate the entry of persons in accordance with their respective internal competences; though the Member States are required to respect whatever obligations are created for them at the EU level.[47] However, when it comes to identifying such obligations, the constitutional position of Ireland is different under EU law from that of the great majority of other Member States. Indeed, the same was true also for the UK while it remained a Member State—certainly, at the time of the referendum and throughout the entire Article 50 TEU negotiation process.[48] Neither Ireland nor the UK fully participated in the Area of Freedom, Security and Justice,[49] since both enjoyed a complex system of opt-out/opt-in rights as regards the policy fields (borders, immigration, asylum, cooperation in civil and criminal matters) covered by the relevant Treaty provisions.[50] In particular, neither Ireland nor the UK fully joined with the other Member States in the Schengen project of abolishing internal passport controls, and for that purpose, constructing a common external border regime.[51] Instead, EU law explicitly recognized the competence of both Ireland

---

[46] Consider, e.g. HMG, *The Process for Withdrawing from the European Union* (Cm 9216 of 29 February 2016), at p 19.

[47] See, in particular, Arts 4(2)(j) and 2(2) TFEU. See further, e.g. Gortazar, 'Abolishing Border Controls: Individual Rights and Common Control of EU External Borders' in E. Guild and C. Harlow (eds), *Implementing Amsterdam: Immigration and Asylum Rights in EC Law* (2001); Pastore, 'Visas, Borders, Immigration: Formation, Structure and Current Evolution of the EU Entry Control System' in N. Walker (ed.), *Europe's Area of Freedom, Security and Justice* (2004); S. Peers, *EU Justice and Home Affairs Law* (2006), at Chapters 2 and 3.

[48] Note that Denmark also has a peculiar legal relationship to the AFSJ: see Protocol No 22 on the position of Denmark. See further on the legal framework for flexibility in relation to the AFSJ, e.g. Monar, 'Justice and home affairs in the Treaty of Amsterdam: Reform at the price of fragmentation', 23 *ELRev* (1998) 320; Hedemann-Robinson, 'The Area of Freedom, Security and Justice with regard to the UK, Ireland and Denmark: The 'Opt-in Opt-outs' under the Treaty of Amsterdam' in D. O'Keeffe and P. Twomey, *Legal Issues of the Amsterdam Treaty* (1999); Fletcher, 'Schengen, the European Court of Justice and Flexibility under the Lisbon Treaty: Balancing the United Kingdom's 'ins' and 'outs'', 5 *European Constitutional Law Review* (2009) 71; Fahey, 'Swimming in a Sea of Law: Reflections on Water Borders, Irish(-British)-Euro Relations and Opting-Out and Opting-In after the Treaty of Lisbon', 47 *CMLRev* (2010) 673.

[49] On the AFSJ, see Title V, Part Three TFEU.

[50] See Protocol No 21 on the position of the United Kingdom and Ireland in respect of the Area of Freedom, Security and Justice. Recall also the UK's option under Protocol No 36 on transitional provisions to repudiate then selectively opt back into EU measures previously adopted under the ex-Third Pillar.

[51] The complex legal relationship of the UK and Ireland to the Schengen system under EU law is laid down in Protocol No 19 on the Schengen *acquis* integrated into the framework of the European Union.

and the UK to retain their own border checks as well as to maintain the CTA in their mutual relations.[52]

Notwithstanding that apparently clear and settled legal position, serious questions were nevertheless raised during and after the UK referendum about the impact of Brexit upon Ireland's competence to continue exercising its own border policy—including the maintenance or renewal of the CTA itself.

In the first place, it was argued that the legal recognition afforded under the Treaties to Ireland's competence to exercise its own border controls, as well as to the existence of the CTA itself, was premised upon two facts: continuing EU membership by both the UK and Ireland; and the continuing maintenance of the CTA between the two countries. The key provision is to be found in Article 2 of Protocol No 20, which provides in effect that, as long as the UK and Ireland maintain the CTA arrangements, the right to exercise its own border controls which is recognized primarily in relation to the UK shall also apply to Ireland under the same terms and conditions as for the UK itself.[53] If either of those facts were to change—either the UK leaves the EU, or the CTA ceases to be a meaningful arrangement—then the relevant Treaty provisions should automatically cease to apply for the benefit of Ireland.[54]

In the second place, it was also argued that Ireland should in any event require the agreement of the remaining Member States and/or EU institutions, in order to maintain or reach any agreement with the UK as regards border controls between the two countries into the future.[55] Indeed, this particular suggestion was to some extent endorsed even in official UK parliamentary reports.[56] It has to be said that no particular legal rationale was offered to back up this second line of argument, unless one counts the idea that the CTA happens to be explicitly referenced in EU law—as if that in itself should be considered enough to determine the constitutional balance of competence between the EU and a Member State.[57]

However, neither of those suggestions ever deserved to be treated as legally robust. To begin with, it surely cannot be the case that the UK's unilateral act of withdrawal from the EU may have the automatic effect of amending or abrogating Union primary law as regards the rights and obligations of another Member State. The particular wording of Article 2 of Protocol No 20 may be rather idiosyncratic, but its clear and unarguable effect is to grant legal respect under EU law for Ireland's power to conduct border checks as well as for its right of continuing participation in the CTA. To suggest that Ireland's own competences are somehow entirely derived from or contingent upon those of the UK, and only in the latter's capacity as a Member State, would not only be an inappropriate interpretation of Union law which seems difficult to reconcile

---

[52] See Protocol No 20 on the application of certain aspects of Article 26 of the Treaty on the Functioning of the European Union to the United Kingdom and to Ireland.

[53] Note that Art 3 also nods towards the conditional nature of Ireland's benefits under Protocol No 20.

[54] This argument is hinted at in evidence cited by the House of Commons Northern Ireland Affairs Committee, *Northern Ireland and the EU Referendum* (HC48 of 26 May 2016), at para 74.

[55] Again, see evidence cited by the House of Commons Northern Ireland Affairs Committee, *Northern Ireland and the EU Referendum* (HC48 of 26 May 2016), at para 74.

[56] In particular: House of Lords EU Committee, *Brexit: UK–Irish Relations* (HL76 of 12 December 2016), especially at paras 110–114.

[57] See House of Lords EU Committee, *Brexit: UK–Irish Relations* (HL76 of 12 December 2016), at para 114.

with respect for Irish sovereignty.[58] It would also be tantamount to allowing the UK to rewrite Ireland's constitutional and substantive position under the Treaties, merely through the UK's own choices about membership, regardless of the views of Ireland itself, and altogether outside the ordinary procedure for amending Union primary law.

Perhaps more importantly: unilateral UK withdrawal from the EU can certainly have no effect whatsoever upon Ireland's entirely distinct prerogatives of opt-out/opt-in as regards the Area of Freedom, Security and Justice in general, and the system of Schengen cooperation in particular, which are also explicitly enshrined in the Treaties.[59] Entirely independently of the membership choices made by the UK, and even regardless of one's interpretation of Protocol No 20, Ireland does not have any obligation to participate in the EU system for abolishing internal borders as regards persons, creating common rules on passage through the external borders of the Schengen zone, or coordinating immigration policies as regards the residency and associated rights of third country nationals. Far from it: the Treaties leave no room to doubt that Ireland remains competent to exercise its own border controls in its relations with both the remaining Member States as well as third countries at large.[60]

From a constitutional perspective, therefore, it was always difficult to understand why UK withdrawal from the EU should change in any material respect the fundamental legal framework governing Ireland's own relationship to the Area of Freedom, Security and Justice.[61] In particular, UK withdrawal could not deprive Ireland of the basic choice it currently enjoys under EU law between deciding to abandon its special status and become a fully-fledged participant in the AFSJ, including even the Schengen policies on internal and external borders; or instead maintaining its existing national competence over its own border and immigration policies, including the possibilities for unilateral action or bilateral agreement with third countries.[62]

However, even if maintaining an open border for the movement of persons across the island of Ireland is primarily a bilateral issue to be resolved between the UK and Ireland, the Union does still have a clear legal interest in the more precise terms of that bilateral relationship, since Ireland would remain bound to comply with any more specific Union law obligations that it has properly assumed under the Treaties: for example, as regards the right of entry into Irish territory for EU nationals and their protected family members, in possession of the appropriate documentation, in accordance with Directive 2004/38.[63]

---

[58] Cp. Art 4(2) TEU.

[59] Precisely under Protocols No 21 and 19 (respectively).

[60] See, in particular, Art 2 of Protocol No 21. Note that, even as regards the great majority of Member States which fully participate in the AFSJ, Protocol No 23 provides that the Union's power to adopt measures concerning checks on persons crossing the external border shall be without prejudice to national competence to enter agreements with third countries (as long as they respect Union law).

[61] See, in a similar sense, the written evidence cited in House of Lords EU Committee, *Brexit: UK-Irish Relations* (HL76 of 12 December 2016), at paras 112–113.

[62] See, in particular, Art 8 of Protocol No 21: 'Ireland may notify the Council in writing that it no longer wishes to be covered by the terms of this Protocol'—in which case, the normal Treaty provisions will apply to Ireland.

[63] Directive 2004/38, OJ 2004 L 158/77. Note Arts 1 and 2 of Protocol No 20, which explicitly refer to these specific obligations. Note also Art 6 of Protocol No 21, as regards specific AFSJ measures that Ireland has chosen to participate in of its own volition.

B. A Common Political Desire to Maintain the CTA

Against that constitutional background, the real question that arose in 2016 was therefore, not whether Union law imposed serious obstacles to the survival of the CTA, but whether Ireland and the UK would be prepared to continue their longstanding mutual understanding and maintain the apparatus required for the CTA's smooth functioning within their respective internal legal and administrative systems.

In that regard, the potential pressures generated by Brexit can be explained as follows. Any cross-border system for the mutual suppression of border controls on persons, such as the CTA or indeed Schengen, is normally regarded as being dependent upon the participating states having closely aligned their external border and immigration systems, as well as establishing close cooperation between their national immigration authorities when it comes to border management and surveillance. Even if the CTA has never been fully aligned in the sense of having identical rules and procedures, the external border and immigration policies of the UK and Ireland were nevertheless regarded as sufficiently similar, and mutual cooperation between the competent national authorities functioned effectively enough, that any discrepancies or divergences were not considered so serious as to call into question the very existence of the CTA.[64]

After withdrawal from the EU, if the UK were to maintain border and immigration policies, as regards both EU and third country nationals, which are more or less equivalent to those that already existed during its period of Union membership, then there would be no reason why the continued existence and smooth operation of CTA itself should come under significant pressure. However, were the UK eventually to adopt an appreciably more restrictive border and/or immigration policy as regards either EU or third country nationals—with Ireland being unable (in the case of EU citizens) or unwilling (in the case of third country nationals) to follow suit—then the emergence of such discrepancies between the two countries' approaches to their common external frontier in respect of persons could put more considerable pressure upon the continued suppression of internal border checks in accordance with the existing CTA.

Having decided that 'taking back control of our borders' provided one of the main drivers behind the Leave vote in 2016, the UK in due course announced that it would impose a significantly more restrictive regime when it came to the future immigration treatment of Union citizens.[65] Since the UK indeed intended to depart from the basic principle of immigration policy alignment at the common external borders of the CTA, three main options were then available (as a matter of principle) to address the implications for relations with Ireland.[66]

First, the CTA could be abandoned in its entirety, and border checks on persons introduced between Ireland and the UK, including at the land border with Northern

---

[64] See further, e.g. House of Commons Library Briefing Paper, *The Common Travel Area and the Special Status of Irish Nationals in UK Law* (No 7661 of 16 October 2019).

[65] E.g. Theresa May, *Lancaster House Speech: The Government's Negotiating Objectives for Exiting the EU* (17 January 2017); HMG, *The United Kingdom's Exit from and New Partnership with the European Union* (Cm 9417 of 2 February 2017).

[66] See, in a similar though not identical sense, House of Commons Northern Ireland Affairs Committee, *Northern Ireland and the EU Referendum* (HC48 of 26 May 2016), at paras 75–80.

Ireland, so as to enable the UK as a whole to enforce its new and more restrictive national border and/or immigration rules as regards EU citizens and/or third country nationals. However, this option raised obvious problems in terms of the sheer costs and practicability of attempting properly to instigate and enforce persons controls along the entire land border between Northern Ireland and the Republic, as well as the serious economic and social repercussions of closing the border; to say nothing of the implications for political stability, particularly having regard to the concerns of the nationalist community.[67]

Secondly, the land border between Northern Ireland and the Republic could be kept open and free of checks, at least when it came to the movement of persons; but with border controls then introduced between the island of Ireland as a whole (on the one hand) and the rest of the UK (on the other hand)—so as to enable the latter territory to enforce its newfound border/immigration restrictions, also when it came to sea and air transport from the former territories. However, this option again raised some obvious problems: it may well have appeared more realistic in terms of costs and practicalities, but it would also have implied the need for Northern Ireland to accept (whether formally or informally) a border and/or immigration policy aligned more with that of the Republic than with the rest of the UK; and again, there would surely be serious political implications, only this time stemming from unionist concerns.[68]

Thirdly, the CTA could be retained in its current form—no entry checks on persons between the Republic and the UK as a whole—notwithstanding the emergence of appreciable differences in Irish and UK border and/or immigration rules as regards EU and/or third country nationals. But in that event, the two countries would have to develop a range of policies—whether in cooperation or unilaterally—to ameliorate the adverse consequences which might arise in practice: for example, through more extensive data sharing between the competent national authorities as regards the movement of persons across the external frontiers of the CTA;[69] and by the UK in particular having to rely on more rigorous internal enforcement of its own immigration restrictions, including as regards access to employment, social security, and public services.[70]

As the withdrawal process unfolded, it became clear that that third and final option would prevail. The UK Government announced that, whatever else might come to pass in terms of relations with the EU as a whole, the CTA with Ireland should be preserved, while also taking measures to protect the integrity of the UK's future immigration system.[71] Naturally, the basic aspiration to maintain the CTA was shared also

---

[67] On which, see House of Lords EU Committee, *Brexit: UK–Irish Relations* (HL76 of 12 December 2016), especially at Chapter 4.

[68] On which, see House of Lords EU Committee, *Brexit: UK-Irish Relations* (HL76 of 12 December 2016), at paras 140–142.

[69] On which, see House of Lords EU Committee, *Brexit: UK-Irish Relations* (HL76 of 12 December 2016), at paras 134–139.

[70] Ultimately, perhaps even some system of national identity cards—with all its attendant concerns about public costs and citizen privacy.

[71] See HMG, *The United Kingdom's exit from and new partnership with the European Union* (Cm 9417 of 2 February 2017), especially at para 4.8 and Annex B; and subsequently HMG, *Position Paper on Northern Ireland and Ireland* (16 August 2017), at Section 2.

by the Irish Government.[72] For its part, the European Council aptly summarized the Union's relevant interests: when it comes to avoiding a hard border across the island of Ireland, the Union 'should recognise existing bilateral agreements and arrangements between the United Kingdom and Ireland which are compatible with EU law'.[73] On that basis, Ireland and the UK conducted bilateral talks concerning the future maintenance of the CTA; while the latter's status was also addressed between the UK and the Union as a whole, through the dialogue on Ireland/Northern Ireland organized under the Article 50 TEU process.

By the time of the Commission–UK Joint Report of December 2017, the matter was effectively resolved, at least from the Union's perspective: the parties recognized that the UK and Ireland may continue to make arrangements between themselves relating to the movement of persons between their territories, while fully respecting the rights of natural persons conferred by Union law, with the UK explicitly accepting that the CTA could continue to operate without affecting Ireland's obligations under Union free movement law.[74] That position was duly translated into what is now Article 3 PINI:

1) The United Kingdom and Ireland may continue to make arrangements between themselves relating to the movement of persons between their territories (the 'Common Travel Area'), while fully respecting the rights of natural persons conferred by Union law.

2) The United Kingdom shall ensure that the Common Travel Area and the rights and privileges associated therewith can continue to apply without affecting the obligations of Ireland under Union law, in particular with respect to free movement to, from and within Ireland for Union citizens and their family members, irrespective of their nationality.

In parallel to Union–UK negotiations over the text of the Withdrawal Agreement, UK–Irish discussions addressed the future maintenance of the CTA also from a bilateral perspective. In May 2019, the two governments signed a Memorandum of Understanding explicitly affirming their joint commitment to uphold the CTA.[75] That Memorandum of Understanding recalls (for example) that the CTA allows Irish and British citizens to move freely between as well as to take up residence in Ireland and the UK (respectively).[76] The two Governments commit to ensuring that their domestic laws facilitate such movement and residency, suggest that they may enter into more detailed bilateral agreements in the future to give effect to specific aspects of the

---

[72] E.g. Irish Government, *Ireland and the Negotiations on the UK's Withdrawal from the European Union: The Government's Approach* (May 2017).

[73] European Council (Article 50), *Guidelines of 29 April 2017*, at para 11.

[74] Joint Report from the EU and UK negotiators (8 December 2017), at para 54.

[75] Memorandum of Understanding between the Government of Ireland and the Government of the UK concerning the Common Travel Area and Associated Reciprocal Rights and Privileges (8 May 2019).

[76] The MoU also records the parties' mutual understanding to maintain various associated rights, e.g. as regards residency, employment, and social security: see the discussion in Chapter 7.

CTA arrangements, and in the meantime undertake to enhance their official dialogue for the purposes of the operation of the CTA. However, the legal basis of the CTA itself remains nothing more than a 'common understanding' between the two states and the Memorandum of Understanding is not of itself intended to create legally binding obligations.[77]

In so far as the British might harbour concerns about Ireland acting as a 'soft underbelly' for illegal entry, residence, or work in the UK by either EU or non-EU nationals—particularly in the light of planned restrictions on the residency and employment rights of Union citizens—the British authorities will simply have to rely on more effective internal enforcement of their own immigration restrictions (for example, at the point of seeking employment or access to public services).[78]

For its part, Ireland will still be obliged to respect any specific obligations imposed or accepted under EU law.[79] For example, no matter what the UK decides in terms of its entry/immigration policies, Ireland must continue to respect the rights of entry and residency available to all EU nationals and their protected family members.[80] Similarly, if Ireland and the UK are minded to enhance their mutual cooperation as regards border surveillance and the exchange of information between national immigration authorities, Ireland would nevertheless have to respect its obligations under the relevant EU data protection legislation, including any applicable restrictions on transferring personal data to third countries.[81]

The CTA, and with it an open border for persons, are therefore safe—at least for now. After all, there is nothing to stop a future UK administration from renouncing the CTA, regardless of the consequences for British–Irish relations in general or the situation of Northern Ireland in particular. But equally, the Republic itself might well decide to terminate the CTA and could then (in addition) exercise its right under Union law to become a full member of the AFSJ—though any such possibility is only conceivable in the future event of reunification with the North and thus the elimination of any threat of a hard border.[82]

5. The Border for Goods

Far more difficult problems were involved in the challenge of avoiding a hard border for the movement of *goods* across the island of Ireland.

---

[77] Memorandum of Understanding between the Government of Ireland and the Government of the UK concerning the Common Travel Area and Associated Reciprocal Rights and Privileges (8 May 2019), especially at para 17.

[78] E.g. HMG, *Position Paper on Northern Ireland and Ireland* (16 August 2017), at para 33.

[79] In which regard, recall the Union rules on granting special authorization for Ireland to contract bilateral agreements with the UK, even in areas falling within exclusive Union competence, as discussed in Chapter 6.

[80] I.e. precisely in accordance with Directive 2004/38, OJ 2004 L 158/77.

[81] The EU's general data protection regime is now contained in Regulation 2016/679, OJ 2016 L 119/1 and Directive 2016/680, OJ 2016 L 119/89.

[82] In accordance with Art 4, Protocol 19 and Art 8, Protocol 21 to the Treaties.

A. Issues of Legal Competence and Empirical Experience

From the perspective of Union law, the constitutional framework applicable to trade in goods is fundamentally different from that applicable to the movement of persons. After all, external customs and trade relations between the Single Market and third countries fall within the Union's exclusive competence: thus, for example, only the Union is entitled to exercise independent regulatory power in respect of the customs union; the Member States are obliged not to engage in autonomous action as regards customs affairs.[83] Finding a solution to the problem of a hard border for goods across the island of Ireland was therefore a matter for the EU and the UK; it was not possible for Ireland and the UK to reach some separate bilateral settlement on this issue.

Moreover, when it comes to understanding the precise nature of the border problem that the Union and the UK would now have to address, it is important to recall that customs frontiers are not just about collecting import or export tariffs. Of course, all customs territories need to perform that basic function: thus, the EU customs union abolishes all internal tariffs between the Member States, then creates a common tariff as regards third countries (in compliance with the rules of the WTO as well as the terms of any preferential trade agreements entered into between the EU and its external partners).[84] But customs frontiers also serve a much broader function: they are an essential part of effective regulatory enforcement for a wide range of substantive policies in fields such as trade, public health, public safety and security, environmental protection, and countering illegal activities like smuggling and counterfeiting.[85]

For those twin reasons—customs and regulatory enforcement—it is inescapable that any given customs territory will entail the erection of some physical frontier for goods in its relations with other distinct customs territories. The real question is: what will be the nature and extent of the system of border controls, checks, and surveillance applied at that external frontier?

In that regard, the EU's handling of customs relations with other third countries already reveals a lot about what is possible and where the limits lie in terms of international cooperation.[86] First, the EU aims in principle to adopt a single approach to customs enforcement across its entire territory, so as to avoid the creation of any 'soft underbellies' that would distort the cohesion of the customs union: national variations should be reduced; customs authorities should act as one. Secondly, the EU system seeks to reduce the need for and intrusive nature of physical inspections at the customs border through a variety of means: for example, widespread use of electronic systems for customs declarations; risk management strategies that identify potential problems and respond in a more targeted manner; a system of 'authorized economic operators' to facilitate ease of customs operations for reliable private actors; distinguishing between commercial transport (which might be required to use

---

[83] Arts 2(1) and 3 TFEU.

[84] See, in particular, Art 28(1) TFEU. Also Arts 30–32 TFEU.

[85] See, e.g. Commission, *The EU Customs Union: Protecting People and Facilitating Trade* (2014).

[86] See Regulation 952/2013 laying down the Union Customs Code, OJ 2013 L 269/1. See further, e.g. L. Gormley, *EU Law of Free Movement of Goods and Customs Union* (2009)—though note that this text is based upon the previous Community Customs Code as laid down in Regulation 2913/92, OJ 1992 L 302/1 and Modernised Customs Code as laid down in Regulation 450/2008, OJ 2008 L 145/1.

specific crossing points) and private traffic (which might be dealt with through more random searches). Thirdly, the EU has concluded a range of international agreements with third countries aimed at facilitating customs cooperation and mutual assistance. Some such arrangements are highly structured within the context of relatively close trading partnerships: for example, as with the EU's own (partial) customs union with Turkey;[87] or as in the case of relations between the EU customs union and the EFTA countries that participate also in the European Economic Area.[88] Other customs agreements between the EU and third countries are less advanced, tending to focus on the mutually beneficial exchange of relevant information.[89]

Indeed, the lessons from the EEA are often considered to be particularly instructive in this context. After all, the EEA provides an example of a special customs relationship based upon the (extensive but not total) abolition of customs duties between the EU Member States and the EFTA–EEA states.[90] At the same time, the EFTA–EEA states are not part of the EU customs union, are not bound by the common customs tariff, and do not otherwise participate in the EU's common commercial policy—thus limiting the benefits of the EEA's preferential tariff system to goods from the participating countries and necessitating the application of 'rules of origin' to ensure the appropriate customs treatment of third country products.[91] That said, the principle of 'dynamic homogeneity' which underpins the entire EEA system—ensuring that the EFTA–EEA states align their legislation to that of the EU itself across a wide range of policy fields—means that the Union's broader concern to ensure effective regulatory enforcement at its external customs frontier is less pressing in this particular context.[92] When it comes to border management, the EEA agreement provides for customs cooperation and mutual assistance, including detailed provisions on issues such as common standards and mutual recognition as regards customs security measures.[93] Specifically in the context of the land border between Norway and Sweden, a bilateral agreement dating from 1959 (and thus applicable even after subsequent Swedish accession to the EU) aims at reducing bureaucracy and duplication while still managing border crossings effectively: for example, providing for a common border zone where each country's customs authorities can operate freely across both territories.[94]

In short, the EU exercises its exclusive competence over the customs union in a way which seeks to limit the burdens and disruption inherent in customs procedures, and

---

[87] See, in particular, Decision No 1/95 of the EC–Turkey Association Council on implementing the final phase of the Customs Union. Note the evaluation of the EU–Turkey Customs Union carried out by the World Bank (Report No 85830-TR published on 28 March 2014).

[88] See, in particular, Agreement on the European Economic Area, OJ 1994 L 1/3. Note the evaluation of the EEA Agreement conducted by Norway (*Outside and Inside: Norway's Agreements with the European Union*, Official Norwegian Reports NOU 2012:2).

[89] The EU currently has customs cooperation agreements with countries including the US, Canada, China, India, and Japan.

[90] See, in particular, Arts 8 and 10 EEA.

[91] See, in particular, Arts 8 and 9 EEA as well as Protocol 4.

[92] See further on the principle of dynamic homogeneity within the legal framework and operation of the EEA since its inception, e.g. Fredriksen and Franklin, 'Of Pragmatism and Principles: The EEA Agreement 20 years on', 52 *CMLRev* (2015) 629.

[93] See, in particular, Art 21 EEA as well as Protocols 10 and 11.

[94] See, e.g. D. Scally, 'Close Sweden–Norway Ties Despite EU Border Dividing Them' (*The Irish Times*, 13 June 2016).

is prepared to cooperate with third countries in order to achieve the same ends, but the fact remains that the existence of separate customs and regulatory territories inherently means the erection and enforcement of corresponding customs and regulatory borders. An ambitious free trade agreement can reduce tariffs between the contracting parties, minimize regulatory discrepancies, and provide for greater cooperation and mutual assistance. But even that will rarely succeed in eliminating all tariffs, or obviate the need to apply 'rules of origin', or extinguish concerns about the effective enforcement of broader regulatory policies—any or all of which still necessitate a customs border in order to safeguard the legitimate interests of the contracting parties.

B. Three Mutually Incompatible Promises by the UK Government

All of those factors and lessons provide part of the essential background to understanding the inherent problems involved in managing tariff and regulatory frontiers between distinct customs territories. But the specific and actual hard border challenges facing the island of Ireland in the wake of the 2016 referendum were entirely of the UK's own making and, in particular, were the direct result of a series of policy decisions and political promises made by the May Government—apparently without much concern for how those decisions and promises might eventually have to be reconciled with each other in practice, given the particular complexities surrounding the position of Northern Ireland vis-à-vis both the Republic and the rest of the UK.

To begin with, after the 2016 referendum, the UK Government announced that the UK would be leaving not just the EU but also the Customs Union and the Single Market.[95] In itself, that announcement implied the creation of separate customs and regulatory territories, together with all their accompanying checks and formalities, not only between the Union and the UK but also between Ireland and Northern Ireland. No amount of tariff reductions, technological innovation, risk management, or cross-border cooperation would eliminate the inevitable disruption that would be entailed by erecting such new frontiers. As we have seen, the adverse consequences would of course be calculated in economic terms, based on the additional costs and inconvenience for businesses and consumers on both sides of the customs border, caused by having to pay any tariffs due on the cross-border movement of goods, as well as having to comply with all the applicable pre- and post-customs processes and formalities, in order for products from one jurisdiction to be treated as having entered free circulation in the other.[96] But in addition, with a more closed physical border for goods would inevitably come a range of broader social and political challenges, including the creation of additional incentives to engage in cross-border smuggling and other forms of illegal activity; the risk that frontier points would once again become an easy target for violent attack by those directly opposed to the peace process; and the danger of

---

[95] In particular: HMG, *The United Kingdom's exit from and new partnership with the European Union* (Cm 9417 of 2 February 2017).

[96] See, in particular, Arts 28(2) and 29 TFEU. And that is besides the additional requirement of lawful marketing within the state of free circulation: see, e.g. Case C-525/14, *Commission v Czech Republic* (EU:C:2016:714).

undermining an important pillar of nationalist identity and cross-community support for the current constitutional settlement.[97]

When it finally dawned upon the May Government that its decision to leave the Customs Union and the Single Market would in fact present direct and serious dangers to economic, social, and political stability in Northern Ireland, the UK made an equally important second promise: there should be no return to a hard border on the island of Ireland.[98] In particular, 'this must mean aiming to avoid any physical border infrastructure in either the United Kingdom or Ireland, for any purpose (including customs or agri-food checks)'.[99] It should be noted that the UK's promise to avoid a hard border was not initially phrased in unconditional terms: the goal was to deliver 'as frictionless a land border as possible' (rather than to guarantee that the current open border arrangements would simply be maintained in any event).[100] It was only later that the UK Government indeed began to promise unconditionally that there would be no physical infrastructure at the border.[101] Moreover, the UK Government evidently believed that it would be perfectly possible for some package of more detailed proposals, based on forms of administrative cooperation and technological innovation, to minimize the need for a physical frontier for either customs or regulatory purposes between Ireland and Northern Ireland.[102] However, it was immediately obvious to many commentators that such complex, novel, and largely untested proposals were unlikely to contain some magical solution to the basic challenges of frontier management that the rest of the world had already been grappling with for many decades. In reality, the only feasible way for the UK to deliver on its second promise, as well as keep the first, would be for Northern Ireland to remain within the Customs Union and at least parts of the Single Market (even if the rest of the UK did not).

However, under pressure from the DUP, upon whose parliamentary votes its very survival now depended, the UK Government also made a crucial third promise: Northern Ireland would be leaving the Customs Union and the Single Market along with the rest of the UK.[103] In particular, the UK argued that negotiations over the Irish goods border should be guided by the principle also of preventing the creation of new barriers to doing business within the UK itself, specifically, between Northern Ireland and Great Britain.[104] According to the Government, 'avoiding a return to a hard border between Northern Ireland and Ireland is one of our top priorities. But the answer as to how to achieve this cannot be to impose a customs border between Northern Ireland and Great Britain .... Imposing new customs barriers

---

[97] See also House of Lords EU Committee, *Brexit: UK–Irish Relations* (HL76 of 12 December 2016), especially at Chapter 3.

[98] That stance was not entirely obvious from HMG, *The United Kingdom's exit from and new partnership with the European Union* (Cm 9417 of 2 February 2017); but was set out more clearly in HMG, *Position Paper on Northern Ireland and Ireland* (16 August 2017), at Section 3—to be read alongside HMG, *Future Customs Arrangements* (16 August 2017).

[99] See HMG, *Position Paper on Northern Ireland and Ireland* (16 August 2017), at para 45.

[100] See HMG, *Position Paper on Northern Ireland and Ireland* (16 August 2017), at para 45.

[101] See, e.g. Prime Minister, *Statement on leaving the EU* (9 October 2017); *Statement on October European Council* (23 October 2017).

[102] See HMG, *Position Paper on Northern Ireland and Ireland* (16 August 2017) read alongside HMG, *Future Customs Arrangements* (16 August 2017).

[103] E.g. HMG, *Position Paper on Northern Ireland and Ireland* (16 August 2017), at para 45.

[104] See HMG, *Position Paper on Northern Ireland and Ireland* (16 August 2017), at para 45.

within the UK would clearly have wider constitutional implications and could not be accepted by the UK Government'.[105] Yet surely the only way to keep that third promise, while still respecting the second, was ... for the UK as a whole to remain within the Customs Union and the Single Market!

Thus was a circle of mutual contradiction completed. But the situation was rendered all the more complicated by a series of other important factors. Recall that a clear majority of the population in Northern Ireland voted to remain within the EU during the 2016 referendum. Yet for most of the Article 50 TEU process, Northern Ireland's devolved political institutions were effectively in abeyance. The two main parties, the DUP and Sinn Féin, hold radically different views on a wide range of issues—not least, they were on directly opposite sides of the argument over UK withdrawal from the Union. Despite those differences, the DUP and Sinn Féin were still expected to co-operate in the co-governance of Northern Ireland—yet power-sharing collapsed in January 2017 following a political row over the DUP's handling of an energy policy scandal.[106] For several years afterwards, the two factions were unable to reach an accommodation that would allow the Belfast institutions to resume work and thus provide Northern Ireland with its own voice in the momentous decisions that were now being made about its own future.[107]

On the contrary, after the 2017 general election, the minority Conservative Government in London was effectively propped up in power only through the support of the DUP and its 10 MPs in the House of Commons. Indeed, it is fair to say that the May Government dropped even the slightest pretence of acting as an 'honest broker' between the two main communities in Northern Ireland: its dependence on the parliamentary support of the DUP offered the latter disproportionate influence over the way that the UK approached negotiations with the EU—not least over the Irish border question.

C. The Joint Report of December 2017

Having promised entirely irreconcilable outcomes to different constituencies of people, the UK Government now found itself obliged to negotiate some more credible solution directly with the Union. The latter's position was clear and (relatively) straightforward: there should be no hard border for goods, and no physical border infrastructure, across the island of Ireland; the UK was expected to bring forward proposals to achieve that objective and the Union would be happy to consider flexible and imaginative solutions; but such solutions had to respect the integrity of the Union's own legal order and could not question Ireland's rightful place within the Customs Union and Single Market.[108]

---

[105] See HMG, *Position Paper on Northern Ireland and Ireland* (16 August 2017), at paras 52–53.

[106] See, e.g. https://www.theguardian.com/politics/2017/jan/09/martin-mcguinness-to-resign-as-northern-ireland-deputy-first-minister.

[107] Power-sharing only resumed in January 2020—after the Johnson Government had completed negotiations with the EU on the terms of UK withdrawal in general, and the treatment of Northern Ireland in particular: see further below.

[108] E.g. European Council (Article 50), *Guidelines of April 2017*; Council Decision of 22 May 2017; Commission, *Guiding Principles for the Dialogue on Ireland/Northern Ireland* (20 September 2017).

Here as elsewhere, the initial period of discussions under Article 50 TEU culminated in the Joint Report of December 2017.[109] It is worth quoting the relevant passages in full:

43. The United Kingdom's withdrawal from the European Union presents a significant and unique challenge in relation to the island of Ireland. The United Kingdom recalls its commitment to protecting the operation of the 1998 Agreement, including its subsequent implementation agreements and arrangements, and to the effective operation of each of the institutions and bodies established under them. The United Kingdom also recalls its commitment to the avoidance of a hard border, including any physical infrastructure or related checks and controls.

44. Both Parties recognise the need to respect the provisions of the 1998 Agreement regarding the constitutional status of Northern Ireland and the principle of consent. The commitments set out in this joint report are and must remain fully consistent with these provisions. The United Kingdom continues to respect and support fully Northern Ireland's position as an integral part of the United Kingdom, consistent with the principle of consent.

45. The United Kingdom respects Ireland's ongoing membership of the European Union and all of the corresponding rights and obligations that entails, in particular Ireland's place in the Internal Market and the Customs Union. The United Kingdom also recalls its commitment to preserving the integrity of its internal market and Northern Ireland's place within it, as the United Kingdom leaves the European Union's Internal Market and Customs Union.

46. The commitments and principles outlined in this joint report will not pre-determine the outcome of wider discussions on the future relationship between the European Union and the United Kingdom and are, as necessary, specific to the unique circumstances on the island of Ireland. They are made and must be upheld in all circumstances, irrespective of the nature of any future agreement between the European Union and United Kingdom.

....

49. The United Kingdom remains committed to protecting North–South cooperation and to its guarantee of avoiding a hard border. Any future arrangements must be compatible with these overarching requirements. The United Kingdom's intention is to achieve these objectives through the overall EU–UK relationship. Should this not be possible, the United Kingdom will propose specific solutions to address the unique circumstances of the island of Ireland. In the absence of agreed solutions, the United Kingdom will maintain full alignment with those rules of the Internal Market and the Customs Union which, now or in the future, support North–South cooperation, the all-island economy and the protection of the 1998 Agreement.

50. In the absence of agreed solutions, as set out in the previous paragraph, the United Kingdom will ensure that no new regulatory barriers develop between

---

[109] Brexit (2017) *Joint report on progress during phase 1 of negotiations under Article 50 TEU on the UK's orderly withdrawal from the EU.* Available at: https://www.gov.uk/government/publications/joint-report-on-progress-during-phase-1-of-negotiations-under-article-50-teu-on-the-uks-orderly-withdrawal-from-the-eu . See further Chapter 4.

Northern Ireland and the rest of the United Kingdom, unless, consistent with the 1998 Agreement, the Northern Ireland Executive and Assembly agree that distinct arrangements are appropriate for Northern Ireland. In all circumstances, the United Kingdom will continue to ensure the same unfettered access for Northern Ireland's businesses to the whole of the United Kingdom internal market.

51. Both Parties will establish mechanisms to ensure the implementation and oversight of any specific arrangement to safeguard the integrity of the EU Internal Market and the Customs Union.

In other words, the Joint Report expressed the parties' aspiration that a hard border for goods across the island of Ireland would best be avoided through an agreement on the overall future EU–UK relationship. However, those negotiations were not due to commence until after British withdrawal was completed; might take a considerable period of time; might not find any workable solution to the Irish border problem; and indeed might not produce any final agreement at all. To guard against those contingencies, the two parties therefore agreed that any withdrawal treaty should include a 'backstop' to prevent the return of a hard border for goods across the island of Ireland in any event—under which the UK (whether as a whole, or in respect of Northern Ireland alone) would maintain full alignment with the Internal Market and the Customs Union as required, now or in the future, to support North–South cooperation, protect the all-island economy, and uphold the Good Friday Agreement.[110]

6. Solving the Irish Goods Border through the Future EU–UK Relationship?

Let's deal briefly with the Joint Report's aspiration that the goods border across the island of Ireland might be resolved as part of some broader agreement on future EU–UK trade relations as a whole. After all, for a considerable time after publication of the Joint Report—in fact, until Boris Johnson assumed office as Prime Minister in summer 2019—the UK Government pinned its hopes on finding some agreed solution that would dissipate any need for customs and regulatory enforcement between the Union and the UK in general and therefore between the Republic and Northern Ireland in particular.[111] Yet so long as the UK maintained its decision to leave both the Customs Union and the Single Market, it was obvious that its Government would struggle to present credible proposals to deliver any such solution.

As we saw in Chapter 4, the main UK proposals were contained in the 'Chequers Plan' of July 2018.[112] In the first place, the Government advocated a 'free trade area for

---

[110] Note also Joint Report from the EU and UK negotiators (8 December 2017), at para 50 and Prime Minister, *Open Letter on Commitments to Northern Ireland* (8 December 2017)—both intended to reassure unionists about Northern Ireland's position within the UK.

[111] Consider, e.g. David Davis, *Statement on EU-UK Article 50 Negotiations* (19 March 2018); Theresa May, *Letter to Donald Tusk* (19 March 2018).

[112] HMG, *The Future Relationship between the United Kingdom and the European Union* (Cm 9593 of 17 July 2018).

goods' based on a common rulebook which would see the UK continue to apply certain EU rules governing trade in goods, though only those strictly necessary to avoid literal border checks between the Union and the UK. In the second place, the UK also suggested a 'facilitated customs arrangement' between the Union and the UK: the latter would adopt its own regime for tariffs on other third country goods as well as its own regulatory standards for a whole range of sectors falling outside the common rulebook of the 'free trade area for goods'; but the UK would also and simultaneously continue to apply and enforce the Union's entirely separate tariff system and potentially divergent product regulations at the very same UK borders. By those means, the Government argued that it was indeed possible to avoid the reintroduction of customs and regulatory controls on the border, not only between UK and EU as a whole, but also between Northern Ireland and the Republic in particular.

However, we know from our previous discussion that those Chequers proposals, for a 'free trade area for goods' and 'facilitated customs arrangements', were soon dismissed as fanciful and unworkable. For example, the 'facilitated customs arrangement' was described as untested and undeliverable—not least since it implied a massive increase in bureaucracy, requiring vast quantities of goods to be categorized, tracked, and verified throughout the various processes of manufacture within, import into, and export from the UK, so as to ensure that they were subject to the correct tariffs and marketed in accordance with the appropriate regulatory standards. And even besides the question of whether the UK's proposals appeared credible from a regulatory and logistical perspective, the Chequers proposals were objectionable to the EU27 on more fundamental political grounds. After all, the UK was proposing to 'take back control' of its borders and money, by expecting the Union to surrender control over its own borders and money to a third country—in effect, allowing the UK to collect the Union's own income and enforce the Union's own public policy regulations. It was also unclear why the UK should enjoy special treatment through continued participation in the free movement of goods, while being free to reject the parallel systems governing natural persons, legal persons, services, and capital (to say nothing of other common policies in fields such as agriculture or external commercial relations); especially since the UK was openly threatening to use its newfound third country status so as to create competitive advantages for its own industries—advantages which could then be immediately and unfairly directed back against the Union's own economy.

That said, however fanciful and unworkable the official proposals of the UK Government, they were still significantly more connected to reality than the approach of many of the leading Leave politicians and campaigners. Among the latter, a surprising number (including within the DUP's contingent at Westminster) simply denied that the problem of a hard border for goods even existed, or at least claimed that it had been massively exaggerated. After all (they claimed) different states apply different internal taxes and apply different regulatory standards all the time, so why (they asked) is it suddenly so hard for different jurisdictions to collect different duties and enforce different rules on goods? Rather than reflect upon their own truly lamentable ignorance about even the basic features of international trade, those Leave politicians and campaigners instead accused the EU (in general) and the Republic (in particular) of 'weaponizing' the goods border so as to punish the

UK for its decision to withdraw and/or to stake an aggressive territorial claim upon Northern Ireland.[113]

Even those Leave enthusiasts who admitted that the goods border was a genuine problem, rather than a figment of the world's collective imagination or the invention of an international anti-British conspiracy, insisted repeatedly that technology could provide a solution to the problem of customs and regulatory enforcement without the need either for convergent tariffs and standards between the Union and the UK; or for any form of physical infrastructure at the border between the Republic and Northern Ireland.[114] When challenged to explain why no other customs territory on earth had managed to develop and deploy the necessary technologies, such Leave campaigners often retorted that the EU itself had already produced a report that proved it was perfectly possible to use available technologies in order to police the Irish border without any physical infrastructure, checks, or controls. And indeed, leading Leave politicians appeared on mainstream news broadcasts brandishing a copy of a report commissioned by the European Parliament into the prospects for a 'smart border' across the island of Ireland.[115] Being generous, one might assume that those politicians had not actually read the report for themselves: after all, the examples and proposals contained in the report produced for the European Parliament each clearly and unmistakably involves the creation of physical infrastructure, and the introduction of customs checks and controls, of precisely the sort the Government had promised to avoid. As the House of Commons Northern Ireland Affairs Committee noted in March 2018: it appears that even the most technologically advanced customs borders in the world are capable only of reducing frontier disruption and delays.[116]

7. Initial Attempts to Design a Backstop

Given the lack of detailed and credible UK proposals that could help provide the basis for an agreed long-term solution, the Union insisted upon holding the UK to its promise of enacting a default or backstop solution: for the UK (as a whole, or least Northern Ireland) to remain fully aligned with whatever EU rules are required, now or in the future, to avoid a hard border. However, trying to work out the details of the backstop proved a tortuous affair.[117] Three main proposals assumed draft or final legal form: first, a proposal from the EU, for a Northern Ireland-only backstop (which the UK refused to endorse); secondly, an alternative model suggested by the May

---

[113] See, e.g. https://www.independent.co.uk/news/uk/politics/brexit-latest-northern-irish-border-problem-weaponised-david-jones-theresa-may-visit-a8454386.html.

[114] Consider, e.g. European Research Group, *The Border between Northern Ireland and the Republic of Ireland post-Brexit* (12 September 2018). Note also the 'report' by Prosperity UK, *Alternative Arrangements Commission: Alternative Arrangements for the Irish Border* (24 June 2019).

[115] L. Karlsson, *Smart Border 2.0: Avoiding a hard border on the island of Ireland for customs control and the free movement of persons* (European Parliament, Policy Department for Citizens' Rights and Constitutional Affairs: PE 596.828 of November 2017).

[116] House of Commons Northern Ireland Affairs Committee, *The Land Border between Northern Ireland and Ireland* (HC 329 of 16 March 2018).

[117] Full details of how the Irish border problem was addressed, within the broader context of the Art 50 TEU negotiations, are contained in Chapters 4 and 5.

Government, for a UK–wide backstop (which was eventually included in the First Withdrawal Package of November 2018); and finally, the backstop model that was re-negotiated at the insistence of the Johnson Government (and which is now contained in the Second Withdrawal Package of October 2019). The final backstop will be discussed shortly. In this section, we will briefly explore the two previous proposals that each failed to survive the rigours of the Article 50 TEU process.

A. The Union's Proposal for a Northern Ireland-Only Backstop

The draft withdrawal agreement published by the Commission in February 2018 included the Union's opening proposal for a dedicated Protocol on Ireland/Northern Ireland, including a plan to avoid a hard goods border across the island of Ireland through the full alignment of Northern Ireland with all relevant EU regulatory regimes.[118]

The Commission's central idea was the establishment of a 'common regulatory area' between the Union and Northern Ireland, i.e. an area without internal borders in which the free movement of goods is ensured and North–South cooperation is protected. That common regulatory area was then fleshed out with more detailed provisions: for example, on Northern Ireland's inclusion within the Union customs territory; continuing the full free movement of goods between the Union and Northern Ireland; maintaining trade in agricultural and fisheries products; protecting the Single Electricity Market; maintaining certain environmental standards, particularly those relevant to cross-border trade in goods; and guaranteeing that Northern Ireland would continue to be governed by the same state aid rules as the Union itself (so as to prevent unfair distortions of competition by unlawfully subsidized goods). The Commission's draft text also contained detailed provisions on governance of the common regulatory area, together with a system for enforcement and dispute settlement; for the adoption of safeguard measures; and for the protection by the Union and the UK of their respective financial interests.

In other words: the Commission proposals would effectively have continued to treat Northern Ireland as part of the Union's own customs territory for all relevant fiscal and regulatory purposes—but would also and inevitably have required the introduction and/or significant expansion of checks on goods travelling by sea and air between Northern Ireland and Great Britain. In effect, the UK could keep its first and second promises (the UK as such leaves the Customs Union and Single Market, though without creating a hard border across the island of Ireland) but only by breaking its third (there should be no new barriers to trade between Northern Ireland and the rest of the UK).

However, the May Government (fully supported, indeed actively encouraged, by its DUP allies) immediately rejected the Union's proposals as an unacceptable attempt to undermine the territorial, constitutional, and economic integrity of the UK.[119] British

---

[118] TF50 (2018) 33.

[119] E.g. https://www.bbc.co.uk/news/uk-politics-43224785; Theresa May, *Letter to Donald Tusk* (19 March 2018). Also: House of Commons Northern Ireland Affairs Committee, *The Land Border between Northern Ireland and Ireland* (HC 329 of 16 March 2018).

opposition appeared to be based essentially on the argument that Northern Ireland simply could not be treated any differently from the rest of the UK for customs and regulatory purposes. However, that argument was rightly greeted with a large degree of scepticism: after all, Northern Ireland is already and self-evidently treated differently from the rest of the UK for all manner of (not only financial and regulatory) purposes.[120] It was therefore difficult for reasonable observers to understand why the Union's proposals for *these specific additional* differences in treatment attracted such hostility from the UK Government—especially since it was manifestly so much easier to conduct customs and regulatory controls (some of which already took place in any case) at a relatively small number of ports and airports connecting Northern Ireland to Great Britain, rather than on road traffic across the entire length of the Irish land border.[121]

B. The UK's Proposal for a (Partly) UK-Wide Backstop

Even if the UK position was not especially convincing, such was the intensity of the May Government's opposition, that it was clear the Commission's plans could not provide the basis for a negotiated solution to the problem of the Irish goods border. And so the Union called upon the UK to bring forward its alternative proposals for the backstop.[122]

The UK's initial proposals for an alternative backstop were greeted with disappointment if not derision—dealing only with the question of customs, not with the problem of regulatory standards; and even then, explicitly presented as a merely temporary arrangement (not the more long-term solution that any default plan is meant and needs to provide).[123] However, as the threat of a 'no deal' outcome loomed and the pressure to reach an agreement under Article 50 TEU intensified, the UK brought forward a new plan which the Union was prepared to talk about in earnest. That plan provided the basis for the Protocol on Ireland/Northern Ireland contained in the First Withdrawal Package of November 2018.[124]

Both sides still hoped (rather optimistically) that the need for a hard border could be avoided, simply through the future trading relationship between the EU and the UK as a whole. In particular, the Union and the UK would use their best endeavours in good faith to negotiate and conclude an agreement on their future relationship with

---

[120] Note that Northern Ireland was only recently brought into line with the rest of the UK on issues such as marriage equality, in the face of the DUP's insistence that Northern Ireland be treated entirely differently.

[121] Points already made by the Union negotiator for some time already, e.g. Commission, *Speech by Michel Barnier at the Centre for European Reform on 'The Future of the EU'* (20 November 2017).

[122] See, e.g. European Council, *Remarks by President Donald Tusk after his meeting with Taoiseach Leo Varadkar* (8 March 2018); Commission, *Speech by President Juncker at the Plenary Session of the European Parliament on the guidelines on the framework of future EU-UK relations* (13 March 2018); *Déclaration par Michel Barnier devant la session plénière du Parlement européen sur les négotiations Article 50 avec le Royaume-Uni* (13 March 2018); *Speech by Michel Barnier at the All-Island Civic Dialogue* (30 April 2018); *Press statement by Michel Barnier following this week's round of negotiations* (8 June 2018).

[123] HMG, *Technical Note on Temporary Customs Arrangement* (7 June 2018); to which the Commission swiftly reacted, e.g. TF50 (2018) 39.

[124] Published at OJ 2019 C 66 I.

a view to its application from the end of the transition period.[125] Or at least through a future agreement dealing more specifically with the Irish border: the Union and the UK would in any event use their best endeavours to conclude, by 31 December 2020, an agreement that could supersede the Protocol on Ireland/Northern Ireland (whether in whole or in part).[126] Moreover, if some sort of future agreement did not appear likely to be in place by the middle of 2020, the UK could still ask for the transition period to be prolonged on a one-off basis.[127] But if and when the transition period were to expire, with no satisfactory alternative solution having been found or at least standing ready to be put into operation, then the UK's alternative backstop would indeed need to be activated.

The centre-piece of that alternative backstop consisted of a 'single customs territory'—a de facto customs union—between the EU and the whole of the UK, so as to remove tariffs in trade between the two parties and thereby solve half of the Irish border problem.[128] Naturally, that customs arrangement was constructed almost entirely on the Union's own terms: for example, the UK would have to comply with the Union's tariff system and much of the latter's trade regime in relations with third countries; as well as respect a wide range of minimum standards in fields like taxation, competition, state aid, environmental, and labour protection—so as to guarantee that UK businesses operated on a level playing field with Union businesses.[129]

But the EU–UK 'single customs territory' would only solve half the Irish border problem. The remaining challenge, of avoiding regulatory checks on goods moving across the island of Ireland, was to be addressed by Northern Ireland indeed remaining aligned with all relevant Single Market rules and processes—ranging from agricultural standards and manufacturing rules, through to state aid controls and VAT/excise duties.[130] The North's regulatory convergence with the Union would allow for the maintenance of an effective zone of free movement for goods with the Republic and indeed the wider Union.[131] But in turn, it would also mean expanding/introducing various checks on goods travelling between Northern Ireland and Great Britain—albeit that the Protocol sought to minimize the burden and visibility of such additional controls.[132]

The final main pillar of the backstop contained in the First Withdrawal Agreement concerned its interpretation, application, and eventual duration. For example: provisions of the Protocol referring to Union law etc were to be interpreted in conformity with all relevant CJEU caselaw (not just that existing at the expiry of the transition period);[133] similarly, references in the Protocol to Union measures would include the relevant measures as amended or replaced also in the future.[134] As regards those Union

---

[125] Art 184 First WA.
[126] Art 2(1) First PINI.
[127] Art 132 First WA and Art 3 First PINI.
[128] Art 6(1) First PINI.
[129] See the detailed provisions contained in the First PINI and its various Annexes.
[130] Art 6(2) First PINI.
[131] See the detailed provisions contained in the First PINI and its various Annexes.
[132] E.g. Art 7 First PINI.
[133] Art 15(3) First PINI.
[134] Art 15(4) First PINI. Note also Art 15(5) First PINI: new Union acts falling within the scope of the Protocol but not amending/replacing existing Union acts should be the subject of a discussion within the

rules applicable specifically to and in Northern Ireland: while their implementation was in principle to be ensured by the UK authorities, the Union institutions (including the CJEU) would continue to exercise certain powers directly, while Union acts were to continue producing the same legal effects in Northern Ireland as they did across the Union itself.[135]

But it was the provisions concerning the proposed duration of the UK's alternative backstop that were among the most significant in determining the eventual fate of the First Withdrawal Package. The Protocol explicitly stressed that its objective was not to establish a permanent relationship between the EU and the UK; it was intended to apply only temporarily unless and until superseded (in whole or in part) by a subsequent EU–UK agreement.[136] If, after the expiry of the transition period, the Union or the UK considered that the existing Protocol was no longer necessary to achieve the objective of preventing a hard border across the island of Ireland, the Joint Committee was empowered to decide (in good faith) that the Protocol should cease to apply (in whole or in part).[137] So this was a backstop with no definite expiry date: the two parties might hope to replace the Protocol with a better alternative in the future; but there was no guarantee that that would happen within any clear timescale or indeed that it would ever happen at all. And in any case, replacing or terminating the proposed arrangements would ultimately require the EU's positive consent.[138]

In short, the UK Government had proposed and agreed to keep its second promise (no hard border across the island of Ireland), but only part of its first promise (the UK as such might be leaving the Single Market, yet it would effectively stay within the Customs Union) and only part of its third promise (Northern Ireland might well be treated the same as the rest of the UK as regards customs, but not for regulatory purposes).

That radically different backstop paved the way for the First Withdrawal Package to be agreed at the political level by both the UK Government and the European Council.[139] But as we know, the deal foundered upon the May Government's persistent failure to secure its domestic approval by the House of Commons in accordance with section 13 of the European Union (Withdrawal) Act 2018.[140] May attributed parliamentary opposition to her deal primarily to the problems associated with her very own backstop model.[141] Of course, it would be wrong to claim that the proposed Protocol on Ireland/Northern Ireland was the only problematic aspect of the First Withdrawal Package or indeed even the main motivation for discontent among

---

Joint Committee with a view to updating the relevant annex or otherwise ensuring the good functioning of the Protocol—in default of which, the Union may take appropriate remedial measures.

[135] Art 14 First PINI.

[136] I.e. under either Art 184 First WA or Art 2(1) First PINI: Art 1(4) First PINI.

[137] Art 20 First PINI.

[138] Though note Art 18 First PINI: reservation of a power for the Union/the UK to adopt certain safeguard/rebalancing measures in accordance with the procedure set out in Annex 10. And also Art 19 First PINI: protection of the Union's/the UK's financial interests against fraud and other illegal activities.

[139] European Council (Article 50), *Conclusions of 25 November 2018*.

[140] See the detailed discussion in Chapter 5.

[141] E.g. Theresa May, *Statement on Exiting the European Union* (10 December 2018); *Statement to the House of Commons* (21 January 2019).

the Government's various and varied political detractors and opponents: the onerous terms of the transition period, or the limited vision for future EU–UK relations as presented in the First Political Declaration, were also controversial among different constituencies of parliamentary opposition; while it was clear that some MPs would never vote for the proposed deal as a matter of ('Hard Leave' or 'Only Remain') principle. Yet unease about the 'backstop' was certainly central to the troubles and ultimately the demise of the May Government, so it is worth here summarizing the main reasons for dissent.

Among Leave supporters, the proposed 'single customs territory' was unacceptable for a range of reasons. For example, while strongly inclined to reject any form of customs union with the EU, they regarded this particular model as a perpetuation of the 'vassalage' that would already be initiated under the transition period—especially given the lack of any unilateral power of termination by the UK itself.[142] Many also believed that the proposed 'single customs territory' would significantly limit the room for 'Global Britain' to negotiate trade agreements with other third countries and in any event (even if this was rarely expressed as such in the public debate) feared that the proposed backstop would limit long-held rightist deregulatory plans across a significant range of domestic social and welfare policy fields.

But the May proposals were hardly less unpopular among many Remain supporters. After all, the 'single customs territory' still fell far short of full and full-blooded UK membership not only of the Customs Union but also of the entire Single Market—the sort of 'soft Brexit' that many felt was the only tolerable alternative to continued membership of the Union per se. And of course, there was an extraordinary disjunction between the May Government's endorsement of the Leave rhetoric about 'taking back control', when set within the context of a backstop that would effectively swop the UK's current position of leadership and influence within the Union for the status of a mere rule-taker—altogether outside the Union's institutions but still effectively bound by many of their rules.

Opposition extended beyond the UK-wide 'single customs territory' to touch also upon the Northern Ireland-specific proposals for regulatory alignment with the Union across various policy fields. Inevitably, the DUP and fellow unionists in the Conservative Party revived the argument which they had first deployed against the Union's original backstop proposals: it was constitutionally, economically, and politically unacceptable for Northern Ireland to be treated any differently from the rest of the UK. Small matter that, under the May proposals, Northern Irish businesses were in many respects being offered a relatively advantageous and indeed privileged relationship straddling both the UK and the EU markets.

Again as we know, May attempted in vain to salvage the First Withdrawal Package in general, and her backstop proposals in particular, by securing additional political assurances from the EU to the effect that neither party regarded the Irish border arrangements as a desirable end-state and both sides would work hard to replace them as soon as possible with some more durable trade model.[143] However, those political assurances did nothing to prevent her first major defeat under section 13 of the

---

[142] On allegations of 'vassalage' under the transition period, see the discussion in Chapter 6.
[143] See the detailed discussion and references in Chapter 5.

European Union (Withdrawal) Act on 15 January 2019;[144] nor her second humiliation by the House of Commons on 12 March 2019.[145] Of similar futility were the various gestures of reassurance and promises of special consideration May offered directly to (primarily the unionist community in) Northern Ireland: for example, proposals to ensure the involvement of Northern Ireland's devolved institutions in the future operation of the backstop, particularly when it came to decisions about whether the UK should agree to keep Northern Ireland aligned also with new Union legislation relevant to the conduct of frontier regulatory controls.[146]

Ultimately, May surely committed a fundamental political error by promising the DUP and her own Tory rebels that she would formally negotiate legally binding amendments to the proposed backstop—either a fixed time-limit on the backstop's lifespan; or a unilateral right for the UK to terminate the backstop of its own free will.[147] After all, it should have been patently clear that the Union would never agree to such radical amendments: not so much because of the jarring political spectacle of the UK Government now denouncing and seeking to rewrite its very own set of proposals; but rather because, to include either a fixed time-limit or a unilateral power of termination, would contradict the very nature and purpose of the backstop as a long-term, all-weather guarantee against the return of a hard border.[148] May's promise was therefore only ever doomed to failure.[149]

8. A New Protocol as Renegotiated by the Johnson Government

Although the Union refused to accede to May's demand to amend the Protocol on Ireland/Northern Ireland—in fact, the European Council insisted that the First Withdrawal Agreement was no longer open for renegotiation at all—the Union did indicate that it would be willing to reconsider the terms of the First Political Declaration: for example, if the UK were amenable to agreeing on a much closer future

---

[144] E.g. European Council (Article 50), *Conclusions of 13 December 2018*; Exchange of Letters between the President of the European Council, the President of the Commission and the UK Prime Minister of 14 January 2019.

[145] 'Strasbourg Deal' of 11 March 2019 (Instrument relating to the Withdrawal Agreement and Joint Statement relating to Political Declaration).

[146] E.g. Prime Minister, *Open Letter on Commitments to Northern Ireland* (8 December 2017); HMG, *Commitments to Northern Ireland and its integral place in the United Kingdom* (9 January 2019); Prime Minister, *Speech in Belfast* (5 February 2019); HMG, *Unilateral Declaration concerning the Northern Ireland Protocol* (12 March 2019).

[147] I.e. following the Government-backed 'Brady amendment' (29 January 2019) to the effect that the House of Commons would support the proposed withdrawal package if the 'Irish backstop' were replaced with alternative arrangements to avoid a hard border. Note that similar proposals had already been flagged up by the UK Government earlier in the Article 50 TEU negotiations, e.g. Dominic Raab, *Statement following negotiation round Thursday 26 July* (26 July 2018); Theresa May, *Statement on Brexit* (15 October 2018) ; Prime Minister, *Statement on European Council* (22 October 2018).

[148] See, e.g. Commission, *Speeches by President Juncker and Chief Negotiator Barnier at the Plenary session of the European Parliament on the occasion of the debate on the United Kingdom's withdrawal from the EU* (30 January 2019).

[149] Note Attorney General's Legal Advice of 13 November 2018; Theresa May, *Statement to the House of Commons on Brexit* (12 February 2019); Attorney General's Revised Legal Advice of 12 March 2019.

economic relationship with the Union, effectively amounting to continued membership of both the Customs Union and the Single Market, such as would eliminate the entire goods problem surrounding the Irish border.[150]

However, the May Government did not choose to pursue that option and its repeated failure to secure parliamentary approval for the First Withdrawal Package made the prospect of a 'no deal' Brexit appear increasingly likely as time rolled by.[151] In the case of the Irish goods border, that outcome appeared especially difficult and unattractive. After all, the prospect of imposing and managing a new customs and regulatory frontier across the island of Ireland was precisely the sort of 'separation issue' that could only be adequately avoided through mutual agreement between the Union and the UK. In the absence of any such agreement, it was obvious that attempting to address the situation, simply through unilateral action by each of the UK and the Union, was never going to do more than mitigate some of the economic, social, logistical, and political challenges that a 'no deal hard border' threatened to bring.[152]

However, in the latter half of 2019, a third and final set of proposals to avoid a hard border for the movement of goods across the island of Ireland did indeed emerge— this time from the new UK Government under Boris Johnson, who approached the entire problem with a very different set of priorities and calculations from those which had so taxed his immediate predecessor.[153]

Those proposals formed the basis of further intensive negotiations,[154] culminating in a new Protocol on Ireland/Northern Ireland within the revised Withdrawal Package of October 2019, on the basis of which UK withdrawal duly occurred.[155] In effect, May's UK-wide backstop was replaced by another Northern Ireland-specific regime: after all that bother, it was indeed the UK's inconvenient third promise that gave way in the end; the UK as such would leave the Customs Union and the Single Market, a hard border would be avoided, but Northern Ireland would become subject to a highly specific trade and regulatory regime compared to Great Britain.[156] However, the final agreement is not quite the same as the Union's original proposals for a 'common regulatory area'. Instead, Northern Ireland will remain formally within the UK customs territory, at the same time as being treated de facto as part of the Union's customs zone, and directly subject to an (albeit more limited) array of Single Market regulation. Moreover, this is no longer merely a default backstop model, to be replaced as soon as possible by some superior arrangement. The new Protocol is intended to endure on an indefinite and potentially permanent basis, albeit subject to a

---

[150] See, e.g. European Council (Article 50), *Conclusions of 10 April 2019*.

[151] See further the more detailed discussion and references in Chapter 5.

[152] Consider, e.g. publication of the UK's plans for (not) managing the Northern Irish goods border in the event of a 'no deal Brexit' (13 March 2019)—which received a less than warm reception, e.g. https://www.theguardian.com/politics/2019/mar/13/brexit-tariffs-on-87-of-uk-imports-cut-to-zero-in-temporary-no-deal-plan.

[153] Prime Minister, *Letter from the Prime Minister to the President of the European Commission* and *Explanatory Note on UK proposals for an amended Protocol on Ireland/Northern Ireland* (2 October 2019).

[154] Having been rejected, in and of themselves, by the Commission: e.g. Michel Barnier, *Statement at the European Parliament Plenary Session* (9 October 2019).

[155] Published at OJ 2019 C 384 I. Note the detailed rules on entry into force of the Protocol contained in Art 185 WA.

[156] Note Democratic Unionist Party, *Statement from the DUP* (17 October 2019).

rolling process of democratic reaffirmation by the devolved institutions in Northern Ireland itself.

Let's now explain those fundamental pillars of the Protocol in greater detail—addressing Northern Ireland's relationship to the Union; its relationship also to Great Britain; and finally, the projected duration of the Protocol's border plans.

A. Northern Ireland and the Union

In the first place, the Protocol makes provision for Northern Ireland's future place within the Union's customs and regulatory area. In particular, Northern Ireland will remain subject to large swathes of Union legislation covering customs, trade, the manufacture and marketing of goods, VAT, excise duties, and state aid.[157] Such legislation will apply to Northern Ireland on a dynamic basis.[158] The Joint Committee will also address the implications of the future adoption of entirely new Union rules that nevertheless fall within the scope of application of the Protocol.[159] Unlike so much of the rest of the Withdrawal Agreement, all relevant Union concepts and provisions must be interpreted fully in accordance with the CJEU's evolving caselaw.[160] In return, Articles 30 and 110 TFEU will continue to apply to Northern Ireland;[161] quantitative restrictions shall be prohibited between the Union and Northern Ireland;[162] and placing Union goods on the market in Northern Ireland shall otherwise be governed by Articles 34 and 36 TFEU.[163]

By those means, the Union succeeds in protecting the basic integrity of the Customs Union and Single Market whilst also avoiding a hard border for the movement of goods across the island of Ireland. But this did involve making some important compromises. For example, as Weatherill has pointed out, the Union was forced to qualify its staunch political mantra that the four freedoms of the Single Market must be regarded as 'indivisible';[164] albeit by reference to the equally important slogan that the unique challenges for Ireland posed by Brexit call for unique solutions.[165] More significantly, the Union has accepted that an external frontier of the Customs Union and Single Market will in future be policed by a third country: many of the Union rules applicable to Northern Ireland will have to be enforced on the ground by the UK authorities.[166] That is an especially noteworthy concession, given that the latter currently

---

[157] In particular: Arts 5, 7, 8 and 10 PINI—which include various specific exceptions/modifications, e.g. Art 5(3) PINI on fisheries and aquaculture products; Art 7 PINI on Northern Ireland matching the VAT exemptions/reductions application in Ireland; Art 10(2) PINI on state aid for Northern Irish agriculture.
[158] Art 13(3) PINI (unless otherwise provided for).
[159] Art 13(4) PINI.
[160] Art 13(2) PINI.
[161] Art 5(5) PINI.
[162] Art 5(5) PINI.
[163] Art 7(1) PINI.
[164] Weatherill, 'The Protocol on Ireland/Northern Ireland: Protecting the EU's Internal Market at the Expense of the UK's', 45 *ELRev* (2015) 222.
[165] E.g. Michel Barnier, *Speech at the William J Clinton Leadership Institute* (27 January 2020).
[166] Art 12(1) PINI. Note a similar acceptance, in a less controversial context, under the Cyprus Protocol. Contrast, e.g. with Michel Barnier, *Speech on German Employers' Day 2017* (29 November 2017).

stand accused of failing to tackle serious border fraud as regards the importation of third country goods into the Single Market.[167]

However, those British authorities enforcing Union law in Northern Ireland will be subject to certain forms of Union supervision—including the duty to provide information on request, the right of Union representatives to be present during relevant activities, and even the power of Union officials to order their UK colleagues to carry out control measures in individual cases for duly stated reasons.[168] Moreover, as regards the core Union rules made applicable to Northern Ireland by the Protocol,[169] the Union's institutions, bodies, and agencies etc shall exercise those powers conferred upon them by or under the Treaties.[170] In that regard, the Protocol specifies several particularly noteworthy features. For example, the relevant Union entities are to exercise their applicable powers in relation to the entire UK, as well as natural and legal persons resident or established anywhere in the UK—not just in relation to, or those located in, Northern Ireland itself. The text also makes particular reference to the jurisdiction of the CJEU—including the possibility that all competent UK courts can make preliminary references as regards relevant provisions of the Protocol or Union law made applicable thereunder.[171] In addition, the relevant acts of competent Union entities must produce the same legal effects for the UK as they do within the Union and its Member States. Poor Brexiters—there really is no escape from direct effect and primacy.[172]

B. Northern Ireland and the Rest of the UK

In the second place, the Protocol also makes provision for Northern Ireland's future place within the UK's own trading system. The starting point is supposedly that Northern Ireland will form part of the customs territory of the UK;[173] and the placing of goods on the Northern Irish market will take place in accordance with UK law.[174] And indeed, the Johnson Government has repeatedly claimed that, under its 'great new Brexit deal', there will be no border of any kind down the Irish Sea.[175] But those initial propositions are entirely subject to (and the UK's political claims are directly

---

[167] Case C-213/19, *Commission v United Kingdom* (pending). But note Art 5(6) PINI: Union customs duties collected by the UK are not remitted to the Union; and (subject to Union state aid rules) the UK may (e.g.) reimburse such duties or compensate undertakings to offset the impact of Union customs legislation. See also Art 7 PINI on the remission of VAT and excise duties.

[168] Arts 12(2)–(3) PINI. Note also Arts 13(5)–(6) PINI on limits to access to Union databases etc/acting as lead authorities etc by UK authorities.

[169] Specifically: Art 5 PINI on customs and goods; Art 7 PINI on technical assessments and approvals etc; Art 8 PINI on VAT and excise; Art 9 PINI on the Single Electricity Market; Art 10 PINI on state aid; and Art 12(2), second subparagraph PINI on monthly information exchanges as regards liability to pay customs duties in accordance with Arts 5(1)–(2) PINI.

[170] Art 12(4) PINI. Note, in particular, Art 13(1) PINI: Part Six of the Agreement shall apply without prejudice to the provisions of this Protocol.

[171] See also Arts 12(6)–(7) PINI.

[172] Art 12(5) PINI.

[173] Art 4 PINI.

[174] Art 7(1) PINI.

[175] See, e.g. https://www.theguardian.com/politics/2019/nov/08/boris-johnson-goods-from-northern-ireland-to-gb-wont-be-checked-brexit.

contradicted by) the explicit obligations contained in the Protocol as well as Union law made applicable to Northern Ireland thereunder.[176] The relevant obligations are sufficiently extensive that Northern Ireland's position within the UK trading system can at best politely be described as 'complicated'.

To begin with, customs and regulatory checks will indeed take place on trade between Northern Ireland and Great Britain—something which we were told no British Prime Minister could ever agree to, because it would destroy the sovereignty and integrity of the UK.[177]

On the one hand, trade *from Great Britain into Northern Ireland* will be subject to all relevant border checks in accordance with Union customs rules; and GB goods must be placed on the Northern Irish market in accordance with the applicable Union legislation.[178] The Joint Committee may make recommendations to avoid or minimize controls at Northern Ireland's ports and airports.[179] But future EU–UK regulatory divergence may well mean (for example) that toys manufactured in England or Scotland, even with no ambition for export beyond the UK, nevertheless still need to be adapted specifically for the Northern Irish market.

On the other hand, as regards trade *from Northern Ireland to Great Britain*, the Johnson Government maintained its predecessor's promise to guarantee 'unfettered market access' to England, Scotland, and Wales.[180] Yet the plain text of the Protocol makes it clear that that is not entirely true: the Agreement specifically envisages certain trade restrictions from Northern Ireland to Great Britain (for example, as regards controlled goods subject to international export requirements).[181] In any case, the UK will still need to know which goods coming from Northern Ireland are in fact of EU rather than purely domestic origin (for example, insofar as necessary to apply UK customs duties in compliance with its WTO obligations).[182]

The highly specific provisions governing Northern Ireland's trade with Great Britain aggravate an already complex and sensitive task: deciding on the future design and operation of the UK internal market itself.[183] Readers may be aware that UK devolution was only created during and within the context of EU membership. The devolved authorities have since been promised that Brexit will lead to a significant increase in their local autonomy.[184] Like any other state divided into territories with independent regulatory powers, the UK now needs to decide which domestic barriers to trade and distortions of competition are to be considered unacceptable; as well as which principles, instruments and institutions will ensure the smooth functioning of its own

---

[176] Arts 4 and 7(1) PINI.

[177] E.g. Theresa May, *Statement on the Salzburg Summit* (21 September 2019).

[178] E.g. Michel Barnier, *Speech at the European Economic and Social Committee: Le choix de la responsabilité, le choix du partenariat* (30 October 2019).

[179] Art 6(2) PINI.

[180] Indeed, in the very text of Art 6(1) PINI. Cp. Joint Report from the EU and UK negotiators (8 December 2017), at para 50.

[181] Art 6(1) PINI.

[182] I.e. the 'most favoured nation' principle.

[183] Further, e.g. https://www.youtube.com/watch?v=kLRMjDUbOA8. We will return to this point in our concluding Chapter 10.

[184] E.g. HMG, *The Future Relationship between the United Kingdom and the European Union* (Cm 9593 of 17 July 2018).

internal market. Those discussions have already proved controversial and remain as yet unresolved—not least given the inherent demographic, economic, and constitutional superiority of England over its smaller and more vulnerable partners.[185] But the fact that Northern Ireland will now be governed by very different domestic trade rules means that the UK internal market will be asymmetrical from the very moment of its birth.

In addition, recall that Johnson insisted on Northern Ireland being formally included within the UK customs territory and thus able to share in the aspirant benefits of an independent UK trade policy (for example, through reduced tariffs on trade with third countries).[186] But as a direct result, Northern Ireland will become subject to two distinct customs regimes running simultaneously in respect of the same territory. The Protocol foresees a nightmarish system for determining and administering which goods pay Union duties, UK duties, or no duties at all.[187] The presumption is that Union duties should apply to all goods entering Northern Ireland from outside the Union itself; unless it is proven (in accordance with more detailed criteria to be adopted by the Joint Committee) that the relevant goods are not at risk of subsequently being moved into the Union (whether by themselves or as part of other goods following processing); in which case they will pay UK duties (if originating from a third country) or no duties (if they come from Great Britain).[188] The Protocol also foresees a system of refunds by the UK authorities, for example, in respect of goods shown not to have entered the Union.[189]

The whole model is reminiscent of the 2018 Chequers Plan for a 'customs partnership' between the EU and the UK as a whole—proposals which were widely dismissed at the time as untested, speculative, massively bureaucratic, and damaging to competitiveness.[190] Yet Northern Ireland is now being used as the guinea pig for precisely such a scheme and risks being left worse off under the Johnson Protocol than it would have been under the previous backstop proposals from either the Commission or Theresa May.

C. Lifespan of the No-Longer-A-Backstop

In the third place, the Protocol ponders its own anticipated longevity and eventual mortality. In theory, the entire system will continue to apply, unless and until replaced

---

[185] Further, e.g. M. Dougan, *Briefing Paper on the UK Internal Market,* Finance and Constitution Committee of the Scottish Parliament (June 2019) available at https://www.parliament.scot/S5_Finance/Meeting%20Papers/Public(6).pdf.

[186] Art 4 PINI. Note the widespread suspicion that one of Johnson's primary motivations in this regard was to allow the UK Government to avoid infringing the statutory limitations imposed under section 55 Taxation (Cross Border Trade) Act 2018. See further the discussion in Chapter 3.

[187] Art 5 PINI.

[188] Art 5 PINI also provides for certain customs exemptions, e.g. personal property of UK residents; consignments of negligible value; goods sent between individuals; goods contained in travelers' personal baggage.

[189] Art 5(6) PINI.

[190] HMG, *The Future Relationship between the United Kingdom and the European Union* (Cm 9593 of 17 July 2018).

in whole or in part by any new EU–UK deal.[191] But in practice, that is unlikely to happen, given the revised preferences of the Johnson Government for the future EU–UK relationship.[192] So in reality, and as the Commission has repeatedly stressed, the border arrangements contained in the Protocol should be treated as permanent.[193]

For that reason, the parties agreed to create not only various dedicated governance tools to help promote the smooth long-term functioning of the Protocol;[194] but also a specific 'consent mechanism' to ensure that the population of Northern Ireland might periodically reaffirm their willingness to remain subject to the border provisions contained in the Protocol.[195] On a rolling basis, commencing four years after the end of the transition period, if the border regime receives cross-community support within the Northern Irish Assembly, it will extend for another eight years, or if there is a simple majority but without cross-community support, the relevant Protocol provisions will extend for another four years; whereas in the event of non-consent, the border arrangements will cease to apply after a further two years of operation (giving at least some time for all relevant parties to decide/prepare for what might happen next).[196]

In effect, for as long as they remain within the UK, and for as long as the latter remains outside the EU, the Northern Irish get to decide whether they would rather have a hard border than continue to live with the Protocol.[197] But at least the consent-conditionality provision in the Protocol makes it easier to reconcile with Article 50 TEU as a legal basis supposedly limited to settling 'orderly withdrawal' issues, rather than establishing long-term future relations.[198]

9. The UK's Implementation Plans

The final Protocol is relatively detailed and precise in its substantive provisions, but it is certainly not entirely self-standing: the full rigour of the regime that will become applicable to and in Northern Ireland now depends upon a range of future choices explicitly reserved to the Joint Committee (for example, about determining when goods entering Northern Ireland from outside the Union are not to be presumed 'at risk' of entering also the Single Market); as well as upon the more detailed implementation plans that inevitably need to be adopted by the competent UK authorities (for

---

[191] Art 13(8) PINI.

[192] See further Chapter 9.

[193] E.g. Michel Barnier, *Remarks at the press conference on the Commission Recommendation to the European Council to endorse the agreement reached on the revised Protocol on Ireland/Northern Ireland and revised Political Declaration* (17 October 2019). In particular, note the deletion, from the final version of the Protocol, of original Arts 1(4), 2–3 and 20 First PINI as agreed in November 2018 (which stressed the purely temporary nature of the 'backstop' provisions): see OJ 2019 C 66 I.

[194] Art 14 PINI (specialized committee) and Art 15 PINI (joint consultative working group).

[195] Specifically: Arts 5–10 PINI.

[196] See the detailed provisions contained in Art 18 PINI. Also: HMG, *Declaration Concerning the Operation of the 'Democratic Consent in Northern Ireland' Provision of the Protocol on Ireland/Northern Ireland* (19 October 2019). Cp. the original consent provisions contained in Joint Report from the EU and UK negotiators (8 December 2017), at para 50.

[197] Note also HMG, *Position of the Government on the Terminability of the Protocol on Ireland/Northern Ireland to the Agreement on Withdrawal of the United Kingdom from the European Union* (17 October 2019).

[198] See further the discussion in Chapter 4.

example, concerning the customs formalities that should be completed by operators in Great Britain in order to place their goods lawfully on the market in Northern Ireland).[199] Needless to say, should the UK's planned implementation fail to meet the Union's own expectations about the obligations prescribed under the Protocol, any such disagreement might well provoke a formal dispute between the parties that would have to be settled in accordance with the mechanisms provided for under the Withdrawal Agreement.[200]

Moreover, those choices and plans need to be adopted in sufficient time for all relevant public and private sector actors to familiarize themselves with, and prepare for the entry into force of, the new trading regime—surely well in advance of the anticipated expiry of the transition period, when the new border arrangements contained in the Protocol are due to take effect. Since the Johnson Government made clear, from the time of the UK general election in December 2019, that it would not be requesting any extension of the transition period as provided for under the final Withdrawal Agreement, that meant the relevant provisions of the Protocol would need to be fully operational by 1 January 2021.[201]

As if that timescale were not challenging enough, the task facing Northern Ireland was further complicated by the fact that the Johnson Government was accused of repeatedly misrepresenting the true nature and actual implications of the border arrangements it had proposed and agreed under the Protocol.[202] Indeed, the Union was obliged to contradict various claims made about the new border arrangements by the UK Government.[203] When the Joint Committee and the Specialised Committee on the Protocol on Ireland/Northern Ireland were then formally inaugurated, the Commission was moved publicly to remind the UK of the overriding need to prepare for and respect its obligations under the Protocol—not least when it came to the publication of the necessary British plans for effective application and enforcement.[204] Moreover, the Commission published a technical note listing the specific obligations the UK was expected to fulfil under the terms of the Protocol—reiterating the importance of full and effective compliance, stressing the urgency to act in order to meet the applicable deadlines, and calling upon the UK to avail itself of the Commission's offers of dialogue and assistance.[205]

On a more positive note, the DUP and Sinn Féin finally agreed to the resumption of power-sharing in January 2020—the former apparently chastened not only by its 'betrayal' at the hands of the Johnson Government, but also by the electoral results of

[199] See section 8C, section 10(1), section 10(2)(b) and Part 1C of Schedule 2 of the EU(W)A 2018 (as amended by EU(WA)A 2020).

[200] See further Chapter 6.

[201] See further the detailed discussion in Chapter 6.

[202] See, e.g. https://www.theguardian.com/politics/2019/nov/08/boris-johnson-goods-from-northern-ireland-to-gb-wont-be-checked-brexit.

[203] See, e.g. https://www.theguardian.com/politics/2020/jan/27/customs-checks-needed-on-irish-sea-trade-after-brexit-eu; referring to Michel Barnier, *Speech at the William J Clinton Leadership Institute* (27 January 2020).

[204] E.g. Commission, *Statement following the first meeting of the EU–UK Joint Committee* (30 March 2020); *Statement following the first meeting of the Specialised Committee on the Protocol on Ireland/Northern Ireland* (30 April 2020).

[205] Commission, *Technical Note on the Implementation of the Protocol on Ireland/Northern Ireland*, UKTF (2020) 16 of 30 April 2020.

December 2019 (when for the first time, unionist parties no longer took a majority of Northern Ireland's seats in Westminster).[206] The Northern Irish institutions were thus operational again by the time the UK Government published its initial proposals for implementation of the Protocol in May 2020.[207] However, the positive atmosphere was not to last: critical scrutiny quickly highlighted several issues and potential problems with the UK's plans.

Some of those issues related to the UK's general framing of the new Northern Irish border and trade arrangements. For example: the UK claimed that implementation of the Protocol should be determined by the Government's 'overall aims of preserving and strengthening Northern Ireland's place in our United Kingdom, and of protecting the huge gains from the peace process and [Good Friday] Agreement'.[208] Whether or not that unusual ordering of priorities was intended to be revealing, it is certainly true that the EU's interest in protecting the integrity of the Customs Union and the Single Market was simply not regarded as falling among the (shared) responsibilities of the UK Government under the Withdrawal Agreement. Moreover, the UK repeatedly argued that the Protocol was not envisaged to be a permanent solution to the border problem (given the requirement for the subsequent grant and periodic renewal of consent by the devolved institutions in Northern Ireland).[209] And putting those two claims together, the UK Government ended up going even further: pending its endorsement by the authorities in Belfast, the Protocol should be treated merely as a provisional arrangement and, until such approval is granted, 'the Government's priority is to ensure that we deliver the Protocol in a way which protects Northern Ireland's place in the UK customs territory'.[210]

Of course, there is no textual basis in the Withdrawal Agreement itself for that interpretation: the UK Government is effectively redefining the multifaceted objectives of the Protocol so as to serve its own particular interests, not least through the filter of some novel temporal rule that seeks to repurpose the entire Protocol during its initial phase of introduction and operation. Yet the UK claimed that—for all those reasons—the relevant provisions of the Protocol now needed to be applied proportionately, flexibly, and pragmatically.[211] Indeed: 'implementation must be consistent with the reality that Northern Ireland may choose in as little as four years' time to disapply these provisions'.[212]

One might well agree that proportionality is an appropriate criterion for exercising discretionary choices and powers within the terms of the Protocol—though as any competent lawyer knows, the meaning and effect of any proportionality assessment are vitally conditioned by one's prior definition of what the very purpose and more

[206] See, e.g. https://www.theguardian.com/uk-news/2020/jan/10/northern-ireland-assembly-to-reopen-after-three-year-suspension.

[207] HMG, *The UK's Approach to the Northern Ireland Protocol* (CP226 of 20 May 2020).

[208] HMG, *The UK's Approach to the Northern Ireland Protocol* (CP226 of 20 May 2020), at para 3.

[209] HMG, *The UK's Approach to the Northern Ireland Protocol* (CP226 of 20 May 2020), at paras 4, 8 and 16.

[210] HMG, *The UK's Approach to the Northern Ireland Protocol* (CP226 of 20 May 2020), at para 14.

[211] HMG, *The UK's Approach to the Northern Ireland Protocol* (CP226 of 20 May 2020), at paras 4, 5, 6 and 10. Note also para 12, which argues for a proportionate application of the Protocol, given the trade statistics between Northern Ireland and Great Britain.

[212] HMG, *The UK's Approach to the Northern Ireland Protocol* (CP226 of 20 May 2020), at para 16.

precise terms of the relevant provisions and powers should be. So, having attempted to repurpose the Protocol in the service of its own internal priorities, the UK's suggestion of a proportionate approach already sounded rather more suspect than a casual reader might suppose. But in any case, the Government's call for a flexible and pragmatic application of the Protocol simply sounded like an ill-disguised effort to depart from or indeed rewrite the existing text and terms of the Withdrawal Agreement—even those provisions which are in fact clear and precise, and regardless of the scope for making discretionary choices or powers—a point well-illustrated by some of the more detailed examples below.

Other problems arising from the UK's initial proposals related more to particular provisions within the Protocol. For example, while the UK was prepared publicly to admit that international law required the imposition of at least certain checks on the movement of particular categories of goods from Northern Ireland to Great Britain,[213] the Government was otherwise at pains to insist that Northern Irish goods would enjoy unfettered access to the rest of the UK market:[214] trade from Northern Ireland should take place as it does now, with no additional processes or paperwork, and no restrictions on Northern Irish goods arriving in England, Scotland, or Wales.[215] Yet the UK proposals gloss over how this blanket promise should relate to the crucial task of distinguishing Northern Irish goods from those originating either in the Union or from elsewhere in the world—since those latter categories of product would not be entitled to enjoy the same privileged treatment when it came to being traded in Great Britain. The UK Government at least admits that that challenge exists: '[t]hese arrangements [on market access for Northern Irish goods] will not cover goods travelling from Ireland or the rest of the EU being exported to Great Britain. The UK's customs and regulatory regime will apply to EU goods and businesses exporting to Great Britain'.[216] But it is rather difficult to see how privileged goods can be separated from non-privileged goods without some form of process or paperwork—as indeed even the UK Government seems to accept, since its proposals explicitly discuss the need to establish and define a 'qualifying status' for goods and businesses in Northern Ireland that will benefit from unfettered access to the market in Great Britain.[217]

Or again, the UK proposals entirely brushed over the crucial fact that goods entering Northern Ireland from outside the Union would be presumed to be 'at risk' of entering also the Single Market, and therefore have to pay customs duties in accordance with the Union tariff regime, unless proven otherwise in accordance with the more detailed criteria that would be decided by the Joint Committee.[218] More importantly, the Government also seemed keen to rewrite the clear provisions of the Protocol, to give effect to the idea that Union duties should only be payable where there was a clear, genuine, and substantial risk of the relevant goods being imported

---

[213] HMG, *The UK's Approach to the Northern Ireland Protocol* (CP226 of 20 May 2020), at para 22.

[214] Indeed: the UK Government reiterates its promise to legislate for that purpose, e.g. HMG, *The UK's Approach to the Northern Ireland Protocol* (CP226 of 20 May 2020), at paras 10 and 19.

[215] See HMG, *The UK's Approach to the Northern Ireland Protocol* (CP226 of 20 May 2020), at paras 17 and 19–21.

[216] HMG, *The UK's Approach to the Northern Ireland Protocol* (CP226 of 20 May 2020), at para 23.

[217] HMG, *The UK's Approach to the Northern Ireland Protocol* (CP226 of 20 May 2020), at para 24.

[218] See Art 5 PINI.

to Northern Ireland then onwards into the Single Market—effectively a reversal of the presumption, as well as an extensive redrafting of the legal test, actually contained under the Protocol.[219] Moreover, the UK also suggested that the grounds upon which goods entering Northern Ireland should be exempt from Union duties might include perishable products and situations where it would be 'uneconomical' for the products in question to be diverted into the Single Market—as if the Republic of Ireland did not also constitute an integral part of the Union, fully capable of receiving perishable goods, and perfectly amenable to cost-effective onward transportation.[220]

Further problems arose from a reading of the UK's proposals on the practical application and enforcement of the border and trade arrangements set out under the Protocol. For example, the UK insisted that, '[a]lthough there will be some limited additional process on goods arriving in Northern Ireland [from Great Britain], this will be conducted taking account of all flexibilities and discretion, and we will make full use of the concept of de- dramatisation'.[221] In particular: when the competent British authorities are applying relevant Union customs rules (say) concerning compliance checks and risk assessments, it would be perfectly legitimate to assume that UK goods did not pose the same level of risk to the Union's legal and financial interests as goods originating from other third countries.[222] Yet neither Union customs law nor the Protocol itself provides the legal basis or justification for any such assumption. If anything, the UK's self-proclaimed determination to engage in regulatory divergence from the Union and its Member States warrants at least equal border vigilance in respect of goods from Great Britain as those from anywhere else.[223]

Or again, the UK promises to make full use of its powers under the Protocol to waive and/or reimburse any customs duties paid on goods entering Northern Ireland from outside the Union, even where such goods are indeed at risk of entering also the Single Market;[224] while at the same time promising to tackle any attempts to exploit the provisions of the Protocol for the purposes of cross-border smuggling and serious organized crime—for which purpose, the UK proclaims its commitment to using the latest technologies and risk/compliance techniques.[225] Details are to be published in due course—but not for the first time, it is unclear how far border technologies will address problems of serious fraud and criminal activity that the rest of the world has thus far been unable to resolve effectively.

Finally, it is worth highlighting the dispute which erupted over the Union's request to open some form of permanent presence at dedicated offices in Belfast, so as to

---

[219] See HMG, *The UK's Approach to the Northern Ireland Protocol* (CP226 of 20 May 2020), at paras 17 and 25.

[220] See HMG, *The UK's Approach to the Northern Ireland Protocol* (CP226 of 20 May 2020), at para 26.

[221] HMG, *The UK's Approach to the Northern Ireland Protocol* (CP226 of 20 May 2020), at para 17. Also paras 29–32; as well as paras 33–35 on agri-food.

[222] See HMG, *The UK's Approach to the Northern Ireland Protocol* (CP226 of 20 May 2020), at para 30. Also para 39.

[223] Curiously, even these very UK proposals boast about the economic opportunities offered by the freedom to diverge from EU standards: see HMG, *The UK's Approach to the Northern Ireland Protocol* (CP226 of 20 May 2020), at paras 58–59.

[224] HMG, *The UK's Approach to the Northern Ireland Protocol* (CP226 of 20 May 2020), at para 27. Note also para 36 on UK tariffs on goods from other third countries.

[225] HMG, *The UK's Approach to the Northern Ireland Protocol* (CP226 of 20 May 2020), at para 28.

facilitate the effective application of the Protocol and, in particular, those provisions authorizing Union participation in the relevant activities of the UK authorities as well as the direct exercise of Treaty-conferred powers by a range of Union institutions and agencies etc.[226] On any objective analysis, the Union's request appeared entirely reasonable, from a logistical and operational perspective, given the nature and extent of the implementation and enforcement powers and obligations clearly set out under the Protocol. However, the UK Government absolutely refused permission for the Union to open any such office in Belfast—arguing that the Union's request was not only unnecessary in order to fulfil the terms of the Protocol, but was in fact politically inappropriate because of the (alleged) risk that it would aggravate community tensions.[227]

The latter claim appeared to be substantiated largely by the objections of hardline unionist politicians—hardly a strong basis upon which a responsible and even-handed government should conceive or manage sensitive community relations, particularly since no weight appears to have been given to the fact that a substantial proportion of the population in Northern Ireland are Union citizens and might well regard it as a serious affront for *their* Union to be barred from maintaining any meaningful presence in Belfast. In any case, there are strong grounds for arguing that, by preventing the Union from opening an office from which its staff could effectively carry out their proper powers and agreed duties under the Protocol, the UK has failed to uphold its own obligations under Article 5 WA—which requires the parties 'in full mutual respect and good faith [to] assist each other in carrying out tasks which flow from this Agreement' and to 'take all appropriate measures, whether general or particular, to ensure fulfilment of the obligations arising from this Agreement and [to] refrain from any measures which could jeopardise the attainment of the objectives of this Agreement'.

On 12 June 2020, the Commission delivered a public statement following the second meeting of the EU–UK Joint Committee, in which it stressed the scale of the tasks that remained to be completed before expiry of the transition period—'in particular with regard to the Protocol on Ireland/Northern Ireland'.[228] Although the Union welcomed publication of the UK's initial proposals for implementation of the new border arrangements, the Commission stressed that those plans still lacked sufficient operational details about how the UK would meet all its obligations under the Protocol, rigorously and effectively, as from 1 January 2021—from putting in place all the necessary checks and controls for goods entering Northern Ireland from Great Britain, to enabling Union officials effectively to exercise their right to be present during relevant activities of the competent UK authorities.

Michel Barnier has been even more explicit in his criticism of the UK's initial proposals for implementation: for example, not only stressing the urgent need for more details to be settled 'if we want to move from aspiration to operation'; but also directly asserting that certain of the UK's specific proposals—including to avoid exit declarations on goods moving from Northern Ireland to Great Britain—are simply

---

[226] See Art 12 PINI.

[227] See HMG, *The UK's Approach to the Northern Ireland Protocol* (CP226 of 20 May 2020), at paras 53–55.

[228] Commission, *Press statement by Vice-President Maroš Šefčovič following the second meeting of the EU-UK Joint Committee* (12 June 2020).

incompatible with the legal commitments accepted by the UK under the Protocol.[229] And if the stakes were not already high enough, the Union has also repeatedly affirmed its view that timely and effective implementation of the Withdrawal Agreement in general, and the Protocol on Ireland/Northern Ireland in particular, are considered an essential prerequisite for building mutual trust and confidence between the Union and the UK as they seek to negotiate the terms of their future relationship in fields such as trade and security.[230]

Yet it is perhaps another unpromising sign that the Johnson Government intends to adopt an uncooperative or even actively obstructionist approach to the operation of the Irish border arrangements, that the UK refused to agree to any of the Union's proposals for the Joint Committee to enact various minor technical amendments to the Protocol on Ireland/Northern Ireland—changes that the Commission argued were necessary in order to correct alleged deficiencies and omissions, made largely as a result of drafting oversights in the annexed lists of Union acts, and deemed relevant to protecting the integrity of the Single Market and facilitating the smooth functioning of the Protocol itself.[231]

10. Concluding Remarks

The Good Friday Agreement was meant to bring relative stability to Northern Ireland—offering time and space for divisions to heal and differences to soften. Although the peace process never explicitly or strictly required the UK to remain a member of the EU, British participation in the Union—alongside the Republic—was certainly an important component in the constitutional and legal environment that facilitated and underpinned the peace process. And so, after the 2016 referendum, anything but the softest of soft Brexits was bound to be a problem for the island of Ireland. Now that the Johnson Government is determined to pursue a hard Brexit (deal or no deal), the challenges facing the North and the Republic have been rendered considerably worse than they need otherwise have been. The common hope is that the revised Protocol will provide a credible and durable solution to the Irish border problem that not only protects the still-fragile peace in Northern Ireland, but also respects the Union's legitimate customs and regulatory concerns, while also satisfying the UK's political demand for an independent trade policy.

But the Protocol contains considerable economic risks for every relevant party.[232] The Union's own external frontier will soon be policed by a third country which has

---

[229] Commission, *Press Statement by Michel Barnier following Round 4 of negotiations for a new partnership between the EU and the UK* (5 June 2020).

[230] E.g. Commission, *Statement by the European Commission following the first meeting of the EU-UK Joint Committee* (30 March 2020); *Press Statement by Michel Barnier following the second round of future relationship negotiations with the UK* (24 April 2020); *Press Statement by Michel Barnier following Round 3 of negotiations for a new partnership between the EU and the UK* (15 May 2020); *Press Statement by Michel Barnier following Round 4 of negotiations for a new partnership between the EU and the UK* (5 June 2020); *Press statement by Vice-President Maroš Šefčovič following the second meeting of the EU-UK Joint Committee* (12 June 2020).

[231] See the Commission's proposed amendments as published in COM(2020) 195 Final. Contrast with the final Decision 1/2020 adopted by the EU–UK Joint Committee as published at OJ 2020 L 225/53.

[232] Even allowing for the various safeguard clauses contained in the Protocol: Arts 13(7), 16 and 17 PINI.

already proven itself unreliable in that task and whose Government has repeatedly made misleading statements about its own obligations under its own Agreement. The Union's concerns can only have been reinforced by the UK's initial proposals for implementing the Protocol, which contain worrying signs that the Johnson Government might indeed be positively intent on distorting and/or evading even its clear legal commitments.

As for the UK, the exceptional provisions concerning Northern Ireland contained in the revised Protocol create additional uncertainty and disruption for the fledgling British 'internal market'—a major constitutional and policy project whose design and operation were already marked by difficult tensions with Wales, but especially with Scotland. The Government's refusal to request an extension to the transition period has created additional pressure to settle as quickly as possible the basic terms of trade within the domestic UK market—pressure that might still result in a solution being imposed unilaterally from London and against the wishes of the administrations in Edinburgh and Cardiff.[233]

And when it comes to Northern Ireland itself, political salesmen like to claim that it will soon occupy a uniquely privileged position, enjoying the best of both worlds by straddling both the EU and the UK markets. But in reality, the Johnson Government has chosen to avoid a hard border across the island of Ireland by necessitating the introduction/expansion of appreciable and potentially significant trading hurdles across the Irish Sea; while the Protocol will introduce Northern Ireland to the experiment of a dual customs regime—an untested novelty once dismissed even by Johnson and his Leave allies as complex, damaging, and unworkable.

More importantly, this Protocol has the inherent potential to damage political stability within Northern Ireland. Of course, anything that impacts upon Northern Ireland's chances of economic growth will also have negative implications for the wider social and political environment within which the peace process must be managed. If the hope was always that greater prosperity would facilitate integration between Catholic nationalists and Protestant unionists, the fear must be that Brexit-induced material hardship will instead risk aggravating cross-community relations. But the problems are not merely economic. In the trade barriers erected across the Irish Sea, loyalists may come to perceive a serious threat to their British identity. Among republicans, Brexit in general and the Protocol in particular could well revive dreams of reunification far sooner than many had expected. It should be a cause of serious concern that the Protocol might effectively reduce the collective incentive to make the Good Friday Agreement work, at the same time as rekindling rather than defusing the tensions of sectarian identity politics.

Even a small risk that the Protocol system may simply break down is still too high— not least since every other pathway leading away from such a scenario would only present even greater problems of its own. For example: what would we do, if the Union were effectively forced to impose a hard border across the island of Ireland, so as to protect its own Customs Union and Single Market, faced with the intolerable provocation of a British government that simply refuses to respect and enforce the terms of

---

[233] See further the discussion in Chapter 10.

the Agreement and shows little concern about the impact of its own behaviour upon Northern Ireland? An unlikely, yet not entirely fanciful prospect. Would a better solution to the entire problem of Brexit and the difficulties of the revised Protocol really lie (as many now believe) in a border poll leading to Irish reunification within the Union? An entirely possible, yet still not straightforward outcome.[234] After all, there are also significant dangers in a premature push for reunification, before both main communities feel genuinely comfortable at the idea, and until we are sure that the Republic itself is willing and able to handle the consequences of such a momentous event.

[234] Note Art 1(1) PINI: 'This Protocol is without prejudice to the provisions of the 1998 Agreement in respect of the constitutional status of Northern Ireland and the principle of consent, which provides that any change in that status can only be made with the consent of a majority of its people'.

9

Future Relations Between the Union and the UK

1. Introduction

This chapter turns our attention away from the legally binding Withdrawal Agreement and instead towards the Political Declaration on future relations between the Union and the UK in fields such as trade and security. At the time of writing, the future EU–UK relationship is still a matter of ongoing negotiation between the two parties.[1] As and when more concrete terms emerge from those or any subsequent talks, those texts will doubtless provide the subject for extensive analysis. But for present purposes, we must be satisfied with highlighting some of the key constraints, preferences, and choices that have already shaped the negotiations thus far and will surely continue to influence their eventual outcomes and future prospects.

Section 2 begins by recalling some of the fundamental contextual points that need to be borne in mind when thinking about the future EU–UK relationship, particularly when it comes to economic affairs, and especially on the Union side: after all, the latter's long and extensive practice of international trade relations has already taught us many valuable lessons about the inherent challenges facing such negotiations, as well as the specific constitutional framework applicable to the Union's relevant activities, and the relative successes and limits reflected in existing third country relationships. Section 3 then provides an overview of the initial stages of the Article 50 TEU process, when both the Union and the UK began to articulate their respective preferences for the future relationship, as part of the pre-withdrawal 'preliminary and preparatory discussions' that had been mandated by the European Council.

Section 4 summarizes the revised Political Declaration of October 2019, that formed an integral part of the final Withdrawal Package endorsed and approved by the Union and the UK. That text foresees only a relatively shallow relationship between the two parties—certainly as compared to the years of UK membership of course, but even when set against other models for third country relations that had been proposed and discussed during the referendum campaign and thereafter. The Political Declaration was never intended to be legally binding or enforceable. Even so, as Section 5 explains, within weeks of the UK's withdrawal from the Union, the Johnson Government published new plans that made clear it did not regard itself even as morally bound by its own revised Political Declaration. Apparently, the already distant relationship foreseen in October 2019 was no longer distant enough for the new UK regime.

---

[1] Readers will recall that the cut-off date for developments to be incorporated into this book was 1 July 2020, i.e. immediately after the deadline for the EU and the UK to agree an extension of the transition period within the Joint Committee (as provided for in Art 132 WA).

The UK's Withdrawal from the EU. Michael Dougan, Oxford University Press. © Michael Dougan 2021.
DOI: 10.1093/oso/9780198833475.003.0009

In Section 6, we will explain how, when formal EU–UK negotiations on their future relations finally commenced, fundamental disagreements emerged almost immediately on a range of key issues: for example, the nature of the 'level playing field' commitments required to ensure fair competition under any free trade agreement; the relationship between continuing access by EU fishing fleets to UK waters (on the one hand) and continuing access by UK fish suppliers to the EU market (on the other hand); as well as the nature of the UK's safeguards for fundamental rights protection, based on the ECHR, as an essential prerequisite for cooperation with the Union in various fields of security, policing, and anti-terrorism.

Yet despite the clear obstacles erected in the path of reaching a meaningful agreement, the Johnson Government absolutely refused to request an extension to the post-withdrawal, status quo transition period (as provided for under the Withdrawal Agreement) in order to create more time for the negotiations. That position was upheld, even despite the onset of the global health and economic crisis caused by the Covid-19 pandemic—thereby risking an abrupt 'no deal Brexit' on 1 January 2021, or at least a major change in the fundamentals of EU–UK trade and security relations, in the midst of an already deeply challenging situation. Readers will know by now and for themselves whether and how far those risks actually materialized.

2. Contextual Considerations

A. A Familiar Agenda for International Cooperation

In any international negotiation aimed at promoting closer cooperation between the parties, particularly in the economic sphere, there are various fundamental issues that need to be addressed and agreed upon.[2]

Some such issues concern the substantive content of the agreement. What will be the basic scope and fields of cooperation covered by the agreement? What will be the ambition for the depth of market integration to be achieved within each relevant field? Which specific techniques and instruments will be employed by the parties in order to realize such ambitions for mutual cooperation? What should be the permissible exclusions from, limits to, or derogations from the planned degree of economic integration between the parties? What range of flanking policies will be necessary in order to prevent distortions of competition, restrict unfair competition, and otherwise ensure a level playing field?

Another set of fundamental issues concerns the governance and legal effects of the agreement. What institutional structures will be agreed, at the political and administrative levels, in order to operationalize the agreement? By which corpus of legal principles and judicial caselaw will the agreement be interpreted? What will be the significance for the smooth functioning of the agreement of any subsequent developments in the relevant legal framework of each party? Which dispute settlement

---

[2] See further, e.g. M. Dougan, *The Institutional Consequences of a Bespoke Agreement with the UK Based on a 'Close Cooperation' Model* (European Parliament, Policy Department for Citizens' Rights and Constitutional Affairs, at the request of the Constitutional Affairs Committee: PE 604.962 of May 2018).

mechanisms will the agreement employ, at a political and/or judicial level? What will be the system of sanctions, safeguards, and balancing measures under the agreement (say) as a consequence of a finding of non-compliance by one party with its obligations? What provisions (if any) will the agreement contain concerning its internal effects within the domestic legal system of each party?

In addition, the parties will be concerned about the compatibility of any agreement with their existing obligations. For example, is the agreement compatible with the internal constitutional requirements of each party? Or again, is the agreement consistent with the existing international commitments of each party (say) as regards obligations undertaken in the context of World Trade Organization membership?

When it comes to addressing that complex agenda of issues for negotiation and agreement, experience has obviously taught us some basic lessons about the underlying nature of and key challenges facing cross-border economic cooperation, particularly when it comes to agreements that aspire to a genuinely more ambitious level of market integration between the parties.

For example: in order to be truly ambitious, the agreement needs to extend beyond enhanced reductions in customs tariffs, basic guarantees of non-discrimination in the treatment of goods and services, and/or standard levels of cross-border regulatory cooperation between public authorities. It must seek also to tackle what is undoubtedly the main challenge in international trade: regulatory barriers to cross-border commerce which arise from mere differences in the way that separate jurisdictions legislate for and supervise the provision of goods and services within their respective territories.[3]

Moreover, such regulatory barriers are difficult enough to address in the field of goods, where the solution will often depend upon some degree of legislative convergence in the applicable public interest standards governing the manufacture and marketing of the relevant products, thereby paving the way for some degree of mutual recognition between the parties based upon a reciprocal principle of home state control. However, regulatory barriers are significantly more challenging to address when it comes to services, especially in highly sensitive and tightly regulated sectors. The relevant barriers generally relate more to intangible standards governing service quality (such as qualifications and competence) as well as amenability to ongoing supervision and effective sanction. A greater degree of legislative convergence, administrative cooperation, and mutual trust is thus required in order to facilitate a workable system of mutual recognition based on reciprocal home state control.[4]

It is therefore obvious that more ambitious agreements, seeking to deliver 'close cooperation' between the parties, involve the assumption of more extensive obligations, leading to commensurately more significant limits on domestic regulatory autonomy: the more ambitious the deal, the more extensive the obligations; the more extensive the obligations, the more a party's theoretical regulatory autonomy may be

---

[3] See further, e.g. A. Dashwood, M. Dougan, M. Ross, E. Spaventa and D. Wyatt, *Wyatt and Dashwood's European Union Law* (6th ed, 2011), at Chapters 14 and 17.

[4] See similarly, e.g. the in-depth analysis by F. Kainer for the IMCO Committee, *The Consequences of Brexit on Services and Establishment: Different Scenarios for Exit and Future Cooperation* (PE 602.035 of June 2017).

constrained in practice. And that is especially true when it comes to the governance and institutional arrangements underpinning the agreement. Indeed, the ambition of any international trade deal is strongly conditioned by the willingness of the parties to agree political, administrative, and judicial arrangements that will operationalize the agreement in a truly effective manner and allow for its smooth functioning even in the face of changing and/or problematic circumstances: for example, allowing for the dynamic evolution of cooperation; providing credible guarantees for even-handed implementation and enforcement; being capable of settling disputes and penalizing non-compliance in a satisfactory manner.[5]

And underpinning all these important lessons is another key reality of international trade negotiations: relative size matters. Put simply, larger economies will naturally seek to exercise a greater degree of influence over the 'rules of the game' upon which the proposed system of cross-border cooperation will be based; for example, when it comes to determining the basis for legislative convergence, setting the expectations for administrative cooperation, or identifying the principles of judicial interpretation. Smaller economies must decide how far that is a price worth paying, particularly for the benefits of an ambitious programme of 'close cooperation'.

B. The Union's Own Model of Cross-Border Trade Relations

When it comes to translating into more practical and detailed terms, both our overall agenda for pursuing greater cross-border economic integration, and our empirical lessons about what it means to pursue an ambitious level of cross-border cooperation, one model stands out from all others: the Union's own system for managing economic relations between its Member States.

After all, that Union model is generally recognized as the 'gold standard' in international trade. It is comprehensive in scope—based on the creation of a fully-fledged Customs Union together with an extensive Single Market covering all 'four freedoms' and extending across all economic sectors. It adopts a high level of ambition: economic integration should extend far beyond guarantees of non-discrimination, so as also to tackle regulatory barriers that arise from mere differences in national law. That ambition is to be achieved through uniquely advanced techniques of market integration, generally based upon complex combinations/degrees of Union-level harmonization, home state control, and mutual recognition. The Union also enshrines strong level playing field guarantees (competition rules, state aid controls, minimum standards of social protection in fields such as employment and the environment etc); as well as detailed flanking policies to facilitate the smooth functioning of the Single Market (in sectors such as data protection and consumer protection). The Union is endowed with autonomous legislative institutions (Council and European Parliament) capable of adopting the measures necessary to deliver the requisite degree of legislative convergence, administrative cooperation, and mutual recognition. The Union is also capable of effective administrative supervision and enforcement through the activities of the

---

[5] See similarly, e.g. Norberg, 'UK–EU relations after Brexit: Which arrangements are possible?', *Europarättslig Tidskrift* [2017] 469.

Commission and Union-level agencies; as well as the creation of close networks of cooperation among, and duties of effective implementation upon, national regulators and other public authorities. Last but not least: judicial supervision and enforcement is entrusted to the Court of Justice acting in partnership with the national courts of each Member State—based upon a highly developed body of principles and rules to govern the relationship between Union law and the domestic legal systems, aimed at securing the effective and uniform application of Union rules.

In the words of the Commission, the Union own model of market integration between the Member States in fact amounts to an 'ecosystem'—aptly capturing the idea of a complex of substantive and institutional rules and structures, which have co-evolved over a period of several decades, and have now become so interdependent and carefully balanced, that they cannot be disaggregated or unpicked, without risking the destabilization of the entire system.[6] Moreover, the unique nature of the Union's own model of market integration between the Member States has been recognized at a constitutional level by the Court of Justice, for example, in its 2014 *Opinion on Union accession to the European Convention on Human Rights*.[7] It is worth quoting the relevant passages in full:

> 157. As the Court of Justice has repeatedly held, the founding treaties of the EU, unlike ordinary international treaties, established a new legal order, possessing its own institutions, for the benefit of which the Member States thereof have limited their sovereign rights, in ever wider fields, and the subjects of which comprise not only those States but also their nationals ...
>
> ...
>
> 166.... [A]s the Court of Justice has noted many times, EU law is characterised by the fact that it stems from an independent source of law, the Treaties, by its primacy over the laws of the Member States ... and by the direct effect of a whole series of provisions which are applicable to their nationals and to the Member States themselves.
>
> 167. These essential characteristics of EU law have given rise to a structured network of principles, rules and mutually interdependent legal relations linking the EU and its Member States, and its Member States with each other, which are now engaged ... in a 'process of creating an ever closer union among the peoples of Europe'.
>
> 168. This legal structure is based on the fundamental premiss that each Member State shares with all the other Member States, and recognises that they share with it, a set of common values on which the EU is founded ... That premiss implies and justifies the existence of mutual trust between the Member States that those values will be recognised and, therefore, that the law of the EU that implements them will be respected.
>
> ...
>
> 172. The pursuit of the EU's objectives, as set out in Article 3 TEU, is entrusted to a series of fundamental provisions, such as those providing for the free movement of goods,

---

[6] See, e.g. Commission, *Internal EU27 preparatory discussions on the framework for the future relationship: 'Services'* (TF50 (2018) 28 of 6 February 2018). Also, e.g. Michel Barnier, *Speech at Hannover Messe* (23 April 2018).

[7] Opinion 2/13, *Accession to ECHR* (EU:C:2014:2454).

services, capital and persons, citizenship of the Union, the area of freedom, security and justice, and competition policy. Those provisions, which are part of the framework of a system that is specific to the EU, are structured in such a way as to contribute—each within its specific field and with its own particular characteristics—to the implementation of the process of integration that is the *raison d'être* of the EU itself.

173. Similarly, the Member States are obliged ... to ensure, in their respective territories, the application of and respect for EU law. In addition ... the Member States are to take any appropriate measure, general or particular, to ensure fulfilment of the obligations arising out of the Treaties or resulting from the acts of the institutions of the EU ...

174. In order to ensure that the specific characteristics and the autonomy of that legal order are preserved, the Treaties have established a judicial system intended to ensure consistency and uniformity in the interpretation of EU law.

175. In that context, it is for the national courts and tribunals and for the Court of Justice to ensure the full application of EU law in all Member States and to ensure judicial protection of an individual's rights under that law ...

It is automatically and inherently the case that—no matter how close—cross-border trade cooperation with third countries will fall short of the exceptional degree of integration provided by the Union's own internal economic model. Since third countries cannot be fully assimilated into the Union's unique substantive and institutional ecosystem, they can neither be subject to the same level of obligations and disciplines, nor enjoy the same range of rights and privileges.

C. Constitutional Concerns Specific to the European Union

Moreover, third countries and other international organizations that wish to negotiate with the Union must accept and live with several inescapable features of the EU's own internal constitutional order that together have an important influence upon the conduct of the Union's external relations. Three key issues are worth highlighting from the outset.

The first issue stems from the fundamental principle of conferred powers laid down in Article 5(2) TEU.[8] That principle requires that every Union action—including in the field of external relations—must find an appropriate legal basis under the Treaties. Each legal basis will prescribe the precise nature of the Union's competence to take external action, as well as the detailed procedure for the exercise of such competence. Each of those features will in turn influence the role (if any) to be played by the Member States themselves, over and above the functions ascribed to the Union's own institutions under the relevant Treaty provisions.[9]

---

[8] See further, e.g. Dashwood, 'The Limits of European Community Powers', 21 *ELRev* (1996) 113.

[9] Note also the important questions that can arise about the competence of the Union's various bodies and agencies to engage in international action/establish relations with third countries and other international organizations. See further, e.g. A. Ott, E. Vos and F. Coman-Kund, *EU Agencies and their International Mandate: A New Category of Global Actors?* (Centre for the Law of EU External Relations: Working Paper 2013/7); Chamon, 'A Constitutional Twilight Zone: EU Decentralised Agencies' External relations', 56 *CMLRev* (2019) 1509.

Of particular relevance here is the distinction—which we have already mentioned previously in Chapter 3—between exclusive and shared Union competence; together with the possibility of an external agreement being classified as a 'mixed agreement'.[10] The latter arises where: either an agreement involves shared competences and the Member States insist upon mixity as a political choice (which is the more common explanation);[11] or an agreement contains provisions falling altogether outside the Union's powers so that mixity becomes a positive constitutional requirement (though that is somewhat rarer).[12] Either way, mixed agreements need to be agreed and ratified also by the Member States themselves.[13] Even though the Treaty of Lisbon broadened the scope of the Union's exclusive external competences,[14] and the Court of Justice has since played its part in confirming their expansive interpretation,[15] rulings such as the *Opinion on the Singapore Free Trade Agreement* remind us that Union competences in general, and exclusive competences in particular, still have their limits and therefore the possibility of mixity remains an important element of Union external relations law.[16]

The second key issue concerns the constitutional principles developed by the Court of Justice so as to safeguard the 'autonomy of Union law'.[17] Those principles act as non-derogable limits to the exercise of Union external competences, with the purpose of protecting the internal functioning of the Union's own institutional system from the impact of any external interference or influence. We have mentioned the Court's caselaw on the autonomy of Union law in passing several times already, but now is the time and place to provide a more detailed outline.[18]

It is worth pointing out immediately that these principles have been developed using a caselaw methodology based on ad hoc judgments delivered over a considerable period of time. The relevant cases often invoke relatively nebulous concepts, which only make full sense when translated into their more fact-specific contexts. Moreover, it can sometimes be difficult to separate the specific principles which protect the 'autonomy

---

[10] See further, e.g. A. Dashwood, M. Dougan, M. Ross, E. Spaventa and D. Wyatt, *Wyatt and Dashwood's European Union Law* (6th ed, 2011), at Chapter 27.

[11] As with the EU–Ukraine Association Agreement or the Comprehensive Economic and Trade Agreement with Canada.

[12] See further, e.g. P. Koutrakos (ed.), *Mixed Agreements Revisited: The EU and Its Member States in the World* (2010).

[13] Subject to the possibility of a Council decision pursuant to Art 218(5) TFEU for provisional application by the Union of an international agreement before its entry into force. See further, e.g. van der Loo and Wessel, 'The Non-Ratification of Mixed Agreements: Legal Consequences and Solutions', 54 *CMLRev* (2017) 735; Driessen, 'Provisional Application of International Agreements by the EU', 57 *CMLRev* (2020) 741.

[14] Arts 3(1) and 3(2) TFEU; but particularly in the field of the common commercial policy under Art 207 TFEU.

[15] On Art 207 TFEU, e.g. Case C-414/11, *Daiichi Sankyo* (EU:C:2013:520); Case C-137/12, *Commission v Council* (EU:C:2013:675); Case C-389/15, *Commission v Council* (EU:C:2017:798). Though note rulings such as Opinion 3/15, *Marrakesh Treaty* (EU:C:2017:114).

[16] Opinion 2/15, *Singapore Agreement* (EU:C:2017:376). Note the clarification in Case C-600/14, *Germany v Council* (EU:C:2017:935).

[17] See, e.g. Opinion 1/91, *EEA Agreement* (EU:C:1991:490); Opinion 1/92, *EEA Agreement II* (EU:C:1992:189); Opinion 1/00, *European Common Aviation Area* (EU:C:2002:231); Cases C-402/05 and C-415/05, *Kadi* (EU:C:2008:461); Opinion 1/09, *European and Community Patents Court* (EU:C:2011:123); Case C-284/16, *Achmea* (EU:C:2018:158).

[18] See, e.g. Chapter 6 on the CJEU's essential role in dispute settlement by arbitration under the terms of the final WA.

of Union law' from other related concepts or rules that happen to arise in the same dispute or ruling.[19] Finally, one must be wary of assuming that extant Union international agreements fully and faithfully reflect the standards and expectations imposed by the caselaw on the autonomy of Union law: the degree of actual compliance might well depend upon various factors, such as the date of the relevant agreement, especially compared to the evolution of the pertinent caselaw; as well as whether any issue of (in)compatibility was specifically raised before the Court of Justice (say) before the agreement was finalized, ratified, and entered into force.[20]

Nevertheless, despite all those caveats, it is certainly possible to identify a core body of binding legal principles. To begin with, an international agreement cannot affect the essential character of the powers conferred upon the Union and the Union's own institutions by the Treaties: for example, by seeking to alter the distribution of competences laid down between the Union and its Member States or the distribution of powers laid down between the Union institutions inter se. In particular: while it is possible for an international agreement to confer additional external functions upon the Union institutions, in relation to the activities, authorities, or natural/legal persons of a third country, such external functions cannot affect the essential character of the powers conferred upon the Union institutions under the Treaties. For example, an international agreement may provide for the courts or tribunals of a third country to make preliminary references to the Court of Justice, concerning the interpretation of that agreement or Union law which is referred to thereunder; but the Court's interpretations delivered pursuant to such preliminary references must be explicitly treated as binding upon the relevant third country courts or tribunals—since the Treaties do not give the Court any power to provide advisory rulings on interpretation and a mere international agreement cannot create a type of judicial competence which does not already exist under the Treaties.[21]

In addition, an international agreement cannot bind the Union institutions to a particular interpretation of Union law as regards the exercise of their internal powers. To be more precise: in principle, an international agreement may well create a court or tribunal for its interpretation and the decisions of such court or tribunal may well be treated as binding upon the Union in general and the Court of Justice in particular. But neither an international agreement nor a court or tribunal created thereunder can infringe upon the Court's exclusive jurisdiction to decide on the definitive interpretation of Union law (both primary and secondary) for the purposes of the Union legal order itself. Nor can an international agreement deprive the Court of its power and

---

[19] E.g. the 'specific characteristics' of the Union legal order referred to in Opinion 2/13, *Accession to ECHR* (EU:C:2014:2454). See further, e.g. Contartese, 'The autonomy of the EU legal order in the ECJ's external relations case law: From the 'essential' to the 'specific characteristics' of the Union and back again', 54 *CMLRev* (2017) 1627.

[20] See further, e.g. de Witte, 'A Selfish Court? The Court of Justice and the Design of International Dispute Settlement beyond the European Union' in M. Cremona and A. Thies (eds), *The European Court of Justice and External Relations Law: Constitutional Challenges* (2016).

[21] However, for an interesting development in Union practice concerning the participation of third countries in the Union's institutional structures, and its relationship to the principles governing the autonomy of the Union legal system, see Bekkedal, 'Third state participation in EU agencies: Exploring the EEA precedent', 56 *CMLRev* (2019) 381.

duty to ensure the effective judicial protection of individual rights within the Union legal order, for example, when it comes to safeguarding respect for fundamental rights.

Furthermore, in its 2019 ruling concerning the compatibility with Union law of the Comprehensive Economic and Trade Agreement between the Union and Canada, the Court introduced another restriction on the powers that the Union may legitimately agree to confer upon courts or tribunals established pursuant to an external agreement with its international partners. Such courts or tribunals cannot be allowed to call into question the level of protection of a public interest that led the Union institutions to introduce restrictions on economic operators within the Internal Market. For example, for an international tribunal to enjoy jurisdiction to order the Union to pay damages to a third country investor based on the level of protection of a public interest established by the Union's institutions could create a financial incentive for the latter to abandon their chosen level of protection. If the Union were to enter into an international agreement capable of having the consequence that the Union (or indeed a Member State in the course of implementing Union law) has to amend or withdraw legislation because of an assessment made by a tribunal standing outside the Union's own judicial system, of the level of protection of a public interest established, in accordance with the EU constitutional framework, by the EU institutions, then such an agreement would undermine the Union's capacity to operate autonomously within its own constitutional framework. It is the task of the Union's own courts to ensure review of the compatibility of the level of protection of public interests established by Union legislation, in accordance with (inter alia) the Treaties, the Charter, and the general principles of Union law.[22]

In any case, the Court has held that ensuring consistency and uniformity in the interpretation of Union law is a joint responsibility shared also by the national courts of the Member States. On that basis, an international agreement cannot affect the autonomy and effectiveness of the preliminary reference procedure under Article 267 TFEU. Similarly, an international agreement cannot deprive the national courts of their power and duty to ensure the effective judicial protection of rights arising under Union law: for example, by purporting to establish a tribunal capable of adjudicating over Union provisions but whose activities (in the event of non-compliance with the standards expected under Union law) would not be subject to the possibility of enforcement proceedings brought by the Commission and/or of incurring liability to make reparation to individuals whose Union law rights were infringed.[23]

The third key issue concerns the particular status of international agreements within the Union legal order itself, which often creates a strong knock-on pressure to ensure reciprocity of internal legal effects (either by levelling-up or by levelling-down) with the Union's international partners. As we saw in Chapter 6, Article 216(2) TFEU provides that international agreements concluded by the Union are binding upon the Union institutions and the Member States and (in accordance with a well-established caselaw) the specific provisions of any given international agreement may be sufficiently clear, precise, and unconditional as to be capable of producing direct effect within the Union legal order as well as the domestic legal systems of the Member

---

[22] Opinion 1/17 (EU:C:2019:341).
[23] Joined Cases C-6/90 and C-9/90, *Francovich* (EU:C:1991:428).

States.[24] The potentially strong legal status offered to its international agreements within the Union's own legal system in turn creates the risk of certain 'enforcement asymmetries' with the Union's negotiating partners—especially in the case of agreements that contain relatively detailed and concrete rights and obligations; and particularly if the other international actor operates as a dualist legal order—giving full legal effect to its international obligations only through the medium of active domestic implementation.[25]

For those reasons, the Union often insists that its international agreements contain specific provisions to determine the appropriate legal status of the treaty within each contracting party: sometimes ruling out any direct internal legal effects; other times insisting upon explicit provisions to ensure such effects, either for the entire agreement or at least as regards parts thereof.[26] 'Levelling up' is particularly important in the case of any relationship aspiring to close cooperation between the Union and a third country, offering a generous degree of market access for the latter's goods and services, invariably based on convergence with the Union's own regulatory standards. As such, the Union will often insist upon clear guarantees to ensure the timely adoption and effective implementation of the relevant Union rules within that third country's domestic legal system.[27]

In certain respects, those various constitutional considerations and constraints—the procedural division between exclusive and shared competence, the substantive need to protect the autonomy of Union law and the enforcement concern to avoid legal asymmetries—act as effective limits on the Union's room for manoeuvre during international negotiations. For example: the prospect of mixity means that the Union must negotiate with third countries mindful of the need eventually to secure the active support of every single Member State, which includes anticipating and addressing the potential concerns and objections of each national (and where relevant regional) parliament.[28] Similarly: respecting the autonomy of Union law places inherent limits on the institutional structures that the Union might possibly be capable of designing under an international agreement—including the scope for third countries to participate in the Union's own decision-making processes; or the degree to which dispute

---

[24] I.e. in the light of the caselaw based on Case 12/86, *Demirel* (EU:C:1987:400).

[25] Though, of course, there are other issues and specific challenges when it comes to the enforcement (say) of level playing field obligations in international agreements: consider, e.g. Bronckers and Gruni, 'Taking The Enforcement of Labour Standards in the EU's Free Trade Agreements Seriously', 56 *CMLRev* (2019) 1591; Marín Durán, 'Sustainable Development Chapters in EU Free Trade Agreements: Emerging Compliance Issues', 57 *CMLRev* (2020) 1031.

[26] Contrast, e.g. the sophisticated enforcement provisions of the EEA Agreement with the limited internal legal effects of the EU–Canada agreement. Sometimes the CJEU itself addresses asymmetries through the criteria for direct internal legal effects of particular international agreements, e.g. as with the WTO agreements in Case C-149/96, *Portugal v Council* (EU:C:1999:574) and Case C-377/02, *Van Parys* (EU:C:2005:121). See further, e.g. Semertzi, 'The Preclusion of Direct Effect in the Recently Concluded EU Free Trade Agreements', 51 *CMLRev* (2014) 1125.

[27] See further, e.g. A. Dashwood, M. Dougan, M. Ross, E. Spaventa and D. Wyatt, *Wyatt and Dashwood's European Union Law* (6th ed, 2011), at Chapter 28.

[28] A point whose importance was reinforced by the experience of both the EU–Ukraine Association Agreement (impact of Dutch referendum) and the Comprehensive Economic and Trade Agreement with Canada (regional parliamentary ratification in Belgium).

settlement bodies can purport to engage in the interpretation of Union legal concepts or acts.[29]

But of course, such constraints may also act as a source of strength in the Union's international negotiations (particularly when combined with its sheer economic size and influence). For example, the need for individual approval from each Member State at the national level can offer the Union a useful backstop for resisting certain third country demands or insisting upon certain exemptions or safeguards. The negotiating potential of mixity is obviously enhanced in the case of agreements aiming at a close level of cooperation: after all, the more ambitious and wide-ranging the agreement, the more likely it will be to touch upon areas of shared competence between the Union and its Member States, and thereby qualify as a mixed agreement requiring individual national ratifications.

Similarly, the caselaw on protecting the autonomy of Union law has the potential to create a mutually reinforcing link between the substantive and the institutional aspects of any international trade agreement. Again, that is particularly true of any agreement providing for close cooperation between the Union and a third country. Such an ambitious degree of market integration can only be achieved through a relatively strong commitment to legislative convergence (as well as administrative cooperation and dispute settlement). Smaller economies will have to accept that such convergence will be based on the Union's own terms. As a matter of constitutional requirement, the core components of those Union terms must be both decided and interpreted autonomously by the Union institutions themselves.

For example: it is standard practice for the administration and implementation of an international trade agreement to be entrusted to a Joint Committee comprising representatives of both parties, able to adopt binding decisions as provided for under the agreement, acting by consensus/mutual agreement between the parties. The responsibilities of the Joint Committee will often include determining the implications for the smooth functioning of the agreement of developments in either the caselaw or the legislation of both the Union and the relevant third country; and acting as a political forum for the settlement of disputes that may arise between the parties concerning the interpretation and application of the agreement.[30]

In the case of a trade agreement characterized by relatively low levels of ambition as regards the promotion of economic integration between the parties (concentrating on the lowering or elimination of tariffs and making provision for limited forms/degrees of regulatory cooperation): Union law will usually play only a marginal role in defining the substantive content of the agreement and the Joint Committee may well perform its functions with little direct reference to Union legislation and caselaw.[31] However, when it comes to agreements which seek to create a stronger degree of cooperation with the Union (by seeking to integrate a third country into elements of the Customs Union and/or Single Market) the terms of engagement will be defined primarily by reference to the relevant provisions of Union law. As a direct result, the

---

[29] As with, e.g. Opinion 1/91, *EEA Agreement* (EU:C:1991:490); Opinion 1/09, *European and Community Patents Court* (EU:C:2011:123); Opinion 2/13, *Accession to ECHR* (EU:C:2014:2454).

[30] As indeed with the EU–UK WA itself: see Chapter 6.

[31] E.g. as with the Comprehensive Economic and Trade Agreement with Canada.

decision-making power and discretion of the Joint Committee will be inherently constrained by the need to respect the underpinning Union frameworks and concepts. For example, the third country may be obliged under the agreement to adapt its national law to new developments in Union legislation: the Joint Committee will generally be expected to update the relevant annexes to the agreement (possibly subject to certain adaptations or exemptions so as to accommodate the needs or interests of the third country) or otherwise to determine the negative consequences of legislative divergence for continued third country access to the Union market.[32] Similarly, in discharging its dispute settlement functions, the Joint Committee will usually be instructed to respect the relevant jurisprudence of the Court of Justice;[33] and (at least in the case of provisions of the agreement which are identical or equivalent in substance to Union rules or concepts) the parties may even be empowered to seek a binding interpretative ruling directly from the Court.[34]

D. Lessons from Existing EU–Third Country Relationships

The Union has concluded a large number of international agreements with third countries and other international organizations. Those agreements are highly diverse in terms of their subject matter, substantive content, governance arrangements, and framework for enforcement. This book is not grounded in external relations law and will not purport to provide a comprehensive analysis (or indeed an analysis based on comprehensive research). It is sufficient, for present purposes, to summarize some of the key common lessons and features shared particularly across those agreements that aspire to an enhanced level of cooperation between the Union and a negotiating partner—especially in the field of trade.[35]

First, and notwithstanding the conclusion of certain more sector-specific relationships, the basic scope of an ambitious cooperation relationship will be broad if not comprehensive. That is exemplified, as regards participation in the Single Market, by the European Economic Area and, as regards participation in the Customs Union, by the customs agreement with Turkey.[36] Secondly, within its scope of application, an ambitious agreement will seek to achieve a relatively high level of market integration with the relevant third country—aiming for as close as possible to the Union's own model of economic relations between the Member States. Thirdly, to deliver on that level of ambition, the techniques and disciplines of market integration need to be of a commensurately sophisticated nature and extent, which in practice means a close degree of alignment to the relevant Union *acquis* (as expressed in the expectation of

---

[32] The prime example being the work of the EEA Joint Committee.

[33] E.g. as with the Multilateral Agreement on the establishment of a European Common Aviation Area (see Art 20 thereof).

[34] Again, as under the EEA Agreement (see Art 111 thereof); or (broader still) the Multilateral Agreement on the establishment of a European Common Aviation Area (see Art 20 thereof).

[35] See further, e.g. M. Dougan, *The Institutional Consequences of a Bespoke Agreement with the UK Based on a 'Close Cooperation' Model* (European Parliament, Policy Department for Citizens' Rights and Constitutional Affairs, at the request of the Constitutional Affairs Committee: PE 604.962 of May 2018).

[36] On the latter, see Decision 1/95 of the EC–Turkey Association Council on implementing the final phase of the Customs Union (22 December 1995).

dynamic homogeneity). Fourthly, to realize an effective implementation and enforcement of those techniques and disciplines, the Union will seek to agree robust governance and institutional provisions. Such provisions must respect the autonomy of the Union's own law and institutions. They must also provide adequate guarantees against asymmetry when it comes to the legal effects of the agreement within the internal system of each party.

The strong Union law basis to such agreements therefore implies a basic trade-off: when it comes to seeking genuinely ambitious forms of cooperation with the Union in the economic sphere, the relevant third country needs to decide how far it is willing to adhere to extensive elements of Union law, with no direct decision-making participation in the formulation of such rules, and only limited opportunities for overall influence (taking into account, of course, also the legal constraints arising from its own constitutional order). The more extensive the alignment to the Union's own regulatory model, the greater the degree of economic integration that will be possible, but the more acute will be the loss of national decision-making autonomy. The less extensive the alignment to the Union model, the greater the degree of national decision-making autonomy, but the more limited will be the potential scope for economic integration with the Union.[37]

If anything, the underlying problems which have been identified with the Union's existing 'close cooperation' agreements—especially the EEA and the customs agreement with Turkey—confirm and reinforce the above analysis. Suffice for present purposes to recall the relevant issues only briefly.

In the case of the EEA,[38] its scope is surely ambitious, though still not comprehensive, since the EFTA–EEA states do not participate in the Customs Union (leading to complaints by Union businesses about the costs of customs procedures). Notwithstanding the central role of the Joint Committee and the characteristic 'two pillar' structure (including the functions and powers of the EFTA Surveillance Authority and EFTA Court), both the fundamental principle of dynamic homogeneity and the autonomy of Union law impose considerable constraints on the scope for deviation from the relevant Union *acquis*. Nevertheless, the goal of dynamic homogeneity can be complicated and/or risks of asymmetry or imbalance may materialize in practice due to a range of operational problems: for example, the Union's persistent concerns about increased EFTA–EEA state requests for adaptations to EEA-relevant acts; and about delays/problems of proper/timely implementation of EEA-relevant acts by the competent EFTA–EEA national authorities. Conversely, although the EFTA–EEA states (exemplified by Norway) regard the agreement as central to their fundamental domestic and foreign policy orientations, they also acknowledge the significant democratic costs entailed by their EEA membership.[39]

---

[37] See further, e.g. Łazowski, 'Enhanced Multilateralism and Enhanced Bilateralism: Integration Without Membership in the European Union', 45 *CMLRev* (2008) 1433.

[38] For examples of the Union's own evaluations of the EEA Agreement, see, e.g. Council, *Conclusions on a homogenous extended single market and EU relatons with Non-EU Western European countries* (16 December 2014); Commission Staff Working Document, *Country reports and info sheets on implementation of EU Free Trade Agreements*, SWD (2017) 364 Final (9 November 2017). See further, e.g. Fredriksen and Franklin, 'Of Pragmatism and Principles: The EEA Agreement 20 Years On', 52 *CMLRev* (2015) 629.

[39] See, in particular, Norwegian Government, *Outside and Inside: Norway's Agreements with the European Union* (Official Norwegian Reports NOU 2012:2 of January 2012).

The experience with Turkey is equally illuminating.[40] The scope of the agreement is limited to the creation of a partial customs union together with associated policies on trade in goods—falling short of a fully-fledged customs union that would eliminate all tariffs and customs processes, while also failing to cover (for example) trade in services or public procurement. The Union has expressed concerns about persistent problems of effective and timely implementation/compliance by the Turkish authorities, exacerbated by relatively underdeveloped governance and institutional structures, especially when it comes to judicial dispute settlement, as well as a marked asymmetry in the internal legal effects of the agreement within the Union as compared to Turkey. For its part, Turkey has also voiced reservations (first) about the strong Union law basis to the agreement, which again entails a significant degree of 'rule taking' by the Turkish authorities, who enjoy only limited opportunities for decision-making influence; and (secondly) about the lopsided effects of the agreement in relations with third countries, i.e. whereby Turkey must abide by the terms of free trade agreements concluded by the Union, without any guarantees of being able to benefit from the relevant preferences in Turkey's own trade relations with the same states. For those reasons, for example, the Commission proposed a significant modernization of the customs and trade relationship with Turkey, aimed at addressing both the Union's and Turkey's concerns, so as to improve the scope, depth, and smooth functioning of the parties' existing cooperation arrangements.[41]

E. Factors Specific to the United Kingdom

For its part, the UK lacks many of the constitutional constraints that make the Union's external relations law so relatively complex.[42] As a general proposition, the power to negotiate and conclude international agreements is vested solely in the central executive. The Westminster Parliament has a limited power of scrutiny, based on the ability (particularly of the House of Commons) to delay ratification of an international treaty;[43] while the devolved institutions in Scotland, Wales, and Northern Ireland lack even that opportunity for influence.[44] Of course, the Westminster Parliament could legislate to confer greater powers upon itself (or the devolved institutions) to

---

[40] See, in particular: Commission, *Study of the EU–Turkey Bilateral Preferential Trade Framework, Including the Customs Union, and an Assessment of Its Possible Enhancement* (Final Report of 26 October 2016). Note also: World Bank, *Evaluation of the EU-Turkey Customs Union* (Report No 85830-TR of 28 March 2014).

[41] See further, e.g. Commission Staff Working Document, *Executive Summary of the Impact Assessment accompanying the Recommendation for a Council Decision authorising the opening of negotiations with Turkey on an Agreement on the extension of the scope of the bilateral preferential trade relationship and on the modernisation of the Customs Union*, SWD (2016) 476 Final; and also European Parliamentary Research Service Briefing, *Reinvigorating EU-Turkey bilateral trade: Upgrading the customs union* (PE 599.319 of March 2017).

[42] See further, e.g. House of Commons Library Briefing Paper, *Parliament's Role in Ratifying Treaties* (No 5855 of 17 February 2017); and the more detailed discussion in Chapter 3.

[43] In accordance with Part Two of the Constitutional Reform and Governance Act 2010.

[44] Though the devolved authorities have various opportunities to exercise more informal influence over UK international affairs: see further, e.g. House of Commons Library Briefing Paper, *The Trade Bill* (No 8073 of 8 January 2018), at Chapter 5.

participate in the conduct and conclusion of international treaties—whether in general or in specific situations. But as the experience of the EU–UK Withdrawal Agreement itself demonstrates, whatever the conventions or statutes that might currently apply or be created anew, concerning the division of labour between executive and legislature, or between the central and devolved authorities, those can easily be overcome or overturned by a London Government possessed of a working Commons majority.[45] And there is no sign of any radical change in the UK's general constitutional approach within the foreseeable future: after winning the general election in December 2019, the Johnson Government immediately reneged upon its previous promise to offer Parliament greater powers to participate in the approval of whatever international agreements might govern future relations between the Union and the UK.[46]

Since a London Government that controls the Commons also enjoys virtually free rein in the conduct of international relations, the UK is not especially perturbed by the sorts of procedural issues (such as competence to ratify) or substantive constraints (like the autonomy of the legal order) that figure so prominently in the Union's calculations. However, there is one constitutional feature of the UK system that might still engage the concern of its negotiating partners: the strictly dualist nature of its domestic legal order requires all international agreements to be implemented into national measures—in the absence of which, such treaties cannot produce independent legal effects within the UK. Dualism makes the UK particularly prone to reservations about enforcement asymmetries, particularly when negotiating with a more monist system such as that of the Union.[47]

Dualism also means that it is at the stage of implementation (rather than negotiation or conclusion) that the Westminster Parliament, as well as the devolved institutions, perform their main constitutional functions in relation to international agreements.[48]

As for the Westminster Parliament, it is worth recalling that the domestic status of any international agreement not only requires a valid legislative basis for its initial implementation, but subsequently remains governed by and subject to the principle of parliamentary sovereignty.[49] Put simply, each Parliament enjoys unlimited legislative authority, such that no Parliament can bind its successors to a particular legislative regime; subsequent legislative measures will therefore take priority over all previous enactments, either through express repeal, or by implied repeal in the event of a conflict or incompatibility. It is constitutionally possible for Parliament to limit the practical possibilities of implied repeal: that was certainly the case with the European

---

[45] As the experience of section 13 EU(W)A 2018 (repealed by section 31 EU(WA)A 2020) so vividly demonstrates: see further Chapter 5.

[46] Contrast the European Union (Withdrawal Agreement) Act as published on 19 December 2019, with the previous version of the Bill as published on 21 October 2019 (especially Clauses 30 and 31 thereof). And with the May Government's plans, e.g. HMG, *Legislating for the Withdrawal Agreement between the UK and the EU* (Cm 9674 of 24 July 2018); Prime Minister, *Commons Statement on New Brexit Deal* (22 May 2019). Again: see further Chapter 5.

[47] As the experience of the Withdrawal Agreement itself demonstrates: see the detailed discussion in Chapter 6 about defining the WA's precise internal legal effects within the UK.

[48] See further, e.g. House of Commons Library Briefing Paper, *Parliament's Role in Ratifying Treaties* (No 5855 of 17 February 2017).

[49] See further, e.g. M. Gordon, *Parliamentary Sovereignty in the UK Constitution: Process, Politics and Democracy* (2015).

Communities Act 1972, which provided the basis for UK membership of the Union and operationalized the principle of primacy within the UK legal system.[50] However, it is not generally regarded as constitutionally possible for one Parliament to rule out the express repeal of its legislation by a subsequent Parliament. In the sphere of international relations, the UK Government accepts that this means the UK could theoretically enter into a state of non-compliance with any of its international obligations—in anticipation of which an appropriate system of sanctions/counter-balancing measures may need to be designed.[51]

As for the devolved institutions, their involvement in the domestic implementation of the UK's international obligations may be engaged either because the relevant treaty creates obligations which fall within the scope of devolved competences and will be implemented through regional legislation; or because the London Government proposes central implementing legislation covering matters that normally fall within the scope of devolved competences—in which case, as a matter of constitutional convention (even if it is not strictly legally enforceable) the devolved administrations must give their prior consent.[52] Efforts to enhance the role of the devolved institutions in external relations, as practised by the central UK authorities, have generally fallen upon deaf ears.[53]

3. Initial Articulation of the Parties' Preferences and Positions

Future EU–UK relations will not be exempt from the standard agenda involved in negotiations to enhance international cooperation. Nor are future EU–UK relations likely to defy the universal lessons experienced over time by every other state or international organization on earth. Just for the sake of the UK, the Union is unlikely to cease referring to its own unique model of market integration between the Member States as the appropriate yardstick against which all other forms of third country deal are to be measured and assessed. And in any case, the Union's own internal constitutional constraints are not suddenly going to be set aside in its external relations with the UK as a third country.[54]

Of course, the British situation does present some highly distinctive features—not least the fact that the UK is undergoing an unprecedented change of status, from being

---

[50] I.e. as interpreted by the UK courts in cases such as *R v Secretary of State for Transport, ex parte Factortame (No 2)* [1990] 3 WLR 818 and *R v Secretary of State for Employment, ex parte Equal Opportunities Commission* [1995] 1 AC 1.

[51] See, e.g. Prime Minister, *Our Future Economic Partnership with the European Union* (2 March 2018).

[52] See, in particular, UK Supreme Court in *R (on the application of Miller) v Secretary of State for Exiting the European Union* [2017] UKSC 5.

[53] Consider, e.g. Scottish Government, *Scotland's Role in the Development of Future UK Trade Arrangements: A Discussion Paper* (30 August 2018).

[54] Further, e.g. Tobler, 'The Institutional Framework of an Alternative Agreement: Lessons from Switzerland and Elsewhere?', 23 *Maastricht Journal* (2016) 575; Norberg, 'UK-EU Relations after Brexit: Which arrangements are possible?', *Europarättslig Tidskrift* [2017] 469; Raitio and Raulus, 'The UK EU Referendum and the move towards Brexit', 23 *Maastricht Journal* (2017) 25; F. Amtenbrink, M. Markakis and R. Repasi, *Legal Implications of Brexit* (Study commissioned by the IMCO Committee of the European Parliament, PE 607.328 of August 2017).

a Member State which fully benefitted from (and indeed played a leading role in creating) the Union's own model of economic integration, to becoming a third country which now needs to decide how far it is willing to trade its own decision-making autonomy as the price for maintaining some alternative form of close relationship with the Union. Yet the underlying calculations remain essentially the same, even if their starting context is rather different. Any new relationship—no matter how close—must automatically and inherently fall short of the exceptional degree of economic integration provided by the Union's own model: the UK might hope to minimize the loss of existing market access, rather than to acquire it de novo; but there can still be no question of a third country outside the Union ecosystem enjoying the same rights and privileges as a Member State.

Indeed, in the absence of an ambitious agreement, it is inevitable that the regulatory conditions governing trade between the Union and UK markets will become substantially less favourable than they have been in past decades—actively creating a potentially vast array of barriers to trade which would (at best) increase costs and (at worst) seal off markets either in law or in fact. Indeed, the potential for economic disruption relates not only to the complex problems surrounding regulatory barriers to trade in goods and services (as a consequence of leaving the Single Market) but extends even to more basic hindrances such as customs checks and related formalities (bound up with departure from the Customs Union).

Against that background, we will now explore the initial positions adopted by the Union and the UK concerning the likely shape of their future relationship.[55] Even though those initial positions were not necessarily or fully carried through, either into the First Political Declaration as agreed with the May Government (November 2018), or into the Second Political Declaration as revised at the insistence of the Johnson Government (October 2019), it is nevertheless worth summarizing and analysing in some detail the respective thinking of the Union and the UK—not least since our analysis will help clarify some of the most important issues and tensions that will inevitably underpin any potential future relationship and certainly continue to enliven the parties' ongoing negotiations.

A. Evolution of the Union's Position

The European Council articulated its overall position towards future relations with the UK in its formative guidelines from April 2017.[56] Bearing in mind the phased approach to negotiations under Article 50 TEU as laid down in those Guidelines, the following key points emerge.

The European Council welcomes and shares the UK's desire for a close partnership. Even though no such partnership can offer the same benefits as Union membership, there is nevertheless a common interest in strong and constructive ties. As regards trade, any agreement should be balanced, ambitious, and wide-ranging. But it cannot

---

[55] For discussion of how the parties' approach to future relations evolved, within the broader context of the overall Art 50 TEU process, see Chapters 3–5.

[56] European Council (Article 50), *Guidelines of 29 April 2017*, especially at paras 18–24.

amount to participation in the Single Market or parts thereof: in particular, the four freedoms are indivisible and there can be no 'cherry-picking' through sector-by-sector participation in the Single Market. Any agreement must also ensure a level playing field (for example, as regards competition and state aid rules), safeguard against unfair competitive advantages (for example, as regards tax, social, environmental, and regulatory measures/practices) and safeguard the Union's financial stability/respect its regulatory regimes.[57] The Union also stands ready to establish partnerships in areas unrelated to trade: in particular, the fight against terrorism and international crime; as well as security, defence, and foreign policy. In any case, the future partnership must include appropriate enforcement and dispute settlement mechanisms—though these cannot affect the Union's autonomy as regards its own decision-making procedures. Finally, no future Union–UK agreement may apply to Gibraltar without an agreement between Spain and the UK.

Having concluded that 'sufficient progress' had been achieved during the 'first phase' negotiations, the European Council meeting in December 2017 adopted additional guidelines elaborating upon important elements of the future (especially economic) relationship between the Union and the UK.[58] First, the European Council affirmed that any agreement on the future relationship can only be finalized and concluded once the UK has become a third country. However, the Union stands ready to engage in preliminary and preparatory discussions with the aim of identifying an overall understanding of the framework for that future relationship, to be set out in a 'political declaration' accompanying and referred to in any eventual withdrawal agreement under Article 50 TEU. Secondly, the European Council intends to issue further guidelines on trade and economic cooperation, to be calibrated in the light of the UK's intention to leave both the Single Market and the Customs Union. Such cooperation must ensure a balance of rights and obligations, preserve a level playing field, avoid upsetting existing relations with other third countries, and preserve the integrity and proper functioning of the Single Market.

And indeed, the European Council meeting in March 2018 saw the adoption of fresh guidelines setting out additional detail concerning the Union's future relationship with the UK.[59] To begin with, the Union must base its position on the UK's stated 'red lines', which will inevitably limit the possible depth of any future partnership—though the European Council remained willing to reconsider its offer, should the UK position evolve in the future. For now, however, the UK's decision to leave the Customs Union and the Single Market would lead to inevitable friction and negative economic consequences—particularly for the UK itself. Moreover, the autonomy of Union decision-making excludes the participation of the UK as a third country in the Union's institutions and the participation of the UK in decision-making by the Union's bodies, offices, and agencies.

As regards the future economic partnership, any free trade agreement should include a comprehensive deal on goods: no customs duties; no quantitative restrictions;

---

[57] On the 'level playing field' under Union external relations law, see further, e.g. Editorial Comments, 'Playing by the Rules: Free And Fair Trade', 55 CMLRev (2018) 373.
[58] European Council (Article 50), *Guidelines of 15 December 2017.*
[59] European Council (Article 50), *Guidelines of 23 March 2018.*

appropriate 'rules of origin'; maintaining existing reciprocal access to fisheries waters and resources; appropriate customs and regulatory cooperation. The agreement should also include a more limited deal on services—based on market access under host state control, to the extent possible and appropriate for a third country. The Union would also seek agreement on other economic issues (including public procurement, intellectual property, and the protection of geographical indications); as well as on cooperation over global challenges (such as climate change, sustainable development, and cross-border pollution). The agreement should include ambitious provisions on the mobility of natural persons, based on reciprocity and non-discrimination between the Member States, as well as agreement on related fields such as social security coordination and the recognition of professional qualifications, plus relevant cross-border cooperation in civil matters (subject to appropriate safeguards for the protection of fundamental rights). The Union and the UK should pursue cooperation on other socio-economic matters, for example, through agreements on aviation and other transport modes as well as UK participation (as a third country) in the Union's various research and educational programmes.

In its March 2018 Guidelines, the European Council placed particular emphasis on the importance of robust guarantees to ensure a level playing field, so as to prevent the UK from engaging in unfair competition, particularly given its geographic proximity and economic interdependence with the EU27. Level playing field guarantees should cover fields such as competition, state aid, tax, social, environmental, and regulatory standards; based on a combination of substantive rules aligned to EU and international standards, measures to ensure effective domestic implementation, agreement-level enforcement and dispute settlement mechanisms, as well as Union autonomous remedies.

Otherwise, the European Council suggests specific partnerships covering law enforcement and judicial cooperation in criminal matters, as well as cooperation in the fields of foreign, security, and defence policy. The former should take into account the UK's position as a third country outside the Schengen zone, and provide strong safeguards for fundamental rights, effective enforcement, and dispute settlement. The latter must respect the autonomy of the Union's decision-making and will require a Security of Information agreement so as to facilitate information sharing. In any case, the future Union–UK relationship would greatly benefit from having rules on data—including the adoption of a Union adequacy decision as regards the sharing of personal data with the UK.

Finally, the governance structures of the proposed Union–UK agreement(s) would need to address management, supervision, dispute settlement, and sanctions/cross-retaliation—taking into account the content and depth of the future relationship, the need for effectiveness and legal certainty, and also the autonomy of Union law (including the role of the CJEU).

It is clear from those various pronouncements of the European Council, that the Union's overall approach to its future relations with the UK remained remarkably stable throughout the formative stages of the Article 50 TEU process. It is worth noting, of course, that the work of the European Council was consistently informed by the more detailed perspectives and input presented by the Commission. For example, Michel Barnier repeatedly stressed the importance of being realistic about the manner in which the UK's own 'red lines' must substantially reduce the prospects for any ambitious model when it comes to the future EU–UK relationship;[60] while the Commission produced copious materials exploring different facets to be explored in the pre-withdrawal discussions and post-withdrawal negotiations.[61] For its part, the European Parliament repeatedly expressed its views on the terms and conditions which should guide internal discussions as well as eventual negotiations with the UK when it came to the future relationship,[62] including a stated preference for the future Union–UK relationship to take the form of a wide-ranging 'association agreement' within the specific terms of Article 217 TEFU.[63]

B. Evolution of the UK's Position

By contrast, much of the UK debate on future relations with the Union evolved almost entirely detached from many of the legal and political realities that would actually and eventually determine the British Government's choices and actions.

Put simply, having settled upon its decision to withdraw from the Union, the fundamental question facing the UK was how to reorientate its position on the world stage. In that regard, it is worth stressing that the victorious Leave campaign never properly defined its vision for the future, preferring instead to make entirely fantastical and mutually contradictory promises in order to win the referendum. Yet the basic choice facing Brexit Britain was relatively simple. Either the UK could aim for a relatively close future relationship with the Union: that would minimize disruption in fields such as trade and security—and also make the Irish border problem less difficult to manage as part of a UK-wide settlement—but it would inevitably come at the price of the UK aligning itself to the Union and its regulatory standards without exercising any appreciable degree of influence. Or instead, the UK could settle for a relatively distant future relationship with the Union. That might appear to tally with the political slogan of 'taking back control', but it would come at the cost of much greater dislocation in

---

[60] Including the (now famous) slide presented to the European Council on 15 December 2017—see TF50 (2017) 21 of 19 December 2017. Note also Commission, *Déclaration presse par Michel Barnier suite à l'adoption d'une 69 ecommendation visant à entamer les discussions relatives à la phase suivante du retrait ordonné du Royaume-Uni de l'Union européenne* (20 December 2017).

[61] In particular: the Commission's detailed slides, prepared for the purposes of the Union's internal preparatory discussions over the framework for a future relationship with the UK, e.g. on fisheries (17 January 2018); aviation (17 January 2018); governance (19 January 2018); security, defence, and foreign policy (24 January 2018); police and judicial cooperation in criminal matters (24 January 2018); level playing field (31 January 2018); international agreements (6 February 2018); services (6 February 2018); mobility (21 February 2018); regulatory issues (21 February 2018); transport (21 February 2018); space-related activities (13 June 2018); foreign, security, and defence policy (15 June 2018); police and judicial cooperation in criminal matters (18 June 2018). Note also the slide on an overall framework for the future EU–UK partnership: TF50 (2018) 37.

[62] E.g. European Parliament, *Resolution on negotiations with the United Kingdom following its notification that it intends to withdraw from the European Union* (5 April 2017); *Resolution on the state of play of negotiations with the United Kingdom* (3 October 2017); *Resolution on the state of play of negotiations with the United Kingdom* (13 December 2017).

[63] E.g. European Parliament, *Resolution on the framework of the future EU-UK relationship* (14 March 2018), at para 5.

trade and security—and also increase the pressure to address the Irish border problem by treating Northern Ireland very differently from the rest of the UK.

But most of all, the prospect of a serious split between the Union and the UK begged the question of what the British would then do with their newfound room for manoeuvre. The Leave Right might well have long dreamt of departing from the hated economic and social model espoused by the Union. But what would replace it? An enthusiastic push for closer alignment to the alternative policies and approaches championed by the US? An optimistically rosy world in which 'Global Britain' acted as its own independent reference point for regulation, trade, and security? A rather more bleak future in which an isolated and exposed mid-ranking power would have to steer a delicate diplomatic course between the world's existing and emergent superpowers and regional blocs?

The basic dilemma thus facing the British may have appeared both stark and obvious. And yet, as we know, the very survival of the May Government depended precisely upon obscuring those very problems and avoiding the difficult but necessary choices for as long as possible.[64]

Building upon Prime Minister May's 'Lancaster House Speech' of 17 January 2017,[65] the UK Government's ideas concerning future relations with the Union were first presented in the White Paper on *The United Kingdom's Exit from and New Partnership with the European Union*.[66] For present purposes, the contents of that White Paper can be boiled down to three important elements. First, the UK imposed its infamous 'red lines' upon future relations with the EU: for example, ending the free movement of persons, rejecting the jurisdiction of the Court of Justice, refusing to make substantial contributions to the Union budget. Secondly and in consequence, the UK had therefore decided to leave both the Customs Union and the Single Market and instead now

---

[64] Even though the basic choices had already been articulated by her predecessor, e.g. HMG, *Alternatives to Membership: Possible Models for the United Kingdom Outside the European Union* (2 March 2016). Consider also, e.g. House of Commons Treasury Committee, *The Economic and Financial Costs and Benefits of the UK's EU Membership* (HC122 of 27 May 2016); House of Lords European Union Committee, *Brexit: The Options for Trade* (HL72 of 13 December 2016); House of Commons Exiting the EU Committee, *The Future UK–EU Relationship* (HC935 of 4 April 2018); House of Lords EU Committee, *UK–EU Relations after Brexit* (HL149 of 8 June 2018). Note that the House of Lords European Union Committee, in particular, produced a lengthy series of substantial reports investigating particular aspects of future EU–UK relations, e.g. *Financial Services* (HL81 of 15 December 2016); *Future UK-EU Security and Police Cooperation* (HL77 of 16 December 2016); *Fisheries* (HL78 of 17 December 2016); *Environment and Climate Change* (HL109 of 14 February 2017); *UK–EU Movement of People* (HL121 of 6 March 2017); *Trade in Goods* (HL129 of 14 March 2017); *Justice for Families, Individuals and Businesses* (HL134 of 20 March 2017); *Trade in Non-Financial Services* (HL135 of 22 March 2017); *Agriculture* (HL169 of 3 May 2017); *The EU Data Protection Package* (HL7 of 18 July 2017); *Farm Animal Welfare* (HL15 of 25 July 2017); *Judicial Oversight of the European Arrest Warrant* (HL16 of 27 July 2017); *Sanctions Policy* (HL50 of 17 December 2017); *Energy Security* (HL63 of 29 January 2018); *The Future of Financial Regulation and Supervision* (HL66 of 27 January 2018); *Competition and State Aid* (HL67 of 2 February 2018); *Common Security and Defence Policy Missions and Operations* (HL132 of 14 May 2018); *Reciprocal Healthcare* (HL107 of 28 March 2018); *The Customs Challenge* (HL187 of 20 September 2018); *Plant and Animal Biosecurity* (HL191 of 24 October 2018); *Chemical Regulation* (HL215 of 7 November 2018); *European Investment Bank* (HL269 of 31 January 2019); *The Erasmus and Horizon Programmes* (HL283 of 12 February 2019); *Road, Rail and Maritime Transport* (HL355 of 21 May 2019); *Refugee Protection and Asylum Policy* (HL428 of 11 October 2019).

[65] Theresa May, *Lancaster House Speech: The Government's Negotiating Objectives for Exiting the EU* (17 January 2017).

[66] HMG, *The United Kingdom's Exit from and New Partnership with the European Union* (Cm 9417 of 2 February 2017).

wants to negotiate a bespoke and ambitious customs and trading relationship with the Union. Finally, the UK wishes to maintain high standards of (particularly operational) cooperation with the Union in the fight against crime and terrorism; and since the UK remains committed to European security, it will also seek to cooperate with the Union in the fields of foreign, security, and defence policy.

The May Government's aspiration for a unique, deep, and special partnership with the Union was reaffirmed by the Prime Minster in her 'Florence Speech' of September 2017.[67] First, the UK affirmed its intention to leave the Single Market and the Customs Union and instead seek a close economic relationship based upon a new balance of rights and obligations. Given that the UK and the Union would be starting from a position of close regulatory convergence, the focus should be on managing future regulatory divergences and their impact on mutual market access. The new economic partnership should be based on a series of shared values: for example, a commitment to high regulatory standards and opposition to anti-competitive practices. But dispute resolution could not be entrusted to the Court of Justice. Secondly, as regards the future security partnership, the UK recognized that no existing third country model matches the scale and depth of cooperation that exists within the Union itself. But the UK still wanted a comprehensive and dynamic framework for cooperation in law enforcement and criminal justice; as well as in defence, security, and development policy. Perhaps aware that some of her Tory colleagues had stoked controversy by suggesting that the British should use security cooperation as a bargaining tool to gain greater concessions in the field of trade, Prime Minister May declared that '[t]he United Kingdom is unconditionally committed to maintaining Europe's security'.

The UK Government's thinking on certain specific issues surrounding future relations with the Union were fleshed out in a series of 'future partnership papers' published shortly before and after the 'Florence Speech'.[68] In early 2018, senior members of the UK Government then delivered a coordinated set of speeches intended to clarify and elaborate upon the UK's official position concerning important aspects of its future relationship with the Union;[69] accompanied by another round of more detailed presentations covering more specific aspects of future EU–UK relations.[70] From those

[67] Prime Minister, *A New Era of Cooperation and Partnership between the UK and the EU* (22 September 2017) available at https://www.gov.uk/government/speeches/pms-florence-speech-a-new-era-of-cooperation-and-partnership-between-the-uk-and-the-eu.

[68] E.g. HMG, *Future Partnership Paper on future customs arrangements* (15 August 2017); *Future Partnership Paper on enforcement and dispute resolution* (23 August 2017); *Future Partnership Paper on the exchange and protection of personal data* (24 August 2017); *Future Partnership Paper on providing a cross-border civil judicial cooperation framework* (22 August 2017); *Future Partnership Paper on collaboration on science and innovation* (6 September 2017); *Future Partnership Paper on foreign policy, defence and development* (12 September 2017); *Future Partnership Paper on security, law enforcement and criminal justice* (18 September 2017).

[69] E.g. Foreign Secretary, *Uniting for a Great Brexit* (14 February 2018); Prime Minister, *Speech at Munich Security Conference* (17 February 2018); Secretary of State for Exiting the European Union, *Foundations of the Future Economic Partnership* (20 February 2018); Secretary of State for International Trade, *Britain's Trading Future* (27 February 2018); Prime Minister, *Our future economic partnership with the European Union* (2 March 2018); Chancellor of the Exchequer, *Speech on Financial Services at HSBC* (7 March 2018); David Davis, *Speech on the future security partnership* (6 June 2018).

[70] E.g. HMG, *Framework for the UK–EU Security Partnership* (9 May 2018); *Framework for the UK–EU Partnership—Science, Research and Innovation* (23 May 2018); *Technical Note on Security, Law Enforcement and Criminal Justice* (24 May 2018); *Framework for the UK–EU Economic Partnership* (24 May 2018); *Framework for the UK–EU Partnership—Data Protection* (24 May 2018); *Technical Note on Consultation*

various interventions, we learned some important detail about the UK's evolving political preferences.

For example, concerning the future economic relationship, the May Government appeared firmly entrenched in its interpretation of the 2016 referendum as a vote to 'take back control' of the UK's borders, laws, and money—which in turn confirmed both the UK's 'red lines' in its negotiations with the Union and its decision to leave both the Single Market and the Customs Union. However, the May Government now recognized that its 'red lines' might need to be softened somewhat, in order to deliver on its ambition of agreeing a 'deep and special [economic] partnership' with the Union. For example, continued UK participation in certain Union agencies would entail recognition of limited Court of Justice jurisdiction and a certain degree of financial contribution.

Moreover, the UK also proposed a more variegated approach to managing its future economic relations with the Union. In some sectors, the 'deep and special [economic] partnership' could mean that the UK would abide by not only the essential objectives of Union policy but also the latter's more precise regulatory techniques and disciplines. In other sectors, the 'deep and special [economic] partnership' could instead mean that, while the UK might share the essential objectives of Union policy, the UK would nevertheless seek to achieve them through its own set of regulatory techniques and disciplines. In a final set of sectors, the UK would not want to participate in either the Union's underlying policy objectives or its more precise regulatory techniques and disciplines—though the May Government accepted that this would have adverse consequences for mutual market access between the two parties.

C. Main Points of Tension in the UK's 'Cake and Eat It' Policy

The core problem afflicting the May Government's efforts at articulating a model for future relations with the Union was that those efforts were founded upon unrealistic expectations—the so-called 'cake and eat it' philosophy—whereby (in general terms) the UK could decide to leave the Union's unique substantive and institutional ecosystem but still retain many of the same rights and privileges as a Member State and/or (in specific terms) the UK could propose to exempt itself from many of the Union's particular regulatory techniques and disciplines but still retain the benefits of mutual recognition based on the principle of reciprocal home state control.[71] The unrealistic nature of the UK's demands can be illustrated by several more detailed examples.

and Cooperation on External Security (24 May 2018); Technical Note on UK Participation in Galileo (24 May 2018); Technical Note on Exchange and Protection of Classified Information (24 May 2018); Framework for the UK–EU Partnership—Transport (7 June 2018); Technical Note on Benefits of a New Data Protection Agreement (7 June 2018); Framework for the UK–EU Partnership—Civil Judicial Cooperation (13 June 2018); Framework for the UK–EU Partnership—Company Law (13 June 2018); Technical Note on Coordination on External Security (21 June 2018); Framework for the UK–EU Partnership—Open and Fair Competition (25 July 2018); Framework for the UK–EU Partnership—Financial Services (25 July 2018).

[71] See further the discussion in Chapter 3.

In the first place, the British request for only partial, sectoral participation in the Single Market conflicted directly with the Union's insistence upon the indivisibility of the 'four freedoms'. In particular, we have noted the UK's suggestion that it should be possible to agree a far-reaching economic partnership with the Union, while nevertheless excluding certain fields from the scope of any agreement, on the basis that the UK shares neither the objectives, techniques, nor disciplines of Union action in the relevant sectors. The main exclusion thus proposed by the May Government concerned the free movement of persons—though the UK made similar suggestions (for example) about not wishing to continue full participation in the Digital Single Market.[72]

In response to the Union's insistence that the integrity of the Single Market must be protected and there can be no 'cherry-picking' through sector-by-sector participation, the May Government implied that the Union position was not only unreasonable but also inconsistent.[73] After all, the UK could point to existing Union-third country agreements to demonstrate how the four freedoms were in fact perfectly divisible: for example, the effective exemption of Lichtenstein from compliance with the full free movement of persons under the EEA Agreement;[74] or the exclusion of any general system to facilitate the free movement of persons under the Association Agreement with Ukraine.[75] Similarly, the UK could refer to existing Union-third country agreements that showed it was possible to enjoy sector-by-sector membership of the Single Market: for example, the complex network of bilateral agreements with Switzerland, that provide for the latter's selective participation in certain Union policies, frameworks, and programmes.[76] Indeed, certain senior UK politicians suggested that the Union's refusal to accede to British demands for selective Single Market participation, in reality reflected a deliberate policy to 'punish' the UK for its decision to withdraw from the Union.[77]

There is a legitimate debate to be had among EU lawyers about whether Union constitutional and/or external relations law positively requires the four freedoms to be treated as indivisible and would thereby preclude the conclusion of certain sectoral agreements purporting to offer unduly selective and preferential degrees of access to the Single Market.[78] However, this is perhaps an issue where the strict question of law is less important than the political imperative that derives from rational self-interest. We know that the Union in general, and the Single Market in particular, form an

---

[72] See further, in particular, Prime Minister, *Our future economic partnership with the European Union* (2 March 2018).

[73] E.g. Prime Minister, *Our future economic partnership with the European Union* (2 March 2018).

[74] Agreement on the European Economic Area, OJ 1994 L 1/3.

[75] Association Agreement between the European Union and its Member States, of the one part, and Ukraine, of the other part, OJ 2014 L 161/3.

[76] See further, e.g. Tobler, 'The Institutional Framework of an Alternative Agreement: Lessons from Switzerland and Elsewhere?', 23 *Maastricht Journal* (2016) 575.

[77] Such language about 'punishment' of the UK by the EU is particularly associated with the UK's (Eurosceptic) International Trade Secretary, Liam Fox: see, e.g. the remarks reported in https://www.theguardian.com/politics/2017/oct/22/britain-not-bluffing-on-no-deal-brexit-says-liam-fox.

[78] See further, e.g. Editorial Comments, 'Is the 'Indivisibility' of the Four Freedoms a Principle of EU Law?', 56 *CMLRev* (2019) 1189. Though note the rather more far-reaching critique of the Union's position on the indivisibility of the four freedoms by Barnard, 'Brexit and the EU Internal Market' in F. Fabbrini (ed.), *The Law and Politics of Brexit* (2017).

ecosystem which is both comprehensive in its scope and unprecedented in the depth of its substantive rules, institutional structures, and enforcement disciplines. The Union has a strong interest in ensuring that any agreement it might reach with a third country does not pose an external threat to the smooth functioning, underlying cohesion, or indeed very legitimacy of the Union's own internal ecosystem. In particular, the Union must ensure that the complex and interdependent elements which together make up the Single Market between its Member States are not undermined or called into question by the possibility of a third country being able to disaggregate, unravel, or pick-and-choose between those very elements.[79]

That is especially true having regard to the symbiotic relationship which exists between the scope and the depth of economic cooperation within the Single Market. It would clearly be easier for the Union to agree on a selective or sectoral approach to economic cooperation with a third country where the degree of market integration pursued between the parties is relatively shallow (say) consisting essentially of reductions in tariffs, mechanisms for bilateral regulatory cooperation, or limited/static regimes on regulatory equivalency. But where the depth of market integration between the parties is to be more profound—approaching closer to that of the Single Market itself—it becomes correspondingly more difficult to justify adopting a selective approach to the overall scope of their economic relationship. Such an approach would directly challenge the network of bargains, balances, compromises, and trade-offs that are eventually required to bind together the entire edifice of a genuinely close trading relationship.

The essentially political (rather than strictly constitutional) imperative for the Union to be seen to protect the integrity of its own Single Market is neither new nor unique to the case of UK withdrawal. For example, that same concept played an explicit role (and was endorsed as such by previous UK Governments) in the Union's management of its bilateral relationship with Switzerland—as we can see in the Council's conclusions of 16 December 2014 assessing the implications for Union–Swiss cooperation of the controversial referendum on restricting 'mass immigration'.[80] Indeed, if anything, the force of the Union's political imperative to protect the integrity of the Single Market has acquired even greater potency in the context of the Article 50 TEU negotiations with the UK: it is self-evidently in the Union's rational self-interest to use its relative bargaining power in order to ensure that a departing Member State is not able to unravel fundamental elements of the Union's unique ecosystem from the outside.

After all, even as a Member State, the UK had secured a series of special privileges as compared to the treatment of its fellows: having voted to leave the Union altogether, there must come a political limit to the Union's willingness to accommodate the British desire for exceptional treatment. As a third country, the UK will remain a major international player and partner: for the Union to make significant concessions to British demands for 'special treatment' could pose substantially greater challenges to the

---

[79] A point repeatedly stressed by Michel Barnier, e.g. *Speech on German Employers' Day (Deutscher Arbeitgebertag) 2017* (29 November 2017).

[80] Council, *Conclusions on a homogenous extended single market and EU relations with Non-EU Western European countries* (16 December 2014), especially at para 45.

coherence and legitimacy of the Union's internal model of economic cooperation than in the case of smaller or less strategically important economies. Moreover, the UK's requests for sectoral exclusions from an otherwise close economic partnership with the Union would be much more likely to provoke political objections and thus serious procedural hurdles, when it comes to securing the ratification of any (mixed) agreement at the domestic level by the national/regional parliaments of the Member States.

In the second place, we discussed how the UK also suggested that, in certain sectors, the UK might share the Union's policy objectives, but seek the freedom to pursue them using its own particular regulatory techniques and disciplines—yet without thereby compromising mutual market access, effectively on Single Market terms, for relevant goods and services. In other words, the May Government proposed requesting the continued benefits of a systematic approach to mutual recognition based on the principle of reciprocal home state control, but without having to comply with the same techniques and disciplines, particularly in terms of regulatory harmonization, and instead offering guarantees that UK law would meet certain equivalent or adequate standards.

Once again, that proposal could never be regarded as particularly feasible. Mutual recognition between states is fundamentally dependent upon the existence of a high level of mutual trust and confidence. Such mutual trust does not self-generate and self-perpetuate somehow spontaneously. It is built and maintained through long and hard labour, often challenged by points of particular tension or even threatened by moments of genuine crisis. It is the purpose of the Union's own model of economic integration to generate and perpetuate sufficient mutual trust between the Member States to allow the Single Market to function on the basis of a uniquely far-reaching programme of mutual recognition. True, that model includes an extensive body of substantive law seeking to harmonize the regulatory standards that protect essential public interests across the Member States. But it is also dependent upon an entire institutional framework that legislates for, implements, and supervises the 'rules of the game'—including the construction of extensive networks and processes (for example) to share information, assess risks, and apportion jurisdiction. It furthermore relies upon a highly developed legal system, common to the Member States, which offers concrete guarantees (for example) that rules of the Single Market can be directly enforced against national public authorities in the event of non-compliance and that the beneficiaries of Union law are entitled to effective remedies before the national courts to vindicate their rights.

A system like the EEA seeks to offer a sufficiently close replication of the Union's own model as to enable its participating states to enjoy a comparable level of mutual trust and thence mutual recognition. But it is simply impossible to imagine that a third country which does not observe the same techniques and disciplines, participate in the same networks and processes, and guarantee the same level of administrative and judicial enforcement etc, can nevertheless claim that sufficient mutual trust exists to install and support a fully-fledged system of mutual recognition, offering the same or even a similar level of market integration as we see within the Union or the EEA.[81] In

---

[81] Again: a point repeatedly stressed by Michel Barnier, e.g. *Speech at BusinessEurope Day 2018* (1 March 2018); *Speech at the Eurofi High-level Seminar 2018* (26 April 2018).

effect, through its 'cake and eat it' proposal, the May Government was actually asking for significantly better treatment and privileges than the Member States are prepared to provide even towards each other within the framework of the Union.[82]

In the third place, even these early discussions about the future Union–UK relationship were dogged by differences, uncertainty, and indeed mistrust about the parties' respective expectations for the level playing field. As the European Council's March 2018 Guidelines stressed, even in the context of a relatively less ambitious trade agreement, ensuring a level playing field is of particular concern in the context of the Union's future relations with the UK—given the latter's geographical proximity, the sheer size of the UK market, and the degree of its interconnection with the Union's economy.[83] And yet the May Government was accused of communicating contradictory messages about its commitment to fair competition based on maintaining high regulatory standards.

As Michel Barnier repeatedly stressed: the Union desired clarity about the scope and depth of the UK's long-term commitment to maintaining a social market economy on the European model.[84] Of course, feelings of uncertainty and suspicion had long been fuelled by the rhetoric (if not genuine policy aspiration) of many leading Leave campaigners, i.e. that withdrawal from the Union would present a golden opportunity to hold a 'bonfire of regulations' and/or to engage in a fundamental reorientation of the UK towards a more aggressively neo-liberal capitalist model based on lower taxes and greater deregulation.[85] But even senior members of the May Government suggested that the UK might 'retaliate' against the Union's failure to agree a satisfactory trade relationship by fundamentally changing the UK's current socio-economic model;[86] though it is fair to point out that subsequent public interventions did seek to reassure the Union that the British would not engage in an outright 'race to the bottom' in

---

[82] Moreover, the legal inter-relationship between mutual recognition and Union membership is not merely an abstract constitutional consideration but can also be seen operating in concrete disputes that come before the Court of Justice. The Court is sometimes called upon to assess the potential justification of prima facie barriers to trade created by a Member State which affect certain third country goods (in free circulation and lawfully marketed within the Union and thus entitled to certain rights of free movement along with Union-origin goods) or third country capital (where the relevant Treaty provisions explicitly protect free movement in/out of as well as purely within the Union). Even in those situations where third country goods/capital enjoy a degree of privileged treatment within the Single Market, the Member States are permitted to justify barriers to trade and thereby limit the principle of mutual recognition in ways which would not be permissible in the case of purely intra-Union disputes—and to do so explicitly taking account of the fact that third countries cannot provide the same (substantive and/or institutional) assurances for the protection of essential public interests as does Union membership itself. Consider recent rulings such as Case C-525/14, *Commission v Czech Republic* (EU:C:2016:714) (concerning goods) and Case C-464/14, *SECIL* (EU:C:2016:896) (concerning capital).

[83] See also Commission, *Internal EU27 preparatory discussions on the framework for the future relationship: 'Level Playing Field'*, TF50 (2018) 27 of 31 January 2018.

[84] E.g. Michel Barnier, *Speech at the Conference 'Obbligati a crescere—l'Europa dopo Brexit'* (9 November 2017); *Speech at the Centre for European Reform on 'The Future of the EU'* (20 November 2017); *Speech on German Employers' Day* (29 November 2017); *Speech at the 'Trends Manager of the Year 2017' event* (9 January 2018); *Speech at BusinessEurope Day 2018* (1 March 2018); *Speech at Green 10, 'Is Brexit a Threat to the Future of the EU's Environment?'* (10 April 2018).

[85] See, e.g. https://www.theguardian.com/politics/2016/dec/07/tory-mps-suggest-firms-draw-up-list-for-bonfire-of-eu-laws-after-brexit; https://www.theguardian.com/politics/2017/jan/04/andrea-leadsom-vows-to-scrap-eu-red-tape-for-farmers-after-brexit.

[86] See, e.g. https://www.politico.eu/article/europes-message-to-theresa-may-play-by-the-rules-or-else-hard-brexit-negotiations-corporate-tax-haven/.

regulatory, social, and environmental standards.[87] And yet uncertainty was not merely a matter of the UK's internal dynamics, but also a product of the UK's future external trade policies with other third countries (such as the USA, China, and India). Whether by conscious design or as the reluctant price for securing more favourable trade terms with other global economic powers, the UK may well agree to market access conditions for foreign goods and services that could have the effect of compromising the maintenance of high regulatory standards,[88] and thus potentially impact upon future regulatory cooperation with/market access to the Union itself.[89]

If those examples illustrate how the May Government's attempts to design a 'deep and special partnership' between the Union and the UK were dogged by unrealistic and indeed undeliverable expectations, it is important to bear in mind that the British position was rendered even more complicated by another crucial part of the withdrawal equation: any agreement on the future economic relationship was intended not just to determine the terms of trade between the Union and the UK, but also to provide a stable and effective framework within which to address the specific problems caused by UK withdrawal for Ireland and Northern Ireland.[90] After all, the Joint Report of December 2017 had expressed the UK's preference for avoiding a 'hard border' for the movement of goods across the island of Ireland through an overall agreement on the future Union–UK relationship. In default of an effective border solution being provided for under that overall agreement, the parties would instead have recourse to the 'backstop' as envisaged by the Joint Report, i.e. an all-weather proposal designed to guarantee that there would be no physical frontier across the island of Ireland under any circumstances.[91] Designing an acceptable backstop was proving at least as complex and controversial as proposing a workable model for future relations—yet for the May Government, the two challenges were effectively interdependent and now needed to be resolved as a package. Otherwise, the entire Article 50 TEU process risked ending in failure.[92]

D. Future Relations Addressed under a First, Then Second, Withdrawal Package

As we have seen in previous chapters, the May Government's 'cake and eat it' policy towards future relations with the Union both reached its apotheosis and found its nemesis in the Chequers Plan of July 2018.[93]

---

[87] E.g. Secretary of State for Exiting the European Union, *Foundations of the Future Economic Partnership* (20 February 2018).

[88] The main example usually cited in this context is the prospect of the UK agreeing to the importation of foodstuffs such as chlorinated chicken from the USA.

[89] As noted repeatedly by Michel Barnier, e.g. *Intervention de Michel Barnier à la conférence 'Obbligati a crescere—l'Europa dopo Brexit'* (9 November 2017); *Speech at the Centre for European Reform on 'The Future of the EU'* (20 November 2017).

[90] See further the detailed discussion in Chapter 8.

[91] Joint Report from the EU and UK negotiators (8 December 2017).

[92] See further the detailed discussion in Chapters 4 and 5.

[93] HMG, *The Future Relationship between the United Kingdom and the European Union* (Cm 9593 of 17 July 2018).

There is no need for us to recount the details of those proposals, or the various critical reactions they prompted both domestically and across the Union.[94] Suffice to recall that the May Government proposed a Union–UK 'free trade area for goods', including a 'common rulebook' based on UK alignment to certain EU rules and policies; together with a Union–UK 'facilitated customs arrangement', whereby the UK would simultaneously administer both the Union's external customs regime and a separate and divergent UK trade policy. The UK also proposed to participate in various Union regulatory agencies and to offer a range of level playing field guarantees. According to the May Government, those plans would maintain frictionless trade at the Union–UK border, thereby also providing a durable solution for the border between Ireland and Northern Ireland, while at the same time allowing the UK to fulfil its ambition of leaving both the Customs Union and the Single Market. But otherwise, there would be significant divergence and future trade barriers between the Union and the UK in fields such as services and digital; and only very limited provisions concerning the future mobility of natural persons between the Union and the UK.

As we know, the Chequers Plan was soon denounced from almost every quarter. Within the UK, hardline Leave campaigners called the proposals a 'betrayal' of the 2016 referendum result, rejecting even this limited degree of economic cooperation with the Union. Supporters of a 'softer Brexit' were also critical: the May Government's plans would still precipitate a serious rupture in trade between the Union and the UK, especially in the economically crucial services sector. Across the EU itself, the British plans were rejected as untried, speculative, and ultimately unworkable. As well as implying a massively complex and costly customs and regulatory bureaucracy, for EU as much as for UK businesses, the Chequers Plan was ridiculed on the basis that the British were demanding to 'take back control' of their borders and money by asking the EU27 to give up control over theirs and hand it to a third country. But most of all, the UK was stubbornly persisting in its attempt to 'cherry-pick' certain elements of the Single Market whilst rewriting or rejecting others, in defiance of one of the core and consistent 'red lines' laid down by the European Council on behalf of the Union as a whole.

After the European Council comprehensively dismissed the Chequers Plan during the informal Salzburg summit in September 2019, it was clear that the May Government would have to re-evaluate its approach to future Union–UK relations as well as its proposals for resolving the Irish border problem.[95] The outcome of that re-evaluation was embodied in the First Withdrawal Package of November 2018: in effect, even if it was not so obvious from a casual reading of the text, the UK had decided to prioritize minimizing EU–UK trade disruption and finding a UK-wide solution to the Irish border problem (at least in the short- and medium-term).[96]

On its face, the First Political Declaration envisaged only a relatively distant future EU–UK relationship. Since the British insisted upon their 'red lines' and remained determined to locate themselves entirely outside the Customs Union and the Single Market, the Union would see through the logical implications of that position when

---

[94] See, in particular, the discussion contained in Chapter 4.
[95] Informal Summit of the Heads of State or Government meeting in Salzburg (19–20 September 2018).
[96] Published at OJ 2019 C 66 I/185.

it came to the scope for and depth of cooperation with the UK as a third country. On goods, the parties would aim for no tariffs or quantitative restrictions across all sectors but there would inevitably be a customs and regulatory frontier and it would need to be managed and enforced accordingly. To help minimize the need for checks and formalities, the UK would consider cooperating with various Union regulatory agencies and consider aligning itself to relevant Union rules. And to justify the total elimination of tariffs and quotas, the UK would also sign up to relatively robust level playing field commitments. But otherwise, future Union–UK cooperation would be much more limited in scope and depth, for example, precisely in fields such as services, digital, and the mobility of natural persons.

However, the entry into force, upon expiry of the transition period, of the 'Irish backstop' as contained in the First Withdrawal Agreement, meant that *in practice* the UK would remain much more closely linked to the EU across a much wider range of policy fields than the approach suggested in the First Political Declaration. After all, the proposed Protocol on Ireland/Northern Ireland provided for a de facto customs union between the Union and the UK, built almost entirely on the Union's own terms, including the UK's adherence to the Union's external trade regime, and thus without any possibility for the British to pursue their independent trade policy. The Protocol also envisaged significant regulatory convergence between the Union and the UK across a wide range of flanking policies; even besides the more detailed provisions, specific to the territory of Northern Ireland, on direct regulatory alignment with the Union—provisions which (if the May Government's promise of unfettered trade between Northern Ireland and Great Britain were to be taken seriously) might end up applying to the rest of the UK as well.[97]

Moreover, it seemed apparent that the 'Irish backstop' (rather than the vision set out in the First Political Declaration) would govern Union–UK relations for at least the foreseeable future and potentially for some considerable time indeed. True, the texts of both the First Withdrawal Agreement and the First Political Declaration repeatedly stressed the parties' determination to find an alternative method of avoiding a hard border across the island of Ireland;[98] while the power to extend the transition period by mutual consent also offered additional time to undertake the relevant negotiations.[99] But the reality was that no effective alternative could even be seen on the horizon. So either the Irish backstop would remain in place, effectively rendering redundant the only-limited degree of cross-border economic cooperation suggested by the First Political Declaration. Or the First Political Declaration did not in fact represent an accurate statement of the full negotiating intentions of the May Government, which in fact contemplated a much more integrated Union–UK relationship of the sort that would eventually be required to replace the backstop. Certainly, the text of the First Political Declaration contained hints that—whatever the UK's insistence upon its 'red lines'—future negotiations might produce a final agreement based on

---

[97] See further the detailed discussion and references in Chapter 8.

[98] Note Art 184 First WA. Also: Exchange of Letters between the President of the European Council, the President of the Commission and the UK Prime Minister of 14 January 2019; 'Strasbourg Deal' of 11 March 2019 (Instrument relating to the Withdrawal Agreement and Joint Statement relating to Political Declaration).

[99] Art 132 First WA.

much closer relations with the Union: for example, the statement that future customs cooperation/border management arrangements, and the UK's level playing field commitments, should each build upon the (already far-reaching) provisions contained in the proposed Protocol on Ireland/Northern Ireland.[100]

Whatever the real and/or apparent understanding and/or intentions of the May Government, we know that the First Withdrawal Package failed repeatedly to secure the necessary approval of the House of Commons—a failure attributed by the Prime Minister (with some justification, though it was no by means a comprehensive explanation) to the backstop and, in particular, its potential to endure indefinitely unless and until the Union itself agreed to its replacement or termination.[101] The European Council was not prepared to reopen negotiations with the May Government over the text of the First Withdrawal Agreement in general or the Protocol on Ireland/Northern Ireland in particular—but the Union did signal that it was willing to redraft the text of the First Political Declaration, should the UK decide to redraw or even abandon its 'red lines', so as explicitly to plan for a much closer future relationship genuinely capable of acting as a satisfactory replacement for the backstop.[102]

The replacement of Theresa May with Boris Johnson radically changed the dynamics of the situation. As we saw in Chapter 5, there was a reasonable suspicion that Johnson's preferred route forward was to conduct a sham renegotiation exercise, blame the Union for its failure, and withdraw from the Union at the earliest opportunity without any negotiated agreement for an orderly withdrawal or any agreed statement on the potential shape of future EU–UK relations. However, any such avenue was effectively closed down when Parliament succeeded in ruling out a 'no deal Brexit' in accordance with Johnson's 'do or die' timetable—which meant that, even if he really did have no serious intention of engaging in proper negotiations with the Union before that point, Johnson was now obliged to seek meaningful revisions to the proposed withdrawal package that could be brought back to Parliament for debate and approval.[103]

For those purposes, we also know that the Johnson Government approached the task of renegotiation with a very different set of priorities compared to those which had dominated the thinking of his predecessor: 'taking back control' demanded that a *genuinely* distant future EU–UK relationship be put in place *as soon as possible*, so that the UK could exercise its freedom to diverge from Union regulatory standards and embark upon its 'Global Britain' trade policy. Significant dislocation and disruption in existing trade and security relations with the Union, as well as the legal and economic segregation of Northern Ireland from the rest of the UK internal market, were regarded by the Johnson Government as prices well worth paying to realize that objective. The Political Declaration was therefore redrafted to dilute still further the ambition for future EU–UK relations;[104] and, notwithstanding the Union's initial insistence that the text of the Withdrawal Agreement had already been settled, the Protocol on

---

[100] See First Political Declaration, at para 79.
[101] See the detailed discussion in Chapters 5 and 8.
[102] See, e.g. European Council (Article 50), *Conclusions of 10 April 2019*.
[103] See the European Union (Withdrawal) Act (No 2) 2019 (known as the 'Benn Act').
[104] Published at OJ 2019 C 384 I/178.

Ireland/Northern Ireland was revised to ensure that the Irish border problem did not stand in Johnson's way.[105]

4. Revised Political Declaration of October 2019

The revised Political Declaration states that the future EU–UK relationship will be based on a balance of rights and obligations, taking into account the 'principles' expressed by each party: for the Union, protecting the autonomy of its own decision-making, respecting the integrity of the Single Market/Customs Union, and upholding the indivisibility of the four freedoms; for the UK, respecting its sovereignty, protecting its own internal market, the development of an independent trade policy, and ending the free movement of people. The future relationship needs to take account of the unique context of EU–UK relations: while it cannot amount to the rights or obligations of Union membership, it should still be approached with high ambition as regards its scope and depth.

The future relationship should be underpinned by shared values—including the UK's continued commitment to respect the ECHR. Given the overall importance of data flows to the future relationship, the Commission will assess the UK's data protection standards with a view to adopting an adequacy decision (in accordance with existing Union law) before 2021. The UK will do the same under its own regulatory framework. The parties will also establish general terms and conditions for UK participation (in accordance with applicable Union legislation) in a range of Union programmes; as well as working together on other joint initiatives such as renewed funding for peace and reconciliation in Northern Ireland; and exploring other options such as the UK's future relationship with the European Investment Bank Group.

However, the bulk of the Political Declaration is dedicated to two main topics. In the first place, an economic partnership between the Union and the UK—based on a Free Trade Agreement and wider sectoral cooperation. In the field of goods, the parties will form separate customs and regulatory territories, but will aim for no tariffs or quantitative restrictions across all sectors, and to engage in customs and regulatory cooperation with a view to minimizing trade barriers. As regards services, the parties will negotiate provisions on market access and national treatment under host state rules, together with arrangements on the temporary entry/stay of natural persons for business purposes, and possibly also rules to govern the mutual recognition of certain professional qualifications. When it comes to financial services in particular, the Union will assess the relevant UK regimes with a view to adopting equivalency decisions (in accordance with existing Union law) before July 2020. The UK will do the same under its own regulatory framework.

There are also more detailed provisions for other specific sectors, for example: digital, intellectual property, public procurement, transport, energy, and global cooperation in fields such as environmental protection and financial stability. Several sections are of particular note. For instance, the Political Declaration reflects the UK's low

---

[105] See the detailed discussion in Chapter 8.

future tolerance for the mobility of people (other than with Ireland): the parties should simply aim for reciprocal visa-free travel for short-term visits, possibly also arrangements on entry/stays for research and study, maybe some cross-border social security coordination and judicial cooperation in family law. Another example concerns fisheries: the parties will cooperate in bilateral and international fora to ensure sustainable fishing and protect the marine environment, including the management of shared stocks; together with a new agreement covering access to waters and quota shares—using best endeavours to reach such an agreement by July 2020, so it can provide the basis for determining fishing opportunities after expiry of the transition period.

Central to the economic partnership provisions of the Political Declaration is the section on a level playing field. The original version agreed by the May Government provided that the future relationship should include provisions on state aid, competition, employment and environmental standards, and relevant tax matters—but building on the corresponding arrangements provided for in the Agreement, in particular, the alignment obligations contained in the UK-wide 'Irish backstop'.[106] However, the revised Political Declaration now states that the future relationship should encompass robust commitments to prevent distortions of trade and unfair competitive advantages—to which end, the parties should uphold the common high standards applicable at the end of transition in the areas of state aid, competition, employment and environmental standards, and relevant tax matters—a less onerous though still important non-regression commitment.[107]

In the second place, the Political Declaration also devotes considerable attention to a security partnership between the Union and the UK. As regards EU–UK cooperation in criminal matters, the parties desire a comprehensive, close, balanced, and reciprocal system of cooperation—but reflecting the commitments the UK is willing to make as regards (for example) regulatory alignment, dispute settlement, and enforcement; and taking into account the fact that the UK will be a non-Schengen third country that does not provide for the free movement of persons. On that basis, the security partnership will address: EU–UK data exchanges, including in fields such as passenger name records and the Prüm system; operational cooperation between law enforcement authorities and cross-border judicial cooperation in criminal matters; and cooperation as regards money-laundering and terrorist financing. The Political Declaration also describes the parties' aspirations in the fields of foreign policy, security, and defence: flexible and scalable cooperation, including appropriate mechanisms for dialogue, consultation, and coordination. Particular provisions address issues such as: sanctions; UK participation in Common Security and Defence Policy (CSDP) missions and operations; UK collaboration in the development of European defence capabilities; thematic cooperation in fields such as cyber-security, illegal migration, and counter-terrorism; and the need for agreements on the protection of classified and sensitive information.

The Political Declaration also sketches out the parties' thinking about the structure and governance of their future relationship. The precise legal form will be determined in due course, but should include an overarching institutional framework, which

---

[106] OJ 2019 C 66 I/185, at para 79.
[107] OJ 2019 C 384 I/178, at para 77.

could take the form of an association agreement, while allowing for more specific governance arrangements in particular areas. As well as dialogue at appropriate levels to provide strategic direction, the parties will also support inter-parliamentary and encourage civil society exchanges. But as usual, the core governance institution will be a Joint Committee; the parties will seek to ensure consistent interpretation and application of their agreements; dispute settlement as necessary through an independent arbitration panel; a preliminary reference system so as to protect the CJEU's exclusive jurisdiction over the binding interpretation of Union law; and a system of sanctions for non-compliance as well as general safeguards and rebalancing measures.

5. Post-Withdrawal Negotiating Positions

The Political Declaration is not intended to be legally binding or enforceable: it is a good faith expression of the parties' common political understanding which 'accompanies' the Withdrawal Agreement and is intended to provide the framework for subsequent formal negotiations.[108] The latter might well produce a new agreement on the future EU–UK relationship either similar to or very different from that envisaged in the Political Declaration itself. Equally, the talks could well lead to no successful outcome; or produce only a very limited set of future arrangements. Moreover, the Political Declaration is in many places so sketchy that it effectively offers no more than a basic checklist for the negotiating agenda but can hardly be said to provide a meaningful guide to what the parties even intended let alone what they might ultimately achieve.[109]

Article 184 WA provides that the Union and the UK shall use their best endeavours in good faith to negotiate and ratify the agreements governing their future relationship with a view to their application from the end of the transition period—permitting the crucial 'single regulatory change' which would at least lessen the disruption caused by Brexit.[110] To help realize that ambitious timetable, the Political Declaration proposes that parallel negotiations covering the various strands of the future relationship should begin as soon as possible after the UK's formal withdrawal and that a high level meeting should convene in June 2020 to take stock of progress—a timescale coordinated with the deadline by which the Joint Committee may agree a one-off extension to the transition period in accordance with Article 132 WA.[111]

The Council adopted the Commission's formal negotiating mandate on 25 February 2020.[112] It contains no great surprises—largely following the European Council's previous guidelines from April 2017 and March 2018 as well as the terms of the revised Political Declaration as approved in October 2019.[113] For its part, the UK published

---

[108] OJ 2019 C 384 I/178, at para 1.
[109] E.g. at para 105: '[t]he Parties should consider appropriate arrangements for cooperation on space'.
[110] See further the discussion in Chapter 6.
[111] See Political Declaration, at paras 135–141.
[112] Council Decision authorizing the opening of negotiations with the United Kingdom for a new partnership agreement (25 February 2020); based on Commission recommendation COM(2020) 35 Final; in turn submitted in accordance with European Council (Article 50), *Conclusions of 13 December 2019*.
[113] See also the Commission's series of slides on internal EU preparatory discussions concerning the future relationship (published in January–February 2020 as UKTF (2020) 1–13).

a parliamentary statement about its negotiating objectives on 3 February 2020 which made clear that the Government did not regard itself even as morally bound to respect the terms of its own revised Political Declaration: Johnson here revives the UK's by-now rather tired 'cake and eat it' act (for example) by peddling the fantasy that the UK should enjoy full tariff-free access to the Single Market without having to undertake anything more than the minimal level playing field commitments contained in standard free trade agreements. But essentially, the UK Government now proposes an extreme form of 'clean break Brexit' which rejects any form of regulatory alignment with the EU, any form of supranational control over UK law in any area, or any constraint upon the future autonomy of the UK legal system in any way.[114] When more details were released a few weeks later, in the UK's official 'Approach to Negotiations', it became clear that the UK was indeed intent on pursuing an even more distant model of future relations with the Union.[115]

The UK position as set out in February 2020 is not only a significant departure from the revised Political Declaration, but also light years away from the Union's negotiating mandate in a variety of important respects.[116]

First and foremost, the parties are embarking from very different (almost philosophically different) starting points. On the one hand, the Union regards its future relationship with the UK as of particular importance in terms of trade, security, and strategic interests: the UK may be a third country, but it is in a unique situation relative to the Union—for a wide range of historical, geographical, demographic, economic, and political reasons—which together call for an especially close relationship, not only in terms of privileges but also as regards obligations. On the other hand, the Johnson Government regards the EU–UK relationship almost with indifference—merely one component in the grand designs of 'Global Britain': trade can be conducted on terms similar to that offered to Canada or Japan; other interests can be managed through ad hoc arrangements, if indeed there need to be any at all. Nothing can intrude upon the sovereignty of the UK once it 'fully recover[s] its economic and political independence'.[117] If anything, we would do well to bear in mind that a substantial proportion of the UK's current ruling party are ideologically hostile to the Union's very existence: far from seeing these negotiations as the route to maintaining close and friendly cooperation, they measure the success of Brexit only relative to the damage it might inflict, and that they can blame, on the despised 'EUSSR'.[118]

---

[114] HMG, *Written Statement to Parliament: The Future Relationship between the UK and the EU* (3 February 2020).

[115] HMG, *The Future Relationship with the EU: The UK's Approach to Negotiations* (CP211 of 27 February 2020).

[116] There are many other detailed issues on which the parties' public positions already reveal actual or potential divergences: e.g. inclusion of audiovisual services; protection of geographical indications of origin; withdrawal of autonomous equivalency decisions on financial services; treatment of Gibraltar.

[117] HMG, *The Future Relationship with the EU: The UK's Approach to Negotiations* (CP211 of 27 February 2020), at para 2. For an earlier insight into Johnson's views, consider HMG, *Uniting for a Great Brexit: Foreign Secretary's Speech* (14 February 2018).

[118] In which regard, note the public rebuke issued by the European Council President on 4 October 2018. Recall that, during the 2016 referendum campaign, Johnson compared the EU to Nazi Germany: see, e.g. https://www.politico.eu/article/boris-johnson-compares-eu-to-nazi-superstate-brexit-ukip/.

Secondly, the UK negotiating position throws the very scope and structure of the future relationship entirely into the air. Whereas the EU bases its mandate on the vision of an overall institutional framework plus broad economic and security partnerships as agreed in October 2019, the Johnson Government now rejects the idea of any such comprehensive framework. Instead, the UK proposes only a free trade agreement, together with a series of more limited and entirely separate agreements on specific issues (providing for cooperation in sectors such as air transport, energy, nuclear, and law enforcement/criminal justice). The concept of a distinct security partnership (including any particular provisions on foreign policy, security, or defence) simply disappears.[119] And the UK shows no particular interest in any more general expression of common values; in institutionalized structures to engage in overall strategic discussions; or in regular opportunities for dialogue on matters of mutual interest. Indeed, the UK has remarkably little to say at all on the entire subject of governance— concentrating its energy on repeatedly asserting the importance of its own untrammelled sovereignty.[120]

Thirdly, even within the economic partnership/free trade agreement, the two parties' negotiating positions stand simply diametrically opposed on the central question of the nature of a level playing field to guarantee free and fair competition. The Union takes the Political Declaration as its starting point but significantly fleshes out the implications and expectations—based on the maxim, 'no tariffs, no quotas, no dumping'.[121] In fields such as employment and the environment, the parties should uphold Union standards as they stand at the end of transition; but there should also be a mechanism for raising standards over time—using Union law as a reference point and with an additional commitment to non-regression for the purposes of encouraging trade/investment;[122] and the Union should be able to take autonomous measures to react quickly against relevant disruptions in competition. In the realm of state aid, the Commission's mandate goes even further: Union law should apply to, and in, the UK on a dynamic basis, enforced by an independent UK authority working closely with the Commission, and amenable to dispute settlement through arbitration (subject to adequate protections for the autonomy of Union law). In stark contrast, the UK entirely downplays the importance of the level playing field and renounces the approach agreed in the Political Declaration: the UK will enact its own state aid regime and disputes over its application should not be amenable to dispute settlement under the agreement; similarly, the UK's autonomous standards on employment and

---

[119] Note concerns that the UK might attempt to use security cooperation as leverage in trade negotiations, e.g. 'Boris Johnson 'is turning security into Brexit trade talks bargaining chip'' (*The Guardian*, 1 March 2020). Note also that other important topics are barely mentioned either, e.g. public procurement; rail and maritime transport; global cooperation; money-laundering and terrorist financing; cyber-security.

[120] HMG, *The Future Relationship with the EU: The UK's Approach to Negotiations* (CP211 of 27 February 2020), especially at paras 4–8 and 83.

[121] E.g. Michel Barnier, *Speech at the European Economic and Social Committee: Le choix de la responsabilité, le choix du partenariat* (30 October 2019); Commission President von der Leyen, *Time for the EU and the UK to build a new future together* (8 January 2020); Commission, *Remarks by Michel Barnier at the European Commission Representation in Sweden* (9 January 2020); Commission, *Von der Leyen sets out the ambition for a free trade agreement with the UK* (11 February 2020).

[122] In line with other recent Union FTAs, e.g. Art 12.1(3) EU–Singapore Agreement; Art 16.2(2) EU–Japan Agreement; Art 23.4 EU–Canada Agreement.

environmental protection should merely be subject to a non-regression duty specifi-cally on grounds of encouraging trade/investment.

Fourthly, an equally wide chasm separates the parties over the vexed question of fisheries. Besides cooperation over the conservation and management of fish stocks, the Union's primary objective is to maintain the status quo as regards reciprocal access to waters and the allocation of quota shares, so as to avoid economic dislocation for Union fishermen that have carried out activities in UK seas—explicitly linking the conclusion of such an agreement to the conditions for UK access to the Single Market. However, the UK wants trade in fisheries products to be dealt with under the proposed Free Trade Agreement (FTA), with an entirely separate agreement on access to waters and cooperation on conservation and management issues—based on annual negoti-ations; rejecting the relative stability mechanism employed under Union law; and with a heavy emphasis on combatting illegal fishing activities.

Fifthly, major divergences in approach are apparent as regards not only the eco-nomic partnership but also security cooperation. For example, the Union insists that, as part of the essential conditions that underpin their entire future relationship, the UK must uphold existing human rights commitments as provided for under the ECHR. In the context of the proposed security partnership, the Commission's mandate goes even further: should the UK denounce the ECHR, the provisions on law enforcement and judicial cooperation in criminal matters should be automatically terminated; while if the UK were to change its domestic law so as to deprive the ECHR of direct internal legal effects, those same provisions should be automatically suspended. The UK Government once again takes a highly sovereigntist approach: its more narrow agreement on security cooperation must not constrain the UK's autonomy in any way, including by specifying how the UK should protect human rights within its own legal system—though the treaty should include a general and unrestricted power for either party to suspend or terminate its provisions in whole or in part.[123]

Last but far from least, the parties hold very different views on the timescales for negotiating their future partnership. While the EU continues both to stress the dif-ficulty of achieving agreement before the end of 2020 and to highlight the possi-bility of extending the transition period in accordance with Article 132 WA, the UK Government declares itself absolutely adamant that there will be no such extension under any circumstances—not only in its general election manifesto,[124] but also in major policy statements since December 2019,[125] and indeed explicitly enshrined in primary legislation.[126] Thus, from the UK's perspective, the transition period will ex-pire on 31 December 2020 and the new EU–UK relationship must commence on the basis of whatever happens to be in place after that date. For the UK, if that means 'no deal' (now disingenuously described as an 'Australia-style' Brexit) then so be it. Indeed, in its 'Approach to Negotiations', the Johnson Government declares that, if the

---

[123] Note the assumption of continued UK adherence to the ECHR which seemed to underpin the CJEU's rulings in Case C-327/18, *R O* (EU:C:2018:733) and Case C-661/17, *M A* (EU:C:2019:53).

[124] According to the Conservative Manifesto 2019: '[w]e will negotiate a trade agreement next year... and we will not extend the implementation period beyond December 2020'.

[125] E.g. HMG, *The Future Relationship with the EU: The UK's Approach to Negotiations* (CP211 of 27 February 2020), at para 9.

[126] See section 15A EU(W)A 2018 (as amended by section 33 EU(WA)A 2020).

June 2020 stock-take cannot identify the broad outlines of an agreement that is capable of being finalized by September 2020, the UK may well walk away from further talks altogether.[127]

6. The Start of Negotiations

Negotiations on the future Union–UK relationship formally commenced on 2 March 2020.[128] The parties then undertook a series of general negotiating rounds—though almost immediately, the logistical arrangements governing talks were seriously affected by the impact of the global pandemic and the imposition of public health lockdowns: the April, May, and June rounds of negotiations had to be conducted virtually.[129] To help provide a focus for negotiations, the Union published its draft texts for an agreement governing future relations with the UK on 18 March 2020, though separating the text relating to foreign and defence policy cooperation from the remainder of the topics covered by the Political Declaration, given the Johnson Government's post-withdrawal decision not to engage in discussions with the Union concerning those particular fields.[130] For its part, the UK was initially willing to share certain proposed texts with the Commission negotiating team, but requested that those texts remain strictly confidential—withheld even from the European Parliament and the Member States.[131] Only on 19 May 2020 did the UK finally publish its own draft texts—envisaging not only a free trade agreement but also a series of separate treaties covering fields such as fisheries, air transport, energy, social security coordination, and police/judicial cooperation in criminal matters.[132]

As foreseen under the Political Declaration, the parties undertook a high level review of the negotiations on 15 June 2020.[133] It came as no surprise that, despite the Commission's repeated invitations for the UK to reconsider its position,[134] the Johnson Government refused to request any prolongation of the transition period as provided for under the Withdrawal Agreement.[135] Instead, the Parties agreed that new momentum was required in the negotiations if any agreement was to be concluded and ratified by 1 January 2021. Talks should therefore intensify from July 2020 with a view (if possible) to finding an early understanding on the principles underlying any agreement—presumably so as to supplement, amend, and/or replace the

[127] HMG, *The Future Relationship with the EU: The UK's Approach to Negotiations* (CP211 of 27 February 2020), at para 9.
[128] See https://ec.europa.eu/info/sites/info/files/agenda-uk-eu-first-round-02-05-march-2020.pdf.
[129] 20–24 April 2020; 11–15 May 2020; 2–5 June 2020.
[130] See UKTF (2020) 14 and 15 (the latter dealing with foreign and defence policy cooperation).
[131] E.g. Commission, *Press Statement by Michel Barnier following the second round of future relationship negotiations with the UK* (24 April 2020); *Press Statement by Michel Barnier following Round 3 of negotiations for a new partnership between the EU and the UK* (15 May 2020).
[132] Available via https://www.gov.uk/government/publications/our-approach-to-the-future-relationship-with-the-eu.
[133] Political Declaration, at para 141.
[134] E.g. Commission, *Press Statement by Michel Barnier following the second round of future relationship negotiations with the UK* (24 April 2020); *Speech by Michel Barnier at the European Economic and Social Committee Plenary Session* (10 June 2020).
[135] See further the detailed discussion in Chapter 6.

understanding which the Union thought it had already reached with the Johnson Government under the revised Political Declaration.[136]

In terms of the key substantive points of divergence between the Union and the UK, it should also have come as little surprise that they would largely correspond to the differences already evident from a comparison of the parties' respective initial negotiating positions. Thus, after the April round of negotiations, Michel Barnier highlighted four main areas where the negotiations had failed to make any significant progress.[137] First, the level playing field: the UK now appeared to deny that factors of economic interconnectedness and geographic proximity could justify robust guarantees against anti-competitive and/or unfair trading practices (despite that point having already been agreed in the Political Declaration itself). Secondly, governance: the UK refused to agree to common governance structures for the future relationship, while the Union would not accept the creation of ad hoc structures that implied duplication, inefficiency, and a lack of transparency. Barnier also noted the existence of particular disagreements (for example) over including some explicit reference to the Union and the UK's common values; continued UK adherence to and domestic implementation of the ECHR; and any role for the CJEU even in protecting the autonomy of Union law in specific fields such as personal data protection. Thirdly, cross-border criminal cooperation: the UK refused to offer firm guarantees (as opposed to vague principles) on the protection of fundamental rights and freedoms; and also insisted upon its power to lower existing standards of data protection. Finally, fisheries: although the Political Declaration had committed the parties to use their best endeavours to reach an agreement by 1 July 2020, Barnier reported that no tangible progress had been made—while reminding the UK that there would be no agreement on the future relationship without a balanced and sustainable long-term solution also on fisheries.

In May 2020, the Commission was again unable to report substantial progress on any of those key issues. Indeed, Michel Barnier highlighted a range of other (less central, but still important) topics where the Union felt obliged publicly to express its disappointment at the British position;[138] and remind the UK that the Union would insist (for example) on robust level playing field guarantees *even if* the parties abandoned their aspiration for a 'zero tariff, zero quota' customs arrangement.[139] The Commission's public summary of the June 2020 negotiating round told a similar story: besides limited progress on the question of continued UK adherence to the ECHR, Barnier described an effective stalemate on all other major points of difference—while also lamenting the fact that the British were refusing even to discuss the entire field of foreign and defence policy.[140] Even when it came to the adoption

---

[136] See Commission, *Addendum to the Terms of Reference on the UK–EU Future Relationship Negotiations* (12 June 2020).

[137] Commission, *Press Statement by Michel Barnier following the second round of future relationship negotiations with the UK* (24 April 2020).

[138] Commission, *Press Statement by Michel Barnier following Round 3 of negotiations for a new partnership between the EU and the UK* (15 May 2020).

[139] Commission, *Reply from Michael Barnier (Chief Negotiator) to David Frost (UK Chief Negotiator)* (20 May 2020).

[140] Commission, *Press Statement by Michel Barnier following Round 4 of negotiations for a new partnership between the EU and the UK* (5 June 2020).

of autonomous decisions on equivalency in the field of financial services—as regards which the Political Declaration had committed each party to complete its necessary internal procedures by the start of July 2020—the Commission was unable to report more than marginal progress by that date, given the UK's limited responses to the Union's requests for relevant information.[141]

Important as those specific areas of substantive disagreement between the Union and the UK positions undoubtedly were, it is also possible to identify a more fundamental and cross-cutting difference in starting assumption and perspective between the two parties when it comes to negotiating the terms for their future relationship.

On the one hand, the UK repeatedly insists upon its status as a 'sovereign equal' to the Union itself—an odd claim, given the fact that the Union is not technically sovereign at all, in the traditional sense of public international law, or as a matter of its own constitutional arrangements—so one assumes that the UK is in fact expressing some political rather than legal point, possibly intended more for domestic consumption than to be taken seriously by the Union and its Member States. Furthermore, the UK has repeatedly complained that the Union refuses to treat the British with proper respect—complaints that seemed to be founded primarily on the fact that the Union is not willing to offer the UK similar terms of Single Market access or cross-border cooperation as might be found scattered here-and-there across a wide range of other third country agreements concluded with various partners over a significant period of time. Instead, the Union has insisted upon 'additional, unbalanced and unprecedented provisions in a range of areas', including obligations that would bind the UK to respect certain EU rules and/or prescribe the institutions required to enforce certain standards, in a manner which (according to the Johnson Government) no democratic country could possibly sign up to.[142]

On the other hand, the Union itself has had little time for the UK's claims and complaints.[143] According to the Union, each party is indeed sovereign over its own territory and exercises that sovereignty to determine the conditions for access to its own market. Indeed, that is the entire point of having negotiations at all. For those purposes, existing relationships between the Union and other third countries do not create any form of binding precedent or legitimate expectation: the Union and the UK must negotiate an agreement tailored to their specific circumstances and needs, according to their respective interests and bargaining power. In reality, according to the Union, it is the UK that is making unrealistic demands and/or failing seriously to

---

[141] E.g. Commission, *Speech by Michael Barnier at the Eurofin General Assembly* (30 June 2020).

[142] See, e.g. HMG, *Letter from David Frost to Michel Barnier* (19 May 2020) available via https://assets. publishing.service.gov.uk/government/uploads/system/uploads/attachment_data/file/886168/Letter_to_ Michel_Barnier_19.05.20.pdf.

[143] E.g. Commission, *Press Statement by Michel Barnier following the second round of future relationship negotiations with the UK* (24 April 2020); *Press Statement by Michel Barnier following Round 3 of negotiations for a new partnership between the EU and the UK* (15 May 2020); *Reply from Michael Barnier (Chief Negotiator) to David Frost (UK Chief Negotiator)* (20 May 2020); *Press Statement by Michel Barnier following Round 4 of negotiations for a new partnership between the EU and the UK* (5 June 2020); *Speech by Michel Barnier at the European Economic and Social Committee Plenary Session* (10 June 2020); *Speech by Michael Barnier at the Eurofin General Assembly* (30 June 2020).

engage in negotiations over key issues. Such frustration includes (but is hardly limited to) the fact that the UK consistently seeks to backtrack on the commitments contained in its very own revised Political Declaration—a text which the Union itself continues to treat as a legitimate, and indeed the primary, reference point for discussion. But the more fundamental problem is that the Johnson Government still clings to its 'cake and eat it' belief that British exceptionalism should allow the UK selectively to maintain the benefits of Union membership without having to comply with the corresponding obligations. The UK might insist it only wants what other third countries already have, but the Johnson Government is in fact asking for significantly more, yet it is simply not open for a third country to pick-and-chose for itself from among the elements that make up the Single Market.

Face-to-face (though still socially distanced) meetings between the Union and UK negotiating teams resumed when the parties held a set of restricted discussions in late June and early July 2020—intended to help intensify talks in accordance with the outcomes of the high level review.[144] However, the Commission's initial assessment was again rather downbeat: serious divergences remained on fundamental sticking points, such as the level playing field, fisheries, and governance/dispute settlement.[145] At the time of writing, negotiations are due to continue across the summer and early autumn. But 1 January 2021 is now the deadline for the entry into force of whatever agreements the Union and the UK might reach—in default of which, the parties will then begin to engage with each other in accordance with their respective internal and external regimes on the default treatment of third countries.

Whatever the outcome of the negotiations on future relations, the Union and the UK still need to complete their preparations for those regulatory and logistical changes that will accompany expiry of the status quo transition period in any event, due to the UK's final departure from a wide range of Union policies and programmes, not least the Customs Union and the Single Market.[146] Equally, the Union and the UK must also finalize their preparations for implementation of the Withdrawal Agreement (particularly as regards the provisions on citizens' rights and the Irish border). After all, the Union has repeatedly asserted that timely and effective implementation of the Withdrawal Agreement is in itself an essential prerequisite for building mutual trust and confidence between the Union and the UK when it comes to negotiations over the terms of their future relationship.[147]

---

[144] 29 June–3 July 2020, in accordance with Commission, *Addendum to the Terms of Reference on the UK-EU Future Relationship Negotiations* (12 June 2020).

[145] Commission, *Press Statement by Michel Barnier following the restricted round of negotiations for a new partnership between the EU and the UK* (2 July 2020).

[146] E.g. Commission, *Press Statement by Michel Barnier following the second round of future relationship negotiations with the UK* (24 April 2020).

[147] E.g. Commission, *Statement by the European Commission following the first meeting of the EU–UK Joint Committee* (30 March 2020); *Press Statement by Michel Barnier following the second round of future relationship negotiations with the UK* (24 April 2020); *Press Statement by Michel Barnier following Round 3 of negotiations for a new partnership between the EU and the UK* (15 May 2020); *Press Statement by Michel Barnier following Round 4 of negotiations for a new partnership between the EU and the UK* (5 June 2020); *Press statement by Vice-President Maroš Šefčovič following the second meeting of the EU-UK Joint Committee* (12 June 2020).

7. Concluding Remarks

It was the UK that decided to lay down various 'red lines', during the tumultuous months after the 2016 referendum and without any serious parliamentary or public debate—the inevitable implication of which was then effectively to rule out any close relationship with the Union into the future. Indeed, the logical consequences of the UK's demand to 'take back control' were a serious dislocation to existing EU trade and security relations and the urgent need to find a workable solution to the problem of a hard border across the island of Ireland. For a considerable period of time, the May Government tried to deny and escape the logical implications of its own policy choices, by claiming that there was no reason why enforcing its 'red lines' should lead to any fundamental negative change in relations with the EU27 or create any long-term problem in maintaining an open border between Ireland and Northern Ireland.

It is fair to say that the Johnson Government reformulated the basic UK position on future relations with the EU (together with its approach to the co-dependent problem of border controls across the island of Ireland) in a way that possessed a greater degree of internal coherence and demonstrated a higher level of political realism (though also, from the perspective of Northern Ireland, a Machiavellian touch of ruthlessness and indeed, from the viewpoint of the DUP, an outright display of disloyalty). However, the cost of such clarity is that the Johnson Government is now driving headlong to-wards a serious rupture in relations with the EU—a far cry from many of the Leave promises made back in 2016 and repeated consistently thereafter—and crucially, that will be true regardless of whether there is a deal or whether there is none.

Yet still, and even within the relatively narrow confines of the future relationship currently being contemplated by the two parties, the Union continues to chide the UK for its 'cake and eat it' philosophy, that the British should enjoy certain benefits without having to suffer any corresponding obligations—a philosophy that appears to have cemented deep differences between the two sides and thus far hampered sig-nificant progress in their negotiations. The UK claims that it sincerely wants to secure a new agreement with the EU, ready to enter into force by the expiry of the transi-tion period. Yet many commentators suspect that the Johnson Government is merely going through the motions of negotiating with the Union, but is in fact indifferent to whether any agreement is reached or not.

Even assuming that the UK is indeed negotiating in good faith, the differences sep-arating the two parties are such as to limit the chance of completing such complex and sensitive negotiations within the limited time available. That is especially true, thanks to the short deadlines effectively imposed by the UK's refusal to request any extension to the transition period under any circumstances. The time pressures become even more acute, if one takes into account the possibility of judicial action before the CJEU about the compatibility of any proposed agreement with Union law;[148] and the po-tential (though currently unlikely) requirement that any agreement that qualifies as 'mixed' may call also for Member State ratifications.[149]

[148] In accordance with Art 218(11) TFEU.
[149] The legal basis of any EU–UK agreement, the division between Union and Member State competences, and the possible need for national ratifications, are all left to be determined in due course: Commission, *Future EU-UK Partnership: Questions and Answers on the Negotiating Directives* (25 February 2020).

Even on an optimistic assessment: if a deal is done, on terms acceptable to both parties, in time for entry into force on 1 January 2021, it would involve such a transformation/downgrading in EU–UK relations that (for many sectors and actors) there may as well be no deal at all. But it seems just as likely that negotiating time will run out and the transition period will expire, with no significant/comprehensive agreement in place—in which case, Johnson's right-wing supporters will have succeeded in procuring the 'hardest of hard Brexits' they have always hoped for. And even if a deal does then eventually emerge at some later point down the line, that will only mean 'two regulatory changes'—something the transition period and the possibility of extension were precisely designed to avoid.[150]

There is an obvious and striking contradiction between Johnson's proud depiction of 'Global Britain' as the champion of free trade versus the reality of a Government poised to commit the single gravest act of economic segregation in modern history. Even besides the damage which will inevitably flow from the UK's decision deliberately to dislocate and distance itself from the Union, that choice also has various important internal consequences for the UK itself. For example, the customs tensions affecting Northern Ireland will only grow in proportion to the degree of Great Britain's divergence from Union law;[151] and the same is true as regards the management of internal trade between England, Scotland, and Wales.[152] But most of all, one wonders why the Johnson Government appears so fixated on the power to diverge from Union regulatory standards, many of which are only minimum in nature and do not prevent the UK from pursuing higher levels of protection. Perhaps 'taking back control' is just an exercise in populist-nationalist political rhetoric.[153] Or maybe the Tories do indeed harbour dreams of dismantling UK adherence to Europe's distinctive socio-economic model.

Moreover, the UK's increasingly abrasive approach to the future relationship also poses serious challenges for the EU itself—above all, the risk of an aggressive competitor on our very doorstep, actively undertaking market deregulation and encouraging social dumping as an alternative economic model; as well as constantly engaging in attempts to undermine the political unity and solidarity of the Member States.[154] Even looking beyond the current generation of Tory politicians in office, the further and harder the UK does drift away from the European norm, the more difficult life will eventually be, even for a new administration more sympathetic to close relations with or indeed renewed membership of the Union. But in the meantime, we should continue firmly to locate the debate on future EU–UK relations within the wider geo-political landscape currently afflicting the developed world: the UK Tories are now fully converted to the cause of hard-right, post-truth populism, in international

---

[150] See further Chapter 6.

[151] On which: see Chapter 8.

[152] On which: see Chapter 10.

[153] Note the (rather disingenuous) claims made by Boris Johnson, *Speech in Greenwich* (3 February 2020).

[154] Note that Michel Barnier has already, for a considerable time, challenged the UK to clarify whether it intends to depart from the European socio-economic model, e.g. Michel Barnier, *Intervention à la conférence 'Obbligati a crescere—l'Europa dopo Brexit'* (9 November 2017); *Speech at the Centre for European Reform on 'The Future of the EU'* (20 November 2017). And continues to do so, e.g. Michel Barnier, *Statement at the presentation of the Commission's proposal for a Council recommendation on directives for the negotiation of a new partnership with the UK* (3 February 2020).

cahoots with their equally dangerous allies in the likes of Trump's USA and Bolsonaro's Brazil. Until the present crisis passes or at least recedes, the Union and its friends are effectively acting in existential defence of liberal social market democracy—and that point should never drift far from the minds of those responsible for negotiations with the UK.

10

Concluding Remarks

This chapter will offer some concluding remarks—highlighting the key themes and lessons that have emerged from our overall study (Sections 2 and 3); and also drawing attention to certain other important and sensitive questions directly raised by UK withdrawal—both for the British (Sections 4 and 5) and for the Union itself (Sections 6 and 7).

1. The Diverse Forces Shaping Withdrawal

This book has deliberately not endeavoured directly to analyse or evaluate the rights or wrongs of the 2016 UK referendum—neither its origins, nor its conduct, nor its outcome. In so far as the referendum has been relevant to our discussion at all, it has generally served to provide a reference point for trying to identify what the Leave campaign, having won the referendum, might actually want the process and terms of withdrawal to look like and/or usefully describe how future EU–UK relations should be constructed. Even in that limited regard, however, Leave's victory in the referendum is fundamentally uninformative and often rather unflattering.

Instead, our focus has been on exploring the main circumstances and factors that influenced the legal process laid down in Article 50 TEU and which culminated in the UK's negotiated departure from the Union on 31 January 2020; together with the overall structure of, and the most significant provisions contained within, the legally binding Withdrawal Agreement concluded between the EU and the UK; as well as the mutual understanding reached between the two parties, about their future relationship in fields such as trade and security, as expressed in the accompanying Political Declaration.

For obvious disciplinary reasons, the factors of greatest relevance and interest to our analysis have been those of a constitutional and legal nature. After all, the 2016 referendum spurred the rapid evolution of an entirely new branch of Union law—'the law of withdrawal'—even if it is a field we hope never to have to study again. From the UK experience, we can now describe with confidence some of the basic parameters that should govern the process of leaving the Union: for example, the fact that Article 50 TEU can provide a valid legal basis only for an agreement addressing the immediate challenges involved in an orderly withdrawal (not for the treaties that will govern relations between the Union and its ex-Member State into the longer term); or the fact that a Member State which has notified its intention to withdraw from the Union may decide to revoke that notification at any point before its own departure has actually taken place (provided that represents a settled decision to remain within the Union on its current constitutional terms and conditions).

The UK's Withdrawal from the EU. Michael Dougan, Oxford University Press. © Michael Dougan 2021.
DOI: 10.1093/oso/9780198833475.003.0010

Similarly, based on the UK experience, we have developed an important set of precedents for how the Union will approach the practical consequences of any Member State's decision to withdraw: for example, about the essentially collaborative 'united front' institutional arrangements that should govern formulation of the Union's overall negotiating position and the subsequent conduct of negotiations; about the precise range of 'separation challenges' that should call for some explicit legal provision to manage the orderly winding-up of the relevant State's existing membership rights and obligations; or about the underlying principles that should govern the detailed methodology for calculating the impact of withdrawal upon the Union's budget and other financial arrangements.

Of course, the UK experience either did not directly address, or at least did not provide definitive answers to, certain other questions involved in 'the law of withdrawal'. Of those, surely the most important is: how far should Article 50 TEU be construed as an exceptional legal basis, capable of deviating from some of the ordinary principles we would expect to apply as a matter of Union constitutional law? The Court of Justice was never called upon (for example) to confirm or deny the Commission and the Council's shared assumption that Article 50 TEU is to be treated as an exclusive Union competence which altogether ousts the ordinary possibilities of shared competence, mixity, and domestic ratifications; or to provide a constitutional justification for treating a third country just as if it were a Member State, for a vast range of legal and regulatory purposes, simply on the basis that it appears convenient to agree a post-withdrawal, status quo transitional period; or to clarify the precise boundary between 'separation issues' connected to the task of delivering an orderly withdrawal, and 'future relationship' questions that fall beyond the permissible reach of Article 50 TEU, particularly where the former arrangements might endure for many years or even decades.

The UK's Withdrawal Package is the product not only of various constitutional and legal constraints, but also of certain empirical facts, together with myriad political choices. Of course, among the empirical facts, one must consider the UK's sheer state of almost total non-preparation for the consequences of taking momentous decisions about its own long-term future; the relative size and strength of the Union and the UK as bargaining actors; and the huge disparity between the likely impacts for each party of failing to reach an agreement at least on facilitating an orderly withdrawal.

As for the political choices, one of the most decisive was the adoption of the European Council's guidelines in April 2017—translating the basic structural premiss underpinning Article 50 TEU into more detailed decisions about the scope, sequence and timing of the UK's withdrawal negotiations. That decision reverberated across the entire remainder of the Article 50 TEU process—not least the division of labour into a legally binding withdrawal agreement, and a non-binding political declaration, straddled by a far-reaching transition period. And though it was bemoaned by the British both at the time and ever since, hindsight has proven that the European Council's approach was indeed instrumental in delivering an orderly withdrawal.

Other important political choices originated not with the Union but rather in the corridors of Westminster and Whitehall. However, those decisions—often motivated by the desire to disguise, defer, or simply avoid the tensions, dilemmas, and problems inherent in the British position—only tended to make an already challenging situation even more difficult to manage. One need only recall the May Government's hasty cobbling-together of the UK's infamous 'red lines', which were to lie at the root of so many problems, not least for the border between Ireland and Northern Ireland; soon followed by the politically disastrous decision to call an early general election resulting in a hung parliament; swiftly succeeded by the equally maladroit choice to eschew any revised policy capable of commanding greater cross-party support, in favour of redoubling the UK Government's dependence upon extreme Leave supporters on the hard right of the Conservative Party together with the equally partisan parliamentary representatives of the DUP. That series of (mis)calculations led directly and predictably to the confusion, obstacles, and difficulties that characterized so much of both the Article 50 TEU negotiations between the Union and the UK and (especially) the chaotic and ultimately doomed process of passing the First Withdrawal Package through the Westminster Parliament.

May's replacement as Prime Minister by Johnson, albeit still working under the constraints imposed upon a minority government in a deeply fractious Parliament, nevertheless significantly altered the dynamics of the final stages in the Article 50 TEU negotiations. Johnson's alliance with the Conservative hard right, combined with his innate political immorality, prompted him effectively to rewrite the terms of British engagement with the problem surrounding the Irish border, and thus also with the mutually interdependent question of how to orientate future EU–UK relations. Yet it was the decision of the UK opposition parties, finally to yield support for Johnson's own longstanding preference of calling another general election, that provided the final momentum to 'get Brexit done'—delivering a Commons majority for the Conservative Party that was capable of steamrollering the Second Withdrawal Package through (what soon was left of) the UK's domestic approval process.

For many in both the Union and the UK itself, ratification of the Withdrawal Agreement was but a sour victory: true, events had finally delivered the UK's signature on a hard-wrought deal aimed at preventing unnecessary disruption, but they had also extinguished any lingering pro-European hopes of staging a second referendum that might reverse the deeply contested 2016 result. Just as importantly, the 2019 general election provided Johnson with a more secure political platform, not only to continue his populist campaign against the institutions and values of liberal democracy in the UK, but also to begin the process of undermining his very own agreements and understandings with the Union itself—despite the fact that he had only just fought and won the 2019 election on the basis that the Second Withdrawal Package was a 'great new', 'oven ready' deal that delivered a 'real Brexit' for the UK. Indeed, the very speed with which Johnson began to repudiate key provisions of the Political Declaration, and to distort or disown important parts of the Protocol on Ireland/Northern Ireland, provides reasonable grounds to suspect that Johnson's strategy may even have been deliberately planned from the outset.

2. Evaluating the Final Withdrawal Package

Against that background, the final Withdrawal Package certainly has its strengths.

To begin with, thanks to the premiss underpinning Article 50 TEU, the decisive nature of the European Council's April 2017 guidelines, and the EU's naturally superior bargaining position, the Withdrawal Agreement provides a much higher degree of legal certainty and predictability to the very act of UK departure and as regards many of its immediate consequences—certainly compared to the confusion and disruption that would otherwise have accompanied an entirely unilateral UK withdrawal from the Union. Thus, the status quo transition period—as was repeatedly said at the time and proved fully correct in hindsight—offered both parties, but especially the UK, invaluable extra time to complete their respective preparations for the full legal and practical consequences of the UK's transformation into a third country. Similarly, the winding up provisions—for example, as regards the resolution of ongoing administrative and judicial processes, or for calculating the balance and scheduling the payments due under the UK's consolidated financial settlement—provided a comparable degree of legal and practical stability for a whole series of transactions which had begun before the end of the transition period.

However, the Withdrawal Agreement also has its weaknesses. Some of those weaknesses are inherent in the Withdrawal Agreement's status as an international legal instrument—though those weaknesses are inevitably more acute when the Union is dealing with a dualist legal order such as that of the UK; and indeed, become particularly worrying in so far as there are reasonable grounds to suspect that the Johnson Government is not entirely committed to full and effective implementation in good faith of the terms of its own negotiated departure from the Union.

Key parts of the Withdrawal Agreement—including sensitive provisions of the Protocol on Ireland/Northern Ireland—depend upon the ability of the Joint Committee to find mutually agreed and timely solutions to a range of problems left outstanding at the close of the Article 50 TEU negotiations themselves. And even as regards those provisions and obligations which are reasonably clear and precise, the Withdrawal Agreement's system of dispute settlement—whether via the CJEU during the transition period, or thereafter, primarily through the Joint Committee and independent arbitration—ultimately depends upon the commitment of both parties to respect not only the substantive content but also the governance mechanisms of their treaty. If the UK Government were (say) to repudiate its financial commitments under Part Five, or unpick its border obligations under the Protocol on Ireland/Northern Ireland—whether in an attempt to secure greater negotiating leverage over future trade and security arrangements or in a deliberate act of further antagonism designed to appeal to their populist-nationalist voter base—it seems unlikely that the UK would nevertheless proceed humbly and quietly to submit itself to the enforcement consequences provided for under the very same international agreement it is deliberately trying to undermine.

However, the Withdrawal Agreement contains other more substantive problems—arguably more serious than its inherent governance and enforcement limitations, not least since these additional problems could have been avoided or at least ameliorated by the parties agreeing different terms for the UK's withdrawal. Two key examples deserve special mention.

In the first place, consider Part Two of the Withdrawal Agreement on the protection of citizens' rights. Such individuals were always going to be the innocent victims of a grave injustice—if nothing else, through being forced to endure years of uncertainty and anxiety, waiting for any form of agreement to be reached and approved, and apprehensive about what might happen to their lives, and those of their families and friends, in the alternative scenario of a 'no deal'. But over and above the cruelty inherent in Brexit, when it comes to the conduct of the Article 50 TEU negotiations and the final terms contained in the Withdrawal Agreement, neither the Union nor the UK can claim to have scored a resounding moral victory in their defence of citizens' rights and interests.

From the outset of the withdrawal process, the UK's approach to citizens' rights was both hypocritical on the 'big picture' and spiteful when it came to the details. The UK Government repeatedly claimed that EU citizens were 'our family, friends and neighbours' and that they were 'welcome to stay on [almost] the same terms as before'— while in the very next breath, adopting and amplifying many of the worst slanders and xenophobic abuses of the Leave campaign: 'free movement' has become an affliction upon UK society, that must be stopped before the 'citizens of nowhere' and European 'queue-jumpers' succeed in stealing more jobs and housing or depleting more public services and resources.

Such public hypocrisy and hostility was mirrored by the UK's conduct throughout the painstaking negotiations over citizens' rights under Article 50 TEU. The UK Government regularly sought to deny or reduce various elements that were included among the Union's existing levels of citizens' rights protection—from rights relating to family life, to the evaluation of criminal conduct, as well as the impact of the transition period—thereby prolonging the negotiations on this crucial issue for far longer than many commentators and individuals had feared. The Union did resist many of the UK's demands but, in the end, the British still succeeded in securing terms that have undeniably made the lives of many Union citizens more difficult and less secure. Consider not only the entire system of compulsory registration for 'settled status' that several million Union citizens were required to undergo (amid regular reports of its various technological and bureaucratic limitations and failings), but also the UK Government's dogged insistence on using Union citizens as the guinea pigs for a novel immigration regime based on issuing digital-only proof of status—a regime that is bound to have entirely predictable consequences, particularly when it comes to accessing private sector jobs and services, with fears that the worst impacts (in terms of confusion, discrimination, abuse, and exclusion) will be experienced by those who are already among the most socially vulnerable.

However, the Union hardly emerges from the Article 50 TEU negotiations entirely free of fault either: not just because it acquiesced in or facilitated various restrictive or obstructive UK demands, but also because the Union itself adopted an essentially legalistic and formalistic approach to defining both the range of individuals who should qualify for protection under the Withdrawal Agreement and the substantive scope/content of their future rights. The Union's approach was grounded in, indeed wedded to, the strict text of existing Union legislation, rather than recognizing the need for a more generous system that would reflect the more complex and fluid realities of so many individual lives—particularly given the fact that Brexit would replace the relatively flexible and renewable rights associated with Union citizenship with a much more static and finite regime under the Withdrawal Agreement. As a result, for many people, their future residency and associated rights in fact rest upon the adoption of more generous policies, or the favourable exercise of discretion, by their host state and its immigration authorities. Such legal insecurity is protracted by the fact that Part Two does not state clearly whether/how far those who benefit from more generous but essentially unilateral treatment in their host state, compared to what is strictly required under the Withdrawal Agreement itself, are nevertheless to be treated as falling within the latter's protective scope and as such entitled to enjoy its full range of material benefits and safeguards.

In the second place, consider the Protocol on Ireland/Northern Ireland. Again, the inhabitants of the island of Ireland were always bound to be the innocent victims of an inherently negative decision that they themselves did not vote for. But as soon as the UK Government expressed its determination to pursue a hard break from the Union, for both the Republic and Northern Ireland, that turned Brexit from 'problem' into 'crisis'. The British departure also from the Customs Union and the Single Market immediately raised the prospect of imposing a hard border across the island of Ireland, which would pose not just serious problems for economic, social, and political stability, but also directly threaten the hard-won yet still-fragile gains made since the Good Friday Agreement.

Delusional Leave campaigners spent several years claiming that the customs and regulatory border problems caused by the UK's preferred 'hard Brexit' had been invented by the Union, or by Ireland, even by Northern nationalists, simply as a means of harming the UK or breaking up Northern Ireland's union with Great Britain; or arguing that, even if those customs and regulatory border problems were real, they could easily be resolved by using modern frontier technologies [that did not actually exist] or waiving some of the rules [that, inconveniently for them, served to protect the EU's core regulatory and territorial integrity]. But back in the real world, it was blindingly obvious that the only way to avoid a hard border across the island of Ireland was either to create instead a stronger border down the Irish Sea, or for the UK as a whole to remain more extensively aligned with the EU. The former option would outrage Northern Irish unionists. But the latter option was unacceptable to the Leave Right: it would endanger their own agenda of pressing the UK to engage in regulatory divergence from the Union and for 'Global Britain' to formulate an independent trade policy.

The May Government's preferred solution was to chop up the available options and mix parts of them together: some Irish Sea borders; some UK-wide alignment to the EU; though hopefully only on a temporary basis; while admitting that the 'Irish backstop' could well endure for a considerable period of time. But far from being viewed as a balanced compromise, this mélange only outraged the Leave Right still further—or at least provided them with a convenient vehicle for opposition that they would probably have raised in any case. The newly installed Johnson Government insisted upon forcing an alternative—even more complex and potentially unstable—settlement upon Ireland and Northern Ireland: an extensive array of customs and regulatory checks across the Irish Sea; combined with an experimental 'dual customs regime' operating in and in respect of Northern Ireland; all of which is no longer explicitly conceived only as a temporary arrangement but is intended to remain in place on a potentially indefinite basis.

Even if Johnson's border plans were to work exactly as they are designed under the Protocol, they are sure to prove economically and politically problematic for Northern Ireland. But more worrying is the mounting evidence that Johnson signed off on this revised Protocol, only in order to 'get Brexit done', with a less than sincere intention of making his own border plans actually work as intended in practice. The question now, is whether the UK government will have so little respect for the rule of law, so little sense of political responsibility or morality, and so little care for the UK's international reputation, that it might deliberately risk undermining those provisions of the Withdrawal Agreement (however imperfect) that would at least avoid the disaster of a hard border across the island of Ireland.

As for the Political Declaration, we know that the May Government had signed off a document that already envisaged only a relatively distant future EU–UK relationship—but those plans were tempered in practice by the commitments made by the UK under the Irish backstop. By contrast, having dumped Northern Ireland by the wayside, Johnson freed himself to insist upon a revised Political Declaration that foresaw an even deeper fracture in future EU–UK relations—more consonant with the dreams of his Leave Right support base, to free up space for UK regulatory divergence and a 'Global Britain' trade policy.

However, even that proved insufficient to satisfy the desires of the triumphant Leave movement. It took only a few weeks after the UK's formal withdrawal for the Johnson Government to set about systematically back-pedalling from many of the commitments and aspirations it had already agreed in principle with the Union. Formal negotiations between the two parties quickly became mired in a series of acrimonious arguments over level playing field commitments, access to waters and markets in the field of fisheries, respect for fundamental rights and freedoms, and governance/dispute settlement structures. At the time of writing, the EU–UK negotiations have yielded little by way of significant, concrete progress—so the Johnson Government's absolute refusal to contemplate extending the transition period beyond 31 December 2020 (even despite the onset of the Covid-19 pandemic and its accompanying public health and economic crises) raised the chances of the Union and the UK experiencing a 'deferred no deal'.

Yet whatever new treaties are concluded between the EU and the UK—whether before the end of transition or in due course thereafter—it is clear that the Johnson Government is determined to force through a far-reaching rupture in EU–UK political, economic, social, cultural, and legal relations. Indeed, for many sectors and actors, whether or not the parties might sooner or later agree to the sorts of minimalist trade and security arrangements preferred by the current UK regime, would prove virtually immaterial.

3. Returning to the Fold?

Of course, neither the Withdrawal Agreement, nor whatever emerges from the ongoing round of trade and security negotiations, will provide the last word in EU–UK relations. At the very least, a future change in the composition of the Westminster Parliament, and therefore of the British government, might well prompt a significant thawing in the UK's current antipathy towards its erstwhile partners—perhaps leading to negotiations over a much closer relationship, more akin to that familiar under the European Economic Area. And one day—whether it be in 10 or 20 years or indeed longer—it is quite possible that a future generation of British (or Scottish) Europeans will manage to steer the UK (or an independent Scotland) back into the Union mainstream.

By that stage, who knows how the Union or indeed the UK might have evolved in terms of their constitutional fundamentals and macro-political preferences. But a short game of speculation, projecting forward based on what we do know from our already familiar world, at least allows us to hint at the sorts of legal questions that might be raised by any future UK (or Scottish) application for accession.

For example, it might be that a future application for UK accession will be premised on a clear political commitment to participate in the Single Currency on the same terms as any other new Member State, together with a voluntary acceptance of the obligation to become fully integrated into the Area of Freedom, Security and Justice. But if future UK accession aspirations are instead framed in terms of trying to resurrect old British membership privileges—in the form of direct opt-outs from any obligation to adopt the Euro and/or to participate fully in the AFSJ, to be enshrined in Union primary law through protocols attached to the Treaties—then the Union would have to make its own essentially political choice about whether and how far to accommodate those demands for special treatment.

If the Union's answer is affirmative, then the challenge will be to find an appropriate legal vehicle for incorporating the parties' mutual political preferences into the negotiated terms of accession—at least without having formally to amend the existing Treaties in advance, in order to make room for a renewed bout of British exceptionalism. In the case of the Euro, the legal challenges might appear more apparent than real: although a commitment to join the Single Currency is a strong political expectation for candidate countries,[1] it is not explicitly identified as a mandatory condition of membership, such that an accession treaty could not legitimately introduce a formal opt-out by way of amendment to existing Union primary law.[2] And in any event, of course, the experience of Sweden is proof that even a 'Member State with a derogation', in the sense of Article 139 TFEU, cannot be forced to join the Euro against its own (essentially political) will.[3]

At first glance, the situation as regards the AFSJ might appear more problematic. After all, existing Union primary law decrees that all candidate states must accept the Schengen *acquis* in full, for the purposes of their own negotiations on future admission to the Union.[4] However, and at least for the time being, there is a strong case for arguing that even that provision need not prevent the existing Member States from agreeing to reinstate a special system of AFSJ derogations specifically for the benefit of the UK (or indeed, of an independent Scotland).

---

[1] In accordance with the longstanding 'Copenhagen criteria' first set out by the European Council, *Conclusions of 21–22 June 1993.*

[2] In accordance with the direct if limited Treaty amendment power conferred under Art 49 TEU.

[3] Sweden is formally a 'Member State with a derogation', but in practice has adopted the position that it will not join the Single Currency, unless that decision is approved by popular mandate.

[4] See Art 7 of Protocol No 19.

The key here lies in the position of Ireland—whose right to maintain its existing Common Travel Area arrangements with the UK is not only affirmed under the Withdrawal Agreement reached under Article 50 TEU,[5] but more importantly, is equally and explicitly recognized as a matter of Union primary law itself.[6] To force the UK (or Scotland) to participate fully and unconditionally in the AFSJ would have the inevitable effect of undermining Ireland's existing right to maintain the existence and operation of the Common Travel Area with those same territories. In other words, Union primary law contains two prima facie conflicting provisions: one that insists upon full AFSJ participation for all future Member States as a precondition for their accession negotiations; and another that preserves Ireland's prerogative to make alternative border arrangements—without distinction as to whether those arrangements are with an existing Member State, a third country, or a candidate state. To insist upon enforcing the former provision would have the inherent consequence of destroying the value and effect of the latter. In such circumstances, it is natural and logical to proceed on the basis that Ireland's concrete constitutional entitlements under Union primary law as an existing Member State must take priority over the expectations that would otherwise be imposed upon contingent negotiations with third country candidates for future accession.[7] There is even a certain pleasing irony in the idea that, one day, it may be Ireland's opt-out from the full Schengen *acquis* that might end up benefiting also any British desire to recapture their right to 'special treatment' as regards the AFSJ, in the UK's capacity as an aspiring Member State.[8]

4. De-Europeanizing the UK Legal System

But future UK re-accession is (if anything) only a longer-term possibility. In the meantime, there are more pressing and equally important questions facing both the UK and the Union itself.

Dealing first with the UK: so far, much of the British debate about the impact of and preparations for Brexit has been focused (understandably) on the immediate challenge of stabilizing the UK legal system, ready for the very act of withdrawal/expiry of the transition period, so that basic conditions of regulatory continuity and legal certainty are preserved for the benefit of both public and private actors. As we saw in Chapter 2, that is the primary function of the 'Brexit legislation' which has been making its way through the Westminster Parliament since 2017: centred around the European Union (Withdrawal) Act 2018 and its complex system for retaining and amending vast amounts of existing Union law within the domestic legal system; but also extending to a range of other important legislative regimes, in situations where

---

[5] See Art 3 WA.

[6] See Protocol No 20.

[7] See further, on resolving clashes of primary law, e.g. K. Sowery, *The Relationship Between the Primary Sources of European Union Law: Is there a 'hierarchy' within Union primary law?* (PhD thesis, University of Liverpool, 2018).

[8] Assuming that, at the relevant time, Ireland has not itself already renounced its own participation in the CTA and fully joined the AFSJ—a scenario only credible in a situation where unification with Northern Ireland had already taken place: see further the discussion in Chapter 8.

the nature and extent of the changes that flow from UK withdrawal have meant that the retention of existing EU rules (even in some amended form) was simply not a feasible approach, and the UK was instead required to fabricate an entirely new replacement regime of its own design.[9]

But however important and taxing the immediate unilateral preparations required by the UK, simply in order to prepare the internal legal system for the inherent consequences of withdrawal, those challenges are merely the basic prelude to the longer-term processes of constitutional change which are set to be unleashed by Brexit. After all, the UK has decided to embark upon the unprecedented process of 'de-Europeanizing' its national legal system after 45-plus years of legal co-evolution with the Union.[10]

In the superficial world painted by Leave activists and the UK Government, de-Europeanization simply means 'taking back control'—allowing Parliament and the devolved legislatures to make their own substantive decisions about which leftover remnants from EU membership they wish to retain, abolish, amend, or replace. But de-Europeanization is obviously a much more far-reaching process: it implies important changes to the methodologies and cultures of the UK's legal and political system and a fundamental reshaping of the balance of power between the UK's legal and political institutions—as well as between its public institutions and concentrations of private (especially economic) power.

For example, the cross-border problems associated with trade, pollution, crime, and terrorism are not going to disappear just because the UK leaves the EU. The British will simply have to find new solutions to those problems—in many cases acting unilaterally, with reduced capacities, and therefore on a manifestly sub-optimal basis. And a reduction in the UK's ability to offer its citizens more effective regulatory solutions will not be limited to direct and obvious changes such as British exclusion from Union-based systems of mutual recognition, coordination, and information sharing. The UK's losses will also extend to more indirect and less immediate, but still potentially significant, changes—not least in the opportunities available for mutual learning through the structured sharing and exchange of ideas, experiences, and personnel.

Or again, what will happen when the UK removes the regulatory safety nets agreed at EU level to provide minimum standards of protection in fields such as the environment, workers, and consumers? Many of the leading Leave campaigners have openly described Brexit as a 'once-in-a-generation' opportunity to engage in the wholesale deregulation of the British economy and society and openly threatened (or fantasized about) how the UK might abandon the European economic and social model of welfare capitalism and instead pursue a US-style strategy of minimal regulation, low taxes, and reduced public services.[11] Of course, such choices will not only be influenced by the UK's own internal deliberations and political preferences, but also be intimately connected to the nature and relative success of its future external policies—not least

---

[9] Including trade; customs; nuclear safety; sanctions; agriculture; fisheries; immigration.

[10] See Dougan, 'Editor's Introduction' in M. Dougan (ed.), *The UK after Brexit: Legal and Policy Challenges* (2017).

[11] Threats repeated (during the Art 50 TEU negotiations) even by supposed 'moderates' such as then-Prime Minister Theresa May and then-Chancellor Philip Hammond.

in the field of trade, where the aspirations of 'Global Britain' will have to be reconciled with the realities of life as a mid-ranking power. Already, contentious debates about US imports of 'chlorinated chicken' and 'hormone-treated beef' demonstrate public concern about the longer-term implications of Brexit for the UK's existing agricultural and environmental standards.[12]

Of at least equal importance, there are myriad questions about the impact of de-Europeanization upon the institutions and inter-institutional relationships (both central and devolved) of the UK state. For example, according to the traditional story, the main winners of Europeanization are the courts, in their relations with both parliament and the executive. The judges are endowed by Union law with a wider range of powers to find state action unlawful. They are entrusted with more penetrating powers of scrutiny over state policy choices, especially through the principle of proportionality. They have strong obligations to ensure the effective judicial protection of individual citizens in their relations with state authority. And of course, they are empowered to disapply primary legislation, in certain circumstances, where it is incompatible with the state's obligations under the Treaties.[13]

But equally, in a constitutional system such as the UK, where the Government already almost entirely dominates Parliament, Union membership may have exacerbated the continuing growth of national executive power at the expense of national legislative power —a situation only partially compensated for by the increasing role offered to national parliaments under Union law itself (particularly since the Treaty of Lisbon) to become more directly involved in Union-level affairs.[14] Naturally, those two phenomena are not unrelated: for many, the bolstering of executive power helps to explain and indeed justify the magnification of judicial scrutiny, so as to help ensure that governmental authority is better held to account, and so as to protect the interests of economic and social minorities.

Against that background, the question now arises: how might 'de-Europeanization' impact upon the future evolution of relations between the courts, the UK Government, and the Westminster Parliament? For instance, will the courts simply resign themselves to life without the direct tools of more effective scrutiny and intervention which were previously provided to them by Union law—relinquishing a significant part of their power to police the proportionality of government action, or to furnish the citizen with suitably effective standards of judicial protection? Or will the courts instead find ingenuous ways to resurrect some of those old powers, through the unwritten codes of common law jurisprudence? Perhaps even proceeding further down the line of challenging for themselves the full force of the traditional doctrine of parliamentary sovereignty?[15]

---

[12] Especially given the UK Government's apparent reluctance to translate its repeated public promises to 'maintain high standards' into any legally binding obligations: see, e.g. https://www.theguardian.com/politics/2020/oct/12/mps-reject-calls-by-campaigners-to-enshrine-food-safety-in-uk-law.

[13] We refer, of course, to core EU doctrines of judicial enforcement such as the general principles of Union law; direct effect and primacy; effective judicial protection and Member State liability to make reparation.

[14] In accordance with Arts 5 and 12 TEU together with Protocols No 1 and 2.

[15] See further, e.g. Dougan, 'The Charter's Contribution to Human Rights in the UK Before and After Brexit' in A. Iliopoulou Penot and Xenou (eds), *La charte des droits fondamentaux, source de renouveau constitutionnel européen?* (2020); Grogan, 'Rights and Remedies at Risk: Implications of the Brexit Process on the Future of Rights in the UK', *Public Law* [2019] 683.

Another major issue, which we touched upon in Chapter 8, but that is now worth saying a few more words about here in our conclusions, is that removing the overarching framework provided by Union law will force the UK to confront difficult issues about managing barriers to trade and distortions of competition within its own 'internal market'. In fact, the regulation of internal UK trade was not considered a significant issue or problem until the UK's decision to leave the European Union (including the Customs Union and the Single Market). After all, when the UK first joined the European Economic Communities, there was no system of devolution allowing Scotland or Wales to engage in their own distinctive legislative activities. And when devolution did occur in the late 1990s, the application of common EU rules helped to structure, not only the UK's trade relations with other Member States, but also the internal operation of the UK market itself.

The problem is now most certainly genuine, even if its precise scale remains (for the time being) uncertain: in any state where autonomous regulatory competences are allocated to different territories, the resultant legislative divergences are capable of creating barriers to trade and distortions of competition that need to be addressed and managed; while the UK Government has repeatedly promised that Brexit will lead to a significant expansion in devolved competences.[16] And yet addressing the future terms of UK internal trade will surely not be a straightforward or uncontroversial process. After all, the starting point of the UK internal market is perhaps unique in the world, thanks to one overriding and undeniable feature: the relatively vast size of the English population and economy, compared to the other three territories within the UK, together with the political and constitutional pre-eminence of the Westminster Government and Parliament over the rest of the UK, in a situation where those central institutions are effectively inseparable from and entirely dominated by English representatives and interests.[17]

Those basic empirical and legal facts render the task of designing the UK internal market unlike that of virtually any other state or regional organization. For example, to base the UK internal market upon a strong system of mutual recognition (with a wide scope of application and limited possibilities for derogation etc) would mean that—whatever the competences of the devolved institutions on paper—the ability of English goods and services freely to access the markets in Scotland or Wales, would make it much more difficult in practice for the devolved institutions to adopt or enforce different/higher regulatory standards of their own. Such standards would effectively disadvantage domestic producers/suppliers; while the potential scale of English imports would, in many circumstances, simply negate any prospect of Scotland or Wales delivering on their desired public interest objectives.

For those reasons, the UK internal market needs to incorporate proper and effective safeguards for the devolved institutions—enabling the latter to adopt different economic and social choices without the risk, not so much that London might directly and formally overrule them at will, as that the free market access of English

[16] See, e.g. HMG, *The United Kingdom's Exit from and New Partnership with the European Union* (Cm 9417 of 2 February 2017).
[17] Thanks, in particular, to the doctrine of parliamentary sovereignty and especially after the UK Supreme Court ruling in *Miller* [2017] UKSC 5.

goods or services might simply render autonomous devolved choices redundant in practice.[18] Otherwise, there is a serious danger that the UK internal market will not merely reflect, but positively reinforce and indeed magnify, the empirical and constitutional facts of English dominance within the UK. At the time of writing, we await the Johnson Government's formal proposals for its UK internal market legislation—with many commentators keen to ascertain just how far those plans will indeed contain adequate safeguards for the meaningful exercise of devolved competences.[19]

5. Life in the Union Without the UK

It is self-evident that Brexit will have significant implications for the longer-term evolution, not just of the UK legal system, but also of the Union's own constitutional order and policy orientations—including the internal dynamics of the Union, within and between its various institutions, as well as in the latter's interactions with the Member States, and indeed, when it comes to relations between the Member States themselves.[20]

Of course, attempting to anticipate or evaluate with any degree of precision the longer-term implications of Brexit for the Union legal system raises significant methodological difficulties. After all, the Union continues to address multiple internal and external policy challenges: for example, creating principles, institutions, and processes of effective and stable economic governance; finding more fruitful pathways to deliver equitable and sustainable growth; managing the internal as well as external pressures of mass migration; tackling the problem of serious democratic backsliding in several Member States; safeguarding European strategic autonomy despite heightened global instability and increasing threats to multilateralism ... And all of those challenges existed, even before the public health crisis and wider economic catastrophe that has just been unleashed by the Covid-19 pandemic. It is virtually impossible to calculate how far and in what ways the Union's responses might have differed, had the UK remained a Member State, as compared to how events have actually unfolded and will continue to evolve.

But even if there is no realistic chance of disaggregating the precise impacts of Brexit from the myriad other factors acting upon the Union's ongoing development, we can still highlight several ways in which it seems reasonable to assume that the

---

[18] See further, e.g. evidence provided by M. Dougan to the Scottish Parliament Finance and Constitution Committee available via https://www.parliament.scot/S5_Finance/General%20Documents/Michael_Dougan.pdf.

[19] On the broader impact of Brexit upon internal relationships between the UK's constituent territories, see, e.g. Hunt, 'Devolution' in M. Dougan (ed.), *The UK After Brexit: Legal and Policy Challenges* (2017); Young, 'The Constitutional Implications of Brexit', 23 *European Public Law* (2017) 757.

[20] Including under the process envisaged by the 'Conference on the Future of Europe': see European Council, *Conclusions of 12 December 2019*, at paras 14–16. Recall previous important moments in the debate about the Union's post-Brexit development, e.g. the Bratislava Declaration of the EU27 (16 September 2016); the Rome Declaration by the EU27 together with the Presidents of the European Council, European Parliament and European Commission (25 March 2017); the Leaders' Agenda, *Building Our Future Together* (October 2017); as well as the Commission's *White Paper on the Future of Europe*, COM (2017) 2025 and its accompanying 'Reflection Papers', e.g. COM(2017) 206, COM(2017) 240, COM(2017) 291, COM(2017) 315, COM(2017) 358.

UK's withdrawal might impact more or less tangibly upon the internal dynamics of the Union legal order.

For example, it is arguable that the departure of the UK, in and of itself, will have a relatively muted impact upon the composition, staffing, and overall functioning of certain Union institutions (including the Commission, the CJEU, the European Central Bank, and the Court of Auditors); as well as various procedures relevant to Union decision-making and its overall institutional balance (such as the 'yellow card' system for monitoring implementation of the principle of subsidiarity via the national parliaments, the functioning of the European Citizens' Initiative, or the work of the Economic and Social Committee and the Committee of the Regions).

By contrast, the UK's departure will almost certainly have a significant impact upon the operation of the remaining Union institutions and, by those means, upon the overall strategic direction of Union decision-making as well as the more detailed elaboration of specific policy activities. In particular, within both the European Council and the Council, while the formal changes to composition and voting thresholds precipitated by Brexit may appear limited, in practice, the total elimination of the once-powerful British presence will obviously lead to a major rebalancing and realignment of the relationship between the remaining Member States—including the leadership orientations of a whole series of smaller Member States that previously took their cue from the UK on a range of major policy questions. Similarly, as regards the European Parliament, UK withdrawal has already led directly to a recalculation of the allocation of seats among the remaining Member States; while also influencing the debate about how far to experiment with novel electoral reforms such as transnational lists; and affecting the overall political balance of the institution (not least) through the removal of the UK's sizable delegation of virulently Europhobic MEPs.[21]

One might also speculate about the more sectoral impacts of Brexit, for particular Union policy fields, over whose historical development the UK had reputedly exercised a significant degree of influence and/or made a distinctive contribution in terms of resources and capabilities. For example, how might the legal character and policy content of Single Market regulation change, without the influence of a major Member State traditionally assumed to have promoted greater economic liberalism and resisted pressure for local as well as international protectionism?[22] What will become of the relationship between the Single Market and the Single Currency, with the elimination of a large Member State that also enjoyed a permanent derogation from eventual participation in the Euro? Will the Union's bargaining position in future trade negotiations with third countries be adversely affected by the loss of the British component to the Single Market, particularly in fields such as financial services? How might the Union's future approach towards (say) employment and social protection evolve without the alleged tendency of the British to resist any and all attempts at more ambitious European harmonization? How will Brexit impact upon the Union's capacities in

---

[21] See, in particular, European Council Decision 2018/937 establishing the composition of the European Parliament, OJ 2018 L 165 I/1.

[22] A question that has attracted particular attention in the field of financial services regulation: see further, e.g. Howarth and Quaglia, 'Brexit and the Single European Financial Market', 55 *JCMS Annual Review* (2017) 149; Moloney, 'Brexit and Financial Services: (Yet) Another Re-Ordering of Institutional Governance for the EU financial system?', 55 *CMLRev Special Issue* (2018) 175.

360 THE UK'S WITHDRAWAL FROM THE EU

the fight against cross-border organized crime, terrorist financing, and terrorist action (the UK having previously been considered a major contributor to police and judicial cooperation in the field of criminal justice); or upon the Union's ambitions for and conduct of the Common Foreign and Security Policy, including the possibility of a common European defence (the UK having been an important actual and potential asset in terms of military and diplomatic capabilities)?

In any case, it is certain that Brexit will prompt a substantial redefinition of both the context and the objectives of the EU's overall neighbourhood policy—posing challenges very different in nature and scale from those previously involved in the management of the Union's relations with its other closest third countries, but surely capable of impacting upon the overall dynamic of pan-European cooperation and co-hesion.[23] And more broadly, the UK's withdrawal raises interesting questions about the future prospects for differentiated policy-making within the Union legal order—especially now that one of the leading advocates of 'flexible integration' has left—whether through the grant of opt-outs and derogations under primary Union law, or through the facility of enhanced cooperation as provided for under the Treaties.[24]

Yet perhaps the most important longer-term impact of Brexit for the evolution of the Union constitutional system lies in the fact that the UK will no longer be able to shape or constrain the reform of primary Union law through its previous power to veto Treaty amendments or to block other major policy decisions.[25] Elimination of the British veto is especially important given the extraordinary and draconian procedural requirements the UK had previously adopted for itself under the European Union Act 2011.[26] The latter legislation required the UK to hold a national referendum before approving virtually any significant attempt at Union constitutional reform (as well as a host of other internal Union initiatives already provided for under the existing Treaties).[27] The 2011 Act was widely viewed as a unilateral attempt by the UK to kill off any prospect of serious Treaty change—potentially forcing the remaining Member States to pursue important constitutional reforms, if at all, through the relatively cum-bersome medium of ordinary international agreements.[28]

The UK's withdrawal therefore opens up various possibilities for future Union re-form, not so much (or at least not just) in terms of specific policy orientations, but also and perhaps more importantly as regards the constitutional processes potentially

---

[23] See further, e.g. F. Dehousse, *The Institutional Consequences of a 'Bespoke' Agreement with the UK Based on a 'Distant' Cooperation Model* (Study commissioned by the AFCO Committee of the European Parliament, PE 604.972 of July 2018).

[24] See further, e.g. Leruth, Gänzle and Trondal, 'Differentiated Integration and Disintegration in the EU after Brexit: Risks and Opportunities', 57 *JCMS* (2019) 1383.

[25] Including those requiring national ratification through the 'organic law' procedure (e.g. Art 42(2) TEU or Art 223(1) TFEU); or indeed those simply requiring unanimity among the Member States within the European Council or the Council.

[26] As mentioned in Chapter 1.

[27] See further, e.g. Dougan and Gordon, 'The European Union Act 2011: 'Who Won the Bloody War Anyway?'', 37 *ELRev* (2012) 3; Craig, 'The European Union Act 2011: Locks, Limits and Legality', 48 *CMLRev* (2011) 1915.

[28] As arguably demonstrated by the experience of the 'fiscal compact', when the UK vetoed any possi-bility of primary law amendment at the European Council meeting on 9 December 2011, effectively forcing the (vast majority of the) other Member States into concluding the 'Treaty on Stability, Coordination and Governance' in the form of an ordinary international agreement instead.

involved in or required for their realization. Of course, that is not to suggest that UK withdrawal will in itself clear the path for more extensive use of the power to amend the Treaties. After all, not just the ordinary but even the various simplified revision procedures provided for under the TEU remain constitutionally onerous and fraught with political risk.[29] The Council's reticence over how far the current plans for a 'Conference on the Future of Europe' should even treat primary law reform as an available option, are a reminder of the Member States' collective anxiety about seeking formally to reopen the Lisbon Treaty settlement in any significant way.[30]

But even if we cannot now specify precisely how or when, we can still feel confident in anticipating that the Union as it will exist in five or 10 or 20 years' time, will be a different Union than it might have been if the UK had remained a Member State. Certainly, having taken back control from the British, after a lifetime of their threats to veto and obstruct, the Union will now evolve according to the wishes of the 27—so if and when the UK finally returns to the fold, it will have to consider rejoining whatever the Union has decided to make of itself, for itself.

6. In Defence of Liberal Social Market Democracy

For many people, the result of 23 June 2016 came as a profound shock. For anyone who had really followed and understood UK politics over the previous years and indeed decades, the outcome may well have been painful, but it could hardly be described as an enormous surprise. Yet for almost everyone, the protracted and laborious process of translating the bare referendum result of 2016 into the actual fact of UK withdrawal in 2020 proved a collective trauma. Moreover, Brexit has produced outcomes, and will continue to generate longer-term impacts, that damage not only the UK itself but also the Union and its remaining Member States. All that said, if there is one benefit to come from the entire debacle, perhaps it is the fact that Brexit has forced many of us to reflect on what it really means to be a Member State of the European Union, and about why we should regard membership as both special and valuable.

Of course, there is a certain specifically legal dimension to those questions. The UK withdrawal process has prompted scholars to evaluate (for example) the constitutional relationship between the nature of state sovereignty and the demands of Union membership, in the context of the *Wightman* litigation over revocation of the intention to leave;[31] as well as the exact meaning and underlying purpose of the 'autonomy of Union law' as a fundamental Union value articulated by the Court of Justice.[32] Similarly, the possibilities and prospects for future EU–UK relations have generated legal debate (say) about whether and how far Union membership should be distilled

---

[29] See Art 48 TFEU.

[30] See, e.g. the Council's agreed position on the Conference on the Future of Europe (24 June 2020) available via https://www.consilium.europa.eu/media/44679/st09102-en20.pdf. Contrast, e.g. with the European Parliament's resolution on the Conference on the Future of Europe (18 June 2020) available via https://www.europarl.europa.eu/doceo/document/TA-9-2020-0153_EN.html.

[31] Case C-621/18, *Wightman* (EU:C:2018:999). See further, e.g. Cuyvers, '*Wightman*, Brexit and the Sovereign Right to Remain', 56 *CMLRev* (2019) 1303.

[32] See the discussion and references in Chapter 9.

into an identifiable and irreducible combination of benefits and trade-offs—such as the indivisibility of the four freedoms within the context of the Single Market—that should not be up for negotiation and compromise with any third country (no matter how strategically important).[33]

But the questions obviously go far beyond the purely legal. Indeed, they are not even limited to the political, the economic, or the philosophical. They also touch upon the psychological and indeed the deeply personal. In fact, when the present author was asked, time and again at public events across the UK and beyond, to define what it was that made Union membership worth fighting for, and why it was that so many UK citizens should feel utterly devastated by the imminent loss of their Union identity, he was surprised and even a little ashamed to realize that those were questions he himself had long neglected to reflect upon in any conscious and articulate manner.

The answers lie well beyond this book. But here are the sort of thoughts I had at least started to offer by way of response to these most direct and obvious, yet complex and revealing of questions.[34] Union membership is, above all else, about peace. Yet peace is about so much more than just the absence of outright and bloody conflict—however fundamental an achievement that surely is, for which the Union deserves its rightful credit and our eternal gratitude. Peace is also about the thousands of opportunities and millions of interactions that allow us—the peoples of Europe—to reach a better understanding of ourselves and of each other; and that furnish our institutions, as well as us as individual citizens, with more effective ways to cooperate together to address our common challenges and to realize our collective ambitions. In doing so, the Union plays a fundamental role in helping us articulate the specifically European experience of what it means to be a liberal social market democracy—indeed, to be a diverse yet cohesive, confident yet dynamic, community of 27 liberal social market democracies. Views might differ about how far the Union's vocation extends to, or rather ends at, promoting the virtues (and vices) of our experience to others across the globe—but the Union certainly has a fundamental role to play in defending those values during a time of increasing instability within an often unsympathetic system of international relations.

The triumph of post-truth political populism that brought about the dramatic demise of the UK as a leading power within the world's largest alliance of liberal social market democracies is a tragic and cautionary tale from which the Union and its Member States must learn some fundamental lessons—not least about the dangers posed by rampant Europhobic propaganda and delusional nationalist fantasies, as well as the risks of pandering to political extremists who will never be satisfied, but only grow more demanding with every concession and more confident with every victory. But our response cannot be only fuelled by fear, inhibited by the defensive, or dampened by uncertainty. We need to generate and experience the confidence and the pride to proclaim, celebrate, and constantly renew our truly great civilizational experiment in peaceful co-existence, fruitful cooperation, and mutual enrichment.

---

[33] See further, e.g. Editorial Comments, 'Is the 'indivisibility' of the four freedoms a principle of EU law?', 56 *CMLRev* (2019) 1189.

[34] See further, e.g. https://www.youtube.com/watch?v=32QwlLPqjcs.

Index